INCENTIVES
Motivation and the Economics of Information

When incentives work well, individuals prosper. When incentives are poor, the pursuit of self-interest is self-defeating.

This book is wholly devoted to the topical subject of incentives from individual, collective, and institutional standpoints. This third edition is fully updated and expanded, including a new section on the 2007–8 financial crisis and a new chapter on networks as well as specific applications of school placement for students, search engine ad auctions, pollution permits, and more.

Using worked examples and lucid general theory in its analysis, and seasoned with references to current and past events, *Incentives: Motivation and the Economics of Information* examines:

- the performance of agents hired to carry out specific tasks, from taxi drivers to CEOs;
- the performance of institutions, from voting schemes to medical panels deciding who gets kidney transplants;
- a wide range of market transactions, from auctions to labor markets to the entire economy.

Suitable for advanced undergraduate and graduate students studying incentives as part of courses in microeconomics, economic theory, managerial economics, political economy, and related areas of social science.

Donald E. Campbell is the CSX Professor of Economics at the College of William and Mary, Virginia. Campbell received a BA from Queen's University in Ontario and his doctorate from Princeton, and previously taught at the University of Toronto for twenty years. He specializes in mechanism design and social choice theory and teaches advanced courses on incentives and information. He has written three books and over 100 articles in leading journals.

Incentives

MOTIVATION AND THE ECONOMICS OF INFORMATION

Donald E. Campbell

College of William and Mary, VA

CAMBRIDGE
UNIVERSITY PRESS

CAMBRIDGE
UNIVERSITY PRESS

University Printing House, Cambridge CB2 8BS, United Kingdom

One Liberty Plaza, 20th Floor, New York, NY 10006, USA

477 Williamstown Road, Port Melbourne, VIC 3207, Australia

314–321, 3rd Floor, Plot 3, Splendor Forum, Jasola District Centre, New Delhi – 110025, India

79 Anson Road, #06–04/06, Singapore 079906

Cambridge University Press is part of the University of Cambridge.

It furthers the University's mission by disseminating knowledge in the pursuit of education, learning, and research at the highest international levels of excellence.

www.cambridge.org
Information on this title: www.cambridge.org/9781107035249
DOI: 10.1017/9781139547390

First published 2018

Printed in the United States of America by Sheridan Books, Inc.

A catalogue record for this publication is available from the British Library.

Library of Congress Cataloging-in-Publication Data
Names: Campbell, Donald E. (Donald Edward), 1943– author.
Title: Incentives : motivation and the economics of information / Donald E. Campbell, College of William and Mary, VA.
Description: Third edition. | Cambridge, United Kingdom ; New York, NY : Cambridge University Press, 2018. | Includes bibliographical references.
Identifiers: LCCN 2017030647| ISBN 9781107035249 (hardback) | ISBN 9781107610330 (paperback)
Subjects: LCSH: Social choice – Mathematical models.
Classification: LCC HB846.8 .C365 2018 | DDC 302/.13–dc23
LC record available at https://lccn.loc.gov/2017030647

ISBN 978-1-107-03524-9 Hardback
ISBN 978-1-107-61033-0 Paperback

For Maggie and Andre

Contents

Preface to the Third Edition

My greatest debt is to Emily Martell, an undergraduate at William and Mary. She was my research assistant for the last eight months of work on the book. Her love of learning, her ability to write good prose, and her extraordinary intellect redounded to my great benefit and to the benefit of anyone who reads this book. Emily contributed to a few of the topics – the Enron debacle among them – and read the new network chapter and some others, each with great care. She responded to requests for help with alacrity and skill. Both her research and her critique of the manuscript were exemplary. She not only identified glitches, she drew my attention to passages that were not sufficiently clear. ("Glitch" is an understatement. She saved me from a horrible blunder in Chapter 4.) Emily even corrected my prose. I am deeply grateful for her help, and blessed to have had her as a colleague. Any defects that remain can be put down to the fact that I did not give her enough time to read the entire manuscript.

I am also thankful for the input of Steven Williams of the Department of Economics, University of Illinois, Lauren Merrill of the Boston Consulting Group, and my longtime colleague Jerry Kelly.

Over the last eight years I have benefitted from the excellent research assistance of Jennifer Boardman, Anthony Guth, Sarah Turner, and Gefoffrey Zinden. They were students in William and Mary's Masters in Public Policy program and my research assistants during their time here. The fruits of their labor can be found in the gray boxes containing the snippets that complement the formal analysis.

A number of William and Mary undergraduates have contributed to the third edition by suggesting improvements to its predecessor. I'm happy to be able to publicly thank Fasil Alemante, Daniel Byler, Bryan Callaway, Jimmy Cao, Sarah Gault, You-Suk Kim, Shane Mangin, Ruoyan Sun, Richard Uhrig, and especially Theresa Long. I'm also grateful to Simon Fung who, as a student at the University of London, drew my attention to an error in the second edition.

I salute my Cambridge University Press editors, Karen Maloney and Stephen Acerra, and editorial assistant Kristina Deusch. Their encouragement and guidance are much appreciated. I am grateful for the assistance of content manager Charles Howell whose speedy responses to my queries helped me enormously.

I thank my copy editor Jennifer Miles Davis for her astuteness and dedication. Development editor Caitlin Lisle was also helpful. I applaud and profusely thank my entire Cambridge team.

I dedicate this book to my two youngest grandchildren, Maggie and Andre. They make the world a better place, especially my world.

1

Equilibrium, Efficiency, and Asymmetric Information

A successful institution, large or small, must coordinate the activities of its individual members. This book examines incentives at work in a wide range of institutions, to see how – and how well – coordination is achieved by informing and motivating individual decision makers. We say that incentives work well when they result in a high level of individual welfare generally. This is problematic when each individual acts to maximize his or her individual payoff, regardless of the implications for the welfare of others. "Societies are most likely to prosper when there are clear incentives to produce and to reap the gains from specialization and trade." (Olson, 2000, p. 1.)

Societies that already have appropriate incentives, and hence are fairly prosperous, nevertheless have regions and groups that do not share in that prosperity to a satisfactory extent. And all prosperous economies have at least a few public policies that have adverse effects on the welfare of many. This book examines incentives to determine the extent to which they prevent the pursuit of self-interest from being self-defeating. We look at an entire economy, as well as a single firm in that economy. Even two-person "institutions" receive attention: a car owner and a mechanic hired to repair the car, for instance. In all cases, a satisfactory outcome requires coordination among the participants, and coordination requires *information transmission and motivation*, as shown in Figure 1.1.

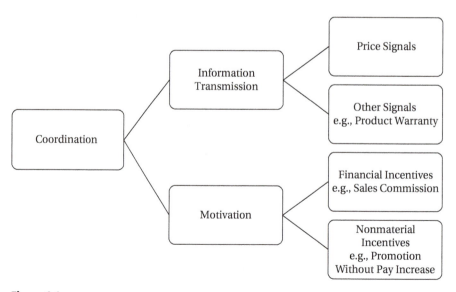

Figure 1.1

The individual members of the institution cannot do their part unless they receive information telling them what their roles are. In the case of a market economy, much of the vital information is transmitted by prices. In a wide range of situations, the consumer's budget constraint and the firm's profit motive give the respective decision makers the incentive to use the information embodied in prices in a way that enhances the welfare of all households. In many political and economic contexts, however, individuals and firms have the relevant information but have no incentive to use that information. The well-being of everyone can fall short of the potential as a result.

If everyone chooses a strategy that benefits himself or herself a little and harms others a lot, the outcome will leave everyone with a lower payoff than the system is capable of delivering. For instance, each individual in a town knows that everyone would benefit from an Independence Day fireworks display if each paid a small fraction of the total cost, but there is no incentive for anyone to use this information in deciding whether to help finance the display. No individual would gain by watching fireworks if he or she also had to pay a large fraction of the entire cost. If the decision were left to the market system there would be no fireworks. This is typically not a good outcome. If the display would cost $100,000 and there are 50,000 townspeople, then the fireworks spectacle could be produced by having each person contribute $2. In many case everyone would be better off if he or she gave up $2 to watch a fireworks display, but an individual would be better off still if the $2 were kept and the fireworks viewed at no cost. (This is the *free rider* problem.) Although everyone knows that there would be a high level of total benefit from the display, no individual has the maximization of overall benefit as his immediate goal. The economic theory of incentives is devoted in part to the design of mechanisms that give the decision taker a higher *individual* payoff when he *does* make choices that lead to a high level of welfare for society as a whole.

> In some cultures a subordinate is *extremely* reluctant to contradict someone in authority, even when the superior is dangerously wrong. Fatal airplane crashes have been traced to mistakes by the pilot that were not corrected by other members of the crew, who spotted the error but only hinted to the captain that something was amiss. Chapter 7 of Gladwell (2008) cites specific instances.

Occasionally there is a natural alignment of the incentives of the decision maker and the rest of the community. For instance, the pilot of an aircraft is just as determined as the passengers to arrive safely at the destination. However, the welfare of an airport security guard or mechanic on the ground is not *directly* linked with that of the passengers. The passengers need to be reassured that the mechanic, say, has a strong incentive to act *as though* his or her chief concern is the passengers' well-being. Without appropriate incentives a mechanic may succumb to the temptation to avoid hard work by doing a superficial job of inspection and repair. (Pilots have committed suicide by deliberately crashing their planes – with passengers aboard – but these cases are extremely rare.)

Incentives are obviously of vital concern to air travelers and are worth studying for that reason alone. But they are also vital to society as a whole. Given the decisions made by others, a worker – whether a mechanic or professor or company president – may find it in his or her interest to expend little effort on the job while drawing a full salary. If a large fraction of the labor force can get away with shirking, the economy's output of goods and services will be greatly diminished and per capita consumption will be very low. In that case, each worker will wish that *everyone* had been prevented from shirking, to enable each to consume less leisure but more produced goods and services. *The pursuit of self-interest is self-defeating in this case.* A more appropriate system of incentives could have prevented this – making everyone better off, even though each individual is maximizing his or her own welfare *given the decisions of others* when everyone shirks as a result of poor incentives.

Appropriate incentives are crucial to the success of any institution, whether large or small. This book examines incentive environments and evaluates each in terms of its ability to promote individual welfare generally. In most cases, the pursuit of self-interest can lead to a high level of individual welfare generally only if the individual taking action incurs a cost equal to the cost that his or her action imposes on the rest of society. We refer to this as *social cost pricing*. Let's see why social cost pricing works: Let U_i be the payoff (or utility) to individual i, who will act to maximize U_i. This will typically affect the payoffs of others, and we let C_i denote the total decline in the payoffs of everyone but individual i, as a consequence of i's decision. Then C_i is the cost that i imposes on the rest of society. We modify the rules of the game so that the payoff to i is now $U_i - C_i$, which is what individual i will now maximize. But the change in $U_i - C_i$ is obviously equal to the change in the sum of the payoffs of everyone in society, including individual i. By imposing a cost on individual i equal to the cost that i's actions impose on the rest of society, we induce individual i to act to maximize the total social payoff, even though i is only directly interested in maximizing his or her own payoff.

DEFINITION: *Social Cost Pricing*

Social cost pricing is employed when each decision imposes a cost on the decision maker i that is equal to the total cost incurred by the rest of the group as a result of that decision. If there is in fact a net benefit realized by everyone else, and hence the "cost" C_i is negative, then the decision maker receives a reward equal to that net benefit.

In a great many economic contexts social cost pricing is key to harnessing self-interest in a way that leads to widespread prosperity. In the presence of uncertainty, however, full social cost pricing is at odds with complete insurance, and a trade-off between insurance and incentives is necessary, as we demonstrate in Section 3.11 of Chapter 3.

This book examines incentive schemes currently in use, and we also attempt to design superior schemes when necessary. We confine attention to situations for which a decision maker D's actions affect a wider group, but D strives to maximize his or her own payoff without taking into consideration any resulting side effects on the other members of the group. If this can be said of each member of the group, the outcome will leave individuals with a lower level of welfare than resources and technology are capable of delivering. That can often be rectified by modifying incentives. This will be tricky because each individual has private information not available to others, including government agencies. For example, the manager of a factory has much better information about the production process and product quality than the firm's consumers or the residents of the neighborhood in which the factory is located. If the government attempts to regulate the firm – to affect product quality or the emission of toxic waste – it can do a much better job if it taps the manager's private information instead of issuing direct commands. If the government orders each factory to modify its production process in the same specific way, it may achieve the desired level of pollution abatement. However, by having different factories adjust in different ways, depending on their specific input requirements and production technologies, it will usually be possible to achieve the same pollution reduction at a lower total sacrifice of resources that have to be diverted from other uses. Doing so requires the provision of incentives to harness the factory manager's self-interest and inside information. We refer to this as *incentive regulation*, and it is coming into increasing use, replacing the old *command and control* approach.

Sometimes, monitoring by customers can be more effective than directives or rewards that come from the head of the firm. If the owner of a pizza shop is not on site she may worry that her staff is pocketing the money from some of the pie sales. If she posts a sign informing customers that their pizza is free if they are not given a receipt, the customer will have an incentive to monitor the workers. In some cases it is possible for an employer to monitor workers from a distance, at low cost. Concessions stands at a baseball park take in vast quantities of money, and it is costly to have an overseer at each stand to prevent the sales staff from diverting some of it into their own pockets. (Moreover, unscrupulous people will self-select into jobs where embezzlement can be accomplished without a significant probability of being caught.) By counting cups before and after the game an employer can easily determine how many drinks were sold, and thus how much money should be in the till.

Transmission of information goes hand in hand with incentives. Market prices have their limitations as conduits of information, but they do a superb job in a wide range of situations. For example, wages are important determinants of individual career choices, and wages contain information about the value of various skills to all consumers. An occupation will command a high wage if it contributes significantly to the production of highly valued goods and services. That's because the high demand for a consumer good translates into high prices and profit for the producer. There will be great demand for workers who are crucial to the production process because they generate substantial revenues for their employers. Competitive bidding in the labor market raises the wage of the most productive workers above that of other workers. A particular wage signals information to the economy as a whole concerning the value of the associated skill. We not only acquire the information that a particular occupation is valuable to consumers as a whole; at the same time, an individual has a strong incentive to take this information into consideration in choosing a career, because higher wages provide more income and thus more consumption opportunities.

In general, the way prices enter our budget constraints gives us the incentive to use the information embodied in those prices. All individuals maximize their own payoffs, but because the prices embody information about the welfare of others, the pursuit of self-interest induces individuals to take the welfare of others into consideration, without realizing that they are doing so.

Traffic congestion in city centers requires motorists to spend significant amounts of time cruising for parking spots. Time is not the only resource affected: fuel consumption per mile is much greater at speeds below 20 miles per hour than at highway speeds. In 2003 an entry fee was imposed on vehicles entering London's city center. The result is a very substantial reduction in traffic and a consequent increase in average speeds of about ten miles per hour. And there are now far fewer car and bus delays. The fee has been changed several times according to a simple rule: it is increased until cruising for a parking spot is eliminated without creating unused parking space. (The fee was £14 in 2016.) See page 87 in Becker and Posner (2009) and pages 7, 92, and 197 in Arnott et al. (2005) for more on the use of entry fees to solve congestion problems.

Information transmission and motivation do not always go hand in hand. Commuters know that traffic is congested during rush hour. If individual driver A joined a car pool, other drivers would benefit from the reduction in the number of cars on the road. But the benefit to A is slight, and A's own welfare would decrease because of the inconvenience of not having his or her own car. Self-interest leads all motorists – well, almost all motorists – to drive their own cars to work. It's plausible that if everyone joined a car pool the improved traffic flow would leave everyone better off, *net* of the inconvenience of carpooling. As it is, everyone knows about the social value of carpooling but no one has an incentive to act on that information. However, information technology now allows municipalities to charge for the use of designated high-speed lanes. Such lanes remain uncongested because their user fee gives motorists for whom time is relatively less valuable the incentive to use the lanes that are free but more crowded.

Information transmission can be more or less costly. Low-cost information transmission is problematic. If the institution is the entire economy, the delivery of information throughout the economy can be exceedingly costly. For one thing, contracts must be enforced, and legal costs can be very high. Prices transmit information at low cost but, as Figure 1.1 indicates, other devices such as warranties are important. An extensive warranty on a manufactured good is a signal that the manufacturer believes that the likelihood of a defect is small. If an entrepreneur set out to deceive

"More than 2000 television sets a year exploded in Moscow alone" before the collapse of the Soviet Union (Milgrom and Roberts, 1992, p. 13).

customers by manufacturing low-quality television sets and passing them off as high-quality sets, he could not offer a good warranty without losing the profits that his deception was designed to yield. He would know that a very high number of sets would be returned for replacement or repair under the warranty. Competition between manufacturers in a private ownership market economy induces each producer of a high-quality appliance to offer an extensive warranty.

Even when the information transmission problem is solved, the motivation problem remains. As with the highway congestion example, there must also be an incentive for the individual to use the information in a way that promotes the goals of the institution – a high level of welfare by commuters generally, in the case of the traffic example. Incentives are essential because individuals' paramount concern is their own welfare, not the welfare of others. This book is devoted to the study of material incentives – incentives that have their impact on the decision maker's welfare through their impact on his or her consumption opportunities. How can they be designed to harness self-interest and prevent the pursuit of self-interest from being self-defeating?

An automobile repair shop illustrates one way that incentives can come into play. A car owner who brings his car to the shop for repair wants a reliable job done at low cost. He has neither the expertise nor the time required to monitor the mechanic. If the car owner suspects that the mechanic has cut corners he is likely to broadcast his suspicions to acquaintances. This implicit threat, along with the existence of other repair shops competing for business, gives the owner of a garage some incentive to ensure that the repairs are well done and that customers are not overcharged. But how does the garage owner motivate the mechanic that she employs? Competition and reputation effects may give the right incentives to the owners of firms, but they are just part of the solution. The owner – in general, the *principal* – now has the problem of providing appropriate incentives to the *agents* (mechanics) that she hires. The private ownership market economy is very sophisticated when it comes to generating devices for solving these principal–agent problems. But there are serious limits to the ability of *any* institution to overcome incentive difficulties in many situations. The difficulties are compounded by the presence of random effects. If the car breaks down a week after it was repaired, should that be attributed to shirking on the part of the mechanic or to bad luck?

In World War II the United States won the race with Germany to develop the atomic bomb. Computers were not available, of course, and the US depended on a team of high school graduates to do a staggering amount of calculating. The productivity of the calculators increased almost tenfold when they were told what they were working on. It was not just a case of working harder. The students invented superior calculating techniques (Dyson, 2012, p. 61 and Gribbin and Gribbin, 1997, p. 97).

Although this book is almost exclusively concerned with material incentives, we acknowledge that nonmaterial incentives play a role in any institution. In one of the first influential articles on the modern economics of information, Kenneth J. Arrow (1963b) noted that the information advantage possessed by physicians in treating their patients has led to the emergence of institutions based on trust and delegation to supplement market incentives. Hence, the code of medical ethics.

Each of us does things that benefit others, at some personal sacrifice. Nevertheless, we employ a model that assumes that each individual always pursues narrow self-interest. One reason for doing so is that we are alerted to potential difficulties if our model predicts low levels of individual welfare generally. By working within this framework we are much less likely to recommend policies that are naively utopian.

The importance of incentives has been documented in many ways and in many contexts, although the specific contractual form derived from economic theory is

Teacher absenteeism is chronic in public schools in poor countries. The absenteeism rate is 25% in rural India and between 15% and 25% in Africa. (*The Economist*, August 1, 2015, p. 9.) A modest financial incentive can make a big difference: a test program in rural India gave the teacher a bonus of $1.15 for each day of attendance after the twentieth day. Attendance was verified by means of a camera with a tamper-proof date and time stamp. The teacher had to submit a picture of herself taken with the class at the beginning of the school day and at the end. Teacher attendance increased dramatically and so did student learning (Duflo et al., 2012). As early as 1931 the Soviet ruler Joseph Stalin deviated from the egalitarian wage ethic, realizing that a high level of economic performance could not be achieved without material incentives. The opportunity to work for the common good was not sufficient motivation (Laffont and Martimort, 2002, p. 23).

not always reflected in contracts as actually written (Chiappori and Salanié, 2003). For the specific case of the relationship between a tenant farmer and the landowner, Allen and Lueck (2002) show convincingly that incentives are central to understanding the nature of the contracts that are employed.

One measure of the importance for public policy of a formal study of incentives is provided by McAfee and McMillan (1988, p. 149). They estimate that switching to appropriate contract design could reduce government costs by at least 8%, and sometimes by as much as 30%. The switch to the *responsibility system* in Chinese agriculture in the 1980s resulted in a remarkable increase in productivity over a short period of time (McMillan, 1992, pp. 96–8 and Naughton, 2007, p. 88). The responsibility system requires each farm to deliver a fixed amount of output to the state, but the farm keeps the proceeds of all output above this quota. This is an example of social cost pricing: the social cost of the farmer's leisure consumption is the output that society loses when the farmer consumes an hour of leisure. But that is also equal to the cost imposed on the farmer under the new system because the farmer would have been allowed to keep the harvest from that hour of labor. Under the old system, the cost to the farmer of an additional hour of leisure consumption was zero because all of the output from an additional hour of labor went to the state. It was the farmer whose return was fixed. The change in incentives that began with agriculture and spread to manufacturing resulted in exceptional economic growth that lifted hundreds of millions of Chinese out of poverty. It has been termed the most successful anti-poverty program in human history.

Another reason why economic models often assume selfish behavior at every turn is that, although it abstracts from important features of the real world, it gives us a simple model with much explanatory power. We have come to accept abstract models in everyday life and should not be reluctant to employ them in economics. A road map, for instance, is a representation of a particular region. It abstracts from almost everything that is important – scenery, the location of shops, and so on. Because it *is* so abstract it is very easy to use to work out a route from one location to another; it can even be used to compute a short route. Similarly, an economic model can be exceedingly abstract and still allow us to determine the effect of an excise tax on a commodity's price or the nature of a salary contract that will be offered when the employer can observe the quality of the employee's work but cannot validate that observation with evidence that would be credible to a third party, such as a judge. Conclusions are drawn from the abstract, formal economic models via theorems.

Many people are impatient with economists for abstracting – and worse, employing assumptions that are at odds with reality. It may comfort you to know that this is standard practice in physics. It can even be useful for a physicist to assume that a cow is a sphere! (See Krauss, 1993, pp. 1–7.) "The set of tools physicists have to describe nature is limited. Most of the modern theories you read about began life as simple models by physicists who didn't know how else to start to solve a problem ... *Before doing anything else, abstract out all irrelevant details* ... Overcoming the natural desire *not* to throw out unnecessary information is probably the hardest and most important part of learning physics" (Krauss, 1993, p. 4). The classical model of the motion of the planets around the sun assumes that the mass of each planet is concentrated at a single point of zero breadth. That's absurd. Nevertheless, the model is extremely useful. It was used to predict the existence of Pluto which was discovered in 1930.

We begin then by assuming that all individuals evaluate outcomes exclusively in terms of the effect on their own well-being. This allows us to work out an individual's response to a change in the incentive environment. The assumption of selfish utility maximization implies that there *will* be a response. Not everyone is able to grasp this point. For example, a lot of people argue against long prison sentences for drunk drivers who kill or maim others: "It could happen to anyone."

> Public drunkenness is not uncommon in Japan, but drunk driving is very rare because of the severe penalties. A professional person can even be disqualified from practicing if convicted of driving while intoxicated.

Well, wouldn't you make sure that it couldn't happen to you if a long prison sentence were the penalty for drunk driving? To adapt a phrase of Dr. Johnson's, the prospect of a long jail sentence focuses the mind wonderfully.

We examine incentives at work to see whether we can expect outcomes that maximize individual welfare generally when individuals are motivated by selfish considerations. We assume that an individual takes whatever available course of action leads to the highest possible personal benefit for himself or herself. Of course, in real life there are situations in which some or all individuals behave altruistically, at least up to a point. But self-seeking behavior is pervasive enough to warrant independent study, particularly when the economy as a whole is our concern. Therefore, our goal is to work out the implications of self-motivated behavior, by means of examples and theorems, and we try to learn from them without being distracted by the many real-world features that are left out of the models. We discover that the need to provide individuals with socially beneficial incentives imposes constraints on the economic system as a whole, forcing us to make trade-offs. For instance, giving individuals an incentive to truthfully reveal their preferences for public goods leads to government budget imbalance. By identifying such trade-offs we can design better public policies. In particular, we won't waste resources trying to accomplish goals that are mutually exclusive.

Links

McMillan (2002) is a superb but nontechnical account of how, and to what extent, markets can provide the incentives that lead to a high standard of living. The role of the CIA in supplying the Bush administration with evidence of Iraq's weapons of mass destruction, prior to the invasion of March 2003, is a reminder that the performance of an organization is a function of worker and management incentives (see *The Economist*, July 15, 2004, "The weapons that weren't".) Baumol (1993) contains many examples of entrepreneurial responses to incentives, some of which reach back to ancient Greece and Rome. See Sappington (1993), Laffont (1994), and Sappington and Weisman (1996) for further discussion of incentive regulation. Stiglitz (1993) has a good discussion of the limits of prices in transmitting information. Chapter 4 of Baumol (1993) has examples of the costs of contract enforcement.

Problem Set

(1) The services of garbage collectors have far more total value to the community than the services of heart surgeons: compare a world without garbage collection – plagues, low life expectancy, only 50 percent of children surviving to the age of five – to a world without heart surgeons – no appreciable difference in life expectancy. But heart surgeons are paid far more per hour than garbage collectors. What information is being signaled by this wage rate differential?

(2) I could buy a safer car – a new Mercedes Benz, for example – than the one I presently drive but I prefer a basket of goods and services that includes my present car and an annual vacation at the ocean to a basket with a safer car but an annual vacation featuring croquet in the backyard. Is it in society's interest for firms to devote enough resources to the production of consumer goods to ensure that there is absolutely no chance of a defective product injuring someone?

(3) A barber will not stay in business long if he gives bad haircuts. Competition among barbers ensures that each attempts to build a reputation for high-quality service. What about an industry in which problems do not show up until long after the commodity has been purchased – housing construction, for instance? Is there a role for some form of government regulation in these cases?

1.1   ASYMMETRIC INFORMATION

When you hire a taxi you are employing an *agent* to carry out an assignment. You, the *principal*, want to get to your destination quickly and at low cost, but the taxi driver wants to maximize his revenue. The driver appears to have an incentive to overcharge, and your ability to monitor this is very limited because you know very little about traffic patterns and expedient routes, if you are a visitor to the city. This is an instance of a *hidden action* problem. The passenger cannot directly determine if the driver has acted in a way that minimizes the travel time.

DEFINITION: *Hidden Action Problem*

A principal hires an agent to carry out a task, but it is impossible or extremely costly for the principal to monitor the agent.

In Section 1.2, we demonstrate that the conventional taxi fare schedule induces the driver (the agent) to choose the route that the principal (the passenger) would select if the principal had as much information about routes and traffic patterns as the agent – even though the principal in fact has very little information, *and the agent knows it*. In general, we investigate the possibility of providing appropriate incentives to agents to induce them to behave in the way the principals would instruct them to act if the principals themselves possessed the relevant information – even though the principal is in fact unable to monitor the agent, and the agent knows this. There are three reasons why the principal may want to employ an agent: the agent may possess a skill that is particularly appropriate to the task at hand. (I hired a specialist to remove a tree that had fallen over my driveway during a storm.) The principal may not have the time to carry out the task herself. (I occasionally eat in a restaurant where the chef is not as good a cook as me.) Finally, even if the principal and the agent are "twins," economies of scale can justify the delegation of some tasks by one to the other.

The principal will strive to motivate the agent by means of an incentive scheme designed to maximize the principal's payoff, subject to two constraints: (i) *Incentive compatibility*. The agent will respond to the incentive scheme by maximizing his or her own payoff. (ii) *The participation constraint*. The agent must be able to reach as high a level of welfare as he or she can achieve in any other employment opportunity.

A second family of hidden information problems concerns the attempts by a principal to elicit some specific information that is known only by the agent, but which affects the principal's welfare. For example, the principal is the owner of an asset that is up for sale. If the owner knew the maximum amount that each potential buyer is willing to pay, the current owner could offer the asset to the individual with the highest willingness to pay at a price that is just below that value. That would clearly maximize the owner's return from the sale. For that very reason, all potential buyers have incentive to conceal their maximum willingness to pay – the hidden information. This is called a *hidden characteristic* problem. In Chapter 6, we show that it is possible to design an auction that motivates the bidders to reveal their true willingness to pay.

DEFINITION: *Hidden Characteristic Problem*

Information possessed by one individual (or firm or institution) is concealed from everyone else, but the welfare of others depends on how that information is used.

In many cases we employ a fictitious principal, usually a surrogate for society as a whole. Maximizing the principal's payoff is then a metaphor for maximizing consumer welfare generally, subject to the limitations imposed by resources and technology. The goal is to provide individuals and firms with an incentive to disclose their private information – specifically, individual preferences and firms' production recipes.

Here are some examples of hidden characteristics:

- An individual's preference scheme, or some statistic based on that preference scheme; the marginal rate of substitution at a point (elicited by some resource allocation mechanisms); the elasticity of demand (elicited by a price-discriminating producer).

- The probability that an automobile driver will have an accident. This information is sought by an insurance company. The probability affects the driver's preference scheme via the expected utility function.

- A voter's most-preferred candidate (required by the plurality rule voting mechanism).

- The cost that would be incurred by a firm if it were to reduce its pollution output by 15 percent.

- A firm's production function.

Sometimes our perspective is global. Worldwide reduction of carbon dioxide (CO_2) emissions would retard global warming. Suppose that each country is required to pay a tax on CO_2 emissions greater than a specified threshold level, which differs across countries. If a country's threshold is a set at a specified fraction of its current CO_2 emission rate it can be expected to overstate its actual emission rate.

The owners of baseball franchises are adept at hiding the team's profit to make it easier to deal with the players' union. For instance if the franchise is owned by a cable TV company that also broadcast the games, the broadcast right could be sold to the TV station at a price well below the market rate, thereby transferring profit from the baseball franchise to the cable TV firm (Zimbalist, 2004, Ch. 4).

All of the models and examples discussed in this book can be placed in either the hidden action or the hidden characteristic category, and many have elements of both. Hidden action problems belong to the family of *principal–agent* models. At the most basic level a single principal hires a single agent to perform a simple task, as when an arriving airline passenger engages a taxi to take her to a hotel. (See Section 1.2.) But "the" principal can also represent a firm's shareholders who number in the tens of thousands, and who are scattered around the world, and "the" agent is the management team. (See Chapter 4.) In neither case can the principal count on the agent to perform the task (or tasks) in precisely the way that the principal would mandate *if* the principal had as much information as the agent *and* had the time and expertise to monitor the agent. Will the taxi driver pad the fare by taking an excessively long route to the hotel? Will the top executives diminish the owners' return by purchasing a fleet of corporate jets for their own comfort? Our investigation of a hidden action problem will begin by asking if the principal can provide the agent with incentives that cause the agent's payoff to reach its maximum when she acts as though she were endeavoring to maximize the principal's payoff. Sometimes these incentives are generated by market forces – over time.

In other situations the principal's welfare depends on the agent's characteristic, which cannot be observed or even verified by the principal. There are two ways in which the principal's payoff can depend on agent characteristics: in general equilibrium resource-allocation models the principal is an abstract planner whose utility is identified with social welfare. Social welfare in turn is a function of the characteristics (preferences and technology) of the economy's agents (consumers and firms). We examine a special case of this in Section 3.1. In Chapters 8 and 11, we investigate this subject thoroughly. In more narrowly focused models the principal may be an insurance company, for instance, and the company's profit depends on the number of claims submitted, and that in turn is a function of the probability that a policyholder has an accident. The potential policyholders are the agents in this case. The agent cannot be relied on to act in the principal's best interest – either to take the appropriate action or disclose the agent's characteristic – because the agent wants to maximize his or her own utility. We see whether and to what extent the agent's self-interest can be harnessed by a judicious deployment of incentives that induce the agent to act in a way that promotes the principal's welfare. In hidden characteristic models, the incentive structure will be deemed a success when the agent's action reveals the agent's characteristic.

The hidden action and hidden characteristic phenomena are often called *moral hazard* and *adverse selection* problems, respectively, echoing insurance terminology. We will use the terms hidden action and hidden characteristic, which are more appropriate for economic applications. The term *moral hazard* will be applied to situations in which there is a hidden action problem that is not handled successfully. Similarly, we use *adverse selection* to refer to welfare losses due to a hidden characteristic problem.

Hidden information problems are everywhere. What guarantee do you have that your instructor devotes a reasonable amount of time to designing the course, preparing lectures, and grading tests? Surely there is a temptation to increase leisure time and reduce preparation time or to substitute consulting or research activity for lecture preparation. In this case the student is the principal and the instructor is the agent. This is clearly a hidden action problem. The committee that *hires* a new faculty member has a hidden characteristic problem, and the characteristic in this case is the prospective employee's quality.

Business travelers sometimes choose unnecessarily expensive flights (paid for by their employers) to get higher "frequent flyer" bonus points, which are then applied to personal travel. (Can you identify the *social* waste in this case?) The United States federal student loans program involves billions of dollars. Private contractors are hired to collect student debts, and some of the collecting companies are financially tied to firms in the profitable secondary loan market, giving the collectors an incentive to allow students to default on the original loans (*Washington Post*, June 19, 1993, p. 2).

Moral hazard can *create* adverse selection! A retail store that did not monitor incoming cash would give employees insufficient incentive to be careful with that cash. This would also invite unscrupulous people to apply for work at this store, in the expectation that they could embezzle easily.

In September of 1995 the web site eBay began life as one of the three pages on its founder Pierre Omidyar's home page. Omidyar did not expect it would become the great success that it is today. He felt that because people are basically good and honest, any conflict that arose between buyer and seller could be policed by the "Feedback Forum" at which people could report their good and bad experiences with sellers. The reports were mostly favorable. However, as the site rapidly grew in popularity it attracted sellers intent on profiting through fraud – the adverse selection problem. (At that point eBay had grown faster than any company in the history of the world.) There was a serious Rolex scam in the spring on 1999. The sale of sports memorabilia was especially rife with fraud. The company now has more than eight hundred people on its full-time security staff – including many former law enforcement officials from around the world (Goldsmith and Wu, 2006, p. 132).

An adverse selection problem can be so severe that the market can disappear completely. Consider the viability of unemployment insurance if it were to be provided by private firms. It would be costly to purchase, so individuals who know that the likelihood of their becoming unemployed is low would not buy it. This would result in a higher number of claims per insured worker, leading to an increase in premiums to enable the insurance companies to offer unemployment insurance without taking a loss. This would lead to more individuals opting out – those who were willing to buy when the premium was lower but who feel that the probability of their being unemployed is not high enough to justify paying the slightly higher premium. As the premium increases, it is always the low-probability individuals within the group of previously insured workers who discover that it is now rational for them to cancel their insurance coverage because of the increase in the premium. This means that the number of claims per insured person will rise after an increase in premiums, resulting in another round of premium increases. The whole market can unravel in this way. And if that's the case and protection against the risk is socially desirable – that is, provides net benefit to workers generally – there is a case for provision by the public sector.

Even in a democracy the legal system exposes its participants to risk. One might be formally charged with a crime that someone else committed. Part of the benefit of a democracy has to do with competition for political office, and the consequent realization of incumbents that they will be punished by defeat at the polls (or worse) if too many constituents are falsely accused of crimes. However, it is in our interest as law-abiding citizens to have arrests made *before* the authorities are perfectly certain that they have identified the culprit. If they waited until they were certain there would be too few arrests and too much crime, and the arrests that were made would be obtained at too high a cost in resources. (What does "too high a cost" mean? How do we know the cost would be too high?) So, there remains some risk that a law-abiding citizen will be arrested and forced to defend himself in court. Why don't private markets insure against that risk by offering policies that pay legal costs? Legal services don't come cheap. (And legal defense insurance

Cardozo Law School's *Innocence Project* pioneered in using DNA evidence to determine the culpability of US defendants who were convicted (primarily of rape and murder) before accurate DNA testing became available in the 1980s. (The project is the brainchild of lawyers Barry Scheck and Peter Neufeld. Cardozo Law School is part of Yeshiva University in Manhattan.) By February of 2016, 337 inmates had been exonerated in the United States. The actual culprits were identified in 140 of those cases. Factors leading to the faulty convictions include mistaken eyewitness reports, coerced confessions, police corruption, poor legal representation, prosecutorial misconduct, and inaccurate laboratory work. (See http://innocenceproject.org. See also Weinberg, 2003, pp. 200–201.) Do police and prosecutors have too strong an incentive to obtain convictions?

would cause legal fees to soar. Why?) The premium would not be trivial and hence not everyone would purchase insurance. But why isn't *some* legal defense insurance provided by the market? The adverse selection problem is quite evident here. The individuals who are most willing to buy this policy would be those who know themselves most likely to be in hot water. This means that the premium would be higher than if everyone in the community purchased a legal defense policy. But, the higher the premium the higher the percentage of lawbreakers among the policyholders. There is no premium at which the claims paid out could be covered by the premiums paid in, and the market breaks down. (Private legal defense insurance is available in the United States – mostly in group form – but it does not provide significant coverage for criminal cases.)

Can a case be made for public provision of legal defense insurance as with unemployment insurance? Probably not. Whether the insurance is provided by the public or private sector, there is a severe moral hazard problem. This doesn't apply to you or me, but a lot of people would increase the scope of their criminal activities if they knew that any necessary legal defense would be funded by taxpayers or holders of private insurance policies. There would be such an increase in the demand for the top spellbinding courtroom orators that their fees would increase and then so would the flow of students into law schools. This waste of resources is perhaps the least of the antisocial effects of the provision of legal defense insurance, a commodity that would substantially increase individual utility were it not for the moral hazard and adverse selection problems. How about insurance to compensate for the trouble and expense of running out of gas? That would diminish the incentive to make prudent visits to the gas pump. And who would buy such insurance? The owners of old, gas-guzzling cars; especially the owners of cars with broken fuel gauges.

Sources

The theory of principal and agent is now central to economic theory. K. J. Arrow (1984) proposed the terms *hidden action* and *hidden information* as substitutes for the terms *moral hazard* and *adverse selection* in widespread use. Arrow (1963b, 1971) was the first to draw attention to the economic significance of moral hazard, called hidden action throughout this book. The modern theory of principal and agent was introduced in Ross (1973) and Stiglitz (1974) and given its modern expression in Mirlees (1999), which debuted in mimeograph form in 1975. The optimal income tax problem, a special case of the principal–agent model with the tax authority as the principal and taxpayers as the agents, was proposed by Vickrey (1945) and examined by Mirlees (1971). The pioneering articles by Akerlof (1970) on the used-car market and Spence (1973) on education as a signal of worker quality are credited with turning the attention of the profession to hidden characteristic problems. Mirlees and Vickrey shared the Nobel Prize in 1996, and Akerlof, Spence, and Stiglitz shared the prize in 2001. K. J. Arrow, considered by many to be the most significant economist of the twentieth century, received the Nobel Prize in 1972.

Links

Stiglitz (2000) and Chapter 1 of Laffont and Martimort (2002) outline the history of the treatment of asymmetric information in economic theory. The former emphasizes the ways in which earlier theory was misleading because of failures to acknowledge problems caused by asymmetric information, and the latter highlights the ways in which modern information theory was anticipated.

1.2   TAXI!

You have just landed at the airport in a city you are visiting for the first time. You hail a cab to take you to your hotel. How can you be sure that the driver chooses the quickest and cheapest route to your destination? You can't, unless you make an investment beforehand – an investment of money to purchase a map and of time to compute the shortest route between your departure point and your destination. Even then, you will not know which streets are normally congested, so it would be very costly to determine the cheapest route. Assuming that you are not prepared to incur that cost, is there any way of ensuring that the taxi driver will not take you out of your way to enhance his or her income at your expense? We need to find a way of providing the driver with an incentive to choose the least-cost route, so that even though you don't know what that route is you will be sure that the driver has chosen it, because that choice maximizes the *driver's* return from operating the cab. This is the purpose of the fixed part of the nonlinear pricing schedule for taxi rides. The fare is $F + cD$ where D is the distance to your destination in miles, c is the charge per mile, and F is the fixed initial fee which is independent of the length of the ride. (In fact, you will be charged for time spent idling in traffic, but let's keep things simple.)

If F is zero, and hence the fare is cD, then the driver has a strong incentive to make each trip as long as possible. That's a consequence of the fact that when passengers are dropped off at their destinations, it takes the taxi driver time to find a new passenger. From the driver's standpoint, it would be better to keep the meter running by keeping the original passenger in the cab, and that requires taking a much longer route than necessary. But if the fixed fee is relatively large – say $3.00 when the average variable cost per ride is $6.00 – then the driver has a strong incentive to maximize the number of trips per day, and maximizing the number of trips per day can be accomplished only by making each trip as short as possible.

The linear fare schedule (with $F = 0$) gives the agent (the taxi driver) incentive to behave in a way that makes a ride unnecessarily expensive. It also wastes the

Example 1.1 The Linear Fare Induces Shirking

$F = 0$ and $c = 1$. Hence the fare is equal to D, the distance of the trip. To simplify, each trip is 5 miles long when the taxi driver takes the short route, and the distance is 10 miles by the long route. The driver can make 30 trips a day of 10 miles each or 55 trips a day of 5 miles each. (Remember, time is lost between trips.) When the driver works efficiently her revenue is $55 \times \$1 \times 5 = \$275$. But when the driver shirks, and takes the long route, her daily revenue is $30 \times \$1 \times 10 = \$300$: she makes more money by shirking.

driver's and the passenger's time. If this fare schedule were used throughout the economy the welfare loss would be enormous.

When F is positive and greater than the value of the time consumed searching for a new passenger, the income maximizing strategy is for the driver to get the passengers to their destinations as quickly as possible: if we assume that L dollars of income is lost every time the driver deposits a passenger and has to wait for another one, working efficiently will give the driver a net gain of $F - L$ over the payoff from shirking. Of course, any particular trip of distance D would cost less if the charge were merely cD instead of $F + cD$, but the fee schedule $F + cD$ results in a lower actual cost to the passenger because it induces the driver to choose a route with the smallest value of D.

Example 1.2 The Nonlinear Fare Motivates the Agent to Perform Well

$F = 3$ and $c = 1$. Hence the fare is $3 + D$. As in Example 1.1, each trip is 5 miles long by the short route and 10 miles by the long route. The driver can make 30 trips a day of 10 miles each or 55 trips a day of 5 miles each. When the driver works efficiently her revenue is $55 \times \$3 + 55 \times \$1 \times 5 = \$440$, but if she shirks her revenue is only $30 \times \$3 + 30 \times \$1 \times 10 = \$390$. The driver's revenue is *lower* when she shirks.

If the driver can make only 50 trips a day when she takes the short route, the revenue would only be $\$400 = 50 \times \$3 + 50 \times \$1 \times 5$. That's only slightly more than the $390 a day that she collects when she shirks. But the point is that the nonlinear fare schedule $3 + cD$ undermines the strong incentive to shirk that is built into the linear fare. The nonlinear fare is an effective solution to the principal–agent problem. The passenger is unable to monitor the driver, and the *driver knows that she cannot be monitored*. Nevertheless, in her own self-interest the driver chooses the action that the passenger would mandate *if* the passenger had the necessary information about the best route.

We said that shirking by taxi drivers wastes both the driver's and the passenger's labor. It is worth noting that the nonlinear fare results in a cheaper ride for the passenger. *Given the length D of the trip*, the fare cD is obviously lower than the fare $F + cD$. However, the latter fare schedule changes the driver's incentive and, because it eliminates shirking, the passenger actually pays less. For Examples 1.1 and 1.2 the passenger is charged $10 for a trip under the linear fare $1 × D but pays only $8 for the same trip when the nonlinear fare $3 + $1 × D is used.

What if the taxi driver is an employee of a firm with many cabs? The franchising section of Chapter 4 (4.5.4) explains how drivers can be motivated to maximize the total amount paid by passengers *in a way that maximizes the income of the owner of the taxi company.*

Links

Camerer et al. (2004); Farber (2005); and Sutton (2000, pp. 1-2 and 87-9) provide different perspectives on the taxi industry.

Problem Set

(1) The fare is $3 + D$, and each trip is 5 miles long by the short route and 10 miles by the long route. The driver can make 30 trips a day of 10 miles each or k trips a day of 5 miles each. Calculate the value of k for which shirking and minimizing the length of a trip are equally profitable, then show that shirking is unprofitable for any higher value of k.

(2) Each trip lasts m miles when there is no shirking and λm miles when the driver shirks. A taxi does s trips per day when the driver shirks and n trips per day otherwise. Of course, $s < n$. The fixed fee is F and the charge per mile is c. Characterize the values of F, c, s, λ, and n for which shirking will not take place.

1.3 PICKING A WINNER

Innovation obviously benefits society as a whole as well as the innovator. Innovators respond to incentives. Many of the patents for agricultural inventions in nineteenth-century Britain can be traced back to prizes that were offered for a specific improvement. Even losing contestants sought patent protection for their ideas, accounting for over 13,000 inventions. In 2006 the online movie rental firm Netflix offered a $1 million prize to the individual or group that devised the best algorithm for generating its online recommendations. By 2009 it had received entries from over 55,000 people in 186 countries. The seven members of the winning team collaborated over the internet, and did not meet until the day they assembled to collect the prize. NASA's recent prize for an improved astronaut glove was awarded to an unemployed engineer, not an aerospace firm.

The development of new products and new production processes is the key to our prosperity. To foster such innovations, capitalist economies provide inventors and product developers with patent protection. A patent gives the holder monopoly power for a limited period of time. This allows the patent holder to charge monopoly prices, whereby research and development costs can be recovered. Patents deliver welfare gains because they provide an incentive to invest in research, leading to improved products and production processes, but there is an associated welfare cost. The monopoly price charged by the patent holder deprives some consumers of the good – those who will not buy the good because of the high price, even though the benefit that they would have derived is high enough to cover the marginal cost of production. This is a public policy dilemma: the longer the life of the patent the greater the incentive to innovate but the higher the welfare cost of missed consumption opportunities.

This section examines a special case of innovation. There is a *sponsor* – perhaps the government – who wants some agent to develop a specific product or production process. Once the research bears fruit the idea will be made available to every firm. What's in it for the firm or individual that first develops the new idea? The sponsor might set up a contest, with a prize going to the winning inventor. This is the approach the government took in 1992 when it offered a thirty million dollar prize to the first firm to develop a new super-efficient refrigerator. To ensure that the new appliance would be valuable to consumers, the prize could not be collected until the winner sold 250,000 new refrigerators. Whirlpool won the contest, but couldn't collect because it sold only 200,000 units. In 1996 the charitable X Prize Foundation offered $10 million dollars for the first private firm to fly a reusable spacecraft to a height of 100 kilometers twice within two weeks. It was awarded in 2004 to a team headed by Paul Allen, the co-founder of Microsoft, and Burt Rutan, an aerospace engineer. The same foundation offered $30 million to the first firm to land a robot on the moon. The offer expired at the end of 2015. In 1714 the British Parliament offered £20,000 for the first person or firm to develop a method for determining longitude on board a ship. At that time mariners had no way of knowing how far east or west they had sailed. Accidental grounding and loss of life sometimes resulted.

Public health provides many examples of opportunities for sponsorship: malaria, for instance, kills over a million people each year, almost all of whom are in low- and middle-income countries. Pharmaceutical companies obviously do not see these populations as a source of profit. There would not be enough revenue from the sale of a malaria vaccine to pay for the research and development costs. For example, the World Health Organization could sponsor the research, with rich countries contributing the funds.

From an overall social welfare standpoint, a contest has two drawbacks. First, a contestant will not be sure of winning, and hence the prize has to be big enough to provide an incentive to invest in research *and* compensate for the uncertainty of being rewarded. Second, because more than one firm invests in research there is duplication of costs and hence wasted resources. (There is also waste, in the form of a lost opportunity to society, if *no* firm invests due to the uncertainty of winning the prize.)

Is there a mechanism that will not only avoid the waste due to duplication of research effort but also induce the firm with the most promise to do the research? The *Vickrey Mechanism* is just such a scheme.

To simplify the discussion we assume that there are only two firms capable of meeting the sponsor's goal. (It is easy to extend the analysis to the case of an arbitrary number of firms.) Let v_1 denote the value to the sponsor of firm 1's innovation, and let v_2 denote the value to the sponsor of 2's innovation. The sponsor knows very little about the inner workings of a firm, and hence does not know v_1 or v_2. Moreover, firm 1 knows v_1 but not v_2, and firm 2 knows v_2 but not v_1. Because firm i will not be able to determine in advance precisely what the results of its research will be, we can think v_i as an *expected* value. And note that v_i is the value to the sponsor, not to firm i itself. For example, if the sponsor is a government then v_i will be the value to the entire country of the new idea. We let c_i be the cost to firm of its research effort. Values and costs will be realized in the future, so we assume that they are both discounted – i.e., present expected values and present expected costs.

The net value to the sponsor of firm 1's research is $v_1 - c_1$, and the net value to the sponsor of firm 2's research is $v_2 - c_2$. For convenience, we set $s_i = v_i - c_i$, the *surplus* generated by firm i. The sponsor wishes to identify the firm with the largest s_i and have that firm alone develop the idea. If the sponsor is the government and the cost c_i will be absorbed by a private firm, and not taxpayers, maximization of $v_i - c_i$ is still the appropriate goal because c_i is a measure of lost welfare as resources are shifted away from the production of other commodities in order to develop the new idea. Maximization of $v_i - c_i$ is certainly appropriate when the sponsor is the government and 1 and 2 are government agencies. In that case the cost will be borne by taxpayers. Finally, the sponsor could be a private firm, with agents 1 and 2 being employees of that same firm. Again, maximization of $v_i - c_i$ is the appropriate goal for the sponsor.

The sponsor wishes to identify the firm with the largest surplus, but the individual firm cannot be expected to reveal its surplus truthfully, unless it has an incentive to do so. The naïve mechanism has each firm reporting its surplus, and the high surplus firm is awarded the contract. In that case each firm will be motivated to vastly overstate its anticipated surplus. By contrast, the Vickrey mechanism provides an incentive for truthful revelation.

DEFINITION: *The Vickrey Mechanism*

Each firm i is asked to report s_i to the sponsor. The sponsor commissions the firm h with the highest reported surplus s_h to develop the idea and pays that firm $v_h - s_j$, where s_j is the second highest reported surplus.

Note that we are assuming that the sponsor can verify v_h after the idea has been developed. It would take time for the value of h's product to be revealed and calculated. Moreover, the costs involved would be incurred at various points in time. We circumvent this difficulty by supposing that v_i and c_i, and hence s_i and the payment $v_h - s_j$, are present values for each firm.

Now we prove that no firm can benefit by deviating from truthful revelation of its surplus s_i, regardless of the reports of the other firms, whether or not a firm knows much or little about the reports of other firms. Suppose initially that there are only two firms. The sponsor does not know whether $s_1 > s_2$ or $s_2 > s_1$ holds, and must rely on the individual firms to reveal their private information truthfully.

Suppose that $s_1 > r_2$, where s_1 is the true surplus of firm 1 and r_2 is the *reported* surplus of firm 2. If 1 reports truthfully it will be given the contract and receive a payment of $v_1 - r_2$. Firm 1's profit would be the payment received minus its cost, which is $v_1 - r_2 - c_1 = v_1 - c_1 - r_2 = s_1 - r_2$, which is positive. Firm 1 cannot profit by misrepresenting s_1 in this case because the payment $v_1 - r_2$ that it receives is independent of the surplus that it reports, *given* that it reports a surplus higher than r_2 and that the actual value v_1 can be verified by the sponsor after firm 1 is given the contract. The only strategy available to 1 that would give it a payoff different from the one arising from truthful revelation is to report a surplus lower than r_2, in which case it would not be awarded the contract and will forego the profit of $s_1 - r_2$ arising from truthful revelation.

Suppose that $r_1 > s_2$, where r_1 is the reported surplus of firm 1 and s_2 is the *true* surplus of firm 2. If firm 2 reports truthfully it will be not be awarded the contract and will neither gain nor lose by submitting its true surplus s_2 or any surplus below r_1. The only strategy yielding a different payoff to 2 would be a report r_2 greater than r_1, resulting in 2 getting the contract and receiving a payment of $v_2 - r_1$, for a profit of $v_2 - r_1 - c_2 = v_2 - c_2 - r_1 = s_2 - r_1$, which is negative. A firm that would not be awarded the contract cannot profit by misrepresenting its true surplus. We formalize this argument as follows, assuming an arbitrary number n of firms competing for the contract:

Theorem:

   The Vickrey Mechanism gives each firm an incentive to report its surplus truthfully.

Proof:

Suppose that firm 1 would be the one reporting the largest surplus *if* it reported its true surplus s_1. Then $s_1 > r_i$ for all $i > 1$, where r_i is the surplus reported by firm i. Give the name 2 to the firm reporting the second highest surplus. Under truthful revelation firm 1 will be selected and will be paid $v_1 - r_2$ to do the research. Because firm 1 will then incur c_1 in cost, firm 1's profit will be $v_1 - r_2 - c_1$. Firm 1's profit would be $v_1 - r_2 - c_1 = v_1 - c_1 - r_2 = s_1 - r_2$. Because $s_1 > r_2$ firm 1 will make a positive profit if it reveals its surplus truthfully. Would a different strategy yield even more profit?

Any reported surplus higher than s_2 will result in firm 1 being selected and receiving a payment of $v_1 - r_2$ for a profit of $v_1 - r_2 - c_1 = s_1 - r_2$, the positive payoff arising from truthful revelation s_1. Any reported surplus *lower* than r_2 will result in firm 1 *not* being selected and missing out on the profit of $s_1 - r_2$ that it could have obtained by revealing s_1 truthfully. We conclude that a firm that would be the high surplus one under truthful revelation cannot profit by deviating from truthful revelation but it can be hurt by doing so. (If $r_1 = r_2$ either firm 1's payoff would equal the one resulting from the report s_1 or else there is a positive probability that firm 1's profit would be zero.)

Suppose that firm j would *not* be the one reporting the largest surplus *if* it reported its true surplus s_j. Then $r_1 > s_j$, where 1 is the name we give to the firm reporting the highest surplus. Under truthful revelation j will not be awarded the contract, resulting in a profit of zero. *Any* report r_j less than r_1 will also give j a payoff of zero. The only strategy that would yield a different payoff is a report $r_j > r_1$. Then j would get the contract and be paid $v_j - r_1$, for a profit of $v_j - r_1 - c_j = v_j - c_j - r_1 = s_j - r_1$ which is negative. A firm that would not be awarded the contract under truthful revelation cannot benefit by deviating from truthful revelation, but it can be hurt by doing so. (If $r_j = r_1$ then either j's payoff would be the same as it would be under truthful revelation s_j or else there is a positive probability that firm j would suffer a loss.)   ∎

The proof pointed out that firm 1 would not be hurt by overstating its true surplus. But that is the case only if 1 knows what number would be reported by the other firm. In practice, firm 1 would not have that information, and would be hurt by over-reporting if its true surplus was below the number reported by its rival.

We continue to refer to the true high surplus firm as firm 1. Firm 1's profit is $v_1 - s_2 - c_1$, which is less than $v_1 - c_1$. Could firm 1 develop the idea on its own and get a profit of $v_1 - c_1$ instead of the lower $v_1 - s_2 - c_1$? Recall that v_1 is the value of the invention to society as a whole, not just to firm 1's customers. Therefore, the private development of the idea by firm 1 might yield far less revenue than v_1. In fact, firm 1's revenue might be zero. The goal of the sponsor might be knowledge, rather than some material good, and once the knowledge is developed it might be acquired by any other firm at virtually zero cost, as in the case of the invention of a clock that keeps accurate time at sea, making it possible to determine a ship's longitude.

Sources

The section is based on Scotchmer (2004). The first paragraph draws from *The Economist*, August 7, 2010, p. 79. The Vickrey mechanism is a special case of the Vickrey auction, which is examined in Chapter 6 and which was introduced into economic theory by Vickrey (1961).

Links

The longitude prize is discussed at length in Sobel (2005). Kremer and Glennersten (2004) outline a promising change in the way that vaccine research is funded for diseases that primarily affect the citizens of low- and middle-income countries.

Problem Set

(1) The discussion in this section does not acknowledge the possibility of a tie. If firms A and B report the same surplus, and all other firms report a lower surplus, then the tie is broken by flipping a coin. The firm that is selected will still be paid an amount equal to its actual value minus the second highest reported surplus. When there is a tie, that will be the same as the surplus

reported by the winner of the coin toss. Prove that it is still not possible for a firm to gain by deviating from truthful revelation.

(2) This question pertains to the model developed in this section. For the following three mechanisms each of the two firms reports its surplus s_i, and the firm with the highest s_h (the winning firm h) is selected to carry out the research. In each case determine whether a firm can ever profit by deviating from truthful revelation. If not, explain why. If it is possible, demonstrate that fact with a numerical example.

  (A) The winning firm is paid a sum equal to its own v_h. The other firm is paid nothing.

  (B) The winning firm is paid a sum equal to 110% of its own c_h. The other firm is paid nothing.

  (C) The winning firm is paid a sum equal to the difference between its own v_h and c_h. The other firm is paid nothing.

(3) This question concerns the government's attempt to determine which of five firms can reduce its emission of carbon dioxide by 1,000 tons per year at the lowest cost. For each of the following five schemes the government will require each firm to report its adjustment cost, and it will impose the burden of adjustment on the firm reporting the lowest cost. In each case, determine whether a firm can ever profit by deviating from truthful revelation. If not, explain why. If it is possible, demonstrate that fact with a numerical example.

  (A) The firm reporting the lowest cost is paid that cost plus 5%.

  (B) The firm reporting the lowest cost is paid the second-lowest reported cost plus 5%.

  (C) The firm reporting the lowest cost is paid the average of the lowest and the second-lowest reported cost.

  (D) The firm reporting the lowest cost is paid an amount equal to 50% of the highest reported cost.

  (E) The firm reporting the lowest cost is paid the second-lowest cost, and all other firms are paid 10% of the lowest reported cost.

1.4 EFFICIENCY

We sometimes advocate taxing household A and using the resulting revenue to enhance the welfare of household B. Whether it's a good idea or not, it's always possible to change the configuration of production and consumption activities to benefit one individual at the expense of another. Clearly, it is not possible to maximize the utility of everyone simultaneously. How, then, can we formalize the notion that an economic system should maximize consumer welfare generally? We can at least insist on the elimination of every conceivable kind of waste. But how can that be formalized? By requiring that it exploit every opportunity to benefit some individuals when that can be achieved without penalizing anyone else. This is the *efficiency* criterion.

DEFINITION: *Efficient and Inefficient Outcomes*

Outcome A is efficient if it is feasible and there is no other feasible outcome B that gives everyone at least as high a payoff as A and gives at least one individual a strictly higher payoff than outcome A. An outcome is inefficient if it is not efficient.

An economic system is efficient if it coordinates individual production and consumption activities so well that it uses every opportunity to increase someone's well-being *without* reducing anyone's well-being. If a system is not efficient, then there are equilibria that could be improved on to the extent of making some people better off without adversely affecting anyone else. Such equilibria would be wasteful because it is extremely costly to identify the individuals in question and to bring about the necessary changes in economic activity. The economic system should not burden public policymakers with this kind of adjustment. The adjustments should be made by the economy itself, before equilibrium is reached.

The efficiency test can be applied to any institution, not just an economic system. Suppose that there are three candidates, A, B, and C, for a political office, and the community's election rules result in A winning even though half of the voters would have been just as happy with C and the rest actually prefer C to A. Then we can say that the result of the election is inefficient, and that the election rules fail the efficiency test. A minimal test of the ability of any system, or institution, to promote individual well-being generally is its ability to eliminate every conceivable kind of waste. There is waste somewhere in the system if it is possible to make at least one person better off without making anyone else worse off. If it is *not* possible to do this we say that the outcome is efficient.

To apply the definition of efficiency we must specify the group of individuals under study and also the set of feasible outcomes. Because the various outcomes are evaluated in terms of the preferences of the members of the group, it is vital to know these preferences. The set of efficient outcomes can change if we change the group whose welfare is being evaluated, or the feasible set changes, or individual preferences change.

Example 1.3 The Movie or the Restaurant?

The group in question is a family of five who must decide whether to spend a total of $50 attending a movie ($M$) or going to a restaurant (R). For this specific group decision problem there are only two feasible outcomes, M and R. If individuals 1, 2, and 3 prefer M to R but 4 and 5 prefer R to M then both outcomes are efficient: a move from M to R would make 1, 2, and 3 worse off, and a move from R to M would make individuals 4 and 5 worse off. Therefore, whatever the feasible outcome, it is not possible to make someone better off without making someone else worse off. Suppose also, that preferences are such that persons 1, 2, and 3 each prefer outcome S to R, where S is obtained from M by taking \$4 from each of the first three individuals and giving \$6 each to persons 4 and 5. Suppose that persons 4 and 5 also prefer S to R. If we *change the decision problem* so that S is now feasible, then R is not efficient in this new context: everyone prefers S to R. Finally, return to the case for which M and R are the only feasible outcomes. Individuals 1, 2, and 3 are the children, and the parents (4 and 5) want the choice of activity to be a function of the children's preferences alone. In that case the relevant group is the set consisting of 1, 2, and 3 only, and hence outcome R is not efficient: each of the three individuals in the group prefers M to R. But suppose that on a different weekend individuals 1 and 2 prefer M to R but person 3 prefers R to M. If the group is {1,2,3} and the only feasible alternatives are M and R then both are efficient. A change in preferences can change the set of efficient outcomes.

If there are 1,000 individuals in the group, the feasible set is {A,B}, and 999 people prefer A to B but the remaining person prefers B to A, then outcome B is efficient, however unfair it might be. Efficiency has to do with the elimination of waste and does not address fairness at all. Consideration of efficiency does not prevent fairness from playing a role: if only 1 of 1,000 individuals prefers B to A then both A and B are efficient. We can argue for the choice of A from the set of efficient outcomes on the basis of *fairness* or *equity*.

There are two sufficient conditions for efficiency that are easy to apply: maximizing total utility yields an efficient outcome, as does maximizing any one person's utility if that can be done in only one way.

Two Sufficient Conditions for Efficiency

(1) A feasible outcome is efficient if it maximizes the total payoff (over the set of feasible outcomes).

(2) A feasible outcome is efficient if some individual strictly prefers it to every other feasible outcome.

Proof:

We show that any feasible alternative that maximizes the total payoff is efficient. Let $U_i(X)$ denote the payoff (or utility) to individual i from generic outcome X. Suppose feasible outcome Z maximizes the total payoff over the set of feasible outcomes but $U_h(Y) > U_h(Z)$ for some feasible outcome Y and some individual h. The inequality

$$U_1(Z) + U_2(Z) + \ldots + U_n(Z) \geq U_1(Y) + U_2(Y) + \ldots + U_n(Y)$$

cannot hold if $U_h(Y) > U_h(Z)$ unless there is an individual j such that $U_j(Z) > U_j(Y)$. In words, if Z maximizes the total payoff it is impossible to increase the payoff to one person without reducing the payoff to someone else.

The second sufficient condition is even easier to apply: if feasible alternative X gives some individual j a strictly higher payoff than any other feasible alternative

Table 1.1

Alternative	U_1	U_2	U_3
A	25	50	25
B	20	25	60
C	25	50	50
D	10	15	70
E	5	10	60

Example 1.4 Three Individuals and Five Feasible Alternatives

Table 1.1 gives the utility of each of the individuals 1, 2, and 3 for each of the feasible alternatives A, B, C, D, and E. U_1 is the utility of person 1. $U_1(A) > U_1(B)$ indicates that individual 1 strictly prefers alternative A to B. U_2 and U_3, the utility functions of 2 and 3, respectively, are interpreted similarly. We know immediately that D is efficient because individual 3 strictly prefers D to every other outcome. Alternative C is efficient because it maximizes total utility: $U_1(C) + U_2(C) + U_3(C) = 125$, which is higher than the total utility from any other feasible alternative. Alternative B is efficient, although we can't use either of our sufficient conditions to prove it. Moving from B to A or C would harm person 3, and moving from B to D or E would harm person 2. Therefore, starting from B, we can't make anyone better off without making someone worse off. Outcomes A and E are inefficient. C gives persons 1 and 2 the same payoff (utility) as A, but C gives person 3 a higher payoff than A, demonstrating that A is not efficient. D gives each person a higher payoff than E, so E is inefficient. Note that A generates more total utility than the efficient alternative D, but A is not efficient. (Of course, A does not maximize total utility.)

then X is efficient. There can't be another feasible outcome that makes one person better off without harming anyone because every other outcome would lower j's payoff. ∎

There typically exist efficient alternatives that do not satisfy either of the sufficient conditions, but any alternative that does satisfy one of them is guaranteed to be efficient.

In *economic* models we typically assume that each individual cares only about the direct impact of an outcome on his own welfare, and that more is better.

DEFINITION: *Self-Regarding and Monotonic Preferences*

Individual i's preference scheme is self-regarding if i cares only about the amount of goods and services that he or she consumes. Monotonicity means that i's utility increases if his or her consumption of each good increases.

The simplest economic model requires a cake to be divided among a fixed group of individuals.

Example 1.5 Dividing a Cake

There are n individuals who are to share one cake. Assume that each person's preference scheme is independent of the amount of cake received by anyone else and that each person always prefers more to less. The feasible set consists of the different ways – *allocations* – of dividing a single cake among the n persons. Allocation x assigns the fraction x_i of the cake to individual i. Of course, $x_i \geq 0$ for all i and $\sum x_i = x_1 + x_2 + \ldots + x_n \leq 1$. These are the feasibility conditions. Our assumption of self-regarding and monotonic preferences implies that individual i will prefer allocation x to allocation y if and only if $x_i > y_i$.

If $\sum x_i < 1$ then x is not efficient because we can set $y_j = x_j + (1 - \sum x_i)/n$ for each j, resulting in a feasible allocation y such that $y_j > x_j$ for all j. On the other hand, if $\sum x_i = 1$ then x is efficient because

$y_j \geq x_j$ for all j and $y_h > x_h$ for some h

implies $y_1 + y_2 + \ldots + y_n > x_1 + x_2 + \ldots + x_n = 1$ and thus y is not feasible. In short, an allocation $x \geq 0$ is efficient for the division of a cake problem if and only if $\sum x_1 = 1$.

If all of the cake has been allocated (the sum of the x_i is 1) we cannot increase one person's utility without decreasing someone else's utility. If all waste has been eliminated it is possible to increase someone's utility only by transferring some cake from someone else. In other words, every allocation x for which the sum of the x_i is 1 is efficient including every allocation that gives one person all of the cake. The division of a cake model has many efficient allocations, as do almost all economic models. (It needs to be emphasized that in this simple model each individual i's utility depends only on x_i, and it increases when x_i increases.)

Assume that $n = 3$ for Example 1.5. Then $x = (x_1, x_2, x_3)$ assigns the fraction x_1 of the cake to person 1, x_2 to person 2, and x_3 to person 3. The allocation (⅓, ⅓, ⅓) is efficient and (0.4, 0.4, 0.1) is not. However, both persons 1 and 2 prefer (0.4, 0.4, 0.1) to (⅓, ⅓, ⅓,). *Therefore, it is false to say that everyone prefers any efficient allocation to any inefficient allocation.* Of course, there is *some* allocation that everyone prefers to (0.4, 0.4, 0.1). For example, everyone prefers the feasible allocation (0.42, 0.42, 0.16) to (0.4, 0.4, 0.1).

Note that (0.2, 0.2, 0.2) is not efficient: the allocation (¼,¼,¼) gives everyone more utility. But (¼,¼,¼) is not efficient either. It represents a movement towards efficiency, but it is not itself efficient because ¾ < 1. *It's false to say that if y gives everyone a higher payoff than x then y is efficient.*

Compare allocations (⅓, ⅓, ⅓) and (1, 0, 0). Both are efficient. Therefore, a move from (1, 0, 0) to (⅓, ⅓, ⅓) will make one person worse off. *But it is false to say that the efficiency criterion stands in the way of such a change.* All that we are entitled to say is that there is no efficiency argument justifying a move from allocation $(1, 0, 0)$ to $(\frac{1}{3}, \frac{1}{3}, \frac{1}{3})$. There may be a strong fairness or equity argument for the change, however.

There is a weak version of efficiency that is often easier to work with. Its advantage lies in the fact that it is an easier definition to apply and that for most economic models the two definitions yield the same set of efficient outcomes.

DEFINITION: *Weakly Efficient Outcome*

An outcome is *weakly* efficient if it is feasible and there is no feasible outcome that would make *everyone* strictly better off.

Obviously, an efficient allocation is weakly efficient in general. If everyone can be made strictly better off then it is certainly possible to make one person better off without harming anyone. Consequently, an outcome cannot be efficient if it is not weakly efficient. However, in noneconomic contexts it is possible to have weakly efficient allocations that are not efficient. Consider, for example, a house party with n guests. One may dress casually or formally. Consequently, there are then 2^n outcomes. Assume that no one cares how anyone else dresses so each person is one of two types: C (someone who prefers to dress casually) or F (someone who prefers to dress formally). There is only one efficient outcome, the one that assigns to each person his or her most-preferred mode of dress. Any other outcome has at least one person in his least-preferred attire. This person can be made strictly better off without affecting anyone else and thus the original outcome is not efficient. However, every outcome but one is weakly efficient. Unless each guest is assigned his or her least-preferred mode of dress the outcome is weakly efficient. If even one person is in his or her most-preferred attire then that person cannot be made better off, so it is impossible to make everyone better off.

In the division of a cake model (Example 1.5) an allocation is efficient if and only if it is weakly efficient. In *any* model, an efficient outcome is weakly efficient. In the case of Example 1.5 we can show that an allocation that is not efficient cannot be weakly efficient: suppose that x is feasible but not efficient. Then there is a feasible allocation y such that $y_j > x_j$ for some j and $y_i \geq x_i$ for all i. Therefore, $\sum y_i > \sum x_i$. Define z by setting $z_h = x_h + (\sum y_i - \sum x_i)/n$ for all h. Then $z_h > x_h$ for all h. Moreover, z is feasible because $\sum z_i = \sum y_i$ and y is feasible. Then x is not even weakly efficient. Alternative z makes everyone better off than under x: any weakly efficient allocation is efficient in the division of the cake model. Hence, efficiency and weak efficiency are equivalent for this model.

We conclude this section by showing that a weakly efficient allocation is efficient in any standard *economic* model – i.e., any model that includes a good such as money (or cake) that can be divided into arbitrarily small amounts, and which everyone wants more of, and such that each person cares only about his own assignment of that good. Suppose that feasible outcome y makes person 1 strictly better off than x and leaves no one else worse off. Construct outcome z from y by having person 1 give up a small amount of money. Make this amount small enough

Table 1.2

| | *Charli* | |
	Opera	Hockey
Nan		
Opera	10,4	2,1
Hockey	0,2	3,9

so that person 1 prefers z to x. Now divide this amount evenly among the remaining individuals to complete the specification of z. Each person likes y at least as well as x. Thus, with the extra money each person $i \neq 1$ will be strictly better off at z than at x. We already know that person 1 prefers z to x. Therefore, everyone strictly prefers z to x. Hence, if it is possible to make one person better off without leaving anyone worse off, then it is possible to make everyone strictly better off.

Problem Set

(1) Two friends Nan and Charli must decide how to spend their evening. Each prefers being with the other to any outcome in which they attend different events, but Nan likes opera better than hockey and Charli likes hockey better than opera. Table 1.2 displays the payoffs, which can be used to recover their preferences. The first number in each cell is Nan's payoff, and the second is Charli's payoff. List the efficient outcomes.

(2) This question concerns a simple economic problem of distribution involving three people, Lilly, Brendan, and Leo. Specifically, there is a six-pound cake to be divided among the three. Assume that *only* the following five assignments are feasible:

$$(6, 0, 0), (2, 2, 2), (2, 1, 2), (1, 2, 3), (2, 0, 4).$$

(The first number is the amount of cake assigned to Lilly, the second is the amount of cake assigned to Brendan, and the third number is the amount of cake assigned to Leo.) Each individual cares only about his or her own consumption of cake and prefers more to less. Of the five specified assignments list the ones that are efficient.

(3) Three siblings, Jeremy, Kerri, and Tom, have jointly inherited three assets: X, a large house; Y, a yacht; and Z, a valuable painting. Each individual must receive one of the assets, so there are six possible assignments of assets to individuals. An individual's utility does not change when the other two swap assets. For each of the following three cases specify the preferences of each of the individuals so that no individual is indifferent between any two assets:

(A) There is only one efficient outcome.

(B) Every outcome is efficient.

(C) There are at least two efficient outcomes and at least one that is not efficient.

(4) Christine, Jay, and Kerri have jointly inherited five assets (call them A, B, C, D, and E). The assets are indivisible – an antique car, a sailboat, and so forth. It is left to the heirs to allocate the assets among themselves. Therefore, the feasible outcomes are the different assignments of the assets to the three individuals. The individual preferences are as follows:

Christine strictly prefers A to B, B to C, C to D, and D to E.

Jay strictly prefers E to D, D to C, C to B, and B to A.

Kerri is indifferent between each pair of assets. (If you took one asset away from her and gave her a different one in its place she would be no better off and no worse off.)

Each person gets positive utility from each asset. (If you gave someone an additional asset, he or she would be better off, whatever the asset.)

(A) List five efficient outcomes that leave Kerri with nothing.

(B) List five efficient outcomes that leave Jay with nothing.

(C) List five efficient outcomes that give each person at least one asset.

(5) This question concerns a situation in which three friends Kyle, Jackson, and Mia, have to choose between the following three alternatives:

X: studying together,

Y: going to a basketball game together, and

Z: going their independent ways.

These three alternatives, and only these alternatives, are feasible. The utility derived by each individual from each alternative is revealed Table 1.3. "Alternative X is efficient yet it does not maximize the sum of individual utilities." Is this statement correct? Explain.

(6) This question asks you to identify the efficient outcomes in a simple model with two individuals, Cathy and Vincent, and six outcomes, F, G, H, J, K, and M. Table 1.4 gives the level of utility obtained by each individual under each outcome. All six outcomes are feasible, and there are no other feasible outcomes. Which of the outcomes are efficient? Suppose that a seventh option

Table 1.3

Alternative	Kyle's utility	Jackson's utility	Mia's utility
X	1	2	3
Y	2	4	1
Z	3	1	0

Table 1.4

Payoff	F	G	H	J	K	M
Cathy's payoff	0	60	200	100	40	205
Vince's payoff	170	60	65	40	110	95

Table 1.5

Utility	A	B	X	Y	Z
U_1	1	2	5	4	3
U_2	50	0	100	1	1
U_3	1	1	1	1	1

becomes available, and it provides utility levels of 206 for Cathy and 172 for Vincent. How would the set of efficient outcomes be affected?

(7) There are three individuals (1, 2, and 3) and five feasible outcomes (A, B, X, Y, Z). Table 1.5 specifies the utility function for each person. List the efficient outcomes and the weakly efficient outcomes.

(8) Return to Example 1.4. Multiply each of the utility numbers for person 3 by 10, leaving the utility numbers of 1 and 2 unchanged. Show that the set of efficient outcomes is unchanged, even though a different outcome now maximizes total utility. This demonstrates that efficiency depends only on individual preference rankings and not on the utility numbers that we use to represent those rankings. To drive this point home, for each individual list the alternatives in order of preference. Now work out the efficient outcomes, using only those rankings. (If two alternatives have the same utility number put them in the same row of your list for the individual in question.)

1.5 EQUILIBRIUM

Each person has a given set of actions from which he or she is allowed to choose. When each person employs a strategy that maximizes his or her payoff, given the choices made by others, we will be at equilibrium. In most situations the strategy that is best for individual A depends on what individual B is expected to do. For instance, in a game of soccer – known as football outside of North America – if a player has a clear shot on goal, whether she kicks to the right or the left depends on whether she expects the goalie to move left or right.

We begin by examining a special family of games in which each person's best strategy *can* be determined independently of what the opponent is expected to do.

1.5.1 Dominant Strategy Equilibrium

This section considers a small but important family of games in which the individual's payoff-maximizing strategy is independent of the strategies that others pursue.

Table 1.6

	Player 2	
	L	*R*
Player 1		
U	5, 5	0, 10
D	10, 0	1, 1

Consider Table 1.6: Player 1 has to choose between two strategies *U* and *D*, and player 2 has to choose between the two strategies *L* and *R*. The first number in a cell is player 1's payoff, and the second number is player 2's payoff. On one hand, if person 1 thinks that her opponent will choose *L* then she'll do better playing *D* than playing *U*. When person 2 plays *L*, player 1 gets 5 by playing *U* but 10 from *D*. On the other hand, if player 1 expects her opponent to play *R* then she'll also do better playing *D* than playing *U*. The former yields 1 but the latter yields 0 when person 2 plays *R*. Therefore, player 1 should play *D*, whatever she thinks her opponent will do. We say that *D* is a *dominant strategy*.

DEFINITION: *Dominant Strategy*

S^* is a dominant strategy for player *A* if, for *any* strategy *T* available to *A*'s opponent, none of *A*'s strategies yield a higher payoff than S^* when *A*'s opponent plays *T*. (We use an asterisk to distinguish a salient strategy or outcome.)

Notice that a dominant strategy does not necessarily give a player the highest possible payoff. It is not even the case that a dominant strategy gives a player the same payoff for each of the opponent's strategies. *D* is clearly a dominant strategy for player 1 in the game of Table 1.6, but when she plays *D* she will get 10 if player 2 chooses *L* but only 1 if player 2 chooses *R*. The payoffs are quite different. But *D is a* dominant strategy because when player 2 plays *L*, player 1's payoff is higher from *D* than from *U*, and when player 2 plays *R*, player 1's payoff is also higher from *D* than from *U*.

Both players have a dominant strategy in the game represented by Table 1.6. Person 2 will do better playing *R*, whichever strategy person 1 has chosen. When player 1 plays *U*, player 2 gets 5 from *L* and 10 from *R*. If player 1 were to play *D*, player 2 would get 0 from *L* and 1 from *R*. Therefore, *R* is a dominant strategy for player 2.

If each individual has a dominant strategy then we can say with confidence that the outcome that has each individual playing his or her dominant strategy is an equilibrium.

DEFINITION: *Dominant Strategy Equilibrium*

If each individual has a dominant strategy then there is a dominant strategy equilibrium, and it results when each person chooses his or her dominant strategy.

The game that we have been analyzing is an example of a *prisoner's dilemma* game, which demonstrates that the pursuit of self-interest does not always lead to an outcome that ultimately benefits the players. In the game of Table 1.6 when each individual is guided by self-interest, person 1 will play D, person 2 will play R, and each will get a payoff of 1. However, if each had chosen the alternative strategy, then the payoff for each would have been 5. The pursuit of self-interest is self-defeating in this game. (If person 1 thinks that person 2 has studied this game and will play L, doing her part so that they can each get 5, then person 1 has a strong incentive to play D because she gets 10 that way.) The prisoner's dilemma is more fully examined in Section 1.6. We remind you that dominant strategies do not often exist. For example, the game resulting from repeated play of the prisoner's dilemma does not have dominant strategies (Section 1.7.1).

1.5.2 Nash Equilibrium

A dominant strategy equilibrium is a special case of a *Nash equilibrium*, in which each person's strategy is a *best response* to the strategies chosen by the other players. We say that S^* is player A's best response to player B's strategy T if there is no other strategy available to player A that gives her a higher payoff than S^*, given that the opponent has selected T. Consider the game described by Table 1.7: (U, L) is a Nash equilibrium because Pat's best response to L is U, and Rob's best response to U is L. It is the only Nash equilibrium, because if Pat were to play D then Rob would respond with R. But D is not Pat's best response to R.

Table 1.7

	Rob	
	L	*R*
Pat		
U	12, 10	15, 5
D	10, 20	5, 25

The unique Nash equilibrium for this game is *not* a dominant strategy equilibrium. Although Pat has a dominant strategy (her best response to L is U, and her best response to R is also U), Rob does not. Rob's best response to U is L, but if Pat were to select D then Rob's best response would be R, not L.

In any two-person game, each player has a set of available strategies, and if player 1 chooses strategy S_1 and 2 chooses S_2, we let $U_1(S_1, S_2)$ represent the resulting payoff to player 1, with $U_2(S_1, S_2)$ denoting player 2's payoff. We say that (S_1^*, S_2^*) is a Nash equilibrium if, given that player 2 plays S_2^*, there is no strategy available to player 1 that gives him a higher payoff than S_1^*, *and* given that player 1 plays S_1^* there is no strategy available to player 2 that gives him a higher payoff than S_2^*.

DEFINITION: *Nash Equilibrium with Two Players*

(S_1^*, S_2^*) is a Nash equilibrium if $U_1(S_1^*, S_2^*) \geq U_1(S_1, S_2^*)$ for every strategy S_1 available to person 1 and $U_2(S_1^*, S_2^*) \geq U_2(S_1^*, S_2)$ for every strategy S_2 available to person 2.

Because the payoff $U_1\left(S_1^*, \ S_2^*\right)$ to player 1 is the highest payoff available to him given that his opponent plays S_2^* we say that S_1^* is a *best response* to S_2^*. Note that a dominant strategy equilibrium is a special case of a Nash equilibrium: a dominant strategy is a best response to *anything* that the opponent might do.

In general, there are n players and each has a set of available strategies. We say that the strategy list $(S_1^*, \ S_2^*, \ S_3^*, \ldots, S_n^*)$ is a Nash equilibrium if for each player i the strategy S_i^* is a best response by i to the choice of S_j^* by each $j \neq i$. We may want an equilibrium to have additional properties but it should at least be self-enforcing in the sense that each person's strategy is a best response to what the others are doing.

1.5.3   The Invisible Hand

The prisoner's dilemma shows that without appropriate incentives the pursuit of self-interest can be self-defeating. Adam Smith identified a range of situations in which the pursuit of self-interest promotes the well-being of everyone, *without the need for regulation by any central authority* – except that there must be some agency to enforce the rules of the game. Consider the game represented by Table 1.8: Person 1 has to choose between two actions U and D, and person 2 has to choose between L and R. If person 2 plays R then person 1 does better playing U than playing D. But when person 1 plays U, person 2 does better switching to L. And when person 2 plays L, the best response for person 1 is to play U. Then we have a Nash

Table 1.8

		Player 2	
		L	*R*
Player 1			
U		5, 5	7, 2
D		2, 7	1, 1

equilibrium with person 1 playing U and person 2 playing L. Although an individual would rather have 7 than the 5 that he or she gets at equilibrium, the temptation to get the big payoff doesn't ruin things. The incentives still take this two-person society to the (U, L) outcome and would still do so if we changed $(7, 2)$ to $(700, 2)$ in the description of the rules of the game: Person 1 has to play U to get 700, but person 2's best response to U is to play L. We don't get an inefficient outcome in this situation, even though each player is pursuing narrow self-interest, as in the prisoner's dilemma game of Section 1.5.1.

It's a matter of incentives. If appropriate incentives are in place the pursuit of individual self-interest leads to an outcome that benefits society as a whole – without the need for a government to guide the participants. We say that we have a decentralized system – that is, the individuals are on their own to follow their self-interest. The games of this section and Section 1.5.1 are both decentralized; in one of them we get the bad outcome and in the other we do not.

1.5.4   The Incentive to Harbor Terrorists

There is a spillover benefit from any effort to eliminate terrorism undertaken by an individual country. The elimination of any terrorist cell by any country reduces the threat to other countries. With many cases of spillover benefits, the resulting game in which the players are involved is a prisoner's dilemma. But not in the case of countries seeking to protect themselves from terrorism. When country X puts more

Table 1.9

	Country B	
	Retaliate	Don't retaliate
Country A		
Retaliate	120, 150	100, 125
Don't retaliate	95, 130	105, 95

Table 1.10

	Country B	
	Retaliate	Don't retaliate
Country A		
Retaliate	120, 150	100, 125
Don't retaliate	95, 130	105, 95
Harbor	140, 75	115, 80

resources into shielding itself from terrorism, country Y becomes more vulnerable, to the extent that terrorists shift their activities away from X and toward Y. (Assume that neither country engages in terrorism.) The cost of attacking a country increases when that country increases its level of protection, and hence the probability of an attack on other countries increases.

Because of the shift in terrorist activity, the specific benefits to country X when it retaliates for acts of terrorism increases with the level of retaliation by country Y. Even if X does not have an incentive to retaliate if Y does not retaliate, if Y *does* retaliate then X is better off retaliating than being passive. Let's examine the resulting two-agent game of Table 1.9. The first number in a cell is country A's payoff, and the second number is country B's payoff. (When a country retaliates, it attacks the terrorists, not the other country.)

Table 1.9 shows that it is to country B's advantage to retaliate, whatever country A does. If A does *not* retaliate, then B's payoff is 130 for retaliation but only 95 for passivity. However, if A *does* retaliate, then B's payoff is 150 for retaliation and only 125 for passivity. Retaliation is a dominant strategy for B. Therefore, we can be sure that country B will choose to retaliate. How will country A respond? Its payoff is 120 if it retaliates, and only 95 if it doesn't. Therefore A will retaliate. We have a unique equilibrium in which both countries retaliate. (Note that A would have an incentive not to retaliate if B did not retaliate. Of course we know that B *will* retaliate.)

Table 1.10 portrays the situation in which country A has a third strategy – to harbor terrorists within its borders, in hopes of winning the terrorists' favor, and in that way shield itself from attack. Often the host country obtains a promise from the terrorists that it will not be attacked. A country that would benefit considerably from a strategy of retaliation – because a terrorist attack could be particularly devastating – might be a country that would also benefit considerably from buying protection – that is, by harboring terrorists. Note that

France, Italy, Greece, and Cyprus are among the many countries that have allowed foreign terrorists to establish a base within their own borders. Cuba has accepted a dozen United Nations' counterterrorist conventions, but it hosts a number of Latin America's most wanted terrorists, in addition to Basque terrorists and Irish Republican Army nationalists *(The Economist,* May 25, 2002, p. 30). Smallpox was eradicated in 1977 by means of a world-wide vaccination program financed by wealthy countries and coordinated by the World Health Organization. Mutual distrust motivated the rival superpowers to store vials of the smallpox virus, posing a terrorist threat (Sandler, 2004).

harboring the terrorist group is now a dominant strategy for A. On one hand, if country B retaliates then A gets a payoff of 140 from harboring, and that is higher than the payoff from either retaliating or being passive, given that B retaliates. On the other hand, if B does not retaliate then A's payoff is 115 from harboring, but A gets only 100 from retaliating and 105 from passivity when B does not retaliate. Therefore, we can expect A to harbor the terrorists. B's best response to that is passivity because it gets a slightly lower payoff from retaliation when A hosts the terrorists. Why does B retaliate in Table 1.9 but not in Table 1.10? Because part of the benefit to any country X from retaliating in the first scenario comes from offsetting the shift in terrorism activities from Y to X that results from Y's retaliation. In the second scenario, country A does not retaliate because it pays A to harbor the terrorists.

The relative magnitude of the numbers that we have used represents just one possible model. In Table 1.9, we can think of B as a country like Israel that is plagued by local terrorists whose objective is to destroy B, whereas country A is victimized by foreign terrorists whose grievances are primarily against B. For that scenario we could increase the 75 in the bottom left-hand cell (excuse the pun) of Table 1.10 to 95, in which case B would be better off retaliating than being passive when A harbors the terrorists.

1.5.5   Dissolving a Partnership

In the spring of 2002 the two co-owners of the New York Mets baseball franchise could not agree on a price at which one could sell his share of the team to the other. A variety of court actions resulted (Zimbalist, 2004). Suppose that two companies, located in different countries, have embarked on a joint project in a third country but one of the founding firms wants to discontinue the joint endeavor. In general, if one of the parties in an ongoing business wants to be released from its commitment at some stage, how should the breakup of the partners be adjudicated?

Before addressing this question, we review the two-person division of a cake problem. (Example 1.5, with $n = 2$.) An allocation x assigns the fraction x_1 of the cake to person 1 and x_2 to person 2. Allocation x is efficient if and only if $x_1 + x_2 = 1$. In particular, the allocation that assigns all of the cake to one person is efficient. (Either $x_1 = 1$ and $x_2 = 0$, or $x_1 = 0$ and $x_2 = 1$.) Such an outcome is far from fair, of course. Let's agree that $x_1 = \frac{1}{2} = x_2$ is the only *fair and efficient* allocation.

Suppose that our aim is to implement the fair and efficient allocation $x_1 = \frac{1}{2} = x_2$ in a decentralized way so that the cake is distributed evenly as the result of selfish utility-maximizing behavior by each individual. We want to design a game for which the unique Nash equilibrium gives exactly half of the cake to each person. This cannot be done without specifying the strategies available to each player and the outcome as a function of the pair of individual strategies. An appropriate mechanism is not hard to find. Let person 1 cut the cake into two pieces. With the sizes of the two pieces determined by individual 1, let person 2 choose one of the two pieces for his own consumption. Person 1 then consumes the remaining piece. The only equilibrium allocation generated by this game is the fair and efficient allocation $x_1 = \frac{1}{2} = x_2$ because person 1 knows that person 2 will choose the larger piece if 1 cuts the pieces unequally. Therefore, person 1 is sure to receive less than half the cake if she cuts the pieces unequally at stage 1. She can prevent this by cutting the cake precisely in half and this, therefore, is the strategy that ensures her the largest payoff. Consequently, person 2's choice becomes irrelevant.

This simple game has an important application in the business world. It often happens that two companies from different countries find themselves involved in a joint business venture in a third country. If at some point one of the parties is presented with a more profitable opportunity elsewhere and wants to abandon the project, there will be considerable uncertainty about the legal resolution that would be handed down by the courts. This prospect could discourage the firms from undertaking the project in the first place, and thus some socially desirable investments may not be adopted.

Some joint ventures have been undertaken after the two participants agreed to settle disputes over withdrawal by the following straightforward variant of the division of the cake mechanism: the partner that wishes to withdraw from the project names a price P at which he is willing to sell his share of the venture to the second partner. If that were all there were to it, the withdrawing partner would have a strong incentive to name an exorbitantly high price (and there would be a strong incentive to withdraw) just as person 1 would have a strong incentive to cut a cake unequally if he were the one to decide who gets the larger piece. But there is a second stage to the game: the second partner now chooses whether to buy the other out at the named price P or to *sell out* to the partner that set the price P. This forces the withdrawing partner to set a price equal to one half of the present value of the project. Here's the proof: suppose that the present value of the project is $\$V$ and the contracting parties have equal ownership shares. If the project is completed then each gets a payoff of $\frac{1}{2}V$. If partner 1 (the company wishing to withdraw) names a price $P > \frac{1}{2}V$ then partner 2 is better off selling to 1 at that price than insisting on completion. If partner 1 sets P below $\frac{1}{2}V$ then partner 2 will want to buy out partner 1 at that price and complete the project at its own expense for a net gain of $V - P > \frac{1}{2}V$. In either case, by choosing a value of P different from $\frac{1}{2}V$, partner 1 will wind up with less that $\frac{1}{2}V$ and can always ensure a payoff of exactly $\frac{1}{2}V$ by setting $P = \frac{1}{2}V$.

Because the only equilibrium solution has the withdrawing partner setting $P = \frac{1}{2}V$, why don't they simply agree in advance that $\frac{1}{2}V$ will be the price at which a partner can be bought out should he or she decide to withdraw before the project is completed? Because there will be disagreement about V. The remaining partner will claim that the project has little likelihood of generating substantial profit and will offer to buy out the other at a very low price,

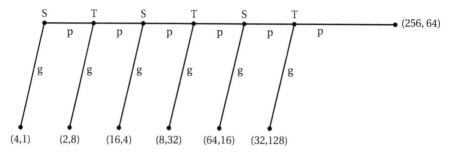

Figure 1.2

claiming that she is offering $\frac{1}{2}V$ but that V is very small. The partner selling his share in the enterprise will have a strong incentive to claim that V is very large, whatever he really believes, and hence $\frac{1}{2}V$ is large. Suppose, however, that partner 1 can name a price P and then partner 2 has the right to buy out the other at P *or* to sell her share to company 1 for P. Then partner 1 could lose heavily by naming a price that was much greater than $\frac{1}{2}V_1$, where V_1 is partner 1's estimate of the present value of the project. If partner 2's estimate of the present value were no higher than partner 1's, then partner 2 would opt to sell to partner 1 at any price P greater than $\frac{1}{2}V_1$ and the net value to partner 1 of the project would then be $V_1 - P$, which is less than $\frac{1}{2}V_1$, the payoff that partner 1 could get just by setting $P = \frac{1}{2}\ V_1$.

1.5.6   The Centipede Game

In spite of the plausibility of Nash equilibrium, there are games that have a single Nash equilibrium that is *not* a reasonable forecast of the game's outcome. One of the niftiest examples is the so-called centipede game characterized by the tree in Figure 1.2. The two players are Samantha and Tyler. As time passes we move from left to right along Figure 1.2.

The players take turns moving, and when it's a player's turn to move he or she has to choose between grabbing the money (g) and passing (p). If he or she passes then the total amount of money available doubles. When one of the players grabs then the game is over and Samantha's payoff is the first number in parentheses and Tyler's is the second number. If each player passes at each turn then the game ends at the extreme right of the diagram with Samantha receiving $256 and Tyler receiving $64. (Note that the only efficient outcomes are this one and the second-last outcome at which Samantha receives $32 and Tyler receives $128.)

What makes analyzing the game tricky is that although the total payoff doubles every time a player passes, the amount that he or she will receive if the other person responds by choosing g is cut in half. Suppose that each player passes every time it is his or her turn to move. Then Tyler will receive $64. But he can get twice as much money by grabbing on his last move instead of passing. Passing at the last stage is not a best response by Tyler to Samantha's strategy of passing at every opportunity. Therefore, the outcome that results when each player passes at each opportunity is not self-enforcing and hence not part of a Nash equilibrium.

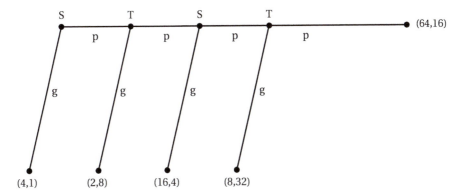

Figure 1.3

Both players can predict that the game will not end with a player passing. Suppose both players anticipate that the game will end after move t with Tyler grabbing at that stage. Then Samantha will not let the game survive to that stage because she can get twice as much money by grabbing on the previous move, instead of passing and letting the game continue. Similarly, if Samantha were expected to end the game by grabbing at stage $t > 1$, Tyler's best response would be to grab at the previous stage because he would double his payoff by doing so. Therefore, the only self-enforcing outcome has Samantha grabbing at the first opportunity and this results in a payoff of $4 for Samantha and $1 for Tyler. This is obviously far from efficient. (The game is called the centipede game because the associated diagram looks like a centipede. Moreover, one could extend the game by adding 94 more moves, with the pot continuing to double each time. The starting point would remain the only equilibrium, but it offers minuscule payoffs relative to those available later on.)

Our intuition tells us that the two players would not end up at the Nash equilibrium. In fact, McKelvey and Palfrey (1992) conducted experiments and found that the players typically finish somewhere near the middle of the centipede, not at either extreme of grabbing at the first opportunity or passing until the last move or two. Therefore, Nash equilibrium is an inappropriate solution concept in this case. Why? To identify the difficulty, we will truncate the game so that each player potentially has only two moves, as illustrated in Figure 1.3. We refer to the later move as the player's second move.

Here is a difficulty: we have implicitly assumed that both players are "rational." Rationality means that agents care only about the effect of an outcome on their own welfare, and they always act to enhance their welfare in any situation where that has an unambiguous meaning. We have also assumed that each player believes that the other is rational. Here is the argument that establishes that the unique Nash equilibrium has Samantha grabbing on the first move and receiving $4, with $1 going to Tyler: if Tyler is rational and he has the opportunity to make the last move – his second move – he will grab rather than pass because he gets $32 by grabbing and only $16 by passing. Nothing remarkable about the background assumptions so far.

Now, suppose that Samantha is rational *and* that Samantha knows that Tyler is rational. Then Samantha can deduce that Tyler will grab if he has a second move. This means that Samantha predicts that she will get $8 if Tyler is given an opportunity to make a second move. Therefore, if Samantha has the chance to make a second move, she knows that she is really choosing between $8 – if she passes – and $16 – if she grabs. She is rational, so she will grab if she has a second move. Now, suppose that Tyler is rational, Tyler knows that Samantha is rational, *and* Tyler knows that Samantha knows that Tyler is rational. Then Tyler can anticipate that Samantha will grab if Samantha has an opportunity for a second move. Then Tyler will wind up with $4 if Samantha has a second move. Therefore, on Tyler's first move – if he has one – he can obtain $8 by grabbing or $4 by passing. He is rational, so he will grab on the first move if Samantha hasn't grabbed first. And so on. The conclusion that Samantha will grab at the first opportunity is based on the following suppositions:

(1) Samantha and Tyler are each rational.

(2) Samantha knows that Tyler is rational.

(3) Tyler knows that Samantha knows that Tyler is rational.

(4) Samantha knows that Tyler knows that Samantha knows that Tyler is rational.

Statement 1 implies that Tyler will grab if he is given a second move. Statements 1 and 2 imply that Samantha will grab if she is given a second move. Statements 1–3 imply that Tyler will grab on his first move if Samantha passes on her first move. Statements 1–4 imply that Samantha will grab on the first move. Therefore, assumptions 1–4 collectively imply that the unique Nash equilibrium has each person grabbing whenever he or she is given an opportunity to move. But these assumptions are extremely unstable. If Samantha actually passes on the first move then Tyler knows that one of the four statements is false – perhaps Samantha is not rational, or perhaps she is unsure that Tyler knows that she knows that Tyler is rational – and the logical chain directing Tyler to grab at the first opportunity is broken. *Anything* can happen now.

The longer the game, the larger is the spread between the payoff a player gets by grabbing early and the payoff that awaits both players if the game ends much later. Moreover, the longer the game, the longer is the chain "I know that he knows that I know that he knows …" that is required to support the backward induction derivation that the game will end on the first move. For long games of this nature – or short ones, for that matter – we don't have a good model for predicting behavior, but at least we can see why results in which the game ends after seven or eight rounds of passing are not inconsistent with our assumption that each agent acts in his or her self-interest. Those results *are* inconsistent with the implicit assumption about what individuals know about what others know.

1.5.7 Subgame-Perfect Nash Equilibrium

The centipede game of the previous section has a single Nash equilibrium, but we don't have much confidence that it would emerge as the outcome when the game is actually played, and that is confirmed by experiments. Now we examine a game with *two* Nash equilibria, one of which is not a sensible forecast of the game's outcome. That equilibrium is implausible because it is based on a threat that is not credible. Simply put, a *subgame-perfect equilibrium* is a Nash equilibrium at which threats, if any, are credible. Before we can present a formal definition we need to prepare the ground.

A *strategy* is much more comprehensive than an *action*. "Steal second base now" is a simple instruction by a coach in a baseball game, and the attempted theft is the action. But a strategy specifies an act as a function of every act made by every participant up to the present stage of the game. "Attempt a theft of second base if we haven't reached the fifth inning, or if it is late in the game and we are behind by two or more runs, provided that the batter has fewer than two strikes and the probability of a pitch-out is less than 0.25" is a strategy. We could specify a single strategy for the manager of a baseball game for the entire game. It would specify a decision for every situation that could arise, as well as the decisions made at the beginning of the game before the opponent has taken any action.

Consider a deterministic two-person game – that is, a game between two individuals that is not affected by any random variables. Let S_1 and S_2 denote, respectively, the strategies chosen by players 1 and 2. Then the pair (S_1, S_2) uniquely determines the outcome of the game. If we display the payoffs awarded to player 1 as a function of the strategies chosen by players 1 and 2, and similarly for player 2, we have what is called the *normal form* representation of the game. The normal form payoffs are simply expressed as functions $U_1(S_1, S_2)$ and $U_2(S_1, S_2)$ of the chosen strategies. Recall that a Nash equilibrium is a pair of strategies (S_1, S_2) such that

$$U_1(S_1, S_2) \geq U_1(T_1, S_2) \text{ for every strategy } T_1 \text{ available to person 1,}$$

and

$$U_2(S_1, S_2) \geq U_2(S_1, T_2) \text{ for every strategy } T_2 \text{ available to person 2.}$$

It is helpful to think of the respective strategies S_1 and S_2 as chosen simultaneously and submitted to a referee who then computes the outcome and assigns payoffs according to the rules of the game. In a nondeterministic game there are points in the game at which a strategy calls for an act to be selected randomly by means of a given probability distribution over a given set of acts. Uncertainty may even be *imposed* on the players – the arrival of rain during a baseball game, for example. The outcome will be random, but the payoff to an individual associated with any configuration of strategies – one for each player – can still be expressed as a single number by using the probabilities as weights on the different payoffs that could arise. (See Section 2.6.1.)

An *extensive form* representation of the game has much more structure than the normal form. The extensive form provides information about the sequences of moves – whose turn it is to move at each stage and what choices that person has. A strategy for an individual prescribes an action for that person for every situation that could arise.

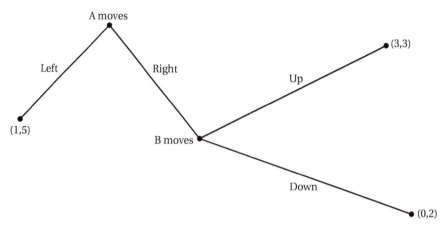

Figure 1.4

DEFINITION: *Individual Strategy*

At any point in the game at which the player is allowed to move, the strategy specifies an action for that player for each potential history of the game to that point and a single action for the game's opening move.

Example 1.6 Extensive Form Two-Person Game

The game is represented as Figure 1.4. At the first stage player A has a choice of moving left or right. If A moves left the game is over with A receiving a payoff of 1 and B receiving 5. If player A moves right at the first stage then player B has the next move and can go up or down. If B chooses up then each gets a payoff of 3, but if B moves down then A's payoff is 0 and B's payoff is 2. Consider the normal form representation of the same game displayed as Table 1.11. $R \rightarrow U$ represents the strategy "B moves Up if A has opened by moving Right," and $R \rightarrow D$ represents "B moves Down if A opened by moving Right." There are two Nash equilibria here: (Right, $R \rightarrow U$) and (Left, $R \rightarrow D$). Confirm that Right is a best response by A to $R \rightarrow U$, and that $R \rightarrow U$ is a best response by B to Right. Note also that Left is a best response by A to $R \rightarrow D$, and that $R \rightarrow D$ is a best response by B to Left.

Table 1.11

	Player B	
	$R \rightarrow U$	$R \rightarrow D$
Player A		
Left	1, 5	1, 5
Right	3, 3	0, 2

The equilibrium (Left, $R \rightarrow D$) of Example 1.6 is not a plausible one. It depends on B's threat to move Down if A moves Right. In plain words, A announces her intention to move Left, whatever B proposes to do should B get a chance to move, and B announces her intention to move Down if A moves Right. If A believes that B is really committed to Down if B gets a chance to move, then

Left is the rational choice for A: Left gives A a payoff of 1, but A gets 0 if he moves Right and B *carries out her threat* to move Down. However, B's threat is not credible. If B *does* get a chance to move it will come after A's move and thus it can have no impact on A's choice. Therefore, the payoff-maximizing move for B is Up, yielding a payoff of 3 instead of 2. A Nash equilibrium that does not depend on an incredible threat is termed a *subgame-perfect Nash equilibrium. Subgame* refers to the game that would be defined if we were to begin play at some advanced stage of the original game. Any node may serve as the origin of a subgame, *provided* that the person who moves at that stage knows the entire history of the game up to that point. The players are assumed to play best responses in the subgame. For Figure 1.4, moving Up is *the* best response for B at the second stage, so a threat to move Down is not credible. The only subgame-perfect Nash equilibrium is (Right, $R \to U$).

DEFINITION: *Subgame*

A subgame of an extensive form game is a game obtained by separating the tree at one node and retaining only that node and all parts of the tree that can be reached from that node by going forward and not backward (in time). Any node may serve as the origin of a subgame, *provided* that the person who moves at that stage knows the entire history of the game up to that point.

The prisoner's dilemma (Table 1.6 in Section 1.5.1) can be represented in extensive form: player 1 moves first and chooses between U and D. At the second node, player 2 chooses between L and R. However, at this point player 2 will not know what choice player 1 made at the first node. Therefore, player 2 will not know the prior history of the game when it is his turn to move. This game has no subgames (except for the entire game itself).

The game of Figure 1.4 has five subgames, including the original game itself: there are three trivial subgames corresponding to the three terminal nodes with respective payoff vectors (1, 5), (3, 3), (0, 2). The trivial subgames do not allow anyone to move, of course. There is only one proper and nontrivial subgame, obtained by eliminating the branches Left and Right.

If the original game includes moves in which the player taking action is not perfectly certain of what has gone before, then a subgame must have an additional property: at the node N where the separation identifying the subgame occurs, any act A by the mover M (the player who moves at N) must be included in the subgame if there is *some* prior history of the game that would make A available to M *if A* is not ruled out by the information available to M at N. A subgame-perfect equilibrium is one that remains an equilibrium for all subgames – with the equilibrium strategies amputated to fit the subgame.

DEFINITION: *Subgame-Perfect Nash Equilibrium*

A Nash equilibrium β is subgame perfect if the strategies specified by β constitute a Nash equilibrium in every subgame.

For the game of Figure 1.4, if we begin at the point where B moves we have a subgame in which B chooses between Up and Down. Clearly, Up is the only Nash equilibrium in this one-player game. Therefore, the equilibrium (Left, $R \rightarrow D$) of the original game is not subgame perfect.

For *finite* games we locate subgame-perfect equilibria by backward induction: begin with the proper subgames that are closest to a terminal node. In Figure 1.4, that would be the subgame beginning with B's move. Replace those subgames with their Nash equilibrium payoffs. For the subgame of Figure 1.4 that begins with B's move, player B has a simple choice between Up, with a payoff of 3 to herself, and Down, which gives her a payoff of 2. She would choose Up, resulting in the payoff vector (3, 3). We replace the entire subgame with (3, 3), as illustrated in Figure 1.5. We continue by induction. Having reduced the size of the game by successively abbreviating it by replacing subgames with their Nash equilibrium payoffs, we have a new game. We then identify the proper subgames that are closest to a terminal node of this new game. Then we replace those subgames with their Nash equilibrium payoffs. If at some stage we have reduced the game to one with a single move, as in Figure 1.5, the Nash equilibrium of that game gives us the subgame-perfect equilibrium of the original game. The unique Nash equilibrium of Figure 1.5 has A choosing Right, leading to a payoff of 3 for A. (His payoff would only be 1 if he chose Left.) Therefore, the unique subgame-perfect equilibrium for the game of Figure 1.4 is (Right, $R \rightarrow U$).

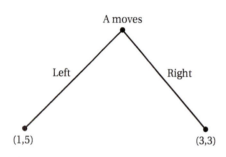

Figure 1.5

Sources

The term *Nash equilibrium* honors the mathematician John Nash, who is the subject of the book *A Beautiful Mind* by Sylvia Nasar (1998). Nash was awarded the Nobel Prize in Economics in 1994. Lee (1988) is the basis for Section 1.5.4 on terrorism. The centipede game was invented by Robert Rosenthal (1981).

Links

Myerson (1999) is an excellent study of the history of Nash equilibrium in economic analysis. Baumol (2002) discusses the contribution of Adam Smith more deeply than our static version of Section 1.5.3. There are other situations, in addition to the centipede game, in which Nash equilibrium does not appear to offer a good forecast of the outcome that would result when intelligent, self-motivated people interact. See Goeree and Holt (2001) for ten important cases. Cramton et al. (1987)

is a very advanced treatment of the problem of dissolving a partnership. See also Levin and Tadelis (2005) on profit sharing in partnerships. Subgame-perfect equilibrium is discussed at length in Binmore (1992), Gibbons (1992), Kreps (1990), and Osborne (2004). Frank (2004) offers an attractive suggestion for enriching the standard economic model in a way that is consistent with observed play of the centipede game.

Problem Set

(1) The utility functions of our two individuals are

$$U_1 = 100(e_1 + e_2) - 150e_1 \ and \ U_2 = 100(e_1 + e_2) - 150e_2$$

where e_1 is the effort contributed by individual 1 and e_2 is the effort contributed by individual 2. Each individual i can set e_i equal to *any number* between zero and one inclusive.

  (A) Given individual 2's choice of e_2, whatever that might be, what is the best response of person 1? Justify your answer.

  (B) What is the Nash equilibrium for this game? Does it result in an efficient outcome?

(2) This time there are n individuals, and e_i is the effort contributed by individual i whose utility function is

$$U_i = \alpha(e_1 + e_2 + \ldots + e_{n-1} + e_n) - \beta e_i$$

Individual i can set e_i equal to *any number* between zero and one inclusive.

  (A) Show that $e_i = 0$ is a dominant strategy for individual i if and only if $\alpha < \beta$.

  (B) For what range of values of α and β will we have $U_i(1, 1, \ldots, 1, 1) > U_i(0, 0, \ldots, 0, 0)$? Justify your answer.

  (C) If $n = 10 = \beta$, for what range of values of α is this a prisoner's dilemma game?

(3) X and Y are on the only candidates on the ballot in an election. Every voter prefers X to Y. Explain why we have a Nash equilibrium if everyone votes for Y and there are at least three voters. Is this a plausible forecast of the outcome? Are there any other Nash equilibria? (Note that each voter has a dominant strategy.)

(4) The airline has lost the luggage of two travelers. Their luggage is identical. Each is invited to submit a claim for any *integer* amount between $10 and $100 inclusive. If the claims are identical then each receives a payment equal to the common claim. If the claims are not the same then the traveler submitting the smaller claim gets that amount plus $5, and the traveler submitting the larger claim receives a payment equal to the smaller claim minus $5. Prove that the unique Nash equilibrium has each person submitting a claim for $10. This game was devised by Basu (1994). (It is noteworthy that experiments reveal a high concentration of claims around $99.)

1.6   THE PRISONER'S DILEMMA GAME

This section discusses a simple situation in which the interplay of incentives leads to an outcome that the participants deeply regret, even though the outcome is the consequence of the pursuit of self-interest: self-interest drives individual behavior but it is self-defeating in this setting. The phenomenon under discussion, the *prisoner's dilemma* paradox, has a wide range of applications; it explains many organizational failures. It is a model of a situation in which individual incentives are *not* well aligned.

> Ninety-seven people died in a Rhode Island nightclub after a fire broke out. "There was nowhere to move" (*Boston Herald*, February 26, 2003). Twenty-one people died in a Chicago nightclub after a fight provoked a panic that resulted in the exits being so completely jammed that the people stuck there couldn't move forward or backward (*Chicago Sun-Times*, February 18, 2003).

If fire is detected in a crowded building almost no one will escape alive if there is panic, and all attempt to get through the exit door at once. But if the crowd is orderly it is advantageous to any one individual to run past everyone else to get to the exit first. Panic will prevail if everyone comes to the same conclusion. However, if everyone runs to the exit then no one can gain anything by walking slowly.

The prisoner's dilemma refers to a simple game involving two players, each of whom must choose one of two options independently of the other. The game can be described abstractly but we will introduce it in its original guise: two individuals *A* and *B* have been arrested and charged with bank robbery. The police are convinced of their guilt but there is no admissible evidence on which they can be convicted of robbery, although they were carrying guns when caught and for this each can be sentenced to one year in jail. To obtain confessions to the crime of robbery the authorities interrogate them separately and offer each his complete freedom if he confesses to the robbery and his partner does not. The partner who does not confess will receive ten years in jail, but if *both* confess then each will receive a five-year sentence. The situation confronting each prisoner is summarized by Table 1.12.

The first number in a cell is *A*'s sentence, and the second number is *B*'s sentence. *A* and *B* cannot communicate with each other – or if they can communicate they can't make binding agreements. (Of course, the goal of each player is to get the lightest sentence.) Suppose that *A* believes that *B* will not confess. Then *A* will receive a sentence of one year if he does not confess, but he will not have to serve any time if he confesses. *A* receives a lighter sentence by confessing. However, suppose that *A* believes that *B will* confess. Then *A* will receive five years if he

Table 1.12

	Player B	
	Don't confess	**Confess**
Player A		
Don't confess	1, 1	10, 0
Confess	0, 10	5, 5

Table 1.13

	Player B	
	Cooperate	Defect
Player A		
Cooperate	20, 20	1, 30
Defect	30, 1	5, 5

confesses but ten years if he doesn't. Again, *A*'s self-interest is served by confessing. Whichever decision the partner in crime is expected to make, an individual does better by confessing than not confessing. They both confess and each receives a sentence of five years. If neither had confessed then each would have been free after only one year.

> US law allows a firm involved in a corporate conspiracy to escape punishment if it is the first to confess (*The Economist*, October 21, 2000, p. 67).

In this situation self-interest drives each person to take a course of action that leaves each worse off than if they had coordinated their strategies. (But notice how strong the incentive is to get one's partner to agree not to confess and then, having also solemnly sworn not to confess, to confess and go free.)

Consider the general formulation of this game, with the outcomes translated to money (or similar) payoffs, which an individual wants to *maximize*. Each person must decide whether to cooperate or to defect without knowing what choice the other will make. The payoff for each of the four possible combinations of strategies is given in Table 1.13. The first number is player *A*'s payoff, and the second number in a cell is player *B*'s payoff.

If *B* is expected to cooperate then *A* can get 20 by cooperating but 30 by defecting. If *B* is expected to defect then *A* can get 1 by cooperating and 5 by defecting. In either case the higher payoff for *A* is obtained by defecting. Defecting is a *dominant strategy*. A dominant strategy is one that is the best course of action for a decision maker regardless of the actions that others are expected to take. *B* is in exactly the same position; both will defect and each receives a payoff of 5. If each had chosen to cooperate then each would have received a payoff of 20. The equilibrium, which is the outcome when both play their dominant strategies, gives each a lower payoff than when both cooperate. The incentive to defect is irresistible, however, assuming that the game is played under two conditions. First, the two players cannot undertake a binding commitment to cooperate. Second, the game is played only once.

If the players can make commitments then the incentives could be quite different. Suppose, for example, that before playing the game the two players anticipated that each would succumb to the temptation to defect and each signed a document that required one person to pay the other a thousand dollars if he defects. This contract could also state that it was binding on a signatory only if the other person signed. This results in a new game in which both can be expected to sign the document and cooperate. (Assume that the payoffs in Table 1.13 are dollar amounts.) Now, suppose that binding agreements are not possible but the same game is repeated a number of times by the same two players. Then we have a different game with different incentives, although the tension that we have uncovered in the "one-shot" game still plays a role in the repeated game. We can still have an equilibrium in which each person defects at each stage, but the justification of this as an equilibrium is feeble compared to the story for the one-shot game. For one thing, there are no dominant strategies in the repeated version of the prisoner's dilemma game which is discussed in more detail in Sections 1.7.1 and 1.7.2.

We now turn to a consideration of seven situations for which the prisoner's dilemma game is applicable. The first five illustrate how the prisoner's dilemma incentive structure can work to the disadvantage of society. But it can also work to society's benefit, as in the case of Sections 1.6.6 and 1.6.7.

DEFINITION: *N-Person Prisoner's Dilemma*

A game with two or more players is a prisoner's dilemma if each has a unique dominant strategy and an inefficient outcome results when each plays his or her dominant strategy.

1.6.1 Economic Sanctions

Shortly after Iraq invaded Kuwait in August 1990 the United Nations Security Council imposed sanctions against Iraq. Most countries endorsed the sanctions and publicly stated a commitment not to allow imports from Iraq or to permit exports to Iraq. By December, observers in the Middle East were reporting serious leakages in the blockade. Let's look at sanctions from the standpoint of the incentives facing a typical country. Oil is the chief export of Iraq. A ban on the purchase of goods from Iraq is costly to an importing country because it reduces its options for acquiring energy. The restriction on exports is costly because trade is mutually advantageous, and to the extent that a country restricts trade it obviously limits the benefits that it receives from trade. The ban on exports would be seen in the legislature and in the press of the banning country as a threat to income and employment in that country. In addition, compliance with the sanctions would have to be monitored by the central government and that involves direct costs.

On one hand, if a large number of countries joined in the imposition of sanctions then country A would be tempted to relax its grip to recapture some of the benefits of trade, hoping that others would maintain the sanctions with sufficient determination to allow A to reap the benefit of sanctions without having to pay the cost. On the other hand, if quite a few countries allow trade to continue then country A will benefit little from any embargo that it imposes, because sanctions have little effect if they are not widely enforced. In short, the dominant strategy for each country is to allow its firms to disregard the sanctions. This is not an argument against multilateral sanctions. However, the prisoner's dilemma problem teaches that sanctions must be implemented with a clear understanding of the incentives facing individual countries and with the determination to use diplomacy and ongoing consultation to maintain compliance.

Although there was less than total compliance with the economic sanctions against Iraq, there was enough of an effect to cause serious hardship among the Iraqi poor. In 1995 the United Nations instituted an oil-for-food program to relieve the suffering. Iraq was allowed to export a limited amount of oil at a limited price. The revenue was paid into a United Nations escrow account, to be used only for essentials – food and medicine, in particular. The program apparently led to a wide range of abuses including smuggling, illegal commissions, bribes, and kickbacks. At least $2 billion wound up in the bank account of the dictator, Saddam Hussein. More surprising are the charges that up to $10 billion found its way into the pockets of officials outside of Iraq (*The Economist*, May 1, 2004, pp. 46–47).

1.6.2 Public Opinion

It is costly for an individual to stay well informed on issues before national legislatures. The cost of investing the time required to develop an intelligent opinion on each critical public event is considerable. Moreover, the personal benefit from the resulting improvement in the quality of public opinion is negligible because a single individual's viewpoint, whether sound or silly, has a negligible effect. Whether others are well informed or not, an individual's own utility is maximized by investing in knowledge up to the point where the benefit *to him or her* from any additional investment would be more than offset by the cost. This results in citizens generally not being well enough informed from the standpoint of their own welfare. If everyone were to invest additional time in studying current events then public opinion would induce better public decisions that would benefit everyone.

1.6.3 Automobile Emissions

Suppose that consumers in a country with an unregulated automobile industry have a choice between cars produced without emission control devices and those that have equipment that eliminates most harmful exhaust but cost $3,000 more than those without. (The emission control equipment costs $3,000 per car to manufacture and install.) Given the choices made by others, whatever they are, the purchase of a pollution-free car would cost the individual $3,000 extra but would not appreciably improve the quality of the air. Clearly, purchasing the cheaper, polluting automobile is a dominant strategy. Everyone makes this choice and thus automobile traffic generates substantial pollution. One could specify the payoffs so that everyone would be better off if each paid a $3,000 charge to eliminate pollution caused by automobile exhaust, but the individual incentives push the society away from this outcome. Knowing this, manufacturers will not install emissions controls in the first place.

The Environmental Protection Agency was formed in the United States in 1970. Before that time pollution was regulated in part by private lawsuits. The prisoner's dilemma phenomenon was involved here as well. Individuals get the benefit of any pollution-reduction strategy financed by their neighbors, whether or not they themselves make a contribution. Declining to help pay the legal costs of a lawsuit is a dominant strategy for each individual. Hence, there is less than the socially optimal amount of pollution abatement when we rely exclusively on private lawsuits to regulate behavior.

1.6.4 Beggar-Thy-Neighbor Policies

The great depression of the 1930s had most industrial countries in its grip, and individual nations were unable to resist the temptation to devalue their currencies. Given the exchange rates of other countries, if one country devalued its currency then its goods would be cheaper to the rest of the world and its own citizens would import less as other countries' goods rose in price in terms of the domestic currency. The result is a stimulus to the devaluing country's industries at the expense of other countries. (It was thus called a beggar-thy-neighbor policy.) But the same temptation confronts each nation. Import restriction is a dominant strategy. Each country attempts to divert demand from imports to domestically produced goods. That leads to a reduction in *each* country's exports, and the worldwide depression deepens.

1.6.5 Disarmament

In this example the players are countries. Defecting in this case is a decision to arm heavily. Cooperation is the decision to maintain only a defensive posture. If country *A* expects others to cooperate *A* has an incentive to obtain an extra measure of security by arming heavily. If the same country expects others to arm heavily then national security demands that the country arm heavily. Arming heavily is a dominant strategy for each country. Alternatively, imagine that war has broken out between *A* and *B* and that defecting corresponds to the use of chemical weapons in combat. Without introducing any other considerations, our analysis predicts that the use of chemical weapons would be commonplace. But that's not what we observe. *Because* defecting is a dominant strategy in these situations, nations generally have a responsibility to convince belligerents that the employment of particularly heinous methods of warfare (or violations of the Geneva conventions on the treatment of prisoners of war, etc.) will be counterproductive. In other words, it has to be brought to bear on *A* and *B* that they are playing a larger game than the immediate one-shot prisoner's dilemma game.

1.6.6 Cartels

Producer cartels form to keep industry supply low and price high. This provides each member of the cartel with more profit than when they compete vigorously against each other. When the firms actively compete then the industry output will be high, and price low, because each firm's output will be relatively high. Cooperation in the cartel context requires a firm to stick to the cartel agreement by restricting its own supply. If each firm does this the market price will be high. If the price is high then an individual firm has a strong incentive to increase its profit by producing more output. If every firm does this the market output will be high and the price low. This is a case where the incentive structure, which leads to an inefficient outcome from the standpoint of the *group of producers*, works to the benefit of society as a whole: individual incentives promote competition in spite of the substantial profits awaiting the shareholders in firms that can get their competitors to agree to cooperate in restricting output. The original prisoners' dilemma, in which suspects are interrogated, is another instance in which society is served although the individuals playing the game deeply regret the outcome.

Table 1.14

	Maggie	
	Hold	Sell 2 shares
Andre		
Hold	36, 36	20, 40
Sell 2 shares	40, 20	30, 30

1.6.7 Hostile Takeovers

DianeCam corporation has two owners, Maggie and Andre, each of whom owns two shares in the firm. The current market value of a share is $10. Maria, an outsider, wants to acquire all four shares in the firm and then replace the current manager with a more effective one. This will raise DianeCam's profit and hence the market value of a share from $10 to $18. Therefore, Maria could offer to buy the outstanding shares at $15 each. This would give Maggie and Andre a nice profit. But, why would they sell if the shares will be worth even more after the takeover?

Maria can get around this difficulty by means of a *two-tier offer*. She offers to pay $20 per share for the first two shares tendered and buy the next two at $10 each, but if Maggie and Andre simultaneously tender two shares each then Maria will pay each owner $20 + $10 for two shares. Maggie and Andre now face a prisoner's dilemma problem represented by Table 1.14.

If Maggie holds onto her shares, waiting for the takeover to drive their value up to $18, then Andre will get at most $18 per share if he also holds out (but only $10 if there is no change in management). Andre would get $20 for each of his two shares if he tenders them to Maria and Maggie doesn't sell. On the other hand, if Maggie tenders her two shares immediately then Andre gets $10 for each of his two shares if he holds out, but a total of $20 + $10 if he also sells right away. (A condition of sale at the $20 price is that DianeCam will be merged with a company Maria already owns, once Maria has 50 percent of the shares, and the outstanding DianeCam shares will be purchased for $10 each.) Whatever Maggie elects to do, Andre does better by selling his shares immediately. Maggie is in the same position vis-à-vis Andre. Because selling is a dominant strategy, the takeover will be consummated. Even if there is no takeover when they both hold out, their shares will be worth only $10 each, so selling is still a dominant strategy. (From an economy-wide perspective, takeovers may improve the performance of managers, who risk being dismissed by a new owner if the firm has been relatively unprofitable. See the discussion in Section 4.1 of Chapter 4.)

Sources

The prisoner's dilemma game was invented by Dresher and Flood at Rand in the 1950s. Professor Albert Tucker of Princeton University immediately recognized its great significance for social studies. The example of Section 1.6.7 is based on Ryngaert (1988).

Links

Poundstone (1992) is an informative book on the history of the prisoner's dilemma game. Both Osborne (2004) and Binmore (1992) provide a thorough analysis of the game. Page 28 of Osborne (2004) gives an excellent account of experiments involving the prisoner's dilemma. See Downs (1957), pages 207–219, for a thorough discussion of the public opinion "game" of Section 1.6.2. Frank (2004) offers an attractive suggestion for enriching the standard economic model in a way that is consistent with observed play of the prisoner's dilemma game.

Problem Set

(1) Table 1.15 gives you enough information to set up three different games. In each case player 1 has two available strategies, U and D, and player 2 also has two available strategies, called L and R in her case. The table gives you each player's payoff (or utility) for each of the four possible pairs of strategies. For each game, determine if it is a prisoner's dilemma game, and defend your answer.

(2) Consider a market served by two firms with identical cost functions $C_i = Q_i$, where Q_i is firm i's output and C_i is the firm's total cost. The market demand curve is $Q = 82 - 2P$.

   (A) Determine the market output and price when the two firms form a cartel that restricts output to maximize industry profit.

   (B) Assuming that the cartel imposes a quota on each firm equal to half the industry profit-maximizing level of output, what is the firm's profit under the cartel arrangement?

   (C) Now assume that consumers will buy only from firm i if it breaks the cartel agreement and charges a price of $15 when the other firm continues to charge the cartel price. What profit will each firm receive if firm i maximizes profit given a price of $15 and given the market demand curve?

   (D) If a firm has a choice of only two strategies – charge $15 or charge the cartel price – show that they are playing a prisoner's dilemma game.

(3) Determine which of the five two-person games defined by Table 1.16 are examples of the prisoner's dilemma game. In each case each individual must choose one of two strategies: A controls the rows and B controls the columns. In other words, A must choose between Up or Down and B must choose between Left or Right. Each combination of strategies determines a payoff to each person as indicated in the table: the first number in a cell is A's payoff and the second number is B's. Each player wants to maximize his or her

Table 1.15

Strategy pair		Game 1		Game 2		Game 3	
S_1	S_2	U_1	U_2	U_1	U_2	U_1	U_2
U	L	-5	10	5	5	10	12
U	R	10	5	7	1	5	5
D	L	-10	5	1	7	5	40
D	R	5	-5	8	2	20	24

Table 1.16

Game	Left	Right
Game 1		
Up	15, 15	2, 8
Down	8, 2	10, 10
Game 2		
Up	12, 12	20, 2
Down	2, 20	5, 5
Game 3		
Up	5, 50	50. 0
Down	0, 500	10, 100
Game 4		
Up	7, 7	4, 10
Down	4, 10	5, 5
Game 5		
Up	100, 100	4, 102
Down	102, 4	5, 5

Table 1.17

	Ryan	
	Cooperate	**Defect**
Jodi		
Cooperate	10, 10	2, 15
Defect	15, 2	5, 5

payoff and the players cannot make binding contracts. (All of which says that we have the standard setting.)

(4) Consider the prisoner's dilemma of Table 1.17. Suppose that Ryan and Jodi play the game three times in succession and each knows that the game will end after three periods. Show that defecting every period is *not* a dominant strategy even though the unique (Nash) equilibrium results in each person defecting each period. (You don't have to prove that a Nash equilibrium results in each person defecting at each stage; you just have to show that the player who always defects is not employing a dominant strategy.)

1.7 REPETITION AND EQUILIBRIUM

A short-run decision can affect a firm or individual's long-run reputation, and that makes it easier to devise incentives under which agents can act to maximize individual payoffs without precipitating an inefficient outcome. Specifically, cooperation can emerge when the players have an opportunity to punish anyone who sacrifices overall group welfare by pursuing short-run personal gain. With repeated play there will be future periods in which the punishment can take place. That means that there are equilibria in which each player faces a *credible* threat of punishment should he or she deviate from the path that results in an efficient outcome. Our intuition will be confirmed by the theory when the number of repetitions is infinite. In fact, just as there are typically many efficient outcomes, there are typically many equilibrium paths if the number of repetitions is infinite. All of this depends on there always *being* a future, which is not the case in the last period if the number of repetitions is finite.

We begin with the repeated prisoner's dilemma game, but first we recall the definition of a strategy from Section 1.5.7.

DEFINITION: *Individual Strategy*

At any point in the game at which the player is allowed to move, the strategy specifies an action for that player for each potential history of the game to that point and a single action for the game's opening move.

1.7.1   Repeated Prisoner's Dilemma with Terminal Date

If we stick to the assumption of selfishness at every turn, then the only equilibrium when the prisoner's dilemma game is played a fixed *finite* number of times has each person defecting at each stage, provided that both players know when play will end.

At each stage the players simultaneously and independently choose between defecting (D) and cooperating (C), and payoffs are then awarded according to Table 1.18, where $\ell < d < c < h$. This game is played exactly T times in succession. We assume that each individual's overall payoff from the repeated game takes the form

Table 1.18

	Player B	
	C	**D**
Player A		
C	c, c	ℓ, h
D	h, ℓ	d, d

$$\alpha_1 u_1 + \alpha_2 u_2 + \cdots + \alpha_{T-1} u_{T-1} + \alpha_T u_T$$

where u_t is the player's payoff in period t and α_t is some positive weight. (The weights can be different for different players.) What will happen? Because the terminal date is known the game unravels with each defecting in each period.

Equilibrium Theorem for the Finitely Repeated Prisoner's Dilemma

Both individuals will defect at each stage if there is a fixed number of repetitions, and both players know when the game will end. This Nash equilibrium is subgame perfect.

Proof:

At the Tth and last stage there is only one possible outcome: both defect because there is no further play, and thus no opportunity for their choices to affect future payoffs, and defecting is a dominant strategy for the one-shot game. Knowing that both will inevitably defect at the last stage, independent of what has happened previously, there can be no advantage to anyone who cooperates at the second-last stage – nothing will induce the opponent to cooperate in the last round. An individual's chosen action in period $T - 1$ then depends solely on the payoffs in that period, and we know that defecting is a dominant strategy in that context. Therefore, both will defect in round $T - 1$. Knowing that both will inevitably defect in the last two rounds, independently of what has happened previously, there can be no advantage to anyone who cooperates in stage $T - 2$. Therefore, both will defect in round $T - 2$, and so on. The only equilibrium has each person defecting at each stage.   ∎

The equilibrium is subgame perfect because the argument of proof works for any subgame. (Section 1.5.7 defines subgame perfection.)

Even though the only Nash equilibrium in the finitely repeated prisoner's dilemma game has each person defecting each period, it is not true to say that defecting each period is a dominant strategy. This is not even true for two repetitions. Suppose that $T = 2$, $a_1 = 1 = a_2$, and we have $c = 20$, $d = 5$, $\ell = 1$, and $h = 30$ as in Table 1.13 at the beginning of Section 1.6. Suppose that A announces his intention to cooperate in the first period, and then to cooperate again in the second period *if* B has also cooperated in the first period, and to defect in the second period if B defected in the first period. (I don't mean to imply that this is a smart decision on A's part; it may or may not be.) This is called the *tit-for-tat* strategy. If B defects in both periods her payoff will be $30 + 5$ but if B cooperates in the first period and then defects in the second period her payoff will be $20 + 30$. (Will that give A second thoughts about playing tit-for-tat?) Given A's tit-for-tat strategy, the cooperate-then-defect strategy gives B a higher total payoff than the defect-then-defect strategy, and therefore the latter is not a dominant strategy. Defecting in both periods is, however, a payoff-maximizing response of B to the announcement by A that he will defect in both periods. Therefore, we have not contradicted the assertion that defection in each period by each player is a Nash equilibrium. (To prove that it is the *only* Nash equilibrium one needs to do more.)

DEFINITION: *The Tit-For-Tat Strategy*

The individual cooperates in period 1 and for any subsequent period t will cooperate in that period if the opponent has cooperated in the previous period, but will defect if the opponent defected in the previous period.

We have seen that the predictions of economic theory based on Nash equilibrium are not always intuitive, and not always confirmed by experiments or observations. An important contribution to the study of the finitely repeated prisoner's dilemma game, and hence to the understanding of the conditions under which cooperation will be induced by rational self-motivated behavior, is the competition devised by Robert Axelrod in which opponents formulated strategies for playing prisoner's dilemma. The strategies competed against each other in a round robin tournament in which each match consisted of repeated play of the prisoner's dilemma game. The tit-for-tat strategy, submitted by Anatol Rapoport, was the winner. Although it did not beat any other strategy it scored highest because it was a survivor: other strategies reduced each other's scores when pitted against each other.

1.7.2 Infinitely Repeated Prisoner's Dilemma

Suppose that neither player knows when the interaction is going to end. We can model this by investigating a supergame in which the one-shot prisoner's dilemma game is played period after period without end. (The one-shot game is also called the stage game.) Even when there is a finite terminal date, having an infinite number of periods in the model is a simple way to embody the fact that the players don't let that terminal date influence their behavior in the early and intermediate stages. We will see that when the game is played an infinite number of times there is an abundance of equilibria. As in any dynamic game, a strategy specifies one's choice at each stage as a function of the possible previous choices of both players, so there is a vast number of strategies and many of these are equilibria.

Players A and B simultaneously and independently choose whether to cooperate or defect in each of an infinite number of periods $1, 2, \ldots, t \ldots$ An individual's preferences are captured by the discounted sum of her payoff each period. That is, her period t payoff u_t is discounted by the factor δ^{t-1}, where $0 < \delta < 1$. Because $\delta < 1$, the discount factor will be close to zero if t is very large. (We simplify by assuming the same discount factor for each individual.) The individual's overall payoff from playing the infinitely repeated prisoner's dilemma game is

$$\sum \delta^{t-1} u_t = u_1 + \delta u_2 + \delta^2 u_3 + \ldots + \delta^{t-1} u_t + \ldots.$$

If the game will end in finite time, but the individual does not know the terminal date, then we can view δ^{t+1} as proportional to the probability that period t is the last time the game will be played. For $0 < \delta < 1$ the more remote the time period the lower is the probability that it will be reached, and far distant dates have a very low probability of being reached.

The discount factor can also be viewed as a measure of patience (or impatience). If $0 < \delta < 1$ but δ is close to 1 then $a\delta^t$ is close to a — the individual is patient: the present value of a dollars received $t + 1$ periods from now, will be close to a: the individual is patient, and distant rewards get almost as much weight as current ones. But if δ is small and, say, $\delta^t < \frac{1}{2}$ the individual gets higher utility from $\frac{1}{2}a$ now than a received $t + 1$ years from now.

If $\delta = (1 + r)^{-1}$ and r is the (positive) rate of interest then we certainly have $0 < \delta < 1$. In fact, if the individual can borrow and lend at the rate of interest r, and the payoffs from the stage game are in money terms, then the individual will act so as to maximize $\sum \delta^{t-1} u_t$ because that maximizes the right-hand side (the wealth term) of the individual's intertemporal budget constraint, without affecting the left-hand side (the expenditure term) of that constraint.

The generic one-shot game is again represented by Table 1.18 of the previous subsection. One equilibrium pair of strategies that induces universal cooperation when δ is sufficiently close to 1 has each person cooperating in the first period and cooperating every period thereafter as long as his opponent cooperated in all previous periods, but defecting every period subsequent to a defection by the opponent. This is called the *grim trigger strategy*.

DEFINITION: *The Grim Trigger Strategy*

The individual cooperates in period 1 and any subsequent period t if the opponent has cooperated in every previous period. The individual defects in every period following a stage in which the opponent defected.

The name derives from the fact that a defection in any period triggers a severe punishment – defection by the other player in every subsequent period.

Consider the special case $c = 20$, $d = 5$, $\ell = 1$, and $h = 30$. Let's see why we have a Nash equilibrium if each adopts the grim trigger strategy and the discount rate is not too low. Suppose that player B uses the grim trigger strategy but player A cooperates in periods 1, 2, ..., $t - 1$ and defects in period t. Then player B will cooperate up to and including period t and defect every period thereafter. Now, compare A's payoffs *discounted to period t* from the grim trigger strategy to the overall payoff from the deviation. The deviation produces a payoff of 30 in period t and at most 5 in every subsequent period. Treating period t as "now," the discounted stream of payoffs, 30, 5, 5, ..., 5, ... is no larger than

$$30 + \delta 5 + \delta^2 5 + \delta^3 5 + \ldots = 30 + \frac{5\delta}{1 - \delta}.$$

Let S_t denote the sum $a\delta + a\delta^2 + \ldots + a\delta^t$ of t terms. Then $\delta S_t = a\delta^2 + a\delta^3 + \ldots + a\delta^t + a\delta^{t+1}$. Then $S_t - \delta S_t = a\delta - a\delta^{t+1}$. We can solve this equation for S_t, yielding

$$S_t = \frac{a\delta - a\delta^{t+1}}{1 - \delta}.$$

If $0 < \delta < 1$ then $a\delta^t$ approaches zero as t gets arbitrarily large. In that case, S_t gets arbitrarily close to $a\delta/(1 - \delta)$ as t gets arbitrarily large. Then we can say that $a\delta/(1 - \delta)$ is the sum of the infinite series $a\delta + a\delta^2 + a\delta^3 + \ldots + a\delta^t + \ldots$ *if* $0 < \delta < 1$. [The sum $\delta 5 + \delta^2 5 + \delta^3 5 + \ldots$ is $5\delta/(1-\delta)$.]

The trigger strategy, which has A and B cooperating every period, yields a discounted payoff of

$$20 + \delta 20 + \delta^2 20 + \delta^3 20 + \ldots = \frac{20}{1 - \delta}.$$

Deviation from the grim trigger strategy can be profitable for A only if

$$30 + \frac{5\delta}{1 - \delta} > \frac{20}{1 - \delta},$$

which is equivalent to $\delta < 0.4$. (To discount to the present multiply the payoffs discounted to period t by δ^{t-1}. That will lead to the same inequality.) Therefore, if $\delta \geq 0.4$ and both play the grim trigger strategy we have a Nash equilibrium. To summarize: if the discount factor δ is small ($\delta < 0.4$) then A is impatient, and gives low weight to payoffs that arrive in the future. Then impatient A will cooperate in the first period but defect in every subsequent period, leading B to defect in every period after the second. If δ is large ($\delta > 0.4$) then the players are patient, in which case a one-time gain from defecting will not be enough to offset the loss from an infinite number of periods in which both players defect.

If $\delta = (1 + r)^{-1}$ then $\delta < 0.4$ is equivalent to $r > 1.5$: only when the interest rate is greater than 150 percent can it be profitable for a player to deviate from the trigger strategy, which induces cooperation in each period. The cooperative outcome can be sustained as long as the players are not inordinately impatient.

The grim trigger strategy equilibrium is not subgame perfect. Consider A's payoff in the subgame following the choice of D by A in period t, with each playing C in each prior period, and B playing C in period t. The trigger strategy has A playing C in the first period of the subgame (period $t + 1$ of the parent game) and B playing D to punish A for the choice of D in period t. Then both will play D in every subsequent period and hence A's payoff stream from period $t + 1$ on will be $\ell, d, d \ldots d, \ldots$ If A were to deviate slightly and play D from period $t + 1$ on then her payoff stream would be $d, d, d, \ldots, d, \ldots$ and, because $d > \ell$, that is better for A for any (positive) value of the discount factor.

We can modify the grim trigger strategy slightly to produce a subgame-perfect equilibrium that sustains cooperation: have each individual cooperate in period 1 and in any period t if the opponent has cooperated in every previous period, but have the individual defect in every period following a stage in which *either* player defected.

If $c > (h + \ell)/2$ then the cooperative outcome also results from the more conciliatory *tit-for-tat* strategy that has a player cooperating in the first period, and in every subsequent period playing whatever strategy the opponent employed in the previous period. We investigate this claim for the generic stage game.

DEFINITION: *The Tit-For-Tat Strategy*

The individual cooperates in period 1 and for any subsequent period t will cooperate in that period if the opponent has cooperated in the previous period, but will defect if the opponent defected in the previous period.

Theorem:

> If $c > (h + \ell)/2$ then both agents playing tit-for-tat constitutes a Nash equilibrium of the infinitely repeated prisoner's dilemma game.

Proof:

We put ourselves in the shoes of player A. Assume that B is playing tit-for-tat. Let's see if tit-for-tat is a best response. When both play tit-for-tat each will wind up choosing C every period, so each will get c every period, and hence A's overall payoff will be $c/(1 - \delta)$. Now, suppose that A chooses D in every period. Then A will get h in the first period but d ever after because B will play D in every period after the first. The resulting overall payoff to A will be

$$h + \delta d + \delta^2 d + \delta^3 d + \ldots = h + \frac{\delta d}{1 - \delta}.$$

The overall payoff from tit-for-tat will be higher if $c/(1 - \delta) > h + \delta d/(1 - \delta)$, and that is equivalent to $\delta > (h - c)/(h - d)$. (Note that $h - c$ is less than $h - d$.) If δ is sufficiently close to 1 (i.e., if A is sufficiently patient) then playing tit-for-tat gives A a higher payoff than defecting every period – when B plays tit-for-tat.

Consider a different strategy for A: suppose that A were to defect in the first period but then cooperate in period 2 and play tit-for-tat thereafter. B is playing tit-for-tat from the start, so A's sequence of actions will be $D, C, D, C, D, C, D, \ldots$ and B's will be $C, D, C, D, C, D, C, \ldots$: they alternate defecting and cooperating, but not in tandem. Then A's sequence of stage-game payoffs will be $h + \ell + h + \ell + \ldots$ resulting in the overall payoff for the repeated game of

$$h + \delta \ell + \delta^2 h + \delta^3 \ell + \ldots = h + \delta^2 h + \delta^4 h + \delta^6 h \ldots + \delta \ell + \delta^3 \ell + \delta^5 \ell + \delta^7 \ell. \ldots$$

The sum of the terms involving h is $h/(1 - \delta^2)$ and the sum of the terms involving l is $\delta l/(1 - \delta^2)$. When do we have

$$\frac{c}{1 - \delta} > \frac{h}{1 - \delta^2} + \frac{\delta \ell}{1 - \delta^2}?$$

Multiplying both sides of the inequality by the positive number $1 - \delta^2$ reveals that it is equivalent to

$$c(1 + \delta) > h + \delta \ell.$$

Because $c > (h + \ell)/2$ (by assumption), $2c > h + \ell$ and hence for $\delta < 1$ arbitrarily close to 1 we have $c(1 + \delta)$ arbitrarily close to $2c$, and hence $c(1 + \delta) > h + \delta \ell$. Therefore, if player B's strategy is tit-for-tat then A cannot do better than tit-for-tat by alternating between D and C.

Suppose that player A waits until period t to begin defecting every period or to begin alternating between D and C. In that case, the deviant strategies will have the same payoff for A as tit-for-tat up to and including period $t - 1$. We can then discount future-stage game payoffs back to period t and this will lead us back to the inequalities of the previous two paragraphs.

For a sufficiently high discount rate, tit-for-tat is a superior response to tit-for-tat than defecting every period or alternating between D and C. What about other strategies? Continue to assume that B plays tit-for-tat but suppose that A plays C in each of the first three periods, then plays D for the next two periods, and then C every period thereafter. Compare A's overall payoff from this strategy to tit-for-tat. Each strategy yields c in each of the first three periods and c in the seventh period and every subsequent period. Therefore, we can begin the comparison at period 4 and end it in period 6, discounting the payoffs to period 4: the deviant strategy yields $h + \delta d + \delta^2 \ell$ and tit-for-tat yields $c + \delta c + \delta^2 c$. We can make $h + \delta^2 \ell$ as close as we like to $h + \ell$ and $c + \delta^2 c$ as close as we like to $2c$ by taking δ sufficiently close to 1. Then with $c > (h + \ell)/2$ we have $c + \delta^2 c > h + \delta^2 \ell$ for δ sufficiently close to 1. And $\delta c > \delta d$ for any $\delta > 0$. Therefore, tit-for-tat is superior to the deviant strategy. If A were to play C for three periods then D for n periods and then C ever after we would have essentially the same argument, except that we would compare $h + \delta^n l$ to $c + \delta^n c$, but again with $c > (h + \ell)/2$ we have $c + \delta^n c > h + \delta^n \ell$ for δ sufficiently close to 1. It is clear that any strategy that elicits a different stream of payoffs from tit-for-tat will be inferior to tit-for-tat if the opponent plays tit-for-tat and if δ is sufficiently close to 1.

There are many other equilibria. For instance, if both players announce that they will defect at every stage regardless of their opponent's behavior then an individual's payoff will fall if he or she does not defect in each period: the opponent will defect in period t, so playing C leads to a lower payoff in that period than D, and hence to a lower overall payoff. Moreover, in this case choosing C will not induce the opponent to act in a future period in a way that enhances the player's overall payoff. Note that this argument is valid for any value of the discount factor δ. Note also that this equilibrium gives each person a payoff of d each period, whereas tit-for-tat leaves each person with c at each stage.

Surprisingly, we can use a variant of the grim trigger strategy to sustain a wide range of overall payoffs at equilibrium. Let S_A be any strategy for A and let S_B be any strategy for B. Player i can threaten to punish player j if the latter doesn't follow the pattern of choices prescribed by S_j.   ∎

DEFINITION: *The Grim Trigger Strategy in General*
Arbitrary individual i performs the actions required by S_i in each period, as long as the other player j has performed the actions required by S_j in each previous period. But if j deviates from S_j in some period then i will defect in every subsequent period.

The grim trigger strategy will induce A to behave according to S_A and B to act according to S_B provided that (i) each would prefer the resulting overall payoff to a payoff of d every period after some time t, and (ii) each is sufficiently patient. The next section clarifies the role of condition (i).

Example 1.7 A Run of Cs and Ds

Suppose that S_A and S_B each have the player cooperating for three periods and then defecting for two periods, and then repeating the cycle indefinitely. The string of payoffs for each is $c, c, c, d, d, c, c, c, d, d \ldots$ If A deviates from S_A in a period t when B chooses C then A will get h instead of c. However, if δ is sufficiently close to 1, we can think of the overall payoff from S_A starting from period t as

$$c + c + c + d + d + c + c + c + d + d + \ldots$$

If B employs the grim trigger strategy we can think of the deviation as precipitating at best

$$h + d + d + d + d + d + d + d + d + d \ldots$$

for player A. The resulting period t gain of $h - c$ from the deviation is swamped by infinite number of periods in which A gets c instead of d by following S_A. Therefore (S_A, S_B) augmented by the grim trigger strategy is a Nash equilibrium for δ sufficiently large.

To turn any Nash equilibrium based on the grim trigger strategy into a subgame-perfect equilibrium we just have to require the individual to play D every period following a deviation from the prescribed behavior S_A or S_B by *either* A or B, respectively.

1.7.3 Equilibrium Theory for Infinitely Repeated Games

The argument of Section 1.7.2, showing that a wide range of strategy pairs can be sustained as a Nash equilibrium of the infinitely repeated prisoner's dilemma game, is easy to generalize to the infinite replication of any n-person game in which each person has a finite number of available actions.

Let's quickly review the prisoner's dilemma case: the strategy "play D every period" yields a payoff of at least d every period – the payoff will be either d or h – and thus yields an overall payoff of at least $d/(1 - \delta)$. Assuming a discount factor δ sufficiently close to 1, the grim trigger strategy, which relegates a player to d one period after a defection *and* every subsequent period, can be used to induce each player to stick to a given strategy, provided that it yields a higher overall payoff than $d/(1 - \delta)$. We refer to d as a player's *security level* in the one-shot prisoner's dilemma game. By playing D an individual is assured of getting at least d, and she could wind up with less by playing C.

To generalize the argument to a replication of an arbitrary one-shot n-person game we need do little more than identify arbitrary player i's security level. We seek a stage game payoff m such that i can guarantee that her payoff is at least m by choosing some action M. Specifically, for each assignment a of actions to the other players, let $\max(a)$ be i's payoff from her best response to a. Now let a^* be the assignment of actions to players other than i that minimizes $\max(a)$. Set $m = \max(a^*)$. (We're assuming that each player has a finite set of available actions.)

DEFINITION: *The Individual's Security Level*

Given a one-shot game, let A denote the set of all logically possible assignments of actions to everyone but i, and for each a in A let max(a) be the highest payoff that i can achieve when the others play a. Then if a^* minimizes max(a) over all a in A we set $m = $ max(a^*) and refer to it as player i's security level.

As in Section 1.7.2 we assume that an individual evaluates the stream of payoffs resulting from an infinite number of plays of a one-shot game by discounting to the present. If the player's period t payoff is u_t (where $t = 1, 2, 3, \ldots$) and δ is her discount factor, then her overall payoff is

$$\sum \delta^{t-1} u_t = u_1 + \delta u_2 + \delta^2 u_3 + + \delta^{t-1} u_t + \ldots.$$

The equilibrium theorem for infinitely repeated games establishes that any pattern of actions in the infinitely repeated game that allows each player to do better than her security level can be precipitated by some Nash equilibrium, provided that all players evaluate their payoff streams with a discount factor sufficiently close to one. That's because the generalized grim trigger strategy can be used to prevent anyone from deviating from the given course of action. To prove this we need to clarify the statement "doing better than" by means of some preliminary notation and definitions.

A strategy profile S for a repeated n-person game assigns a strategy S_i to each player i. Given a strategy profile S, for arbitrary individual i, and arbitrary period t we let $U_i^t(S)$ be i's payoff stream from period t on, discounted to period t, assuming that each individual j employs S_j. Let $\overline{U}_i$ be the value of the stream of i's *security-level* payoffs, received every period, discounted to period t.

Equilibrium Theorem for Infinitely Repeated Games

Let S be a strategy profile such that $U_i^t(S) > \overline{U}i$ for each individual i for each period t. If each individual is sufficiently patient there is a subgame-perfect Nash equilibrium in which each individual i behaves according to S_i at equilibrium.

Proof:

To show that S is sustained by a Nash equilibrium we just have each individual employ a generalized trigger strategy. Each individual i follows S_i provided that no individual j has deviated from S_j in the past. After a deviation by any individual, every other person employs the action that, collectively, drives the deviating individual to his or her security level and takes that action in every subsequent period, ad infinitum. This typically does not give us a *subgame*-perfect equilibrium, but it is possible to refine the strategies to give each player an incentive to punish anyone who does not do his or her part in punishing someone who deviates from the behavior prescribed for him or her by S, and thereby to justify the use of the adjective *subgame perfect*. (This is easy to do for the repeated prisoner's dilemma because the individual security levels emerge from the unique Nash equilibrium of the stage game.) ∎

To bring out the significance of the equilibrium theorem we explore a version of the prisoner's dilemma game that gives rise to a continuum of Nash equilibria in the infinite replication game, even though the stage game has a single dominant strategy equilibrium: each player must choose *a level of cooperation between zero and one* – not necessarily just an extreme point, zero (defect) or one (full cooperation).

Example 1.8 The Continuum Dilemma

In the stage game player A selects a fraction $\alpha(0 \leq \alpha \leq 1)$ and B selects a fraction $\beta(0 \leq \beta \leq 1)$. Each person's fraction expresses the degree of cooperation chosen. The payoffs are defined so that $\alpha = 0$ is a dominant strategy in the stage game for A, and similarly $\beta = 0$ is a dominant strategy for B. Set

$$u_A(\alpha, \beta) = 2\beta - \alpha \text{ and } u_B(\alpha, \beta) = 2\alpha - \beta.$$

These payoff functions can be given a simple interpretation. A and B are neighbors, and each is bothered by the amount of debris that motorists deposit as they drive by. If either A or B supplies e units of effort to cleaning up the trash then *each* will receive $2e$ units of utility from the improved appearance of the neighborhood. But cleanup is costly, and for each unit of effort expended by A there is a utility cost of 3 units and similarly for B. If A devotes α units of effort to cleanup while B contributes β then A's utility is $2(\alpha + \beta) - 3\alpha$ and B's utility is $2(\alpha + \beta) - 3\beta$. This gives us the displayed payoff functions. Whatever the value of β, player A can increase u_A by reducing α. Therefore, $\alpha = 0$ is a dominant strategy for A in the stage game. Similarly, $\beta = 0$ is a dominant strategy for B. The security level is zero for each player.

What are the feasible payoff vectors for this game? They comprise the entire diamond OKLM in Figure 1.6 (including the interior). Consider point x, which is a convex combination of $(-1, 2)$ and $(1, 1)$. That is, $x = \lambda(-1, 2) + (1 - \lambda)(1, 1)$ for some value of λ between zero and unity. In plainer terms, the first component of x (A's payoff) is $\lambda(-1) + (1 - \lambda)(1)$ and the second (B's payoff) is $\lambda(2) + (1 - \lambda)(1)$. Can we have

$$2\beta - \alpha = -\lambda + (1 - \lambda) \text{ and } 2\alpha - \beta = 2\lambda + (1 - \lambda)?$$

The solution of these equations is $\alpha = 1$ and $\beta = 1 - \lambda$, and both are admissible strategies.

Consider $y = \lambda(1, 1) + (1 - \lambda)(2, -1)$. Set

$$2\beta - \alpha = \lambda + 2(1 - \lambda) \text{ and } 2\alpha - \beta = \lambda - (1 - \lambda).$$

The solution is $\alpha = \lambda$ and $\beta = 1$ and both are admissible. Verify that

$w = \lambda(2, -1) + (1 - \lambda)(0, 0)$ *results from* $\alpha = 0$ *and* $\beta = \lambda$,

$p = \lambda(-1, 2) + \theta(1, 1) + (1 - \lambda - \theta)(2, -1)$ *if* $\alpha = \lambda + \theta$ *and* $\beta = 1 - \lambda$,

$q = \lambda(-1, 2) + \theta(2, -1) + (1 - \lambda - \theta)(0, 0)$ *if* $\alpha = \lambda$ *and* $\beta = \theta$.

In each case $0 \le \lambda \le 1$, and for p and q we have $0 \le \theta \le 1$ and $0 \le \lambda + \theta \le 1$ as well.

To summarize, any point in the diamond OKLM in Figure 1.6 is a feasible payoff assignment for the one-shot version of the game. The equilibrium theorem says that any point (u_A, u_B) in the shaded part of the diamond, excluding the lines OH and OJ, can be sustained as a subgame-perfect Nash equilibrium in which A gets u_A each period and B gets u_B each period in the infinitely repeated game if the discount rate is sufficiently high. We have seen why these payoffs can be supported by a Nash equilibrium. The grim trigger strategy permanently reduces an opponent to a utility of zero if he once deviates from the equilibrium degree of cooperation. It is easy to see why a point outside of the shaded area cannot be sustained, even with infinite replication and a high discount rate. Outside of the shaded area one person receives less than zero, but a player can always guarantee a payoff of at least zero per period by selecting a cooperation level of zero each period.

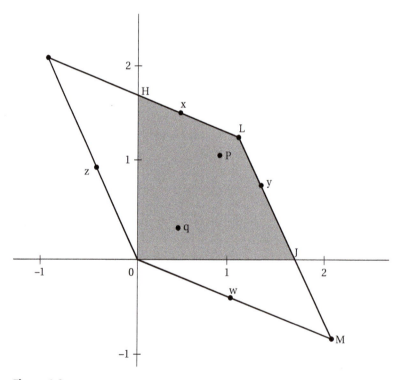

Figure 1.6

Although we can show how cooperation might be sustained in an infinitely repeated game, we have not shown that cooperation is inevitable. There are many other equilibria as well.

1.7.4 Terminal Date and Unknown Type

Section 1.7.1 demonstrated that if the repeated prisoner's dilemma game has a known finite terminal date then each player will defect each period. That depends on the supposition that player B knows that A will always play a best response to B's strategy, and A knows that B knows this, and that B knows that A knows that B knows this, and so on. What if B believes that there is a small but positive probability that A is committed to the tit-for-tat strategy, even when it is not a best response to what B has done? We now show how this opens the door for cooperation by *both* even when both players know the finite terminal date. (See Section 1.7.2 for a definition of tit-for-tat.)

We again begin with the generic one-shot prisoner's dilemma game of Table 1.18 in Section 1.7.1. Recall that $\ell < d < c < h$. We simplify by not discounting: each player wants to maximize the sum of the payoffs over the lifetime of the repeated game. Player A is one of two types, but B does not know which type A actually is when play begins. There is a positive probability π that A is a cooperative type who can only play the *tit-for-tat* strategy. Tit-for-tat cooperates in the first period and for every subsequent period duplicates the move made by the opponent at the previous stage. In that case we say that A is type Q. With probability $1 - \pi$ player A is

Table 1.19

Period 1		Period 2
Opponent	Player	Player
D	D	D
D	D	C
C	D	C
C	D	D
D	C	C
C	C	D
D	C	D
C	C	C

"rational" (type R), which means that R can play any strategy, and R knows that this is also true of B. (Section 1.7.1 showed that if both players are rational, and both know this, then the unique Nash equilibrium has each player defecting each period.) Player B is assumed to be risk neutral, which means that B wants to maximize $\pi q(s) + (1 - \pi)r(s)$, where $q(s)$ is the payoff that B gets from strategy s if he's actually playing against Q, and $r(s)$ is his payoff from s should he be playing against R.

With two choices available to each player there are four logically possible pairs of first-round decisions, and for each there are two possible responses for a given player. These eight cases are displayed as eight rows in Table 1.19. The first four cases will not arise when the player is type Q because Q always begins by cooperating. The tit-for-tat strategy is represented by the last two lines with Q as the player. What will R do in equilibrium? R could begin by cooperating to fool B into thinking that she (player A) is type Q. But in a two-period model this will not work. R knows that B will defect in period 2. Therefore, R will defect in both periods. Q will cooperate in the first period and select X in the second period, where X is B's first period choice. It remains to determine B's first period move X.

Table 1.20

	Period 1		Period 2			
A's type	A	B	A	B	B's total payoff	Probability
Q	C	C	C	D	$c + h$	π
R	D	C	D	D	$\ell + d$	$1 - \pi$
Q	C	D	D	D	$h + d$	π
R	D	D	D	D	$d + d$	$1 - \pi$

There are two possibilities: $X = C$ (cooperate) and $X = D$ (defect). For each of these R's move is uniquely determined in each period and so is Q's move in each period. Therefore, there are 2×2 cases, displayed as Table 1.20. If B cooperates in period 1 his overall payoff is $\pi(c+h) + (1 - \pi)(l+d)$ the sum of the first two rows of the column 4 payoffs weighted by the probabilities. But if B defects at the outset his overall payoff is $\pi(h+d) + (1 - \pi)(d+d)$. Cooperation in period 1 leads to a higher payoff for B when $\pi(c+h) + (1 - \pi)(\ell+d) > \pi(h+d) + (1 - \pi)(d+d)$, and this reduces to $\pi > \frac{d-\ell}{c-\ell}$. Set $\pi^0 = (d - \ell)/(c - \ell)$. As long as $\pi > \pi^0$ the equilibrium strategies for the two-period game are as follows:

> Q: tit-for-tat.

> R: defect each period, whatever B does.

> B: cooperate in the first period, then defect, whatever A has done.

Because d is smaller than c, the threshold π^0 decreases when ℓ increases. (If $0 < \delta < y < z$ then $(y - \delta)/(z - \delta)$ is less than y/z. Set $y = d - \ell$ and $z = c - \ell$, then increase l by δ. That will reduce the threshold $\pi^0 = (y - \delta)/(z - \delta)$.) If ℓ is sufficiently close to d, but larger than d, we only need a tiny probability that A is tit-for-tat to sustain *some* cooperation in equilibrium. That's because the cost to B of cooperating in the first period against someone who defects is very small if ℓ is close to d.

Consider a three-period replication. It is conceivable that R will open by cooperating to build a reputation for cooperating and so induce B to cooperate. We know that R and B will both defect in the last period, so there is no value to R in cooperating beyond the first period. Either R will defect every period or else R will cooperate in period 1 and defect in the other two periods. Therefore, the only decision to be specified for R is the first-period move. But if R defects on the first move B will know for sure that he is not playing against Q and will thus defect in each of the last two periods (because he will know that A will defect in each of the last two stages). Let's see if cooperation by R on the first move can be sustained at equilibrium. There are two possibilities, and for each of these there are four possible moves for B. (We know that B will defect on the last round.) Therefore, there are 2×4 cases to consider, represented by Tables 1.21A–1.24B. For each of the four table numbers, the A and B tables differ only with respect to R's first period move.

Table 1.21A

Type	Period 1	Period 2	Period 3	Payoff
Q	C	D	D	$\ell + d + d$
B	D	D	D	$h + d + d$
R	C	D	D	$\ell + d + d$
B	D	D	D	$h + d + d$

Table 1.21B

Type	Period 1	Period 2	Period 3	Payoff
Q	C	D	D	$\ell + d + d$
B	D	D	D	$h + d + d$
R	D	D	D	$d + d + d$
B	D	D	D	$d + d + d$

Table 1.22A

Type	Period 1	Period 2	Period 3	Payoff
Q	C	D	C	$\ell + h + \ell$
B	D	C	D	$h + \ell + h$
R	C	D	D	$\ell + h + d$
B	D	C	D	$h + \ell + d$

Table 1.22B

Type	Period 1	Period 2	Period 3	Payoff
Q	C	D	C	$\ell + h + \ell$
B	D	C	D	$h + \ell + h$
R	D	D	D	$d + h + d$
B	D	C	D	$d + \ell + d$

Table 1.23A

Type	Period 1	Period 2	Period 3	Payoff
Q	C	C	C	$c + c + \ell$
B	C	C	D	$c + c + h$
R	C	D	D	$c + h + d$
B	C	C	D	$c + \ell + d$

Table 1.23B

Type	Period 1	Period 2	Period 3	Payoff
Q	C	C	C	$c + c + \ell$
B	C	C	D	$c + c + h$
R	D	D	D	$h + h + d$
B	C	C	D	$\ell + \ell + d$

Table 1.24A

Type	Period 1	Period 2	Period 3	Payoff
Q	C	C	D	$c + \ell + d$
B	C	D	D	$c + h + d$
R	C	D	D	$c + d + d$
B	C	D	D	$c + d + d$

Table 1.24B

Type	Period 1	Period 2	Period 3	Payoff
Q	C	C	D	$c + \ell + d$
B	C	D	D	$c + h + d$
R	D	D	D	$h + d + d$
B	C	D	D	$\ell + d + d$

Table 1.23A has R cooperating in the first period and B cooperating in the first two periods. Let's work out the conditions on π such that Table 1.23A is observed at equilibrium. The strategies underlying this table are as follows:

S_R: R cooperates in the first period and defects in each of the other two periods, whatever B does.

S_Q: Q cooperates in the first period and then imitates B's previous move in each of the subsequent periods.

S_B: B cooperates in period 1 and defects in the other two periods if A defects in period 1: if A cooperates in the first period then B will cooperate in the second period and defect in the last period.

Will it be profitable for R to deviate from S_R? If R defects in period 1 then B will know in period 2 that A is type R and will defect in periods 2 and 3. Therefore, a deviation by R will take us to Table 1.24B. This deviation will be unprofitable for R if $h + d + d < c + h + d$, and that is equivalent to $d < c$, which is always the case for a prisoner's dilemma game. We don't have to consider a deviation by Q from S_Q because, by assumption, Q can only play tit-for-tat.

Will B deviate from S_B, given that R plays S_R? Note that R opens by playing C, which restricts us to the A tables. The four A tables differ only with respect to B's actions (and

Table 1.25

B's strategy	B's payoff
From Table 1.21A	$\pi(h + 2d) + (1 - \pi)(h + 2d) = h + 2d$
From Table 1.22A	$\pi(2h + \ell) + (1 - \pi)(h + \ell + d) = h + \ell + \pi h + (1 - \pi)d$
From Table 1.23A	$\pi(2c + h) + (1 - \pi)(c + \ell + d) = c + \pi(c + h) + (1 - \pi)(\ell + d)$
From Table 1.24A	$\pi(c + h + d) + (1 - \pi)(c + 2d) = c + d + \pi h + (1 - \pi)d$

any effect that may have on the tit-for-tat player's actions). Table 1.23A has B playing S_B. The other three S_B tables present the three possible deviations from S_B. Note that B's payoff from S_B is $\pi(c + c + h) + (1 - \pi)(c + l + d) = c + \pi(c + h) + (1 - \pi)(l + d)$ from Table 1.23A. Table 1.25 gives B's payoff from each of the four A tables, given that R cooperates in the first period and defects in the other two, regardless of what B does. The third line results from S_B, and the other three lines result from the possible deviations by B.

Consider the deviation from S_B represented by Table 1.21A, which results in a payoff to B of $\pi(h + 2d) + (1 - \pi)(h + 2d) = h + 2d$. We have $c + \pi(c + h) + (1 - \pi)(\ell + d) > h + 2d$ as long as

$$\pi > \frac{h + d - \ell - c}{h + c - \ell - d}. \qquad [1]$$

Consider the deviation from S_B represented by Table 1.22A, which results in a payoff to B of $\pi(h + \ell + h) + (1 - \pi)(h + \ell + d) = h + \ell + \pi h + (1 - \pi)d$. We have $c + \pi(c + h) + (1 - \pi)(\ell + d) > h + \ell + \pi h + (1 - \pi)d$ as long as

$$\pi > \frac{h - c}{c - \ell} \qquad [2]$$

Consider the deviation from S_B represented by Table 1.24A, which results in a payoff to B of $\pi(c + h + d) + (1 - \pi)(c + d + d) = c + d + \pi h + (1 - \pi)d$. We have $c + \pi(c + h) + (1 - \pi)(\ell + d) > c + d + \pi h + (1 - \pi)d$ as long as

$$\pi > \frac{d - \ell}{c - \ell} \qquad [3]$$

Therefore, we have an equilibrium with cooperation in the early stages of the game (for one period by R and two periods by B) as long as [1], [2], and [3] hold. Notice that [3] is the condition for cooperation by B in the first period of a two-period game.

We have examined reputation building as a motivation for behavior that promotes social welfare. Is R creating a *false* reputation by cooperating on the first move? No. Defecting every period is implied by rationality only when there is a finite number of repetitions with a known terminal date and R's opponent knows that he is rational. But if B doesn't know A's type then the optimal strategy for rational A will be affected. In the two-period model it is only B who cooperates at all (for one period). But as the three-period case shows, if B can be induced to cooperate – because of his uncertainty about A's type – then A has an incentive to build a reputation as a cooperative player, even if A is actually type R.

Let's apply conditions [1], [2], and [3] to the case $c = 20$, $d = 5$, $\ell = 1$, and $h = 30$. We get $\pi > 7/22$, $\pi > 10/19$, and $\pi > 4/19$. Therefore, B has to believe that the probability of A being tit-for-tat is greater than $10/19$ to be induced to cooperate in the first two periods. However, as the number of repetitions increases the greater the long-run payoff to cooperative behavior, and hence smaller values of π will sustain cooperation. Note that $\pi > 4/19$ is sufficient to induce B to cooperate in the first period of the *two*-stage game, whereas $\pi > 10/19$ is the sufficient condition for (S_R, S_Q, S_B) to be an equilibrium in the three-stage game. Don't be misled into thinking that cooperation is *more* problematic when the time horizon is longer. We get *more* cooperation – two periods instead of one period – when $\pi > 10/19$.

Sources

The repeated prisoner's dilemma competition devised by Robert Axelrod is reported in Axelrod (1984). An early version of the equilibrium theorem for infinitely repeated games was proved by Friedman (1971). The treatment of the prisoner's dilemma game when individual types are unknown is based on Gibbons (1992, p. 225). Kreps et al. (1982) actually prove that, given π, if there is a large number of periods then the players will cooperate in every period until they are close to the terminal period.

Links

For more on the prisoner's dilemma game replayed many times see Rapoport (1989). See Calvert (1986, pp. 47–54) for related treatments of reputation in economics and politics. Osborne (2004, pp. 439–441) provides a very good assessment of Axelrod's tournament. Fudenberg and Maskin (1986) and Wen (1994) develop significant generalizations of the equilibrium theorem, which is called the folk theorem in the literature.

Limitations in the information processing capacity of the players can eliminate a lot of Nash equilibria of the infinitely repeated game, appearing to make cooperation more likely in the prisoner's dilemma case. In particular, see Rubinstein (1986 and 1998) and Binmore and Samuelson (1992).

Problem Set

(1) Prove that the grim trigger strategies constitute a Nash equilibrium of the generic version of the infinitely repeated game provided that each individual is sufficiently patient.

(2) Let A's discount rate be 0.9 and let B's be 0.7. Find a condition guaranteeing that cooperation every period by both players is the outcome of a subgame-perfect Nash equilibrium when the payoffs in the stage game are given by Table 1.13 in Section 1.6.

(3) Rework the argument of Section 1.7.2 for the specific case $c = 20$, $d = 5$, $l = 1$, and $h = 30$.

(4) Does the analysis of Section 1.7.4 change if we replace tit-for-tat with the strategy "cooperate every period whatever the opponent does?"

2

Basic Models and Tools

2.1   MAXIMIZING A QUADRATIC

There are about a hundred worked examples in this book, and many of them entail finding the value of x that maximizes a quadratic function of the form $Px - Qx^2 + R$, a very simple procedure that does not require calculus. This section shows how to determine whether that function has a maximum, and if it does how to quickly compute that maximizing value of x as a simple function of P and Q. We begin by assuming that x is unconstrained and then determine the solution to the constrained maximization problem, for which x must lie between the numbers a and b, inclusive.

> **Danger**: The formula for the *root* of the quadratic
>
> $$ax^2 + bx + c \text{ is } x = \frac{-b \pm \sqrt{b^2 - 4ac}}{2a}.$$
>
> This gives the two values of x at which the value of the function is *zero*. In this section we seek to *maximize* the value of the quadratic.

2.1.1   Unconstrained Maximization

Consider the basic consumer decision problem, which requires the maximization of a utility function $U(x, y)$ subject to the simple budget constraint $p_1 x + p_2 y = \theta$. We can turn that into an unconstrained maximization problem by solving the budget constraint for y as a function of x. Then we can substitute this expression for y in the utility function to get a function of a single variable x.

Example 2.1 Consumer Choice with Quadratic Utility

The budget constraint is $4x + 2y = 12$. Then $2y = 12 - 4x$ and thus $y = 6 - 2x$. The given utility function is

$$U(x, y) = 64x - x^2 + 3y.$$

If we substitute $6 - 2x$ for y in the utility function we get

$$U = 64x - x^2 + 3[6 - 2x] = 64x - x^2 + 18 - 6x = 58x - x^2 + 18.$$

The final expression depends on x alone because the budget constraint is built in. If we maximize

$$f(x) = 18 + 58x - x^2$$

then we will have solved the problem of maximizing utility subject to the budget constraint.

The function $f(x) = 18 + 58x - x^2$ is called a *quadratic* because there is only one unknown, and the highest power of the unknown is a squared term. Functions of a single variable will also come up in other contexts, such as profit maximization by firms and the determination of the efficient level of output of a public good. The purpose of this section is to teach you how to quickly find the value of x that maximizes a quadratic of the form

$$Px - Qx^2 + R \quad \text{where } Q > 0.$$

That is, P, Q, and R are given real numbers, and Q is positive.

Example 2.2 Maximizing the Function $25 - (x - 3)^2$

Note that $f(x) = 25 - (x - 3)^2$ and if x is not equal to 3 then $(x - 3)^2$ is positive, which means that we subtract a positive amount from 25. Therefore, the best that we can do, if we want to maximize $f(x)$, is to make sure that $(x - 3)^2$ is zero. There is only one value of x for which $(x - 3)^2 = 0$, and that is $x = 3$. Therefore, $x = 3$, and only $x = 3$, maximizes f. Note that this function can be written in the form $Px - Qx^2 + R$: Because $(x - 3)^2 = x^2 - 6x + 9$ we have

$$f(x) = 25 - (x - 3)^2 = 6x - x^2 + 16.$$

That is, $P = 6$, $Q = 1$, and $R = 16$.

When there is one and only one value that maximizes $f(x)$ we say that it is a unique global maximum.

DEFINITION: *Global Maximum*

The number x^* is a global maximum of f if $f(x^*) \geq f(x)$ for every real number x. And x^* is a *unique* global maximum if $f(x^*) > f(x)$ for every real number x distinct from x^*.

The function $f(x) = 6x - x^2 + 16$ can be rewritten as $f(x) = 25 - (x - 3)^2$ to allow us to apply the argument of Example 2.2. What about other cases?

Example 2.3 Maximizing the Function $6x - \frac{1}{2} x^2 + 82$

We are given $f(x) = 6x - \frac{1}{2} x^2 + 82$. But $6x - \frac{1}{2} x^2 + 82 = 82 - \frac{1}{2}(x^2 - 12x) = 82 - \frac{1}{2}(x - 6)^2 + 18$. Hence $f(x) = 100 - \frac{1}{2}(x - 6)^2$.

If $x \neq 6$ then $(x - 6)^2$ is positive, and hence a positive amount is subtracted from 100. Therefore $f(x)$ has a unique global maximum at $x = 6$.

Return to our generic function $Px - Qx^2 + R$ with $Q > 0$. Rewrite this as

$$f(x) = R - Q\left(x^2 - \frac{P}{Q}x\right).$$

Note that $[x - (P/2Q)]^2$ is similar to $x^2 - (P/Q)x$. In fact

$$\left(x - \frac{P}{2Q}\right)^2 = x^2 - \frac{P}{Q}x + \frac{P^2}{4Q^2}.$$

Therefore, if we replace $-Q[x^2 - (P/Q)x]$ in $f(x)$ by $-Q[x - (P/2Q)]^2$ we have to add $Q \times (P^2/4Q^2)$ to preserve the value of $f(x)$. To summarize, we have

$$f(x) = R - Q\left(x^2 - \frac{P}{Q}x\right) = R + \frac{P^2}{4Q} - Q\left(x - \frac{P}{2Q}\right)^2.$$

The only part of this that is influenced by x is $-Q[x - (P/2Q)]^2$, and because Q is positive we maximize $f(x)$ by making $[x - (P/2Q)]^2$ as small as possible. Therefore, we set $x = P/2Q$, which gives us a unique global maximum. It is unique because any x different from $P/2Q$ will cause $[x - (P/2Q)]^2$ to be positive.

Formula for Maximizing a Quadratic

If $f(x) = Px - Qx^2 + R$ and $Q > 0$, then for $x^* = P/2Q$ we have $f(x^*) > f(x)$ for all $x \neq x$.

Note that $f(x)$ does not have a maximum if $f(x) = Px - Qx^2 + R$ and $Q < 0$. That's because we can write

$$f(x) = R + \frac{P^2}{4Q} - Q\left(x - \frac{P}{2Q}\right)^2,$$

and when $-Q$ is positive we can make $-Q[x - (P/2Q)]^2$ arbitrarily large by making x sufficiently large.

2.1.2 Constrained Maximization

In this subsection we want to maximize $f(x) = Px - Qx^2 + R$ subject to the constraint $a \leq x \leq b$. Restrictions of the form $a \leq x \leq b$ arise in consumer theory because we cannot have $x < 0$ or $y < 0$. (The budget constraint $p_1 x + p_2 y = \theta$ implies $y < 0$ when expenditure on commodity X exceeds income - i.e., when $p_1 x > \theta$, which is equivalent to $x > \theta/p_1$. Therefore, when we find the global maximizing value x^* we have to check to make sure that the inequality $0 \leq x^* \leq \theta/p_1$ is satisfied.)

If $f(x) = R + (P^2/4Q) - Q[x - (P/2Q)]^2$ and $Q > 0$ then $f(x)$ decreases as x increases *if we use $x = P/2Q$ as the starting point.* That's because $Q[x - (P/2Q)]^2$ is zero when $x = P/2Q$ and $Q[x - (P/2Q)]^2$ increases when x increases if $x \geq P/2Q$ initially. Using $x = P/2Q$ as the starting point $f(x)$ decreases as x decreases because $Q[x - (P/2Q)]^2$ is zero when $x = P/2Q$ and $Q[x - (P/2Q)]^2$ increases when x decreases through values less than $P/2Q$. We have established that the graph of f is hill shaped, with the peak occurring when $x = P/2Q$ (Figure 2.1, with $x_4 = P/2Q$).

We have just learned that $f(x)$ is increasing (the graph is uphill) to the left of $x = P/2Q$ and $f(x)$ is decreasing (the graph is downhill) to the right of $x = P/2Q$. If $P/2Q > b$ then the solution of the problem

$$\text{maximize} \quad f(x) = Px - Qx^2 + R \quad \text{subject to } a \leq x \leq b$$

must be $x = b$. That follows from the fact that $P/2Q > b$ implies that $f(x)$ increases when $x < b$ and x increases (Figure 2.1, with $x_2 = b$). However, if $P/2Q < a$ then the solution to the constrained maximization problem is $x = a$ because $a > P/2Q$ implies that $f(x)$ increases when $x > a$ and x decreases (see Figure 2.1, with $x_6 = a$).

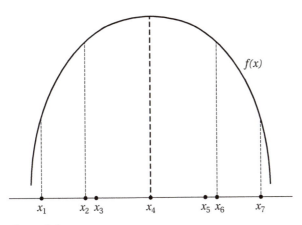

$$x_1 \qquad x_2\ x_3 \qquad x_4 \qquad x_5\ x_6 \qquad x_7$$

Figure 2.1

Formulas for Constrained Maximization of a Quadratic

The given function is $f(x) = Px - Qx^2 + R$ and $Q > 0$. And a and b are given numbers, with $a < b$.

If $a \leq P/2Q \leq b$, then $x^* = P/2Q$ maximizes $f(x)$ subject to $a \leq x \leq b$.

If $P/2Q > b$, then $x^* = b$ maximizes $f(x)$ subject to $a \leq x \leq b$.

If $P/2Q < a$ then $x^* = a$ maximizes $f(x)$ subject to $a \leq x \leq b$.

∂2.2 OVERVIEW OF CALCULUS

This section establishes the first-order conditions for maximization of a function of one real variable, with and without constraints. The derivation is self-contained, but some of the applications in this book assume that you know more than is presented in Section 2.2.1. For instance, it is taken for granted that you know the power rule: the derivative of x^n is nx^{n-1}. Also, the chain rule is used on occasion. Nevertheless, the basic theory is developed rigorously in Section 2.2.1 because many readers will benefit from a refresher course. Moreover, we highlight the intuition underlying the use of calculus. We use $f'(x)$ to denote the first derivative f at x, although on occasion $\frac{df}{dx}$ or even $\frac{dy}{dx}$, with $y = f(x)$, make an appearance.

Consider the standard consumer choice problem:

$$\text{maximize} \quad U(x, y) \quad \text{subject to } p_1 x + p_2 y = \theta.$$

U is the utility function, and utility depends on the amounts x and y of the two goods consumed. The prices of goods X and Y are p_1 and p_2, respectively, and θ is the individual's income. The budget constraint $p_1 x + p_2 y = \theta$ can be solved for y as a function of x:

$$y = \frac{\theta}{p_2} - \frac{p_1 x}{p_2}.$$

Now, substitute this value of y into the utility function. We want to maximize

$$V(x) = U\left(x, \frac{\theta}{p_2} - \frac{p_1 x}{p_2}\right)$$

and V is a function of only one variable, x, because θ, p_1, and p_2 are constants – they are outside of the control of the consumer at the time the consumption decision is made. This means that we can apply elementary calculus to the problem and maximize $V(x)$. We no longer have to worry about the budget constraint because that is built into V. With one stroke we have eliminated one variable and the budget constraint as well. Once we have obtained the number x^* that maximizes V, we simply use the budget constraint to solve for y.

2.2.1 Unconstrained Maximization

Let $f(x)$ represent the function to be maximized, with x a real variable. This means that x can be any real number, and for any choice of x the function f specifies another real number $f(x)$. Initially, we assume that there is no constraint of any kind on the range of values that x can assume. We'll show that $f'(x^*) = 0$ must hold if f is maximized at x^*.

Now let x^* represent any real number that maximizes the function f. Formally, this means that $f(x^*) \geq f(x)$ holds for every real number x. Another way of saying this is $f(x^*) \geq f(x^* + \epsilon)$ for every real number ϵ. (Just replace x by $x^* + \epsilon$, defining ϵ as the quantity $x - x^*$.) We can think of ϵ as an increment, positive or negative, taking us away from x^*. Because f is maximized at x^*, this increment, or step, cannot increase the value of f. More formally, we write

$$f(x^* + \epsilon) - f(x^*) \leq 0 \quad \text{for all } \epsilon. \tag{1}$$

Condition [1] is just another way of saying that f is maximized at x^*. This is pretty obvious, but we only need to pursue this a little further to get a striking and useful result.

Multiplying an Inequality by a Constant

Let α, β, ϵ, and ϕ be real numbers. If $\epsilon > 0$ and $\phi > 0$ then $\epsilon\phi > 0$. Therefore, if $\alpha > \beta$ then $\alpha - \beta > 0$, and thus $\epsilon(\alpha - \beta) > 0$ if $\epsilon > 0$. This implies that if $\alpha > \beta$ and $\epsilon > 0$ we have $\epsilon\alpha > \epsilon\beta$. It follows that if $\epsilon < 0$ and $\alpha > \beta$ then $-\epsilon\alpha > -\epsilon\beta$, which in turn implies $\epsilon\alpha < \epsilon\beta$. Finally, if $\epsilon > 0$ and $\alpha \geq \beta$ then $\epsilon\alpha \geq \epsilon\beta$, and if $\epsilon < 0$ and $\alpha \geq \beta$ then $\epsilon\alpha \leq \epsilon\beta$.

If ϵ is positive (strictly greater than zero) then $f(x^* + \epsilon) - f(x^*)$ will still be less than or equal to zero after we multiply that expression by ϵ^{-1}. We state this formally as Condition [2]:

$$\frac{f(x^* + \epsilon) - f(x^*)}{\epsilon} \leq 0 \quad \text{for all } \epsilon > 0. \tag{2}$$

As ϵ approaches zero through positive values, the limit must also be less than or equal to zero as a consequence of Condition [2]. For future reference, we state this as Condition [3]:

$$\text{The limit of } \frac{f(x^* + \epsilon) - f(x^*)}{\epsilon} \text{ is} \leq 0 \text{ as } \epsilon > 0 \text{ approaches 0.} \tag{3}$$

Similarly, if we multiply $f(x^* + \epsilon) - f(x^*)$ by ϵ^{-1} for any $\epsilon < 0$ the inequality sign will change direction, and hence

$$\frac{f(x^* + \epsilon) - f(x^*)}{\epsilon} \geq 0 \quad \text{for all } \epsilon < 0. \tag{4}$$

As ϵ approaches zero through *negative* numbers the limit must be nonnegative because each term is nonnegative by Condition [4]. This is represented as Condition [5]:

$$\text{The limit of } \frac{f(x^* + \epsilon) - f(x^*)}{\epsilon} \text{ is} \geq 0 \text{ as } \epsilon < 0 \text{ approaches 0.} \tag{5}$$

If f has a derivative at x then, by definition, the limit of $[f(x^* + \epsilon) - f(x^*)]/\epsilon$ must be the same when ϵ approaches zero through positive values as it is when ϵ approaches zero through negative values. But [3] and [5] can both be satisfied only if the limit is zero in both cases. In short, $f'(x^*) = 0$ is a necessary condition for f to have a maximum at x^*. The function f in Figure 2.1 is maximized at $x^* = x_4$. We see that the first derivative of f is zero at x_4 because the graph of f is perfectly horizontal at x_4.

Necessary Condition for an Unconstrained Maximum

If $f(x^*) \geq f(x)$ for all real numbers x then $f'(x^*) = 0$.

Here is an alternative derivation of the fact that $f'(x^*) = 0$ if f is maximized at x^*. (You don't need to master both treatments; just adopt the one with which you are more comfortable.) Suppose that $f'(x) > 0$. We show that f cannot have a maximum at x. Let δ represent $f'(x)$. We have $\delta > 0$. Intuitively, a small move to the right will increase the value of f. It may have to be a very small move if x is close to the top of the hill, as is the case with $x = x_2$ in Figure 2.1. A move to x_7 will lower the value of f, but a sufficiently small move to the right, such as the one taking us from x_2 to x_3, will increase f.

Here is the formal argument: the limit of $[f(x + \epsilon) - f(x)]/\epsilon$ is δ, and we assume that $\delta > 0$. For $\epsilon > 0$ sufficiently close to zero we can get $[f(x + \epsilon) - f(x)]/\epsilon$ close enough to δ to guarantee that the ratio is greater than $\frac{1}{2}\delta$. But then

$$f(x+\epsilon) - f(x) > \epsilon \times \tfrac{1}{2}\delta > 0.$$

This means that $f(x + \epsilon) - f(x) > 0$, or $f(x + \epsilon) > f(x)$, establishing that x is not the maximizing value of f.

Next we show that f cannot have a maximum at x if $f'(x) < 0$. Let δ again represent $f'(x^*)$, with $\delta < 0$ this time. Intuitively, a small move to the *left* increases the value of f. It may have to be a very small move as in the case $x = x_6$ in Figure 2.1. A move to x_1 lowers $f(x)$, but a sufficiently small move to the left, such as the one taking us from x_6 to x_5, will increase $f(x)$. Consider: Because the limit of $[f(x + \epsilon) - f(x)]/\epsilon$ is δ, for $\epsilon < 0$ sufficiently close to zero we can get $[f(x + \epsilon) - f(x)]/\epsilon$ close enough to δ to guarantee that ratio is algebraically smaller than $\frac{1}{2}\delta$. Therefore, $[f(x + \epsilon) - f(x)]/\epsilon < \frac{1}{2}\delta$ for ϵ sufficiently close to zero and negative. Now if we multiply this last inequality on both sides by $\epsilon < 0$ we change the sign, yielding

$$f(x+\epsilon) - f(x) > \epsilon \times \tfrac{1}{2}\delta > 0.$$

(We have $\epsilon \times \frac{1}{2}\delta > 0$ because both ϵ and δ are negative.) But then $f(x + \epsilon) - f(x) > 0$, or $f(x + \epsilon) > f(x)$. Again x does not yield the maximum value of f, because $f(x + \epsilon)$ is larger than $f(x)$. Therefore, if f is maximized at x we can rule out both $f'(x) > 0$ and $f'(x) < 0$.

Example 2.4 Maximizing the function $f(x) = 10x - x^2 - 25$

We want to find the point at which f is maximized. Note that $f(x) = -(x-5)^2$, which can never be positive. When $x = 5$ the value of the function is zero, so that is the point at which f reaches a maximum. Every other value of x will yield $f(x) < 0$. We don't need calculus in this case but let's see how calculus brings us to the same conclusion. We need to calculate the first derivative of f.

$$f(x+\epsilon) = 10(x+\epsilon) - (x+\epsilon)^2 - 25$$
$$= 10x + 10\epsilon - x^2 - 2\epsilon x - \epsilon^2 - 25 = f(x) + 10\epsilon - 2\epsilon x - \epsilon^2.$$

Therefore,

$$f(x+\epsilon) - f(x) = 10\epsilon - 2\epsilon x - \epsilon^2$$

and hence

$$\frac{f(x+\epsilon) - f(x)}{\epsilon} = \frac{10\epsilon - 2\epsilon x - \epsilon^2}{\epsilon} = 10 - 2x - \epsilon.$$

Clearly, $10 - 2x - \epsilon$ approaches $10 - 2x$ as ϵ approaches zero. Therefore, $f'(x) = 10 - 2x$, the first derivative of f. We said that $f'(x) = 0$ is necessary for a maximum. Set $f'(x) = 0$ and solve for x: We get $10 - 2x = 0$, and thus $x = 5$.

Next we look at consumer choice.

Example 2.5 A Simple Consumer Choice Problem

We want to maximize $U(x, y) = xy$ subject to the budget constraint $5x + 2y = 1000$. The utility of a basket with x units of commodity X and y units of commodity Y is the product of the two numbers x and y. (It may help at this point to draw a typical indifference curve, for instance the set of consumption plans (x, y) that yield a utility of 12.) The price of good X is 5 and the price of good Y is 2. Income is 1000. Solving the budget constraint for y yields

$$y = \frac{1000}{2} - \frac{5x}{2} = 500 - 2.5x.$$

Now, substitute this value of y into the utility function. We want to maximize

$$V(x) = x(500 - 2.5x)$$

$$V(x) = 500x - 2.5x^2, \text{ and thus } V'(x) = 500 - 5x.$$

Then $V'(x) = 0$ yields $500 - 5x = 0$, and thus $x^* = 100$, the only value of x that gives $V' = 0$. Therefore, there can be only one utility-maximizing value of x, namely $x = 100$. Finally, use the budget constraint to solve for y:

$$y = 500 - 2.5x = 500 - 2.5(100) = 500 - 250 = 250.$$

Therefore, the chosen basket has $x = 100$ and $y = 250$.

We can use the technique of Example 2.5 to solve for the *demand functions*. All we have to do is represent prices and income symbolically, but treat them as numbers.

Example 2.6 Deriving a Demand Function

$U(x, y) = xy$, which we maximize, subject to the budget constraint $p_1x + p_2y = \theta$, where prices and income are parameters. We solve for the demands x and y as a function of prices and income. Then $y = \theta/p_2 - p_1x/p_2$, and we substitute this into the utility function:

$$V(x) = x \times \left(\frac{\theta}{p_2} - \frac{p_1x}{p_2} \right).$$

We have $V = \theta x/p_2 - p_1x^2/p_2$ and thus $V'(x) = \theta/p_2 - 2p_1x/p_2$. When $\theta/p_2 - 2p_1x/p_2 = 0$ we have $x = \theta/2p_1$. This is the only value of x that gives $V' = 0$, so the consumer choice problem has a unique solution: $x = \theta/2p_1$. From the budget constraint, $y = \theta/p_2 - p_1x/p_2$ and if in addition $x = \theta/2p_1$ we must have $y = \theta/2p_2$. (Note that $p_1x = \frac{1}{2}\theta = p_2y$, and thus $0 < x < \theta$ and $0 < y < \theta$ both hold if $\theta > 0$.) The expressions $x = \theta/2p_1$ and $y = \theta/2p_2$ are the demand functions for commodities X and Y respectively.

If we are given particular values for prices and income we can plug them into the demand functions to get the *amounts* demanded at that price and income regime. (Verify that $x = 100$ and $y = 250$ when $p_1 = 5$, $p_2 = 2$, and $\theta = 1000$.)

Note that we have $V''(x) < 0$ for all x when V is derived from the utility function $U = xy$ by solving the budget constraint for y and substituting. (Section 2.2.3 introduces the second derivative and explains its role in maximization.)

2.2.2 Constrained Maximization

Suppose that we want to maximize f subject to the restriction $a \leq x \leq b$. It is vital that you pay attention to the difference between $a < x$ and $a \leq x$ and similarly to the distinction between $x < b$ and $x \leq b$. Our first observation is that if we actually have $a < x^* < b$ at the point x^* where the constrained maximum is achieved, then $f'(x^*) = 0$ remains a necessary condition for f to be maximized at x^*. The proof of that is actually embedded in the discussion of the unconstrained case. If $f'(x) > 0$ then for $\epsilon > 0$ sufficiently close to zero we will have $[f(x + \epsilon) - f(x)]/\epsilon > 0$ and hence $f(x + \epsilon) > f(x)$. Review Section 2.2.1 to confirm that we will have $[f(x + \epsilon) - f(x)]/\epsilon > 0$ if we make $\epsilon > 0$ smaller still. Therefore, if $f'(x) > 0$ and $x < b$ then we can find $\epsilon > 0$ small enough so that we get *both* $x + \epsilon < b$ and $f(x + \epsilon) > f(x)$. And we will certainly have $x + \epsilon \geq a$ if $x \geq a$. Therefore, if $a \leq x < b$ and $f'(x) > 0$ the function f cannot be maximized at x even if we are not allowed to consider values of x larger than b or smaller than a. (In Figure 2.1, f is not maximized at x_2, even when the constraint $x_1 \leq x \leq x_7$ must be observed.)

Similarly, we can show that f cannot be maximized at x if $f'(x) < 0$ and $a < x \leq b$, even if we are not allowed to go below a or above b. (In Figure 2.1, f is not maximized at x_6, even with the restriction $x_1 \leq x \leq x_7$.) We have proved the following: If x^* maximizes f subject to the constraint $a \leq x \leq b$ and $a < x^* < b$ actually holds, then we can't have $f'(x^*) > 0$ and we can't have $f'(x) < 0$. This means that $f'(x^*) = 0$ must hold.

Be careful! There is nothing to guarantee that $a < x^* < b$ will actually hold at the solution value x^*. (Try maximizing $f(x) = 2x$ subject to $0 \le x \le 100$. Clearly, the solution is $x^* = 100$, but $f'(100) = 2$ because f' is constant at 2.) But *if* $a < x^* < b$ *does* hold at the solution point then we must have $f'(x) = 0$. The function f is maximized at $x = x_4$ in Figure 2.1, with or without the constraint $x_1 \le x \le x_7$. The first derivative of f is zero at x_4. Another caveat: $f'(x_2) > 0$ and thus f can be increased by increasing x at x_2. That is not to say that any increase in x will increase f. Note that $x_7 > x_2$ but $f(x_2) > f(x_7)$. We *can* say that if $f'(x) > 0$ there will be some increase in x that will increase the value of f. Similarly, if $f'(x) < 0$ there will be some decrease in x that will increase the value of f. (Note that $f'(x_6) < 0$ and $x_1 < x_6$, but $f(x_1) < f(x_6)$.)

What if we do have $x^* = a$ or $x^* = b$ at the point x^* where f is maximized, subject to the constraint $a \le x \le b$? Calculus is still a big help here, but you have to know how to use it. In general, calculus is not a formula for cranking out an answer to a problem but rather a useful device for finding the solution.

We know that if f is maximized at x^* and $a < x^* < b$, then $f'(x^*)$ must equal zero. Therefore, if we want to maximize f subject to the constraints $a \le x \le b$ then either f will achieve its maximum at a point where its first derivative is zero or else the solution value of x will be a or b.

First-Order Conditions for Constrained Maximization

If $f(x)$ is maximized at x^* subject to $a \le x \le b$ then either $f'(x) = 0$ or $x^* = a$ or $x^* = b$.

This means that in solving the constrained maximization problem we can confine our attention to a limited number of values of x: points where the first derivative is zero, and the values $x = a$ and $x = b$. Then compute $f(x)$ at these points to see which gives the highest value of $f(x)$.

Example 2.7 Consumer Choice with Nonnegative Consumption

Let $U(x, y) = (x + 5)(y + 2)$, which we want to maximize subject to $Px + y = \theta$, $x \ge 0$, and $y \ge 0$. (We fix p_2 at 1 and set $P = p_1$ to simplify computation.) We have $y = \theta - Px$ from the budget equation, and substituting this into the utility function yields

$$V(x) = (x + 5)(\theta - Px + 2) = (\theta + 2 - 5P)x - Px^2 + 5\theta + 10.$$

$V'(x) = \theta + 2 - 5P - 2Px$. Then $V''(x) = -2P$, which is always negative. Therefore, the graph of the function V is hill shaped, and if $V'(x) = 0$ yields a unique value of x satisfying $0 \le x \le \theta/P$ this will be the demand for x. Of course, $\theta + 2 - 5P - 2Px = 0$ implies $x = [\frac{1}{2}(\theta + 2 - 5P)]/P$. If $P = 1$ and $\theta = 100$ then $x = 97/2 = 48.5$, which certainly satisfies $0 \le x \le 100$. (How much Y will be demanded in that case?) If $P = 25$ and $\theta = 100$ then $V'(x) = 0$ implies $x = -0.46$, which is inadmissible. The consumer will either set $x = 0$ or $x = 100/25$. We have $V(0) = 5 \times (100 + 2) = 510$, and $V(4) = (4 + 5) \times (100 - 100 + 2) = 18$. Therefore, the consumer will demand 0 units of X and 100 units of Y when $p_1 = 25$, $p_2 = 1$, and $\theta = 100$.

In solving the earlier problem of Example 2.5 we ignored the constraint $0 \le x \le 200$ that is required to ensure that neither x nor y is negative. Here's why we could do that: In this case utility is zero when x or y is zero. That is, $U = xy = 0$ if $x = 0$ or $y = 0$. Even a tiny amount of money spent on each good will yield a positive product xy, so we know that the consumer can do better than zero utility. Therefore, the utility-maximizing basket will have $x > 0$ and $y > 0$. But if y is positive we can't have $x = 200$; we must have $x < 200$. Therefore, the solution value x^* will have to satisfy $0 < x^* < 200$. We know that in this case we must have $V'(x^*) = 0$. We saw that only one value of x gives $V' = 0$. The solution to the consumer choice problem *must* have $V' = 0$. The same argument works for the derivation of the demand functions in Example 2.6. Corner (or boundary) solutions can be ruled out a priori for many other utility functions that you will encounter.

Example 2.8 Corner Points Need Not Apply

Maximize $U(x, y) = x^2 y$ subject to $5x + 2y = 60$. From the budget equation we have $y = 30 - 2.5x$. Substitute this for y in the utility function to obtain

$$V = x^2(30 - 2.5x) = 30x^2 - 2.5x^3.$$

We want to maximize this function of x subject to $0 \le x \le 60/5$. $V'(x) = 60x - 7.5x^2$ and we know that $x > 0$. Also, $V''(x) = 60 - 15x$. Setting the first derivative equal to zero yields

$$60 - 7.5x = 0 \quad \text{or} \quad x = 8.$$

Because $U = 0$ if $x = 0$ or $y = 0$, utility will be maximized at a point where x is strictly greater than 0 and strictly less than 12. Therefore, $V'(x) = 0$ at the solution to the consumer choice problem, implying that $x = 8$ is the optimal value of x. The budget constraint yields $y = 10$.

You will probably have encountered other techniques for generating consumer demand. We will apply each of them to the problem

$$\text{maximize} \quad U(x, y) = x^2 y \quad \text{subject to} \quad 5x + 2y = 60$$

to confirm that they yield the same solution. The first (in Section 2.2.5) is expressed in terms of the tangency of the indifference curve through the chosen bundle to the budget line. (The other approaches are found in Section 2.2.6 and Section 2.3.)

2.2.3 Strictly Concave Functions

We now confine our attention to a special class of functions that often arises in economics, namely functions for which the *second derivative* $f''(x)$ is negative at all values of x. These are called *strictly concave* functions.

DEFINITION: *Strictly Concave Function*

   The function f of a single variable x is strictly concave if $f''(x) < 0$ for all x.

By definition, f'' is the derivative of the derivative. For $f(x) = 10x - x^2 - 25$ we have $f'(x) = 10 - 2x$ and hence $f''(x) = -2$, which is negative. The second derivative tells us how the first derivative changes as x changes. If we always have $f''(x) < 0$ then $f'(x)$ gets smaller (algebraically) as x increases. This has two important implications. First, if $f'(x^*) = 0$ then there is no other value of x for which f' is zero: To the right of x^* the first derivative is negative. Why? Because $f'(x)$ falls as x increases and it is zero at x^*, so $f'(x) < 0$ for all $x > x^*$. Therefore, we cannot find any $x > x^*$ for which $f'(x) = 0$. Now, consider $x < x^*$. The first derivative decreases as we move to the right, so it increases as we move to the left. If f' is zero at x^* and it increases as we move to the left then $f'(x)$ is positive for all $x < x^*$. Therefore, we cannot have $f'(x) = 0$ for any $x < x^*$. In short, if f'' is negative at all points then there is at most one value of x for which f' is zero.

If $f'(x) = 0$ we know that f' is positive to the left of x^* and f' is negative to the right of x^*. When f' is positive the value of the function f itself is increasing. We know that because $f'(x) > 0$ is just another way of saying that f is increasing at x. To the right of x^* we have $f'(x) < 0$ and hence the value of f falls as x increases beyond x^*. This is a consequence of the fact that f' is negative to the right of x^*, and $f'(x) < 0$ is just another way of saying that f is falling at x. (In Figure 2.1, $x^* = x_4$ and $f'(x)$ is strictly positive to the left of x_4 and $f'(x) < 0$ to the right of x_4.)

Let's summarize: Suppose f'' is negative everywhere and $f'(x^*) = 0$. Then f' is not equal to zero for any other value of x. Moreover, f falls as we move to the right of x^* and f rises as we move *toward* x^* from the left. This means that the graph of f is a hill with the peak at x^*, as in Figure 2.1 with $x^* = x_4$. In other words, f has a unique global maximum at x^*.

Global Maximization with a Negative Second Derivative
If $f''(x) < 0$ for all x and $f'(x^*) = 0$ then $f(x^*) > f(x)$ for all $x \neq x^*$. In other words, f has a unique global maximum at x^* if $f'(x^*) = 0$ and $f''(x) < 0$ for all x.

Suppose, however, that we are restricted to the region $a \leq x \leq b$. If we find some x^* in that interval such that $f'(x^*) = 0$ then we are sure that is the unique solution to our problem. Why? Because $f'(x^*) = 0$ implies that $f(x^*) > f(x)$ for *all* other x, and therefore we certainly have $f(x^*) > f(x)$ for all $x \neq x^*$ satisfying $a \leq x \leq b$ (Caveat: This depends on $f'' < 0$ holding everywhere.) Suppose, however, that the value of x for which f' is zero is outside of the interval $a \leq x \leq b$.

Consider first the case $f'(x^*) = 0$ and $x^* > b$. We know that f is rising to the left of x^*. Therefore, f is increasing at all x in the constraint region, because $a \leq x \leq b$ implies that x is to the left of x^*. Therefore, $f'(x^*) = 0$ and $x^* > b$ implies that $x = b$ is our solution: $f(b) > f(x)$ for all x satisfying $a \leq x < b$, as illustrated in Figure 2.1 with x_1 representing a and x_2 representing b (and $x^* = x_4$). Now suppose that $f'(x^*) = 0$ and $x^* < a$. Because $f'' < 0$ at every point, f is falling to the right of x^*. Therefore f is decreasing at all x in the constraint region because $a \leq x \leq b$ implies that x is to the right of x^*. Therefore, $f'(x^*) = 0$ and $x^* < a$ implies that $x = a$ is our solution:

$f(a) > f(x)$ for all x satisfying $a < x \le b$, as illustrated in Figure 2.1 with $a = x_6$ and $b = x_7$ (and $x^* = x_4$).

2.2.4 Minimization

If x^* minimizes $f(x)$ over all real numbers x, then by definition $f(x^*) \le f(x)$ for all x. It follows that $-f(x^*) \ge -f(x)$ for all x. In other words, if x^* minimizes f then x^* maximizes $-f$. It follows that the derivative of $-f$ is zero at x^*. But for any function f, the derivative of $-f$ is the negative of the derivative of f. Therefore, $f'(x^*) = 0$ if f is minimized at x^*. Similarly, $f'(x^*) = 0$ if $a < x^* < b$ and x^* is the solution to problem

$$\text{minimize } f(x) \text{ subject to } a \le x \le b.$$

Finally, we say that f is *strictly convex* if its second derivative is positive at every point. But if $f''(x) > 0$ for all x then the function $-f$ has a negative second derivative at every point. In that case, $-f'(x^*) = 0$ implies that $-f(x^*) > -f(x)$ for all $x \ne x^*$. It follows that $f(x^*) < f(x)$ for all $x \ne x^*$. Because $-f'(x^*) = 0$ implies $f'(x^*) = 0$, we have demonstrated that for any strictly convex function f, if $f'(x^*) = 0$ then f has a unique global minimum at x^*.

Conditions for Minimization

If $f(x^*) \le f(x)$ for every real number x then $f'(x^*) = 0$. If $f(x)$ is minimized at x^* subject to the constraints $a \le x \le b$, then either $f'(x^*) = 0$ or $x^* = a$ or $x^* = b$. If f is strictly convex and $f'(x^*) = 0$ then f has a unique global minimum at x^*. If f is strictly convex and we minimize f subject to $a \le x \le b$, then $f'(x) = 0$ and $x > b$ implies that the solution is $x = b$, and the solution is $x = a$ if $f'(x) = 0$ implies $x < a$.

2.2.5 The Tangency Approach

Recall that the marginal rate of substitution (MRS) at a point (x^0, y^0) is the absolute value of the slope of the indifference curve through (x^0, y^0). Let C be that indifference curve. C is defined by $U(x, y) = c^0$, where c^0 is the constant $U(x^0, y^0)$, and it implicitly gives us y as a function of x. For many utility functions we can explicitly solve for y as a function of x. For other cases, we use the implicit function theorem: the derivative dy/dx of the implicit function is the negative of the ratio of the partial derivatives of U.

Example 2.9 Tangency and Consumer Choice

We reconsider Example 2.8: Maximize $U(x, y) = x^2y$ subject to $5x + 2y = 60$. Notice that utility is zero if either $x = 0$ or $y = 0$, so the solution will have $x > 0$ and $y > 0$. In that case, the economic argument based on indifference curves reveals that the MRS equals the price ratio at the chosen consumption plan. To derive the MRS we set utility equal to a constant ℓ. That gives us the equation of a generic indifference curve: $x^2y = \ell$ in the present case. Solve for y to get $y = \ell x^{-2}$. Then $dy/dx = -2\ell x^{-3}$. Because $\ell = x^2y$ we have

$$\frac{dy}{dx} = -2x^2yx^{-3} = -\frac{2y}{x}$$

The MRS is the negative of the slope of the indifference curve, and hence if $U = x^2y$ the MRS at the generic bundle (x, y) is $2y/x$. The price ratio is $5/2$. Therefore, the solution will satisfy $2y/x = 5/2$, which implies $4y = 5x$. This equation does not have a unique solution, nor should we expect one. We can't pin down the choice without the budget equation. Substituting $4y$ for $5x$ in the budget equation yields $4y + 2y = 60$ and hence $y = 10$. Then $4y = 40 = 5x$. Therefore, $x = 8$. (Verify that $x = 8$ and $y = 10$ satisfies the budget equation and equates MRS and the price ratio.)

2.2.6 The Total Derivative and the Chain Rule

If f is a function of x and y, and y itself is a function of x, say $y = g(x)$, then the chain rule gives us df/dx in terms of the partial derivatives of f and the derivative of g. Specifically

$$\frac{df}{dx} = \frac{\partial f}{\partial x} + \frac{\partial f}{\partial y} \times \frac{dy}{dx}$$

$$= \frac{\partial f}{\partial x} + \frac{\partial f}{\partial y} \times g'(x).$$

In words, the rate of change in f with respect to x is the rate of change of f with respect to x when y is held constant, *plus* the rate of change of f with respect to y (with x held constant) multiplied by the rate of change of y per unit change in x, determined by the function g. It is easy to grasp the idea by looking at linear functions.

Example 2.10 The Chain Rule With Linear Functions

Suppose $f(x, y) = 2x + 5y$, and $y = 3x$. Of course, $\partial f/\partial x = 2$ and $\partial f/\partial y = 5$, with $g'(x) = 3$. According to the chain rule $df/dx = 2 + 5 \times 3 = 17$. We can confirm this by substituting $3x$ for y in f. We get $f = 2x + 5(3x) = 17x$. Clearly, $df/dx = 17$.

Example 2.11 The Chain Rule and Consumer Choice

Maximize $U(x, y) = x^2y$ subject to $5x + 2y = 60$. We have $y = 30 - 2.5x$ from the budget constraint, and thus $dy/dx = -2.5$. Because $U(x, y)$ depends on x and y we let U_x denote the partial derivative of U with respect to x and let U_y denote the partial derivative of U with respect to y. If we think of y as a function of x, then the total derivative of U with respect to x is

$$\frac{dU}{dx} = U_x + U_y \times \frac{dy}{dx}.$$

We have $U_x = 2xy$ and $U_y = x^2$. Therefore, $dU/dx = 2xy - 2.5x^2$. Now, set this equal to zero to find a maximum:

$$2xy - 2.5x^2 = 0.$$

Dividing through by x yields

$$2y - 2.5x = 0 \text{ and } 4y = 5x.$$

(Do we have to worry about dividing by zero?) Substituting $4y$ for $5x$ in the budget equation yields $y = 10$, and thus $x = 8$.

Sources

The material in this section is very standard and is the subject of hundreds of mathematics books, including Strang (1991). Dozens more texts with economic applications have been written by and for economists, including Novshek (1993) and Binmore and Davies (2001).

Problem Set

(1) Draw the graph of a function that has a unique global maximum at $x^* > b$ although the solution to the problem "maximize $f(x)$ subject to $a \le x \le b$" is $x = a$. In other words, the solution to the constrained maximization problem is not the point in the constraint region that is closest to x^*.

(2) Solve for the demand functions of a consumer whose preferences can be represented by the utility function $U(x, y) = x^\alpha y^\beta$, where α and β are positive constants.

(3) Solve for the demand functions of a consumer whose preferences can be represented by the utility function $U(x, y) = (x + 1)y$.

(4) Solve for the demand functions of a consumer whose preferences can be represented by the utility function $U(x, y) = \sqrt{x} + y$.

2.3 LAGRANGIAN MULTIPLIERS

In Section 2.2 we were able to solve constrained maximization problems involving two variables x and y because there was only one constraint, and that could be solved to express y as a function of x. The resulting function was then substituted for y in the function being maximized, leaving us with an unconstrained one-variable problem. That technique suffices for all of the applications in this book. However, if you want to know more about the use of prices – that is, Lagrangian multipliers – in solving constrained maximization problems you will benefit from this section. The Lagrangian technique requires verification of a constraint quali-fication, but we will not address that issue because our examples will use functions for which the qualification is met. Moreover, that is also the case with virtually all economic applications.

∂2.3.1 The Lagrangian Multiplier with a Single Resource Constraint

We return to Example 2.8, this time using the Lagrangian technique to obtain the solution.

Example 2.12 The Lagrangian Approach to Consumer Choice

We want to maximize $U(x, y) = x^2 y$ subject to $5x + 2y = 60$. Instead we maximize

$$\mathcal{L} = x^2 y - \lambda(5x + 2y - 60).$$

Let $\mathcal{L}_x$ denote the partial derivative of $\mathcal{L}$ with respect to x and let $\mathcal{L}_y$ denote the partial of $\mathcal{L}$ with respect to y. Setting the first partials equal to zero yields

$$\mathcal{L}_x = 2xy - 5\lambda = 0 \text{ and } \mathcal{L}_y = x^2 - 2\lambda = 0.$$

The first equation yields $\lambda = 2xy/5$ and substituting this value of λ into the second equation leads to

$$x^2 - 2 \times \frac{2xy}{5} = 0,$$

or $5x = 4y$ after dividing both sides by x. (We know that x will not be zero at the chosen consumption plan.) We solve $5x = 4y$ and the budget equation to obtain $x = 8$ and $y = 10$.

Now, substitute the solution values of x and y into the equation $\mathcal{L}_x = 0$ to solve for λ. We get $2(8)(10) - 5\lambda = 0$, and hence $\lambda^* = 32$ at the solution point $(x^* y^*)$. To interpret λ^*, write the budget equation with income m as a variable:

$$5x + 2y = m.$$

Solve once more for the consumer's chosen basket. We still get $5x = 4y$ whatever solution technique is employed. Substituting into the budget equation yields $4y + 2y = m$, or $y = m/6$. Because $4y = 5x$ we have $5x = 4m/6$, or $x = 4m/30$. This gives us the demands as a function of income: $x^* = 4m/30$ and $y^* = m/6$, given $p_1 = 5$ and $p_2 = 2$. Now, substitute these demands into the utility function. We get

$$U = \left(\frac{4m}{30}\right)^2 \times \frac{m}{6} = \frac{16m^3}{5400}.$$

Then $dU/dm = (16 \times 3m^2)/5400 = 8m^2/900$. When $m = 60$ this yields $dU/dm = 32 = \lambda^*$. This generalizes: the Lagrangian multiplier always gives the increase in utility per unit increase in income.

∂2.3.2 Remark on Planning and Lagrangians

The function of price in a market system is in part to signal marginal values to producers and consumers. Example 2.12 illustrates the fact that Lagrangian multipliers are also marginal values. If we maximize $U(x, y)$ subject to the constraint $px + qy = c$, the value of U at the solution point (x^*, y^*) will, of course, be a function of c. If p and q are positive constants, the larger is c the larger U will be. Specifically, $dU/dc = \lambda^*$ if λ is the multiplier associated with the constraint. That means that the Lagrangian can be interpreted as a price. This will be true even if the constraint is nonlinear. Therefore, prices are intrinsic to the solution of constrained maximization problems, even in the case of problems that appear to have nothing to do with economics. For optimization problems that arise from economic considerations, the fact that Lagrangians are marginal values is of great significance.

Suppose that $U(x, y)$ is an economic planner's objective function, representing the social value of output in the economy, and the equation $px + qy = c$ represents a resource constraint on the capacity of the economy to produce x and y. Then the solution value λ^* of the Lagrangian multiplier associated with a particular constraint is the marginal value of the associated scarce resource. If Δc additional units of the resource were obtained, and the maximization problem was solved again, the value of U would increase by approximately $\lambda^* \Delta c$. Therefore, even if the planner has no intention of deferring to the market system, prices are embedded in the mathematical logic of constrained maximization. They can be used to guide the system to the socially optimal menu of goods and services – that is, the one that maximizes U subject to resource and technology constraints. Moreover, when prices are used to guide decision making, it is far easier to design incentives to get producers and consumers to do their part in arriving at the optimal menu.

When there are many variables and many constraints the Lagrangian technique is by far the most efficient. And, as Example 2.12 demonstrates, once the planners start using Lagrangians they are using prices. The Lagrangian is the marginal value of an additional unit of the scarce resource that gives rise to the constraint, as we explain in greater depth in the next section.

∂2.3.3 Lagrangian Multipliers with More than One Resource Constraint

Consider the problem

$$\text{maximize } f(x, y) \quad \text{subject to } g(x, y) \le a \text{ and } h(x, y) \le b.$$

We will not consider functions that depend on more than the two variables x and y, nor will we have more than the two constraints g and h. The two-variable, two-constraint case will provide sufficient insight.

The function f represents the goal or objective, and we want to pick the values of x and y that maximize f. But constraints g and h restrict the values of x and y that can be selected. For instance, f might refer to the value to society of the plan (x, y) with g and h reflecting resource utilization by the plan of two inputs A and B – labor and capital, say. Then a and b denote the total amounts available of A and B, respectively. The plan (x, y) uses $g(x, y)$ units of labor, and that cannot exceed the total amount of labor, a, in the economy. Similarly, the plan (x, y) uses $h(x, y)$ units of capital but the economy has only b units of capital available. In different application $f(x, y)$ is a firm's profit from the production of x units of commodity X and y units of commodity Y. The constraints represent limitations such as warehouse and transportation capacity.

DEFINITION: *Resource Utilization*

The plan (x, y) requires $g(x, y)$ units of resource A as input and $h(x, y)$ units of resource B.

The solution of our constrained maximization problem can be characterized by means of two Lagrangian variables α and β associated with the respective constraints g and h. If x^* and y^* constitute a solution to the problem then there exist $\alpha \geq 0$ and $\beta \geq 0$ such that

$$\frac{\partial f(x^*,y^*)}{\partial x} - \alpha \times \frac{\partial g(x^*,y^*)}{\partial x} - \beta \times \frac{\partial h(x^*,y^*)}{\partial x} = 0 \qquad [6]$$

and

$$\frac{\partial f(x^*,y^*)}{\partial y} - \alpha \times \frac{\partial g(x^*,y^*)}{\partial y} - \beta \times \frac{\partial h(x^*,y^*)}{\partial y} = 0. \qquad [7]$$

Notice that we arrive at the same two necessary conditions if (x^*, y^*) is the plan that maximizes

$$\mathscr{L} = f(x,y) - \alpha g(x,y) - \beta h(x,y),$$

provided that we treat α and β as given constants. That is, if we take the partial derivatives of $\mathscr{L}$ and equate them to zero we get the first-order conditions [6] and [7]. The interpretation of α and β as prices is not a mere contrivance: Lagrangian variable α is a price in the sense that it is the marginal value of a unit of the resource A underlying constraint g, and similarly for β and resource B. In other words, if additional units of A can be obtained then α is the rate at which f will increase per unit of A added. Therefore, α and β are *social cost prices*. (Recall the definition in the introductory section of Chapter 1.) Hence $\mathscr{L}(x, y)$ is the gross value $f(x, y)$ of the plan (x, y) minus the cost of employing the scarce resources.

We need to *prove* that there exists α and β such that [6] and [7] have to hold if (x^*, y^*) is a solution to our original problem. Why can we use prices to characterize the solution to a problem that at the outset may have nothing to do with prices or at least is articulated without any reference to prices? The remainder of this subsection explains, but if you want to make a smaller investment of time you may be satisfied with the following numerical example.

Example 2.13 Linear Functions

Maximize $f(x, y) = 4x + 7y$ subject to $x + 3y \leq 34$ and $2x + y \leq 18$. Figure 2.2 shows that the solution will occur at the plan (x^*, y^*) where the lines $x + 3y = 34$ and $2x + y = 18$ meet. Solving these two equations yields $x^* = 4$ and $y^* = 10$, and thus $4x^* + 7y^* = 86$, the maximum value of f.

The solution is the plan $(4, 10)$ where the lines $x + 3y = 34$ and $2x + y = 18$ intersect because the slope of the line $4x + 7y = 86$ is in between the slopes of the lines $x + 3y = 34$ and $2x + y = 18$. (The absolute values of the slopes of g, f, and h are respectively $1/3 < 4/7 < 2$.) For the present problem, [6] and [7] become

$$4 = \alpha + 2\beta \quad \text{and} \quad 7 = 3\alpha + \beta$$

the solution of which is $\alpha = 2$ and $\beta = 1$. Our claim is that if we obtain one more unit of resource A and replace the constraint $x + 3y \leq 34$ with $x + 3y \leq 35$ then the solution value of the objective function will increase by $\alpha = 2$. Let's confirm this. The solution

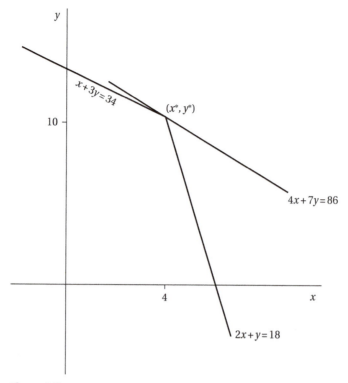

Figure 2.2

is now $x = 3.8$ and $y = 10.4$ where the lines $x + 3y = 35$ and $2x + y = 18$ meet. The value of the objective function f is $4 \times 3.8 + 7 \times 10.4 = 88$, an increase of 2 over the solution value of f for the original problem. Now let's have b increase by 1, with a at its original level of 34. Does the maximum value of the objective function increase by $\beta = 1$? The solution to this new constrained optimization problem is $x = 4.6$ and $y = 9.8$ at the intersection of the lines $x + 3y = 34$ and $2x + y = 19$. This time, the value of the objective function is $4 \times 4.6 + 7 \times 9.8 = 87$, an increase of 1.

Consider the simple linear equation $5x + 2y = 0$ represented in Figure 2.3 where we see that the vector of coefficients $(5, 2)$ makes a ninety-degree angle with the line generated by those coefficients. This always holds: the vector (p, q) makes a ninety-degree angle with the line $px + qy = 0$. Look at the specific case $5x + 2y = 0$ first. If $x = 2$ then $y = -5$ if the point (x, y) is on the line. (Just solve $5 \times 2 + 2y = 0$ for y.) Then we have a triangle with the three vertices $(5, 2)$, $(2, -5)$, and $(0, 0)$ and with sides a, b, and c as depicted in Figure 2.3. We want to show that angle θ is a right angle, so we need to prove that $a^2 + b^2 = c^2$, the Pythagorean equality. (Section 2.3.4 shows why θ is a right angle *if* the Pythagorean equality holds.)

$$a^2 = (5 - 0)^2 + (2 - 0)^2 = 25 + 4 = 29.$$
$$b^2 = (2 - 0)^2 + (-5 - 0)^2 = 4 + 25 = 29.$$
$$c^2 = (2 - 5)^2 + (-5 - 2)^2 = 9 + 49 = 58.$$

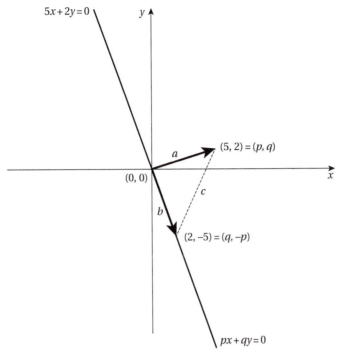

Figure 2.3

Therefore, $a^2 + b^2 = c^2$, and hence θ is a right angle. In general, the point $(q, -p)$ is on the line $px + qy = 0$ so we have a triangle with the three vertices (p, q), $(q, -p)$, and $(0, 0)$. Consult Figure 2.3 again:

$$a^2 = (p - 0)^2 + (q - 0)^2 = p^2 + q^2,$$
$$b^2 = (q - 0)^2 + (-p - 0)^2 = q^2 + p^2,$$
$$c^2 = (q - p)^2 + (-p - q)^2 = q^2 - 2qp + p^2 + p^2 + 2pq + q^2 = 2(p^2 + q^2).$$

Therefore, $a^2 + b^2 = c^2$, and hence θ is a right angle.

Because (p, q) makes a right angle with the line $px + qy = 0$, if we start at a point (x, y) on the line $px + qy = \Omega$ and move in the direction (p, q) then we are increasing the value of $px + qy$ at the fastest rate, as illustrated by Figure 2.4. The directions A_1 and A_2 do not make right angles with the line ℓ_0, and they get us onto the respective level curves ℓ_1 and ℓ_2, which are below the level curve ℓ_{pq} associated with the direction (p, q). (We have normalized the arrows so that they all have unit length.)

Consider the generic constrained optimization problem for linear functions:

$$\text{maximize } f_1 x + f_2 y \quad \text{subject to } g_1 x + g_2 y \leq a \text{ and } h_1 x + h_2 y \leq b.$$

In this case, f_1, f_2, g_1, g_2, h_1, and h_2 are given *constants*. We deal with the family of problems for which the solution occurs at the plan (x^*, y^*) where the lines $g_1 x + g_2 y = a$ and $h_1 x + h_2 y = b$ meet (Figure 2.5a). The vector (f_1, f_2) must lie between (g_1, g_2) and (h_1, h_2) otherwise (x^*, y^*) would not be the solution (Figure 2.5b). This means that (f_1, f_2) can be expressed as a linear combination of (g_1, g_2) and

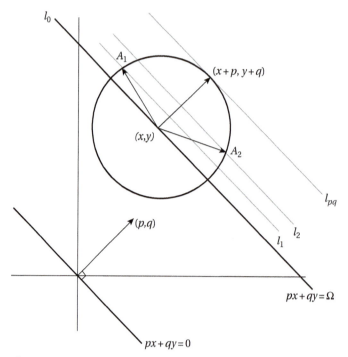

Figure 2.4

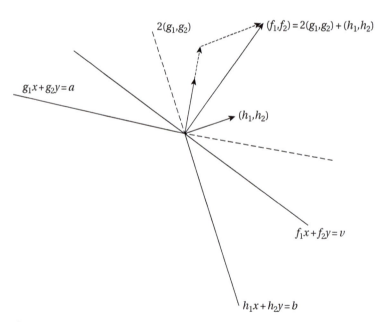

Figure 2.5a

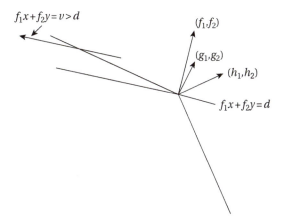

Figure 2.5b

(h_1, h_2) *and* that the weights α and β will be positive (or at least nonnegative). For the example of Figure 2.5a we have $(f_1, f_2) = 2(g_1, g_2) + 1(h_1, h_2)$. That is,

$$f_1 = 2g_1 + h_1 \quad \text{and} \quad f_2 = 2g_2 + h_2.$$

(When we apply these two conditions to Example 2.13 we get $4 = 2 \times 1 + 1 \times 2$ and $7 = 2 \times 3 + 1 \times 1$.)

Consider two special cases. Case (i): the lines $f_1x + f_2y = v$ and $g_1x + g_2y = a$ coincide, where v denotes the solution value of the objective function. Then the arrows (f_1, f_2) and (g_1, g_2) point in the same direction, and we must have

$$f_1 = \alpha g_1 + 0h_1 \quad \text{and} \quad f_2 = \alpha g_2 + 0h_2$$

for $\alpha > 0$. What does this tell us? Consult Figure 2.6. An increase in the B resource, shifting the boundary of the h constraint out from ℓ_b to ℓ_{b+1}, will not lead to any increase in the value of the objective function f. The diagram shows that there is no production plan in the expanded feasible region that puts us on a higher level curve. Clearly, the marginal value of resource B is zero: additional amounts of it are not beneficial. This is why $\beta = 0$.

Case (ii): the lines $f_1x + f_2y = v$ and $h_1x + h_2y = b$ coincide, so (f_1, f_2) and (h_1, h_2) are colinear. Hence

$$f_1 = 0g_1 + \beta h_1 \quad \text{and} \quad f_2 = 0g_2 + \beta h_2$$

for $\beta > 0$. This time an increase in the A resource will not increase the solution value of the objective function. You can confirm this by drawing a diagram analogous to Figure 2.6. The marginal value to society of resource A is zero in this case.

Consider the typical situation with α and β both positive. Suppose that (f_1, f_2) is close to (g_1, g_2) as depicted in Figure 2.7a. Then α will be large relative to β, and this tells us that an increase in resource A will have a bigger impact on the objective function than an increase in resource B. We demonstrate this by considering in turn what happens when the amount available of input A increases from a to $a + 1$ and then when the amount of input B increases to $b + 1$. When input A increases to

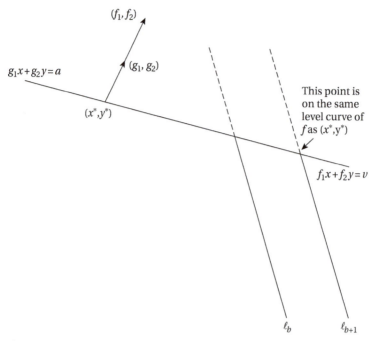

Figure 2.6

$a + 1$ the boundary of the g constraint, involving resource A, shifts up from ℓ_a to ℓ_{a+1}, as Figure 2.7a shows. The other boundary line is unchanged, because b has not changed. We can move to a higher level curve, reflecting an increase in the solution value of f. The optimal plan moves from S^0 to S^{a+1}. Figure 2.7b shows what happens when the amount available of input B increases to $b + 1$. The boundary of the h constraint, involving resource B, shifts out, from ℓ_b to ℓ_{b+1}, and ℓ_a is unchanged. We again move to a higher level curve (from S^0 to S^{b+1}) but the move is not nearly as great as when we get an additional unit of resource A. Resource A is substantially more valuable than resource B: there is a much bigger increase in the solution value of f when we get an extra unit of A, and thus α is much bigger than β. To convince yourself that α is *precisely* the rate at which the solution value of f increases per additional unit of resource A – and analogously for B – go back to the calculation of Example 2.13.

The Lagrangian variables α and β are prices in the sense that they equal the value of additional units of the respective resources. For the planning interpretation of the constrained maximization problem, the variable α is the cost imposed on society by a firm using a unit of A. This unit of A could be employed elsewhere to generate α additional units of "social welfare" – assuming that is what f measures. Imposing a cost on the firm of α per unit of A employed by the firm promotes efficiency in that it forces the firm to provide at least α units of social welfare per unit of A employed. Otherwise its profit would fall when it increased its employment of A. It would take a loss. The unit cost (or price) α reveals to the firm the consumer benefit lost when that firm employs a unit of A, thereby diverting it from the production of other commodities. The profit motive gives the firm incentive to

(a)

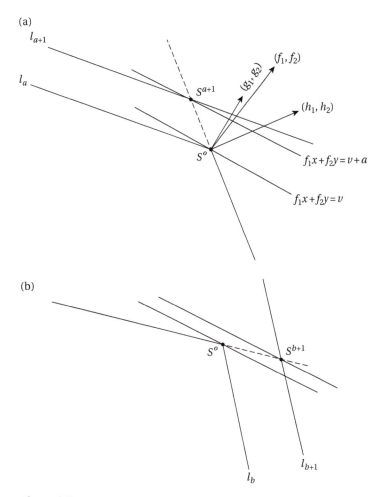

(b)

Figure 2.7

incorporate that social cost into its decision making. The same holds for β with respect to resource B. (Chapter 4 investigates the problem of motivating the manager of the firm to maximize profit.) We haven't discussed incentives in this section, but we have seen that prices can in principle be used to guide an economy, or a firm within an economy, to an efficient outcome. We didn't begin with the determination to employ prices. The prices were forced on us by the mathematics.

If the functions f, g, and h are nonlinear, then the preceding argument goes through if we interpret f_1 as the partial derivative of f with respect to x, evaluated at the optimal plan, with f_2 representing the partial of f with respect to y, also evaluated at the optimal plan, and similarly for g_1, g_2, h_1, and h_2. Confirm that [6] and [7] are the first-order conditions associated with the maximization of

$$\mathscr{L} \equiv f(x, y) - \alpha g(x, y) - \beta h(x, y).$$

Recall that $g(x, y)$ is the amount of A used as input by the plan (x, y). If the price α is the cost to society of employing one unit of A, then $\alpha g(x, y)$ is the cost to society of the amount of A required by the production plan (x, y). Similarly, $\beta h(x, y)$ is the cost to society of the amount of B required by the plan (x, y). Therefore, maximization of $\mathscr{L}$ can be interpreted as the maximization of the value to society of the plan (x, y) net of the cost to society of the resources consumed by that plan.

2.3.4 The Converse of the Pythagorean Theorem

The Pythagorean theorem states that $a^2 + b^2 = c^2$ if θ is a right angle (see Figure 2.3). To prove that θ is a right angle *if* $a^2 + b^2 = c^2$, drop a line from the vertex at the intersection of sides a and c, so that the line meets side b at a right angle (Figure 2.8). Call this line d, and let e represent the third side of the right triangle, which has as its other sides a and d. Let the same letters represent the *lengths* of the sides, and consider the following equations:

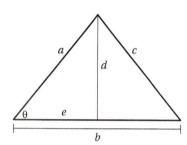

Figure 2.8

$$a^2 + b^2 = c^2, \tag{8}$$

$$d^2 + e^2 = a^2, \tag{9}$$

$$d^2 + (b - e)^2 = c^2, \tag{10}$$

We are given [8] and the other two statements are derived from the Pythagorean theorem. Rewrite [10], after replacing d^2 with $a^2 - e^2$ (from [9]) and c^2 with $a^2 + b^2$ (from [8]). We get

$$a^2 - e^2 + b^2 - 2be + e^2 = a^2 + b^2,$$

which reduces to $2be = 0$. We are given $b \neq 0$, and hence $e = 0$. Therefore, a and d coincide. It follows that θ is a right angle. (Could θ be greater than ninety degrees? That would put the line d to the *left* of side a? In that case, draw a new diagram by extending the base b of the original triangle to the left so that it meets the line d, which is perpendicular to the extended base line. Equations [8] and [9] still hold but [10] is replaced by $d^2 + (b + e)^2 = c^2$, and the three equations still yield $2be = 0$.)

Sources

The eighteenth century French mathematician Joseph-Louis Lagrange showed how multipliers (later called Lagrangian multipliers) can be used to derive necessary conditions for the maximization of a function subject to *equality* constraints. Kuhn and Tucker (1950) extended this to *in*equality constraints that satisfy a simple regularity condition, and the multipliers came to be known as Kuhn-Tucker multipliers before it was discovered that their work was anticipated by William Karush (1939). They are now called Karush-Kuhn-Tucker multipliers.

Links

A good introductory treatment of the general problem of maximizing a function of an arbitrary number of variables subject to an arbitrary number of constraints can be found in Chapter 12 of Weintraub (1982). Chapters 5 and 6 of Novshek (1993) provide a more thorough account, as does Chapter 6 of Binmore and Davies (2001). Koopmans (1957) remains a superb elucidation of the lessons of constrained optimization theory for resource allocation.

Problem Set

(1) Given the constants f_1 and f_2, use an algebraic argument to show that if we take a step of unit length in any direction from the point (x, y) then we will obtain the greatest increase in the value of $f_1 x + f_2 y$ if we move in the direction (f_1, f_2).

(2) $(f_1, f_2) = (0, 1)$, $(g_1, g_2) = (2, 2)$, and $(h_1, h_2) = (1, 0)$. Draw a diagram to show that (f_1, f_2) does not lie between (g_1, g_2) and (h_1, h_2). Now use algebra to show that we cannot have $(f_1, f_2) = \alpha(g_1, g_2) + \beta(h_1, h_2)$ for nonnegative α and β.

(3) Repeat 2 with $(f_1, f_2) = (4, 1)$, $(g_1, g_2) = (1, 2)$, and $(h_1, h_2) = (2, 1)$.

(4) $(f_1, f_2) = (2, 2)$, $(g_1, g_2) = (0, 1)$, and $(h_1, h_2) = (1, 0)$. Draw a diagram to show that (f_1, f_2) lies between (g_1, g_2) and (h_1, h_2), and then find $\alpha > 0$ and $\beta > 0$ such that $(f_1, f_2) = \alpha(g_1, g_2) + \beta(h_1, h_2)$.

(5) Repeat 4 with $(f_1, f_2) = (2, 1)$, $(g_1, g_2) = (1, 2)$, and $(h_1, h_2) = (4, 1)$.

(6) Consider the standard consumer choice problem:

maximize $U(x, y) = xy$ subject to the budget constraint $x + 4y \leq 24$.

Of course, U is the utility function. Utility depends on the amounts x and y consumed of the two goods. The price of X is \$1 and the price of Y is \$4. Income is \$24. The upper bound on the constraint is the budget line.

(A) Draw the indifference curve through $(4, 3)$ and the indifference curve through $(4, 5)$. Try to be reasonably accurate.

(B) Use calculus to find the consumption plan (x, y) that maximizes utility subject to the budget constraint. To turn this into a one-variable problem, first express the budget constraint as an equality, solve it for y as a function of x, and then substitute this expression for y into the utility function.

(C) Let $g(x, y) = x + 4y$ represent the left-hand side of the budget constraint. Compute the following four partial derivatives: $\partial U(x, y)/\partial x$, $\partial U(x, y)/\partial y$, $\partial g(x, y)/\partial x$, and $\partial g(x, y)/\partial y$. Remember: the partial derivative of f with respect to x, denoted by $\partial f/\partial x$, is obtained by treating y as a constant. (For instance, if $f(x, y) = x^2 + yx + y^2$ then $\partial f/\partial x = 2x + y$.) Similarly, the partial derivative of f with respect to y, denoted by $\partial f/\partial y$, is obtained by treating x as a constant.

(D) Evaluate the partial derivatives of part C at the chosen consumption plan. Find a positive number α such that

$$\frac{\partial U(x^0, y^0)}{\partial x} = \alpha \times \frac{\partial g(x^0, y^0)}{\partial x} \text{ and } \frac{\partial U(x^0, y^0)}{\partial y} = \alpha \times \frac{\partial g(x^0, y^0)}{\partial y}$$

where (x^0, y^0) represents the chosen consumption plan from part B.

(E) Now solve this problem:

$$\text{maximize} \quad U(x, y) \equiv xy \quad \text{subject to } x + 4y = \theta.$$

Note that we have just replaced income in the budget constraint with the parameter θ. The chosen plan (x^*, y^*) will now be a function of θ. Substitute x^* and y^* into the utility function $U = xy$ to get utility as a function of θ, then take the derivative of this function (with respect to θ) and evaluate it at $\theta = 24$. The number you get will equal the value of α from part D.

2.4   THE COMPOSITE COMMODITY MODEL

This section justifies the two-commodity model of consumer choice. To do so we must test it against the complete model with a large number of goods – an arbitrary number, in fact.

In the contrived, composite commodity model X is a conventional good, which we also refer to as the zero*th* good, with x denoting the amount of commodity X demanded. Assuming that the prices of all goods other than X are constant, we let y denote total expenditure on all goods other than X. The second good, Y, is called a *composite commodity*. In fact there is a total of $n + 1$ commodities from which to choose.

2.4.1   The Budget Constraint and Preferences

Let p_0 be the price of X and let θ denote the individual's income. The budget constraint is "total expenditure = income," and this is equivalent to

expenditure on X + expenditure on all other goods = income.

In symbols, $p_0 x + y = \theta$.

Therefore, we can express the individual's budget constraint in terms of the conventional good X and the contrived, composite commodity Y.

What about individual preferences? Let (x', y') and (x'', y'') be two different commodity bundles in the composite model. We say that the individual prefers (x', y') to (x'', y'') if and only if the individual prefers (x', b') to (x'', b'') where b' is the most desirable basket of the n goods other than X that the individual can buy with y' dollars, given that he or she will consume x' units of X, and b'' is the most desirable basket of goods other than X that the individual can buy with y'' dollars, given that he or she will consume x'' units of X. Note that b' itself is a collection of n commodities (involving everything but X) and so is b''. The individual's primitive preferences have been compressed into a preference for bundles in the composite commodity model. We lose a lot of information in the process. The consumption plan (x^*, y^*) is the most-preferred of all the plans satisfying the budget constraint. It identifies expenditure y^* on all goods other than X, but we have no idea how y^* is distributed across the individual commodities. The composite commodity model *does* tell us that the individual demands exactly x^* units of commodity X.

2.4.2 The Composite Commodity Theorem

Section 2.4.1 showed rigorously that the budget constraint can be expressed in terms of x and y, given the price p_0 of X and the individual's income θ. It also suggested that the consumer's preferences can be squeezed into this mold. We now give a rigorous proof that the resulting preferences can be used to identify the amount of commodity X that the individual would actually demand in the real world of $n + 1$ goods.

Let x_c denote the amount of commodity c consumed, for $c = 0, 1, 2,\ldots, n$, and let p_c denote its price. Let $u(x_0, x_1,\ldots, x_n)$ represent the individual's utility function. The consumer will choose the consumption plan $(x_0, x_1,\ldots, x_n)$ that maximizes utility subject to the budget constraint. We refer to this as problem B.

DEFINITION: *The Basic Problem*

Problem B: find the values $x_0, x_1, x_2,\ldots, x_n$ that maximize $u(x_0, x_1, x_2,\ldots, x_n)$ subject to $p_0x_0 + p_1x_1 + p_2x_2 + \cdots + p_nx_n \le \theta$.

We want to solve this and show that the solution value of x_0 is equal to the solution value of x in the composite commodity model – assuming that we use the same income and the same prices in both cases.

Before we can even state the maximization problem for the composite commodity model we have to derive the two-commodity utility function U from the primitive utility function u of the basic problem. Simply put, $U(x, y)$ is the utility from consuming x units of X along with the best combination of the other goods and services that costs y dollars.

DEFINITION: *The Contrived Utility Function U*

$U(z_0, y)$ is the value of $u(x_0, x_1, x_2,\ldots, x_n)$ when we choose $x_0, x_1, x_2,\ldots, x_n$ to maximize $u(x_0, x_1, x_2,\ldots, x_n)$ subject only to the restrictions

$$x_0 = z_0 \text{ and } p_1x_1 + p_2x_2 + \cdots + p_nx_n \le y.$$

As we will see, the basic problem is closely related to the maximization of U subject to the restriction that expenditure on X and Y cannot exceed θ.

DEFINITION: *The Contrived Problem*

Problem C: Choose α and β to maximize $U(\alpha, \beta)$ subject to $p_0\alpha + \beta \le \theta$.

The solutions to problems B and C are related in the following way.

The Composite Commodity Theorem

If $(z_0, z_1, z_2, \ldots, z_n)$ is a solution to problem B then for $\alpha = z_0$ and $\beta = p_1 z_1 + p_2 z_2 + \cdots + p_n z_n$, the two-commodity bundle (α, β) is a solution to problem C. Conversely, if (α, β) is a solution to problem C there is some solution $(z_0, z_1, z_2, \ldots, z_n)$ to problem B such that $z_0 = \alpha$ and $p_1 z_1 + p_2 z_2 + \cdots + p_n z_n = \beta$. Moreover, for any solutions $(z_0, z_1, z_2, \ldots, z_n)$ and (α, β) to the respective problems B and C we have $u(z_0, z_1, z_2, \ldots, z_n) = U(\alpha, \beta)$.

Proof:

Part 1. Suppose that $(z_0, z_1, z_2, \ldots, z_n)$ is a solution to problem B. We show that (α, β) solves problem C if $\alpha = z_0$ and $\beta = p_1 z_1 + p_2 z_2 + \cdots + p_n z_n$.

Set $\alpha = z_0$ and $\beta = p_1 z_1 + p_2 z_2 + \cdots + p_n z_n$. We have $U(\alpha, \beta) \geq u(z_0, z_1, z_2, \ldots, z_n)$ by definition of U, because $\alpha = z_0$ and $p_1 z_1 + p_2 z_2 + \cdots + p_n z_n \leq \beta$ certainly hold. Clearly, $p_0 z_0 + \beta \leq \theta$ holds. Therefore, (α, β) satisfies the constraints of problem C. Suppose that (α^*, β^*) maximizes U subject to the two constraints of problem C. Then $U(\alpha^*, \beta^*) \geq U(\alpha, \beta)$ because (α, β) is feasible for problem C. By definition of U, there is some $(x_0, x_1, x_2, \ldots, x_n)$ such that

$$U(\alpha^*, \beta^*) = u(x_0, x_1, x_2, \ldots, x_n),$$

with $x_0 = \alpha^*$ and $p_1 x_1 + p_2 x_2 + \cdots + p_n x_n \leq \beta^*$.

But $p_0 x_0 + p_1 x_1 + p_2 x_2 + \cdots + p_n x_n \leq p_0 \alpha^* + \beta^* \leq \theta$. This means that $(x_0, x_1, x_2, \cdots, x_n)$ is feasible for problem B. Therefore

$$u(z_0, z_1, z_2, \ldots, z_n) \geq u(x_0, x_1, x_2, \ldots, x_n)$$

because $(z_0, z_1, z_2, \ldots, z_n)$ gives the maximum value of u subject to the feasibility constraints of problem B. We have proved the following:

$$u(z_0, z_1, z_2, \ldots, z_n) \geq u(x_0, x_1, x_2, \ldots, x_n) = U(\alpha^*, \beta^*) \geq U(\alpha, \beta) \geq u(z_0, z_1, z_2, \ldots, z_n).$$

This can only hold if all of the inequalities are satisfied as *equalities*. Then $U(\alpha, \beta) = U(\alpha^*, \beta^*)$. Note that (α^*, β^*) is the name we have given to an arbitrary solution to problem C and (α, β) satisfies the constraint of problem C. Therefore, (α, β) is also a solution to problem C. We have thus proved the first part of our claim.

Part 2. Suppose that (α, β) is a solution to problem C. We prove that there is a solution $(z_0, z_1, z_2, \ldots, z_n)$ to problem B such that $z_0 = \alpha$ and $p_1 z_1 + p_2 z_2 + \cdots + p_n z_n = \beta$. By definition of U there is some $(z_0, z_1, z_2, \ldots, z_n)$ such that $\alpha = z_0$, $\beta \geq p_1 z_1 + p_2 z_2 + \cdots + p_n z_n$, and

$$U(\alpha, \beta) = u(z_0, z_1, z_2, \cdots, z_n) \geq u(x_0, x_1, x_2, \ldots, x_n)$$

for all $(x_0, x_1, x_2, \cdots, x_n)$ such that $x_0 = \alpha$ and $p_1 x_1 + p_2 x_2 + \cdots + p_n x_n \leq \beta$. Because (α, β) satisfies the constraint of problem C we have

$$p_0 z_0 + p_1 z_1 + p_2 z_2 + \cdots + p_n z_n \leq p_0 \alpha + \beta \leq \theta$$

and hence $(z_0, z_1, z_2, \cdots, z_n)$ satisfies the constraint of problem B. Next we show that $(z_0, z_1, z_2, \cdots, z_n)$ is actually a solution to problem B. Let $(x_0, x_1, x_2, \cdots, x_n)$ be any consumption plan satisfying the constraints of problem B. Set $\alpha^* = x_0$ and $\beta^* = p_1 x_1 + p_2 x_2 + \cdots + p_n x_n$. Then

$$p_0 \alpha^* + \beta^* = p_0 x_0 + p_1 x_1 + p_2 x_2 + \cdots + p_n x_n \leq \theta.$$

Therefore, by definition of U we have

$$u(x_0, x_1, x_2, \ldots, x_n) \leq U(\alpha^*, \beta^*).$$

Note that $p_0 \alpha^* + \beta^* \leq \theta$, and therefore $U(\alpha^*, \beta^*) \leq U(\alpha, \beta)$, because (α, β) solves problem C and (α^*, β^*) is feasible for C. We have

$$u(x_0, x_1, x_2, \cdots, x_n) \leq U(\alpha^*, \beta^*) \leq U(\alpha, \beta) = u(z_0, z_1, z_2, \cdots, z_n).$$

Therefore, $u(x_0, x_1, x_2, \cdots, x_n) \leq u(z_0, z_1, z_2, \cdots, z_n)$ for any values of $x_0, x_1, x_2, \cdots, x_n$ that satisfy the constraint for problem B. This proves that $(z_0, z_1, z_2, \cdots, z_n)$ is a solution to problem B.

Part 3. We have to show that the maximum utility for problem B equals the maximum utility for problem C. We have already done that because Part 1 established that $u(z_0, z_1, z_2, \cdots, z_n) = U(\alpha, \beta)$ holds for any two solutions $(z_0, z_1, z_2, \cdots, z_n)$ and (α, β) of the respective problems. ∎

In some applications, X is also a composite commodity: in an economic analysis of health care, x would be total expenditure on health care and y would be expenditure on everything else. You can see that the justification for employing a composite commodity Y would also be valid for X when x is expenditure on health care, or education, or food, and so forth.

Sources

The composite commodity theorem was discovered independently by Hicks (1939) and Leontief (1936).

2.5 QUASI-LINEAR PREFERENCES

Having simplified things by reducing the number of commodities to two, we now show how a simple family of utility functions can be used to bring additional clarity. Suppose the individual's utility function $U(x, y)$ has the special form $B(x) + y$. This function is linear in y but not necessarily in x.

DEFINITION: *Quasi-Linear Function*
A quasi-linear function of two variables x and y has the form $B(x) + y$, where B can be any function of x.

Quasi-linear preferences endow economic models with some very nice properties. They will be used to uncover basic principles with relatively little effort.

We assume throughout this section that Y is a private good that is divisible. This means two things: (i) an individual cares only about his or her own consumption of Y (but not anyone else's) and prefers more Y to less; and (ii) any amount of any individual i's consumption of Y can be transferred to any individual j. Assumption (i) implies that if x is unchanged but individual i's consumption of Y increases then individual i's utility increases, regardless of how anyone else's consumption of Y changes. Assumption (ii) implies that if individual i has a positive amount ϵ of the private good, however small, any positive fraction of ϵ can be transferred from individual i to someone else. If X is a private good, then x specifies an assignment of some amount X to each individual. If X is a public good, then x denotes the level of that good provided to all. It is also possible that x denotes some mix of public and private goods.

One of the advantages of assuming quasi-linear preferences is that efficiency is equivalent to maximization of the sum of individual utilities (subject to the limitations inherent in resource constraints, etc.). This is demonstrated in two subsections. Subsection 2.5.1 offers a short, easy proof, but it does not incorporate the constraint that an individual's consumption of Y cannot fall below zero. Using calculus, and assuming that consumption is strictly positive, Subsection 8.1.2 of Chapter 8 establishes the equivalence of efficiency and total utility maximization when preferences are quasilinear.

2.5.1 Efficiency with Quasi-Linear Utility

Assuming that Y is a divisible private good and that individual preferences are quasilinear, we show that an allocation is efficient if and only if it maximizes total utility. We have already seen that for *any* model, any outcome that maximizes total utility is efficient (Section 1.4 of Chapter 1). Without quasi-linear preferences, an outcome can be efficient without maximizing total community utility, as Example 2.16 demonstrates. The next example highlights the role of the divisibility assumption.

Table 2.1

Outcome	U_1	U_2
A	2	20
B	100	15

Example 2.14 Efficiency Without Divisibility

There are two feasible outcomes, A and B, and two individuals whose utility functions are displayed in Table 2.1. A is efficient, because a move to B would lower person 2's utility. But A certainly does not maximize total utility. *If* a divisible private good were available, some of it could be transferred from person 1 to person 2 at outcome B to increase U_2. And *if* both U_1 and U_2 were quasi-linear the transfer could be accomplished in a way that left both 1 and 2 with more utility than they would have at A. But this transfer would create a new outcome C, contradicting the assumption that only A and B are feasible in the present case. In this example there is no divisible commodity in the background.

Table 2.2

	1	2	3	Total
$U_i(F)$	15	20	29	64
$U_i(G)$	29	14	28	71
$U_i(H)$	17	22	32	71

This section explains why, when every individual's utility function is quasi-linear, and Y is a divisible private good, every efficient allocation maximizes total utility. We do this by showing how everyone's utility can be increased at any allocation that does *not* maximize total utility.

Each individual i's utility has the form $U_i(x, y_i) = B_i(x) + y_i$. Therefore, if y_i changes to $y_i + \Delta y_i$ but x remains the same, then the change in the individual's utility is

$$\Delta U_i = B_i(x) + y_i + \Delta y_i - [B_i(x) + y_i] = \Delta y_i.$$

In brief, if x does not change, then for each individual i we have $\Delta U_i = \Delta y_i$. In words, the change in individual i's utility is equal to the change in i's consumption of Y if x is unchanged. Now, suppose that outcomes F and G are both feasible, but total utility is higher at G than at F. Then we can create outcome H from G by redistributing commodity Y without changing the value of x at G. Because x does not change, there is no transfer of resources from the production of Y to the production of X. Consequently, the total amount of Y available for consumption will be the same at G and H. When we create H from G simply by redistributing Y the new outcome H will be feasible. And because total utility is higher at G than at F the redistribution can be done in a way that increases everyone's utility.

Example 2.15 Three Individuals

Outcomes F and G are given, and the individual utility levels realized at each are specified by Table 2.2. F is not efficient, but outcome G by itself does not demonstrate that because persons 2 and 3 have lower utility at G than at F. However, if we create H from G by setting $\Delta x = 0$, $\Delta y_1 = -12$, $\Delta y_2 = +8$, and $\Delta y_3 = +4$ then the sum of the changes in Y is zero. Therefore, H is feasible. Because $\Delta x = 0$ we have $U_1(H) = U_1(G) + \Delta y_1 = 29 - 12 = 17$. And $U_2(H) = U_2(G) + \Delta y_2 = 14 + 8 = 22$. Finally, $U_3(H) = U_3(G) + \Delta y_3 = 28 + 4 = 32$. Outcome H gives everyone more utility than F, and we have demonstrated that F is not efficient.

There will be more than one efficient allocation because if (x, y) maximizes total utility then it is efficient. Then (x, y') is efficient for any y' such that $\sum_{i \in N} y'_i = \sum_{i \in N} y_i$. That's because x has not changed and total consumption of Y has not changed, and thus total utility is still maximized. Thus (x, y') must be efficient.

Example 2.15 does not specify the consumption y_1 of individual 1 at G. Therefore, we cannot be sure that $y_1 - 12$ is not negative. Our argument was perfectly rigorous, provided that $y_i \geq 0$ is not required. In many models, the original consumption levels of the private good are assumed to be high enough so that there is no danger of driving someone's consumption of that good below zero. We continue to assume that there is no nonnegativity constraint on individual Y consumption. (Section 8.1.2 of Chapter 8 imposes the constraint $y_i \geq 0$.)

Efficiency Theorem for Quasi-Linear Utility Functions
> *If each individual's preference scheme can be represented by a quasi-linear utility function and y_i is allowed to have any value (positive, negative, or zero) then an allocation is efficient if and only if it maximizes total utility.*

Proof:

There are n individuals, indexed by $i = 1, 2, \cdots, n$. $\sum$ will always denote summation over all n individuals. Our argument works for any interpretation of the variable x.

We will show that an outcome cannot be efficient if it does not maximize total utility. Each individual i has a utility function of the form $U_i(x, y_i) = B_i(x) + y_i$. It follows that if x does not change then $\Delta U_i = \Delta y_i$.

Suppose that A and Z are feasible outcomes but $\sum U_i(Z) > \sum U_i(A)$. Create a new outcome Q that is identical to Z except that we change each y_i by an amount Δy_i. (Q and Z have the same value of x.)

$$\text{Set } \Delta y_i = U_i(A) - U_i(Z) \text{ if } i > 1.$$

Then $U_i(Q) = U_i(Z) + \Delta y_i = U_i(A)$ if $i > 1$. Feasibility of Q is assured if $\sum \Delta y_i = 0$.

$$\text{Set } \Delta y_1 = \sum U_i(Z) - U_1(Z) - \sum U_i(A) + U_1(A).$$

We have $\sum \Delta y_i = 0$. And

$$U_1(Q) = U_1(Z) + \Delta y_1 = U_1(Z) + \sum U_i(Z) - U_1(Z) - \sum U_i(A) + U_1(A).$$

$$= U_1(A) + \sum U_i(Z) - \sum U_i(A)$$

which is positive, and thus $U_1(Q) > U_1(A)$. Because $U_i(Q) = U_i(A)$ for all $i > 1$, we have increased one person's utility without lowering anyone else's. Outcome A is not efficient. ∎

It is easy to modify the proof to give everyone strictly greater utility than at A: just have person 1 share some, but not all, of his Y increase with everyone else. Our proof clearly depends on the divisibility of Y – think of Y as money – but X could be available only in discrete units, although the argument applies equally well when X is divisible. We conclude this subsection by showing that the quasi-linear assumption is crucial.

Example 2.16 Counterexample When One of the Utility Functions is Not Quasi-Linear

There are two individuals, 1 and 2. $U_1(x, y_1) = \frac{1}{2}x + y_1$ and $U_2(x, y_2) = xy_2$. Person 1's utility function is quasi-linear, but 2's is not. The feasible outcomes are values of x, y_1, and y_2 such that $x + y_1 + y_2 = 4$. Outcome A has $x = 2$, $y_1 = 1$, and $y_2 = 1$. Then A is feasible. It is also efficient. To prove that A is efficient we begin by trying to increase U_2 without changing U_1. To keep U_1 constant set $\frac{1}{2}x + y_1 = 2$. We also have to satisfy the feasibility requirement $x + y_1 + y_2 = 4$. If we subtract $\frac{1}{2}x + y_1$ from the left-hand side of the last equation and we subtract 2 from the right-hand side we get $\frac{1}{2}x + y_2 = 2$. This means that $y_2 = 2 - \frac{1}{2}x$. Therefore, we want to maximize $U_2 = xy_2$ subject to $y_2 = 2 - \frac{1}{2}x$. That is equivalent to maximizing $x(2 - \frac{1}{2}x) = 2x - \frac{1}{2}x^2$. You can use calculus to get the solution value $x = 2$. Alternatively, note that $2 - \frac{1}{2}x^2 = 2 - \frac{1}{2}(x - 2)^2$. To maximize $2 - \frac{1}{2}(x - 2)^2$ we have to set $x = 2$; otherwise we will be subtracting a positive number from 2 to get the value U_2. We have $x = 2$ and $y_2 = 2 - \frac{1}{2}x$. Therefore, $y_2 = 1$. If $x = 2$, $y_2 = 1$, and feasibility requires $x + y_1 + y_2 = 4$, we must have $y_1 = 1$. That is precisely outcome A. We have demonstrated that if U_1 must equal its value at A then any feasible outcome other than A must yield a lower value of U_2 than the value of U_2 at A. This implies that, starting from A, we cannot increase U_2 without lowering U_1. It also implies that, starting from A, we cannot increase U_1 without lowering U_2. (Why?) Therefore, A is efficient. But A does not maximize $U_1 + U_2$ over the set of feasible allocations. At A we have $U_1 + U_2 = 2 + 2 \times 1 = 4$. If B has $x = 2 = y_2$ and $y_1 = 0$, then at B we have $U_1 + U_2 = 1 + 2 \times 2 = 5$. A is efficient, but it does not maximize the sum of utilities. This does not depend on the fact that y_1 is 0 at B: Set $x = 2$, $y_1 = \epsilon$, and $y_2 = 2 - \epsilon$ to create outcome C. Then C is feasible. We can take $\epsilon > 0$ sufficiently small so that $U_1 + U_2$ is as close as we like to 5.

Our proof of the efficiency theorem did not acknowledge the possibility that when Δy_i is negative the resulting consumption of the private good by individual i, which is $y_i + \Delta y_i$, could be negative. Fortunately, there are many applications in which we do not need to worry about the constraint $y_i \geq 0$, simply because there is reason to believe that no one's consumption of the private good will be driven to zero. For completeness and rigor, Section 8.1.2 of Chapter 8 explicitly imposes $y_i \geq 0$ for each individual i.

∂2.5.2 Quasi-Linear Preference and Demand

We now drop the subscript i and focus on a single individual, whose utility depends only on his or her own consumption of X and Y. The utility function has the quasi-linear form $U(x, y) = B(x) + y$. We also assume diminishing marginal utility, which means that $B''(x) < 0$ at all x. We show (in Section 2.5.3) that the function B can be recovered from the individual's demand function for X.

We will demonstrate that, beyond a minimum income level, when the individual's income increases he or she will not change the consumption of X if prices do not change. Assuming that the price of X is not so high that the individual demands zero units of X, maximization of utility subject to the budget constraint implies that $B'(x)$ equals the price ratio. Let x^* be the value of x for which this holds. As income increases, we will still have $B'(x^*)$ equal to the price ratio, so x^* will still be the individual's demand for X. (*This claim is true only for quasi-linear preferences.*)

Income Effect with Quasi-Linear Utility Functions

If $U = B(x) + y$, and both x and y are positive at the chosen consumption plan, then the demand for X will not change when income increases.

Proof:

Maximize $B(x) + y$ subject to $p_1x + p_2y = \theta$, *and* $x \geq 0$ and $y \geq 0$: we can solve the budget constraint for y. We have $y = (\theta - p_1x)/p_2$. Therefore we maximize

$$V(x) = B(x) + \frac{\theta - p_1x}{p_2},$$

a function of x, subject to $0 \leq x \leq \theta/p_1$. (Note that $y = (\theta - p_1x)/p_2$ will be nonnegative if and only if $x \leq \theta/p_1$.) Assume that $0 < x^* < \theta/p_1$ at the maximizing value of x. Then the first derivative of $V(x)$ must equal zero at x^*. That is, $B'(x^*) - p_1/p_2 = 0$, which of course implies $B'(x^*) = p_1/p_2$. The solution x^* will be unique because $B''(x) < 0$ at all x. Moreover, $B'(x^*) = p_1/p_2$ will still hold if income increases and prices do not change. Therefore, the demand for X does not change when income changes. ∎

We can view this in terms of the tangency condition for consumer choice: the indifference curve is tangent to the budget line at the chosen bundle. This means that the marginal rate of substitution (MRS) equals the price ratio. To determine the MRS we start with the fact the utility is constant along an indifference curve. Therefore, the equation of an indifference curve is $B(x) + y = \ell$, where ℓ is a constant. We have $y = \ell - B(x)$. The derivative of this function is $-B'(x)$, which is thus the slope of the indifference curve at the point (x, y). Because the MRS is the absolute value of the slope of the indifference curve, the MRS is $B'(x)$. The MRS is independent of y so, with x on the horizontal axis, the MRS is constant along any vertical line. If we have a consumer optimum (x^*, y^*) that does not occur at a corner point of the budget region we will have MRS $= p_1/p_2$, and that can occur at only one point on the budget line. As income increases and the budget line shifts out parallel to itself the new optimum will also occur at a point where MRS $= p_1/p_2$. The MRS doesn't change. This can only happen on the vertical line through x^*: there is no change in the demand for X. (The demand for X *does* change when p_1 or p_2 changes.)

Now, suppose that $B'(x) = p_1/p_2$ implies $x < 0$. Because $B'' < 0$ we have $B'(0) < p_1/p_2$ and thus $V'(0) = B'(0) - p_1/p_2 < 0$. Because $V'' = B'' < 0$, we have $V'(x) < V'(0) < 0$ for all $x > 0$, and hence $V(x) < V(0)$ for all $x > 0$. The solution to the constrained utility maximization problem is $x = 0$. If θ (income) increases we will still have $B'(0) < p_1/p_2$, and thus $x = 0$ will still solve the constrained utility-maximization problem. There is no income effect on the demand for X in this case as well.

There can be an income effect on the demand for X only if $B'(\theta/p_1) > p_1/p_2$, and this inequality will fail for θ large enough, because B' falls as x increases. Let θ^* satisfy $B'(\theta/p_1) = p_1/p_2$. For $\theta > \theta^*$ there is no income effect on the demand for x, and even when $\theta \leq \theta^*$ there is no income effect if $B'(0) < p_1/p_2$. But beyond a minimum income level θ^* there is absolutely no income effect.

Example 2.17 Consumer Choice with Quasi-Linear Utility

$U(x, y) = \ln(x + 1) + y$. Now maximize utility subject to $p_1 x + p_2 y = \theta$. (If y is a composite commodity set $p_2 = 1$.)

Because the budget constraint implies $y = (\theta - p_1 x)/p_2$ we can maximize $V(x) = \ln(x+1) + (\theta - p_1 x)/p_2$ subject to $0 \le x \le \theta/p_1$. The first derivative is $(x+1)^{-1} - p_1/p_2$ and the second derivative is $-(x+1)^{-2}$, which is always negative. If $V'(x^*) = 0$ and $0 \le x^* \le \theta/p_1$ then x^* is our solution (see Section 2.2). Then we will have $(x^*+1)^{-1} - p_1/p_2 = 0$, which implies $x^* = p_2/p_1 - 1$. If $p_2/p_1 - 1 < 0$ or $p_2/p_1 - 1 > \theta/p_1$ we know that $p_1/p_2 - 1$ cannot be the demand for X. In either case the consumer will demand either zero or θ/p_1 units of X. V'' is negative everywhere so (from Section 2.2) if $V'(x) = 0$ implies $x > \theta/p_1$ then $x = \theta/p_1$ maximizes V subject to $0 \le x \le \theta/p_1$. If $V'(x) = 0$ implies $x < 0$ then $x = 0$ is our solution. We can now display the demand function for x:

$$x(p_1, p_2, \theta) = 0 \qquad \text{if } \frac{p_2}{p_1} < 1,$$

$$x(p_1, p_2, \theta) = \frac{p_2}{p_1} - 1 \qquad \text{if } 1 \le \frac{p_2}{p_1} \le 1 + \frac{\theta}{p_1}, \text{ and}$$

$$x(p_1, p_2, \theta) = \frac{\theta}{p_1} \qquad \text{if } \frac{p_2}{p_1} > 1 + \frac{\theta}{p_1}.$$

By solving the budget constraint $p_1 x + p_2 y = \theta$ for y and substituting X's demand function for x we can obtain the demand function for Y.

$$y(p_1, p_2, \theta) = \frac{\theta}{p_2} \qquad \text{if } \frac{p_2}{p_1} < 1,$$

$$y(p_1, p_2, \theta) = \frac{\theta + p_1 - p_2}{p_2} \qquad \text{if } 1 \le \frac{p_2}{p_1} \le 1 + \frac{\theta}{p_1} \text{ and}$$

$$y(p_1, p_2, \theta) = 0 \qquad \text{if } \frac{p_2}{p_1} > 1 + \frac{\theta}{p_1}$$

Fix p_1 and p_2 and allow θ to vary. If p_1 is larger than p_2 then we have $x(p_1, p_2, \theta) = 0$ for all values of θ. The income effect on the demand for X is zero. If $p_2/p_1 > 1 + \theta/p_1$ then all income is spent on X, and this continues to be the case as θ rises until it reaches $p_2 - p_1$. At this point we have $x = \theta/p_1 = (p_2 - p_1)/p_1 = p_2/p_1 - 1$. As θ rises beyond $p_2 - p_1$ all additional income is spent on commodity Y. Note that if either inequality $1 \le p_2/p_1$ or $p_2/p_1 \le 1 + \theta/p_1$ holds then it continues to hold as θ rises. In summary, for $\theta \ge p_2 - p_1$ or $p_1 > p_2$ there is no increase in the demand for X when income increases. There is an income effect on the demand for X only when $p_1 < p_2$ and even then only in the extreme case of incomes less than $p_2 - p_1$ (or less than $1 - p_1$ if y is a composite commodity and $p_2 = 1$).

∂2.5.3 Consumer Surplus

Now we show that if utility is quasi-linear then the demand function for commodity X can be used to estimate the utility function. Specifically, if $U(x, y) = B(x) + y$ then the demand curve for X can be used to recover the benefit function $B(x)$. For convenience we assume that $B(0) = 0$. Quasi-linear utility also means that the area under the demand curve and above the line $P = p_1$, where p_1 is the given price of X, is equal to the utility gain from being able to purchase X at the price p_1. We refer to this utility increase as the *consumer surplus*.

DEFINITION: *Consumer Surplus*

The consumer surplus is $U(x, \theta - p_1 x) - U(0, \theta)$, where θ is the individual's income and x is the amount of commodity X that maximizes U subject to the budget equation $p_1 x + y = \theta$. (We simplify by setting $p_2 = 1$.)

Because $p_2 = 1$, the budget equation implies that $y = \theta - p_1 x$. Therefore, $U(x, \theta - p_1 x) - U(0, \theta)$, is the utility from being able to purchase X at the price p_1 minus utility when only commodity Y is available (in which case the budget equation implies $y = \theta$).

Let's see how the consumer surplus can be recovered from the demand function for X. We begin by deriving that demand function. Maximize $B(x) + y$ subject to $p_1 x + y = \theta$ and $x \geq 0$ and $y \geq 0$. Equivalently, maximize $B(x) + \theta - p_1 x$ subject to $0 \leq x \leq \theta/p_1$. We assume a range of prices such that the demand for X satisfies $0 < x < \theta/p_1$, which implies that the first derivative of $B(x) + \theta - p_1 x$ equals zero. That is, $B'(x) = p_1$ is satisfied at the solution to the consumer decision problem. It follows that if we plot $B'(x) = p_1$ on a diagram with x on the horizontal axis and p_1 on the vertical axis we will portray the individual's demand curve for X. Given p_1, the curve shows us the value of x for which $B'(x) = p_1$ and that is in fact the demand for X at the price p_1. (Strictly speaking, $B'(x)$ is the *inverse* demand function. However, when we plot the graph of $B'(x)$ we can interpret it as the demand curve by taking a given price and finding the value of x on the graph at that price. It will be the quantity demanded at that price because it will be the quantity x at which $B'(x)$ equals the given price.)

We can't observe the function B directly, but we can observe prices and quantities, so we can estimate the demand curve. Let $P(x)$ be the function represented by that demand curve. Suppose, for convenience, that P and B' are identical. (The demand curve has been estimated with precision.) Using the fundamental theorem of calculus we have

$$B(x) = \int_0^x B'(t) \, dt = \int_0^x P(t) \, dt.$$

Because $\int_0^x P(t) \, dt$ is the area under the curve $P(t)$ from 0 to x, we can use the observable demand curve to compute $B(x)$.

Assuming for convenience that $B(0) = 0$, the consumer surplus is $B(x) + \theta - p_1 x - [B(0) + \theta]$, which equals $B(x) - p_1 x$. The consumer surplus $B(x) - p_1 x$ is the area under the demand curve from 0 to x minus $p_1 x$. Now, $p_1 \times x$ is the area of a rectangle with height p_1 and length x and thus is the area under the line $P = p_1$ between 0 and x. We have shown that the consumer surplus is the area under the demand curve from 0 to x minus the area under the horizontal line $P = p_1$ between 0 and x. In other words, the consumer surplus is the area below the demand curve and above the price line, and between 0 and x.

Measuring Consumer Surplus with Quasi-Linear Utility Functions

If $U = B(x) + y$ and $p_2 = 1$, then the surplus from consuming X at price p_1 is equal to the area under the demand curve for X and above the horizontal line drawn p_1 units above the horizontal axis.

Example 2.18 Consumer Surplus with Quasi-Linear Utility

$U(x, y) = \ln(x + 1) + y$, as in Example 2.17. We saw that the individual's demand function is $x = P^{-1} - 1$, if $p_2 = 1$ and P denotes p_1. (Again, we are assuming a range of prices for which the amount of commodity X demanded is strictly between 0 and θ/P.) Of course, $x = P^{-1} - 1$ implies $P = (x + 1)^{-1}$. This is the inverse demand function, which we want to integrate to determine the area under the demand curve. $\int P\, dx = \int (x + 1)^{-1} dx = \ln(x + 1) + c$, for arbitrary constant c. Note that $B(x) = \ln(x + 1)$, and if $B(0) = 0$ we must have $c = 0$. We have recovered the function $B(x)$ from the demand curve. The consumer surplus is $B(x) - Px$, which equals the area between the demand curve and the horizontal line at height P.

We conclude this section by showing that if each individual i has a quasi-linear utility function then the area under the *market* (or total) demand curve is equal to the aggregate consumer surplus and hence is equal to the total utility realized by the community when each individual is able to purchase X at a price of P. Individual i's utility function is $U_i = B_i(x_i) + y_i$, where x_i is the amount of X consumed by household i and y_i is the amount of Y consumed by i. The function B_i can be different for different individuals, hence the i subscript.

Individual i's consumer surplus is

$$\int_0^x P_i(t)\, dt - Px_i,$$

the area below i's demand curve P_i and above the horizontal line at height P. But we can also integrate along the vertical axis: the area under the individual demand curve and above the horizontal line at P is

$$\int_P^\infty x_i\, (\rho)d\rho$$

where x_i is consumer i's quantity demanded as a function of the price ρ. Total market demand q is the sum of the individual demands, so we can write $q(\rho) = \sum_{i \in N} x_i(\rho)$, where N is the set of consumers. Therefore,

$$\sum\nolimits_{i\epsilon N} \int_P^\infty x_i(\rho)\, d\rho = \int_P^\infty q(\rho)\, d\rho.$$

But $\int_P^\infty q(\rho)\, d\rho$ can be expressed as $\int_0^q P(t)\, dt$, where $P(q)$ is the inverse market demand curve – that is, the price at which a total of q units would be demanded in total by all consumers. Clearly, $\sum\nolimits_{i\epsilon N} Px_i = Pq$. Therefore,

$$\sum\nolimits_{i\epsilon N} \int_P^\infty x_i(\rho)\, d\rho = \int_0^q P(t)\, dt - Pq.$$

The area under the market demand curve and above P is the sum of the areas under the individual demand curves above P. Because the sum of the areas under the individual demand curves is equal to the total utility, we can say that total utility is exactly equal to the area under the market demand curve when each individual's utility function is quasi-linear. Similarly, the total consumer surplus equals the area under the market demand curve and above a line P units above the horizontal axis.

Measuring Total Consumer Surplus with Quasi-Linear Utility Functions

If each individual's utility function has the form $U_i = B_i(x) + y_i$ and $p_2 = 1$, then the total surplus from consuming X at price P is the area under the market demand curve for X and above the horizontal line drawn P units above the horizontal axis.

Example 2.19 Total Consumer Surplus with Quasi-Linear Utility

To simplify the calculations we will assume n identical consumers, each with the utility function $U(x, y) = \ln(x + 1) + y$, as in Example 2.17. When each individual begins with $x = 0$ and then is able to purchase X at price P, the individual increase in utility is $\ln(x + 1) - Px$. Therefore, the total increase in utility over the entire community is $n\ln(x + 1) - nPx$. We will show that this equals the area between the market demand curve and the horizontal line at height P.

The individual demand function is $x = P^{-1} - 1$ (Example 2.17), so market (or total) demand is n times that. If q denotes market demand we have

$$q = nP^{-1} - n \text{ and thus } P = n(q+n)^{-1},$$

which is the inverse market demand function. Integrate the inverse market demand function:

$$\int P dq = \int n(q+n)^{-1} dq = n\ln(q+n) - n\ln n.$$

(By subtracting $n\ln n$ we get an area of zero when q is zero.) Therefore, the area under the market demand curve and above the horizontal line at P is

$$n\ln(q+n) - n\ln n - Pq.$$

(The area from 0 to q between the horizontal axis and the line of height P is a rectangle of height P and width q, and thus has area Pq.) Now, $q = nx$, and thus $n\ln(q+n) - n\ln n = n\ln(nx+n) - n\ln n = n\ln[(nx+n)/n] = n\ln(x+1) = nB(x)$. Therefore, the area under the market demand curve and above the horizontal line at height P is equal to $n[B(x) - Px]$, the total consumer surplus. (Compare to Example 2.18.)

Source

The efficiency condition of Section 2.5.1 first appeared in Samuelson (1954).

Links

See Campbell and Truchon (1988) for a general characterization of efficiency with quasi-linear preferences covering allocations for which $y_i = 0$ for some individuals i. See also Conley and Diamantaris (1996). See Katzner (1970, p. 152) for the general result on demand functions and consumer surplus when preferences are not necessarily quasi-linear.

2.6 DECISION MAKING UNDER UNCERTAINTY

When uncertainty is featured in this book it is typically assumed that there are only two possible random events, "bad" and "good," and that the decision maker knows the probability of each event. Therefore, we begin with a study of choice under uncertainty when an action leads to one event with probability π and an alternative event with probability $1 - \pi$. Of course, $0 \leq \pi \leq 1$. The bad event leads to a low payoff x, and the good event yields a high payoff y. Think of x and y as the decision maker's wealth in the respective events. To standardize the terminology we refer to the prospect of getting x with probability π and y with probability $1 - \pi$ as an asset, even though there will be other applications, such as the purchase of insurance.

DEFINITION: *Asset*
  An asset is any opportunity that yields a specified low payoff x with probability π and a specified high payoff y with probability $1 - \pi$.

We allow x to be negative. In some cases we want the payoffs to be reported net of the purchase price of the financial instrument.

2.6.1 Asset Preferences

An individual with a current wealth of θ is confronted with a choice between a safe asset (money) that preserves his or her wealth at θ with certainty and a risky asset (an investment) that reduces his or her wealth to x with probability π but will cause wealth to increase to y with probability $1 - \pi$. Of course, $x < \theta < y$. One important element – but not the only element – of the decision process is the expected payoff.

The expected monetary value of an asset is the weighted sum of the monetary payoffs, where each payoff's weight is its probability.

DEFINITION: *Expected Monetary Value (EMV)*

If x dollars is received with probability π and y is received with probability $1 - \pi$ then the expected monetary value of the asset is $\pi x + (1 - \pi)y$.

Example 2.20 EMV when the Bad Outcome is a Burglary

An individual's current wealth of $100 will be reduced to $40 if he or she is robbed, and that will happen with probability 0.3. Then the EMV of wealth (without insurance) is $0.3 \times 40 + 0.7 \times 100 = 82$.

A risky asset would leave the individual with x with probability π and y with probability $(1 - \pi)$, with $x < \theta < y$. For most of us there is a value of π sufficiently close to 0 (perhaps *extremely* close) that would induce us to choose this risky asset. And there would be a value of π sufficiently close to 1 that would prompt us to choose the safe asset, with a guaranteed θ. But what about more realistic, intermediate, values of π? Clearly, the decision would depend on the magnitudes θ, x, y, on the probability π, and on the individual's preferences under uncertainty. For a wide range of circumstances it is possible to model an individual's preferences by means of a utility-of-wealth function $U(w)$, where w is the market value of the individual's wealth. The utility function represents the individual's preferences in the sense that he or she would prefer the risky asset if and only if

$$\pi U(x) + (1 - \pi)U(y) > U(\theta).$$

The expected utility (EU) of an asset is the weighted sum of the payoff utilities, where each weight is the probability of the associated payoff.

DEFINITION: *Expected Utility (EU)*

If U is the utility-of-wealth function and x dollars is received with probability π and y is received with probability $1 - \pi$ then

$$EU = \pi U(x) + (1 - \pi)U(y).$$

Example 2.21 EU when the Bad Outcome is a Burglary

The individual's utility-of-wealth function is $U(w) = 4\sqrt{w}$. Then for the situation of Example 2.20

$$EU = 0.3 \times 4\sqrt{40} + 0.7 \times 4\sqrt{100} = 35.6.$$

Under fairly mild assumptions on the nature of individual preference, one can prove that for each preference scheme there is a utility-of-wealth-function such that the individual will always choose the asset that leads to the highest expected utility of wealth. In other words, the individual acts so as to maximize his or her expected utility.

DEFINITION: *Expected Utility Maximization*

The market will provide the individual with a range of affordable assets, and the individual will choose the one that yields values of x and y that maximize $\pi U(x) + (1 - \pi)U(y)$ over all affordable assets.

This means that the individual can be represented as an expected utility maximizer. The quantity $\pi U(x) + (1 - \pi)U(y)$ is called the expected utility of an investment that results in a wealth level of x with probability π and a wealth level of y with probability $1 - \pi$. In general, given a choice between an investment I that yields x with probability π and yields y with probability $1 - \pi$ and an investment J that yields a with probability ρ and b with probability $1 - \rho$, the individual will choose I if

$$\pi U(x) + (1 - \pi)U(y) > \rho U(a) + (1 - \rho)U(b)$$

and will choose J if

$$\rho U(a) + (1 - \rho)U(b) > \pi U(x) + (1 - \pi)U(y).$$

We are *assuming* expected utility maximization but, as we have said, it is possible to deduce this property from mild assumptions about individual preference. This book does not present the proof, however.

Example 2.22 Individuals with Different Preferences make Different Choices

Dale's utility-of-wealth function is $U(w) = 10\sqrt{w}$ and Joanne's is $U(w) = 2w$. Each has to choose between a safe asset A that leaves the individual with $196 for sure, and a risky asset B that yields $36 with probability ½ and $400 with probability ½. For Dale we have

$$EU(A) = 10\sqrt{196} = 140$$

and

$$EU(B) = ½ \times 10\sqrt{36} + ½ \times 10\sqrt{400} = 130.$$

For Joanne,

$$EU(A) = 2 \times 196 = 392$$

and

$$EU(B) = ½ \times 2 \times 36 + ½ \times 2 \times 400 = 436.$$

Dale chooses A but Joanne chooses B.

Outcomes can be tested for efficiency even in an uncertain environment. One applies the standard definition (of Chapter 1, Section 1.4) but the individual's payoff is *expected* utility. (If your town built so many parking garages that you can always find a spot, no matter where or when you arrive, the outcome would not be efficient. Can you explain why?)

Source

Von Neumann and Morgenstern (1944) introduced the notion of expected utility. They also showed how it could be used to represent a very wide family of preference schemes.

Links

The axioms that imply expected utility maximization are introduced and explained in Chapter 5 of Kreps (1988), where a fairly elementary proof that the axioms imply EU maximization can also be found. A more general result is Herstein and Milnor (1953). Chapter 6 in Mas-Colell et al. (1995) also contains a very general theorem and proof, along with a discussion of the associated economics.

2.6.2 Risk Aversion and Risk Neutrality

Suppose that you are offered a choice between your annual salary of $40,000 for sure, and a chance of getting double that salary with probability ½ accompanied by an equal chance of winding up with zero. Most of us would choose the sure thing because the two options have the same expected monetary value ($40,000), but the plunge from $40,000 to zero is far more devastating than a drop from $80,000 to $40,000.

Example 2.23 A Chance to Double your Salary

If the individual's utility-of-wealth function is $U(w) = 4\sqrt{w}$ then the EU of $40,000 for sure is $4\sqrt{40,000} = 800$. The EU of a gamble that yields $80,000 with probability ½ or zero with the same probability is

$$\tfrac{1}{2} \times 4\sqrt{80,000} + \tfrac{1}{2} \times 4\sqrt{0} = 565.7.$$

This individual prefers $40,000 for sure because it yields a higher level of expected utility than the gamble.

We say that individuals are *risk averse* if they prefer having w for sure to an uncertain wealth level with an expected monetary value that is no higher than w. If asset A yields a high outcome y with probability ½ and a low outcome x with probability ½, and asset B yields $y + \delta$ with probability ½ and $x - \delta$ with probability ½ and $\delta > 0$, then B is unambiguously the riskier asset. The two have the same mean, but B's payoffs have a wider spread than A's.

DEFINITION: *Risk Aversion*

Individuals are risk averse if for any payoff w they would always prefer w dollars for sure to an asset under which their wealth would have an expected monetary value of w but which would leave them with less than w with positive probability. In general, if assets A and B provide the individuals with the same expected monetary value of wealth, but A is unambiguously less risky, risk-averse individuals will always prefer A to B.

The individual would prefer θ for sure if the opportunity of obtaining a higher level of wealth brought with it the chance of winding up with a lower level of wealth *and* θ is at least as high as the average (expected) wealth associated with the gamble.

We conclude this section by showing that risk aversion is equivalent to diminishing marginal utility of wealth: we let MU_w denote the marginal utility of wealth at the level w. Suppose that we have $MU_x > MU_y$ for any x and y such that $x < y$. In other words, the marginal utility of wealth is always positive, but it is smaller at higher levels of wealth. Consider an asset that pays $w - \delta$ with probability ½ and $w + \delta$ with probability ½, where $\delta > 0$. The EMV of this asset is w. Let L denote the potential utility loss, $U(w) - U(w - \delta)$, and let G denote the potential utility gain, $U(w + \delta) - U(w)$. Diminishing marginal utility of wealth implies that L is larger than G, because L involves a change in wealth at a lower level than G. Therefore, ½G < ½L, which can be written

$$0.5[U(w+\delta) - U(w)] < 0.5[U(w) - U(w - \delta)].$$

Add ½$U(w)$ + ½$U(w - \delta)$ to both sides of this inequality. We get

$$0.5[U(w+\delta) + U(w-\delta)] < 0.5[U(w) + U(w)] = U(w).$$

Therefore, the EU of an asset that yields $w + \delta$ with probability ½ and $w - \delta$ with probability ½ is less than the EU of w dollars for sure. This is a consequence of diminishing marginal utility of wealth, and it holds for every wealth level w and every positive δ. We've shown algebraically that diminishing marginal utility of wealth implies risk aversion.

Figure 2.9 portrays the graph of a utility-of-wealth function with diminishing marginal utility. Diminishing MU causes the graph to bow up, away from the horizontal axis, so that the straight line connecting any two points on the graph lies entirely below the graph, except at the endpoints. Let x be the wealth level at the left end with y denoting the wealth at the other end. The wealth level at the halfway point on the line is ½x + ½y. Note that this is the expected monetary value of an asset that leaves wealth at x with probability ½ and at y with probability ½. The coordinate on the vertical axis for the halfway point on the straight line is the average utility, ½$U(x)$ + ½$U(y)$. Of course, this is the EU of an asset that leaves wealth at x with probability ½ and at y with probability ½. Because of the curvature of the graph of U, $U($½x + ½$y)$ is greater than ½$U(x)$ + ½$U(y)$. In other words, the

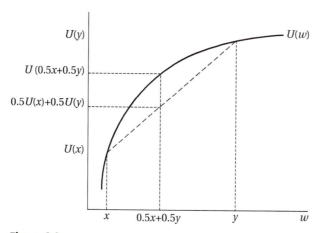

Figure 2.9

utility from ½ x + ½y for sure is greater than the expected utility of an asset with an EMV of ½x + ½y, if the probability of receiving x is positive. We've shown graphically that diminishing marginal utility of wealth implies risk aversion.

It is easy to show that risk aversion implies diminishing marginal utility of wealth. We just have to "press rewind." By definition of risk aversion, we have

$$0.5[U(w+\delta) + U(w - \delta)] < U(w) = 0.5[U(w) + U(w)]$$

for every choice of positive w and δ because the EMVs are equal. This implies

$$U(w+\delta) - U(w) < U(w) - U(w - \delta).$$

But $U(w + \delta) - U(w)$ is proportional to the marginal utility of wealth at w, and $U(w) - U(w - \delta)$ is proportional to the marginal utility of wealth at the lower level $w - \delta$. Therefore, risk aversion implies that the marginal utility of wealth is lower at higher levels of wealth.

A *risk-neutral* individual is insensitive to the degree of risk. He or she will always choose the asset with the higher EMV and will be indifferent between two assets with the same EMV, even if one has a much bigger spread between the two payoffs.

DEFINITION: *Risk Neutrality*

An individual is risk neutral if for any two assets A and B he or she prefers A to B if and only if A has a higher expected monetary value than B.

In general, to determine which asset an individual will choose we have to determine how each asset will affect an individual's wealth and then calculate the resulting expected utility. The asset that results in the highest EU from the final wealth portfolio will be the one that is chosen. However, in the case of a risk-neutral decision maker, we just have to calculate the expected monetary value of each asset. The one with the highest EMV will be chosen. That follows from the fact that

EMV (original wealth + new asset) = EMV (original wealth) + EMV (new asset).

The asset with the highest EMV will be the asset that leads to the highest EMV of the new wealth portfolio.

We have shown – albeit informally – that risk aversion is equivalent to diminishing marginal utility of wealth. The next subsection uses elementary calculus to establish this rigorously.

∂2.6.3 Risk Aversion and a Negative Second Derivative

If $y \geq x$ then a risk-averse individual is one who would prefer an asset A that yielded y with probability ½ and x with probability ½ to an asset B that yielded $y + \delta$ with probability ½ and $x - \delta$ with probability ½, as long as δ is positive. Notice that A and B have the same EMV, $\frac{1}{2}x + \frac{1}{2}y$. For a risk-averse individual asset B will have a lower expected *utility* because there is a greater spread between the low outcome and the high outcome. The definition of risk aversion leads directly to a proof that risk-averse individuals have utility functions with negative second derivatives.

The Risk-Aversion Theorem

> *An individual with a twice differentiable utility-of-wealth function U is risk averse if and only if the second derivative of U is negative at every point.*

Proof:

Suppose that $y > x$ and $\delta > 0$. By the definition of risk aversion $\frac{1}{2}U(y) + \frac{1}{2}U(x) > \frac{1}{2}U(y + \delta) + \frac{1}{2}U(x - \delta)$ and therefore $U(x) - U(x - \delta) > U(y + \delta) - U(y)$, which implies

$$\frac{U(x) - U(x - \delta)}{\delta} > \frac{U(y+\delta) - U(y)}{\delta}$$

because δ is positive. As δ approaches zero the left-hand side of this inequality approaches $U'(x)$ and the right-hand side approaches $U'(y)$, establishing that $U'(y) \leq U'(x)$ holds whenever $y > x$. But we can do better.

Suppose that $U'(x) = U'(y)$ and $x < y$. Then $U'(x) = U'(z) = U'(y)$ for $x \leq z \leq y$ because we have just proved that U' cannot increase as wealth increases. That is, $U'(x) \geq U'(z) \geq U'(y) = U'(x)$ implies $U'(x) = U'(z) = U'(y)$. Consider the asset that yields $x^0 = x + \frac{1}{4}(y - x)$ with probability ½ and $y^0 = y + \frac{1}{4}(y - x)$ with probability ½. For a risk-averse individual this must have a higher expected utility than the asset that yields x and y each with probability ½ because the latter has the same expected monetary value as the former but a lower low outcome and a higher high outcome. Therefore, for $\delta = \frac{1}{4}(y - x)$ we have

$$\frac{1}{2}U(x) + \frac{1}{2}U(y) < \frac{1}{2}U(x+\delta) + \frac{1}{2}U(y - \delta)$$

and thus

$$U(y) - U(y - \delta) < U(x+\delta) - U(x).$$

But this is inconsistent with U' being constant on the range of values between x and y. The inconsistency arises from the fact that constant U' implies $U(y) - U(y - \delta) = \delta U'(x) = U(x + \delta) - U(x)$. We must conclude that $U'(x) > U'(y)$ actually holds for a risk-averse person whenever $x < y$.

Figure 2.9 in the previous section is used to sketch a proof of the converse: a utility-of-wealth function with a negative second derivative everywhere represents preferences that exhibit risk aversion.   ∎

Because a risk-averse individual gets higher expected utility from asset A than asset B if they have the same EMV but A is unambiguously less risky, it is clear that a risk-averse individual will pay a premium – large or small, depending on preference – to avoid risk. This is one of the foundations of the insurance industry. (The other is the law of large numbers.) In fact, the prominence of insurance in almost all aspects of our economy is strong evidence for the prevalence of risk aversion. Individuals have even been known to buy insurance against the possibility that an existing insurance opportunity will disappear.

Because a risk-neutral person is indifferent between two assets with the same EMV, we have

$$0.5\ U(x) + 0.5\ U(y) = 0.5\ U(x + \delta) + 0.5\ U(y - \delta)$$

for all values of x, y, and δ. Therefore,

$$\frac{U(y) - U(y - \delta)}{\delta} = \frac{U(x + \delta) - U(x)}{\delta}$$

for all $\delta \neq 0$, and thus $U'(x) = U'(y)$ for all x and y. If the first derivative is constant the function U must be of the form $U(x) = \alpha x + \beta$. If utility is increasing in wealth we must have $\alpha > 0$. Therefore, maximizing expected utility is equivalent to maximizing expected monetary value in the case of a risk-neutral individual.

2.6.4 The Market Opportunity Line

In the absence of uncertainty the individual's consumption plan $(x,\ y)$ must be chosen from a budget line determined by equating expenditure and income. When the individual chooses in an uncertain environment the market also determines the combinations of x and y from which the decision maker is able to choose. Although these pairs $(x,\ y)$ can't always be represented by a straight line, almost all of the examples in this book are elementary enough to be so depicted, and we will refer to the *market opportunity line*.

DEFINITION: *Market Opportunity Line*

The market opportunity line is the set of pairs $(x,\ y)$ from which the individual is allowed to choose.

Example 2.24 An Investment

Kristina has current wealth of $160. She has an opportunity to invest in a project that will be successful with probability 0.7, in which case she will receive $4 for every dollar invested. There is a probability 0.3 that the project will fail and she will get back only twenty cents on the dollar. Let C be the amount invested. If the project fails Kristina's wealth will be $160 - C + 0.2C = 160 - 0.8C$. If the project were to succeed, wealth will be $160 - C + 4C = 160 + 3C$. Therefore, $x = 160 - 0.8C$ and $y = 160 + 3C$. From the first of these equations we have $C = 200 - 1.25x$. Now substitute the right-hand side of this equation for C in $y = 160 + 3C$. We get

$$y = 160 + 3(200 - 1.25x) = 760 - 3.75x.$$

Finally, the market opportunity line can be expressed as $3.75x + y = 760$. Confirm that $x = y = 160$ satisfies the equation.

Because $3.75x + y = 760$, if y increases the value of x must fall to preserve equality. In plain terms, an individual who wants a bigger payoff when the project succeeds must commit more of her funds, accepting the fact that she will lose more if the project does poorly.

Example 2.25 Insurance

Lindsey has current wealth of $100, but will have 70 percent of it stolen with a probability of 0.3. She can purchase insurance for forty cents per dollar of coverage. If C is the amount of coverage purchased, then Lindsey's wealth will be $x = 30 + C - 0.4\,C$ if there is a burglary, and $y = 100 - 0.4\,C$ if there is no burglary. Because $x = 30 + 0.6\,C$ we have $C = (1/0.6)x - 50$. Therefore,

$$y = 100 - 0.4\left(\frac{1}{0.6}x - 50\right) = 120 - \frac{2}{3}x.$$

The market opportunity line is $\frac{2}{3}x + y = 120$. Note that this equation is satisfied when Lindsay buys no insurance, in which case $x = 30$ and $y = 100$.

The coefficients of x and y on the left-hand side of the market opportunity line are both positive, and thus y must fall if x increases, to preserve equality. In plain terms, if an individual wants more insurance coverage – i.e., a bigger claim check and hence a higher level of wealth if she has an accident – she must pay a higher premium, reducing the level of wealth she would have if she does not suffer an accident.

When π is the probability of receiving x and $1 - \pi$ is the probability of receiving y, *and* the market opportunity line has the form $\pi x + (1 - \pi)\,y = \theta$, we say that the odds are *fair*.

DEFINITION: *Fair Odds Line*

A fair odds line is any market opportunity line that can be written in the form

$$\pi x + (1 - \pi)y = \theta$$

where π is the probability of actually receiving x, $1 - \pi$ is the probability of actually getting y, and θ is some constant.

If $2\pi x + 2(1 - \pi)y = \theta$ we still have fair odds because we can divide both sides of the equation by 2 to get $\pi x + (1 - \pi)y = \theta/2$. In general, if the market opportunity equation is $p_1 x + p_2 y = \theta$ then we have fair odds if and only if $p_1/p_2 = \pi/(1 - \pi)$. In that case, multiply both sides of $p_1 x + p_2 y = \theta$ by π/p_1 and use the fact that $p_2\pi/p_1 = 1 - \pi$ to prove that the equation can be expressed in the form $\pi x + (1 - \pi)y = \theta\pi/p_1$.

Note that we do not have fair odds in Example 2.24 because $p_1/p_2 = 3.75/1$ but $\pi/(1-\pi) = 0.3/0.7 > 0.428$. Nor do we have fair odds in Example 2.25 because $p_1/p_2 = 2/3$ but $\pi/(1-\pi) = 0.3/0.7 < 0.429$.

Example 2.26 Insurance with Fair Odds

Cindy has current wealth of $100, but will have 70 percent of it stolen with probability 0.2. Every dollar of premium paid to the insurance company results in $5 being received in case of an accident. If P is the premium paid, then $x = 30 + 5P - P$ and $y = 100 - P$. This last equation yields $P = 100 - y$ and thus $x = 30 + 4P = 30 + 4(100 - y)$. Therefore, the market opportunity line is $x + 4y = 430$. The ratio of probabilities is $0.2/0.8$, which is equal to ¼, the ratio of the coefficients of the market opportunity line. Cindy faces fair odds.

The next two sections relax the assumption that there are only two possible outcomes. We briefly consider a finite sample space then assume an infinite number of possibilities.

2.6.5 The Uniform Probability Distribution

There is a finite number of possible outcomes. When each outcome has the same probability of being realized as any other, we say that the random variable has the uniform probability distribution. If there are ten balls in a hopper and each bears a different number then we have a model of the uniform probability distribution, assuming that the balls are of the same size and weight, and thus have the same probability of being selected. The probabilities must sum to 1, so the common probability must be 0.1. However, if the sample space is infinite then the sum of the probabilities cannot be unity. It cannot even be finite if the probabilities are all the same. But there is nonetheless a way of embodying the notion of uniform probability.

Suppose that the random variable x could turn out to be any of the real numbers between zero and one inclusive. Assume further that each value is as likely as any other. How do we characterize this *uniform probability distribution*? Because there are an infinite number of values between 0 and 1, the most useful way of representing the uniform distribution is in terms of the probability that x is between 0 and β, for a given value of β (not exceeding 1). For the uniform probability distribution on $[0, 1]$, the probability that the random variable x is between 0 and β (i.e., $0 \leq x \leq \beta$) is β itself. The probability that $0 < x < \beta$ is also β. Now, consider the uniform probability distribution on the interval $[a, b]$, which is the set of x such that $a \leq x \leq b$.

DEFINITION: *The Uniform Probability Distribution*

If x is a random draw from the interval $[a, b]$ then the probability that $a \leq x \leq \beta$ is $(\beta - a)/(b - a)$ if x is governed by the uniform probability distribution on $[a, b]$.

For instance, if you are submitting a bid in a sealed-bid auction with one other participant, and you view your opponent's bid as a random draw from the uniform probability distribution on the interval $[0, 100]$ then the probability that you will win with your bid of β is the probability that the other person's bid is below β. Therefore, the probability of your winning with a bid of β is $\beta/100$.

∂2.6.6 The Continuum Case in General

Suppose that the random variable x is drawn from the interval $[a, b]$ of real numbers, where $[a, b]$ denotes the set of all numbers x such that $a \leq x \leq b$. We use a probability density function $f(x)$ to determine the probability that x belongs to the subinterval $[\alpha, \beta]$. The function f is integrable, and given real numbers α and β such that $a \leq \alpha < \beta \leq b$,

$$\text{Prob} \left[\alpha < x < \beta\right] = \int_{\alpha}^{\beta} f(x) \, dx.$$

Of course, $\text{Prob}[\alpha < x < \beta]$ denotes the probability that $x > \alpha$ and $x < \beta$ both hold. In the continuum case, $\text{Prob}[\alpha < x < \beta] = \text{Prob}[\alpha < x \leq \beta] = \text{Prob}[\alpha \leq x < \beta] = \text{Prob}[\alpha \leq x \leq \beta]$.

Given the utility-of-wealth function U, the expected utility of the random variable x over the interval (α, β) is

$$\int_{\alpha}^{\beta} U(x) f(x) \, dx.$$

In the case of the uniform probability distribution on $[a, b]$, $f(x) = 1/(b - a)$ for all x. Hence

$$\text{Prob}[\alpha < x < \beta] = \int_{\alpha}^{\beta} \frac{1}{b - a} dx = \frac{\beta}{b - a} - \frac{\alpha}{b - a} = \frac{\beta - \alpha}{b - a}.$$

Therefore, if $a = 0$ then x is drawn from the uniform probability distribution on the set of numbers between 0 and b, in which case the probability that x is less than β is β/b. For the uniform probability distribution on $[a, b]$, we have $f(x) = 1/(b - a)$, and thus the expected utility of the random variable x over the interval (α, β) with respect to the utility function U is $\int_{\alpha}^{\beta} \frac{U(x)}{b-a} \, dx.$

Link

See Sheffrin (1993, p. 51) for an instance of the purchase of insurance against the possibility that an existing insurance opportunity will disappear.

2.6.7 The Binomial Distribution

The binomial distribution was introduced by the seventeenth-century Swiss mathematician Jacob Bernoulli in the following form: there are two possible outcomes, S (success) and F (Failure), and π is the probability of S. An experiment consists of n trials, and the outcome of one trial is statistically independent of the outcome in any other trial. In other words, π is the probability of S in any of the n trials. (This will be generalized later.)

We denote the outcome of the experiment by a sequence of S and F statements. For instance, $(S, F, F, S, F, \ldots)$ denotes the fact that S was the outcome in trial number 1, F was the outcomes in trials 2 and 3, with S occurring in trial 4, and so on. Let $p(x)$ be the probability that S will be the outcome in exactly x of the trials. For any probability distribution the expected value, or mean, is a measure of central tendency. In the case of the binomial distribution this is $n\pi$, the *expected number* of successes over n trials. That is, if there are n trials then

$$n\pi = 0 \times p(0) + 1 \times p(1) + 2 \times p(2) + 3 \times p(3) + \ldots + (n-1) \times p(n-1) + n \times p(n).$$

Example 2.27 The Probability of One Success in Three Trials

$n = 3$. Then $x = 1$ can occur in three different ways: (S,F,F) or (F,S,F), or (F,F,S). The probability of (S,F,F) is $\pi(1-\pi)(1-\pi)$. The probability of (F,S,F) is $(1-\pi)\pi(1-\pi)$, and the probability of (F,F,S) is $(1-\pi)(1-\pi)\pi$. It follows that $p(1) = 3\pi(1-\pi)^2$ when $n = 3$.

What is $p(1)$ for arbitrary n? The probability of $(S,F,F, \ldots,F,F)$ is $\pi(1-\pi)^{n-1}$. The probability that S occurs only once, and on trial number t, is $\pi(1-\pi)^{n-1}$. There are n different ways in which the experiment can result in exactly one success: it can happen on the first trial, or the second trial, or the third trial, and so on. Therefore, $p(1) = n\pi(1-\pi)^{n-1}$ for an experiment with n trials.

What is $p(x)$ for arbitrary x and n? In words, what is the probability of exactly x successes in n trials? The probability of S on the first trial and on the second and on the third, and so on down to trial number x on which S also occurs, and then observing F on the remaining trials, is $\pi^x(1-\pi)^{n-x}$, the product of the probabilities for the individual trial events. But that's not the only way that exactly x successes in

n trials can occur. The probability $p(x)$ is $\pi^x(1-\pi)^{n-x}$ multiplied by the number of ways that exactly x successes can occur. For *each* occurrence of x successes the probability is $\pi^x(1-\pi)^{n-x}$, because S on a particular trial occurs with probability π and there are x such trials, and F on some other trial occurs with probability $(1-\pi)$ and there are $n-x$ such trials. To find $p(x)$ we need $C_n(x)$, the number of ways that exactly x successes can occur in n trials.

To calculate $C_n(x)$ begin by arbitrarily choosing one trial on which S occurs. There are n ways of doing that. Having made that choice, select another trial on which S occurs. There are $n-1$ trials left and thus $n-1$ ways of making the second choice. That means there are $n(n-1)$ ways of arbitrarily choosing two particular trials on which S will occur. Choose another trial. There are now $n-2$ trials left and hence $n-2$ ways of choosing a third trial on which S can occur. Then there are $n(n-1)(n-2)$ ways of choosing three trials on which S will occur. It follows that there are

$$T_n(x) = n(n-1)(n-2)(n-3) \times \ldots \times (n-x+2)(n-x+1)$$

ways in which exactly x successes can occur in n trials. Suppose $n=3$. Then $T_3(2) = 3 \times 2$. But getting exactly two successes is identical to getting exactly 1 failure, and that can happen in only *three* ways: on the first trial or the second trial, or the third trial. What went wrong? $T_3(2)$ double counts the event "failure is observed on the first trial followed by two successes." If in computing $C_3(2)$ we first choose trial 2 on which S occurs and next choose trial 3 on which another S occurs we have two successes. If instead we had first chosen trial 3 on which S occurs and next chosen trial 2 on which another S occurs we have two success but exactly the same scenario as in the previous sentence. We see that $T_3(2)$ counts each scenario twice. Therefore, $C_3(2) = 0.5T_3(2) = 3$.

In general, to calculate the number of ways of getting exactly x successes we must divide $T_n(x)$ by the number of different ways of ordering x objects. The result will be the number of different ways that x successes can occur - i.e., the total number of experiments in which exactly x successes occur. We denote this number by $C_n(x)$. The number of different ways of ordering x distinct objects is

$$x(x-1)(x-2)(x-3) \times \ldots \times (2)(1)$$

which is represented by $x!$ and pronounced x *factorial*. (For convenience, $0!$ is taken to be 1.) Then $C_n(x) = T_n(x)/x!$. Of course, $n! = n(n-1)(n-2)(n-3) \times \ldots \times (2)(1)$ and thus we can write $T_n(x)$ as $n!/(n-x)!$. It follows that

$$C_n(x) = \frac{n!}{x!(n-x)!}.$$

The probability of any one instance of x successes (for example, S occurs on trials 1 through x and F occurs on the other trials) is $\pi^x(1-\pi)^{n-x}$ and thus

$$p(x) = C_n(x)\pi^x(1-\pi)^{n-x}.$$

The Probability of x for the Binomial Distribution

The probability of exactly x successes in n statistically independent trials is $\frac{n!}{x!(n-x)!}\ \pi^x(1-\pi)^{n-x}$ if the probability of success in any one trial is π.

Now we can compute E_n, the expected number of successes in n trials. We begin with two examples:

Example 2.28 Expected Value with Two Trials

There will be zero or one or two successes. Then $E_2(X) = 0 \times p(0) + 1 \times p(1) + 2 \times p(2)$. Of course, $p(1)$ is the probability of (S,F) or (F,S) and is thus $\pi(1-\pi) + (1-\pi)\pi = 2\pi(1-\pi)$. (Confirm that $C(1) = 2$ when $n = 2$.) And $p(2)$ is the probability of (S,S) which is π^2. Therefore,

$$E_2(X) = 0 \times (1 - \pi)^2 + 1 \times 2\pi(1 - \pi) + 2 \times \pi^2 = 2\pi - 2\pi^2 + 2\pi^2 = 2\pi.$$

We will show that $E_n = \pi n$ in general. First, consider $n = 3$.

Example 2.29 Expected Value with Three Trials

The experiment can result in exactly one success in three different ways: (S,F,F) or (F,S,F) or (F,F,S) and the respective probabilities are $\pi(1-\pi)^2$, and $(1-\pi)\pi (1-\pi)$, and $(1-\pi)^2\pi$. The sum of the probabilities is $3\pi(1-\pi)^2$, and thus $p(1) = 3\pi(1-\pi)^2$ when $n = 3$. The experiment can result in exactly two successes in three different ways: (S,S,F) or (S,F,S) or (F,S,S) and the respective probabilities are $\pi^2(1-\pi)$, and $\pi(1-\pi)\pi$, and $(1-\pi)\pi^2$. The sum of the probabilities is $3\pi^2(1-\pi)$ and thus $p(2) = 3\pi^2(1-\pi)$ when $n = 3$. Finally, there will be three successes only when we have (S,S,S) and this will occur with probability π^3. That is, $p(3) = \pi^3$ when $n = 3$. Therefore

$$E_3(X) = 0 \times (1 - \pi)^3 + 1 \times 3\pi(1 - \pi)^2 + 2 \times 3\pi^2(1 - \pi) + 3 \times \pi^3 = 3\pi.$$

Theorem: The Mean of n Trials

If each trial in an experiment with n trials consists of a draw from a binomial distribution that will yield 1 with probability π and zero with probability $1 - \pi$, and the trials are statistically independent, then $n\pi$ is the mean of the random variable x, the number of successes in n trials.

Proof:

Recall that for arbitrary n and $x \leq n$ we have $p(x) = \frac{n!}{x!(n-x)!} \pi^x (1-\pi)^{n-x}$.

By convention, 0! is the number 1. Therefore,

$$E_n(X) = 0 \times \frac{n!}{0!(n-0)!} \times \pi^0 (1-\pi)^{n-0} + 1 \times \frac{n!}{1!(n-1)!} \times \pi^1 (1-\pi)^{n-1}$$

$$+ 2 \times \frac{n!}{2!(n-2)!} \times \pi^2 (1-\pi)^{n-2} + \ldots$$

$$+ x \times \frac{n!}{x!(n-x)!} \times \pi^x (1-\pi)^{n-x} + \ldots + n \times \frac{n!}{n!(n-n)!} \times \pi^n (1-\pi).$$

$$[11]$$

Note that $xp(x) = x \times \frac{n!}{x!(n-x)!} \times \pi^x (1-\pi)^{n-x} = 1 \times \frac{n!}{(x-1)!(n-x)!} \times \pi^x (1-\pi)^{n-x}$.

The last expression is obtained from its predecessor by employing the fact that $\frac{x}{x!} = \frac{1}{(x-1)!}$.

Because $n! \times \pi^x = n\pi(n-1)!\pi^{x-1}$ we have

$$xp(x) = n\pi \frac{(n-1)!}{(x-1)!(n-x)!} \pi^{x-1} (1-\pi)^{n-x}.$$

Let m denote $n-1$ and let w denote $x-1$. Then $n-x = m-w$ and we have

$$xp(x) = n\pi \frac{m!}{w!(m-w)!} \pi^w (1-\pi)^{m-w}$$

$$[12]$$

Because $0p(0) = 0$, statement [11] can be simplified by summing from $x = 1$ to $x = n$ instead of from $x = 0$ to $x = n$. Then w ranges from 0 to m and thus [11] and [12] yield

$$E_n(X) = \sum \frac{n!}{x!(n-x)!} \pi^x (1-\pi)^{n-x} = n\pi \sum x \frac{(n-1)!}{(x-1)!(n-x)!} \pi^{x-1} (1-\pi)^{n-x}$$

$$= n\pi \sum_{w=0}^{m} \frac{m!}{w!(m-w)!} \pi^w (1-\pi)^{m-w}$$

$$= n\pi [p(0) + p(1) + p(2) + \ldots + p(m-1) + p(m)].$$

Of course $p(0) + p(1) + p(2) + \ldots + p(m-1) + p(m)$ equals 1 because it is the sum of the probabilities over all possible outcomes of an experiment with m trials. We have proved that $E_n(X) = n\pi$. ∎

It is straightforward to generalize this result when the outcome of a single trial is the value a with probability π and z with probability $1 - \pi$. (Think of z as the current value of your house, and a as the value when the house is damaged by a fire, which will occur with probability π.) The expected value μ of a single trial is $\pi a + (1-\pi)z$.

The Mean of n Trials in General

If each trial in an experiment with n trials consists of a draw from a binomial distribution that will realize the value a with probability π and z with probability $1 - \pi$, and the trials are statistically independent, then $n\mu$ is the mean of the random variable obtained by summing the outcomes of the n trials, where μ is the expected value of a single trial.

Proof:

Let x denote the number of times that the value a is realized in an experiment with n trials. (A single trial would be the exposure of your house to the risk of fire over a twelve-month period, and there are n periods.) What is the expected value for the experiment? When $x = 0$ the value is nz, and that will occur with probability $(1-\pi)^n$. When $x = 1$ the value is $a + (n-1)z$ and that will occur with probability $n\pi(1-\pi)^{n-1}$. For arbitrary x the value is $xa + (n-x)z$, which occurs with probability $\frac{n!}{x!(n-x)!}\pi^x(1-\pi)^{n-x}$. Therefore,

$$E_n(X) = \sum_{x=0}^{n} [xa + (n-x)z] \frac{n!}{x!(n-x)!} \pi^x(1-\pi)^{n-x}$$

$$= \sum_{x=0}^{n} [nz + x(a-z)] \frac{n!}{x!(n-x)!} \pi^x(1-\pi)^{n-x}$$

$$= nz\sum_{x=0}^{n} \frac{n!}{x!(n-x)!} \pi^x(1-\pi)^{n-x} + (a-z)\sum_{x=0}^{n} x \frac{n!}{x!(n-x)!} \pi^x(1-\pi)^{n-x}$$

$$= nz + (a-z)n\pi = n[\pi a + (1-\pi)z]$$

Therefore, the expected value of the experiment with n trials is n times the expected value of a single trial. ∎

Note that when $a = 1$ and $z = 0$ then $\mu = \pi$ and the expected value of n trials is $n\pi$.

The *variance* of a random variable X is $E(X-\mu)^2$, the expected value of $(x-\mu)^2$, where μ denotes $E(X)$. In words, the variance of a random variable is the expected value of the squared deviations from the mean. While the mean μ is a measure of central tendency, the variance σ^2 is a measure of the dispersion of the random variable. We use $E(X-\mu)^2$ instead of $E(X-\mu)$ because $E(X-\mu)$ is zero for a symmetric distribution, however wide the spread around the mean. (If the random variable X is symmetrically distributed, then for every value x above the mean there is a value that is $x-\mu$ units below the mean, and the two occur with equal probability. If $x = 10^6$ with probability ½ and $x = -10^6$ with probability ½ then $E(X) = \mu = 0$ and $E(X-\mu)$ is also zero, but there is substantial dispersion about the mean, reflected in the fact that the variance $E(X-\mu)^2$ is 10^{12}.)

We conclude this section by proving that the variance of the binomial distribution is $n\pi(1-\pi)$.

Theorem: The Variance of the Binomial Distribution when there are n Trials

If each trial in an experiment with n trials consists of a draw from a binomial distribution that will yield 1 with probability π and zero with probability 1 − π, and the trials are statistically independent, then nπ(1−π) is the variance of the random variable obtained by summing the outcomes of the n trials.

Proof:

First we prove that for any random variable X we have

$$E(X - \mu)^2 = E(X)^2 - \mu^2$$

This is a consequence of the fact that $(X-\mu)^2 = X^2 - 2\mu X + \mu^2$ and

$$E(X^2 - 2\mu X + \mu^2) = E(X^2) - 2\mu E(X) + E(\mu^2) = E(X^2) - 2\mu^2 + \mu^2$$

$$= E(X)^2 - \mu^2.$$

For the binomial distribution we have $\mu^2 = (n\pi)^2$ so it remains to work out $E(X^2)$. By definition,

$$E_n(X^2) = \sum_{x=0}^{n} x^2 \, \frac{n!}{x!(n-x)!} \, \pi^x (1-\pi)^{n-x}.$$

Because $x^2 = x(x-1) + x$ we have

$$E_n(X^2) = \sum_{x=0}^{n} [x(x-1) + x] \frac{n!}{x!(n-x)!} \, \pi^x (1-\pi)^{n-x}$$

$$= \sum_{x=0}^{n} x(x-1) \frac{n!}{x!(n-x)!} \, \pi^x (1-\pi)^{n-x} + \sum_{x=0}^{n} x \, \frac{n!}{x!(n-x)!} \qquad [13]$$

$$= \sum_{x=0}^{n} x(x-1) \frac{n!}{x!(n-x)!} \, \pi^x (1-\pi)^{n-x} + \mu$$

If $x = 0$ or 1 then $x(x-1) = 0$. Therefore, we only need to sum the terms in [13] from 2 through n.

$$E_n(X^2) = \sum_{x=2}^{n} x(x-1) \frac{n!}{x!(n-x)!} \, \pi^x (1-\pi)^{n-x} + \mu$$

$$= \sum_{x=2}^{n} \frac{n!}{(x-2)!(n-x)!} \, \pi^x (1-\pi)^{n-x} + \mu.$$

If we factor out $n(n-1)\pi^2$ this becomes

$$E_n(X^2) = n(n-1)\pi^2 \sum_{x=2}^{n} \frac{(n-2)!}{(x-2)!(n-x)!} \, \pi^{x-2} (1-\pi)^{n-x} + \mu. \qquad [14]$$

But $n - x = (n-2) - (x-2)$. Therefore, if we set $w = x-2$ and $m = n-2$ in [14] we have

$$E_n(X^2) = n(n-1)\pi^2 \sum_{w=0}^{m} \frac{m!}{w!(m-w)!} \; \pi^w (1-\pi)^{m-w} + \mu.$$

Of course $\sum_{w=0}^{m} \frac{m!}{w!(m-w)!} \; \pi^w (1-\pi)^{m-w}$ is the sum of the probabilities over all possible outcomes of an experiment with m trials and hence that sum is unity. Note that w increasing from 0 to m is equivalent to x increasing from 2 to n. Therefore,

$$E_n(X^2) = n(n-1)\pi^2 + \mu = n^2\pi^2 - n\pi^2 + n\pi = \mu^2 - n\pi^2 + n\pi.$$

Recall that for *any* distribution the variance $E(X-\mu)^2$ is equal to $E(X)^2 - \mu^2$. Therefore, for the *binomial* distribution,

$$E_n(X-\mu)^2 = \mu^2 - n\pi^2 + n\pi - \mu^2 = n\pi - n\pi^2 = n\pi(1-\pi),$$

the variance of the binomial distribution.   ∎

2.6.8   The Law of Large Numbers

When a polling agency randomly samples a population to predict the outcome of an election it will contact only a small fraction of the voters. The result will give some indication of the strength of the various candidates, but will not provide the actual fraction of the votes that each candidate will ultimately get. A larger sample will be more reliable in the sense that the sample result will be closer to the actual outcome with high probability. Intuitively, the larger the sample the more likely the poll is to get close to the actual fraction of the population that supports a given candidate. This section proves that claim.

The general statement is known as the *law of large numbers*. The theorem applies to a wide range of situations, not just to sampling voters. It applies to industrial quality control: testing a sample of manufactured goods as they come off the assembly line to estimate the total number of defective items as a fraction of the total number produced. In fact, the law applies to virtually any random variable that can be expressed as a nonnegative number. (In the voting context we assign 1 if the individual plans to vote for the candidate, and zero otherwise.) To express the law of large numbers theorem we need some notation.

X is the random variable, and $p(x)$ is the probability that it will take on the value x. (We confine attention to cases for which x can have only a finite number of values, but it is easy to generalize the theorem.) The *expected value* of X, denoted $E(X)$, is the "average" value and is computed by multiplying each x by its probability $p(x)$ and summing the result over all values of x.

DEFINITION: *The Expected Value of a Random Variable*

$$E(X) = \sum_A x p(x)$$

where summation is over A, the sample space. $E(X)$ is also referred to as the mean of the random variable X and denoted by the Greek letter μ.

Example 2.30 Three Events

$A = \{\alpha, \beta, \gamma\}$. That is, $x = \alpha$ or β or γ with probability $p(\alpha)$, $p(\beta)$, $p(\gamma)$ respectively. By definition of a random variable $p(\alpha) + p(\beta) + p(\gamma) = 1$. In this case

$$E(X) = \alpha p(\alpha) + \beta p(\beta) + \gamma p(\gamma).$$

The random variable might itself be the result of n trials of an experiment that can yield either success or failure on each trial.

Example 2.31 Calculating Probability with Three Trials

$A = \{0, 1\}$ where 0 represents failure and 1 denotes success. The probability π of success on a single trial is 0.8. Assume that there are three trials ($n = 3$) and the result of each trial is statistically independent of any other trial. The number x of successes is 0 or 1 or 2 or 3. Then

$$p(x) = \frac{3!}{x!(3-x)!} \; \pi^x(1-\pi)^{3-x} = \frac{3!}{x!(3-x)!} \; 0.8^x \times 0.2^{3-x}.$$

Thus, $p(0) = 1 \times 0.2^3 = 0.008$, $p(1) = 3 \times 0.8 \times 0.2^2 = 0.096$, $p(2) = 3 \times 0.8^2 \times 0.2 = 0.384$, and $p(3) = 1 \times 0.8^3 = 0.512$. Note that the sum of these probabilities is 1.

Another key population parameter is the variance, which measures the dispersion of the random variable around the mean. It is computed by squaring $x - \mu$, the deviation from the mean, multiplying the result by $p(x)$, and then summing over all values of x.

DEFINITION: *Variance*

$$E(X - \mu)^2 = \sum_A (x - \mu)^2 p(x)$$

is the *variance* of the random variable X and is often denoted by $\text{Var}(X)$ or σ^2.

If the distribution is symmetrical around the mean then $E(X-\mu) = 0$, however wide the spread of X around the mean. For instance, if $x = 10^6$ with probability ½ and -10^6 with probability ½ then $E(X) = \mu = 0$ and $E(X-\mu)$ is also zero, but there is great dispersion about the mean, reflected in the fact that $E(X-\mu)^2$ is 10^{12}. Therefore, we use $E(X-\mu)^2$ instead of $E(X-\mu)$ as a measure of the dispersion of the random variable X.

Example 2.32 The Variance with One Trial

If $x = 1$ with probability 0.8 and $x = 0$ with probability 0.2 then $E(X) = 1 \times 0.8 + 0 \times 0.2 = 0.8 = \mu$. Thus, $E(X-\mu)^2 = (1-0.8)^2 \times 0.8 + (0-0.8)^2 \times 0.2 = 0.16 = \sigma^2$.

We need to establish some preliminary properties of the mean and the variance before proving the law of large numbers. First, we show that if all values of X are nonnegative then for any positive number ω we have Prob $(x \geq \omega) \leq \frac{E(X)}{\omega}$. In words, the probability that the draw x is at least as high as ω cannot exceed $E(X)/\omega$. Because $E(X)$ is a specific number, the bigger is ω the smaller is the probability that one realization of the random variable will yield a value that is at least as large as ω. That much is quite intuitive. We will prove that the probability cannot be bigger than $\frac{E(X)}{\omega}$.

Markov's Inequality

X is a nonnegative random variable and ω is a given positive number. Then

$$\text{Prob}(x \geq \omega) \leq \frac{E(X)}{\omega}$$

Proof:

Recall that A denotes the sample space – the set of possible outcomes. Given the positive number ω let B denote the set of x in A such that $x \geq \omega$.

$$E(X) = \sum \left\{ xp(x) : x \text{ is in } A \right\} \geq \sum \left\{ xp(x) : x \text{ is in } B \right\} \geq \omega \times \sum \left\{ p(x) : x \text{ is in } B \right\}.$$

The first inequality is a consequence of the fact that B is a subset of A and the random variable is nonnegative. We obtain the second inequality from the first by replacing $xp(x)$ with $\omega p(x)$, and exploiting the fact that $x \geq \omega \geq 0$ and $p(x) \geq 0$. It follows that $E(X) \geq \omega \sum \{p(x) : x \text{ is in } B\}$.

But $\sum \{p(x) : x \text{ is in } B\}$ is Prob$(x \geq \omega)$, the probability that x is at least as large as ω. Therefore, we now have $E(X) \geq \omega \times \text{Prob}(x \geq \omega)$ and hence Prob $(x \geq \omega) \leq \frac{E(X)}{\omega}$ because ω is positive. ∎

Next we use Markov's inequality to show that the probability that the *absolute value* of the deviation of X from the mean μ will be larger than a given ω gets smaller as ω increases.

Chebyshev's Inequality

X is a nonnegative random variable and ω is a positive number. Then

$$\text{Prob}\left(|X - \mu| \geq \omega^2\right) \leq \frac{\sigma^2}{\omega^2}.$$

Proof:

We start with $(X - \mu)^2$ which is algebraically easier to deal with than $|X - \mu|$. Note that $(X - \mu)^2$ is itself a random variable. In fact, it's a nonnegative random variable. Therefore, Markov's inequality implies that

$$\text{Prob}\left((X-\mu)^2 \geq \omega^2\right) \leq E(X-\mu)^2/\omega^2 = \sigma^2/\omega^2.$$

But $\text{Prob}\left((X-\mu)^2 \geq \omega^2\right) \leq \sigma^2/\omega^2$ is equivalent to

$$\text{Prob}\left(|X-\mu| \geq \omega\right) \leq \frac{\sigma^2}{\omega^2}$$

because $\omega > 0$, and hence if $x - \mu < 0$ then $|x - \mu| \geq \omega$ is equivalent to $\mu - x \geq \omega$ which in turn is equivalent to $(x-\mu)^2 = (\mu-x)^2 \geq \omega$ if $\mu - x \geq \omega$. ∎

We are ready to state the law of large numbers formally: there is a single random variable X and we are going to draw a value of the variable at random n times in succession. If one thinks of drawing numbered balls from a hopper then we record the value x_1 from the first draw, then replace the ball and stir the hopper (so the probabilities don't change), then draw a second ball, record its value x_2 and replace the ball and so on. We wind up with a sequence of values $x_1, x_2, \ldots, x_n$. We can think of this as a set of realizations of n random variables, but they obviously have the same mean μ and the same variance σ^2. The law of large numbers states that for any positive number ε, however small, if we take a large enough sample then the probability that the sample average $(x_1+x_2+\ldots+x_n)/n$ is more than ε above or below the mean can be made as small as we like. Specifically, as the sample size n gets arbitrarily large

$$\text{Prob}\left(\left|\frac{x_1+x_2+\ldots+x_n}{n} - \mu\right| > \varepsilon\right)$$

approaches zero.

The proof depends on the fact that the expected value of a sum of random variables is the sum of the expected values, the expected value of λX is λ times the expected value of X, and the variance of λX is λ^2 times the variance of X. We prove this in two stages.

Theorem

$$E(\lambda X) = \lambda E(X) \text{ and } E(\lambda X)^2 = \lambda^2 E\left(X^2\right).$$

Proof:

$E(\lambda X) = \sum_A \lambda x p(x) = \lambda \sum_A x p(x) = \lambda E(X)$ and $E(\lambda X)^2 = \sum_A \lambda^2 x^2 p(x) = \lambda^2 \sum_A x^2 p(x) = \lambda^2 E(X^2).$ ∎

Suppose that X is a random variable on sample space A and Y is a random variable on sample space B. We say that X and Y are *statistically independent* if for any x and y (in X and Y respectively), the probability of observing x and y is $p(x)p(y)$, the product of the probabilities. Suppose that you flip a coin and the person sitting beside you draws one card from a deck of fifty-two playing cards. The probability of heads is 0.5 and the probability of drawing a spade is 0.25. Therefore, the probability of you tossing heads *and* your neighbor drawing a spade is $0.5 \times 0.25 = 0.125$

because the two events are statistically independent. The probability of drawing a black card is 0.5 and the probability of drawing a spade is 0.25. The probability of drawing a black card *and* a spade is 0.25, not 0.5 × 0.25. The two events are not statistically independent.

DEFINITION: *Statistical Independence*

If X is a random variable on sample space A and Y is a random variable on sample space B we say that X and Y are statistically independent if the probability of observing x and y is $p(x)p(y)$ for every x and y.

Theorem: Mean and Variance of a Sum

If random variable X on sample space A and random variable Y on sample space B are statistically independent real random variables then E(X+Y) is E(X) + E(Y). If we also have A = B then the variance of X + Y is the variance of X plus the variance of Y.

Proof:

By definition

$$E(X+Y) = \sum_{AB}(x+y)\text{Prob}[x+y] \text{ which equals } \sum_{AB}(x+y)p(x)p(y)$$

when X and Y are statistically independent. (AB denotes the set of all pairs (x,y) such that x is in X and y is in Y.) Then

$$E(X+Y) = \sum_{AB}[xp(x)p(y) + yp(x)p(y)]$$
$$= \sum_{A}p(x)[x\sum_{B}p(y) + \sum_{B}yp(y)]$$
$$= \sum_{A}p(x)[x + E(Y)]$$
$$= E(X) + E(Y)\sum_{A}p(x) = E(X) + E(Y).$$

The last two equalities exploit the fact that $\sum_{A}p(x) = 1 = \sum_{B}p(y)$, and $E(\lambda X) = \lambda E(X)$ for $\lambda = E(Y)$.

Now, suppose that $A = B$. Then

$$Var(X+Y) = E[X+Y-E(X+Y)]^2 = E[X+Y-E(X)-E(Y)]^2$$
$$= E[X+Y-2\mu]^2 = E[X-\mu+Y-\mu]^2$$
$$= E[(X-\mu)^2 + (Y-\mu)^2 + 2(X-\mu)(Y-\mu)]$$
$$= E[(X-\mu)^2] + E[(Y-\mu)^2] + 2E[(X-\mu)(Y-\mu)]$$
$$= Var(X) + Var(Y) + 2E[XY - \mu X - \mu Y + \mu^2]$$
$$= Var(X) + Var(Y) + 2[E(XY) - \mu E(X) - \mu E(Y) + \mu^2]$$
$$= Var(X) + Var(Y) + 2[E(XY) - \mu^2 - \mu^2 + \mu^2].$$

Because X and Y are statistically independent, $E(XY) = E(X) \times E(Y) = \mu^2$ and thus $E(XY) - \mu^2 = 0$. We have proved that $\mathrm{Var}(X+Y) = \mathrm{Var}(X) + \mathrm{Var}(Y)$ if X and Y are independent random variables on the same sample space.   ∎

The Law of Large Numbers

If X is a random variable and each x_t $(1 \le t \le n)$ is a single draw from X's distribution, then for any two positives numbers δ and ε there exists a value of n large enough so that

$$\mathrm{Prob}\left(\left|\frac{x_1 + x_2 + \ldots + x_n}{n} - \mu\right| > \varepsilon\right) < \delta.$$

provided that each of the n samples is statistically independent of the others.

Proof:

Because $E(X_t / n) = \mu / n$ we have

$$E[(X_1 + X_2 + \ldots + X_n)/n] = E(X_1)/n + E(X_2)/n + \ldots + E(X_n)/n$$
$$= \mu/n + \mu/n + \ldots + \mu/n = \mu.$$

And $\mathrm{Var}\,[(X_1 + X_2 + \ldots + X_n)/n] = Var(X_1 + X_2 + \ldots + X_n)/n^2$

$$= \sigma^2/n^2 + \sigma^2/n^2 + \ldots + \sigma^2/n^2$$
$$= n\sigma^2/n^2 = \sigma^2/n.$$

We want to show that for any two positive numbers δ and ε, however small, there is a sample size n such that the probability that the sample mean differs from the population mean by more than ε is less than δ. This follows from Chebyshev's inequality, which implies

$$\mathrm{Prob}\left(\left|\frac{x_1 + x_2 + \ldots + x_n}{n} - \mu\right| > \varepsilon\right) \le (\sigma^2/n)/\varepsilon^2 = \sigma^2/n\varepsilon^2.$$

But σ^2 is the variance of the single random variable X, and it doesn't change as the sample size increases. And ε is our chosen bound on the deviation of the sample size from the mean, so it is also fixed. Therefore, $\sigma^2/n\varepsilon^2$ decreases as we increase the sample size n, and given $\delta > 0$, however small, we can find n large enough so that $\sigma^2/n\varepsilon^2$ is less than δ, our bound on the probability.   ∎

Note that we have actually proved something more general: if $X_1, X_2, \ldots, X_n$ are n random variables that are statistically independent and identically distributed then for any positive number ε

$$\mathrm{Prob}\{|(x_1 + x_2 + \ldots + x_n)/n - \mu| > \varepsilon\} \le \sigma^2/n\varepsilon^2.$$

Link

Ghahramani (2002) is an accessible yet rigorous treatment of the foundations of probability theory.

Problem Set

(1) The individual's utility-of-wealth function is $U(w) = \sqrt{w}$ and current wealth is \$10,000. Is this individual risk averse? What is the maximum premium that this individual would pay to avoid a loss of \$1,900 that occurs with probability ½? Why is this maximum premium not equal to half of the loss?

(2) An individual has a utility-of-wealth function $U(w) = \ln(w + 1)$ and a current wealth of \$20. Is this individual risk averse? How much of this wealth will this person use to purchase an asset that yields zero with probability ½, and with probability ½ returns \$4 for every dollar invested? (When the asset pays off, a \$1 investment returns \$3 net of the original outlay.)

(3) The utility-of-wealth function is $U(w) = \ln(w + 1)$ and the individual's current wealth is θ. As a function of π, r, and θ how much of this wealth will the individual invest in a project that yields zero with probability π, and with probability $1 - \pi$ pays rC dollars to an investor who has sunk C dollars into the project?

(4) For $U(w) = \sqrt{w}$ prove that $U(½ x + ½y) > ½U(x) + ½U(y)$ for $x \neq y$.

(5) For $U(w) = \sqrt{w}$ prove that $U(\pi x + (1 - \pi)y) > \pi U(x) + (1 - \pi)U(y)$ for $0 < \pi < 1$ and $x \neq y$.

(6) Diane has a utility-of-wealth function $U(w) = \sqrt{w}$ and a current wealth of \$2000.

    (A) Will Diane invest in a scheme that requires an initial capital outlay of \$2,000 and returns nothing with probability ½ (i.e., the initial outlay is lost and there is no revenue) and returns \$6,000 with probability ½?

    (B) Cathy is identical to Diane in every respect. If Diane and Cathy can share the investment (this is called *risk spreading*) will they do so? In this case sharing means that each puts up \$1,000 and they split the proceeds of the investment.

(7) Leo, who has a utility-of-wealth function $U(w) = \ln(w + 20)$, has \$100 of income before tax and is taxed at a rate of 40 percent of earned income. If he is caught underreporting his income he will have to pay the taxes owed and in addition will pay a fine of \$1 for every dollar of income he failed to report. How much income will he conceal (i.e., fail to report) if the probability of being caught is 0.2? (Let C denote the amount of income concealed.)

(8) Clara, who has a utility-of-wealth function $U(w) = \ln(w + 100)$, would have an *after-tax* income of \$100 *if* she reported all her income. She is taxed at a rate of 50 percent of earned income (just to keep the calculations simple). If she is caught underreporting her income she will have to pay the taxes owed, of course, but in addition will pay a fine of F dollars for every dollar of income she failed to report.

(A) How much income will she conceal (i.e., fail to report) if $F = 2$ and the probability of being caught is 0.10? Let C denote the amount of income concealed.

(B) Determine C as a function of the fine F and the probability of being caught ρ. Show that C falls when either F or ρ increases.

(9) Jacob, who has a utility-of-wealth function $U(w) = \sqrt{w}$, has an initial wealth of $52. He has an opportunity to invest in a project that will cause him to lose his capital with probability 0.75, but with probability 0.25 will provide a net return of $4 for every dollar of capital he puts up. How much will he invest? (Let A denote the amount invested – i.e., the amount of capital he puts up. He loses A if the project fails, but if it succeeds it will pay him $5 gross for every dollar invested.)

(10) Determine the market opportunity line for questions 2, 3, 7, 8A, and 9.

(11) A standard measure of the degree of risk aversion at wealth level w is $-U''(w)/U'(w)$. (It is called the *Arrow-Pratt* measure.)

(A) Show that if $U(w) = w^{\alpha}$, where α is a positive constant less than one, then the degree of risk aversion decreases as w increases.

(B) Show that if $U(w) = K - e^{-\alpha w}$, where $\alpha > 0$, then degree of risk aversion is independent of the level of wealth.

(The idea of the Arrow-Pratt measure is that the faster the marginal utility of wealth declines, the more risk averse the individual is. The first derivative of U is used as the denominator because we would otherwise have a change in the measure if we replaced U with λU for $\lambda > 0$. That would be undesirable because the underlying preferences can be represented by either U or λU: if the EU of asset A exceeds that of asset B according to U then the EU of A will be greater than the EU of B according to λU, and vice versa.)

(12) The host of the television game show *Wheel of Fortune* tells contestants that it would be irrational to risk $15,000 for a $12,000 car because the probability of losing everything is one-half. The "asset" in this case yields zero with probability ½ and $27,000 with probability ½. If the individual stands pat and takes the safe asset, he or she will have $15,000 for sure.

(A) Explain why any risk-averse individual would stand pat.

(B) Find a utility-of-wealth function U such that the EU of the risky asset is greater than the expected utility of $15,000 for sure. Of course, U will not have diminishing marginal utility.

(I have oversimplified the position in which the contestants find themselves, but not in ways that vitiate the point that the gamble is not irrational for *some* people.)

(13) Generalize Markov's inequality to the case of a random variable that can take on an infinite number of possible values.

(14) Prove that $E(X - \mu) = 0$ if X is symmetrically distributed around the mean μ.

2.7 INSURANCE

In this section we work out the equilibrium of a competitive insurance market when the probability of an accident is the same for any two individuals and no individual has an opportunity to reduce the probability of an accident by devoting effort to preventive care. These two extreme assumptions establish a benchmark case. We relax the latter in Section 3.9 of Chapter 3 when we take account of the fact that if everyone takes preventive care there will be far fewer accidents and hence a higher level of expected utility for everyone. However, with insurance coverage no *individual* has incentive to invest in preventive care. Section 5.7 of Chapter 5 examines a competitive insurance market when individuals have different accident probabilities. That information is hidden from the insurance companies and that can also result in inefficiency. But in this chapter everyone has the same probability of an accident, and that probability is independent of any choice made by any individual. We begin by showing that a risk-averse decision maker will set $x = y$ when confronted with fair odds.

The simplest form of insurance is a barn raising. The term refers to an implicit contract binding farmers in a community. If a family's barn burns down its neighbors will contribute time and materials to replacing it. This imposes a cost on each member of the community – the "insurance premium" – but the contract provides a net gain to all. Each family is better off than it would be without the contract but with the risk of losing everything in case of fire.

2.7.1 The Complete Insurance Theorem

When risk-averse individuals choose under fair odds they will set $x = y$. This will allow us to identify their decision quickly: if the market opportunity line is $\pi x + (1 - \pi)y = \theta$, then $x = y$ implies $\pi x + (1 - \pi)x = \theta$, and thus $x = \theta = y$.

Complete Insurance Theorem

   A risk-averse individual will maximize expected utility by setting $x = y$ whenever the odds are fair.

We say that we have *complete insurance* whenever $x = y$ because the individual's wealth is the same in either event. Without complete insurance, the low payoff (which occurs with probability π) will be lower than the payoff that occurs with probability $1 - \pi$.

2.7.2 Sketch of the Proof of the Complete Insurance Theorem

We test the bundle (x, y) to see if it maximizes expected utility subject to the fact that x and y must be on the opportunity line. With x as the initial level of wealth, let MU_X denote the increase in U per unit increase in wealth in the "accident" state.

Similarly, starting from the level y, let MU_Y denote the increase in U per unit increase in wealth in the "no accident" state.

Under fair odds the choice of x and y must satisfy $\pi x + (1 - \pi)y = \theta$. We get

$$y = \frac{\theta}{1 - \pi} - \frac{\pi}{1 - \pi}x.$$

Therefore, if we change x and y by Δx and Δy, respectively, we must have $\Delta y = -[\pi/(1 - \pi)]\Delta x$. The resulting change in EU will be

$$\Delta EU = \pi MU_X \Delta x + (1 - \pi)MU_Y \Delta y.$$

Replace Δy in this last expression by $-[\pi/(1 - \pi)]\Delta x$. We get

$$\Delta EU = \pi \times MU_X \times \Delta x + (1 - \pi) \times MU_Y \times - \frac{\pi}{1 - \pi}\Delta x$$

$$= \pi\Delta x(MU_X - MU_Y).$$

Therefore, a fair odds market opportunity line implies that $\Delta EU = \pi\Delta x(MU_X - MU_Y)$. If $MU_X > MU_Y$ then we can increase ΔEU by setting $\Delta x > 0$, in which case both $\pi\Delta x$ and $MU_X - MU_Y$ will be positive, and thus ΔEU will also be positive. Therefore, if $MU_X > MU_Y$ we have not maximized EU. If $MU_X < MU_Y$ then we can increase ΔEU by setting $\Delta x < 0$, in which case both $\pi\Delta x$ and $MU_X - MU_Y$ will be negative, and thus ΔEU will be positive. Therefore, EU is not at its maximum if $MU_X \neq MU_Y$. We have established that MU_X must equal MU_Y at the values of x and y that maximize EU. Diminishing marginal utility of wealth implies that $MU_X > MU_Y$ if $x < y$ and $MU_X < MU_Y$ if $x > y$. Therefore, $MU_X = MU_Y$ holds if and only if $x = y$. Consequently, maximization of EU subject to fair odds implies that $x = y$. When we set $x = y$ the opportunity line $\pi x + (1 - \pi)y = \theta$ yields $x = \theta = y$.

∂2.7.3 Calculus Proof of the Complete Insurance Theorem

We want to maximize $EU = \pi U(x) + (1 - \pi)U(y)$ subject to $\pi x + (1 - \pi)y = \theta$. First we solve the market opportunity equation for y. We get $y = \theta/(1 - \pi) - [\pi/(1 - \pi)]x$. Then $dy/dx = -\pi/(1 - \pi)$. The variable y appears in the expression for EU, but we will treat it as a function of x. Then we can set

$$V(x) = \pi U(x) + (1 - \pi)U(y)$$

and use the chain rule to find the first derivative of V. We have

$$\frac{dV}{dx} = \pi U'(x) + (1 - \pi)U'(y) \times \frac{dy}{dx}$$

$$= \pi U'(x) + (1 - \pi)U'(y) \times \pi(1 - \pi) = \pi U'(x) - \pi U'(y).$$

The first derivative must be equal to 0 at a maximum of V. But $V' = 0$ and $V' = \pi U'(x) - \pi U'(y)$ imply $U'(x) = U'(y)$ if $\pi > 0$. (What can we say if $\pi = 0$?) Finally, because $U'' < 0$ at every point (by the risk-aversion assumption) we can have $U'(x) = U'(y)$ if and only if $x = y$. (If $U'' < 0$ at every point then the first derivative of U falls as the wealth level increases. Therefore, if $x < y$ then $U'(x) > U'(y)$, and if $x > y$ we have $U'(x) < U'(y)$.)

To confirm that $V' = 0$ takes us to a *maximum*, let's compute the second derivative of V. With fair odds the first derivative of V is $\pi U'(x) - \pi U'(y)$. Then

$$V'' = \pi\, U''(x) - \pi\, U''(y) \times \frac{dy}{dx} = \pi\, U''(x) - \pi\, U''(y) \times -\frac{\pi}{1-\pi}$$

$$= \pi\, U''(x) + \frac{\pi^2}{1-\pi}\, U''(y).$$

Because π and $(1-\pi)$ are both positive and U'' is negative at every point (by risk-aversion) we have $V''(x) < 0$ for all x. Therefore, $V' = 0$ at the point where V achieves its unique global maximum.

Example 2.33 A Specific Utility-of-Wealth Function

$U(w) = \ln(w+1)$. The individual will receive x with probability ¼ and y with probability ¾. We are told that $¼x + ¾y = 10$ is the individual's market opportunity equation. Therefore, he or she faces fair odds. Now, maximize $¼\ln(x+1) + ¾\ln(y+1)$ subject to $¼x + ¾y = 10$. The market opportunity equation implies $y = 40/3 - ⅓x$. Then we wish to maximize

$$V(x) = ¼\ln(x+1) + ¾\ln(40/3 - ⅓x + 1).$$

We have

$$V'(x) = ¼(x+1)^{-1} + ¾(y+1)^{-1}(-⅓) = ¼(x+1)^{-1} - ¼(y+1)^{-1}.$$

Note that $V'' < 0$ at all points. Therefore, if $V'(x) = 0$ yields nonnegative values of x and y the equation $V'(x) = 0$ will provide the solution. But $V'(x) = 0$ gives us $¼(x+1)^{-1} = ¼(y+1)^{-1}$. Multiply both sides by $4(x+1)(y+1)$. This yields $y + 1 = x + 1$, and hence $x = y$. Substituting x for y in the market opportunity equation yields $x = 10$. Thus $x = 10 = y$ and we have complete insurance.

The next three examples demonstrate that different risk-averse individuals will purchase different levels of insurance coverage if the odds are not fair, but the same individuals will choose complete insurance when the odds are fair.

Example 2.34 Insurance Without Fair Odds

Rosie's utility-of-wealth function is $U(w) = \sqrt{w}$. Her current wealth is $100, but with probability 0.3 an accident will reduce her wealth to $30, as summarized by Table 2.3. Suppose that a dollar of insurance coverage costs forty cents. Therefore, if Rosie has an accident and has C dollars of coverage her wealth will be

$$x = 30 + C - 0.4\,C = 30 + 0.6\,C.$$

(She gets a claim check for C dollars but still has to pay her premium in a year when she has an accident.) With C dollars of insurance she will have wealth of

$$y = 100 - 0.4\,C$$

if she doesn't have an accident. Let's calculate the market opportunity line: We have $y = 100 - 0.4C$ and thus $C = 250 - 2.5y$. Now substitute $250 - 2.5y$ for C in the expression $x = 30 + 0.6C$. We get $x = 30 + 0.6 \times (250 - 2.5y) = 30 + 150 - 1.5y$. That is, $x = 180 - 1.5y$. Then

$$x + 1.5y = 180$$

is the equation of the market opportunity line. We do not have fair odds because the ratio of the x coefficient to the y coefficient is 2/3 but the ratio of probabilities is 3/7.

Let's determine how much insurance Rosie will purchase. We want to maximize

$$EU = 0.3 \sqrt{x} + 0.7\sqrt{y} = 0.3 \sqrt{30 + 0.6C} + 0.7 \sqrt{100 - 0.4C},$$

a function of C. The first derivative is

$$\frac{0.3 \times 0.6}{2\sqrt{30 + 0.6C}} + \frac{0.7 \times -0.4}{2\sqrt{100 - 0.4C}}$$

We maximize EU by setting the first derivative equal to 0. (Confirm that the second derivative is negative for all $C \geq 0$.) After setting the first derivative equal to 0 and multiplying both sides of the equation by 200 we get

$$\frac{18}{\sqrt{30 + 0.6C}} - \frac{28}{\sqrt{100 - 0.4C}} = 0.$$

This implies $9\sqrt{100 - 0.4C} = 14\sqrt{30 + 0.6C}$. We square both sides and solve for C, yielding $C^* = 14.8$. If Rosie has an accident her wealth will be $x^* = 30 + 0.6 \times 14.8 = 38.88$. If there is no accident her wealth will be $y^* = 100 - 0.4 \times 14.8 = 94.08$. With insurance, Rosie's EU will be $0.3\sqrt{38.88} + 0.7\sqrt{94.08} = 8.66$. Without insurance her EU is $0.3\sqrt{30} + 0.7\sqrt{100} = 8.64$.

Let's see what a different individual will choose with the same market opportunity.

Example 2.35 The Same Odds but a Different Utility-of-Wealth Function

Soren's utility-of-wealth function is $U(w) = \ln(w + 1)$. Except for the utility-of-wealth function, the data are the same as for Example 2.34: Soren's wealth will be $100 with probability 0.7 and $30 with probability 0.3. A dollar of insurance coverage costs forty cents. To determine how much insurance Soren will purchase we maximize

$$EU = 0.3\ln(x + 1) + 0.7\ln(y + 1) = 0.3\ln(30 + 0.6\,C + 1) + 0.7\ln(100 - 0.4\,C + 1).$$

The first derivative is

$$\frac{0.3 \times 0.6}{31 + 0.6C} + \frac{0.7 \times -0.4}{101 - 0.4C}.$$

(Confirm that the second derivative is negative for all $C \geq 0$.) When we set the first derivative equal to 0 and solve for C we get $C^* = 39.58$. This is substantially more coverage than Rosie would purchase under the same terms. Evidently, Soren is more risk averse than Rosie. If Soren has an accident his wealth will be $x^* = 30 + 0.6 \times 39.58 = 53.75$. If there is no accident his wealth will be $y^* = 100 - 0.4 \times 39.58 = 84.17$. With insurance, Soren's expected utility will be $0.3\ln(53.75 + 1) + 0.7\ln(84.17 + 1) = 4.31$. Without insurance his EU is $0.3\ln(30 + 1) + 0.7\ln(100 + 1) = 4.26$.

Both individuals buy some insurance, even though it lowers the EMV of their wealth. With $x = 30 + 0.6C$ and $y = 100 - 0.4C$ we have EMV $= 0.3(30 + 0.6C) + 0.7(100 - 0.4C) = 79 - 0.1C$. Then without insurance we have $C = 0$ and $EMV = 79$. When C is positive then EMV is less than 79. Risk-averse individuals typically buy some insurance even when it lowers the EMV of their wealth because the reduction in exposure to risk more than makes up for the loss in EU resulting from the lower EMV. (Of course, under fair odds the EMV of wealth is the same with insurance as without.)

Table 2.3

State	Probability	Wealth
No accident	0.7	100
Accident	0.3	30

Now, suppose that the cost of a dollar of insurance coverage falls to thirty cents. This leads to fair odds. Let's check. We now have

$$x = 30 + C - 0.3\,C = 30 + 0.7\,C \text{ and } y = 100 - 0.3\,C.$$

From the second equation we get $C = 100/0.3 - y/0.3$. When we substitute the right-hand side for C in the equation $x = 30 + 0.7\,C$ we get

$$x = 30 + \frac{70}{0.3} - \frac{0.7y}{0.3}.$$

Multiply both sides by 0.3, resulting in $0.3x + 0.7y = 79$. We do indeed have fair odds.

Example 2.36 The Chosen Coverage under Fair Odds

As shown in Table 2.3, the individual faces the same risk as in the previous two examples but a dollar of insurance coverage now costs thirty cents. Rosie will now maximize

$$EU = 0.3\sqrt{x} + 0.7\sqrt{y} = 0.3\sqrt{30 + 0.7C} + 0.7\sqrt{100 - 0.3C}$$

The first derivative is

$$\frac{0.3 \times 0.7}{2\sqrt{30 + 0.7C}} + \frac{0.7 \times -0.3}{2\sqrt{100 - 0.3C}}.$$

Note that the derivative is 0 when $C = 70$. Rosie chooses $70 of coverage. In that case, $x = 30 + 0.7 \times 70 = 79$ and $y = 100 - 0.3 \times 70 = 79$. Rosie chooses complete insurance. Note also that the expected value of her wealth is $79 with insurance, and it is also \$79 without insurance ($0.3 \times 30 + 0.7 \times 100 = 79$). With complete insurance Rosie's EU is $0.3\sqrt{79} + 0.7\sqrt{79} = 8.89$.   To determine how much insurance Soren will purchase under fair odds we maximize

$$EU = 0.3\ln(x+1) + 0.7\ln(y+1) = 0.3\ln(30 + 0.7C + 1) + 0.7\ln(100 - 0.3C + 1).$$

The first derivative is

$$\frac{0.3 \times 0.7}{31 + 0.7C} + \frac{0.7 \times -0.3}{101 - 0.3C},$$

which will be zero when $C = 70$. The two risk-averse individuals make the same choice when the odds are fair. With complete insurance, Soren's expected utility is $0.3\ln(79 + 1) + 0.7\ln(79 + 1) = 4.38$.

2.7.4   Competitive Insurance Markets

Assume a large number n of individuals and that an individual's wealth will fall from z to a with probability π. Each has the utility-of-wealth function $U(w)$, and we assume diminishing marginal utility of wealth because each person is assumed to be risk averse. Because there are n identical individuals, we can treat the n experiences as the result of n statistically independent experiments in which the probability of failure is π in each case. The law of large numbers assures us that the actual number of failures will be very close to the expected number πn with very high probability. (See Section 2.6.8 of this chapter.) In that case we save ourselves the trouble of saying that our results hold with probability extremely close to one by claiming that there will be "exactly" πn accidents. It follows that there will be πn individuals with wealth a and $n - \pi n$ who do not suffer an accident and have wealth z. Therefore, the community's actual wealth will be $\pi n a + (n - \pi n)z$, *with or without insurance*.

Suppose that an individual pays a premium of p per dollar of *net* coverage. That is, if coverage of c is purchased then the individual's wealth will be $a + c$ with probability π and $z - pc$ with probability $(1 - \pi)$. (Note that the individual pays the premium pc whether or not there is an accident. Therefore, in case of accident the policy holder receives a check for $c + pc$ dollars.) In short, $x = a + c$ and $y = z - pc$. Because the individual ultimately cares about x and y we let the terms of the policy be implicit and refer to an insurance policy as a pair (x, y). We can always use (x, y) to derive the terms of the policy because $c = x - a$ and $p = (z - y)/c$. In other words, given the pair (x, y), the total premium is $z - y$ (the difference between wealth if there is no accident and no insurance and wealth if there is insurance but no accident). The net coverage (the claim check minus the premium) is the difference between an insured person's wealth if there is an accident and wealth if there is an accident but no insurance. The premium per dollar of net coverage is, of course, the total premium divided by net coverage.

DEFINITION: *The Simple Model*

There are n identical individuals, and each is risk averse. The probability of an accident is π for each, and they have the same utility-of-wealth function U. Without insurance, all individuals have wealth a if they have an accident and z otherwise. With insurance, an individual's wealth is x in case of an accident and y otherwise.

We show that a competitive insurance market leads to complete insurance. Specifically, in our simple model we have $x = y$ at equilibrium for each policy holder. Moreover, x and y are each equal to the expected monetary value of individual wealth without insurance. Therefore, (x, y) is on the fair odds line at equilibrium. To prove this we first show that insurance companies enjoy a positive economic profit if (x, y) is below the fair odds line for everyone, and they sustain losses if (x, y) is above the fair odds line for everyone. This is quite intuitive: if (x, y) is below the fair odds line then y is low and hence the premium is high, and if (x, y) is above then y is high so the premium must be low. The next step is to show that competition and profit maximization combine to maximize individual expected utility, even though that is not at all what profit-seeking companies are trying to do.

Competitive Equilibrium Theorem for the Simple Model

At equilibrium each insurer offers a policy that results in $x = y = EMV$, the expected monetary value of individual wealth, and each individual purchases that policy.

Proof:

Figure 2.10 portrays a typical indifference curve for a risk-averse individual. It is bowed in towards the origin. The point E where $x = y$ on the fair odds line has a

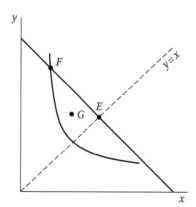

Figure 2.10

higher expected utility than any other point on that line. (Recall the complete insurance theorem.) Policy E is above the indifference curve through F because expected utility is higher at E than at F. We have $\pi x + (1 - \pi)y = \pi a + (1 - \pi)z$ at F because F is on the fair odds line. Then $(1 - \pi)(z - y) = \pi(x - a)$ at F. If we multiply both sides of that equality by m, the number of individuals who purchase the "policy" (x, y), we get

$$(m - m\pi)(z - y) = m\pi(x - a)$$

at F. In words, the number of individuals who don't have an accident multiplied by the premium that each of those individuals pays is equal to the number of individuals who do suffer an accident multiplied by the net amount of money paid out to each by the insurer. (Money paid in equals money paid out.) Therefore, profit is zero. But at G, below the fair odds line, we have $\pi x + (1 - \pi)y < \pi a + (1 - \pi)z$ and hence $(m - m\pi)(z - y) > m\pi(x - a)$ at G: the insurer has a positive economic profit at G. Losses are sustained above the fair odds line because $(m - m\pi)(z - y)$ is less than $m\pi(x - a)$ there.

The industry is not at equilibrium if any insurer is selling a policy that puts a substantial number of individuals above the fair odds line because the insurer will take steps to eliminate those losses. An insurer that sells a policy that puts its customers at a point such as F is not suffering losses, but the insurer can turn a profit by withdrawing those policies and replacing them with one that leads to G, where profits are positive. Consumers will buy it in preference to F because it puts them above the indifference curve through F. (Because expected utility is not maximized at F, the indifference curve through F cuts across the fair odds line. Even if individuals have different utility of wealth functions, there will be a point such as G that is below the fair odds line and above everyone's indifference curve through F.)

We used G to show that equilibrium does not occur at F. But a policy that leads to G is not consistent with equilibrium either: policy G is below the fair odds line. Therefore, there is a policy G' that is directly above G (with the same value of x but a larger y than at G) but still below the fair odds line. Therefore, G' is profitable, but not as profitable as G. An insurance company selling G has no incentive to withdraw it and substitute G'. However, because G' yields a positive economic profit there is an incentive for new capital to enter the industry by offering G' and drawing customers away from firms selling G. We have established that equilibrium cannot occur at a point such as F on the fair odds line, where the indifference curve cuts across the line, nor at a point such as G below the fair odds line but above the indifference curve through F. What's left? Equilibrium must occur at E, the point on the fair odds line where individual expected utility is maximized, and hence the indifference curve through E is tangent to the line. And $x = y$ at E by the complete insurance theorem.

We have $\pi x + (1 - \pi)y = \pi a + (1 - \pi)z$ at every point (x, y) on the fair odds line. If we also have $x = y$ then $x = y = \pi a + (1 - \pi)z$, the expected monetary value of individual wealth without (and with) insurance. ∎

Example 2.37 A Simple Case

The probability of an accident is $\pi = \frac{1}{4}$ for each person. Then $1 - \pi = \frac{3}{4}$, the probability that the individual does not have an accident. Each person's wealth is $a = 4$ if there is an accident and no insurance, and $z = 12$ if there is no accident and no insurance. In a competitive insurance market the individual's opportunity equation is

$$0.25x + 0.75y = 0.25(4) + 0.75(12) = 10.$$

Because complete insurance under competitive conditions yields $x = y$, we have $x = 10 = y$. The insurance premium is z minus wealth when there is insurance but no accident. Specifically, the premium is $12 - 10 = 2$. In case of an accident individuals would receive claim checks for $8, and their wealth would be a + claim check − premium = $4 + 8 - 2 = 10$.

We would expect that, even with complete insurance, the individual's wealth would be lower if the probability of an accident were higher. The next example illustrates.

Example 2.38 A Higher Probability of an Accident

The probability of an accident is ½, which is also the probability that there is no accident. We again assume that wealth is $a = 4$ if there is an accident and no insurance and $z = 12$ if there is no accident and no insurance. The competitive equilibrium per capita opportunity equation is

$$0.5x + 0.5y = 0.5(4) + 0.5(12) = 8.$$

Then $x = y$ gives us $x = 8 = y$. The insurance premium is now $12 - 8 = 4$, and if there is an accident individuals receive claim checks for $8, and their wealth would be $4 + 8 - 4 = 8$.

2.7.5 Efficiency of Competitive Insurance Markets with Full Information

To establish a benchmark case, we are assuming away all hidden action and hidden characteristic problems. Specifically, we suppose that no individual can reduce the probability of an accident by devoting effort to prevention – no potential moral hazard problem – and also that the probability of an accident is the same for everyone – no possibility of adverse selection. We continue to assume a large number n of risk-averse individuals, each with a probability π of his wealth declining from z to a. We have seen that the competitive equilibrium results in $x = y = \pi a + (1 - \pi)z$ for each. We now prove that this outcome is efficient. We do so by showing that any outcome that gives everyone higher expected utility than the competitive equilibrium is not feasible because it requires more total wealth than the community has available.

Suppose that each individual's expected utility is higher at (x', y') than it is at the competitive equilibrium. Because the latter maximizes individual EU on the market opportunity line $\pi x + (1 - \pi)y = \pi a + (1 - \pi)z$, an allocation delivering even higher EU must be above that line. Therefore,

$$\pi x' + (1 - \pi)y' > \pi a + (1 - \pi)z.$$

If we multiply both sides of that inequality by n we get $n\pi x' + (n - n\pi)y' > n\pi a + (n - n\pi)z$. Because $n\pi$ individuals will have an accident, $n\pi x' + (n - n\pi)y'$ is total community wealth as a result of giving each person (x', y'), and $n\pi a + (n - n\pi)z$ is actual community wealth. Then $\pi x' + (1 - \pi)y' > \pi a + (1 - \pi)z$ tells us that we *can't* give everyone (x', y') because it requires more wealth to be distributed than the community actually has. (Insurance, whether it is provided by private firms or the government, cannot create wealth; it can only redistribute it.) Therefore, there is no feasible outcome that gives everyone higher expected utility than the competitive equilibrium.

The preceding argument is incomplete because it ignores the possibility of giving individuals different levels of insurance.

Example 2.39 A Highly Unlikely Scenario

Suppose that $a = 40$ and $z = 60$ with $\pi = \frac{1}{2}$. Consider two policies, $A = (46, 56)$ and $B = (50, 54)$. If everyone got policy A the outcome would not be feasible because the expected value of per capita wealth with insurance would be $\frac{1}{2} \times 46 + \frac{1}{2} \times 56 = 51$, which exceeds $50 = \frac{1}{2} \times 40 + \frac{1}{2} \times 60$, the expected value of per capita wealth without insurance. Similarly, B is not feasible if everyone gets B because its expected value is $\frac{1}{2} \times 50 + \frac{1}{2} \times 54 = 52$. Suppose, however, that half the people get A and the other half get B. The "actual" number of accidents will be $n/2$. Suppose that all the people with A have an accident, but none of the people with B suffer an accident. Then the actual wealth per capita will be $\frac{1}{2} \times 46 + \frac{1}{2} \times 54 = 50$, and that *is* feasible.

There is something seriously wrong with the argument of Example 2.39. We can discount this challenge to the competitive equilibrium because, with a large number of individuals, the probability of it happening is virtually zero: if we give $n/2$ individuals policy A and the rest policy B we can't count on only those holding policy A to have an accident. The outcome is feasible only if a very specific – and very improbable – pattern of accidents occurs. If no one holding the policy that pays a high claim has an accident then the premiums can be sufficient to cover the claims paid out. Feasibility calculations should not be so contrived. To impose a more meaningful test we will say that a mix of policies is feasible if the *expected* amount of revenue from premiums is at least as large as the expected amount paid out in claims. We conclude this section by showing that there is no feasible set of policies – according to this new definition – that would give everyone more expected utility than the competitive equilibrium. We do that by showing that if a set of policies S *does* give everyone more expected utility than the competitive equilibrium, then S must not collect enough premium revenue on average to pay the claims that will be paid out on average.

Suppose that n_1 individuals get (x_1, y_1), a different group of n_2 persons get (x_2, y_2), and n_3 get (x_3, y_3), and so on. Suppose that there are k different groups. Of course, $n_1 + n_2 + \ldots + n_k = n$. Suppose that the expected utility of each individual in group i is higher at (x_i, y_i) than it is at the competitive equilibrium. Because the latter maximizes individual expected utility on the market opportunity line $\pi x + (1 - \pi)y = \pi a + (1 - \pi)z$, an allocation delivering even higher expected utility must be above that line. Therefore,

$$\pi x_i + (1 - \pi)y_i > \pi a + (1 - \pi)z \text{ for } i - 1, 2, \ldots, k.$$

If we multiply both sides of that inequality by n_i we get $n_i\pi x_i + (n_i - n_i\pi)y_i > n_i\pi a + (n_i - n_i\pi)z$. Because $n_i\pi$ individuals will have an accident, the number $n_i\pi x_i + (n_i - n_i\pi)y_i$ is total group i wealth as a result of giving (x_i, y_i) to each person in group i, and $n_i\pi a + (n_i - n_i\pi)z$ is actual group i wealth. Therefore, the total wealth allocated to all individuals (over all groups) exceeds actual total wealth summed over all individuals. This tells us that we *can't* give (x_i, y_i) to everyone in group i for all groups because it requires more wealth to be distributed than the community actually has. Note that

$$n_i\pi x_i + (n_i - n_i\pi)y_i > n_i\pi a + (n_i - n_i\pi)z$$

is equivalent to

$$n_i\pi(x_i - a) > (n_i - n_i\pi)(z - y).$$

The second inequality says that the total net claim paid to the individuals in group i who have an accident exceeds the total money collected in premiums from the people in group i who do not suffer an accident. Therefore, there is no feasible outcome that gives everyone higher expected utility than the competitive equilibrium, establishing that the competitive equilibrium is efficient.

Sufficient Condition for Efficiency

If there is a large number of individuals, each with probability π of having wealth level a and probability $(1 - \pi)$ of wealth z then the outcome at which each person has $x = \pi a + (1 - \pi)z = y$ is efficient.

Example 2.40 Expected Premiums and Expected Claims

Suppose $a = 40$ and $z = 60$ with $\pi = \frac{1}{2}$. Half of the n individuals get $A = (46, 56)$ and the other half get $B = (50, 54)$. Therefore, A pays a net claim of $46 - 40 = 6$, and B pays a net claim of $50 - 40 = 10$. A's premium is $60 - 56 = 4$ and B's premium is $60 - 54 = 6$. The expected number of accidents in each group is $0.25n$. The expected amount of premium income from the individuals who don't suffer an accident is $0.25n (4) + 0.25n (6) = 2.5n$. The total expected value of claims paid out to those who do have an accident is $0.25n (6) + 0.25n (10) = 4n$. Expected claims paid out $(4n)$ exceeds expected premium income $(2.5n)$.

Problem Set

(1) Prove that the competitive equilibrium is efficient (not just weakly efficient) by showing that if it is possible to give one person higher *EU* without lowering anyone else's *EU* then it is possible to give everyone higher *EU*.

Questions 2 to 5 pertain to Dana, whose utility-of-wealth function is $U(w) = 1 - 1/(w + 1)$, and Harry, whose utility-of-wealth function is $U(w) = \ln(w + 1)$. Each has a current wealth of \$100 and in each case there is a probability of 0.2

that $60 of it will be destroyed in an accident. (If an insured individual has an accident and has $C of coverage then he or she will get a claim check for $C.) For the remainder of the questions:

- **(A)** Derive the market opportunity line. Does it exhibit fair odds? Explain.
- **(B)** How much insurance coverage will Dana purchase? What will Dana's wealth be if she has an accident, and what wealth will she have if she does not have an accident?
- **(C)** How much insurance coverage will Harry choose? What will his wealth be if he has an accident, and what wealth will he have if he does not have an accident?

(2) Are Dana and Harry each risk averse? Explain.

(3) Insurance can be purchased for twenty-five cents per dollar of coverage.

(4) Insurance can be purchased for forty cents per dollar of coverage.

(5) Insurance can be purchased for twenty cents per dollar of coverage.

3

Hidden Action

This chapter and the next investigate the extent to which an agent can be motivated to act in the principal's interest when the principal cannot determine whether the agent has in fact taken the appropriate action. Agents' behavior is problematic because their goal is to maximize their own utility. The next chapter is devoted to the specific hidden action problem of motivating workers and management in a firm, with the top executives receiving most of our attention. This chapter examines a wide variety of other issues. In many of these the principal is a surrogate for society as a whole, and the principal's utility is maximized when the agents – the producers and consumers – are all motivated to do their part in contributing to an efficient outcome.

As with all hidden information problems, there are hidden characteristic elements as well as the hidden action element. In fact, some of the topics could have been presented as hidden characteristic problems. For instance, we could study resource allocation from the standpoint of inducing consumers to reveal their hidden preferences and firms to reveal their hidden production technologies so that an efficient outcome can be identified. However, the approach taken in the first section is that of inducing each individual to *choose* a bundle of goods and services at which his or her marginal rate of substitution equals that of the other consumers. Similarly, when discussing pollution abatement in Section 2, we begin with the fact that the adjustment cost of an individual firm – the firm's characteristic – is hidden from the government. If the firm were simply asked to report its adjustment cost we would have a hidden characteristic problem, belonging in Chapter 5. However, we instead look at an incentive scheme that harnesses the profit motive to induce firms to coordinate their actions so that the adjustment burden falls on the firms that can reduce pollution at the lowest cost to consumers.

Hidden action problems are complicated by the presence of uncertainty. If your car breaks down a week after you bring it home from the repair shop you do not know whether you are the victim of bad luck or shirking by the mechanic. This makes it hard to design efficient, incentive-compatible contracts. Consider the case of a principal who owns farmland and hires a worker – the agent – to operate the farm. Suppose that the landlord charges a fixed rent and hence allows the agent to keep all the proceeds of the farm over and above the rental payment. Then the agent has maximum incentive to run the farm efficiently. That's because the agent is the *residual claimant* under the rental contract: once the rent is paid every additional dollar of profit goes directly into the agent's pocket. This should result in the maximum possible payoff for both the principal and the agent. The rent can be set at a level that leaves each with a higher return that can be achieved through any alternative contract – that is, sharing arrangement – that results in a lower profit.

We have implicitly assumed, however, that the agent is risk neutral. The farm's profit is affected by uncertainty in many ways. The weather, the activity of pests, and so forth can be viewed as random variables from the standpoint of both the principal and the agent. It is reasonable to assume that the farm worker is risk averse. Because the profit derived from the farm has a random component, when the agent is the residual claimant, he not only has maximum incentive, he also has maximum exposure to risk. The rent will have to be reduced sufficiently to keep the agent on the farm and prevent him from taking a fixed-wage job in the city. The owner of the land will find that she can get more income by sharing the risk with the agent – by offering a contract that reduces the rental payment when events beyond the control of the agent reduce the harvest.

We still haven't identified all the ways in which uncertainty affects the nature of the contracts that principals offer their agents. There are things that the agent can do to mitigate the effect of harmful events. For instance, keeping fences in good repair makes it unlikely that the crop will be trampled by the neighbor's cattle. By devoting effort to keeping rodents out of the barn, less seed will be consumed by these intruders. In some cases a contract can be structured so that the agent's rent is reduced in bad times only if he has devoted effort to keeping pests away. However, if the owner of the land does not live on the farm then she can't observe whether the agent has expended effort to that effect. In that case, the contract cannot be written so that the agent's return is conditional on his supply of effort. In other cases, the agent's effort is observable by the principal but not by a third party such as a judge.

> When you buy a new car the warranty is kept in force only if the periodic maintenance has been done properly. It is fairly easy for the manufacturer to determine whether the maintenance was proper.

For instance, if the owner lives on the farm she can see whether the agent puts effort into keeping rodents out of the barn. But the owner's observations would not be admissible in court, which would require independent evidence of shirking by the agent. Therefore, the conditional contract could not be enforced, so it would not be written in the first place. When the agent's effort can't be observed by the principal or by a judge or jury, a fixed rent would leave the worker with maximum exposure to risk but minimum incentive to shirk. However, a fixed income would provide the worker with maximum shelter from risk but minimum incentive to work. The principal will maximize her return from the contract by finding the optimal trade-off between providing incentive and providing shelter from uncertainty. In this case farming often takes the form of *sharecropping*, particularly in developing countries: the worker gets a fixed share of the farm's profit, say one-half. If profit falls by 100 then the worker's share falls by 50, not by 100, so there is some insulation from uncertainty. When profit increases by 120 as a result of the agent's effort the agent's income increases by 60, so there is some incentive for the agent to supply effort, although it is not the maximum incentive.

The effect of risk on efficiency is not treated explicitly until Section 9, although uncertainty plays a supporting role in Sections 3 through 6.

Source

The rationale for sharecropping is based on Stiglitz (1974), a seminal contribution to the theory of incentives.

3.1 RESOURCE ALLOCATION

A necessary condition for efficient resource allocation is the requirement that an individual does not consume a good up to the point at which it adds very little to that person's welfare when it could provide substantial additional benefit to someone else. This section considers the possibility of giving individuals an incentive to consume only up to a certain point – a point that depends on the preferences of others. The aim is to arrive at an efficient allocation of consumer goods. (Chapter 11 considers production and consumption simultaneously.)

To get a handle on the conditions for efficiency in the allocation of consumer goods we'll begin with the simplest case of two individuals, A and B, and two commodities, 1 and 2. Suppose that A's marginal rate of substitution (MRS) is 2 at her current consumption plan, and B's MRS is ½ at his current plan. That means that if A sacrificed less than 2 units of commodity 2 but received an additional unit of commodity 1 she would be better off as a result. If B lost a unit of the first good he would wind up better off if he received more than half a unit of the second good as compensation. Then if we arrange for A to give B one unit of the second good in return for one unit of the first good they would both wind up better off. In general, if $MRS_A > MRS_B$ then A and B could each gain by trading, provided that A exported the second good and imported the first good, and B did the reverse, *and* the amount of commodity 2 exchanged per unit of commodity 1 is between MRS_A and MRS_B. Similarly, they could strike a mutually advantageous trade if $MRS_A < MRS_B$. Efficiency requires equality of the marginal rates of substitution for any two individuals and any two commodities that each actually consumes.

Example 3.1 Two Consumers with Unequal Marginal Rates of Substitution

A's utility function is $U_A = x^2 y$, and $U_B = xy^2$, where x is the amount of the first good consumed and y is the amount of the second good. Suppose that each person is currently consuming 4 units of each good. Then $U_A = 64 = U_B$. We don't actually have to compute each MRS here to construct a trade that increases the utility of each. Note that A's utility function puts extra weight on the first good and B's puts extra weight on the second good. In other words, the first good gets more weight in A's preference scheme and the second good gets more weight in B's preference scheme. Surely $MRS_A > MRS_B$ and both would be better off if A gave one unit of good 2 to B in return for one unit of the first good. Let's check: $U_A(5, 3) = 5^2 \times 3 = 75$ and $U_B(3, 5) = 3 \times 5^2 = 75$. The trade increases the utility of each.

Resources have been wasted when an economic system delivers an inefficient outcome. Moreover, it would be extremely costly to bring about the changes in economic activity that would benefit some without harming anyone – even if individuals could be relied on to reveal their private information truthfully. The economic system should not burden public policy with this kind of adjustment.

It is easy to show that at an equilibrium of an exchange economy is efficient if one person's consumption does not directly affect the welfare of another. Before giving the brief (but rigorous) proof of that claim we give the intuition: consider two people, A and B, and two goods. Suppose that each consumes some of each good at equilibrium. Then each individual's MRS will equal the price ratio P_1/P_2, the price of good 1 divided by the price of good 2. The price ratio plays a central role in A's determination of her preferred consumption plan. But the price ratio equals B's MRS, so without realizing it A is taking B's preferences into consideration when determining her own consumption plan. It's as though A says, "I've studied economics. When my MRS is greater than the price ratio my MRS is greater than B's. Because I place a higher intrinsic value on commodity 1, I am justified in consuming more of it. I'm not wasting resources. But I don't want to consume up to the point where my MRS is below the price ratio. If that happened I *would* be wasting resources. I would be consuming units of the good that have less intrinsic value to me than they do to person B." In fact, it is in A's *self-interest* not to consume good 1 beyond the point where her MRS equals the price ratio. The prices transmit information to A about the preferences of other consumers, *and* the budget constraint gives A the incentive to take that information into consideration when planning her consumption. This results in an efficient allocation of resources.

Now here's the general proof. Consider two individuals: A, who lives in Allentown, and B, who lives in Bozeman. They haven't met, and because the market economy is *decentralized*, with no central agency making sure that individuals do get together when something mutually advantageous might ensue, we have to ask if it is possible for A and B to trade in a way that would leave both better off. We're assuming that the system has reached an equilibrium before the trade takes place because we're testing the market economy for efficiency. Let's suppose that we have found a mutually advantageous trade. This assumption will quickly be shown to be untenable.

The trade must be balanced if we want to leave the consumption of others unchanged. (We want to increase U_A and U_B without harming anyone else.) The trade will be balanced if every increase in A's consumption comes at the expense of B and vice versa. Let a denote the list of exports and imports for individual A. For instance, if $a = (+7, -3, -6, \ldots)$ then A receives (imports) 7 units of the first good from B, but delivers (exports) 3 units of the second good and 6 units of the third good to B, and so on. We'll let b represent the list of B's exports and imports. Hence, our example requires $b = (-7, +3, +6, \ldots)$ because B exports 7 units of the first good to A and imports 3 units and 6 units, respectively, of the second and third goods. In brief, $b = -a$. Let pa denote the value of all A's imports minus the value of all A's exports, calculated using equilibrium prices. Similarly, pb is the value of all B's imports minus the value of all B's exports.

Suppose this trade makes both A and B better off. Because the trade makes A better off, we must have $pa > 0$. If $pa \leq 0$ then these changes would already have been incorporated into A's consumption plan at equilibrium. For instance, if $a = (+7, -3, -6)$ and each good costs \$2 (so $pa < 0$) then by reducing consumption of good 2 by 3 units and reducing consumption of good 3 by 6 units, individual A would have reduced her expenditure by enough to enable her to purchase 7 units of the first good. We're claiming that these changes would leave her better off, and that she could afford to make the changes on her own. (If the cost of the goods that A is acquiring is \$14, and the cost of the goods that A is giving up is \$18, then A can effect the change unilaterally.) That contradicts the notion that at equilibrium individual maximize utility subject to the budget constraint. It follows that $pa > 0$.

Similarly, because the changes specified by b leave individual B better off they must not have been affordable when B chose his consumption plan. In other words, $pb > 0$. We also have $a + b = 0$ because every unit of a commodity imported by A is exported by B and vice versa. But $a + b = 0$ is inconsistent with a and b both having a positive market value: That is, we can't simultaneously satisfy $a + b = 0$, $pa > 0$, and $pb > 0$. For instance, if $a = (+7, -3, -6)$, $b = (-7, +3, +6)$, and each good costs \$2 at equilibrium, then $pb = +4$ but $pa = -4$. We are forced to abandon the supposition that there is a trade between A and B that would leave both better off than they are at the market equilibrium.

Once the market system reaches equilibrium, if someone in Allentown telephoned everyone in Bozeman, hoping to find an individual with whom to strike a mutually advantageous trade, he or she would be disappointed. (How do we account for eBay then? Preferences have changed: People are trading things they no longer want. There is also a lot of retail activity on eBay — it is part of the market process.)

In any market, the price has three functions:

(1) *Rationing:* The price adjusts until demand equals supply, which means that for every unit of the good that someone wants to buy there is a unit that someone wants to sell and vice versa.

(2) *Information transmission:* The equilibrium price ratio transmits information to each consumer (and each firm) about the marginal rate of substitution of other individuals.

(3) *Incentive compatibility:* The budget constraint gives all individuals the incentive to take that information into consideration when planning their consumption.

Suppose that you are vacationing 900 miles from home when a temporary disruption in the supply of crude oil causes the price of gasoline to rise by 20%. You haven't been following the news, but you've taken an introductory course in economics and the spike in the price of gas informs you that there has been a large reduction in its supply. Do you worry that you won't be able to obtain enough gas for your drive home? No. Independent truckers will drive at a lower speed, to reduce their gas consumption per mile, as if they were altruistically sacrificing leisure time to make gas available for your trip home. In fact they are governed by self-interest and the impact of the increase in price on their budget constraints. Some families will respond to the price increase by cancelling a planned vacation trip, thereby ensuring that there will be enough gas for your trip home. Of course, those decisions are also motivated by self-interest. You might well brood about the effect of the price increase on your consumption in general, but you won't be concerned about the trip home.

We can easily extend the argument of this section to any number of consumers. Let's organize a trade involving n individuals. Let t_1 be the list of exports and imports for individual 1, with t_2 denoting the list of exports and imports for individual 2, t_3 the list of exports and imports for individual 3, and so on. If this trade makes individual i better off, then we have $pt_i > 0$. If the trade makes everyone better off than under the market equilibrium, we have $pt_i > 0$ for each individual i. But if we add over all n individuals we get $pt_1 + pt_2 + \ldots + pt_n > 0$. This tells us that the total value of imports exceeds the total value of exports. That is inconsistent with the fact that for every unit of a good imported by someone there is a unit of the same good exported by someone. (We are not changing any production plans at this stage. That will be considered in Chapter 11.) Therefore, it is not possible to have *any* number of individuals trade among themselves in a way that leaves everyone better off than they are at the market equilibrium.

Would it be possible to change the consumption of a subset of the individuals in a way that doesn't raise or lower the level of well-being of any member of the subset but do so in a way that generates a surplus that can be used to make someone else better off? No. Section 1.4 of Chapter 1 showed that if the menu of produced goods can be reallocated in a way that makes *some* individuals better off, and leaves others with the same level of welfare as before, then it is possible to make *everyone* strictly better off. (Just have the individuals who gain share some of the gain with the rest.) But we have just proved that there is no feasible outcome that makes everyone better off.

We said at the outset that the key assumption is that one person's consumption does not have a direct effect on another's welfare. Where did this assumption get used? If, say, person C's welfare were affected by the consumption of A and B, we could construct an example of an economy such that, starting at equilibrium, we could have A and B trade in a way that neither increased nor decreased the welfare of either but increased the welfare of C. We can't say that C would have brought about the change as part of his or her own consumption plan, because the increase in C's utility requires A and B to act in very specific ways.

If we use the term *private good* to refer to a commodity that is immune to external effects, then we have shown that there is no change in the market equilibrium allocation of the produced private goods that could be used to make some individuals better off without harming others.

DEFINITION: *Private Good*

A commodity is private if a change in the amount of it consumed by one individual has no direct effect on the welfare of any other individual whose own consumption does not change.

Links

Chapter 4 of this book examines the problem of giving a firm's manager the incentive to choose the production plan that contributes to efficiency. Koopmans (1957) is a classic and very readable exposition of the connection between

Table 3.1

	CASE 1			CASE 2	
	Commodity X	Commodity Y		Commodity X	Commodity Y
Person A	4	8	Person A	2	2
Person B	6	2	Person B	8	8

efficiency and the competitive market system. Pages 1–126 are especially recommended.

Problem Set

The two cases presented in Table 3.1 give you the amounts of two commodities X and Y consumed by two individuals A and B. Individual A's utility function is $U_A(x, y) = xy$ and thus A's MRS at consumption plan (x, y) is y/x. Individual B's utility function is $U_B(x, y) = x^2 y$ and the MRS at (x, y) is $2y/x$. Answer each of the following questions for each case.

(1) Report the utility level and the MRS for each individual at the given consumption plan.

(2) Construct a trade between A and B that *increases* the utility of each. Make sure that the trade is balanced – that is, the total consumption of X remains at 10 and the total consumption of Y also remains at 10.

(3) Report the exchange rate for your trade of question 2. (The exchange rate is the amount of commodity Y exchanged per unit of commodity X.) Notice that the exchange rate is between the two marginal rates of substitution.

(4) Using the exchange rate of question 3, construct a trade that *reduces* the utility of both A and B by making the trade "too big" – that is, with a large amount of exports and imports.

(5) Assume the exchange rate of question 3, but with *trade flowing in the opposite direction* (have A export the good that he or she imported in your answer to question 2). For each of the two cases displayed in Table 3.1, show that both individuals have *lower* utility than they had to start with (in question 1) as a result of trade.

3.2 MARKETABLE POLLUTION RIGHTS

Incentive regulation allows the regulated party to choose from a menu that is determined by the regulatory authority. It has replaced command and control regulation in many cases. If the menu items are cleverly chosen, a superior outcome can emerge, because the regulated agent has better information than the regulator. The local decision makers are on the scene day after day. They typically have far

Command and control regulation can be daunting: the US Department of Defense requires thirty-five pages of small print to define a T-shirt in its guide for firms supplying that garment to military personnel (Stiglitz, 1993).

more at stake than the regulator, and that gives them a strong motive for acquiring information. A successful incentive scheme can tap this information by judiciously harnessing the self-interested behavior of the regulated agent.

This section presents a scheme for giving producers an incentive to cooperate in achieving the least-cost method of reducing pollution. The pollutant in question could be any toxic or noxious substance that is released into the air or water during the production process. We will use sulphur dioxide to illustrate.

The production of electricity releases large amounts of sulphur dioxide (SO_2) into the air when fossil fuel is burned to produce the steam that runs the turbines. The SO_2 by-product can be reduced only if the firms that make electricity modify their existing equipment or install new equipment. Suppose that the regulatory agency wants to reduce the amount of SO_2 in the air in a way that minimizes the value of resources that have to be diverted from the production of other goods and services in order to modify the process of generating electric power. The agency would have to acquire specific information about the production technology of individual electricity firms if it is to identify the ones that can adjust at lowest cost – i.e., at the minimum diversion of resources away from the production of other commodities, and hence the smallest sacrifice by consumers. Without proper incentives these firms will not disclose the information willingly and accurately. For instance, if firms are asked to report their cost schedules – i.e., the cost incurred for each level of abatement – and the low cost firms are required to undertake the lion's share of the emissions reduction then each firm, including those whose adjustment costs are relatively low, has a strong incentive to overstate costs in an attempt to shift the adjustment burden to other firms.

3.2.1 The Economic Argument

When marketable pollution permits are employed to reach the target reduction of harmful emissions at lowest cost, the regulatory authority issues a number of permits equal to the target level of emissions. (The media refer to the use of pollution allowances as the "cap-and-trade" technique.) Suppose for instance that a total of 30 tons of SO_2 was dumped into the air last year, and the regulatory authority wants to reduce that amount by 10 tons this year. It would issue 20 permits, and a firm would have to surrender one pollution permit for each for each ton of SO_2 that it emits. Each firm would have a permit allowance – the number of permits that it received from the regulatory authority. These permits can be bought and sold in a competitive market, and if the firm wanted to dump an amount of SO_2 that exceeded its allowance it would have to buy additional permits. But *every* ton of SO_2 released has an opportunity cost. When a firm uses a permit that was part of its allowance it loses the opportunity to sell it at the market price. When the firm has to buy the permit, the opportunity cost is also an accounting cost.

The command and control approach to regulation is best represented as a uniform requirement across all firms. For instance, if there are two firms X and Y and the authority wants to reduce total emissions by 10 tons it would require X and Y to each reduce emissions by 5 tons. That is almost certain to be inconsistent with efficiency: suppose that the cost to X of reducing its emissions by 6 tons would be $100 greater than the cost of a 5 ton reduction, but the cost to Y of reducing its emissions by 4 tons would be $140 less than the cost of a 5 ton reduction. Then the total cost of reaching the target would fall by $40 = $140 − 100 if the adjustment burden were shared unequally, with X reducing by 6 and Y reducing by 4. But X has every incentive to overstate its adjustment cost to avoid shouldering more of the adjustment burden.

Even if the regulatory authority imposed an unequal adjustment burden, with X required to reduce its emissions by 7 tons and Y by 3 tons, inefficiency is still likely. The marginal cost of adjustment could still be lower in X than Y, or it could be the other way round. Unless the authority has accurate information about individual firm adjustment costs – and the firm has no incentive to provide that information truthfully – any arbitrary assignment of adjustment burdens is almost certain to be inefficient. We will see that the use of marketable pollution permits gives the low-cost firm an *incentive* to assume the lion's share of the total emissions reduction.

DEFINITION: *Marketable Pollution Permits*

Each firm in the industry is given a number of pollution permits. Each permit entitles the bearer to dump one ton of sulphur dioxide into the air, and the total number of permits issued by the government equals the target *level* of SO_2 output. (The difference between the previous year's SO_2 output and the total number of permits issued in the current year is the target SO_2 *reduction*.) The individual firm can buy any number of entitlements and can sell as many of its own permits as it chooses, at a price determined by a competitive market.

There will be a demand for permits, and the demand increases when the price of permits falls. At a lower price more firms can profit by reducing their abatement effort and purchasing additional permits at the market price to support the higher level of emissions. If P is the price of a permit we will have $P > MC_L$ for low-cost firm L, where MC_L is the addition to cost of reducing its emissions by another ton. The permit market is not at equilibrium because firm L has not maximized profit: L's profit will increase by $P - MC_L$ when it sells an additional permit and reduces its emissions by another ton. A high cost of adjustment firm H will find that P is less than MC_H. That firm's profit will increase by $MC_H - P$ if it reduces its abatement effort by one ton and thereby increases its emissions. The cost of doing so is the price of the permit that it will have to buy, and the benefit is the saving, MC_H, resulting from the reduced adjustment burden. The low-cost firm has no incentive to pass the adjustment burden onto another firm because doing so would cause it to forego the extra profit of $P - MC_L$ it realizes by accepting its role in reducing the total cost of reaching the industry target emissions level. This illustrates how the US program of marketable pollution permits has worked to not only reduce sulphur dioxide emissions by 50% since 1990, but to do so at a substantially lower cost than would be incurred by alternative pollution reduction policies.

People on the left of the political spectrum often oppose the use of marketable pollution permits because it allows firms to pay to pollute. But that misses the point: Imposing an opportunity cost of polluting gives the low-cost firm an incentive to pollute less. Commentators on the right often oppose the use of marketable pollution permits because it imposes a new tax on producers. But it's not a tax, it's a price; a price for using pure air and water, valuable and scarce resources. A decentralized system such as a private ownership market economy cannot perform at its best if a decision maker can use a scarce resource without incurring a cost. Marketable pollution permits extend the virtues of the price system to the use of air and water. (One of the many reasons for the failure of the Soviet economy is that capital was not appropriately priced, and hence was misallocated.)

Assume (temporarily) that a firm's revenue is unaffected by any policy that constrains its level of pollution. The policy will have a significant effect on cost because the production process will have to be modified to comply with the abatement requirement. It is easy to prove the following:

Efficiency Theorem
  Regardless of how the given number of pollution allowances is allocated to firms, when the market for these allowances reaches an equilibrium the total industry cost of achieving the given reduction in emissions is lower than for any other policy that would achieve the same abatement level.

The formal proof of this claim is presented in Section 3.2.4. Section 3.2.3 presents the intuition behind the theorem.

3.2.2 Bargaining

To clarify the role of incentives, we assume in this section that the transfer of permits is achieved by direct negotiation between firms X and Y. If revenue is constant, cost minimization is equivalent to profit maximization.

Given any pattern of emissions levels that achieve the target pollution reduction goal, let L_X denote the fall in X's profit when it transfers a pollution permit to Y and reduces its SO_2 emissions by one more ton, incurring additional cost of L_X. The extra permit allows Y to reduce its *abatement* effort by one ton. In other words, Y can increase its SO_2 emissions by one ton, and thus reduce cost by, say, G_Y. If L_X is less than G_Y then that transfer of the adjustment burden from Y to X would lower the industry-wide cost of reaching the target by $G_Y - L_X$.

We now abandon the assumption that revenue is unaffected by any policy that constrains a firm's pollution output. When L_X is less than G_Y we don't have to rely on a central authority to arrange the transfer of the adjustment burden from Y to X. If $L_X < D < G_Y$ both firms gain when X transfers one permit to Y for a payment of D. The increase in X's profit would be $D - L_X$ and the increase in Y's profit would be $G_Y - D$.

Bargaining Theorem

Total industry profit is maximized, subject to the target abatement goal, when the transfer of permits from one firm to another results from bargaining between the two firms, at a price determined by these negotiating firms.

Why do we use profit as a measure of the net benefit that consumers derive from a firm's activities? Revenue is a good measure of the *gross* benefit that consumers receive from a unit of the commodity produced by the industry in question. (Budget-constrained utility maximization implies that the price of the industry's output equals the marginal rate of substitution when the second good is a composite good – total expenditure on all other commodities.) The cost of production is equal to the market value of inputs used, and that in turn is a rough measure of the value to consumers of other goods that could have been produced with the resources that were employed instead in firm X. The difference measures the *net* value to consumers of the firm's activities. Because we want to impose emission reductions on firms in a way that maximizes the net benefit to consumers, we want to maximize total industry profit subject to the total pollution emissions not exceeding the target.

The use of carbon permits to reduce carbon dioxide (CO_2) emissions is gaining momentum. However, the World Bank reports that 80 percent of emissions are still untaxed. The European Union has a fairly extensive permit program. Chile, China Columbia, Costa Rica, Indonesia, Thailand, Turkey, and Vietnam are developing "cap-and-trade" programs. South Korea has begun a program. Ten US states operate cap-and-trade programs, focusing on electricity generation. California's is the most effective and covers a wide swath of industries. In Canada, the provinces of Alberta, British Columbia, and Quebec have extensive programs.

Trade in pollution rights allows the two firms to maximize their total profit *and to share that total in a way that gives each more profit than if the government had insisted on them sharing the burden of pollution abatement equally – or according to some other arbitrary formula.* Why do we claim that this holds regardless of how the given number of pollution allowances is allocated to firms? Because our informal "proof" didn't make any assumption about the allocation of pollution rights. It is valid for any distribution of a given number of permits.

Would it always be possible for the two firms to benefit from an exchange of permits if the allowances from the regulatory authority were not consistent with the allocation of emissions levels that maximized industry profit subject to reaching the target? Yes. The proof is a simple application of the following "pizza theorem": A pizza (representing total industry profit) is to be shared by n individuals (representing the n firms in the industry). No matter how the pizza is divided – equally, very unequally, fairly equally – if a larger pie becomes available (representing maximum industry profit) it is possible to divide it so that everyone has more than he or she had with the given division of the smaller pizza. No matter how the large pie is divided, the n individuals can trade among themselves so that each winds up with a bigger piece than she had with the given division of the small pie.

Example 3.2 Two Firms, Each with a Quadratic Profit Function

We let x denote the amount of SO_2 released by firm X as a by-product of its production process. The higher is X's output of goods and services, the larger is x. We let $f(x)$ denote the profit realized by X when the SO_2 output is x and emissions are unconstrained. Specifically

$$f(x) = 190x - 5x^2.$$

Using calculus (or the formula for maximizing a quadratic) we see that f is maximized when $x = 190/(2 \times 5) = 19$. The reason why profit declines as x increases beyond 19 is that higher levels of SO_2 result from higher sales of the firm's product, and because marginal cost of production is increasing and marginal revenue is non-increasing, there is a point when profit falls as output increases — and consequently, profit falls when SO_2 increases beyond that point.

We let $g(y)$ be firm Y's profit when y tons of SO_2 are emitted by that firm and emissions are unconstrained. Specifically

$$g(y) = 110y - 5y^2.$$

Firm Y's profit is maximized when $y = 110/(2 \times 5) = 11$.

If each firm can maximize profit without constraint we will have $x = 19$ and $y = 11$, in which case a total of 30 tons of SO_2 will be released into the air. But suppose that the regulatory authority wants to restrict the total emissions to 20 tons. To incorporate this constraint we can set $y = 20 - x$. Now, maximize total profit, $f + g$ when $y = 20 - x$. We maximize

$$190x - 5x^2 + 110(20 - x) - 5(20 - x)^2 = 280x - 10x^2 + 200.$$

This is maximized when $x = 280/(2 \times 10) = 14$. We have $x = 14$ and $y = 6$. (Remember, $y = 20 - x$.) Confirm that $f(14) = 1680$ and $g(6) = 480$. However, if the government required the firms to share equally the burden of reduced SO_2 emissions, each firm would have to reduce its pollution to 10 tons per year (for a total of 20). In that case $f(10) = 1400$ and $g(10) = 600$ are the respective profit figures. Table 3.2 summarizes.

Suppose that instead of insisting that each firm reduce its SO_2 output to 10 tons, the government gave each firm the right to release 10 tons into the air and allowed each firm to sell all or part of that right. If Y sells firm X the right to dump 4 tons of SO_2 for a price between 120 and 280 each firm would have more profit than under the equal burden formula. (X would pay up to $f(14) - f(10) = 1680 - 1400 = 280$ for

Table 3.2

x	y	$X's$ profit	$Y's$ profit	Total profit
10	10	1400	600	2000
14	6	1680	480	2160

4 permits, and Y would have to be paid at least $g(10) - g(6) = 600 - 480 = 120$ to part with 4 permits.) The total amount of pollution would still be 20. If, instead, X had been given the right to dump 15 tons of SO_2 and Y the right to dump 5 tons, the target of 20 would still be reached. This time firm X would sell Y the right to dump 1 ton, resulting in the maximum total profit once again (subject to $x + y = 20$). The minimum that X would accept in payment is the difference between profit at $x = 15$ and profit at $x = 14$, which is $f(15) - f(14) = 45$. The maximum that Y would be prepared to pay is the difference between profit at $y = 6$ and profit at $y = 5$, which is $g(6) - g(5) = 55$. Tradeable pollution rights give the two firms the chance to share the maximum total profit in a way that makes each better off than under a rigid assignment of individual firm pollution limits, however the rights are initially assigned.

3.2.3 Market Allocation

Example 3.2 assumes that the two firms would negotiate to find the exchange of pollution permits that maximizes industry profit. This is unrealistic for two reasons. First, the negotiation could break down as each firm tried to hold out for a larger share of the gain from trade. Second, there will be more than two firms – perhaps many – and it will be costly for the firms to negotiate until each finds a partner with whom it would be profitable to trade. (With n firms each would have $n-1$ potential trading partners. There is a total of $n(n-1)/2$ pairs of potential partners.) Both problems are circumvented when permits exchanges are realized anonymously, through a market: A firm's decision to buy or sell permits is based only on its own calculation of its own profit.

Here is an informal proof that the cost of achieving the target is minimized when permits are bought and sold at the equilibrium price: to bring out the intuition we simplify by assuming that the effect on total industry revenue is tiny, and can be ignored. Suppose that the total cost of reaching the target has *not* been minimized. We show that the market for permits can't be at equilibrium. If total cost can be reduced there must be two firms I and J with different marginal costs of abatement. In other words $MC_I < MC_J$ at the current configuration of emissions levels. Let P denote the price of a permit. If $P > MC_I$ we can't be at equilibrium because firm I will increase its profit by $P - MC_I$ if it sells one more permit or buys one less). If $P < MC_J$ we can't be at equilibrium because firm J will increase its profit by $MC_J - P$ if it buys one more permit (or sells one less). But $P \leq MC_I$ and $P \geq MC_J$ cannot both

Example 3.3 Equilibrium in the Market for Permits

We feature the two firms X and Y of Example 3.2, with the same unconstrained profit functions, $f(x) = 190x - 5x^2$ and $g(y) = 110y - 5y^2$, respectively. Let P denote the price of one permit. X receives α permits initially and Y receives β permits. If $x > \alpha$ then X buys $x - \alpha$ permits and its profit becomes

$$f_\alpha(x) = 190x - 5x^2 - P(x - \alpha).$$

This equals $190x - 5x^2 + P(\alpha - x)$, the profit realized by X if $x < \alpha$ and it sells $\alpha - x$ permits. Therefore

$$f_\alpha(x) = (190 - P)x - 5x^2 + P\alpha$$

is the profit of X whether it buys or sells permits. Similarly, Y's profit is

$$g_\beta(y) = (110 - P)y - 5y^2 + P\beta$$

whether it buys or sells permits. To derive the demand for permits by each firm we simply choose the values of x and y that maximize the respective profit functions. We get

$$x(P) = (190 - P)/10 \text{ and } y(P) = (110 - P)/10,$$

where $x(P)$ and $y(P)$ are the respective permit demand functions of the two firms. The supply of permits is fixed (by the regulatory authority) at 20, the target emissions level. Equilibrium is reached when $x(P) + y(P) = 20$. (Demand equals supply). We have $(190 - P)/10 + (110 - P)/10 = 20$, the solution of which is $P^* = 50$. When we substitute 50 for P in X's demand function we get $x = 14$, which is the value obtained by maximizing industry profit (Example 3.2). And when we substitute 50 for P in Y's demand function we get $y = 6$. Industry profit is maximized when the market for pollution permits reaches equilibrium. Note that the values of x and y at equilibrium are independent of the way that the permits are initially allocated. That is, we get $x = 14$ and $y = 6$ at equilibrium regardless of the values of α and β, as long as $\alpha + \beta = 20$.

hold because $MC_I < MC_J$. In other words, the total cost of achieving the target is not at its minimum the permit market is not at equilibrium.

Return to Example 3.2. When $\alpha = 10 = \beta$ and 4 permits are traded both the buyer (X) and the seller (Y) benefit if X pays less than 280 and Y receives more than 120. If the payment is determined in a competitive market for permits the equilibrium permit price is 50 and those bounds are respected: Note that $120 < 50 \times 4 < 280$.

We see that marketable pollution permits achieve the target SO_2 reduction. The regulatory authority determines the number of permits, and a firm must surrender one permit for every ton of SO_2 released. The permits achieve that target in the way that is most beneficial to consumers — reducing SO_2 output requires resources to be diverted from the production of goods and services so that the electric utility can modify its production technology, and we have seen that, if revenue is unaffected, the lower cost firms will do the adjusting. The low-cost firms maximize profit by selling some of their permits, requiring them to further reduce their SO_2 output. The high-cost firms maximize profit by buying additional permits, allowing them to release more SO_2 than their initial allotment of permits allows. Marketable pollution permits give each firm the incentive to implement the production plan that would be assigned to it by a central planning authority *if* the planning authority were able to obtain reliable information about the firm's adjustment cost.

3.2.4 A Formal Proof of Efficiency at Equilibrium

Suppose (temporarily) that a policy to reduce emissions will increase a firm's cost but will not affect revenue. It follows that minimizing the cost of reaching a particular abatement level is equivalent to maximizing profit, subject to the attainment of that abatement level. We now show that total industry profit is maximized when the abatement target is reached by employing marketable pollution permits. But why assume constant revenue? Any policy that affects firms' costs will affect the price of the industry output, and hence *will* change total industry revenue. Because a firm's revenue is a measure of the benefit that consumers derive from the firm's activities, and the firm's cost is a measure of the value to consumers of the output lost when resources are transferred to the firm in question, the firm's profit is a measure of the *net* value to consumers of a firm's activities. Accordingly, it is in consumers' interest for the regulatory authority to employ an emissions policy that maximizes total industry profit subject to the emissions target being reached.

We begin with a simple model with only two firms, X and Y. If firm X has an allowance of α permits but $x > \alpha$ then it will have to purchase $x - \alpha$ permits at price p and, given x, its profit will fall from $f(x)$ to $f(x) - p(x - \alpha)$. If x is less than α then X will be able to sell $\alpha - x$ permits, adding $p(\alpha - x)$ to revenue. X's profit would increase from $f(x)$ to $f(x) + p(\alpha - x)$. In either case, X's profit would be $f(x) - p(x - \alpha)$ if it produces x units of output and permits can be bought and sold. Of course, $f(x)$ is the profit it would realize at output level x if pollution was not regulated in any way. Similarly, Y's profit is $g(y) - p(y - \beta)$ at y units of output when its permit allowance is β.

The Two-Firm Model

Firm X emits x tons of the pollutant, resulting in a profit of $f(x)$ before incorporating the effect on revenue or cost that results from the purchase or sale of permits. Firm Y emits y tons of pollutant, resulting in a "before" profit of $g(y)$. The permit allowances of X and Y are α and β respectively, and $\alpha + \beta = T$, the target level of total emissions. Accounting profit, taking into consideration revenue or cost from the purchase or sale of permits, is $f(x) - p(x - \alpha)$ for X and $g(y) - p(y - \beta)$ for Y, where p is the permit price. Let x^*, y^*, and p^* denote the values of x, y, and p respectively when the market for permits reaches equilibrium.

Note that $f(x) - p(x - \alpha)$ is X's accounting profit but $f(x) - px$ is its economic profit: Every permit that X purchases requires an expenditure of p, but the use of a permit that is part of its endowment, and hence was obtained free of charge, involves an opportunity cost of p because the permit could have been sold for p. Note also that maximization of $f(x) - p(x - \alpha)$ is equivalent to maximization of $f(x) - px$ because the two functions differ only by a constant. The two functions are maximized at the same value of x.

Example 3.4 Accounting and Economic Profit

Suppose that $f(x) = 190x - 5x^2$, $\alpha = 10$, and $p = 50$. If $x = 14$ then
accounting profit $= 190(14) - 5(14)^2 - 50(14 - 10)$ and
economic profit $= 190(14) - 5(14)^2 - 50(14)$.

It is easy to prove that industry profit is maximized, subject to the constraint that total emissions not exceed the target, when the market for permits reaches equilibrium.

Efficiency Theorem for the Two-Firm Model
$f(x^*) + g(y^*) \geq f(x) + g(y)$ for all x and y subject to $x + y \leq T$,
where x^* and y^* are the output levels of X and Y when the permit market is in equilibrium.

Proof:

At equilibrium each firm maximizes profit. Therefore,

$$f(x^*) - p^*(x^* - \alpha) \geq f(x) - p^*(x - \alpha) \qquad [1]$$
$$g(y^*) - p^*(y^* - \beta) \geq g(y) - p^*(y - \beta) \qquad [2]$$

hold for all x and y. The inequality is preserved when we add the left-hand side of [1] to the left-hand side of [2] and then do the same with the right-hand sides. That gives us

$$f(x^*) - p^*(x^* - \alpha) + g(y^*) - p^*(y^* - \beta) \geq f(x) - p^*(x - \alpha) + g(y) - p^*(y - \beta) \qquad [3]$$

Every ton of the pollutant requires the transfer of one permit from firms to the regulatory authority. And every permit is used at equilibrium because an unused or unsold permit incurs an opportunity cost of p^*. Therefore, $x^* + y^* = \alpha + \beta$. It follows that

$$p^*(x^* - \alpha) + p^*(y^* - \beta) = p^*(x^* + y^*) - p^*(\alpha + \beta) = 0.$$

Hence, the left-hand side of [3] reduces to $f(x^*) + g(y^*)$.

Recall that T, the target emissions level, equals $\alpha + \beta$. If $x + y \leq T = \alpha + \beta$ then

$$-p^*(x - \alpha) - p^*(y - \beta) = -p^*(x + y) + p^*(\alpha + \beta) \geq 0.$$

Hence, the right-hand side of [3] is no smaller than $f(x) + g(y)$ when $x + y \leq T$. Then [3] can be read as $f(x^*) + g(y^*) \geq f(x) + g(y)$. We have proved that $f(x^*) + g(y^*)$ maximizes $f(x) + g(y)$ subject to $x + y \leq T$. ∎

Suppose that either [1] or [2] holds as a strict inequality when $x \neq x^*$ or $y \neq y^*$. Then [3] will also hold as a strict inequality. It follows that $f(x^*) + g(y^*)$ will be strictly greater $f(x) + g(y)$ for any x and y such that $x + y \leq T$ and $x \neq x^*$ or $y \neq y^*$.

Finally, we consider a model with n firms, where $f_j(y_j)$ denotes the profit of firm j when it emits y_j tons of SO_2. Specifically, $f_j(y_j)$ is firm j's profit before deducting the cost (if any) of purchasing additional permits, and before adding the revenue (if any) from the sale of permits. The goal is to find the assignment of SO_2 emissions $y_1, y_2, \ldots, y_n$ that maximizes the sum of the $f_j(y_j)$ over all n firms, which we denote by $\Sigma f_j(y_j)$, subject to the constraint $y_1 + y_2 + \ldots + y_n \leq T$. The amount T is the target – the level of total SO_2 emissions to which the industry will be limited. We show that the solution is obtained at the equilibrium in the market for pollution permits when exactly T permits are issued. The claim is true no matter how the T permits are distributed to the firms.

The n-Firm Model

There are n firms, and $f_j(y_j)$ denotes j's profit (before factoring the effect of any purchase or sale of permits) when it emits y_j tons of SO_2. The permit allowance of j is q_j and $q_1 + q_2 + \ldots + q_n = T$, the target level of total emissions.

We might have $q_j = 0$. A new firm may not be given any permits at all, and be required to purchase the permits it needs.

If $y_j > q_j$ then j will have to buy $y_j - q_j$ permits, at a cost of $p(y_j - q_j)$. In that case its accounting profit will be

$$f_j(y_j) - p(y_j - q_j). \qquad [4]$$

If $y_j < q_j$ then j will be able to sell $q_j - y_j$ permits and that will add $p(q_j - y_j)$ dollars to the firm's revenue. Its accounting profit will be

$$f_j(y_j) + p(q_j - y_j). \qquad [5]$$

Clearly, [4] and [5] are identical: Accounting profit is $f_j(y_j) + p(q_j - y_j)$, whether $y_j \leq q_j$ or $y_j \geq q_j$.

We conclude this section by showing that when the market for permits has reached equilibrium total industry profit is maximized subject to the constraint that total emissions not exceed the target level.

Efficiency Theorem for the General Model

If the output level of firm i is x_i when the market for permits is at equilibrium at price p then

$$f_1(x_1) + f_2(x_2) + \ldots + f_n(x_n) \geq f_1(y_1) + f_2(y_2) + \ldots + f_n(y_n)$$

for all y_1, y_2, ... y_n satisfying $y_1 + y_2 + \ldots + y_n \leq T$.

Proof:

At equilibrium each firm *j* maximizes *its own* profit, and hence

$$f_j(x_j) + pq_j - px_j \geq f_j(y_j) + pq_j - py_j \quad \text{for any } y_j \qquad [6]$$

Adding the left and rights sides of [6] over all *n* firms, we get

$$\sum f_j(x_j) + p\sum q_j - p\sum x_j \geq \sum f_j(y_j) + p\sum q_j - p\sum y_j \qquad [7]$$

Inequality [7] holds for any y_1, y_2, ..., y_n. At equilibrium the demand for permits equals the supply. Therefore, we have $p\sum q_j = p\sum x_j$ because $\sum q_j = T = \sum x_j$. Therefore, [7] yields

$$\sum f_j(x_j) \geq \sum f_j(y_j) + p\sum q_j - p\sum y_j \text{ for any } y_1, y_2, \ldots, y_n. \qquad [8]$$

Now, suppose that y_1, y_2, ..., y_n is an assignment of SO_2 emissions that meets the target. That is, $y_1 + y_2 + \ldots + y_n \leq T$. Then $y_1 + y_2 + \ldots + y_n \leq T = q_1 + q_2 + \ldots + q_n$. It follows that $p\sum q_j - p\sum y_j \geq 0$. Therefore, inequality [8] implies $\sum f_j(x_j) \geq \sum f_j(y_j)$ for any assignment y_1, y_2, ..., y_n of SO_2 emissions that meets the target. ∎

Links

Stoft (2008) compares the performance of the market for pollution allowances in mitigating the effect of climate change to that of a carbon tax. The fact that the distribution of emissions levels across firms is independent of the way that rights are initially allocated across firms (given total emissions) is a special case of the Coase theorem (Coase, 1960). Schmalensee et al. (1998) and Stavins (1998) provide good overviews of the success of the American pollution allowance program. Joskow et al. (1998) provide a deeper, more technical analysis. For an application of the pollution permit idea to carbon regulation see Cramton and Kerr (1999). For global perspectives see Schmalensee et al. (1998) and Chichilnisky and Heal (1993, 1999). Hannesson (2004) discusses the use of transferrable fishing quotas.

Problem Set

(1) Show that for any total SO_2 output *T*, for any assignment *A* of emissions levels to the individual firms that totals *T*, at the assignment of emissions levels that maximizes total profit (subject to total emissions being *T*), the total profit can be shared in a way that gives each firm more total profit than under *A*.

For the remaining questions, x denotes the amount of SO_2 released by firm X as a by-product of its production process, with $f(x)$ denoting the resulting (unregulated) profit of firm X. Similarly, let $g(y)$ be firm Y's (unregulated) profit when y tons of SO_2 are emitted by firm Y. For each of the following five cases answer the following three questions.

    (A) Assuming that the firms are not regulated in any way, find the profit-maximizing levels of x and y for firms X and Y, respectively. Determine the profit realized by each firm.

    (B) The regulatory authority gives α pollution allowances to firm X and β to Y, but allows either firm to sell some or all of its right to pollute to the other firm. Assuming that the firms negotiate directly to exchange permits, determine the resulting equilibrium values of x and y and the profit realized by each firm before taking into consideration the money that changes hands as a result of the exchange of pollution rights. Which firm sells pollution rights and which firm buys them? How many rights are exchanged? What are the lower and upper bounds on the amount of money that the buying firm pays the selling firm?

    (C) Let P denote the price of a right to dump one ton of SO_2. Derive each firm's demand function for permits. Solve for the values of P, x, and y at equilibrium.

(2) $f(x) = 144x - 4x^2$ and $g(y) = 120y - 5y^2$. In this case $\alpha = 15$ and $\beta = 6$.

(3) $f(x) = 144x - 4x^2$ and $g(y) = 120y - 5y^2$, as in question 2. This time $\alpha = 12$ and $\beta = 9$.

(4) $f(x) = 300x - 10x^2$ and $g(y) = 120y - 5y^2$. In this case $\alpha = 12 = \beta$.

(5) $f(x) = 300x - 10x^2$ and $g(y) = 120y - 5y^2$, as in question 4. This time $\alpha = 13$ and $\beta = 11$.

(6) Let $f(x) = 1200x - 10x^2$ and $g(y) = 4000y - 20y^2$. This time leave α and β as parameters such that $\alpha + \beta = 50$.

3.3 INCENTIVE REGULATION OF THE TELECOMMUNICATIONS INDUSTRY

Incentive regulation allows the regulated party a choice from a menu that is governed by the regulatory authority. We use the telecommunications industry to illustrate. *Rate of return regulation* has been used for decades to curtail the market power of the suppliers of telephone services. It allows the regulated firm to set prices high enough for its revenue to cover all costs of production and to provide a reasonable return on capital as well. But the return on capital cannot exceed the limit set by the regulatory authority. The implicit restraint on the firm's price reduces the consumer welfare losses that arise when a firm with substantial market power sets a price well above marginal cost. However, the firm that is governed by rate of return regulation has little incentive to innovate or reduce cost if it is a monopolist, because the resulting increase in profit would result in a rate of return above the limit, which in turn would force a reduction in price.

The failure to take advantage of productivity gains, or cost reductions in general, can result in consumer welfare losses that swamp any gains from lower prices. Allowing the firm to operate as an unregulated monopolist would seem to eliminate that problem because a reduction in cost of a dollar results in an increase in profit of a dollar. However, the discipline of competition is an important factor in driving a firm to reduce cost or to innovate. Monopolies tend to be sluggish, in spite of the fact that a dollar in the pocket of a shareholder of a monopoly is no less welcome than a dollar in the pocket of an owner of a firm operating under intense competition.

Price cap regulation eliminates the excessively high prices associated with monopoly power without eliminating the incentive to reduce cost or improve product quality. The regulated firm is required to reduce prices annually by a fraction x determined by the regulatory authority. This fraction, called the *productivity offset*, is an estimate of the industry's future productivity growth. If the value of input required per unit of output falls by $x\%$ then the price can decrease by that same $x\%$, without causing revenue to fall short of cost. This gives the firm a strong incentive to innovate, in order to realize the productivity gain that will keep it from insolvency. Moreover, once that goal is reached, any additional dollar of profit – from further cost reductions or product improvements – is retained by the firm. Hence there is a strong incentive to innovate and cut costs under price cap regulation, which was imposed on British Telecom in 1984 and on AT&T in the United States in 1989. The drawback is that the regulatory authority cannot predict future productivity increases with certainty. If they impose too stringent a price reduction on the firm it may be plunged into insolvency. The result is job loss and perhaps a disruption in supply.

The dilemma can be solved by giving the firm a choice between a price cap and rate of return regulation. If a firm cannot achieve a satisfactory rate of return on capital under a price cap, it will choose rate of return regulation because it not only allows the firm to raise prices to a level sufficient to cover costs – and hence avoid insolvency – but also a modest rate of return on capital is allowed. The firm that would *not* have its rate of return driven below an acceptable level under price cap regulation will choose a price cap: if r is the maximum return allowed under rate of return regulation, and the firm can obtain a higher return under price cap regulation, it will obviously choose the price cap. The superior consumer benefits of price cap regulation will be realized in most cases but not at the cost of killing off the firms that would go bankrupt under the price cap.

Here is a simple model that shows that adding the option of returning to rate of return regulation delivers higher consumer welfare than mandatory price cap regulation: let $F(x)$ be the probability that the firm's actual productivity gain is less than the productivity offset x imposed by the regulatory authority. If a price cap is mandated, and the firm is rendered insolvent, the level of consumer welfare will be A. However, if the firm remains healthy under the price cap, the benefit to consumers will be $B \times (1 + x)$. We assume, as is reasonable, that B is greater than A. Of course $B(1 + x)$ is higher when the productivity offset x is higher. If the firm that would be insolvent under a price cap chooses to be governed by rate of return regulation then the consumer benefit level is B, which is less than $B(1 + x)$ but greater than A.

The probability that the firm would be insolvent under price cap is $F(x)$, the probability that its actual productivity increase is smaller than the mandated price reduction x. Therefore, $1 - F(x)$ is the probability that the firm would be solvent under a price cap. The expected consumer benefit under a mandatory price cap is

$$V(x) = F(x)A + [1 - F(x)]B(1 + x).$$

The expected consumer benefit if the firm has the option of choosing rate of return regulation when it would otherwise go broke is

$$W(x) = F(x)B + [1 - F(x)]B(1 + x).$$

We see that $W(x) > V(x)$ for any $F(x) > 0$, because $B > A$.

If price cap is mandatory, the regulatory authority chooses x to maximize $V(x)$. Let x_M denote the solution. If price cap is optional, the authority chooses x to maximize $W(x)$, and we let x_O be the solution. $W(x_O)$ is larger than $V(x_M)$. In other words, consumer welfare is higher when a price cap is optional. That follows from the fact that $W(x_O) \geq W(x_M) > V(x_M)$. We have $W(x_O) \geq W(x_M)$ because x_O maximizes W. And $W(x_M) > V(x_M)$ follows from $B > A$.

Example 3.5 *F* is the Uniform Distribution

We suppose that x is uniformly distributed on the interval 0 to β, with $\beta > 1$ and hence $F(x) = x/\beta$. (Review Section 2.6.5 of Chapter 2.) Consequently

$$V(x) = \frac{x}{\beta} \times A + \left(1 - \frac{x}{\beta}\right) B(1 + x)$$
$$= \frac{1}{\beta}[Ax + B(\beta - x)(1 + x)] = B + \frac{1}{\beta}[(A + B\beta - B)x - Bx^2].$$

Calculus (or the formula for maximizing a quadratic from Section 1 of Chapter 2) yields the solution value

$$x_M = \frac{A}{2B} + \frac{\beta - 1}{2}.$$

Now we maximize

$$W(x) = \frac{x}{\beta} \times B + \left(1 - \frac{x}{\beta}\right) B(1 + x)$$
$$= \frac{B}{\beta}[x + (\beta - x)(1 + x)] = B + \frac{B}{\beta}[(\beta x - x^2].$$

The solution is

$$x_O = \frac{\beta}{2}.$$

When a firm that is in danger of going broke can choose rate of return regulation, the regulatory authority can impose a more stringent (higher) productivity offset, resulting in lower prices set by firms operating under price cap. That is reflected in this example, because $x_M < x_O$. That is a consequence of the fact that $A < B$ and thus $A/2B < 1/2$. Therefore, $x_M < 1/2 + (\beta - 1)/2 = \beta/2 = x_O$.

Source

Much of this section is based on Sappington and Weisman (1996).

Links

Leibenstein (1966, 1976) discusses the effect that the discipline of competition has on innovation. Scotchmer (2004) is a comprehensive treatment of innovation and incentives.

3.4   THE US SAVINGS AND LOAN DEBACLE

A savings and loan firm (*S&L*, or *thrift*), like a bank, takes in depositors' money, paying interest on those deposits, and then lends their money for a fee. Until the early 1980s its profit came mainly from the difference between the interest rates on lending and borrowing. Loans by an S&L were essentially limited to residential mortgages until the Depository Institutions Act of 1982 eased restrictions.

Maximization of general consumer welfare requires monitoring of borrowers to ensure that the funds are devoted to the installation of capital equipment with the highest rate of return to society. And it is certainly in the interest of depositors as a whole to monitor their creditors to ensure that the funds will yield the maximum monetary return. However, no *individual* has an incentive to do the monitoring.

Deposit insurance eliminates the lender's (i.e., depositor's) incentive to comparison shop. Deposit insurance means that even if the institution holding your money fails, the balance in your account will be covered by the insurer. Consequently, depositors have no incentive to shop for a bank or S&L that will be careful with their money, thereby diminishing the borrower's incentive to avoid excessive risk. So why not eliminate deposit insurance? Because it is key to preventing bank runs. (There was an epidemic of them after the 1929 stock market crash.) If I anticipate that many of my bank's depositors are going to withdraw their money, and my deposit is not insured, then it is in my interest to try to get to the bank first to withdraw my deposit, before the bank's cash reserves are exhausted. This is true whether or not I think that the others are foolish for wanting to withdraw their money in the first place. Thus, deposit insurance provides a clear social benefit – stability of the banking system. But there is a cost: even solvent banks or S&Ls will undertake more risky loans if their depositors do not penalize them for doing so by withdrawing their money. And, as we will discuss, S&Ls that are insolvent but are allowed to continue operating have a very strong incentive to assume risks that significantly diminish social welfare.

Prior to 1980 the thrift industry was a sleepy one, protected and coddled by Congress and state governments. A thrift's primary – almost exclusive – source of income was long-term home mortgages. The loan paid a fixed interest rate for a thirty-year period – sometimes for a shorter period – determined when the mortgage was obtained. The thrift's deposit liabilities were primarily savings accounts that could be withdrawn at any time. This made it vulnerable to an *interest rate squeeze*: If rates increased significantly, competition for deposits forced the institution to raise the interest paid on deposits, while the bulk of its income came from low-interest mortgage loans many years from maturity. Some breathing room was provided by the fact that competition with other lenders was limited by law, restricting a thrift's lending ability to a 100-mile radius. In fact, post-World War II economic growth, especially in housing construction, kept the industry fairly healthy. S&L failures were rare. When interest rates increased in the 1960s and the thrifts were squeezed, Congress responded by placing a ceiling on the rate that an S&L could pay on deposits. This eliminated price competition within the industry – as long as the equilibrium rate was above the ceiling – and the firms then competed by offering gifts to anyone who would open a deposit. When Congress limited the value of those gifts, the thrifts competed by staying open longer. The interest rate ceiling protected the industry from the interest rate squeeze for the rest of the 1960s and most of the 1970s.

By 1980 30 percent of the nation's thrifts reported losses as a result of sharply rising interest rates during the period 1979 to 1982. The worst year was 1982, in which 80 percent reported losses. Congress responded by deregulating the industry, allowing a thrift to make a wide variety of new loans. An S&L could now offer variable rate mortgages, make car loans, and issue credit cards, among other new opportunities. They were also allowed to have a higher fraction of their loans in the business sector. The interest rate ceiling was phased out, thrifts were allowed to pay interest on checking deposits, and the amount of deposit insurance was increased to $100,000 per account. All of this could have rescued the industry if deregulation had not been accompanied by incentives to assume excessive risk. Accounting standards were relaxed. For instance, an asset purchased with depositors' money could be kept on the books at its original value for several years after a drop in that value, and a thrift could record $10,000 as current income if a borrower seeking $100,000 for a project was given $110,000 on the understanding that the extra $10,000 was to be used to pay the first year's interest. S&L deregulation also meant a reduction in monitoring by the government board charged with overseeing the industry. (The term deregulation refers not to the elimination of all kinds of oversight but to the substitution of regulation by consumers for regulation by a government agency. As we have noted, consumers – depositors – had little incentive to monitor the S&Ls.)

Diversification gave a thrift new opportunities for increasing its income but also new opportunities for risk taking. The wave of failures in the 1980s included a disproportionate number of S&Ls with heavy investments in land loans, direct equity (i.e., the purchase of stocks), and commercial mortgages. Fraud also played a role but in a minority of cases: false statements were made to the regulatory authority, inappropriate loans were made to relatives and business partners of the thrift's officers, a borrower's assets were dishonestly valued to justify large loans, and sometimes excessive amounts of money were spent on the offices and other amenities of the thrift's chief executives.

The *Federal Savings and Loan Insurance Corporation* (*FSLIC*) is the federal program that guarantees customers' deposits. If a thrift failed then FSLIC covered any part of a deposit that couldn't be collected from the failed institution. The wave of S&L failures beginning in the 1970s led to a crisis in which more than $30 billion of deposits had to be redeemed in this way. Depositors who had to be bailed out had placed their money in S&Ls which had used the money to purchase assets that subsequently fell in value. In fact, these assets collectively fell by more than $30 billion in market value. This was an enormous waste in resources. For instance, if a thrift used $10 million of depositors' money to finance the construction of an apartment building for which few tenants could be found, then the market value of the building would be far less than $10 million. If the money had been invested more wisely, the value of consumer goods and services would have increased not decreased.

The initial S&L failures have their explanation primarily in the drop in oil prices, which had serious implications for real estate values and business activity in the "oil patch," particularly Oklahoma and Texas. But there was a slump in real estate generally, and a rise in interest rates that left many S&Ls locked into long-term mortgages yielding low rates of return while paying high interest rates to current depositors. However, we do not examine the onset of the crisis. Rather, we ask, "Given the original conflagration, why was gasoline poured on the flames instead of water?"

In 1981 almost 4,000 thrifts were insured by FSLIC. Seventy percent of US thrifts reported losses that year, and the entire industry's net worth was negative – the market value of assets fell short of the dollar deposit liabilities. Here was a clear warning sign. Yet in 1986 the President's Council of Economic Advisors was still trying to get the attention of the president, the Congress, and the country, calling for reform and warning of the potential bill that would be presented to taxpayers.

Here is the key to understanding how we managed to pour gasoline on the flames: *Zombie* institutions – thrifts that were insolvent and should have been pronounced dead – were allowed to *gamble for resurrection*. They took in more money from depositors and sunk it into risky investments in desperation. The risky investment would probably fizzle, but in the unlikely event that it succeeded it would restore the company to financial health. Why did depositors entrust their wealth to zombie institutions? Why did the regulatory agency overseeing the thrift industry (the Federal Home Loan Bank Board) permit zombie thrifts to continue gambling? And finally, why did the owners of the S&Ls want their firms involved in wildcat schemes?

First, why didn't depositors do a better job of monitoring the thrifts that borrowed from them? Because the federal deposit insurance program removed the incentive for depositors to do comparison shopping. Lenders still had a strong incentive to look for the highest interest on their deposit, but they had little reason to care about financial insolvency or imprudent thrift managers. If the deposit were lost as a result of the thrift's insolvency then US taxpayers, through the federal government, would replace the money. The Canadian banking system did not have a formal deposit insurance scheme until 1967. The stability of the Canadian system before 1967 can be partly attributed to the

Between 1890 and 1966 only twelve Canadian chartered banks failed, and in only six of those failures did depositors lose any money. The stability can be traced to the monitoring incentive, as well as to portfolio and geographical diversification of Canadian branch banks. (Nationwide branch banking is severely limited by regulation in the United States; Carr et al., 1995.)

incentive for monitoring by lenders and to market discipline on the part of the individual bank. There is little incentive for lenders to monitor US banks – in addition to the family of savings and loan institutions. The crisis was confined mainly to the thrift industry because banks were subject to more stringent regulation. However, the value of outstanding loans to Latin America by nine giant US banks was almost double the capital of those banks, and repayment of the loans was problematic. The US government and Federal Reserve indirectly rescued the banks by assisting Mexico and other Latin American countries.

Why was the regulation of the thrift industry much more permissive than that of the banking industry? In particular, why did the regulatory agency (FHLBB) not put a stop to gambling for resurrection in the thrift industry? Because Congress generally favored regulatory forbearance. Why would a federal regulatory agency be sensitive to the mood of Congress? Because Congress can restrict the powers of a regulatory agency. Also, many who serve on the regulatory board look forward to lucrative careers in Washington when they leave the agency – counseling firms on how to approach Congress, for example. So, even an independent agency is wary about defying Congress. Congress can cut the agency's budget as well as its powers. In fact it refused to increase the fund that FSLIC used to redeem the deposit liabilities of failed thrifts, even though the fund was not large enough to cover the deposits held in zombie S&Ls. The regulators faced a dilemma: if they shut down the zombie S&Ls there would not be enough money to rescue the stranded depositors. If they allowed the zombies to continue operating the crisis would deepen. They chose the latter. Finally, the 1982 Depository Institutions Act changed the accounting rules to allow ailing S&Ls to hide their insolvency, making them appear healthy. Before we consider why Congress wanted a permissive regulatory climate, let's see why the owners of a thrift would be in favor of gambling for resurrection in the first place.

Example 3.6 A Zombie S&L and a Solvent One

Firm S is solvent, with the current market value of its assets exceeding deposit liabilities by $1,500. Zombie firm Z has a $200 shortfall, which means that its liabilities to depositors exceed the current market value of its assets by $200. Each contemplates an investment that would require taking in $1,000 of fresh deposits on which 6 percent interest is paid. Each S&L has to choose one of two investements, PI (the prudent one) or WS (the wildcat scheme), each of which requires a $1,000 capital outlay. After one year PI would return $1,080 with probability ½ and $1,070 with probability ½. After one year WS would return $1,700 with probability ½ and $100 with probability ½.

Look at the choice from the point of view of the owner of the Zombie firm: if *WS* is a success then the owner will clear $440. The investment returns $1,700 but out of that $1,060 (principal plus 6 percent interest) must be paid to the depositor of the $1,000. In addition, the $200 shortfall can be covered by the return on *WS* when it is successful. That leaves $440 in increased equity for the owners of the S&L, which would then be solvent. If *WS* fizzles only $100 will be recovered, and thus $960 will be added to the shortfall $(1060 - 100 = 960)$, and the firm would be even "more dead." But the zombie owner's equity doesn't change when an investment flops. It remains at zero. The shortfall increases, but that will be covered by deposit insurance. The zombie owner's equity was zero, and it stays at zero. The expected change in equity when *WS* is chosen is

$$\tfrac{1}{2} \times 440 + \tfrac{1}{2} \times 0 = 220$$

in the case of a zombie owner. The *PI* investment returns $1,800 or $1,070, each with probability ½. In each case there is a small amount left over after the obligation of $1,060 to depositors, but whether the difference is $20 or $10, there will be no change in the zombie owner's equity: the $20 (or $10) will have to be used to reduce the shortfall - i.e., to honor the obligation to the original depositors. The zombie owner has a strong incentive to choose *WS* because it results in an expected gain to the owner of $220, but *PI* offers nothing to the owner.

The situation is quite different for the solvent firm. The owner has positive equity, which will have to be tapped if a new investment does not return enough. Therefore, the return to solvent owner who undertakes *WS* is $1,700 - $1,060 if it succeeds, but $100 - 1060 = -960$ if it fizzles. The expected change in equity when *WS* is undertaken by a solvent firm is

$$\tfrac{1}{2} \times 640 + \tfrac{1}{2} \times -960 = -160.$$

WS would significantly reduce the expected value of a solvent owner's equity. Because *PI* returns $1,800 or $1,070, and only $1,060 is claimed by depositors, that investment has increased the solvent owner's equity with certainty. (The expected change in equity is ½ × 20 + ½ × 10 = 15 for a solvent owner, who will choose *PI* over *WS*.)

Recall that the deposit insurance fund was exhausted before the S&L crisis, and thus any increase in a zombie's shortfall would be honored by taxpayers. Therefore, the *WS* choice by a *single* zombie firm results in a change in claims on taxpayers of −$200 with probability ½ and +$960 with probability ½, for an expected increase of $380. With many zombie institutions gambling for resurrection we can use the law of large numbers and assert that, with near certainty, one half of them would see their wildcat schemes yield the high return while the other zombies would see them fizzle, for an actual return to society of

$$\tfrac{1}{2} \times n \times 1700 + \tfrac{1}{2} \times n \times 100 = 900n,$$

where *n* is the number of zombies gambling for resurrection. The system as a whole begins with wealth of $1,000n$ (the fresh deposits) and ends with wealth of $900n$,

Table 3.3 Prudent Investment (*PI*) by a Solvent Firm

Values	Depositors	Owners	FSLIC	Society
Initial outlay	1000	0	0	1000
High return	1060	20	0	1080
Low return	1060	10	0	1070
Average return	1060	15	0	1075
Rate of return	6%			7.5%

Table 3.4 Wildcat Scheme (*WS*) Undertaken by a Zombie

Values	Depositors	Owners	FSLIC	Society
Initial outlay	1000	0	−200	1000
High return	1060	440	+200	1700
Low return	1060	0	−1160	100
Average return	1060	220	−480	900
Rate of return	6%			−10%

for a negative rate of growth. The zombie owner has a strong incentive to invest in wildcat schemes, but that is adverse to society's interest. Clearly, the "dead" S&Ls should not have been allowed to continue operating – certainly not to the extent of taking in fresh deposits.

The solvent part of the S&L industry had an incentive to undertake schemes that imposed no burden on taxpayers – prudent investments did not lead to shortfalls – and which promoted economic growth. If there are n solvent firms and each undertakes *PI* then

$$\tfrac{1}{2} \times n \times 1800 + \tfrac{1}{2} \times n \times 1700 = 1075n$$

is the return to society from an investment of $1000n$. In other words, the solvent part of the S&L industry brings a positive expected return to society of 7.5 percent. These data are summarized in Tables 3.3, 3.4, and 3.5.

The *WS* is valuable to the zombie S&L only because it has no assets that can be used to honor its deposit liabilities in case the project fails. Calculation of the rate of return for the solvent S&L is quite different because it would have to reduce its asset holdings by enough to pay its depositors. Table 3.5 shows how drastically that affects the owners' rate of return. Given a choice between *PI* and *WS*, the zombie chooses *WS* but the solvent bank chooses *PI*.

Return to our examination of the zombie firm. The deposits that are used for either of these schemes would be fresh deposits, brought in to allow the S&L to undertake new investments. If the firm has outstanding deposit liabilities that it is unable to honor and it is in danger of being shut down by the FHLBB, then the *WS* offers the zombie S&L a last chance for financial health. In the unlikely event that the risky investments pay off, there will be plenty for everyone – depositors and

Table 3.5 *WS* When Undertaken by a Solvent Thrift

Values	Depositors	Owners	FSLIC	Society
Initial outlay	1000	0	0	1000
High return	1060	640	0	1700
Low return	1060	−960	0	100
Average return	1060	−160	0	900
Rate of return	6%			−10%

The selling of naked call options on bonds is a good example of a wildcat scheme. When *A* sells a naked call option to buyer *B*, *B* has the right to purchase bonds from *A* at any time in the future, at a fixed price determined when the call option is sold. It is a naked call option if *A* doesn't actually own any bonds! This was the only "asset" of an S&L that failed after only a year in business (Milgrom and Roberts, 1992, p. 174).

owners. If they fail to pay off, the owners do not lose because the institution is already insolvent, which means that they could not recoup any of the wealth they invested in their firm, even without *WS*. Gambling for resurrection is comparable to a basketball team deliberately fouling when it is behind by seven points with a minute remaining in the game. If the opposing team fails to make its free throws, then the other team has a chance of taking the ball down court and scoring. The strategy rarely works, but it gives the trailing team *some* chance of winning or at least sending the game into overtime. There is a high probability that the strategy will fail, but losing by ten points is no worse than losing by seven points. There is no chance of winning without a desperation move and some slight chance with it. This logic made things tougher on responsible thrifts. The firms that were gambling heavily offered higher interest rates on deposits to attract new funds to finance the wildcat schemes. Competition forced the responsible firms to pay higher interest rates too, making them more vulnerable.

If depositors had cared how an S&L was managed, many would have accepted lower interest rates to have their money stored in a safer place. As it was, the higher interest rates even influenced the size of the national debt. This consideration apart, gambling for resurrection constitutes a significant welfare loss for consumers because valuable resources are employed in ways that yield a much lower return to society than they are capable of providing. If only one firm gambled for resurrection it would be difficult to claim that the decision was bad from an overall social welfare perspective. It might turn out very badly, but it might turn out very well. But when more than a thousand S&Ls undertake this sort of plunge, we can say that the outcome will be harmful for sure.

Why would members of Congress want a milder regulatory climate? We have to assume that they failed to understand the impact on the efficacy of markets when the incentive for comparison shopping is diminished. And Congress itself would have had more incentive to work at understanding the banking industry if it had not been playing a version of the prisoner's dilemma game. To simplify, suppose that a member of Congress only has a choice between stringent regulation of the thrift industry and mild regulation. Consider the implications of these two strategies for the legislator's own constituency. With *WS*, US taxpayers have to shell out an additional $960 when the scheme fails. The scheme will fail half the time, so if there is a large number of gambling S&Ls in the legislator's state the actual number of failures per investment will be close to the average. Therefore, we can assume that US taxpayers have to contribute $480 per *WS*. ($480 = \frac{1}{2} \times -200 + \frac{1}{2} \times 1160$. (When *WS* is successful the $200 shortfall is eleiminated.) But only one-fiftieth of that will come out of the pockets of the legislator's constituents – the other forty-nine states receive 98 percent of the bill. So, when *WS* is successful it will rescue an S&L in the legislator's home state, and when it fails 98 percent of the costs are passed on to other states. This argument may explain the temptation that induced some members of Congress to intervene in the regulatory process on behalf on local thrifts, especially when it is coupled with the intense lobbying for regulatory forbearance by the thrift industry. However, it does not fully explain the creation of a milder regulatory climate via legislation. When it comes to the framing of legislation, we must think in terms of group decision making rather than the independent individual choice that can lead to the prisoner's dilemma. (But don't lose sight of the fact the legislation results from *individual* voting behavior.)

New regulations were introduced at the end of the 1980s. One effect was to increase the deposit insurance premiums paid by individual thrifts. (These premiums are used to build up the fund that is tapped when an S&L fails and depositors have to be bailed out.) However, thrifts that take bigger risks are still not charged higher premiums. The life insurance counterpart would be to charge smokers the same premium as nonsmokers or to charge drivers who have speeding tickets and accidents on their records the same premium for car insurance as people with clean records. The careful person would be subsidizing the careless. More significantly, society would lose an opportunity to give risky decision makers incentive to modify their behavior.

There is an important hidden characteristic element to the thrift debacle. The 1982 Depository Institutions Act broadened the scope of activities available to an S&L. At the same time the thrift regulators lowered the capital-asset requirements on individual thrifts. The new regulatory climate attracted entrepreneurs who saw an opportunity to raise easy money to finance their personal get-rich-quick schemes. This is the *adverse selection* phenomenon: incentives are such that characteristics that are least beneficial to society are selected.

In addition to exacerbating the adverse selection problem, the new regulatory environment made it easier to profit through fraud. In some cases, an S&L that was managed by its largest shareholder would make a loan to a friend of the manager on terms guaranteed to result in a loss to the thrift. But the borrower would make a secret payment to the manager, resulting in a net gain for both – at the expense of the other owners, of course. This is referred to as *looting*, to distinguish it from gambling for resurrection, which at least offered some hope of restoring the health of the S&L.

Sources

The introduction to this section is based on White (1991). Although they were not the first to highlight the critical role of gambling for resurrection, Romer and Weingast (1991) take the analysis further than others in tracing the problem back to Congress. Part of this section is based on their article.

Links

For additional discussion of the S&L debacle, see Kane (1989), Demirgüç-Kunt and Kane (2002), Milgrom and Roberts (1992, pp. 170-176), Chapter 11 in Mishkin (1992) on the crisis in banking regulation, and Litan (1991), a comment on Romer and Weingast (1991). Dewatripont and Tirole (1994, p. 95) discuss the regulators' dilemma: allow the crisis to deepen or shut down the zombie S&Ls at a time when the insurance fund was insufficient to meet all the deposit liabilities. See Mishkin (1992, p. 260) on the scandal surrounding Charles H. Keating Jr. and Lincoln Savings & Loan for a case of adverse selection. Akerlof and Romer (1994) discuss looting. Dewatripont and Tirole (1994, p. 94) touch on the indirect rescue of US banks by the US government and the Federal Reserve when they assisted Latin American countries. Shoven et al. (1992) show that the increases in interest rates caused by zombie S&Ls attracting new deposits even increased the national debt.

Problem Set

(1) How would a private insurance carrier respond to a client that always took extreme risks and frequently submitted large claims?

(2) Rework Tables 3.3-3.5 when the high return occurs with probability 0.25 and the low return occurs with probability 0.75. Which investment would a solvent S&L choose and which would be chosen by a zombie?

(3) Rework Tables 3.3-3.5 when the high return occurs with probability 0.75 and the low return occurs with probability 0.25. Which investment would a solvent S&L choose and which would be chosen by a zombie?

Questions 4 and 5 each pertain to a pair of investments, X and Y. Each investment requires a $1,000 capital outlay, $100 of which must be funded by the owners of the S&L, with the rest coming from the cash entrusted to the S&L by depositors. An interest rate of 10 percent is paid on deposits. For each investment, prepare a table (similar to the ones in this section) and fill in the cells. Determine which of the pair of investments would be selected by a solvent S&L and which would be selected by a zombie firm that began with a $200 shortfall.

(4) Investments X and Y are given by Tables 3.6 and 3.7.

Table 3.6 Investment X

Return	Probability	Payoff
Low	0.4	500
High	0.6	1500

Table 3.7 Investment Y

Return	Probability	Payoff
Low	0.2	1100
High	0.8	1200

(5) Investments X and Y are given by Tables 3.8 and 3.9.

Table 3.8 Return on Investment X

Probability	Payoff
1.0	1200

Table 3.9 Return on Investment Y

Return	Probability	Payoff
Low	0.5	600
High	0.5	2000

3.5 THE GREAT RECESSION OF 2007–2009

What happened? Why did it happen? What should be done to prevent a recurrence? We will answer the first two questions and then direct the reader to some excellent books for insightful discussions of the last question.

What happened? US house prices were essentially at the same level in January of 2000 as in the year 1950. There were spikes along the way, reaching peaks in 1979 and again in 1989, but the housing price index at each of those peaks was only about 18 percent above the 1950 level. Housing prices began to soar in the year 2000, and by 2005 they were more than 80 percent above the year 2000 level. They stopped their swift rise in 2006 after months of widespread defaults on home mortgages, and then began their perilous slide. This was quickly followed by declining bond prices and defaults on many types of loans, in addition to mortgages. Stock markets were next. The vulnerable US credit system had all but collapsed, and there were sufficient links with capital markets around the world to bring about a global crisis. Jobs disappeared, incomes tumbled, pensions and college savings plans lost considerable value. In short, the crisis caused widespread misery, even as many – albeit, a relative handful – earned staggering bonuses for their role in the fiasco.

The easiest part of the story to explain is why a global credit freeze can lead to a severe economic downturn with widespread reductions in material wellbeing and collateral suffering: consumer spending declines when it becomes difficult to borrow. People save at a greater rate to provide a cushion for the future, and spending that would have been loan financed does not take place. Businesses that have difficulty getting short-term funding to meet payrolls and finance inventory cut back. Firms that supply those businesses suffer a drop in demand. Layoffs and wage cuts become epidemic. A downward spiral results. Consumers and producers respond to falling demand and output by further reducing demand

and output. The severity of the contraction depends on the magnitude of the initial shock. The 2007–2008 credit crisis was not the largest in US history, but it was one of the larger ones and it was devastating.

Why did it happen? For the same reason that the "unsinkable" Titanic went down in 1912. Many serious blunders were made, more-or-less simultaneously. The Great Recession was triggered by excesses in mortgage markets in the US and the resulting impact on world bond markets. These excesses can be traced to inappropriate incentives, and could have been tamed by responsible regulation. Reckless lending behavior fueled a housing price bubble which then provoked a bubble in bond prices. By 2005 20 percent of new mortgages were *subprime* – granted to households that could not meet conventional credit-worthiness standards – and subprime mortgage balances were close to $1.25 trillion. During the euphoria preceding the crisis it was not unusual for mortgages to be granted with little or no documentation to individuals who were financially illiterate. This massive increase in lending to home buyers was coupled with a corresponding increase in demand, followed by increasing housing prices. That lead to speculation that there will be further price increases, which can lead to a self-sustaining cycle of price increases triggering increases in demand. This is referred to as a *bubble* when price increases keep fueling speculation that there will be further increases to the extent that the speculation becomes self fulfilling. The bubble bursts when enough people become convinced that the bubble will soon burst.

The four agencies charged with regulation of US banks did not intervene to put a stop to extremely risky and sometimes fraudulent lending practices because the individuals appointed to those institutions believed that markets could do no wrong. They may also have been under political pressure not to intervene. If the regulators had acted to put an end to the worst excesses in the market for home loans, the housing bubble would have done far less damage when it burst.

Firms that make loans but, unlike banks, do not take in deposits comprise the *shadow banking sector*, which is even larger than the banking sector proper. Shadow banks are essentially unregulated. In addition to making loans, they are involved in creating and selling *derivatives*, the value of which are only indirectly linked to assets like stocks and bonds. Stocks and bonds have value because they are claims on something fundamental – the profits of firms that produce the economy's goods and services. When the credit bubble burst many investors discovered that they did not understand the derivatives markets in which they had speculated. If senior officials at the Federal Reserve and the Treasury had not been hostile to arguments that the derivatives markets should be regulated, the recession would not have been so great. If the top executives of the large commercial and investment banks had fostered better risk management practices the panic might have been contained. The US economy was too frail to withstand the shock it received on September 15, 2008 when the giant investment bank Lehman Brothers filed for bankruptcy. Real US GDP growth, which had been dismal, became negative. The shock waves caused damage around the world.

Through most of the twentieth century a bank that issued a mortgage would retain ownership of the loan. The bank received monthly payments from borrowers and could adjust the payments if the home owner suffered a temporary setback.

Before granting a loan bank officials examined the homeowner's background and credit worthiness, and hence were in a good position to determine if the bank would fare better by adjusting the payments than by foreclosing on the house. (Foreclosure rarely recovers anything close to the original market value of the property.) Things were very different in the new century. The housing boom of 2000 to 2005 was accompanied by the *securitization* of mortgages: conventional mortgages were sold by the mortgage broker to a second company that bundled many mortgages together and then sold shares in these bundles. The shareholder would get a fraction of the returns, which came from the monthly payments by the homeowners who took out the original mortgages. Securitization itself was not new, but the bundling of vast numbers of sub-prime mortgages was indeed novel. (A sub-prime mortgage is one issued to a borrower whose credit-worthiness is problematic.) The buyers of securitized mortgages were scattered around the world, making it impossible for a homeowner in distress to renegotiate terms. The securities turned out to be very risky, largely because a significant fraction of the underlying mortgages defaulted. Securitization transmitted the credit crisis to other countries. The agent who brokered the original mortgage had no incentive to look into the borrower's background and credit-worthiness because the risk of default was passed on to the purchaser of the security – the bundle of mortgages. The mortgage broker *did* have incentive to maximize the number of loans that he or she arranged because each transaction earned the broker a substantial fee.

There were other sources of unusual risk: the insurance industry exists to allow households and firms to hedge risk. The shadow banking sector created instruments, such as credit default swaps (CDS), that were akin more to gambling than insurance. A CDS *is* an insurance policy. But it's a very unusual kind of insurance, and not just in its name. A CDS is not insurance against a house catching fire or a car being stolen. It's insurance that pays off only if a particular bond defaults. In itself, that can be a good thing. Economic growth depends to a great extent on the production and installation of new machinery – i.e., real capital formation. That in turn depends on the ability of the firm installing the machines to find the money to pay for them. The funds are often obtained by borrowing – by issuing bonds. Bonds pay the purchaser (the lender) a fixed amount per year plus repayment of the principal at maturity. Real capital formation is encouraged when the lender can obtain insurance against default by the borrower, making loans less risky. The astonishing thing about a CDS is that you don't have to be a holder of a General Motors bond to buy insurance against default by GM. (That qualifies a CDS as a derivative.) Giant financial firms such as AIG sold billions of dollars' worth of credit default swaps to individuals and firms who were betting on default. AIG sold these "swaps" because its sales agents convinced management that default on the bond to which a CDS was linked was virtually a zero-probability event, and thus AIG would be collecting billions in premiums on insurance policies on which it would never have to pay claims. By 2008 AIG had sold about $500 billion in credit default swaps. When default rates on bonds rose, AIG discovered that it could not renew its funding because of widespread doubt about its ability to pay claims. Because almost all of the world's major financial firms were AIG clients policymakers were concerned that if AIG failed it would cause a financial tsunami affecting the large financial firms *and* holders of ordinary insurance policies. In September of 2008 the US government determined that there *would* be massive claims by holders of credit default swaps that AIG would be unable able to honor. It bailed out AIG at taxpayer expense.

A frenzy of *leveraging*, in home ownership and in asset purchases in general, was part of the run up to the great recession. Leverage is the term used in the financial industry for the practice of borrowing part of the money used to purchase an asset, with the remainder covered by the buyer's own funds. Leverage increases the asset holder's gains, when the asset price increases, but it also increases the loss when the price falls. This magnification of gains and losses has implications for the amount of leverage in an economy and for the vulnerability of the economy to panics. A transaction is *more* leveraged if a larger fraction of the payment is obtained by borrowing. A simple example illustrates the effect of leverage on the rate of return.

Example 3.7 Leveraged Home Ownership

Andre and Maggie buy a house for $300,000. Each has an inheritance that they had invested in Treasury Bills paying $15,000 a year in interest. That's a safe 5% return. Suppose that they sell those bonds and buy the house for $300,000 cash. If the couple sells the house one year later and it has increased in value by 12% then their investment has yielded a 12% return. However, if it falls in value by 12% then they sustain a 12% loss. Suppose instead that Andre and Maggie sell only $20,000 worth of their T-Bills and use that as a down payment, borrowing the remaining $280,000. If the house increases in value by $36,000 (i.e., 12%) their $20,000 housing investment yields a return of 80% after one year. That's substantially more than 12%, even after factoring in interest on the loan. However, if the house falls in value by $36,000 the couple could sell it for only $264,000, not enough to pay off the $280,000 mortgage. They lose all of their equity – and more, if the mortgage gives the lender a claim on other assets held by the borrower. With the mortgage, the upside is an 80% gain but the downside is a 100% or more loss. Leverage magnifies gains and losses.

Note that Andre and Maggie can cash in $300,000 worth of T-Bills and purchase *fifteen* houses, each with a down payment of $20,000 accompanied by a $280,000 mortgage. If the houses increase in value by 12% they get an 80% return on $300,000. But if housing prices fall by 12% they are wiped out – they will have borrowed $4.2 million but have assets of only $3.96 million ($264,000 multiplied by 15). However, we have overlooked the possibility of diversification: if the fifteen houses were located in different parts of the country a fall in housing prices in one region would not typically be accompanied by falling values in any of the fourteen other areas. If even six of the houses gained 12% in value and the other nine lost 12% then the $300,000 leveraged investment would have yielded an overall 12%

return: $6 \times 36{,}000 - 9 \times 20{,}000 = 36{,}000$, and 36,000 is 12% of 300,000. (This calculation assumes that in case of default on a mortgage Andre and Maggie only lose the $20,000 down payment.)

Diversification by mortgage lenders did not mitigate the financial crisis that lead to the Great Recession. Housing prices were carried aloft by the bubble throughout most of the US. The subsequent crash in *values* was widespread. Moreover, the mortgage securities were not as diversified as many were lead to believe. For one thing mortgage securities were particularly concentrated in California.

American accounting rules, which are less stringent than those governing financial statements in the European Union, made it possible for banks to conceal some of their exposure to risk by removing it from their balance sheets. The technique is called *synthetic leveraging*, and makes use of a *Structured Investment Vehicle* (SIV), as illustrated in the next example.

Example 3.8 Synthetic Leveraging

The BUSB balance sheet of Table 3.10 is on the books of the Big US Bank, which has raised funds by selling shares for a total of $10 billion and taken in deposits of $90 billion. (The unit for Tables 3.10 and 3.11 is one billion dollars.) This bank then sells $50 billion of its loans to SIV, which pays $49 billion in cash, obtained by borrowing in the commercial paper market, and gives BUSB $1 billion worth of shares in SIV, resulting in the SIV balance sheet of Table 3.10. Although SIV has only $1 in equity for every $50 in loans, it apparently has almost no exposure to risk because BUSB has guaranteed the loans purchased by SIV. The $49 billion in cash it received from SIV is loaned out, and the books that BUSB shows to the world features the new BUSB Balance Sheet of Table 3.11. The ratio of assets to equity remains at 10 to 1. In financial jargon, both the before and after balance sheets of BUSB show that it is leveraged 10 to 1. However, if we include the loans that it sold to SIV *and guaranteed* we get the final balance sheet of Table 3.11, showing that BUSB is actually leveraged 14.9 to 1.

The BUSB financial statements claim that its owners have $1 of their own money at stake for every $10 of outstanding loans. But when we incorporate the off balance sheet loans guaranteed by BUSB we see that the owners have $1 of their

Table 3.10

BUSB Balance Sheet		Balance Sheet of BUSB's SIV	
Assets	**Liabilities & Net Worth**	**Assets**	**Liabilities & Net Worth**
Loans $100	Deposits $90 Equity $10	Loans $50	Commercial paper $49 Equity $1

Table 3.11

	New BUSB Balance Sheet		Consolidated Balance Sheet of BUSB & SIV
Assets	**Liabilities & Net Worth**	**Assets**	**Liabilities & Net Worth**
Loans $99	Deposits $90	Loans $149	Deposits $90
Stock in SIV $1	Equity $10		Commercial paper $49
			Equity $10

own at stake for every $14.9 of outstanding loans, or 67 cents at stake for every $10 in outstanding loans. We can expect the owners to be that much less concerned about their bank's exposure to risk.

Example 3.8 underestimates the incentive of a bank's owners to use subterfuge to increase their leverage if much of the downside risk would be shouldered by innocent bystanders. Translation: if BUSB is considered *too big to fail* – i.e., bankruptcy would lead to substantial unemployment and income loss – its owners might expect to be bailed out by the government, and hence by taxpayers. The market system can't do its job well if the costs arising from an important decision are not borne by the agent making that decision.

The financial industry lobbied intensively against regulation, and shares blame with the industry's regulators themselves for lax oversight of banking and shadow banking in the US. Whether deliberate or not, bank lobbyists used the word "capital" in a confusing way, to engender the belief that economic growth could only be achieved if the government made no attempt to reduce the financial industry's exposure to risk. Reducing banking sector risk does not require an increase in the fraction of bank assets held in cash reserves. It can be achieved by decrease in the fraction of a bank's invested funds that come from borrowing by means of an increase in *equity*, without reducing the bank's lending. In other words, a bank could issue new ownership shares. That would make the banking system as a whole safer, without making credit less available and thus without jeopardizing economic growth. An increase in equity funding makes the financial system safer because bank owners have more of their own money at stake, and hence have a greater interest in making loans that are not at high risk of default. (The *cash reserve* is the fund that a bank has on hand to meet an unusually large withdrawal by depositors. Bank *capital* is the value of assets supplied by the bank's owners.)

Bank lobbyists pointed out that a higher equity requirement increases a bank's costs, but they failed to mention that in a high-risk environment part of the financial industry's costs are borne by the taxpayer: to the extent that a big bank or shadow bank is considered too big to fail, bailout follows bankruptcy.

The salesperson and the scientist are two extreme approaches to investigation. The salesagent highlights arguments that tend to support the hypothesis that he or she wishes to see confirmed, and downplays, or even dismisses, arguments to the contrary. The scientist on the other hand has an obligation to attack his or her *own* hypothesis as vigorously as possible. The purest form of the scientific approach is found in mathematics, which does not allow one to claim something as true until one can rigorously dismiss every logical possibility to the contrary. Lobbyists use the sales approach.

Adverse incentives also infected the industry that grades individual stocks and bonds. The grades are used by investors, particularly in Europe and Asia, as a guide to reliability. On the eve of the crisis only six American corporations had earned the coveted AAA rating. Astonishingly, a significant fraction of the securitized mortgage bundles were graded AAA. There are three major rating agencies in the United States: Fitch, Moody's, and Standard and Poor's. In each case the firm seeking to have its stock or bond issue graded is the one that pays for the evaluation, resulting in a serious conflict of interest. Because each rating agency had two competitors, a firm could shop for a good rating. A firm would sometimes negotiate a rating by asking the agency what it could do to get a better grade. When the bond bubble burst, investors were shocked to discover how badly the rating agencies had performed. It was not only a problem of adverse incentives. Incompetence played a role: the agencies had fitted their models with only three years of data.

Sources

This section is based on Blinder (2013), Admati and Hellwig (2013), and to some extent on Rajan (2010), and Stiglitz (2010). Example 3.8 is due to Blinder (2013). The housing price index referred to in the second paragraph is the Case-Shiller Index: http://us.spindices.com/index-family/real-estate/sp-corelogic-case-shillerdata.

Links

Admati and Hellwig (2013), Blinder (2013), and Rajan (2010) each provide a wealth of detail and insight into the great recession and are equally informative and insightful in explaining how to minimize the magnitude of future crises.

3.6 PERSONAL BANKRUPTCY

Personal bankruptcy filings in the United States have increased fourfold in the past thirty years. At present about 5 percent of consumer loans will not be repaid. The default of some borrowers raises the cost to those who repay their loans. (If half of all borrowers defaulted then lenders would have to double the interest rate charged to get the same return on loans as they would if there were no default.)

To the extent that default is a consequence of a loss of income beyond the control of the borrower – due to ill health or unemployment, for example – we can think of the higher interest charge as an insurance premium. Moreover, the availability of such insurance – via the right to file for bankruptcy – enhances individual welfare, just as automobile or health insurance does. And it's financed in the same way. Those who do not make a claim pay a tiny amount of money – the insurance

If insurance against being unable to pay one's debts is a good thing, why isn't it provided by the private sector? If an individual's income were guaranteed by insurance there would be a severe moral hazard problem: one would have very little incentive to work effectively. An insurance contract that paid a claim only on the condition that the individual supplied appropriate effort on the job could not be enforced because there is no way for a third party - a judge - to verify the policyholder's effort level. If the contract couldn't be enforced it wouldn't be offered.

premium or the increase in the interest rate - that's pooled and used to pay a large sum to those who do have a claim. In the case of a drastic loss of income, the claim payment is the discharge of the debt. We choose to buy car insurance because we're better off giving up the small annual fee in return for the guarantee of receiving a large sum in case of a serious loss.

If default only occurred after a loss of income due to events beyond the control of the borrower then the higher interest charge is the insurance premium, and the availability of a bankruptcy procedure enhances individual welfare. However, a large fraction of bankruptcy filings are made by individuals who have not suffered a severe financial setback. These individuals file simply because the financial benefits of doing so exceed the financial costs. How can that be?

The cost of filing for bankruptcy is the $400 filing fee and the increased difficulty of borrowing in the future. To compute the benefit of filing we need to examine the US bankruptcy law. It is a federal law, and one can file under Chapter 7 or Chapter 13. Chapter 7 leaves future income untouched but requires the individuals to turn over their assets to their creditors - up to the value of the outstanding debts. Chapter 13 leaves assets untouched but requires the individuals to submit a plan to commit a share of future income to repay debts. However, individual states are allowed to impose asset exemptions for Chapter 7 filings. Some states exempt the entire value of one's house. Most states have some level of exemption on retirement accounts and the cash value of life insurance, in addition to the homestead exemption.

Suppose state X has an unlimited homestead exemption and a borrower can cash in other assets and put them into housing just before filing for bankruptcy. Suppose also that courts do not check to see whether an individual is in dire financial straits. Then an individual in state X with $200,000 worth of stocks and bonds, a $300,000 house, and $500,000 of debt can sell his assets for $500,000, purchase a new $500,000 house, and then file for bankruptcy. The entire debt will be discharged, and the house will not be touched. Seventy percent of all bankruptcies are filed under Chapter 7.

If the individuals who purchased automobile collision insurance took advantage of the fact that any damage was covered by the insurer and drove carelessly in parking lots, there would be a great many more dented fenders to be repaired. The overall increase in claims would increase everyone's premium. That's why the deductible is part of the insurance contract. Otherwise, individuals would devote far less than the efficient amount of effort to preventive care. Similarly, the fact that bankruptcy filing can be beneficial for someone who has not suffered a financial setback means that more than the socially optimal amount of "bankruptcy insurance" is supplied. Note that these *strategic* bankruptcy filings increase the default rate on loans and result in

Since 1988 twenty American steel companies have declared bankruptcy. Bethlehem Steel, the second-largest US steel firm, did so because it was able to receive additional bank financing and other benefits (*The Economist*, October 20, 2001, p. 62).

an additional increase in interest rates. One might expect to see lenders offering lower interest rates to borrowers who waived their right to file for bankruptcy, but that waiver could not be enforced because it is contrary to the bankruptcy act. (Chapter 7 has recently been modified to make bankruptcy less attractive.)

Sources

This section is based on White (1999) and Fay et al. (2002).

3.7 MANDATORY RETIREMENT

Mandatory retirement is the practice of an employer preventing an employee from working beyond a specified age. Employees must retire at the specified time, no matter how able they are to work or how eager to continue working. For the first three-quarters of the twentieth century, US firms typically required workers to retire at age sixty-five. The 1978 Age Discrimination in Employment Act outlawed compulsory retirement before seventy. The 1987 amendment to the act eliminated the practice for most US employers, regardless of the worker's age. (Coverage was extended to college and university professors in 1994.) It is doubtful that involuntary retirement at age sixty-five or seventy is discriminatory. A worker obviously cares about the entire profile of lifetime earnings, and if all workers coming on stream are treated in the same way – as far as retirement is concerned – where is the discrimination? We won't debate that issue, however. Our main purpose is to reveal an economic rationale for mandatory retirement in a society in which there are hidden action and hidden characteristic problems on the job.

3.7.1 Posting a Bond

Hidden action problems arise whenever work is performed in a team and it is difficult or impossible to identify the contribution made by a particular member of the team, as is the case with modern manufacturing processes. In the long run, malingerers can be detected in a number of ways. However, firing malingerers when they are identified is not by itself enough to discourage shirking if workers can switch jobs with impunity. But by accepting employment in a firm that pays its workers less than the competitive wage (i.e., the value of the marginal product) in the early years and more than the competitive wage in later years the worker is in effect posting a bond. The bond is forfeited if the worker is caught persistently shirking, because he or she will be fired. And a worker who is fired won't be around to collect the deferred pay. The boss must monitor occasionally for the threat of bond forfeiture to have force, but the existence of the threat substantially reduces monitoring costs.

DEFINITION: *Compensation*

The worker's compensation is his or her annual income plus other benefits such as the employer's contributions to the employee's health insurance plan.

In an economy that did not solve this hidden action problem, workers in general would perform poorly, total output would be low, and everyone's utility would be far below what it would have been if everyone had contributed more effort and had more consumer goods and services in return. How do we know? After all, an increase in individual effort involves a cost – lower leisure consumption – in addition to the benefit of increased consumption of other goods. But when workers in general have no disincentive to shirk, the cost to an individual of reducing effort is zero. But the cost to the society – reduced output of goods and services – is positive and large. When social cost pricing is not used, outcomes are typically inefficient.

Even when there is a single worker, such as a hired hand on a farm, it is impossible to determine the extent of the worker's contribution by observing output if that output is affected by random events (weather, insects, etc.) in addition to the worker's effort. Over a long period of time the law of large numbers can be used by the employer to determine the worker's average effort from average output. In other words, the worker's actions do not remain hidden in the long run, and shirking is penalized by forfeiture of the "bond." Posting a bond in the form of deferred compensation also brings the labor market closer to the efficient level of on-the-job training. An otherwise profitable investment in worker training will be unprofitable if workers leave the firm after the new skills have been acquired. This problem will be mitigated if the worker posts a bond with the firm that pays for the training.

Inefficiency can still result if effort levels are observable but not verifiable. It may be quite evident to a manager that a worker is shirking, even though the manager is unable to prove this with objective evidence that would convince a judge or jury. In that case, it will not be possible to employ a contract that directly penalizes a worker for shirking. The contract could not be enforced because the employer could not prove in court that shirking did in fact occur. An example of an observable but unverifiable shirking is discourteous behavior by a waiter to a restaurant customer.

There is also a hidden characteristic element to the employer–employee relationship. Even if there is no shirking there are more talented and less talented workers. Again, team production makes it very costly to identify less talented workers in the short run. These workers may know who they are but they would not voluntarily identify themselves and accept less pay. However, if compensation is below the competitive level in the early years and above the competitive level in later years a less talented worker would not accept a contract designed for a talented worker. Such a contract would be beneficial only if the worker collected the late-career high pay, but the worker would be dismissed or kept on at lower pay when it became clear that he or she were not a high-quality worker. The compensation profile can be used to sort less talented workers from talented workers even though the former attempt to conceal their identity. The compensation profile induces the less talented workers to *self-select*. This also promotes efficiency.

The fact that pay is low at the beginning of the career, when young people want to start a family and buy a home, might prevent the deferred compensation formula from persisting in equilibrium were it not for the possibility of borrowing against future income by taking out a home mortgage. Lenders will know that compensation increases over time and take that into account when reviewing the loan application.

We have argued that the standard compensation profile, paying below competitive levels early and above competitive levels later in one's tenure in the firm, has an economic rationale. However, this compensation profile could be unprofitable for employers if workers were able to collect the high late-career pay indefinitely into old age, hence the mandated cut-off age.

Let's illustrate with a simple model of labor supply.

3.7.2   The Formal Argument

There are two goods, leisure consumption X and a composite commodity Y, which is total expenditure on all goods other than X. Let x and y denote the respective amounts consumed of the two goods. The worker's utility function is $U(x, y) = B(x) + y$. It is assumed that MB_X, the marginal utility of X, is positive but diminishing. That is, $MB_X(x)$ is positive for all $x \geq 0$, but $x' > x''$ implies $MB_X(x') < MB_X(x'')$. The production of Y is represented by a production function $f(E)$, with labor as the input, and E as the total labor employed (over all workers). Thus, E is the number of years' worth of labor used in production. It is assumed that $MP(E)$, the marginal product of labor, is positive for all $E \geq 0$, but beyond some value of labor input it is diminishing in the sense $E' > E''$ implies $MP(E') < MP(E'')$ for values of E' and E'' beyond the threshold. (When discussing retirement it is appropriate to measure time in years.)

We put the spotlight on a particular individual J, and let L_J denote J's labor supply. An individual can't control the amount of labor supplied by others, so we take that as given and denote it by L_O. Therefore, $E = L_J + L_O$ and thus $f(E) = f(L_J + L_O)$. Because we are treating L_O as a constant, we can view f as a function of L_J, which means that MP is also a function of L_J. In fact, we simplify by writing $MP(L)$, which is the increase in output when individual J works one more year, given that J has worked for L years and that the total amount of additional labor employed is L_O. We begin by showing that efficiency requires $MB_X(x) = MP(L)$.

If $MB_X(x) < MP(L)$ we can have individual J supply an additional unit of labor, resulting in the production of $MP(L)$ additional units of Y, which we give to J. This will increase utility, but the net change in J's utility must reflect the loss of one unit of leisure consumption. The reduction in the utility derived from leisure is $-MB_X(x)$, and hence the net change in utility is

$$-MB_X(x) + \Delta y = -MB_X(x) + MP(L),$$

which is positive when $MB_X(x) < MP(L)$. We have increased one individual's utility without affecting the utility of anyone else. The worker's extra consumption of Y

was generated by increasing that worker's time on the job. No one else's consumption changed, and no one else's labor supply changed.

Suppose now that $MB_X(x) > MP(L)$. Then we can increase individual J's utility without affecting anyone else by increasing J's leisure consumption by one unit and letting J's consumption of Y fall by the resulting drop in output, which is $MP(L)$ because an increase in leisure of one year reduces labor input by one year. Again, we made one person better off without harming anyone else. Therefore, efficiency is incompatible with $MB_X(x) < MP(L)$ and also with $MB_X(x) > MP(L)$. It follows that efficiency requires $MB_X(x) = MP(L)$ for an arbitrary individual J. Assume that ninety is the time endowment. That is, the individual does not anticipate living longer than ninety years. Then once we specify J's leisure consumption x we have determined J's labor supply L. It's $90 - x$. Consequently, $MB_X(x) = MP(L)$ can be written $MB_X(x) = MP(90 - x)$. Let x^* be the solution of this equation. We can say that x^* is the efficient leisure consumption for J, and $L^* = 90 - x^*$ is J's efficient retirement date. (Different consumers would have different B functions, and hence different efficient levels of X, even with the same production function.)

Efficiency Theorem

If in every period the worker's compensation equals the worker's marginal product in that period then that worker will choose the efficient retirement date.

Proof:

Here is the calculus derivation of x^*: The utility function of individual J is $U(x, y) = B(x) + y$. Let L_O denote total amount of labor contributed by everyone but J. If the outcome is efficient it must maximize U given the labor supply and the consumption plan of every other individual. Therefore, we can derive a necessary condition for efficiency by maximizing

$$V(x) = B(x) + f(L + L_O) - y_O$$

where y_O is the total Y consumption of everyone but individual J. Use the chain rule and the fact that $dL/dx = -1$ to take the derivative of V with respect to x. The first derivative is $B'(x) - f'(L_O + L)$, and when we set this equal to zero we get equality between J's marginal utility of X and the marginal product of J's labor. Let x^* denote the solution of that equation. We know that the first derivative will equal zero at the maximum because we can assume that $x = 0$ won't maximize the individual's utility nor will $L = 0$. That is, there will not be a corner solution.   ■

The efficient labor supply is $90 - x^*$, which is represented as L^* in Figure 3.1. Because MB_X falls as leisure consumption increases, when the marginal utility of leisure is plotted as a function of L (which is on the horizontal axis), it increases as L increases. $MP(L)$, the marginal product of labor, increases early in the career, as the individual learns on the job, and then declines after a point, as age takes its toll.

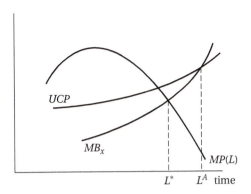

Figure 3.1

If there were no hidden information problems, a compensation profile equal to the marginal product of labor schedule would induce the individual to retire at the efficient date L^*. Consider: When the compensation C equals $MP(L)$, the marginal product of labor, at each date L, if the worker were to retire at date $L < L^*$ then $x > x^*$. An increase in L of one year would cause the worker's utility to change by

$$-MB_X(x) + C$$

(Remember, J's utility function is $B(x) + y$, and $\Delta y = C$ if time on the job were to increase by one year.) $C - MB_X(x)$ is positive when $x > x^*$ because $C = MP(L)$, $MB_X(x^*) = MP(L^*)$, and $MB_X(x)$ decreases as x increases and $MP(L)$ increases as L decreases. (Utility maximization cannot occur at a value of L at which $MP(L)$ is increasing.) Therefore, if J were free to choose he or she would not retire before L^*. However, if $L > L^*$ then J can increase utility by reducing L by one year. The change in utility is $MB_X(x) - C$, which is positive when $x < x^*$. Hence J would not retire later than L^* if the decision were J's to make. To summarize: if there is no hidden information problem and at each point in time the worker's compensation is equal to the marginal product of labor, the utility-maximizing consumer will choose the efficient retirement date L^*.

The compensation profile represented by $MP(L)$, the marginal product of labor, in Figure 3.1 is rarely observed. Much more typical is the upward sloping compensation profile represented by the curve UCP. We can find an upward sloping UCP such that the consumer is indifferent between UCP and retirement at L^* on the one hand, and on the other hand a compensation package equal in value to the current marginal product of labor at each date. There *is* some UCP that gives exactly the same utility at the retirement date L^* as the profile $MP(L)$. This follows from the fact that if UCP is sufficiently low the individual will prefer $MP(L)$ and if UCP is sufficiently high the individual will prefer UCP. There must be some intermediate upward sloping compensation profile to which the individual is indifferent, and this is represented in Figure 3.1.

At L^* the actual compensation (located on UCP) is above $MB_X(x^*)$ and the individual will want to keep working at the current rate of pay. An upward sloping compensation profile is in society's interest, because it helps solve hidden information problems, leaving everyone with more utility. Consequently, mandatory retirement is in society's interest because the upward sloping profile will not be offered by profit-maximizing firms if workers continue on the job beyond L^*. If UCP and the marginal product compensation profile $MP(L)$ have the same present value *when each is truncated at L^**, the firm will prefer the marginal product schedule to the UCP schedule if the worker chooses the retirement date. The worker will choose to retire at L^A with compensation schedule UCP. Between L^* and L^A the value of compensation is above the marginal product of labor and the firm loses the compensation minus $MP(L)$ on each unit of additional labor employed.

The overall outcome could be very unprofitable with UCP and no mandated retirement date. Therefore, the equilibrium will not include firms offering an upward sloping compensation profile without specifying the retirement date. If we look at labor supply only, we see that the equilibrium could include firms that offer the marginal product compensation profile with the retirement date chosen by the worker and contracts that offered an upward sloping compensation profile with retirement mandated at L^*. Firms that employ the latter will be more profitable because they will have fewer hidden information problems. These firms will be able to set lower prices and drive the other firms out of the market. Therefore, when we look at labor demand as well as supply, we see that the equilibrium will feature only firms that offer an upward sloping compensation profile with mandatory retirement at L^*.

Have we seen a change in US compensation profiles since legislation forced the end of mandatory retirement? No, because there are other reasons for requiring the employee to post a bond. Moreover, workers often choose to retire before seventy and even before sixty-five. Decades of economic growth have made that possible.

3.7.3 The Intertemporal Budget Constraint

This section shows why there are many compensation profiles that provide the same level of utility to a given worker. Initially, assume that there are only two periods: period 0 (the present) and period 1 (which is one year from now). Let C_0 be the number of dollars available for consumption now and let C_1 be the number of dollars available for consumption one year from now. We assume an interest rate of r that is the same for lenders and borrowers. We express r as a decimal fraction. (If the interest rate is 7 percent, then $r = 0.07$.) To specify the budget constraint we need to know current income, which we denote by I_0, and income one year from now is I_1.

To derive the intertemporal budget constraint put yourself in the position of the consumer one year from now, and ask simply, "How much money can I spend on goods and services in period 1?" If the consumer saved in period zero that number will be

Period 1 Income + Savings + Interest on Savings.

Saving is, by definition, equal to the amount of income not spent on consumption. Therefore, saving equals $I_0 - C_0$. Interest earned on saving is the amount saved multiplied by the interest rate, which is $(I_0 - C_0) \times r$ in this case. Therefore, the amount that a saver can spend on consumption in period 1 is

$$I_1 + I_0 - C_0 + (I_0 - C_0) \times r = I_1 + (I_0 - C_0)(1+r).$$

Therefore, a saver is constrained by the following equation in period 1:

$$C_1 = I_1 + (I_0 - C_0)(1+r).$$

What about someone who borrows initially? How much money can someone who borrowed in period 0 spend in period 1? The answer is clearly

Period 1 Income - Amount of the Loan - Interest on the Loan.

The principle has to be repaid in period 1 in a two-period model, and so does the interest on the loan. It is easy to determine the amount borrowed; it will be equal to the amount spent on consumption in period zero in excess of period zero income. That is, borrowing $= C_0 - I_0$. The interest charge is the interest rate times the amount of the loan, or $(C_0 - I_0) \times r$. Therefore, the amount that a borrower can spend on consumption in period 1 is

$$I_1 - (C_0 - I_0)(1 + r) = I_1 + (I_0 - C_0)(1 + r).$$

Therefore, borrowers and savers are governed by the same intertemporal budget constraint:

$$C_1 = I_1 + (I_0 - C_0)(1 + r). \qquad [9]$$

Of course, if the individual neither lends nor borrows in period 0 we will have $C_0 = I_0$ and hence $C_1 = I_1$, which also satisfies [9]. Therefore, [9] is *the* two-period intertemporal budget constraint.

Suppose the individual will live $T + 1$ periods. We claim that the individual's consumption opportunities are governed by

$$C_T = I_T + (1 + r)(I_{T-1} - C_{T-1}) + (1 + r)^2(I_{T-2} - C_{T-2}) + (1 + r)^3(I_{T-3} - C_{T-3}) + \ldots$$
$$+ (1 + r)^{T-1}(I_1 - C_1) + (1 + r)^T(I_0 - C_0). \qquad [10]$$

To prove that [10] is the correct representation of the constraint that the market places on the individual's lifetime consumption plan $(C_0, C_1, \ldots, C_{T-1}, C_T)$ we suppose that we have already proved it for $T = t$. We then demonstrate that that supposition implies the claim for $T = t + 1$. Because we have already established the claim for $T = 1$, we will then have proved by induction that [10] holds for any finite number of years.

If the right-hand side of [10] for $T = t$ is the available purchasing power in period t, given the previous consumption levels $(C_0, C_1, \ldots, C_{t-2}, C_{t-1})$, then the amount of purchasing power R_t left over after C_t is spent in period t is the right-hand side of [10] minus C_t. That is,

$$R_t = I_t - C_t + (1 + r)(I_{t-1} - C_{t-1}) + (1 + r)^2(I_{t-2} - C_{t-2})$$
$$= (1 + r)^3(I_{t-3} - C_{t-3}) + \ldots + (1 + r)^{t-1}(I_1 - C_1) + (1 + r)^t(I_0 - C_0).$$

R_t is available to be distributed over period $t + 1$ and subsequent periods.

Note that If R_t is positive it will add to the individual's purchasing power in the next period. In other words, saving is carried over to the next period, with interest of course. If R_t is negative, debt is carried forward to the next period and will have to be paid back, with interest. In either case, the purchasing power available in the next period is $I_{t+1} + (1 + r)R_t$, When we set $C_{t+1} = I_{t+1} + (1 + r)R_t$ we get [10] for $T = t + 1$. Therefore, [10] is the intertemporal budget constraint for any lifetime $T + 1$, for any value of T.

If we divide both sides of [10] by $(1 + r)^T$ and move the consumption terms to the left of the equal sign we get

$$C_0 + \frac{C_1}{1+r} + \frac{C_2}{(1+r)^2} + \frac{C_3}{(1+r)^3} + \ldots + \frac{C_{T-1}}{(1+r)^{T-1}} + \frac{C_T}{(1+r)^T}$$

$$= I_0 + \frac{I_1}{1+r} + \frac{I_2}{(1+r)^2} + \frac{I_3}{(1+r)^3} + \ldots + \frac{I_{T-1}}{(1+r)^{T-1}} + \frac{I_T}{(1+r)^T} \qquad [11]$$

We refer to [11] as the *present value* form of the intertemporal budget constraint. The right-hand side is the present value of the income stream $(I_0, I_1, \ldots, I_{T-1}, I_T)$, and the left-hand side is the present value of the consumption stream $(C_0, C_1, \ldots, C_{T-1}, C_T)$. Clearly, there are many different income streams that will have as their present value the number on the right-hand side of [11]. All such streams provide the consumer with the same consumption opportunities. If two income streams A and B have the same present value, then a consumption stream will be affordable with A if and only if it is affordable with B. Suppose A delivers high levels of income in the early years and relatively low levels later on. If it's the other way around with B but they have the same present value, then by borrowing and lending the consumer can finance a particular consumption stream with A if and only if the consumer can finance that consumption stream with B. Consequently, a particular consumer will wind up with the same utility with either income stream.

Source

The economic rationale for mandatory retirement is based on Lazear (1979).

Links

See Carmichael (1989) for more on this problem. The mandatory retirement story doesn't fit US data perfectly. See Stern and Todd (2000). For example, pension funds should be included in the model because they also play the role of bonds posted by the employees. See Lazear (1992). Since mandatory retirement was outlawed in 1978 for US workers under the age of seventy, the increase in the average retirement age has been slight (Costa, 1998, p. 24).

Problem Set

All of the questions refer to Figure 3.2.

(1) What is the efficient retirement age if H is the value of the worker's marginal product as a function of time, K is the marginal utility of leisure, and J is the compensation profile?

(2) What is the efficient retirement age if H is the value of the worker's marginal product as a function of time, J is the marginal utility of leisure, and K is the compensation profile? What retirement age would the worker choose?

(3) What is the efficient retirement age if K is the value of the worker's marginal product as a function of time, J is the marginal utility of leisure, and H is the compensation profile?

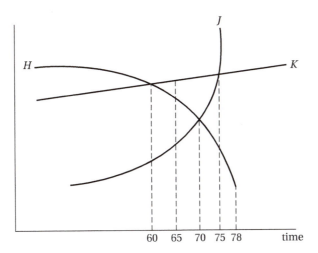

Figure 3.2

(4) What retirement age would the worker choose if H is the worker's compensation profile, J is the value of the worker's marginal product as a function of time, and K is the marginal utility of leisure?

3.8   TENURE AND THE PERFORMANCE OF PROFESSORS

The principal is a university administration and the agent is a professor at that institution. The spotlight is on the professor's hiring, promotion, and sometimes dismissal. The promotion regimen employed in colleges and universities in Canada, the United States, and many other countries is an example of an *up-or-out* policy, which is also used in law and accounting firms organized as partnerships. After a probationary period of six or seven years, the employee is either given permanent employment or is released. But why up or out? If workers are found to be of low quality, why not offer them continued employment at a lower wage? Why terminate employment? In general, the up-or-out policy gets around the problem of the *employer* giving the worker a false low rating to cut labor costs. If other firms could observe the worker's quality, this wouldn't work. But because information is hidden it would be a serious possibility and a serious problem: if the university administration were to systematically underrate professors, they might respond by working less, because the return to hard work is reduced.

In the case of colleges and universities, a professor's performance is reviewed after six years by members of his or her own department. Outside evaluations of the candidate's research are obtained. Evidence of teaching effectiveness is also examined, but the candidate's contributions to scholarship receive almost all of the weight in the top research universities. If the decision is negative, the teacher must leave the university. Even if he or she offers to stay on at a big cut in pay, the teacher will not be retained after a negative tenure decision. If the decision is favorable, the professor is granted lifetime tenure in the department. This means that the professor can't be fired for poor performance, only for moral turpitude or extreme dereliction of duty. The only other way that a university can dismiss a tenured professor is to close down the entire department. Assuming no serious moral lapses, a tenured professor has a lifetime job; his or her position in the department is terminated only by death – the professor's death (or retirement) or the department's, whichever comes first.

What benefit could come from a policy that prevented an employer from firing a worker for shirking or incompetence? Given the roster of faculty members in a particular university department, it would seem to be in society's interest to allow the employer to fire low-quality workers at any time and replace them with higher quality faculty. The university would decide the relative weight to place on teaching and research and then rank the members of a department. The poor performers could then be identified and released. However, if this policy were adopted by universities, the departments themselves would make different hiring decisions in the first place. The established department members would be reluctant to hire the best young people available. These high-quality young people might outperform the original department members by such a wide margin that the university would want to reduce the pay of the incumbents or even fire them. Therefore, there would be a strong incentive for departments to hire low-quality newcomers. The net result of allowing the university to fire low-quality professors at any time and replace them with higher quality faculty would be departments with very low-quality workers! The overall result of abolishing tenure could well be lower quality colleges and universities. But why let the department members themselves hire their new colleagues? Because the individual academic disciplines are so specialized that members of a particular department are the only people in the university community capable of judging the candidates for an opening in that department.

Compare the university system with professional sports: in both cases performance declines significantly with age. The public has an interest in seeing that workers are replaced when the quality of their performance falls below that of newcomers waiting in the wings who not only have the benefit of youth but also the most up-to-date tools. In athletics, management *can* replace one worker with a superior one. Magagement *is* better able to evaluate candidates for a position on the team than the athletes on the field. There is no efficiency argument for awarding tenure to professional athletes. The case for academic tenure does not apply here.

In academe the weak performers can be identified by the administration with the passage of sufficient time – a decade or two, say. Why not allow the university to replace them at that point? We come back to the hiring decision. Professors will have a strong incentive to hire weak newcomers if there is a possibility that a strong candidate could eventually replace the incumbent.

Compare university hiring with the way it's done in the legal profession: the senior partners in a law firm do not seem to be reluctant to hire the best young people. But this is a field in which newcomers bring revenue to the firm in addition to talent. The better the lawyers the more their clients will be billed for their services. The new lawyers create room for themselves without displacing the incumbents. A university department, on the other hand, has a limited number of positions. In a law firm, a bad hire will diminish the firm's revenue and hence the income of those making the hiring decision. In a university, a bad hire may eventually diminish the quality of the students admitted, but if the original department members get to keep their jobs by making bad hires they will realize a net gain. They may notice the deterioration in student quality, but that is more than compensated for by the increased probability of holding onto their jobs.

Granting lifetime job security to professors may be necessary to ensure that they do not have an incentive to hire weak newcomers. But that should not prevent the university from periodically examining the performance of a faculty member to ensure that the individual's *own* rate of productivity is maintained or from having a department compete for its share of the money available for pay raises.

Although lifetime tenure is desirable, why base teachers' promotion decisions even partly on their research output? If the creation of new knowledge is *not* an important part of teachers' jobs, as in the case of pre-university education, then the instructor is just passing on the discoveries of others. New hires can be evaluated by the administration and the case for tenure vanishes. At the university level, research is an important part of the professor's job – and not just because it adds to the stockpile of knowledge. Professors who are not sufficiently interested in their subjects to go beyond what is already known will probably be less than inspiring in the classroom. Moreover, if the instructors are not engaged in intensive research it is very hard for them to pick up the new tools and pass breakthroughs on to students.

In general, writing a paper for publication in a leading scholarly journal requires skills that are closely related to the talents needed for effective teaching at the university level: intelligence, thorough knowledge of one's field, intellectual discipline, creativity, and an interest in the subject. Less-talented scholars take a lot longer to prepare an article that's suitable for the high-quality journals. Therefore, it is less costly for the high-quality workers to signal their quality – in this instance, a signal is publication of an article in a high-prestige journal. Basing hiring, firing, and promotion decisions heavily on the individual's publication record has a rationale as a partial solution to a principal–agent problem, which in this case has both hidden characteristic and hidden action elements. The university could not take job applicants' word that they are diligent scholars with a keen interest in the discipline, a determination to work long hours learning more about the subject, and the intelligence to keep up with the other scholars in the field. Even if the university and society in general had no interest in scholarly research there would be a signaling rationale for using publication records in employment decisions. (Of course, if research had no social value it would receive much less funding and there would be less of it.) If you wish to test the proposition that publication has its uses apart from the scientific value of the output, you need to go well beyond estimating the correlation between teaching ability and success in publishing that you observe at your own college. You need to compare the present situation with what you would expect to find if universities were unable to use a fairly objective quality signal such as publication.

Sources

The role of the up-or-out contract in solving the problem of the principal (employer) falsifying information was pointed out by Kahn and Huberman (1988). The economic argument for awarding tenure to professors is based on Carmichael (1988).

Links

Carmichael (2001) explains why professors' unions are highly undesirable if professors also have tenure. Hoxby (2014) argues that the practice of awarding tenure to teachers in US public schools and grade schools stands in the way of changes in hiring and retaining teaches that could lead to a vast increase in the productivity of public schools.

3.9 UNIVERSITY PERFORMANCE IN EUROPE AND THE US

The *Shanghai Ranking* of the world's top 500 universities uses six criteria to score the research output of a university's faculty members. Five economists – Philippe Aghion, Mathias Dewatripont, Caroline Hoxby, Andreu MasColell, and André Sapir – used that ranking to create an index of country-wide university research performance relative to a country's population. The US level, which is the highest of all the relative performance scores, is arbitrarily set at 100. Switzerland is second with a score of 97. Then comes the UK (72), Canada (39), The Netherlands (20), Japan (13), EU15(13), EU25(10), Sweden (7), and France (3). (EU15 is comprised of the fifteen countries that belonged to the European Union on April 30, 2004. EU25 is the result of the expansion to twenty-five countries on May 1, 2004.) The index value is zero for any individual European country other the UK, The Netherlands, Sweden, and France.

The low scores for all but a handful of European countries is a concern because of three decades of disappointing growth in the *EU*. Could improved university performance lead to more rapid growth? Could enhanced funding of universities lead to greater and better research output? The European Union spends 1.3 percent of GDP on higher education, while the US spends 3.3 percent. Moreover, European universities are not sufficiently autonomous and incentives are often perverse.

At many European universities, tenure, which essentially gives the professor lifetime job security, is too easy to get. (Lifetime job security has adverse incentives, but a case can be made for making it available to academics, provided that there is a lengthy and demanding probationary period. See the previous section.) Adverse incentives can jeopardize university performance when the government takes an active role in hiring faculty. Suppose, for instance, that a university department is required to submit three approved job candidates from which a government agency will select the department's new faculty member. (This is not unknown in Europe.) A department may be tempted to put forward two inferior candidates along with the individual it would really like to recruit, opening the door to the possibility that political considerations lead to the appointment of one of the inferior individuals.

Aghion et al. (2010) use the number of patent awards to gauge the contribution that a region's universities make to economic productivity in that region. Specifically, they use US data to estimate the extent to which increased funding for higher education will lead to an increase in patent awards. Some states within the US have more generous funding than others. The data reveal that funding has a positive effect on performance. Moreover, universities within the US differ with respect to their degree of budget autonomy. The data not only show that greater autonomy is associated with better research performance, but also that a given increase in funding has a greater impact on research when there is greater autonomy.

Source

This section summarizes Aghion et al. (2010).

Link

Hoxby (2014) finds that greater autonomy even leads to greater productivity in the case of US public high schools and grade schools when these schools face at least a modicum of competition. School productivity is measured in terms of student achievement relative to expenditure per student.

3.10 PAY AND PERFORMANCE IN US PUBLIC SCHOOLS

American public schools have a dismal reputation. American universities are the envy of the world. Students from around the world come to the United States for their postsecondary education. The situation for grades 1 through 12 is remarkably different. In 1995, American seventh- and eighth-grade students ranked twenty-third in mathematics and twelfth in science out of the forty countries involved in the third International Math and Science Study. (Ireland ranked seventeenth in math, and Canada ranked eighteenth.) Moreover, the standing of American students is even lower at higher grade levels. High school seniors ranked below those of every country except Lithuania, Cyprus, and South Africa. In addition to these data we have a steady stream of media reports of egregious conditions in public schools.

Fifty-two US universities are among the world's top 100 universities when rated by research performance, according to the Shanghai Ranking produced by Shanghai Jiao Tong University. (www.shanghairanking.com/ARWU2015.html. More data can be found in Section 3.9 of this chapter.) In 1997, 29% of the PhDs awarded by American universities were earned by noncitizens, and 43% of the degrees in mathematics and computer science went to noncitizens (Ehrenberg, 2000, p. 4). Contrast those data with the reputation of US schools in the grade range 1 through 12: 67% of low-income parents say that they would be inclined to take their children out of the public school system if the alternatives were not so costly (Moe, 2001).

This section argues that the way that teachers are paid in the public school system creates serious moral hazard and averse selection problems that exacerbate the performance problem – and may be the main obstacle to correction. (There is strong evidence that increasing expenditure on education will not lead to improved student performance in the presence of these hidden information problems.) We begin with the hidden action story.

In the vast majority of school districts in the United States, teachers' pay depends on the number of years of college attained, the number of graduate courses taken, and especially the number of years they have been employed as teachers. The quality of the colleges that the teachers attended is irrelevant in determining their salary, as is the nature of the courses taken. The teacher's performance in the classroom is *not* part of the salary formula. The largest teacher's union, the NEA (National Education Association), has always traditionally resisted – very successfully – the idea that good performance be rewarded and bad performance be punished. This creates a severe moral hazard problem: two things that have a profound effect on the performance of workers in other sectors of the economy – the carrot and the stick – are not employed in the public school system. Instead, teacher pay is determined by factors that have little bearing on the quality of teaching.

Most professionals – physicians, professors, public school teachers, lawyers, and so forth – claim to do the best job that they can as a matter of pride and integrity, whether or not that is reflected in their pay. There is strong evidence to the contrary. For instance, physicians recommend more expensive treatments in cities with more doctors per capita. (See Section 3.11.1 of this chapter.)

In addition to the moral hazard problem that is created when pay is independent of performance, there is a serious adverse selection problem. Highly motivated, hard-working, and talented individuals are discouraged from entering a field that does not increase the person's pay when those qualities are manifest in superior performance. (The educational quality of US teachers has been steadily declining over the past quarter century. That is in part, but only in part, a consequence of the relative decline in the supply of talented women to the teaching profession as barriers to entry for women into law, medicine, academe, and other professions have fallen.) The quality problem is compounded in the public school system because science and math teachers are paid no more than others, although they receive an 8 percent bonus in the private sector. Many school districts are forced to hire unqualified math and science teachers.

The core of the NEA's attack on pay-for-performance is that good performance by teachers is very hard to measure. However, it can't be any harder to measure the quality of teaching by American college and university instructors, although merit pay is a crucial part of their salary formula. In fact, 90 percent of large public and private sector organizations attempt to measure the quality of an individual's work and adjust pay accordingly, in spite of the measurement problems. Inequities are inevitable, but there is far more harm done by the inefficiency of a pay schedule that includes no incentive for good work.

The performance of American students on international tests, the argument that moral hazard and adverse selection problems are built into the pay formula of American teachers, and the groundswell of parental dissatisfaction with the performance of public schools have prompted the NEA to propose an additional program of certification. Mastery of certain skills and/or knowledge would be certified and a teacher's pay would increase with the number of certificates presented. However, less than three-tenths of a percent of North American firms use certification in that way. The NEA proposal is not an improvement on the present system but just more of the same. It is noteworthy that only 1 percent of private school teachers have the certification demanded by public school boards.

How do we know the system would respond to a change in the incentive environment? Evidence comes from a comparison of the performance of public schools that face serious competition with schools that do not. The city of Boston has seventy school districts accessible from the city center within half an hour, whereas Miami has but a single district. Some public schools face competition from relatively inexpensive Catholic schools, and many do not. Some school districts employ the voucher system or have a charter schools program, both of which provide stiff competition for the local public school. Public schools that face competition perform better than those that do not, after adjusting for factors such as the level of parental education and income that would otherwise cloud the results. When even a single low-cost alternative arrives on the scene, the productivity of the public school increases profoundly, even without additional funds. And the increase is greater the larger the fraction of parents who had been without an alternative to the public system — typically because of low income. Competition provides disincentive to the public schools authorities to stand pat, for fear of losing enrollment and then government revenue. Presumably, one of the consequences is the provision of better incentives for teachers.

Concluding note on the voucher system and charter schools: The voucher system gives parents the right to transfer the amount of money that would have been given to a public school for the child's education to the private school of their choice. Any difference between the private school fee and value of the voucher comes out of the parent's pocket. The system greatly expands the family's range of choice, especially if the difference between the private fee and the value of the voucher is small. The NEA claims that vouchers will drain the public school system of the best students and consequently further disadvantage those left behind. That has not happened. In Michigan and Milwaukee the poor and minority students remaining in the public system have made impressive gains – presumably as a result of the schools responding to competition. And the fraction of poor students in the public system has not changed. Charter schools are largely publicly funded but have considerable autonomy and find it much easier to respond to parental concerns.

Sources

The lack of a meaningful link between teacher pay and teacher performance has been thoroughly studied by Dale Ballou and Michael Podgursky. See for example, Ballou and Podgursky (1997, 2001). Data on the standing of US students in international tests are taken from Hanushek (2002) and Woessman (2001). The effect of competition on public schools has been intensively researched by Caroline Hoxby (2001a, 2001b, 2002, 2003). Hoxby measures school productivity in terms of student achievement relative to expenditure per student.

Links

See Hanushek (2002) for a review of the evidence revealing that increasing expenditure on education will not lead to improved student performance with conventional compensation formulas in place. Lazear (2003) points out that the educational quality of US teachers has been steadily declining over the past quarter century.

3.11 MORAL HAZARD AND INSURANCE

The term *moral hazard* was first used in the insurance industry to refer to the fact that individuals with insurance coverage have diminished incentive to devote effort to preventive care. Preventive care reduces the probability of the kind of accident that is covered by insurance. This is a concern for insurance companies because diminished preventive care results in a larger number of accidents and hence more claims paid by the insurer. It is a concern for society as a whole because, although insurance coverage increases individual welfare, it also induces individuals to devote less than the *efficient* amount of effort to preventive care.

Effort is costly to the individual, and efficiency calculations always require benefits to be weighed against costs. Why would expected utility-maximizing individual decisions not lead to an efficient outcome? After all, this book does not consider the effort that people devote to vacuuming their carpets to determine whether an efficient outcome results from self-regarding individual decisions. That's because there are no direct effects on the welfare of anyone else when you vacuum your carpet. Admittedly, there is an *indirect* effect on the welfare of others. The electrical energy that you used is not available to others. But you pay a price for that electricity. Your budget constraint induces you to take the welfare of others into consideration when you purchase goods and services because, in most cases, the prices that you face embody information about the preferences of other households.

Return to the case of accident insurance. You could lower the probability of an accident by having your car brakes inspected every quarter – in general, by increasing the effort that you devote to accident prevention. But the cost to you of the extra time and effort is not accompanied by a sufficiently high benefit. If you do have an accident, the loss will be financed by the other policyholders. Their premiums provide the money with which the insurance company pays your claim. But every policyholder has diminished incentive to invest in prevention, and that increases the total number of accidents and the total value of claims paid. That in turn results in a higher insurance premium. No *individual* can reduce his or her premium by investing in prevention, however. When *everyone* devotes effort to preventive care the probability of an accident is lower for everyone. There are fewer accidents and less real wealth thereby destroyed. It is easy to construct examples in which everyone would have been better off if each had devoted more effort to preventive care, although no one has an incentive to do so. That is precisely what we do in Sections 3.11.3–3.11.5.

Having your car's brakes inspected every week would reduce the probability of an accident, thereby benefitting you and other motorists. But that would *create* inefficiency: The required resources – your time and the mechanic's – could generate even more benefit if the time spent on brake inspection were significantly reduced. The efficient level of preventive care is not zero, but it is not unbounded either.

DEFINITION: *Moral Hazard with Insurance Coverage*

Moral hazard refers to the fact that insurance coverage drives a wedge between the net benefit to the individual and the net benefit to the society when the individual acts to reduce risk. The former falls far short of the latter. Contracts that condition a claim payment on the individual's actions cannot be enforced when the amount of effort devoted to preventive care cannot be verified in court.

You may feel that an individual has sufficient incentive to invest in preventive care even with insurance coverage when there is also the potential for personal injury or even loss of life – burglary, fire, automobile insurance, and so forth. Don't jump to the conclusion that a person would employ every available device for minimizing the chance of accident and injury, independent of any financial incentive. You probably drive a car that is not as safe as a more expensive car that you might have purchased instead – perhaps with the aid of a car loan. You chose a less expensive car because, even after factoring in the probability of an accident and injury, you have higher expected utility with that vehicle and a larger basket of other goods and services. It is obviously not in our interest to spend all our money, or all our time, on preventive care. If we did, each household would want to live next to a hospital, and no one would ever take a vacation because the money saved on vacations could be devoted to increased fire protection for the home. Why not hire a night watchman for your home to reduce the probability that you will die in your bed in a fire?

When drivers of police cars and rescue vehicles are monitored by means of devices similar to the "black box" (flight data recorder) installed on commercial aircraft, the frequency of accidents goes down dramatically, giving us additional evidence that individuals left on their own do not devote maximum effort to preventive care – not even when life and limb are at stake. (Monitoring is effective even when it takes the relatively primitive form of a loud noise going off inside the vehicle when speed is excessive.)

We first look at some examples of moral hazard and then offer a formal model (in Section 3.11.2). Sections 3.11.3 and 3.11.4 calculate the equilibrium level of prevention resulting from individual choice and then the efficient level of preventive care. We see that the latter is substantially higher.

3.11.1 Overview

The most striking example of moral hazard would be an individual who commits suicide so that his family can collect the life insurance benefits. This possibility is in fact eliminated by the insurance contract, which releases the insurance company from its obligation to pay when death is the result of suicide. (That provision

By exploiting the different lengths of the suicide exemption period in OECD countries economists Y. J. Choi, J. Chen, and Y. Sawada (2015) discovered a significant number of cases of individuals who committed suicide after purchasing life insurance but who had no intention of ending their lives before obtaining the insurance. The data also reveal that some individuals purchase life insurance *because* they intend to commit suicide.

usually lapses a year or two after the insurance is purchased. Why?) It is costly for the company to determine if the insured did commit suicide, but the costs are typically small relative to potential claim.

In many cases the costs of verifying moral hazard are too high for it to be part of the contractual relationship: homeowners' insurance pays the cost of replacing objects stolen when your home is robbed. The most severe loss is sometimes the utility destroyed when an article with extremely high sentimental value but low market value is taken. Why can't the policyholder be compensated financially for the loss in sentimental value? Because there would be no way for the insurance company to verify that it would take $5,000 to compensate for the loss of great grandmother's button collection. It would be extremely costly – and in most cases impossible – to determine if an object really was treasured by the policyholder.

Why can't you buy insurance to protect against a loss of home equity should the market value of your house fall below the price you paid for it? Because of the extreme moral hazard. The insurance would all but eliminate the incentive to keep your house in good repair. It would also diminish the incentive to work hard to get a good price when selling it. (Writing the insurance contract so that a claim is paid only when the home owner has maintained the house well and fought to get the best price wouldn't work. Why?) However, basing the coverage on the average value of houses in the surrounding neighborhood will restore appropriate incentives: if the average value falls by 10 percent then you can claim 10 percent of the original purchase price of your house when you sell it. If the owner has actually increased the value of the house through maintenance and renovation then the owner will realize the fruits of that effort because the claim is based on the neighborhood average selling price. This type of equity insurance is only available in a few areas in the United States at present, but it could become commonplace.

"Laurie and Norm: I had to go out for an hour. The key is under the mat. Make yourself at home." Would you leave this note on your front door if you weren't covered by burglary insurance? Some homeowners with fire insurance will burn leaves in the driveway but would not do so if they were not insured against fire.

I once went to the emergency ward of an Ottawa hospital to get a prescription for our son's medication, which had been forgotten at home in Toronto. The hospital visit was covered by insurance but it could have been avoided by taking a tiny amount of preventive care – checking to make sure we had the medicine before leaving home. Sensible insurance coverage would not allow me to pass the costs of that visit on to the rest of the community. I want to make it clear that I'm not proud of this example.

Health insurance is fraught with moral hazard. That is not to say that people who have health insurance allow their health to deteriorate. But there are often a number of ways of successfully treating a given health problem. If the alternative methods impose different burdens on the community's resources and these social costs are not reflected in the *private* costs incurred by the individual making the decision then the private decisions will not likely contribute to efficiency.

What exacerbates moral hazard in health care is that the key decisions are usually made by a third party – the physician. Doctors know that the patient will pass the costs of health care onto the insurance carrier *and* that patients typically have almost no expertise in determining the appropriate treatment of their condition. Economists use the term *induced demand* to refer to a treatment prescribed by a physician that does not benefit the patient but which augments the physician's income, but it is difficult to interpret the data on inducement. If patients receive more medical treatment in areas with a high ratio of doctors per capita, is this because doctors have fewer patients and regulate their incomes by prescribing unnecessary procedures or is it the case that communities with a high demand for medical care attract more physicians per capita?

In the 1980s escalating health care costs in the US – due in part to the moral hazard and perceived induced demand – motivated insurance companies to play a role in the selection of the method of treatment. Until then, the typical scenario was that the physician would recommend a course of treatment, the patient would approve, and the insurance company would pay whatever costs were incurred. Patients had little incentive to shop for the least expensive provider of a specific treatment or to elect a simple procedure when a more complicated one had been recommended by the doctor. This remains true today, and it can lead to the doctor overprescribing medical care. According to one medical study, 20 percent of the heart pacemaker implants in the United States were not endorsed in retrospect as the most appropriate treatment, and 36 percent of the implants were recommended on the basis of an extremely optimistic forecast of expected benefits (Hsiao et al., 1988).

> There tends to be a higher frequency of baby deliveries by Caesarian section in communities that have more obstetricians relative to the number of women of child-bearing age (Gruber and Owings, 1996).

Medical practitioners in Western Europe often rely on drug therapy to treat heart disease and Americans are more likely to recommend surgery. Of course, surgery is more expensive. Americans spend far more per capita on health care than Canadians but have about the same health status. (Canadians have a slightly higher life expectancy in fact. And virtually all Canadians are covered by some form of comprehensive health insurance, whereas 13 percent of Americans are not covered at all.) And because the direct cost to the recipient of medical services is typically very low, hospitals have very little incentive to compete on the price dimension. They tend to appeal to consumers by publicizing the acquisition of high-cost, high-tech equipment, even when it has little overall effect on the community's health status. The equipment does have a big impact on health care costs, of course.

Insurance companies try to mitigate moral hazard by requiring the insured party to pay a small fraction of the loss. Very often the patient will have to pay 20 percent of the health care costs – the *copayment* – while the insurance company pays 80 percent. Compared to someone without any health care insurance the patient's financial burden is lightened considerably, but at the same time the

An influential study by the RAND corporation tracked more than six thousand individuals. Some of them received free medical care and the others were charged significant copayments. The two groups were equally healthy after five years, in spite of the fact that the treatments given to those receiving free care were 30 percent more expensive. (See Dranove, 2000, pp. 30–31, for a discussion of this research.)

patient pays a fee that is proportional to the social cost of medical care. This makes it costly for individuals to incur expenses that add little to their utility. If medical care is free to individuals then they have an incentive to consume any health care service as long as it adds *something* to their utility, regardless of the cost to society.

Deductibles also eliminate the gap between private and social cost in the case of a small loss. The deductible clause makes the insured party liable for any expenses under the deductible limit, which is usually around $200 for automobile collision coverage. The individual is protected against big losses, but for small losses, which are often the ones that can be easily avoided, the individual suffering the loss is the one who pays. Private costs are equal to social costs for the small losses below the deductible limit. In addition, the deductible is used by the insurance carrier as a screening device. If two policies are offered, one with a low premium and a high deductible and the other with a high premium and a low deductible, drivers who know they are prudent and careful will choose the former. This menu also provides some incentive for motorists to improve their driving habits. The high-deductible, low-premium policy could provide drivers with more expected utility *if* they drive safely.

Automobile insurance companies use experience rating to encourage careful driving. Drivers pay higher premiums if they have speeding tickets or accidents on their records. Some companies won't accept business at any price from drivers with very poor records. This gives a financial incentive to take preventive care. Health insurance companies use experience rating to determine the amount of premium paid by firms that purchase group policies. Firms in industries in which the incidence of AIDS is unusually high sometimes cannot purchase health insurance at all. If insurance companies were able to sort us into risk categories with perfect precision and charge higher premiums to individuals in higher risk groups they would do so.

Up to a point, sorting by risk is socially beneficial because it reduces the moral hazard problem. But if it is taken too far then each risk category contains relatively few individuals, and the law of large numbers will not apply. That diminishes the social benefit of insurance. In a large pool of insured individuals the number of accidents varies little from year to year. (If twenty classmates each tossed a coin 1,000 times, there is a very high probability that very close to 10,000 heads would be recorded.) Therefore, the premium can be more or less constant and still generate just enough revenue for the insurance carrier to pay off on claims. In a small pool, the number of accidents would vary considerably from year to year, requiring significant changes in the premium from one year to the next. The individual is less insulated against risk. If everyone belongs to a small pool then everyone's expected utility could be increased by aggregating many of the pools.

However, if insurance companies did not sort into risk categories they would face a serious adverse selection problem. Consider health insurance: if all policyholders paid a common premium the most healthy of them might find that their expected utility was higher without insurance (or with a small amount of coverage). Then the remaining policyholders would have a higher probability of submitting a claim, and the premium would have to rise to cover the value of claims paid. In that case, healthy policyholders who benefitted from insurance under the lower premium might find that *their* expected utility is now higher without insurance. When they opt out, the riskiness of the remaining group increases yet again, resulting in another increase in claims and premiums. And so on. This unraveling is prevented by *group insurance* coverage, which requires a participating firm to enroll all of its employees.

Experience rating and risk sorting for health care insurance can go well beyond a due consideration of incentives. On one hand, it is in society's interest to make individuals who choose to smoke pay higher health insurance premiums. On the other hand, an individual with a genetic predisposition to breast cancer should be treated as a victim of bad luck, not as someone who has made a bad choice. "Genetic testing may become the most potent argument for state-financed universal health care" (*The Economist*, October 19, 2000, cited in Wheelan, 2002, p. 90). Society should insure risks over the individual's lifetime, but at the same time charge higher premiums to individuals who are in a higher risk category *because of behavior over which the individual has control.*

If one were able to get more than 100 percent fire insurance coverage, the moral hazard problem would be particularly acute: if the building were completely destroyed by fire then the value of the insurance claim would exceed the market value of the building. The owners would have a strong financial incentive to torch their own buildings. This would definitely affect the probability of a loss and would have a big impact on the size of fire insurance premiums. Insurance companies will not give more than 100 percent coverage. (There is one astonishing and egregious exception, discussed in Section 3.5 on the great recession of 2007–2009.)

The market system often provides its own solution to a hidden action problem. We have discussed the example of taxi fares (Section 1.2 of Chapter 1). Health maintenance organizations (HMOs) came into prominence in the 1980s and 1990s in response to rapidly rising health care costs. HMOs provide comprehensive medical care to the individual in return for a fixed annual fee. The HMO monitors costs – and hence claims – by giving the physician a strong financial incentive to keep the patient in good health, in part by heading off problems before they require expensive treatment by specialists. The pay of a physician under contract to an HMO has two components. First, the HMO pays the doctor a fixed monthly fee for each patient registered with that doctor. Second, there is an adjustment based on the frequency with which the doctor's patients visit specialists or hospitals: the doctor is given a monthly allowance of F dollars. The HMO reduces that allowance by C dollars for every such visit by a patient. At the end of the month the doctor is paid a bonus equal to F minus all these deductions. This may be a negative number, in which case the physician pays that amount to the HMO. This discourages the physician from making too many referrals to specialists. But it also discourages the doctor from delaying a vital referral – the illness could become more severe and require more expensive treatment.

It is inevitable that health care costs will rise at a substantially greater rate than prices in general, due to the fact that productivity increases at a slower rate in the health care industry than in the overall economy. However, those same economy-wide productivity gains ensure that non-medical consumption will grow at a significant rate even as the fraction of GDP devoted to health care will increase dramatically (Baumol, 2012).

Are patients getting lower quality care under HMOs? The evidence is mixed. Has the HMO system (and other managed care programs) had a mitigating effect on US health care costs? There was indeed a drop in the rate of growth of health care expenses in the early 1990s, so that it was roughly the same as the rate of growth of the US gross domestic product. However, by 2000 the differential was again positive – and widening (Reinhardt et al., 2004).

Sometimes the government can nudge consumers toward the efficient effort supply. A law requiring insurance companies to give a premium discount if a silent alarm is installed can enhance social welfare. Consider burglary insurance. A homeowner with insurance is less inclined to check that the windows are locked before leaving the house and certainly less likely to install an expensive security device – unless the insurance contract provides some inducement. Even the *type* of security device has efficiency implications. Some provide protection for others, and some shift criminal activity to others. On one hand, if bars are placed on the windows, burglars will pass up that house and move on to the next one. On the other hand, a silent burglar alarm, which rings in the police station, may discourage thieves from attempting to rob any house in the neighborhood because they will not know which houses have silent alarms. Suppose that a thief breaks into two houses per week in your city. Even if 1 percent of the houses have silent alarms the probability is 0.65 that he will be caught before the year is out. The probability is only 0.35 that none of the houses he enters will have a silent alarm. If 5 percent of the houses have a silent alarm then the probability of not entering a house with an alarm in 104 burglaries is 0.005.

These calculations show that invisible security devices provide a substantial spillover benefit to individuals in addition to the one installing the device. Suppose that the homeowner has a choice between a visible security device that costs $25 and an invisible system that costs $700 but provides a total of $7,000 of benefit to everyone, including the individual who installs it. (The invisible device reduces the value of automobiles stolen by an average of $7,000 per device.) If the visible device merely shifts criminal activity to others then it provides a net social benefit of zero but has a positive social cost. The invisible device adds $6,300 to social benefit, net of cost. The individual has a strong incentive to purchase the cheaper, crime-shifting technology, and thus society has an interest in promoting the invisible, crime-reducing technology.

In fact it has been estimated that a $700 investment in the silent car alarm Lojack does result in an average $7,000 reduction in losses due to automobile theft. One alternative is the much less expensive Club, which attaches to the steering wheel and primarily shifts crime to others because it is visible to the thief. Automobile theft in Boston, Massachusetts, has fallen by 50 percent since the enactment of a state law requiring insurance companies to provide a 25 percent discount to any policyholder with a silent alarm. (Although a $300 discount – on a

$1,200 insurance premium – does not provide a net gain to the buyer *after one year*, the annual discount offers a significant net gain over the life of the policy.)

Why didn't insurance companies take the initiative and introduce the discount scheme on their own? Because no insurance provider wanted to be the first to offer the discount. Suppose that company X does go first – in a region where there is no law requiring the discount. If many of the car owners insured with X install the device, then the probability of being caught steeling *any* car increases, and hence there will be a community wide reduction in the total value of cars stolen. But that reduction may not be very significant because the probability of a thief being caught will not increase nearly as much as it would if all insurance carriers provided an incentive to install the silent alarm, resulting in a much larger increase in purchases. Moreover, *whatever* the reduction in automobile theft, only a fraction of the resulting claims reduction will be captured by X itself. Most of the cars thus spared will be owned by households that carry insurance with other companies. The positive effect on X's profit due to reduced claims will not be enough to offset the reduction in revenue resulting from the discount to its policyholders who install the silent alarm. However, if all automobile insurance companies simultaneously offer the discount, firm X will benefit from the much larger increase in the probability of a thief being caught, and will see its claims fall, not only because many of its own customers install the silent alarm, but more so from the devices installed by the customers of all the other automobile insurance firms. The industry may have needed the nudge provided by the Massachusetts law.

We conclude with a moral hazard story from a very different industry. In the 1940s American movie producers began giving major stars a share in the profits from their movies. This gave the stars an incentive to avoid the silly temper tantrums that cause production delays and escalate the costs of the movie. When profit sharing became a common practice some movie producers began disguising the profit earned by the most lucrative movies – for instance by charging them with some of the fixed costs, such as set construction, from other projects. Contracts that offered the performers a cut of the profits were less rewarding as a result, and many responded by holding out for a percent of the *gross* – that is, they demanded a cut of the picture's revenue instead of its profit.

3.11.2 The Formal Model

We use a simple model to investigate the conditions for efficiency when there is moral hazard. There are only two commodities, W, wealth, and L, leisure. Preferences are quasi-linear, and thus

$$U(w, \ell) = B(w) + \ell,$$

where $B(w)$ is the utility of w dollars of wealth, and ℓ is the amount of leisure consumed. We assume that the individual is risk averse, so that the marginal utility of wealth is positive but diminishes as wealth increases. The individual is endowed with T units of leisure but if he or she devotes e units of effort to preventing accidents then $\ell = T - e$. Because we want to highlight effort supply we express utility as

$$U = B(w) + T - e.$$

The effort supply e is determined by the individual and is not a random variable. Of course uncertainty does affect the individual's wealth, which is either partially destroyed with probability $\pi(e)$ or remains intact with probability $1 - \pi(e)$. The probability that the individual suffers a loss in wealth is a function of his or her effort supply e. We assume that $\pi(e'') < \pi(e')$ for all $e'' > e'$: An increase in effort reduces the probability of an accident.

Let a represent the value of an individual's wealth when there is an accident but no insurance has been purchased, and let z represent the value of the same individual's wealth when there is no accident and no insurance. Of course, $a < z$. The actual wealth will be different from both a and z if insurance is purchased. Let x denote the individual's actual wealth when he or she suffers an accident, taking into account any insurance benefits that may be paid. Let y denote wealth when there is no accident but the individual has paid an insurance premium. The individual's expected utility (EU) is

$$EU = \pi(e)B(x) + [1 - \pi(e)]B(y) + T - e.$$

The individual will choose e, x, and y to maximize EU. The values of x and y are subject to the individual's market opportunity equation, but the market places no restrictions on the choice of effort level e. Section 3.11.3 simplifies the calculations by assuming that e can be set equal to zero or one but nothing in between. (The individual either does or does not devote effort to preventive care.) In the final two sections (3.11.4 and 3.11.5) the individual chooses from a continuum of effort supply levels.

DEFINITION: *The Basic Model*

Without insurance, an individual's wealth is a if he or she has an accident and z otherwise. With insurance, the individual's wealth is x in case of an accident and y otherwise. The individual's EU is

$$EU = \pi(e)B(x) + [1 - \pi(e)]B(y) + T - e.$$

where e is the amount of effort that the individual devotes to preventive care, and $\pi(e)$ is the probability of an accident as a function of e. The number T is the maximum possible effort supply.

The next two sections show that the individual will set $e = 0$ if he or she is insured, and that the resulting outcome is inefficient. Devoting zero effort to preventive care is a consequence of the fact that we are abstracting from the possibility of personal injury – by carelessly operating a chain saw, say. In our model, an accident merely reduces individual wealth. There are lots of situations in which an injury *can* occur with positive probability and the individual devotes some effort to preventive care as a result. However, our analysis of the extreme case can be applied here to demonstrate that the level of preventive care chosen by individuals will not result in an efficient outcome. *Without* insurance, the individual *will* invest in preventive care, even if only wealth is at risk, but that will yield less expected utility than complete insurance even with zero investment in preventive care.

Section 2.7.4 of Chapter 2 proves that individuals will demand and obtain complete insurance ($x = y$) under competitive conditions. This theorem is exploited in the next two sections (3.11.3 and 3.11.4), although the value of x will depend on the amount of preventive care supplied by individuals. In employing the complete insurance theorem in this way we greatly simplify the calculations. However, doing so requires us to ignore the fact that insurance companies will provide less than complete insurance to partially offset the diminished incentive to reduce risk. This oversight is corrected in the last section, 3.11.5.

3.11.3 The Binary Choice Model of Moral Hazard

This subsection assumes that you are familiar with the economics of insurance without moral hazard – that is, the material in Sections 2.7.1, 2.7.2, and 2.7.4 of Chapter 2. To obtain quick insight, we initially suppose that there are only two possible effort supply levels: either $e = 1$, which means that the individual devotes effort to prevention, or $e = 0$, which means that no effort is made. Assume a competitive insurance market and hence that the individual purchasing insurance faces fair odds. Competition forces insurance companies to offer the contract on the fair odds line that maximizes EU, as we showed in Section 2.7.4 of Chapter 2. Therefore, $x = y$ by the complete insurance theorem. The fair odds line is

$$\pi(e)x + [1 - \pi(e)]y = \pi(e)a + [1 - \pi(e)]z.$$

When we set $x = y$ we get $x = y = \pi(e)a + [1 - \pi(e)]z$. Set

$$w(e) = \pi(e)a + [1 - \pi(e)]z.$$

Then $w(e)$ is the individual's wealth, whether there is an accident or not, when insurance is purchased under fair odds. Note that $\pi(e)B(w(e)) + (1 - \pi(e))B(w(e)) = B(w(e))$. Therefore, the individual's utility after purchasing insurance is

$$\mu(e) = B(w(e)) + T - e.$$

We have implicitly assumed that individuals are identical. (All are risk averse. They have the same a and z values, and the same $\pi(e)$ function.) This is unrealistic, but it simplifies our calculations without generating any misleading conclusions. All that remains is to calculate individual effort supply and to determine if we have an efficient supply of effort at the market equilibrium. If the individual sets $e = 0$ we have

$$\mu(0) = B(w) + T.$$

We have used w instead of $w(0)$ as the argument of B because the effort supply of the *other* policyholders will determine their probability of an accident, which in turn influences the number of dollars in claims that have to be paid and hence the per capita level of wealth w that is available with insurance. Before working out the individual's utility when $e = 1$ we introduce one more assumption: there is a large number of policyholders, and hence a change in one individual's probability of an accident does not appreciably affect the premium charged because it does not appreciably affect the value of claims paid per capita. Hence, if our individual sets $e = 1$ his or her wealth with insurance will still be w. Therefore, if $e = 1$ we have

$$\mu(1) = B(w) + T - 1.$$

Clearly, $B(w) + T$ is larger than $B(w) + T - 1$, so the individual will set $e = 0$. Then everyone will set $e = 0$, and hence $w = w(0) = \pi(0)a + [1 - \pi(0)]z$ at equilibrium.

Equilibrium Theorem

No individual has an incentive to devote effort to prevention, and thus each individual's utility is $B(\pi(0)a + [1-\pi(0)]z) + T$ at the competitive equilibrium.

Because the individual is risk averse, this utility level will be significantly higher than $\pi(1)B(a) + [1 - \pi(1)]B(z) + T - 1$, the utility without insurance. (Note that without insurance the individual typically *does* have incentive to set $e = 1$.)

Will the competitive equilibrium be efficient? *If* everyone were to set $e = 1$, then with complete insurance the individual utility level would be $B(\pi(1)a + [1 - \pi(1)]z) + T - 1$. For many real-world applications (and for the example to follow) we would have

$$B(\pi(1)a + [1 - \pi(1)]z) + T - 1 > B(\pi(0)a + [1 - \pi(0)]z) + T,$$

in which case the competitive equilibrium is not efficient.

Example 3.9 An Inefficient Effort Supply at Equilibrium

Let $B(w) = 2.4\sqrt{w}$ and $T = 1$. Therefore, $U = 2.4\sqrt{w} + 1 - e$. If $e = 1$ suppose that the probability of an accident is ⅓, but if $e = 0$ the probability of an accident is ½. That is, $\pi(1) = ⅓$ and $\pi(0) = ½$. Finally, $a = 30$ (individual wealth is 30 if there is an accident but no insurance), and $z = 72$ (individual wealth is 72 if there is no accident and no insurance). There are n identical individuals, where n is a large number. Now, $w(0) = ½ \times 30 + ½ \times 72 = 51$. Therefore at the competitive equilibrium (where everyone sets $e = 0$) individual utility is $2.4\sqrt{51} + 1 - 0 = 18.14$. *If* everyone were to set $e = 1$ then individual wealth would be $w(1) = ⅓ \times 30 + ⅔ \times 72 = 58$, and individual utility would be $2.4\sqrt{58} + 1 - 1 = 18.28$. Because each individual's utility is higher when each sets $e = 1$, the competitive equilibrium is inefficient.

When insurance is supplied under competitive conditions the individual will set $e = 0$ (in this example). But if insurance is not available the individual will set

$e = 1$, as we now show. He or she will maximize $\pi(e) \times B(30) + [1 - \pi(e)] \times B(72) + 1 - e$. Because the only choice is $e = 1$ or $e = 0$ we just have to compare $\frac{1}{3} \times 2.4\sqrt{30} + \frac{2}{3} \times 2.4\sqrt{72} + 0$ with $\frac{1}{2} \times 2.4\sqrt{30} + \frac{1}{2} \times 2.4\sqrt{72} + 1$. The former is 17.96, and the latter is 17.75. Therefore, when there is no insurance the individual chooses $e = 1$, the efficient amount of preventive care. *That does not mean that we get an efficient outcome without insurance.* Note that individual utility is 18.14 at the competitive equilibrium and that is higher than 17.96, the utility without insurance. Therefore, everyone is better off with insurance – because individual risk is diminished – even though the individual has no incentive to invest in preventive care when insured and without insurance the individual supplies maximum effort.

∂3.11.4 A Continuum of Effort Supply Levels

It is assumed that you are familiar with the material in Sections 2.7.1, 2.7.2, and 2.7.4 of Chapter 2. We employ the model of Section 3.11.2 but this time with effort continuously variable between zero and one: $0 \le e \le 1$. Think of e as fraction of one's leisure time – time not spent working or sleeping – devoted to preventive care. The individual's *EU* (expected utility) is

$$EU = \pi(e)B(x) + [1 - \pi(e)]B(y) + T - e.$$

The derivative of π with respect to e is negative because preventive care reduces the probability of an accident.

As in the previous subsection, we exploit the fact that the competitive insurance results in the individual receiving the contract on the fair odds line that maximizes *EU*, given that the individuals are identical and everyone chooses the same level of e. Therefore, $x = y$ by the complete insurance theorem, and hence the individual's wealth is

$$w(e) = \pi(e)a + [1 - \pi(e)]z$$

whether there is an accident or not. (This is explained at the beginning of the previous subsection.) Because $\pi(e)B(w(e)) + [1 - \pi(e)]B(w(e)) = B(w(e))$, the individual's utility after purchasing insurance is

$$\mu(e) = B(w(e)) + T - e.$$

To determine the choice of effort supply by the individual at equilibrium, we set wealth equal to w, independent of one individual's effort supply, because a change in the probability of an accident by a single individual will not have an appreciable effect on the terms on which insurance can be offered. Therefore, the individual will choose e to maximize $B(w) + T - e$. Obviously, this is achieved by $e = 0$. Everyone is in the same position, so each individual sets $e = 0$. Therefore, at the competitive equilibrium individual wealth is $w(0) = \pi(0)a + [1 - \pi(0)]z$, whether or not the individual has an accident. Then each individual's utility is $B(w(0)) + T$. This will be inefficient if there is an effort level e such that

$$B\Big(w(e)\Big) + T - e > B\Big(w(0)\Big) + T.$$

Example ∂3.10 Calculating the Efficient Effort Supply

$B(w) = 4\ln(w + 3)$ and $T = 1$. Therefore, $U = 4\ln(w + 3) + 1 - e$. Note that we have $B' > 0$ and $B'' < 0$ for all w. (You may prefer to set $B(w) = 4\ln(w + 3) - 4\ln3$ to ensure that $B(0) = 0$.) Assume that $a = 24$, $z = 96$, and $\pi(e) = \frac{1}{2} - \frac{1}{4}e$, with $0 \le e \le 1$. At equilibrium, $e = 0$ and thus expected wealth is $\frac{1}{2} \times 24 + \frac{1}{2} \times 96 = 60$. Individual utility at equilibrium is $4\ln63 + 1 = 17.57$.

Calculate the efficient level of preventive care: The end of Section 2.7.2 of Chapter 2 shows why setting $x = y$ maximizes EU on the individual fair odds line. We are assuming that the probability of an accident is the same for everyone, and that a and z are the same for everyone. Given e, the probability $\pi(e)$ of an accident is determined. Given the probability of an accident, individual EU is maximized by complete insurance. Therefore, the individual's wealth will be

$$w(e) = 24\pi(e) + 96[1 - \pi(e)] = 24(\tfrac{1}{2} - \tfrac{1}{4}e) + 96(\tfrac{1}{2} - \tfrac{1}{4}e) = 60 + 18e$$

whether there is an accident or not. Hence, individual utility is

$$G(e) = 4\ln(60 + 18e + 3) + 1 - e.$$

Now, choose e to maximize $G(e)$. We have $G'(e) = (4 \times 18)(63 + 18e)^{-1} - 1 = 72(63 + 18e)^{-1} - 1$. The second derivative is $G''(e) = -72(63 + 18e)^{-2} \times 18$, which is negative for all e. Therefore, if $G'(e) = 0$ gives us a value of e between 0 and 1 it will maximize G subject to $0 \le e \le 1$.

$72/(63 + 18e) - 1 = 0$ implies $72 = 63 + 18e$, the solution of which is $e = \frac{1}{2}$. Therefore, the equilibrium, with $e = 0$, is not efficient. To test this claim compute individual utility when $e = 0$ and utility when $e = \frac{1}{2}$. (Recall that $w(e) = 60 + 18e$.)

$$G(0) = 4\ln[w(0) + 3] + 1 - 0 = 4\ln(63) + 1 = 17.57$$
$$G(\tfrac{1}{2}) = 4\ln[w(\tfrac{1}{2}) + 3] + 1 - \tfrac{1}{2} = 4\ln(72) + \tfrac{1}{2} = 17.61$$

Individual EU is 17.57 at equilibrium but would be 17.61 if everyone could be induced to set $e = \frac{1}{2}$. The competitive equilibrium is not efficient.

If insurance were not available at all then the individual of Example 3.10 would choose e to maximize

$$(\tfrac{1}{2} - \tfrac{1}{4}e)4\ln27 + (\tfrac{1}{2} + \tfrac{1}{4}e)4\ln99 + 1 - e.$$

The first derivative of this function is $- \ln27 + \ln99 - 1 = +0.299$. The individual will increase e until it reaches the upper bound of one. In other words, if insurance is not available then the individual will set $e = 1$, in which case the probability of an accident is $\frac{1}{4}$ and EU is $\frac{1}{4} \times 4\ln27 + \frac{3}{4} \times 4\ln99 + 1 - 1 = 17.08$. Note that individual

EU is higher when insurance is purchased in a competitive market, even though the individual then has a strong incentive not to devote effort to preventive care.

The difference between maximization of $B(w) + T - e$ and maximization of G is that in the former case we are modeling individual decision making, and we have to be careful not to give the individual control over the effort supply of others. Consequently, we don't have x and y change when the individual changes e. However, when we maximize G we are not modeling individual decisions but rather determining the highest level of per capita expected utility that the economy is capable of producing. Therefore we are free to change everyone's effort supply simultaneously.

∂3.11.5 Incomplete Insurance

With fair odds the individual will devote no effort to prevention. We can expect insurance companies to modify the contract to give individuals some incentive to take steps to reduce the probability of an accident. Let c denote the net insurance coverage. That is, $x = a + c$. If p is the cost of insurance per dollar of net coverage, then pc is the policy premium and thus $y = z - pc$.

The consumer will choose e and c to maximize *EU*, which is

$$V(e, c) = \pi(e)B(a + c) + [1 - \pi(e)]B(z - pc) + T - e,$$

subject to the constraints $0 \le c \le z/p$ and $0 \le e \le T$. Assume that the solution value of c lies strictly between 0 and z/p.

Let's rewrite *EU* as $V(e,c) = \pi(e)B(x) + [1 - \pi(e)]B(y) + T - e$, with $x = a + c$ and $y = z - pc$. We will use the chain rule, and the fact that $dx/dc = 1$ and $dy/dc = -p$. Then

$$\frac{\partial V}{\partial c} = \pi(e)B'(x) + [1 - \pi(e)]B'(y) \times -p$$

and

$$\frac{\partial V}{\partial e} = \pi'(e)B(x) - \pi'(e)B(y) - 1 = \pi'(e)[B(x) - B(y)] - 1.$$

When $p = \pi/(1 - \pi)$ the individual faces fair odds. Let's check: we have $x = a + c$ and $y = z - pc$. The first equation implies $c = x - a$, and when we substitute $x - a$ for c in the second equation we get $y = z - p(x - a)$. This can be expressed as $px + y = pa + z$. And if $p = \pi/(1 - \pi)$ we can multiply both sides of the equation by $1 - \pi$ yielding $\pi x + (1 - \pi)y = \pi a + (1 - \pi)z$. In summary, if $p = \pi/(1 - \pi)$ then the individual's market opportunity line embodies fair odds.

We know that with fair odds a risk-averse individual will maximize *EU* at the point where $x = y$. In that case $\partial V/\partial e = -1$. In other words, the individual can always increase expected utility by reducing e. Therefore, the individual will set $e = 0$, as we discovered in the two previous subsections.

With moral hazard, fair odds will not likely be offered, even under competitive conditions. However, if p is close to fair – that is, close to the ratio of probabilities – then x will be close to y and $-\pi'(0)[B(y) - B(x)]$ will be positive but small. (Recall that π' is negative at all effort levels. We have $y > x$ because without complete insurance the individual's wealth will be smaller when he or she suffers an accident, even with insurance.) Then $\partial V/\partial e$ will be negative when $e = 0$. If we assume diminishing returns to effort supply (or just nonincreasing returns), then $\partial V/\partial e$ will be negative for all e. In that case, the individual will still set $e = 0$ to maximize expected utility.

We have discovered that, even without fair odds, the individual will not devote any effort to prevention if the odds are close to fair. What is the efficient effort supply? Again, we maximize per capita EU. Efficiency implies fair odds. (Review the first two paragraphs of Section 2.7.5 of Chapter 2.) Fair odds and risk aversion imply complete insurance, and hence $x = y$. Then the individual will have wealth $w(e) = \pi(e)a + [1 - \pi(e)]z$, whether or not there is an accident. Note that $dw/de = -\pi'(e)(z - a)$. We maximize

$$G(e) = B(w(e)) + T - e.$$

The first derivative is $G'(e) = B'[w(e)] \times -\pi'(e)(z - a) - 1$. Because B', $-\pi'$, and $(z - a)$ are all positive, we would expect $-B'[w(0)] \times \pi(0)] \times [z - a]$ to be large and positive. That is, $G'(0)$ is positive in all but rare cases, and the efficient effort supply is positive (where $G'(e) = 0$).

Example 3.11 Equilibrium Effort Supply When Odds are Not Fair

$U = 4ln(w + 3) + 1 - e$ as in Example 3.10, with $a = 24$, $z = 96$, and $\pi(e) = \frac{1}{2} - \frac{1}{4}e$. ($0 \le e \le 1$.) In Example 3.10 we calculated the efficient effort supply by maximizing $G(e) = 4In(63 + 18e) + 1 - e$. We concluded that $G(e)$ is maximized at $e = \frac{1}{2}$. Will the individual set $e = \frac{1}{2}$ when the odds are not fair? Note that $\pi(\frac{1}{2}) = \frac{3}{8}$ and $1 - \pi(\frac{1}{2}) = \frac{5}{8}$. Fair odds would require $p = (3/8)/(5/8) = 0.6$. Suppose, instead, that $p = 0.8$. What effort will the individual supply? Because $B(w) = 4ln(w + 3)$, $\pi'(e) = -\frac{1}{4}$ for all e, and $\pi(\frac{1}{2}) = \frac{3}{8}$ we have

$$\frac{\partial V(\frac{1}{2}, c)}{\partial c} = \frac{3}{8}B'(x) + \frac{5}{8}B'(y) \times -0.8 = 0.375B'(x) - 0.5B'(y)$$

$$= 0.375 \times \frac{4}{27 + c} - 0.5 \times \frac{4}{99 - 0.8c}.$$

$$\frac{\partial V(\frac{1}{2}, c)}{\partial e} = 0.25[B(x) - B(y)] - 1 = 0.25[4ln(y + 3) - 4ln(x + 3)] - 1$$

$$= ln(99 - 0.8c) - ln(27 + c) - 1.$$

If we set $\partial V/\partial c = 0$ we get $[1.5/(27 + c)] - [2/(99 - 0.8c)] = 0$, the solution of which is $c = 29.5$. When we substitute $c = 29.5$. into $\partial V/\partial e$ we get $\partial V/\partial e = -0.71$. That is, at $e = \frac{1}{2}$ we have $\partial V/\partial e < 0$, which means that the individual would not set $e = \frac{1}{2}$ but would reduce effort supply.

Sources

The claim that the frequency of accidents goes down significantly when the drivers of police cars and rescue vehicles are electronically monitored is based on Nalebuff and Ayres (2003, pp. 107-108). Data on the net social benefit of the silent alarm

Lojack are taken from Ayres and Levitt (1998). The notion that home equity insurance would be viable if the claim were based on average house prices originated with Shiller and Weiss (1999). The sketch of HMOs is based on Dutta (2000, pp. 304–305.) Reinhardt et al. (2004) track the rate of change of health care expenditure as a fraction of GDP.

Links

Baumol (2012) explains why technological progress ensures that the fraction of GDP devoted to health care will continue to increase dramatically. The book also demonstrates that non medical consumption will also increase significantly, due to that very same technological progress. See Zeckhauser (1970) for an important early contribution to the study of deductibles and similar devices. Lazear (1992) contains additional examples of market-generated solutions to hidden action problems. Dranove (2000) provides a thorough (and nontechnical) economic analysis of the US health care industry. See Diamond (1992) for more on the social significance of the difference between risks that individuals can modify with their behavior and those that they cannot. See Dranove (2000) for a review of the evidence on the quality of care under HMOs. See Chapter 5 (especially pages 131 and 132) of Kotlikoff and Burns (2004) to see why the US government's attempt to control Medicare and Medicaid costs by enrolling participants in HMOs has not worked.

Problem Set

The first two questions assume that $T = 1$ and each individual can set $e = 0$ or 1 but not any intermediate value. If $e = 0$ then the probability of an accident is ½ but if $e = 1$ the probability of an accident is ¼.

(1) $B(w) = 2.5\sqrt{w}$, $a = 30$, and $z = 72$ for each individual. Find the competitive equilibrium and determine whether it is efficient.

(2) Each individual's utility-of-wealth function is $B(w) = 5\ln(w + 1)$ when there is no insurance. If there is an accident then the individual's wealth will be 40 but if there is no accident wealth will be 120.

    (A) If insurance is not available determine the value of e chosen by the individual, the individual's wealth if there is an accident, wealth if there is no accident, expected wealth, and EU.

    (B) If insurance is available in a competitive market determine the value of e chosen by the individual, the individual's wealth if there is an accident, wealth if there is no accident, expected wealth, and EU.

    (C) What is the efficient level of effort? Determine the resulting wealth if there is an accident, wealth if there is no accident, expected wealth, and expected utility.

The remaining questions assume that $T = 1$ and e can assume any value between 0 and 1, inclusive. Utility is $B(w) + 1 - e$.

(3) If an individual devotes e units of effort to preventive care then the probability of an accident is $1 - 0.8e$. Each individual has the expected utility function

$$\pi\sqrt{x}+(1-\pi)\sqrt{y}+1-e,$$

where π is the probability of an accident, x represents wealth if there is an accident, and y represents wealth if there is no accident. If there is no insurance then $x = 3$ and $y = 8$.

    (A) Assuming complete insurance, show how wealth depends on e.

    (B) Demonstrate that individual expected utility is higher when everyone sets $e = 0.25$ than when everyone sets $e = 0$, or everyone sets $e = 1$. Why does that establish that the competitive equilibrium is not efficient?

    (C) Assuming that everyone can be made to employ the same level of preventive care, find the value of e that maximizes per capita EU.

(4) Each individual's utility-of-wealth function is $B(w)=2\sqrt{w}$. If there is an accident then the individual's wealth will be 36 but if there is no accident then wealth will be 72. The probability of an accident is $\frac{1}{2} - 0.2e$. Answer questions A, B, and C of question 3 for this model.

(5) Let $B(w) = 10\ln(w + 1)$, and $\pi(e) = \frac{1}{2} - \frac{1}{4}e$. Show that the individual will set $x = y$ and $e = 0$ at the competitive equilibrium.

(6) Let $B(w) = \beta\ln(w + 1)$, $\pi(e) = \frac{1}{2} - \frac{1}{4}e$, and $U(x,y,\ell)=\pi B(x) + (1 - \pi)B(y) + a\ell$. Find a condition on the positive parameters α, β, a, and z that implies inefficiency of the competitive equilibrium of the insurance market.

The last three questions do not assume fair odds. Each dollar of net claim costs p dollars.

(7) Prove that a risk-averse individual will set $x < y$ if $p > \pi/(1 - \pi)$.

(8) If $B(w) = 4\ln(w + 3)$, $a = 24$, $z = 96$, and $\pi(e) = \frac{1}{2} - \frac{1}{4}e$, for what values of p will the *individual* set $e > 0$?

(9) Prove that if $p < \pi(1 - \pi)$ then the policy will not generate enough premium revenue to pay all of the claims submitted.

4

Corporate Governance

This chapter investigates incentives in firms. We explore the hidden action problems of a modern corporation. Section 4.1 compares firms in several leading industrialized countries. Section 4.2 examines the relationship between two senior executives who share the firm's profits and is followed by a brief look at the relationship between the owner and employees in an owner-managed firm (Section 4.3). The rest of the chapter is devoted to the hidden action problem confronting a widely dispersed group of shareholders whose objective is to have the firm that they jointly own maximize the value of their shares. Can they rely on the board of directors to provide the appropriate incentives to the company's management team, even though it is extremely costly for the shareholders to monitor the management and the board members as well?

4.1   A BRIEF TOUR OF SEVERAL COUNTRIES

We are primarily concerned with the attempt of a firm's owners to obtain a satisfactory return on the capital they supply to the firm. The owners provide financing when they purchase shares in the firm. They also contribute passively every time the firm uses retained earnings to purchase equipment. Firms also borrow financial capital, and in many industrialized countries bank loans are a much more important source of finance than in the United States. All the suppliers of finance want management to function in a way that brings them a high return. However, a chief executive may act in a way that benefits himself or herself at the expense of the suppliers of capital. We refer to this as the *agency problem*.

DEFINITION: *The Modern Corporation's Agency Problem*
The firm's owners and creditors seek a high return on their investments but the daily decisions that determine that rate of return are made by the firm's management team, and the managers may be assumed to have their own welfare at heart.

One striking difference between the pattern of ownership across countries lies in the role of the financial sector. US banks were prohibited from holding equity in corporations until the repeal of the Glass-Steagall Act in 1999. In the United States only 5 percent of shares are held by banks and other financial institutions, but in France, Germany, Japan, and the United Kingdom the fraction is closer to 30 percent. In fact, a Japanese corporation has a long-term relationship with a particular bank, called its *main bank*. The main bank is expected to play a significant role in monitoring the firm with which it is associated. In practice, the bank lets the firm have its way, except in times of crisis. The United States and United Kingdom are quite similar in that a firm's owners are expected to do the monitoring through their representatives, the board of directors. Apart from those in Canada, Britain, and the United States most corporations are private – their shares are not traded on a public exchange – and even the ownership of some public firms is highly concentrated, often with family ownership and control.

The fraction of shares held by *individuals* is much higher in the United States than in other countries. And the level of top executive pay is much higher in the United States, as is the fraction of executive pay that is received in the form of bonuses. (It may not be a coincidence that 43 percent of the total investment in research and development – R&D – by the leading industrial countries comes from the United States. See Baumol, 2002, for data on R&D.)

German firms have a supervisory board of directors, half of whom are elected by shareholders. The others are elected by employees. Daily operations are directed by a management board, appointed by the supervisory board. Firms in Canada, the United States, and Great Britain have a single board of directors with outside members, elected by shareholders, and inside members, the firm's top executives. The CEO (chief executive officer) is the head of the management team and is often the chairman of the board. Because the outside directors are typically nominated by the incumbent management they usually remain loyal to those chief executives. French law allows a firm to choose between the Anglo-Saxon corporate form and the German form. Japanese law makes it relatively easy for shareholders to nominate and elect directors, but the board is large and unwieldy, and in practice the owners have less influence over management than in the United States. In part that is because Japanese management is expected to give higher priority to stable employment for the firm's workers than dividends for the owners.

> In the 1960s the value of IBM shares listed on the New York Stock Exchange exceeded the entire value of the German stock market, as measured by the Frankfurt Stock Exchange.

Allen and Gale (2000) conclude that the agency problem is substantial regardless of the form of corporate governance or corporate finance. "Managers seem to get their way most of the time" (Vives, 2000, p. 2). However, Carlin and Mayer (2000) find considerable evidence that corporate governance and finance can be a significant factor for a *country*'s economic performance.

In the next section we begin our in-depth study of the agency problem by examining a simple two-person production team. By cooperating with each other, the pair can take advantage of a production technology that is superior to the one available to an individual working alone. But as soon as two or more individuals are involved, incentives come into play. Is one worker motivated to consider the effect that his or her actions have on the welfare of the other members of the team?

Sources

Allen and Gale (2000) and Vives (2000).

4.2 PARTNERSHIPS

In this section we discover why few firms are organized as partnerships. The key workers in a partnership are also the firm's *residual claimants*, who share the profits. (When we use the word partner in this chapter we actually mean what is referred to in law as an *equity* partner.)

DEFINITION: *Residual Claimant*

A firm's residual claimant is entitled to whatever money is left in the firm after all the contractual obligations have been met – workers' pay, the purchase of intermediate goods, etc.

Sometimes one partner puts more capital into the firm than the others and receives a larger share of the profits, but the essential point is that each partner shares in the income created by the effort of the other partners. By the same token, the partner receives only a fraction of the income generated by his or her own effort and thus each partner contributes less than the efficient amount of effort. The owner–employee relationship (Section 4.3) results in each person receiving a leisure-income package that the individual prefers to the one obtained in a partnership. Why, then, are partnerships are observed at all? We provide the answer at the end of the next section.

In the 1960s the Cuban government used state stores to provide citizens with equal rations of food and clothing. Housing was almost free, and every family was provided with a free vacation at the beach. Absenteeism on the job soared and productivity and product quality declined precipitously. The government reluctantly implemented a complicated and comprehensive system of monitoring (Kohler, 1977).

Why does production take place in *teams* in the first place? Because there is more output per worker in a team than when individuals work independently. In other words one-person firms generate far less output per unit of labor input than do multiperson firms. We examine these issues by means of a simple framework.

4.2.1   The Model

There are two consumer goods, leisure and income. Income is a composite commodity – the total number of dollars available for expenditure on goods other than leisure. Let x be the amount of leisure consumed and let y be the income level. $U(x, y)$ is the individual's utility function. Let T denote the length of a period, in hours. ($T = 168$ if the time period is a week.) The income generated by a production team depends on the amount of effort expended by each of the team members. If e is the amount of effort contributed by an individual, then $x = T - e$. Note that x is not just T less the number of hours "worked." An individual may show up for work but not put in much effort, consuming leisure on the job. This will affect the amount of output and income generated by the firm and also the individual's utility through its effect on leisure. Therefore, we need to keep track of effort, not hours on the job. (The quality of effort is just as important as the quantity, but we simplify the analysis by focusing on only one dimension of the principal–agent problem, the incentive to work rather than shirk.)

When individuals work on their own (in one-person firms) the equation $y = \alpha e$ represents the production technology of a single firm. It expresses the income available when e units of effort are expended. The positive constant α is the income generated per unit of effort. Because $x = T - e$ we have $y = \alpha(T - x)$ for a one-person

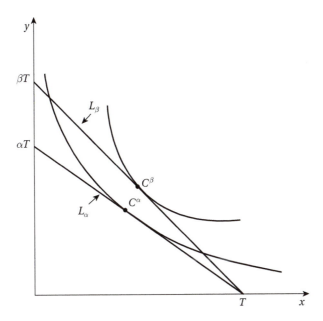

Figure 4.1

firm. The individual chooses the bundle (x, y) to maximize U subject to the production constraint $y = \alpha(T - x)$, or $\alpha x + y = \alpha T$. The chosen point $C^\alpha = (x^\alpha, y^\alpha)$, illustrated in Figure 4.1, is a point of tangency of the indifference curve and the production line L_α. In economic terms the marginal rate of substitution at C^α equals α, which is the opportunity cost of leisure – that is, the amount of income sacrificed per hour of leisure consumed. (Of course, individuals can observe their own effort levels.)

Now consider a two-person firm. Let β denote the income generated per unit of effort when two individuals cooperate in production. Let e_i denote the effort expended by i with x_i denoting the leisure consumed by i, and y_i the income of individual i $(i = 1, 2)$. Then $y_1 + y_2 = \beta(e_1 + e_2)$. Of course $\beta > \alpha$. In other words, output *per worker* is greater when production takes place in teams.

We abstract from a lot of real-world phenomena to focus on the role of incentives. For one thing, we assume that the individuals in our firm have identical preferences, and $U(x, y)$ will again represent the individual's preference scheme. And we only study firms with two-person management teams, although the generalization to n persons is straightforward. If the individuals have identical consumption then $x_1 = x_2$ and $y_1 = y_2$, and hence $e_1 = e_2$. Then $y_1 + y_2 = \beta(e_1 + e_2)$ implies $2y_i = \beta(2e_i)$ and thus $y_i = \beta e_i$. This allows us to contrast the two-person firm with the one-person firm (Figure 4.1). The *per capita* production line $y_i = \beta e_i = \beta(T - x_i)$, denoted L_β, lies above its one-person counterpart L_α at every point except where $x = T$ because $\beta > \alpha$ and L_β and L_α meet on the horizontal axis. The two-person firm can provide a higher level of per capita income than the one-person firm.

Let x, e, and y denote, respectively, individual leisure consumption, effort, and income. The time endowment is T and thus $e = T - x$. Individual utility U is a function of x and y. The per capita production function is $y = \beta e$.

Let $C^\beta = (x^\beta, y^\beta)$ denote the utility-maximizing bundle available with a two-person firm assuming that the team members consume the same bundle. That is, C^β maximizes $U(x, y)$ subject to $y = \beta(T - x)$. The marginal rate of substitution at C^β equals β, which is the opportunity cost of leisure per person in a two-person team. We can also say that C^β maximizes $U(x, y)$ subject to $y \leq \beta(T - x)$: if $y < \beta(T - x)$ we can increase utility by increasing *both* x and y without violating $y \leq \beta(T - x)$.

We can call the outcome that gives each person the bundle C^β *fair* precisely because both people have identical preferences and receive identical consumption under C^β. Because the outcome is also efficient it is a reasonable standard by which to measure the performance of a contractual arrangement, particularly if we expect each of the team members to have identical consumption and utility levels, as in the case of the simple model of this section.

Efficiency Theorem

For any number of identical workers, the outcome that gives C^β to each person is fair and efficient.

Proof:

The outcome C^β is fair by definition. To prove efficiency, let (x_1, y_1) and (x_2, y_2) be two bundles that give one person more utility than C^β and the other person at least as much. Say,

$$U(x_1, y_1) > U(x^\beta, y^\beta) \quad \text{and} \quad U(x_2, y_2) \geq U(x^\beta, y^\beta).$$

Because C^β maximizes U subject to $y_i \leq \beta (T - x_i)$ anything that gives higher utility than C^β must violate the inequality $y_i \leq \beta(T - x_i)$. Therefore $y_1 > \beta(T - x_1)$. If we actually had $y_2 < \beta(T - x_2)$ then we could increase both y_2 and x_2 to satisfy $y_2 = \beta(T - x_2)$, and that would result in an increase in utility for person 2. This new utility level would be higher than $U(x^\beta, y^\beta)$ because we already have $U(x_2, y_2) \geq U(x^\beta, y^\beta)$. In that case we have contradicted the fact that (x^β, y^β) maximizes U subject to $y = \beta(T - x)$. Therefore we have

$$y_1 > \beta(T - x_1) \quad \text{and} \quad y_2 \geq \beta(T - x_2),$$

and hence $y_1 + y_2 > \beta(T - x_1 + T - x_2) = \beta(e_1 + e_2)$. Then the new outcome that assigns (x_i, y_i) to each i is not feasible: the total income allocated exceeds $\beta(e_1 + e_2)$, the total available income generated by the effort supplied. Similarly, $U(x_1, y_1) \geq U(x^\beta, y^\beta)$ and $U(x_2, y_2) > U(x^\beta, y^\beta)$ cannot hold for any feasible pair (x_1, y_1) and (x_2, y_2). Therefore, the outcome assigning C^β to each is efficient – there is no feasible outcome that gives both persons at least as much utility as C^β and one person strictly more. ∎

Note that the argument easily extends to a team of more than two individuals.

Can C^β in fact be realized? C^β is feasible, but only when the two individuals cooperate. But then one person's income depends on the total income of the team, which in turn depends on the amount of effort contributed by *both* persons. Will there be incentive for each to contribute the required amount of effort? Consider the partnership case.

4.2.2 A Two-Person Partnership

The rules of partnership are simple. The partners share equally in the income that is created by their joint effort, and any losses are absorbed equally by the individual partners.

DEFINITION: *Partnership*

A firm that is managed by the residual claimants who share the profits. The firm's constitution specifies the share of profit going to each partner. For convenience, we assume that the shares are equal.

Professional service industries employ the partnership method of team organization more than any other contractual form. Partnership is the typical form for accounting firms, law firms, and medical clinics. Apart from professional services, however, large firms are rarely organized as partnerships. (By 1900 investment banking had largely converted from partnerships to the standard corporate owner–employee form, although partnerships may return to that industry in a limited way as a result of the great recession of 2007–2009.) Why are partnerships widely employed in the professional service industries but rarely in evidence elsewhere? To answer that question we need to focus on the amount of effort contributed by a utility-maximizing partner.

We assume $n = 2$ until further notice. If effort is unobservable, how can a team member determine the effort supplied by the other partner at equilibrium? By working out the utility-maximizing responses to the incentives governing the partner's behavior. Also, the individual can determine the total effort supplied by others simply by observing total output y, inferring the total effort supplied, and then subtracting the person's own effort.

We put the spotlight on partner 1. Person 1 chooses (x_1, y_1) to maximize $U(x_1, y_1)$ subject to the sharing rule $y_1 = \frac{1}{2}\beta(e_1 + e_2)$ that determines a partner's income. Partner 1 cannot control e_2, so we take it as fixed, at c. That is, when partner 1 changes her effort supply we assume that partner 2's effort level does not change. But y_1 changes as a result of the change in e_1. We will be at equilibrium if each partner's effort level maximizes his or her own utility given the other partner's effort level. We have $e_1 = T - x_1$ so partner 1 will endeavor to maximize $U(x_1, y_1)$ subject to $y_1 = \frac{1}{2}\beta(T - x_1 + c)$. The constraint can be expressed as $\frac{1}{2}\beta x_1 + y_1 = \frac{1}{2}\beta(T + c)$, which is

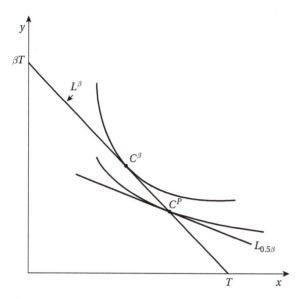

Figure 4.2

$L_{0.5\beta}$ in Figure 4.2. This is a budget line. (The line $L_{0.5\beta}$ extends to both axes, with intercepts $(x_1, y_1) = (T + c, 0)$ and $(x_1, y_1) = (0, \frac{1}{2}\beta(T + c))$ but the diagram does not show that.) The individual opportunity cost of leisure is $\frac{1}{2}\beta$ under the partnership sharing rule. It is the ratio of the "prices" of the two goods. If person i consumes one more hour of leisure the *firm* loses one hour of effort and thus β dollars of income, but individual i loses only $\frac{1}{2}\beta$ dollars of income because the β dollars of income generated would have been shared with the other person. Therefore, utility maximization requires equality between the marginal rate of substitution (MRS) and the opportunity cost $\frac{1}{2}\beta$. Compare this with our derivation of C^{β}: in that case the constraint line was $y_1 = \beta e_1$, or $y_1 = \beta(T - x_1)$, or $\beta x_1 + y_1 = \beta T$. Because at C^{β} the social (or team) opportunity cost of leisure is β, and the marginal rate of substitution equals β.

Because the partners are identical, we can drop the subscript. The variables will pertain to one of the partners – either one, but only one. Let $C^P = (x^P, y^P)$ be the individual's choice at equilibrium under the partnership arrangement. The partners will have the same consumption at equilibrium because they have the same preferences and are confronted with the same incentives. We know that $C^P \neq C^{\beta}$ because the MRS is $\frac{1}{2}\beta$ at C^P and double that at C^{β}. We also know that the utility of C^{β} exceeds the utility of C^P because C^{β} *maximizes* utility subject to $y \leq \beta e$, and C^P is one of the bundles that satisfies $y \leq \beta e$. To prove the latter claim note that $y^P + y^P \leq \beta(e^P + e^P)$ because the partnership outcome is feasible. (Recall that the partners make the same choices at equilibrium, and whenever we fail to employ a subscript it is implicit that the variable applies to each individual.) Therefore, $y^P \leq \beta e^P$. Hence the partnership outcome gives each person less utility than C^{β}, which is feasible. Not only that, C^P provides more leisure but less income than C^{β}. The increased consumption of leisure at C^P is due to the fact that the opportunity cost of leisure to the individual in a partnership is half of the opportunity cost to the team: half of the β dollars lost to the firm when i consumes another unit of leisure would have been given to the other partner.

To show that leisure consumption is higher under C^P than under C^β try placing C^P *above* C^β on L_β by increasing y and decreasing x. Now draw the indifference curve through C^P. It has an MRS of $\frac{1}{2}\beta$ at C^P so the curve is flatter than L_β at C^P. The indifference curve through C^P is flatter than L_β at C^P, and it gets flatter as we move to the right. The MRS at C^β is equal to β, and thus the indifference curve through C^β is tangent to L_β at C^β, and it gets steeper as we move to the left. Consequently, the two indifference curves would have to intersect, which is logically impossible. The following is a formal proof:

Inefficiency Theorem for Partnership

Individual utility is higher at the fair and efficient outcome C^β than at the partnership equilibrium C^P, and each partner supplies less effort than at the fair and efficient outcome.

Proof:

If $x^\beta = x^P$ then $C^\beta = C^P$ because both are on the negatively sloped line L_β. That contradicts the fact that the MRS at C^β is double the MRS at C^P.

Suppose that $x^\beta > x^P$ actually holds. Find the point y on $L_{0.5\beta}$ that is directly above C^β. That is, find the point y such that (x^β, y) is on $L_{0.5\beta}$. The point (x^β, y) will satisfy $\frac{1}{2}\beta x^\beta + y = \frac{1}{2}\beta x^P + y^P$. When we solve this for y we get

$$y = \frac{1}{2}\beta x^P + y^P - \frac{1}{2}\beta x^\beta. \tag{1}$$

Because C^β and C^P are both on the budget constraint L_β we also have $\beta x^P + y^P = \beta x^\beta + y^\beta$ and thus $y^P = \beta x^\beta + y^\beta - \beta x^P$. When we substitute the right-hand side of this last equation for y^P in [1] we get

$$y = \frac{1}{2}\beta x^P + \beta x^\beta + y^\beta - \beta x^P - \frac{1}{2}\beta x^\beta = y^\beta + \frac{1}{2}\beta\left(x^\beta - x^P\right).$$

It follows that $x^\beta > x^P$ implies $y > y^\beta$. Then $U(x^\beta, y) > U(x^\beta, y^\beta)$ because (x^β, y) has the same amount of X as C^β but more Y. And $U(x^\beta, y^\beta) \geq U(x^P, y^P)$ also holds because C^β maximizes U on L_β. Therefore, $U(x^\beta, y) > U(x^P, y^P)$, contradicting the fact that $U(x^P, y^P)$ maximizes U on $L_{0.5\beta}$. We have to drop the supposition that $x^P \leq x^\beta$. ∎

The proof implicitly assumes that U has a well-defined MRS at each point, and hence for any downward sloping line L the indifference curve through (x, y) is tangent to L if (x, y) maximizes U on L.

We used the theory of consumer choice to derive C^P. We did so by determining the individual's demand for each commodity. But commodity 2 is income. Why doesn't the individual have an infinite demand for income? Because he or she has to pay for each dollar of additional income with an increased supply of effort and hence a sacrifice of leisure.

Example 4.1 A Specific Case with Two Partners

Let $U(x, y) = xy$, $\beta = 2$, and $T = 24$. (We'll ignore the subscript at first.) To find C^β we maximize U subject to $y = 2 \times e = 2(24 - x)$. Replace y in the utility function with $48 - 2x$ and then maximize $x(48 - 2x) = 48x - 2x^2$. This quadratic is maximized at $x^\beta = 48/4 = 12$. (The first derivative is $48 - 4x$ and the second derivative is negative.) Then $y^\beta = 48 - 24 = 24$. We have $C^\beta = (12, 24)$. (Confirm that this is feasible: total effort is 24 and thus total income is 48, which is shared.)

To find C^P, the partnership equilibrium, we solve

$$\text{maximize } x_1 y_1 \text{ subject to } y_1 = \tfrac{1}{2} \times 2(24 - x_1 + e_2).$$

Substitute $24 - x_1 + e_2$ for y_1 in the utility function, and then maximize $x_1(24 - x_1 + e_2)$, treating e_2 as a constant. Then we maximize $x_1(24 - x_1 + e_2) = (24 + e_2)x_1 - x_1^2$. This quadratic is maximized when $x_1 = (24 + e_2)/2$. (The first derivative is $(24 + e_2) - 2x_1$ and the second derivative is negative.) Setting $e_2 = e_1 = 24 - x_1$ and substituting $24 - x_1$ for e_2 yields $x_1 = 12 + 12 - \tfrac{1}{2}x_1$ and hence $x_1 = 16$. Therefore, $y_1 = y_2 = 16$. At the partnership equilibrium, $x^P = 16$, $y^P = 16$, and $e^P = 8$ for each person.

Compare utility levels: at the fair and efficient allocation C^β each person's utility equals $x^\beta \times y^\beta = 12 \times 24 = 288$. At the partnership equilibrium C^P utility equals $x^P \times y^P = 16 \times 16 = 256$ for each, which is about 11% less than the utility at C^β.

If we set $e_2 = e_1$ too early (i.e., before taking the derivative) we ascribe to partner 1 the ability to control the effort supply of partner 2, and we will not arrive at the equilibrium.

The partnership outcome is not efficient; there is another *feasible* outcome that would give each more utility. Section 4.3 shows that a different contractual arrangement can give each team member the incentive to supply the amount of effort required by the fair and efficient outcome C^β. First, we consider whether incentives are different in a long-term partnership relationship.

4.2.3 Reputation and Repeated Interaction

Section 1.7.3 of Chapter 1 showed that an efficient level of cooperation can be sustained in a relationship that is repeated indefinitely. We now apply this reasoning to partnerships. (This section is self-contained, but it might be wise to read the concluding section of Chapter 1 – particularly 1.7.3.) The infinite horizon assumption is a good way to model a long-term business relationship in which the finite lifetime of a business has no bearing on individual decision making in the early stages or even the intermediate term.

The two partners interact repeatedly for an infinite number of periods, $1, 2, \ldots, t, \ldots$. We represent the individual's preferences by discounting the sum of the single period utilities. If δ is the discount rate and u_t is the partner's period t utility, then the individual maximizes

$$u_1 + \delta u_2 + \delta^2 u_3 + \ldots + \delta^{t-1} u_t + \ldots$$

where $0 < \delta < 1$. The discount rate δ is less than 1 to reflect the fact that more distant periods get less weight when we formulate plans today for work and consumption today and into the future. An individual who is relatively patient – who requires a lower premium to be induced to postpone consumption – will have a higher discount factor. But because $\delta < 1$ the discount factor δ^t will be close to zero if t is sufficiently large, reflecting the fact that very remote periods get almost no weight in current decision making. Recall that the infinite sum $a + a\delta + a\delta^2 + \cdots + a\delta^{t\cdots}$ equals $a/(1 - \delta)$ when $0 < \delta < 1$ (Section 1.7.2 of Chapter 1).

As in the static partnership model we simplify the analysis by assuming that the partners have identical utility functions. In the static (one-shot) case we found that there is an efficient individual effort supply e^β that is larger than the effort supply e^P at the partnership equilibrium. The individual partner maximizes utility by choosing $e^P < e^\beta$ because the individual opportunity cost of leisure consumption is only half the opportunity cost to the two-person team. The effort supply e^P by each partner results in each consuming $C^P = (x^P, y^P)$ where $x^P = 24 - e^P$ and $y^P = \frac{1}{2}\beta(e^P + e^P)$. The efficient effort supply e^β supports the commodity bundle C^β. Although $U(C^\beta) > U(C^P)$, the consumption plan C^β does not emerge at equilibrium in a one-period model because e^β is not a best response by one partner to the supply of e^β by the other. However, when the partnership relationship is repeated period after period, one partner has an opportunity to punish the other for deviating from the efficient effort supply. The punishment takes place in future periods of course and, unless the discount rate is very low, the one-period gain to a deviating partner will not be large enough to offset the very large number of rounds of future punishment.

Specifically, if the discount rate is sufficiently large then we have a Nash equilibrium where each partner supplies e^β in the first period, and e^β in any period t provided that the other supplied e^β in the previous $t - 1$ periods, *and* a partner threatens to supply e^P every period following any period t in which the other partner failed to supply e^β.

Example 4.2 Infinitely Repeated Version of Example 4.1

Let $U(x, y) = xy$, $\beta = 2$ and $T = 24$. We derived $C^\beta = (12, 24)$ with $e^\beta = 12$ in the one-shot case (Example 4.1). At the one-period partnership equilibrium we have $e^P = 8$ with $C^P = (16, 16)$. Note that $U(C^\beta) = 288$ and $U(C^P) = 256$. One Nash equilibrium for the infinitely repeated partnership has each partner supplying 12 hours of effort in the first period and every subsequent period as long as the other partner supplied 12 hours in each previous period, but will supply 8 hours of effort in period t and every subsequent period if the other partner did not supply 12 hours of effort in period $t - 1$.

Suppose that partner 1 deviates from $e = 12$ in period t. What's the highest one-period utility that a partner can achieve when the other partner supplies 12 hours of effort? The answer is obtained by maximizing $U(x, y)$ when $y = \frac{1}{2} \times 2 \times (24 - x + 12)$. That is, we maximize $x(24 - x + 12) = 36x - x^2$. Using the formula for maximizing a quadratic (Section 2.1 of Chapter 2) or calculus yields $x = 36/2 = 18$. Then partner 1 will supply 6 hours of effort. Each individual's income will be $\frac{1}{2} \times 2(6 + 12) = 18$ and partner 1's period t utility will be $U(18, 18) = 324$. (One can also solve for x by setting the MRS, which is y/x, equal to partner 1's opportunity cost of leisure, which is $\frac{1}{2} \times 2$, and then using the budget constraint $y = 24 - x + 12$.)

By deviating in period t, partner 1 gets an increase in utility of at most $324 - 288 = 36$. But he is then punished by partner 2 in period $t + 1$ and every subsequent period. Partner 2 supplies 8 hours of effort in period $t + 1$ and beyond. We already know what partner 1's best one-shot response is because we have a unique Nash equilibrium of the one-shot game when each supplies 8 hours of effort. Therefore, each will supply 8 hours of effort from period $t + 1$ on. Hence the deviating partner will get a utility of at most 256 in each of those periods. Had he not deviated, utility would have been 288 each period. Therefore, by deviating partner 1 gets a utility bonus of at most 36 in period t but suffers a utility penalty of at least $288 - 256 = 32$ in every period after the tth. Discounting to period t, we find that deviating will not be profitable if

$$36 - 32\delta - 32\delta^2 - 32\delta^3 - \ldots \leq 0$$

And this simplifies to $36 \leq 32\delta/(1 - \delta)$. Therefore, deviating cannot benefit a player if $36 - 36\delta \leq 32\delta$, or $\delta \geq 36/68 = 0.53$.

If the discount rate is 0.53 or higher then the trigger strategy specified in the first paragraph of Example 4.2 is a Nash equilibrium. The efficient outcome can be sustained if the partnership lasts many periods and the partners are not too impatient. However, it is just *one* of the Nash equilibria in the infinitely repeated partnership. There are many other equilibria. At the other extreme, if each announces his intention to supply e^P in each period of the repeated game, whatever the other does, then we have a Nash equilibrium of the repeated game whatever the discount rate. (e^P is the amount of effort that emerges in the one-shot Nash equilibrium.)

Sources

Alchian and Demsetz (1972). The discussion of repeated interaction in a partnership is based on Radner (1991).

Links

See Milgrom and Roberts (1992, pp. 522–523) on the conversion of investment banks from partnerships. See Kandel and Lazear (1992) on the role of peer pressure in partnerships. See Aoki (2000) for a perspective on the computer industry in the Silicon Valley. Levin and Tadelis (2005) provide an in-depth examination of a partnership extending over time. Williams and Radner (1995) show how the introduction of uncertainty *improves* the prospects for risk-neutral partners achieving an efficient outcome.

Problem Set

(1) Find the fair and efficient outcome and the partnership equilibrium for Example 4.1 by using the theory of consumer choice. This means that you have to set the MRS equal to the price ratio for the appropriate budget line. For the utility function $U = xy$, the MRS at generic bundle (x, y) is y/x.

(2) Find the partnership equilibrium in a two-person firm with the following features: $T = 24$, and each individual has the utility function $U = 5\ln(x + 1) + y$. Each dollar of income generated by the firm requires a total of two hours of effort per day as input.

(3) Determine the equilibrium of a two-partner firm in which each partner has the utility function $U(x, y) = 8\sqrt{x} + y$, $T = 24$ and the output/input ratio is two. Show that the outcome is inefficient.

(4) Determine the equilibrium of a two-partner firm in which each partner has the utility function $U(x, y) = 16\sqrt{x} + y$, $T = 24$, and the output/input ratio is two. Show that the outcome is inefficient.

(5) A firm has *four* partners and each has the utility function $U(x, y) = \sqrt{x} \times y$, with $T = 24$. An individual's MRS at the bundle (x, y) is $y/2x$. The firm's profit, before deducting the partners' pay, is \$50 multiplied by the total effort supplied. Prove that the partnership equilibrium is $C^P = (16, 400)$. That is, prove that at the equilibrium, each partner has $x = 16$ and $y = 400$.

(6) Consider a model of team production in which total income is four times the total amount of effort supplied. There are two individuals on the team and each individual i has the utility function $U(x, y) = x^2 y$ and $T = 24$.

  (A) Determine the commodity bundle that maximizes person 1's utility subject to the production technology constraint and the requirement that the partners wind up with identical utility levels.

  (B) Determine the partnership equilibrium. Make sure you identify the amount of each good consumed by each person.

(7) $U(x, y) = xy$ and $T = 24$ as in Example 4.1. Show that x^β, leisure consumption at the fair and efficient outcome, is 12 for any positive value of β. Explain why that is the case. (*Hint*: Express the per capita production function $y = \beta e$ as the budget constraint $\beta x + y = 24\beta$ involving the two commodities X and Y, and then use income and substitution effect analysis to explain what happens to x when β increases. Note that β appears on the right-hand side of the budgets constraint as well as on the left.)

(8) Using the parameters of Example 4.2 show that there is a Nash equilibrium of the infinitely repeated partnership in which each partner supplies 10 hours of effort each period.

(9) Translate the condition on δ into a condition on the interest rate, guaranteeing that the Nash equilibrium of Example 4.2 is in fact a Nash equilibrium of the infinitely repeated partnership. Do the same for the equilibrium of question 7.

4.3   THE OWNER–EMPLOYEE RELATIONSHIP

We continue with the simple case of a two-person production team without repetition. The previous section showed that the partnership sharing rule resulted in an inefficient outcome. Under that formula, the individual's opportunity cost of leisure consumption is half of the opportunity cost to the team. (The opportunity cost of leisure consumption to an individual partner, β/n, falls as n, the number of partners, increases.) Therefore, each partner overconsumes leisure – in the sense that the resulting outcome is inefficient. We are about to see that an efficient outcome can be reached if one of the team members is singled out as the owner, and then pays the other person – the worker - a high income, but only if the worker supplies a high level of effort. The owner then keeps every dollar of profit after paying the worker. That makes the *owner* the residual claimant, with an individual opportunity cost of leisure consumption of β, the opportunity cost to the team. Because the individual and the social (i.e., team) opportunity costs of leisure consumption are identical, the owner is motivated to supply the amount of effort that leads to the fair and efficient outcome. The worker is also induced to deliver that effort supply because he or she doesn't get paid otherwise.

DEFINITION: *Residual Claimant*

A member of a production team is the residual claimant if that person has title to all of the revenue left over after all contractual obligations are met. In everyday language, the residual claimant gets the enterprise's profit.

Suppose that person 1 is the sole owner of the two-person firm of Section 4.2, and she hires individual 2 as the second member of the team. The two individuals work together as in a partnership but the reward scheme is quite different: person 1 pays person 2 an income of y_2 with the residual income going to the owner person 1. That is $y_1 = \beta(e_1 + e_2) - y_2$. To determine e_1 and e_2 we need to be more explicit about the worker's contract. The owner agrees to pay the worker exactly y^β, no more and no less, provided that the worker, person 2, supplies *at least* e^β units of effort. Recall that $C^\beta = (x^\beta, y^\beta)$ is the bundle that maximizes individual utility on the per capita production line $y = \beta e = \beta(T - x)$. If person 2's effort supply is less than e^β he is not paid at all.

DEFINITION: *The Worker's Contract*

The worker's pay y_2 equals y^β if $e_2 \geq e^\beta$ and $y_2 = 0$ if $e_2 < e^\beta$.

Note that this contract requires monitoring by the owner to ensure that the threshold effort level e^β is reached. We assume initially that monitoring is costless. When we turn to the case of significant monitoring costs, at the end of this section, we will see that the higher these costs are, the more likely it is that the firm will be organized as a partnership.

Assuming that the worker's utility at (x^β, y^β) is at least as high as he can obtain by working elsewhere – or by staying home and consuming leisure – it is in the worker's interest to supply exactly e^β units of effort and receive the income y^β. If $e_2 < e^\beta$ the worker is dismissed. Even if he gets a new job, there will be costs associated with the transition, and consequently the worker's utility will fall below $U(C^\beta)$.

Now consider the owner's situation. The owner wishes to maximize $U(x_1, y_1)$ subject to the two constraints $y_1 = \beta(e_1 + e^\beta) - y^\beta$ and $x_1 = T - e_1$. Recall that $y^\beta = \beta e^\beta$. Then person 1 will maximize $U(x_1, y_1)$ subject to $y_1 = \beta e_1 + \beta e^\beta - y^\beta = \beta e_1 = \beta(T - x_1)$. But $y_1 = \beta(T - x_1)$ is the equation of the line L_β in Figure 4.1, and we already know that C^β maximizes utility on that line. Therefore, it is in the owner's interest to choose C^β, which means that she supplies e^β units of effort. We have designed a contract regime such that each person has an incentive to supply e^β units of effort and as a result each receives the bundle C^β, and this outcome is efficient. (Efficiency of C^β was proved in Section 4.2.1.) We have established the following:

Efficiency of the Owner-Employee Relationship

The fair and efficient outcome can be implemented by a contract that makes one member of the team the residual claimant, whereas the other gets paid the fair and efficient income level, but only if he or she supplies the fair and efficient level of effort.

Instead of a contract that pays the worker y^β if his effort is e^β or more and zero otherwise, the owner could simply offer a wage of β and let the worker choose his utility-maximizing basket (x_2, y_2) subject to the budget constraint $\beta x + y = \beta T$. The line representing this budget constraint is L_β of Figure 4.2. Therefore, the offer of a wage of β leads the worker to choose C^β as in the case of the "contribute e^β or else" contract. Either contract is effective, although they have slightly different monitoring consequences. (What are the differences?)

Why do the owner and employee receive the same level of utility, $U(x^\beta, y^\beta)$, at equilibrium? The owner does not get a bonus for risk taking, because there is no risk in our simple model. Imagine a community in which many of the individuals have access to the technology that converts input into output at the rate of β dollars of income per unit of effort. If *all* firms pay their workers less than y^β then owners must get more than y^β. Workers can leave the firm and start their own businesses in which they receive

Silicon Valley engineers average only eleven months in one job. They often brainstorm with employees of other firms. There is more loyalty to one's profession than to one's firm (McMillan, 2002, pp. 113-114). In general, the benefits of technological progress are not all captured by suppliers of capital because the owners of firms compete with each other for the skilled labor needed to implement the technological innovations. This drives up wages, passing on part of the fruits of progress to workers.

$U(x^\beta, y^\beta)$ as owner. The Silicon Valley of California is celebrated for this. However, if the workers do better than the owners, the latter can be expected to sell their businesses and seek jobs as workers. This will increase the supply of workers and lower their pay.

Example 4.3 A Large Number of Workers and Costless Monitoring

Let $U(x, y) = xy$, $\beta = 2$, and $T = 24$, as in Example 4.1, but this time we assume that there are n workers. With n team members the per capita production line is still $y = 2e = 2(24 - x)$, and thus we still have $C^\beta = (12, 24)$. If person 1 is the residual claimant and pays each of the other $n - 1$ individuals $24 provided that they supply 12 units of effort, then each worker will accept such a contract. (Suppose that the only alternative is staying home and consuming the bundle (24, 0), which delivers zero units of utility.) The owner then chooses x and y to maximize $U = xy$ subject to

$$y = 2[e + 12(n - 1)] - (n - 1)24.$$

This equation reflects the fact that the total effort supply is $e + 12(n - 1)$, where e is the owner's effort, and the owner has to pay $24 to each of the $n - 1$ workers, hence the subtraction of $24(n - 1)$ from the team revenue of $2[e + 12(n - 1)]$. The equation $y = 2[e + 12(n - 1)] - (n - 1)24$ clearly reduces to $y = 2e$, and we know that $C^\beta = (12, 24)$ maximizes $U = xy$ on the line $y = 2(24 - x)$. Therefore, the owner also supplies 12 units of effort. Each team member receives the fair and efficient bundle (12, 24).

Next we work out the partnership equilibrium: to find C^P we solve

$$\text{maximize } x_1 y_1 \text{ subject to } y_1 = \tfrac{1}{n} \times 2(24 - x_1 + c)$$

where c is the sum of everyone's effort supply except individual 1. That's not something that person 1 can control, so we treat c as a constant. Replace y_1 in the utility function with $(1/n) \times 2(24 - x_1 + c)$ and maximize

$$V(x_1) = x_1 \times \frac{1}{n} \times 2(24 - x_1 + c) = \frac{2}{n} \times (24 + c)x_1 - \frac{2}{n} \times x_1^2.$$

This quadratic is maximized at

$$x_1 = \frac{(48 + 2c)/n}{4/n} = 12 + \frac{c}{2}.$$

At equilibrium everyone supplies the same effort and hence consumes the same amount of leisure. Therefore, $c = (n - 1)(24 - x_1)$. We now have

$$x_1 = 12 + \frac{(n - 1)(24 - x_1)}{2}$$

the solution of which is $x_1 = 24n/(n + 1)$. (Confirm that $x_1 = 16$ when $n = 2$.) Because $T = 24$, effort supply is zero when $x_1 = 24$. Therefore, for large n an individual partner's leisure consumption is close to 24 and effort supply is close to zero. Specifically, $e_1 = 24/(n + 1)$. Total effort supply is $n \times 24/(n + 1)$. Therefore, the total profit to be shared by the partners is $2 \times [n/(n + 1)] \times 24$. Individual income is thus $48/(n + 1)$. What is individual utility at C^P where

$$x^P = \frac{24n}{n+1} \quad \text{and} \quad y^P = \frac{48}{n+1} ?$$

(At equilibrium $x_1 = x_2$ and $y_1 = y_2$, and we denote these by x^P and y^P respectively.)

$$U(C^P) = [24n/(n+1)] \times [48/(n+1)] = 12 \times 24 \times 4n/[(n+1)(n+1)].$$

Recall that 12×24 is individual utility at the fair and efficient bundle (Example 4.1). Because $n < n + 1$ we have

$$\frac{4n}{(n+1)(n+1)} < \frac{4}{n+1}.$$

Therefore, $U(C^P)$ is less than $4U(C^\beta)/(n + 1)$. When n is large, $U(C^P)$ is a small fraction of $U(C^\beta)$. The differential between $U(C^P)$ and $U(C^\beta)$ increases with n. In fact, $U(C^P)$ is close to zero for large n.

Very few firms are organized as partnerships. That's because each partner receives only a fraction — $(1/n)$th if there are n partners - of the income generated by his or her own effort. Thus there is an incentive to undersupply effort, and hence the equilibrium leisure–income bundle consumed by each partner provides a lower level of utility than the ideal plan C^β, which can be realized by the owner-worker regime. This utility differential is greater the larger is the number of partners, because the individual's opportunity cost of leisure consumption falls as n increases. Then why do partnerships exist at all? The answer has to do with the costs of monitoring the worker to ensure that the threshold level of effort e^β has been supplied. In some enterprises the manager (or the manager's agent) need do little more than ascertain that the worker is on the job and at the appropriate workstation to determine that there is no shirking (i.e., that $e_i \geq e^\beta$). If bicycle wheels are being produced and a sample reveals wheels with missing spokes it is a relatively easy matter to determine the source of the problem. The costs of monitoring are low in these cases. (A worker's output can be tracked electronically in some production processes.) Even when the per capita monitoring cost m is subtracted from C^β there is still substantially higher utility, $U(x^\beta, y^\beta - m)$, than is provided by the partnership outcome C^P.

However, monitoring costs are very high in firms that provide sophisticated consulting or diagnostic services. Consider a team of accountants, lawyers, or physicians. If one member of the team is to verify that another has done a good job for a client then the former would essentially have to retrace the latter's steps. In that case the per capita technological income-leisure trade-off line L_m *for the owner-worker regime* will be parallel to L_β but strictly below it, the vertical distance between the two providing a measure of the per capita monitoring cost m. The utility-maximizing bundle on L_m is C^m, assuming that the two individuals receive the same bundle (Figure 4.3). The partnership scheme does not require monitoring

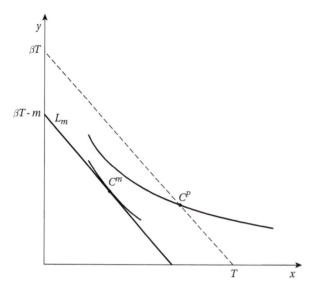

Figure 4.3

so L_β remains the appropriate trade-off line in that case. Figure 4.3 shows that $U(C^P)$ will exceed $U(C^m)$ if m is sufficiently large. However, given the per capita monitoring cost m, the per capita partnership utility level $U(C^P)$ falls as n increases. Therefore, large firms are much less likely to be organized as partnerships than small firms. (Do you tend to study in a team of two or three people or in a larger group?)

Theorem: The Owner–Employee Equilibrium with Costly Monitoring

There are n team members, person 1 is the owner and residual claimant, and k is the cost of monitoring an individual worker. The preferences of each team member can be represented by a common utility function $U(x,y)$. At equilibrium, x maximizes $U(x,(\beta(24-x) - (n-1)k/n))$ and $e_i = e_1$ for each $i \geq 2$, with $y_i = \beta e_i - \frac{(n-1)k}{n}$ for each $i \geq 1$.

Proof:

We begin by demonstrating that the owner will share the total monitoring cost with the workers. (The owner does not require monitoring of course.) In our simple model each of the n team members is just as productive as any other team member and their preferences can be represented by a common utility function. Therefore, the owner's utility cannot be less than a worker's utility at equilibrium, because that would motivate the owner to dissolve the firm and join another enterprise as a worker. The original situation could not have been an equilibrium. If a worker's utility is less than an owner's the former would be motivated to quit and start his or her own firm. We can't have equilibrium in that case either. Therefore, the total cost of monitoring the $n-1$ workers is shared by the n team members. The cost per individual is $\frac{(n-1)k}{n}$. (There are $n-1$ workers.)

Let x^* maximize $U(x,(\beta(24-x)-(n-1)k/n))$. Set $e^* = T - x^*$, where T is the time endowment, and set $y^* = \beta e^* - \frac{(n-1)k}{n}$. If each of the n workers supplies e^* hours of effort and is paid y^* then person 1, as residual claimant will receive

$$y_1 = \beta(e_1 + (n-1)e^*) - (n-1)y^* - (n-1)k$$

which is profit R, before deducting the income of any of the team members, minus what is paid to the $n-1$ workers and the total monitoring cost $(n-1)k$. Then

$$y_1 = \beta e_1 + (n-1)\beta e^* - (n-1)\beta e^* + \frac{(n-1)^2 k}{n} - (n-1)k$$

$$= \beta e_1 - \frac{(n^2 - 2n + 1 - n^2 + n)k}{n} = \beta e_1 - \frac{(n-1)k}{n}.$$

Therefore, person 1 will maximize $U(x_1, \beta(24-x_1)-(n-1)k/n)$. We know that this is maximized at $x_1 = x^* = T - e^*$. Therefore, at equilibrium each worker will be offered a contract that pays $\beta e^* - \frac{(n-1)k}{n}$ provided that at least e^* hours of effort is supplied; otherwise pay is zero. The worker will accept the contract and supply e^* units of effort because he or she cannot do better as the owner of a firm. The owner of the firm in question will respond by also supplying e^* units of effort. Profit will be $\beta n e^* - (n-1)k$ and it will be shared equally by the n team members. ∎

The next example works out the equilibrium in a special case. Monitoring cost needs to be factored in when working out the owner-employee equilibrium, but not when determining the partnership equilibrium which is enforced by means of incentives: a partner chooses the effort level that maximizes his or her utility, given the effort choices of the other partners. The section ends with a brief discussion of monitoring in partnerships, however.

Example 4.4 Costly Monitoring with a Two-Person Team

$U(x, y) = xy$ for each of the n team members. The time endowment (T) is 24, and total profit (R) before deducting the incomes paid to the team members is 12 times the total effort supplied. If workers have to be monitored the cost is 36 per *worker*.

If $n = 2$ and the team forms a partnership the individual partner maximizes $x[6(24 - x + c)]$ where c represents the effort supplied by the other partner. The first derivative is $144 - 12x + 6c$. Set this equal to zero. (Confirm that the second derivative is negative.) We have $144 - 12x + 6c = 0$. *Now* we can set $c = e = 24 - x$, where x is the leisure consumption of the individual whose utility we are maximizing. We get $144 - 12x + 6(24 - x) = 288 - 18x$. When we set this equal to zero and solve for x we get

$$x^P = 16, \text{ and hence } e^P = 8 \text{ and } y^P = 96.$$

This is C^P, the partnership equilibrium when $n = 2$. $U(C^P) = 16 \times 96 = 1536$ if $n = 2$. Under the *owner-employee relationship* with costly monitoring each team member absorbs half of the \$36 cost of monitoring the worker. To find the owner-employee equilibrium C^M we maximize $x[12(24 - x) - 18]$. The first derivative is $288 - 24x - 18$ and the second derivative is negative. When we set $288 - 24x - 18$ equal to zero and solve for x we get $x^M = 11.25$, and hence $e^M = 12.75$ and $y^M = 12 \times 12.75 - 18 = 135$. The owner-employee equilibrium C^M has one of the team members as the owner and residual claimant who offers to pay the other person (the worker) 135 if he or she supplies at least 12.75 hours of effort; otherwise the pay is zero. Then $U(C^M) = 11.25(135) = 1518.75$. We have $U(C^P) = 1536 > U(C^M)$. When $n = 2$, individual utility is higher under the partnership sharing formula than under the owner-employee relationship with costly monitoring.

The next case is identical to Example 4.4 except that we have a three-person team.

Example 4.5 Costly Monitoring with a Three-Person Team

As in the previous case, $U(x, y) = xy$, $T = 24$, R is 12 times the total effort supplied. Monitoring cost is 36 per *worker*.

If $n = 3$ the individual partner maximizes $x[4(24 - x + 2c)]$, where c represents the effort supplied by each of the other two partners. The first derivative is $96 - 8x + 8c$. Setting this equal to zero yields $96 - 8x + 8c = 0$, and the second derivative is negative. *Now* we can set $c = e = 24 - x$, where x is the leisure consumption of the individual whose utility we are maximizing. We get $96 - 8x + 8(24 - x) = 288 - 16x$, the solution of which is $x^P = 18$, and hence $e^P = 6$ and $y^P = 72$, the partnership equilibrium C^P when $n = 3$. $U(C^P) = 18 \times 72 = 1296$. Under the *owner-employee relationship* with costly monitoring each team member absorbs a third of the cost of monitoring two workers, or $\frac{1}{3} \times 2 \times 36$. To find the owner-employee equilibrium C^M maximize $x[12(24 - x) - 24]$. The first derivative is $288 - 24x - 24$. Therefore, $264 - 24x = 0$. (The second derivative is negative.) We have $x^M = 11$, $e^M = 13$, and $y^M = 12 \times 13 - 24 = 132$. At C^M, the owner-employee equilibrium, one of the team members is the owner and residual claimant who offers pay of 132 to each of the other two team members, provided that he or she supplies at least 13 hours of effort; otherwise the pay is zero. Then $U(C^M) = 11(132) = 1452 > 1296 = U(C^P)$, when $n = 3$. In that case individual utility is *lower* under the partnership sharing formula than under the owner-employee relationship with costly monitoring.

The owner-employee relationship is likely to deliver more individual utility than a partnership the larger is the size n of the management team. That's because β/n, the cost of leisure consumption to an individual partner, falls rapidly as n increases, and hence so does the incentive to supply effort. Of course, when the team is governed by the owner-employee relationship the cost of monitoring borne by each individual rises as n increases. In general it is $\frac{n-1}{n}k$, where k is the cost of monitoring an individual worker. But that cost increases relatively slowly as n increases. If there are economies of scale in monitoring then that cost will increase more slowly still.

For any value of n the partnership is inefficient and so is the owner-employee equilibrium when monitoring is costly. To demonstrate that, derive the fair and efficient outcome for Example 4.4: maximize $U = xy$ subject to $y = 12e$ and $e = 24 - x$. The first derivative of $x[12(24 - x)]$ is $288 - 24x$ and the second derivative is negative. Then $288 - 24x = 0$ and thus $x^\beta = 12$, $e^\beta = 12$ and $y^\beta = 144$, the outcome C^β. We have $U(C^\beta) = 12(144) = 1728$, which exceeds $U(C^P)$ for any $n \geq 2$ and exceeds $U(C^M)$ for any positive monitoring cost. That is not to say that we are able to present an institutional regime that would lead to an efficient outcome!

Note that $x^\beta > x^M$ and x^M is smaller the greater is the monitoring cost borne by each team member. That's due to the fact that the function that is maximized to find C^M is the same as the one that is maximized to find C^β except for the subtraction of a monitoring cost from y when we derive C^M. The team opportunity cost of leisure consumption is β in both cases. Hence, there is no substitution effect: the price of leisure is the same in both situations. But there is a negative income effect because the monitoring cost reduces income. The individual will demand less of every commodity, including leisure, hence the reduction in the value of x. Because the absolute value of that income effect is greater the greater is the monitoring cost ($\frac{n-1}{n} k$ increases with n) the value of x decreases as the size of the team increases.

Professional service firms do not require enormously large teams, in contrast to most manufacturing processes. Therefore, $U(C^P) > U(C^M)$ is plausible in the professional service field where the partnership format is employed. In fact, there will be some minimal monitoring in a partnership. Why would the partners in a medical clinic invest the time necessary to monitor each other even a little? Malpractice can be very costly to the client, and hence to the partnership, and because the partners share losses as well as profits, each member is extremely vulnerable to the shirking of the others. This gives the partners a strong incentive to monitor each other, in contrast to the position of senior executives in a limited liability corporation. The personal assets of an owner cannot be tapped to pay the creditors or legal penalties of a limited liability corporation. (Large law and accounting firms typically have *salaried* partners who, unlike equity partners, do not have a legal claim on a fraction of the firm's profits. Salaried partners are liable when creditors or clients successfully sue.)

Source

Alchian and Demsetz (1972) provide the key insight for this section.

Problem Set

(1) Compute the equilibrium outcome for a firm that has ten workers, one of whom is the owner who manages the firm. The firm's net income (net of the cost of materials, etc.) is always five times the total amount of effort contributed. (The total effort includes the effort contributed by the owner.) Each individual has the utility function $U_i(x_i, y_i) = x_i^2 y_i$. Where x_i is the number of hours of leisure consumed by i per week, and y_i is i's income per week. Assume that monitoring is costless.

> The remaining three questions pertain to an n-person production team. The preferences of each member of the team can be represented by the utility function $U(x, y) = x(y - 36)$, where x is individual leisure consumption and y is individual income. The time endowment (T) is 24. The team's total profit (R) before deducting the incomes paid to the n team members is 10 times the total effort supplied.

(2) Derive the fair and efficient outcome.

(3) Suppose that $n = 2$.

    (A) Derive the partnership equilibrium and show that it is not efficient.

    (B) Determine the equilibrium that results from the owner–employee organizational form of corporate governance when the monitoring cost is 24 per *worker*. Show that individual utility is *higher* under the partnership sharing formula than under the owner–employee relationship.

    (C) Show that if monitoring were costless then individual utility would be higher under the owner–employee relationship than under the partnership sharing formula.

(4) Suppose that $n = 3$.

    (A) Derive the partnership equilibrium and show that it is not efficient.

    (B) Determine the equilibrium that results from the owner–employee organizational form of corporate governance when the monitoring cost is 24 per *worker*. Show that individual utility is *lower* under the partnership sharing formula than under the owner–employee relationship.

4.4   THE OWNER–MANAGER RELATIONSHIP IN PRACTICE

In the next section we derive the managerial contract that maximizes the owners' return. This section surveys the US corporate landscape. A modern US corporation has many shareholders. To take advantage of the economies of scale in production and advertising, the contemporary firm must be extremely large, beyond the capacity of all but a handful of individuals to finance on their own. Even if most firms were to have only one owner, risk aversion would motivate providers of capital to diversify their portfolios – in other words, to own a small fraction of many different companies rather than large fractions of a few companies. We will examine a firm that is owned by a large number of unrelated shareholders.

A firm's owners appoint a manager to run the company on their behalf. The owners do not make the daily decisions that determine how successful the firm will be. Those are made by the managerial team, which answers to a board of directors, who are supposed to represent the owners. The directors and the managers are agents of the owners, and we speak of an *agency problem* because the managers and the directors will, at least to some extent, act so as to enhance their own welfare, not that of the owners. The shareholders want the managers to make decisions that lead to the maximum value of shares in the company, and that requires high annual profits. However, the owners will not know when the highest possible profit is attained. If it were obvious how to maximize profit then the shareholders could issue the appropriate orders directly to the workers. As it is, the shareholders need to hire an agent.

The owners want the board to design a contract that provides every incentive for the manager to maximize shareholder value, even though the manager's immediate concern is his or her own material well-being, which will depend on factors such as the manager's future prospects that are not perfectly correlated with the firm's profit. Even if a portion of managers' wealth is held in the form of shares in the firms that they manage, the other shareholders cannot be sure that the managers will do all they can to maximize profits. The firm's long-run profitability will not be the only aspect of managers' stewardship that affects their welfare. For example, the managers' prospects for future employment and income may be enhanced if they increase the size of their present enterprise, and this may induce them to increase the firm's output beyond the point at which profit is maximized. The managers may expose the firm to more risk than is in the best interest of the owners. They may even negotiate a merger that provides them with tens of millions of dollars in consulting fees but does nothing (or less than nothing) for the owners of the firm that spearheads the merger.

4.4.1 How Managers are Disciplined

The severity of the agency problem is mitigated by a variety of things that impose discipline on the managers. The devices by which managers are regulated can be grouped into four categories:

Regulation by *shareholders*:
through contracts that provide performance incentives and via direct oversight by the board of directors.

Regulation by the *capital market:*
If the firm performs poorly, a financier can buy a controlling interest in the company and replace the incumbent management. This is called a *hostile takeover*. The motivation for the takeover springs from the fact that if the company subsequently does well, the market value of the financier's shares will increase. The implicit *threat* of a hostile takeover gives managers substantial incentive for doing their jobs well.

Regulation by the *legal system*:
In most countries the manager of a firm is legally responsible to the firm's owners. The degree of investor and creditor protection afforded by the legal system varies appreciably across countries, although it is usually substantial, at least in theory.

Regulation by *product markets*:
If competition is intense, profit margins will be small and a firm can be driven out of business if cost (and hence price) increases or product quality declines because of management shirking. The probability of bad decisions costing the top executives their jobs if the firm goes under will factor into managerial decision making.

We discuss each of these sources of discipline in turn, but most of our attention is given to regulation by shareholders and by capital markets.

The Legal System

The US legal system may place managers under more intense scrutiny than in any other country, but its role is still rather limited. First, American courts do not intervene in a company's internal business decisions. Shareholders *can* sue the *directors* if the directors do a bad job of oversight. American courts are also willing to adjudicate allegations of self-dealing and challenges to the CEO's compensation package. However, practical obstacles stand in the way of significant judicial review of compensation packages. Nevertheless, relative to other countries, both the UK and the US legal systems give investors and creditors substantial protection. One fairly simple technique by which owners of firms in other countries can purchase American or British legal protection is by listing their stock on the exchanges of those two countries. Some firms in emerging markets and in the European Union have done this (Shleifer, 2000).

> Before the reunification of Germany, some East German automobile manufacturing plants were so poorly run that the value of the cars that they produced fell short of the value of the inputs used (Wheelan, 2002, p. 27). A full 92 percent of all East German workers produced commodities whose variable costs exceeded their international market value (Akerloff et al., 1991).

Alternatively, a firm operating in a country whose legal system affords investors little protection from mismanagement can adopt the legal environment of a country that is more protective of investors by being acquired by another firm that already operates in such an environment. This becoming quite common in Western Europe (Shleifer, 2000). Suppose for instance that firm X is controlled by a small group of owners who also manage the firm, and these managers divert a significant fraction of the profits into their own bank accounts. If a dollar lost by the other shareholders results in a gain of less than a dollar by management an outsider can buy a controlling interest in X at a price that will leave the incumbent owner-management team better off and still leave a net gain for the company that takes over firm X and the other shareholders as well.

Example 4.6 Transplanting the Legal System

Iliad Corp. is managed by Homer, the founder of the company, who also owns 60 percent of the shares. The annual profit is $1,000 of which Homer is entitled to $600. Not all of the $400 to which the outside shareholders are entitled reaches them. They get only $100, because Homer diverts $300 of their share to himself. However, the diverted funds are used to buy a painting for the board room. Homer is indifferent between having $120 in cash and having the painting in the board room. If Virgil purchased the firm for the equivalent of an annual payment of $900, with $760 of that going to Homer and $140 going to the incumbent outside owners then everyone gains. Virgil pays $900 for something worth $1,000. The outside owners get $140 instead of $100, and Homer gets $760 instead of $720.

Why can't the shareholders pay the incumbent manager $150 to leave the $300 in the firm? Even assuming that the owners could do the math (and that is problematic, with the manager controlling the flow of information), we would then have a situation in which the manager could repeatedly threaten to act adversely to the owners' interest, inviting them to bribe him not to do so.

Product Markets

How important is competition in product markets in disciplining top executives? The manager will lose his or her job if the firm suffers losses year after year, and this gives the manager incentive to avoid losses. This is a long way from claiming that the manager will make every effort to maximize profit, but it will prevent extreme abuse. Moreover, the more intense is the firm's competitive environment the more efficient the management team has to be for the firm to stay afloat. Each of the world's major industrialized countries is host to firms that are among the world's leaders – even countries that do not appear to provide managers with strong motivation. This suggests that product market competition has substantial impact. But note that even if competition in the product market does prevent profit from declining, it doesn't stop the top executives from adopting strategies that transfer profit from the owners to management.

Performance Bonuses

We turn to the possibility of paying managers in ways that motivate them to look out for the owners' interests, even though the managers cannot be closely monitored. In the United States, not only are CEOs paid twice as much on average as their counterparts in other countries, but they also receive a much higher fraction of that pay in the form of performance bonuses – 50 percent in the United States. Other countries are slowly approaching US practice, however (Murphy, 1999).

It is important to understand that a performance bonus doesn't necessarily provide an incentive to perform. When the CEO or the board announces, "We had a great year so everyone gets a big bonus," it is past performance – or perhaps good luck – that is being rewarded, and that is not necessarily an inducement to do well in the future. A contract that permanently ties senior executives' pay to profit is a much better incentive device.

What kind of performance bonus would induce a manager to maximize profit? A substantial bonus that is paid only if the manager realizes maximum profit would provide the appropriate incentive. However, if the shareholders know how much profit the firm is capable of generating they can simply write a contract so the manager's continued employment is conditional on the firm reaching its potential. How can the owners induce profit maximization when they don't know what the maximum profit is?

Stock options are a partial answer. A stock option is a commitment by the shareholders to the manager, allowing the latter to purchase a specified number of shares in the company in a specified time interval at a fixed price, usually the price of the stock at the time the option is granted. This gives the manager a strong incentive to take actions that lead to the largest increase in the value of the stock

The Walt Disney Corporation was run by family members for several years after the death of the founder in 1966, and the family members did a poor job. Profits were dismal, and the managers even used $31 million of the owners' wealth to repurchase the shares of a financier attempting to buy a controlling interest in the company in hopes of being able to turn it around. (They paid $31 million more than the shares were worth on the stock market.) When Michael Eisner was hired to run the company in 1984 he was given a bonus of 2% of all profits in excess of a 9% return on equity. Under Eisner's leadership, the return on equity soared to 25%. (It was well below 9% when he was hired.) Over a five-year period, Eisner received about $10 million a year in performance bonuses, a tiny fraction of what he delivered to the company's owners (Milgrom and Roberts, 1992). Eisner resigned in 2005 under pressure from shareholders following a number of disappointing movie releases.

over that time interval, and this is usually accomplished by generating the maximum profit for the firm. Increases in the firm's profit will be noticed by investors and will result in an increase in the demand for the firm's shares. That in turn causes the share price to increase.

Stock options can be abused, however, especially because managers are not usually required to hold the stock for any period of time. The chief executives can cause a temporary increase in the share price by overstating current profit. They can exercise their stock options and sell their stock before the actual profit is discovered. When the truth is revealed, investor confidence can be undermined to an extent that the resulting collapse in the share price can bring many shareholders to ruin. Also, the board of directors sometimes weakens the incentive effect of stock options by *repricing* them after a fall in the share price. (If the price was $100 a share two years ago when the option was offered to the CEO, and the price is currently $90, the option price may be lowered to $90!) Repricing *can* benefit owners if it is done after a drop in the share price that is unrelated to the manager's performance. In that case, repricing would restore the incentive effect of stock options. (If the price decline was sufficiently large, it may be extremely unlikely that the stock price would rise above the exercise price of the option, no matter how hard the manager strives to increase profit.)

Too often bonuses and stock options are given to reward service in the past. But it is future performance that the shareholders want to inspire; it is too late to affect past performance. In fact, poor performance may be the result of unfavorable random events – changes in exchange rates and so forth – that are beyond the control of the manager. The manager may have been exceptionally industrious and creative. The aim is to reward effort, and effort is imperfectly correlated with performance and profit. Paradoxically, it may be smart to give a stock option to a manager after a period of *low* profits, giving the manager a strong incentive to work more effectively in the future. That won't work with cash bonuses of course. In fact,

Example 4.7 Stock Options and Managerial Incentive

Suppose the share price of firm X is currently $100 and firm X's CEO is given the option to buy shares at that price. If the share price were to increase to $250 after a time, the CEO could buy shares for $100 each, resulting in an increase in his or her wealth of $150 per option exercised.

cash bonuses are usually tied to the *office* – with a chairman receiving more than a vice president. So, performance bonuses are a potentially useful tool in the shareholders' attempt to induce the manager to maximize profit, but they are often used inappropriately. Moreover, shareholders often view these sort of financial devices as bribes to get the managers to do something that they are paid large salaries to do in the first place. Accordingly, shareholders sometimes oppose the use of stock options on ethical grounds and will sometimes sue the manager if the firm's board of directors agrees to this type of compensation. Nevertheless, performance bonuses of one kind or another are ubiquitous.

When the price of the company's shares is used to connect the manager's pay to managerial performance – whether or not a stock option is used – the manager can profit from an economy-wide increase in share price levels. This happened during the bull market of the 1990s. The median pay of the CEOs of the top 500 firms (Standard and Poor's 500) increased by about 150 percent from 1992 to 1998 (Perry and Zenner, 2000). Tying the manager's performance to the *difference* between the firm's share price and a general stock market price index might be a more effective incentive device.

Why aren't incentive schemes that condition the manager's pay on the firm's performance more widespread? On average, an increase of $1,000 in the market value of a company's shares increases the CEO's compensation by only about $3.25, most of which is attributable to stock ownership (Jensen and Murphy, 1990a, 1990b). Using more recent data (from the period 1980 to 1994) and taking the stock *option* component of pay into account, Hall and Liebman (1998) discover that pay is substantially more sensitive to performance. (See also Perry and Zenner, 2000.) Moreover, Haubrich (1994) demonstrates that when the manager's risk aversion is taken into account, contracts come much closer to the predictions of theory – the theory of Section 4.5, that is.

It may not be necessary to have close to maximum incentive to induce close to maximum CEO performance. It might be appropriate to divide the set of managers into good guys and bad guys. Even the good guys will disappoint the owners if they are not rewarded for walking the extra mile – but they certainly won't ruin their principals by driving the firm into bankruptcy, even if that would add significantly to the agents' wealth. The good guys will deliver maximum performance if they are generously rewarded for doing so, even if they get much less than a dollar at the margin for every dollar of extra profit realized by the firm. The bad guys, however, are governed only by material incentives. If they can increase their wealth from extraordinarily high to fanciful levels by exploiting a loophole in their contract, they will do so – even if that impoverishes many of the firm's owners.

Shleifer and Vishny (1988) suggest that the members of the *board of directors* be paid in the form of stock in the company rather than salary. The practice of tying a director's pay to the company's stock is making significant inroads. In 1997, 81 percent of the Standard and Poor's 500 firms awarded either stock or stock options (or both) to their board members (Bebchuk et al., 2002, and Bebchuk and Fried, 2004). In theory this would align the interests of the board and the shareholders. Although the board of directors represents the shareholders, and shareholders sit on the board, it is often dominated by the manager. (In fact, managers often control the selection of the board members. And they can arrange to have their firms award lavish consulting contracts to board members. Brickley et al. (1994) marshal evidence suggesting that shareholders do better when the board contains a large number of directors who have no significant business ties with the company.) However, "it has been widely agreed that the board of directors is an ineffective way of dealing with this [agency] problem" (Allen and Gale, 2000, p. 76).

An increasingly commonplace device for inducing performance that generates the maximum increase in the value of the company's shares is the *franchise* arrangement, discussed in Section 4.5.

Capital Markets

How do capital markets discipline top executives? Debt financing has the potential for disciplining the management team. If the firm were committed to pay out substantial interest on debt, the executives would be motivated to avoid shirking and also to minimize the amount of revenue diverted to their own bank accounts (Grosssman and Hart, 1982; Jensen, 1986). However, American corporations rely on retained earnings to finance expansion far more than debt.

When an outside interest purchases a controlling interest in a firm we refer to this as a *takeover*. When the incumbent management is replaced we refer to it as a *hostile takeover*. If the firm's performance had been poor, then the price of its shares will be low. If the new owners replace the management team with a more effective one, and there is a big increase in profit as a result, the share price will increase due to the increase in the demand for them. The new owners will have realized a handsome return, justifying the takeover. Note that the *threat* of a takeover and subsequent dismissal may provide an incentive for managers to maximize profit in the first place. (This process can also correct deviations from profit maximization caused by management error, as opposed to management shirking.) Hostile takeovers were relatively rare until the 1960s (Hansmann, 1996). They remain rare outside of Anglo-Saxon countries.

If an outsider can determine when the management team is underperforming, why can't the firm's current owners? The research required to evaluate a firm's performance is costly. If each owner has a small fraction of the shares, the cost of research to an individual will be greater than any increase in the value of the individual's holdings as result of that research. However, if an outside interest purchases a significant fraction of the shares, it will realize a net gain if the firm's performance does in fact improve. (See Examples 4.8 and 4.9 in Section 4.4.4.)

Takeovers are not inevitable when the management team does a bad job. Easterbrook (1984) estimates that it takes an anticipated 20 percent increase in the value of shares to trigger a takeover. The threat of a takeover does little to discourage management from diverting profit away from the owners when the potential gain is below this threshold. (A 15 percent increase in the CEO's pay would result in a tiny drop in the value of shares. Bebchuk et al., 2002, p. 26). Also, managers often restrict the flow of information concerning the internal operation of the firm, making it even harder to determine its potential. Moreover, it often happens that dismissed managers have contracts with the original owners that provide them with multimillion-dollar parting gifts (*golden parachutes*) in case they are fired as a result of a takeover. The fact that boards of directors offer this sort of compensation may point to the unwillingness of directors to properly monitor managers. However, golden parachutes can be socially beneficial if they induce managers to accept hostile takeovers.

Some acquisitions serve the managers' interests by entrenching their positions. Shleifer and Vishny (1988) report that managers sometimes initiate takeovers. If some managers have strong reputations in the railroad industry, say, and their firm acquires a railroad, then they will be much more valuable to the shareholders. They have strengthened their positions at the head of the firm, even if the acquisition diminishes the present value of shareholder wealth.

In spite of the obstacles, takeovers are far from rare in the United States (and the United Kingdom). Almost 10 percent of the US firms listed in the Fortune 500 in 1980 have since been taken over in a hostile transaction – or one that started out hostile (Prowse, 1995). These takeovers left a trail of data that should allow us to determine if takeovers have provided a significant corrective. For takeovers during the period 1976 to 1990, the increase in the value of shares in the target companies was about $750 billion according to Jensen (1993). Scherer (1988) is skeptical about the social value of takeovers, but Lichtenberg (1992) finds strong evidence that a firm's total factor productivity increased after a takeover. And in a review of the empirical work on this question, Jarrell et al. (1988) conclude that takeovers induce a beneficial restructuring of real capital. According to Jensen (1986), restructuring of the firm following a merger sometimes eliminates projects with negative net present value. The contemporary consensus is that the takeovers of the 1980s precipitated significant efficiency gains (Holmström and Kaplan, 2001).

There is a free rider problem that could undermine takeovers as a device to discipline managers. Existing shareholders stand to benefit from any improvement in profitability that a takeover would bring. This could make them reluctant to sell to the takeover group at the current market price or at a price low enough to render the takeover profitable to the new owners. Consequently, it could become difficult or impossible to find enough current shareholders willing to sell their shares (Grossman and Hart, 1980). That is why the constitutions of many firms include a *dilution* provision. This allows the new owner to sell part of the firm's assets to another company belonging to the new owner at terms that are beneficial to takeover group and disadvantageous to the firm's minority shareholders. Dilution can also take the form of the new owners issuing themselves new shares. Why would the original owners of the firm place such a provision in their constitution when it is potentially to their disadvantage? Because it makes takeovers more credible and thus serves to discipline the firm's manager. If the discipline is strict enough then the incumbent manager will work assiduously to maximize profit, vitiating the need for dilution. A two-tiered offer can also eliminated the free rider problem, as we showed in Section 1.6.7 of Chapter 1.

Are there any other techniques that can be used to provide managers with appropriate incentives? One surprising possibility is *insider trading* (Manne, 1965,

1966). This term refers to the managers of firm A using important information about A's prospects that is not available to the general public, or even to trading specialists, to purchase or sell A's shares in a way that benefits the managers or their friends. It seems very unfair for those on the inside to profit from their privileged position. Indeed, the US Securities and Exchanges Commission declared insider trading unlawful in 1961, and the courts have ratified this position. (Insider trading is not unlawful if it is based on information that is available to the general public.) Is it harmful enough to outsiders to warrant its prohibition? Banerjee and Eckard (2001) examine data from mergers that took place during "the first great merger wave" (1897 to 1903), before insider trading was outlawed. They discovered that outsiders appear not to have benefitted significantly from the ban on insider trading.

One form of insider trading is clearly harmful to society in general. If managers were able to take short positions in the shares of their own company they would have a strong incentive to ensure that their firms did *badly*. Selling short consists in selling something you don't own (shares in this case) at a price agreed upon now for delivery at a specified time in the future. The person selling short is betting that the asset will fall in value. When it is time to deliver the promised number of units of the asset and the price *has* fallen, the seller buys the required number of units on the "spot" market and delivers them, collecting the high price specified in the original contract. If managers could do this with shares in the companies they run they could get rich by mismanaging their companies to cause the stock to fall in value. The flow of goods and service to consumers would be correspondingly diminished. It is clearly in our interest to have short sales by managers declared illegal, as has been the case in the United States since 1936.

> In July 1929 the head of the large Chase bank sold short more than 42,000 shares of Chase stock in advance of the October crash (Malkiel, 2003, pp. 47–48).

4.4.2 Examples of Managerial Shirking

Managers' immediate concern is their long-run well-being. Unless incentives or personal integrity take them in a different direction, their performance will be designed to enhance their present income, nonmonetary rewards, and future monetary rewards on the job, perceived value to other companies (to enhance job prospects elsewhere), and retirement package. Studies of the agency problem have uncovered a long list of avoidable deviations from profit maximization. Some are deliberate, and some are the result of poor judgment. Ideally, both can be corrected by means of contracts that provide appropriate incentives to the decision makers.

We present a variety examples of departures from profit maximization under four headings: deliberate mismanagement, wealth diversion from the owners to the manager, bad judgement, and sins of omission. (Examples from the recent great recession can be found in Section 3.5 of Chapter 3.)

Deliberate Mismanagement

Managers have been known to restrict the flow of information to the board of directors to make it harder to determine whether the managers are acting in the interest of the shareholders. Managers may even reduce the present value of the annual profit stream by tapping a source of profit slowly, so that it provides a steady flow of acceptable returns over the long haul. This can yield an annual profit that is high enough to survive owner scrutiny but not so high as to raise expectations for a repeat of the previous year's record return. (This form of shirking was said to be a common practice of managers in the former Soviet Union.) In the 1970s the management of H. J. Heinz delayed declaring some of its profit in one year so that profit in subsequent years would be artificially higher, to allow bonuses to kick in. (If a bonus is paid in any year in which profit increases by 5%, and profit is increasing at the rate of 4% a year, then by declaring a 2% increase in one year and a 6% increase the next, the executives qualify for a bonus in the second year.) It is not uncommon for managers to delay an announcement that would have a positive effect on the share price – for instance, the discovery of a new drug – until after they have been granted stock options (Yermack, 1997).

Between 2009 and 2015 inclusive Volkswagen programmed about 11 million diesel automobiles to cause certain emission controls to be to activated only under laboratory testing conditions. Under normal driving conditions these cars emitted forty times as much nitrous oxide, one of the primary greenhouse gases, as they did during a test.

The threat of a hostile takeover imposes considerable discipline on managers, but it is undermined when managers adopt strategies to make takeovers costly. In some cases they can even block them. There is evidence that their defensive strategies often work (Jarrell et al., 1988). Because managers control the flow of information, they may be able to persuade shareholders that the company attempting a takeover is not offering enough for the shares and that they should continue with the present management or wait for a better offer. Managers can use shareholder wealth – that is, company cash – to buy back the shares acquired by a firm attempting a takeover. This usually requires a payment in excess of the market value of the shares. In the 1980s the Disney management paid $31 million in excess of market value to buy back shares. This is called *greenmail*. Managers have also used their time and shareholder wealth to lobby state governments for antitakeover legislation. They have been enormously successful. More than 50 percent of US states have passed legislation making hostile takeovers more costly.

The constitutions of many firms include provisions that are activated when the firm is taken over without the endorsement of the board of directors. The purpose of these *poison pill* clauses is to preempt a hostile takeover by substantially reducing the value of the company to an outsider. Poison pills appeared for the first time in 1982. By making hostile takeovers excessively costly, poison pills entrench management at the expense of shareholders, as Malatesta and Walking (1988) and Ryngaert (1988) have demonstrated. (Both papers are good introductions to the poison pill technique; in particular they have insightful examples.) One poison pill strategy requires the new owner to make large payments to the incumbent management of the company. By far the most common strategy is *dilution* – a clause in the firm's constitution that permits the board of directors of the target firm to sell new shares to incumbent owners, at 50 percent of current market price, when an offer is made for the company. With more outstanding shares, the firm attempting the takeover finds that control of the target company would be worth less because it gets a smaller fraction of profits. Some have argued that this benefits the shareholders of the target firm because it gives its management bargaining power: management can threaten dilution unless the shareholders are given a better deal by the takeover firm. If that were the case we would expect to see a company's shares rise in value after the adoption of a dilution clause, but the share price usually *falls* on the stock market. Another significant poison pill strategy gives the board the power to reject any offer that it considers not in the company's interest. If the board is in thrall to incumbent management it may use that provision to block a takeover that would benefit the shareholders but cause the incumbent management to be dismissed. (These examples are taken from Dutta, 2000, p. 172.) Comment and Schwert (1995) report that 87 percent of firms listed on the New York Stock Exchange have a poison pill statute of some kind on the books. A recent court decision in the state of Delaware (where many US corporations are based) did away with *dead hand* pills that remained in effect even after an entire board was dismissed (*The Economist*, June 1, 2002, p. 61).

Self-Dealing

Even when the managers do everything they can to maximize profit, there is much that they can do to increase the share of that profit going to the top executives by decreasing the share going to owners. In 1985 Victor Posner of Miami held a controlling interest in DWG, but he was not the sole shareholder. He extracted $8 million in salary from DWG that year, even though the firm did not make a profit (Shleifer and Vishny, 1997, p. 742). However, most of the US examples of wealth diversion from shareholders to CEOs are less direct, thanks in part to the intervention of the courts.

Management may buy an expensive fleet of corporate jets and use them primarily to fly executives to a trendy resort, or buy an expensive apartment in Manhattan for the use of the executives when in New York on business. Both purchases can often be justified as sound business practice but sometimes they are made to enhance the executives' leisure consumption. It is not unheard of for corporate jets to be used to fly executives to Superbowl games, baseball spring training sessions, and the like (McMillan, 1992, p. 121). As head of RJR Nabisco in the 1980s F. Ross Johnson bought ten corporate jets and hired thirty-six pilots. That was just the tip of the Johnson iceberg (Milgrom and Roberts, 1992, p. 493). In some firms the executives reward themselves with exquisite amenities, such as an opulent executive dining room, that cost the company millions of dollars a year. At least one CEO is known to have kept celebrities and athletes on the payroll for retainers of a million dollars a year, apparently for no other reason than to give the executives an opportunity to play golf with the luminaries.

Armand Hammer, the founder and CEO of Occidental Petroleum, used $120 million of company funds to build a museum to house his personal art collection despite being challenged in court by the shareholders (Milgrom and Roberts, 1992, p. 493). (The dispute was settled out of court.) The direct approach is for a manager to persuade the firm's board to grant an enormous pay raise, far beyond what has been established by convention or is required for appropriate incentives. There are a number of reasons why this strategy often succeeds. For one thing, the board members are often CEOs of other companies, and if they grant an extravagant raise to the manager under their aegis, the bar is raised and thus so is the probability that their own salary will be matched. (The manner in which CEO pay is determined is intensively studied in Bebchuk et al., 2002.)

Suppose a bank manager, who is also the bank's largest shareholder, makes a loan to a friend on terms guaranteed to result in a loss to the bank. If the borrower makes a secret payment to the manager there can be a net gain for both – at the expense of the other owners, of course. See Akerlof and Romer (1994) for evidence of this kind of fraud. The manager of manufacturing firm M can establish a company to supply M with key inputs. If these are priced above the market level – that is, more than other suppliers charge – then the manager will have successfully transferred some of the profit from M to the company the manager owns (Vives, 2000, p. 4). Russian oil companies have been known to sell their oil at absurdly low prices to companies owned by the managers of the oil companies. Korean conglomerates (called *chaebols*) have sold entire subsidiaries to relatives of the founder at low prices. Similar stories have surfaced from Italy (Shleifer and Vishny, 1997, p. 742). For the most part, American courts thwart this extreme form of self-dealing.

As Section 4.4.3 on the Enron story demonstrates, the top executives can manipulate the price of their company's stock to take advantage of stock options. This is not a new practice. Early in the history of the Ford Motor Company, Henry Ford announced that the company would soon cease paying dividends so that it could provide enhanced benefits to the firm's workers. This maneuver was successfully challenged in court by the shareholders. It appears that Ford had no intention of carrying out his plan but was attempting to manipulate the price of shares so that he could purchase Ford stock at a reduced price (Allen and Gale, 2000, p. 26). Also see Miller (1992), p. 72.

Bad Judgement

In 1921 Ford made 55% of the cars sold in the United States and General Motors (GM) made 11%. GM's business strategy had a number of fundamental flaws. The divisions (Chevrolet, Pontiac, Buick, Oldsmobile, and Cadillac) made very similar cars, so the divisions were competing with each other. The economy was in recession, and car sales were sluggish. Nevertheless, each division continued to overproduce, resulting in unprofitable inventory accumulation. The company did not have a strategy for inducing division managers to take into consideration the cost that inventory accumulation imposed upon GM.

When Alfred P. Sloane took the helm at GM the company was transformed. Decision making was decentralized. The head of GM made policy – for instance, each division was told to make a car targeted to a particular segment of the market – and each division manager was required to maximize the division's profit subject to guidelines set by the head. In particular, the division's inventory was charged to the division as a cost. Henry Ford, who was still the chairman of Ford and its largest stockholder in the 1920s, vigorously resisted the notion of decentralization. Ford felt that absolute control should flow from the top down. However, a large firm runs more efficiently if it takes advantage of the reduction in agency costs when decentralization is used. (All large modern corporations decentralize, at least to some extent.) By 1940 Ford's market share had fallen to 16% and GM's had risen to 45%. (The last two paragraphs are based on Milgrom and Roberts, 1992, pp. 2–4.)

Between 1980 and 1990 GM spent $67.2 billion on research and development. GM could have purchased Toyota *plus* Honda for that, but by 1990 equity in GM was only $26.2 billion. The CEO was fired in 1992. General Tire (owned by General Corporation) had substantial excess capacity in 1985 due primarily to the introduction of radial tires, which last three to five times longer than bias-ply tires. Nevertheless, the General Tire management *expanded* capacity.

Incentives can be too strong. Consider the case of Salomon Brothers, the bond trading firm. In the 1980s they had a very comprehensive bonus system involving employees from top to bottom. The firm calculated an employee's contribution to profit from almost every transaction, and bonuses were based to a great extent on an employee's annual contribution to profit. This induced people to work very hard, but it did not yield the best outcome for the firm as a whole. Department *A* might withhold key information from Department *B* if disclosure would benefit *B*. On occasion, a department would "steal" another department's profit. In 1990 Salomon hired Myron Scholes, a Stanford professor who would win the Nobel Prize in Economics seven years later, to reform the incentive system. Scholes's key innovation was to have the employee's bonus money used to buy company stock, with the proviso that it could not be sold for five years. This gives the employee a sufficient interest in the profit of the firm as a whole, eliminating the incentive for dysfunctional behavior (Milgrom and Roberts, 1992, pp. 10–11).

We explain in Section 4.5 why a firm's owners may be assumed to be risk neutral: they want the firm to maximize the expected value of profit. The managers, however, are risk averse because a large fraction of their income comes from the firm that they manage. If the managers' pay is a function of their firms' profit, they may avoid decisions that increase the expected value of profit when that would result in a big increase in the variability of profit. This may be the rationale behind *golden parachutes*, which give a manager who is dismissed a huge severance payment. However, if the manager's pay is not sufficiently sensitive to profit then he or she may cause the firm to take *excessive* risk. In the 1980s, managers in the oil industry spent billions of dollars exploring for oil when proven reserves could have been purchased for less than a third of the money. Alternatively, the money could have been passed on to shareholders (Jensen, 1986; see also, McConnell and Muscarella, 1986).

Inertia – Sins of Omission

Managers who sacrifice shareholder value for personal gain are more likely to take it easy than engage in empire building (Bertrand and Mullainathan, 2003). Profit maximization is a journey into uncharted territory. Managers have to put pressure on themselves to be creative in many dimensions. They have to be on the lookout for new products, new production techniques, and so on. Just because profit is high doesn't mean it has been maximized. Sometimes, an opportunity for increasing profit has already been demonstrated by another firm, yet the manager doesn't adopt it. For instance, banks in Australia and the United Kingdom offer personal accounts that automatically move a customer's money into the highest yielding account – including paying down one's mortgage. This service is available to business customers in the United States but not to individuals (Nalebuff and Ayres, 2003). This personal service has been a great success in countries that have tried it. One would think that an American bank could attract customers away from rivals by introducing it. Why don't they? Surely a bank's owners would favor such an innovation.

Providing appropriate incentives to the firm's other workers is a key part of the management team's assignment. Managers can be considered to be shirking if they do not put much effort into solving the problem of shirking by the firm's other employees. Here are two examples: the Safelite Glass Corporation, which installs car windshields, began using piece rates in the mid-1990s. It now pays a worker according to the number of windshields installed. The firm's productivity (output per worker) increased by 44 percent as a result, and profit also went up. This was due in part to the incentive to work quickly, and in part to self-selection: workers who knew themselves to be unwilling or unable to pick up the pace left the firm for jobs that did not involve piece rates. The danger with piece rates is that workers might skimp on quality to increase the rate of output. But Safelite used a computer chip to tag a windshield so that the worker who installed it could be identified. US shoe manufacturers switched *away* from piece rates to an hourly wage because of problems such as unreliable quality. (The Safelite story is based on Lazear, 2000, and the shoe manufacturing story is from Freeman and Kleiner, 2005.) Motivating workers is becoming increasingly important to the modern firm because human capital is becoming more and more central to the firm's operations (Rajan and Zingales, 2000).

Less than half of the value of stock options granted to employees in the United States are awarded to individuals in or near the top executive category. This means that more than half of the stock options are granted to workers who have little or no ability to affect the firm's overall performance. Moreover, this is an expensive form of compensation for the firm. Hall and Murphy (2000, 2002) estimate a firm's cost of granting an option to one of its employees – essentially, the revenue that would have been earned by selling the option on the market – and compare it to the value to the employee receiving the option, which is roughly half of the cost to the firm. Why is the value to the employee so much lower? Because the employee is undiversified and is prevented by law and employer policy from hedging the risk of holding so much in the stock of one company. Why are stock options granted to sub-executive workers when they are so costly to the firm and have no incentive effect? Hall and Murphy (2003) argue that it is because managers and boards of directors are too enamored of the fact that granting options does not require an *immediate* cash outlay. (Other accounting considerations play a role as well.)

4.4.3 The Enron Debacle

According to its own financial statements, Enron was the seventh-largest American corporation in December of 2000 when its shares were trading for $84.87. At that point Enron stock had returned 500 percent since 1995 (Grove et al., 2004). By November 28, 2001, the share price was below $1 after its accounting practices came under public scrutiny, and the company filed for bankruptcy a few days later.

Enron's profit came primarily from arbitrage – buying energy where it was priced low and selling it where it commanded a high price. The Enron management team explicitly adopted the arbitrage strategy, in preference to actually *producing* electricity, which requires a large stock of expensive equipment. The company was able to supply energy to utilities under long-term, fixed-price, contracts.

Arbitrage can be very profitable, as it was initially for Enron which got a head start in newly formed energy markets of the 1980s, as the United States and many other countries restructured their former state monopoly energy industries. However, as other companies followed suit, learning from their own experience and from Enron's, the opportunities for Enron to buy cheap and sell dear greatly diminished. Couple that with the emphasis that Wall Street placed on revenue growth in the 1990s, and you have the conditions for the debacle.

Arbitrage *per se* is socially valuable: a commodity will command a high price where it is in short supply, and its price will be low where it is abundant. The arbitrageur corrects the imbalance by buying in the low-price market and selling where the price is high. (A high price reflects a high marginal rate of substitution, and thus additional units of the good have a relatively high intrinsic value to consumers.)

Enron executives exploited the considerable discretion available to them under GAAP (generally accepted accounting practices). For instance, they reported gross revenue from future electricity deliveries as if it were net revenue – that is, they did not deduct the cost of buying the electricity. They made a large sale to at least one company while promising to reverse the transaction at a future date but recorded the proceeds of the sale as revenue. They produced an indecipherable balance sheet and took advantage of Wall Street's preoccupation with revenue growth. In many cases, Enron covered losses from particular ventures by borrowing hundreds of millions of dollars, adding the proceeds of the loan to reported profit while keeping the loss off its books by attributing it to a "partnership" (Malkiel, 2003, pp. 99–100). By 1999 well over 3,000 off balance sheet affiliates and subsidiaries had been established by the company. (Grove et al., 2004. Example 3.8 in Chapter 3 shows how a firm can move remove some of its liabilities from the balance sheet.)

"The desire of Enron's management to maintain initial revenue and profit growth rates despite the growing sophistication of its competitors created very strong incentives for its management to engage in many of the dubious accounting practices and risky business ventures that ultimately led to Enron's bankruptcy" (Wolak, 2002). Some Enron executives received prison sentences. Obviously, the victims of the duplicity of the top executives included the employees who lost their jobs and the Enron shareholders – including present and former workers whose pensions were vested in company stock – who lost their investments. In addition, many affiliates were hurt by the demise of Enron, creditors lost billions, and purchasers' contracts were not honored (Trinkaus and Giacalone, 2005).

Because Enron's management strategy led to bankruptcy it was certainly not in the owners' long-run interest. How did it benefit the top executives? Enron's spurious claims of high revenue growth led initially to large increases in the price of Enron shares. That made it enormously profitable for management to exercise stock options, making the top executives fabulously wealthy. In principle, stock options give management the incentive to maximize profit because increases in profit lead to increases in the price of the shares on the stock exchange. Because managers are rarely required to hold their shares for any length of time, they have an inordinate interest in short-run profit maximization. They can "earn" tens of millions of dollars in a few years, and when that is a possibility the interests of the executives and the owners diverge. Not that every CEO will exploit the opportunity to acquire vast wealth with reckless disregard for the value and long-run viability of the firm. Presumably, most executives strive to carry out their responsibilities faithfully, and the stock option carrot works in the shareholders' interest if management feels itself ethically constrained to exploit stock options in a way that also enhances the welfare of the firm's owners. However, the stock option carrot can attract unscrupulous individuals whose guiding principle in life is to take as much as they can get away with.

> Of course, mismanagement is not exclusive to private enterprise. Argentina's state-owned telephone company was so inefficient in the 1980s that many companies hired someone whose only job was to put a telephone receiver to an ear until a dial tone was heard. This sometimes took hours (Rajan, 2010, p. 54). Corrupt politicians and regulators in Japan colluded with the Tokyo Electric Power Company to suppress safety concerns over a period of years. In 2011 an earthquake and tsunami led to a nuclear disaster that could have been, and should have been, prevented (Admati and Hellwig, 2013, p. xi).

Source
The subsection is based on Wolak (2002).

Links
See Healy and Krishna (2003) for thorough examination of the downfall of Enron. Holmström and Kaplan (2003) demonstrate that in spite of the corporate board and governance scandals that shook the public's faith in the management of American companies, the system has performed well overall, both in comparison with periods before and after the scandals broke in 2001 and relative to other countries. (Bengt Holmström and Oliver Hart shared the 2016 Nobel Prize in Economics.)

4.4.4 Why Shareholders Allow Managerial Shirking
Why are managers able to take decisions that enhance their own financial positions at the expense of the owners? Why don't the directors prevent it? In part because executives control the flow of information about their company and can sometimes

withhold information from the board if it reflects adversely on management. Also, managers often award consulting contracts to directors and the firms with which they are associated. CEOs often select the directors themselves, and these directors are often CEOs of other companies. Moreover, they frequently serve on a large number of boards and are stretched thin. Directors with a reputation for challenging CEOs will find their invitations to serve on boards drying up (Bebchuk et al., 2002).

A key point is that a shareholder who owns a small fraction of the company has no incentive to incur the costs of monitoring a management team – the potential benefit to the group of shareholders as a whole is enormous, but the gain to a small individual shareholder will be small. If monitoring requires a high fixed cost and yields a relatively small benefit to the individual, then no owner can gain by absorbing the monitoring cost. But the net gain to the owners as a whole can be vast. A *group* of owners could share the monitoring cost in a way that would allow each member of the group to gain, net of the cost. However, an individual has an incentive not to join, knowing that any increase in the share price that resulted from monitorong financed by others would benefit the abstainer in equal measure. This is an instance of the *free rider problem:*

Example 4.8 No Owner has an Incentive to Monitor the Manager

Firm X has a large number of shareholders, each of whom owns 2,500 shares. The shares of firm X are currently trading for $40. Therefore, the value of each person's holding is $2500 \times \$40 = \$100,000$. Monitoring the manager would increase the value of shares by 50 percent, but monitoring would cost $120,000. (A consulting firm would have to be engaged to conduct in-depth research.) No single shareholder is willing to pay $120,000 to increase his or her wealth by $50,000.

Suppose that there is a total of 100 shareholders. If each were to contribute $1,200 the consultant could be hired and each owner would gain $50,000 at a cost of $1,200. But an individual owner would have an incentive to contribute nothing to the fund. There would be no way of preventing someone who didn't contribute from benefitting from the increase in the stock price that resulted from the monitoring financed by others.

Clearly, if any owner had enough at stake the entire cost of monitoring could be absorbed by that person and still leave him or her with a net gain.

Example 4.9 A Firm with a Large Stakeholder

Firm Y has many shareholders, one of whom (individual J) holds 12,500 shares. Y's shares are currently trading for $40, and thus J's holdings are worth $12,500 \times \$40 = \$500,000$. If J incurred the $120,000 monitoring cost, and the value of each share rose by 50 percent as a result, J's wealth would increase by $250,000 − \$120,000 = \$130,000$.

Firm Y will be monitored by one of the owners, but firm X will not be. Is there evidence for this? Bertrand and Mullainathan (2000) examined CEO contracts before and after the introduction of legislation that made it more costly for an outsider to mount a successful hostile takeover. (More than half of the states in the United States have adopted such laws.) When hostile takeovers become more costly, managers are subject to weaker discipline. Will the owners substitute another form of discipline, or will the CEOs seize the opportunity to increase their pay? Firms with at least one owner holding a fairly substantial fraction of the shares responded to the change in the legal environment that diminishes the market discipline on CEOs by increasing the incentive component of executive contracts, but other firms tended not to do so. In fact, in firms without a large shareholder the salary part of the manager's pay tends to increase when external discipline weakens. (See also Shleifer and Vishny, 1986, and Bertrand and Mullainathan, 2001.)

Performance bonuses have *some* effect on pay and hence on performance. In the United States, however, the effect on performance is too narrowly focused on the short run. From the standpoint of both consumer and shareholder welfare, it is long-run profit that should be maximized. If the US stock market is sensitive to short-run profit maximization more than long run, then to the extent that changes in the value of a company's stock affect its managers' performance, it is short-run profit maximization that is encouraged. (We might expect to see a reduction in research and development spending by newly acquired US firms. The evidence is mixed, according to Hall, 1988.) Why might the US stock market be too insensitive to the long run? More than 50% of the common stock is held by pension funds, mutual funds, educational endowments, and charitable foundations, and these institutions account for 80% of the trading (Bernstein, 1992). A mutual fund seldom holds more than 1% of the outstanding stock of a company, and – to ensure diversification – it is illegal for a mutual fund or pension fund to hold more than 10% of the stock of its sponsoring company. The significance of this is demonstrated by Examples 4.10 and 4.11. Management would be more intensely scrutinized if ownership were more concentrated.

In short, most of the stock in a large US company is held by institutions who hold only a tiny fraction of its shares and who trade them frequently. This means that the majority of owners have only a very short-run interest in the company, and the executives themselves stay with the company for only five years on average. (In Japan it is typically a lifetime. Worker-managed firms are springing up across the United States, and the worker-managers typically have a long-term interest in their business. See Harrison, 1993.) Who, then, will put pressure on management to consider the long view? In the United States only 21% of research·and development funding in the private sector is targeted for long-run projects; this contrasts with 47% in Japan and 61% in Europe. (The profitability of a randomly selected firm may not increase by anything close to 10% as a result of an investigation of management practices. But firms that are suspected of being poorly managed may well be capable of yielding 10% more profit.)

Sources

More than a hundred articles were used in preparing Section 4.4, so the citations have been inserted into the text at the relevant points.

Links

Kotowitz (1989) is a general but brief introduction to hidden action problems. Radner (1992) examines the role of hierarchy in the managerial process. See Easterbrook (1986); Jarrell et al. (1988); Jensen (1988); Leland (1992); Scherer (1988); and Shleifer and Vishny (1988) for more on takeovers. Hall and Murphy (2003) provide a thorough examination of the role of stock options in American executive compensation and employee compensation in general. See Kanter (1989) for examples of other devices for motivating workers. Carmichael and McLeod (2000) is a superb treatment of one aspect of this issue. Bebchuk et al. (2002) consider the extent to which managers are governed by incentives and the extent to which they are able to get their own way. They conclude that managers often set the terms of their own compensation, constrained only by the fear of provoking public outrage. Murphy (2002) examines their argument carefully and finds it inadequate.

4.5   AGENCY THEORY

Consider fictional Hightech Corporation. The manager is the agent, and the set of shareholders constitute the principal. Each owner holds a fraction of the outstanding shares of Hightech, as well as ownership shares in other firms. That is, each Hightech owner has a diversified portfolio. Thus, we assume that "the" principal is risk neutral and simply wants the manager to maximize expected profit.

Example 4.10 The Benefits of Diversification

Lilly is risk averse and owns one share each in 50 separate but financially similar firms. For any of these firms, if a manager's strategy is passive the profit will be 105 with probability ½ and 95 with probability ½. However, if the manager's strategy is aggressive a firm's profit will be 180 with probability ½ and 60 with probability ½. A passive strategy is less risky but it results in an expected value of 100, whereas the expected value of the aggressive strategy is 120. On one hand, if the manager of each firm is aggressive, then with very high probability close to half of the firms will have profit of 180 and the rest will have 60. Therefore, with very high probability the profit per firm will be close to 120. With very high probability the owner will get a share in a total profit of $50 \times 120 = 6000$ if each manager is aggressive. On the other hand, if each manager is passive, the total profit will be very close to $50 \times 100 = 5000$. Lilly is much better off when each manager pursues the risky strategy, even though Lilly is risk averse. Diversification reduces the risk of the *portfolio*, even when the individual shares incorporate a lot of risk. Therefore, the diversified owner may be assumed to be risk neutral from the standpoint of the performance of the firms in which she owns shares.

In most cases, the *manager's* consumption and utility depends crucially on the pay received for managing the firm. Hence, the manager is typically risk averse. The manager's effort has a strong influence on the firm's profit but so do random forces. If the manager's pay went up by a dollar every time profit went up by a dollar, and went down by a dollar every time profit fell by a dollar, then the manager would have the strongest possible incentive to maximize expected profit. We say that the manager has *maximum incentive* in that case. But when the manager's pay moves perfectly in step with the firm's profit, that pay is most strongly influenced by the random component of profit. Because the manager is risk averse, that will lower his or her expected utility (*EU*) unless the manager is compensated in the form of higher expected pay. The higher expected pay can lower the expected return to the firm's owners.

With maximum incentive, the gross expected profit is highest, but the manager's share of that profit would have to be higher on average because of the manager's exposure to risk. The owner's *net* expected return – profit net of the manager's compensation – is not maximized under maximum incentives when the manager is risk averse. Shareholders face a trade-off between incentives and risk spreading. Compared to a contract in which variations in profit have their full effect on the manager's pay, the shareholders do better when they reduce the manager's exposure to risk by providing an insurance element in the pay package. This weakens the manager's incentive, of course. The insurance market provides an extreme example. The consumer who purchases health insurance can influence the size of claims submitted by means of preventive medicine and by eschewing frills when illness does strike. But the random forces that select one person as a victim of ill health rather than another play a vastly more important role in determining individual medical expenses. Therefore, insurance contracts give relatively little scope for incentives and go a long way toward protecting the individual from random events. (This is discussed in more detail in Section 3.9 of Chapter 3.) At the other extreme, fast food chains commonly employ franchising: the manager of the local outlet absorbs much of the risk to enable incentives to have a big impact, giving the owners of the parent company more profit. (See Section 4.5.4 in this chapter.)

When we model the principal–agent relationship, we assume that effort is one dimensional. The agent can supply an additional unit of effort by reducing leisure consumption by one unit. This is the only way that the manager can affect the firm's profit in our formal model. In the real world, managers' activities can deviate substantially from maximizing the owner's return even when managers put in long hours. For instance, a manager can devote considerable effort to concealing data from the directors and shareholders, knowingly undermining the principal's welfare. Happily, we can draw a great deal of insight from a model in which the manager has a simple one-dimensional trade-off between effort and leisure.

4.5.1 A Diagrammatic Introduction

We model the principal–agent relationship by abstracting from everything but the inability of shareholders to determine the amount of effort contributed by the manager of their firm, even though effort is correlated with profit. Because profit is also influenced by random forces, the correlation between managerial effort and the firm's profit is not perfect. The owner can only observe profit and thus has to offer the manager a pay schedule that features a dependence of the compensation package on profit alone and will endeavor to structure compensation in a way that induces the manager to apply a high level of effort – not the highest possible level of effort, but the level that maximizes the return to the owners.

Although we speak in terms of a manager in relation to the firm's owners, the analysis applies just as well to any principal–agent relationship. The principal can be a university designing a contract for its agent, a football coach. The manager of a privately owned firm is the principal when he or she employs a salesperson. Should the salesperson be paid on commission, and if so at what rate? The agent could be a professor hired by a university, the principal, and so on. In any principal–agent relationship there will be a wide variety of opportunities for shirking. In spite of the fact that shirking is multifaceted, it is modeled here as a one-dimensional sacrifice of effort in return for increased leisure consumption.

We begin by supposing that profit has no random component. It is easy to adapt the argument to cover uncertainty with risk-neutral individuals after we have analyzed the deterministic case. The firm's profit R is βe if the manager supplies e units of effort. T is the time endowment, and x is the manager's consumption of leisure. Of course $x = T - e$.

DEFINITION: *Profit in the Agency Model*
When we use the term profit (R) in this section we mean revenue minus all costs except the manager's pay. The owner's *net return N* is profit in the usual sense – revenue minus all costs, including the manager's pay.

Figure 4.4 shows the profit function $R = \beta e$ as line L. (Although x not e is on the horizontal axis we have $e = T - x$, and thus L represents the line $R = \beta(T - x)$.) The owner's net return N is the difference between gross profit R and the payment y to the manager. Maximization of the owner's net return keeps the manager on the indifference curve u^0, representing the utility that would be realized by the manager in her best alternative. (This is explained in Section 4.5.2.) The diagram shows three net return levels N_1, N_2, and N_3 corresponding to three respective budget constraints for the manager, B_1, B_2, and B_3. For any budget line B, the owner's net return N the vertical distance between L and the point where B is tangent to the indifference curve; this gives us $R - y$, where y is the manager's pay. If $-p$ is the slope of the budget line then the line can be expressed as $px + y = m$, or $y = p(T - x) + F$, or $y = pe + F$, where F is the constant $m - pT$.

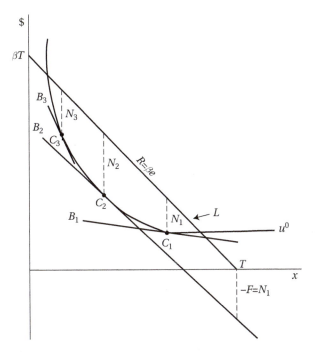

Figure 4.4

It is clear that the owner's net return is highest with budget line B_2 parallel to L. Here's why: assume temporarily that effort is observable and can be mandated in a contract offered by the owner. Consider B_1, which is tangent to u^0 at C_1. In other words, the manager will choose basket C_1 if his or her budget line is B_1. The owner's net return is N_1. Now, increase the manager's input of effort by changing the budget line, making it steeper, so that the manager has a new consumption plan a little bit north-west of C_1 on u^0. The line B_1 is flatter than L, which means that, beginning at C_1, an increase in effort (i.e., a reduction in x) will cause R to increase faster along L than y does along u^0. It follows that profit R increases faster than the manager's pay y. Therefore, the owner's net return will increase. This argument applies at any point on u^0 to the right of C_2. (At C_2 the tangent to u^0 is parallel to L.) Therefore, to the right of C_2 the owner's net return $N = R - y$ increases with e because the manager's consumption plan moves north-west along u^0 and R increases at a faster rate than y.

To the right of C_2 on u^0, the tangent to u^0 (the manager's budget line) gets steeper as we move toward C_2 by increasing the amount of effort required by the agent. Increasing p for budget line $y = pe = p(T - x) + F$ is equivalent to increasing the manager's reward per unit of effort supplied. This increase in p is advantageous to the principal because it allows $N = R - y$ to increase. But if we move in a north-west direction beyond C_2 on u^0 by making p larger than β, the owner's profit will fall. Why? Because u^0 is steeper than L north-west of C_2, and thus as we move the manager along u^0 above C_2 the manager's compensation y will increase faster than R. Even though R increases, because the manager supplies more effort, y increases at a faster rate so the owner's net return falls to the left of C_2. (A glance at Figure 4.4 reveals that N_3, the owner's net return at C_3, is less than N_2, the owner's net return at C_2. Similarly, N_1, the owner's net return at C_1, is less than N_2.)

The owner's net return is highest with budget line B_2 parallel to L, which is expressed algebraically as $R = \beta e = \beta(T - x)$. (Exercises 8–10 at the end of this section take you through an algebraic proof.) Lines B_2 and L have the same slope, so B_2 has slope $-\beta$. Then we can write B_2 as $y = \beta(T - x) + F = \beta e + F = R + F$ where R is the firm's realized profit. R depends on the manager's effort, and the manager knows the relationship between R and e. (The manager knows that $R = \beta e$ plus a random term, and she knows the value of β.) Therefore, the contract $y = R + F$ offered by the owner will induce the manager to supply the amount of effort that leaves N_2 for the owner, *even if the owner cannot observe and enforce e*. The contract $y = R + F$ reads "the manager gets all the profit R after delivering the fixed amount $-F$ to the owner."

We now drop the assumption that effort is observable, because the contract $y = R + F$ transfers all of the social gains or losses from a change in the manager's effort level directly to the manager, who is now the sole residual claimant on the firm's profit. In other words, $y = R + F$ is optimal for the owners because, under that contract, the cost of leisure consumption to the manager is equal to the cost to the firm.

Note that F is negative (Figure 4.4). The manager pays a *franchise fee* of $-F$ to the owner and then keeps all profit net of the fee.

DEFINITION: *Residual Claimant*

If the members of a production team share an amount of revenue that is a function of the input of the members of the team, and the share of all but one of them is determined independently of the amount of revenue generated, then the remaining individual is the residual claimant, receiving whatever revenue is left after all contracts have been honored, including the payments to the other team members.

This argument applies to production with uncertainty as long as the manager and the owner are risk neutral and the expected value of the random component is zero. Suppose that $R = \beta e + \xi$, where ξ is a random variable with expected value zero. Then the expected value of R is βe, and we apply the analysis to the expected value of R, which the owner wants to maximize, net of the payment to the manager. If the manager is risk neutral then y enters the manager's utility function linearly. That is, $U(x, y) = B(x) + y$. If y is the expected value of the manager's pay then $B(x) + y$ is the manager's expected utility, and the argument above goes through. In fact, this holds even if $E(\xi)$ is not zero. We assume that $E(\xi) = 0$ to simplify the calculations. (Even if $E(\xi)$ is non-zero, it is a constant, and

Recall the story of Chinese agricultural reform of the 1980s (p. 8 in Chapter 1). Before the reform, the farm had to deliver all of its surplus to the state and hence agricultural output was very low. When the rule changed, allowing the farm to keep the surplus after delivering a fixed amount to the central government, output soared. Under the new rule the agent – the farmer – is the residual claimant and hence has maximum incentive to work efficiently. Consequently, the central government collects more output because it can require a fairly high fixed quota to be supplied by the farm. The same principle explains contemporary amusement park pricing: the rides are free, so visitors to the park derive a high level of consumer benefit. This allows the park owner to collect a high entry fee at the gate. The owner receives more revenue by giving the rides away and collecting a large fixed fee as the patron enters the park.

Fruit pickers in orange groves are paid a piece rate – a fee per box of oranges. This motivates them to pick quickly. (If they were on salary they would have an incentive to dawdle.) They supply maximum effort in the everyday sense of the word. But the piece rate formula gives workers an incentive to pick the ground fruit first, although oranges on the ground are high in bacteria. Also there is a tendency to take the most accessible fruit from the branches and leave the rest to rot on the tree. Hence, there is shirking in a more general sense, and it is handled by direct monitoring of the workers (McPhee, 1966, p. 55).

hence will not affect the value of e and x at which the owner's net return is maximized, nor will it affect the value of e and x at which EU is maximized.

We can apply this discussion to *any* of the firm's workers. The optimal contract requires a wage $W = R + F$, where F is negative. But would we really expect the worker to pay the employer? This incentive scheme would actually provide more utility for the worker. Because it induces efficiency there would be more output per capita in the economy, and competition among employers for workers would result in a higher u^0 (utility from alternative employment). But suppose there is a cash constraint preventing a payment by workers to employers, or hidden information problems standing in the way of a loan of F dollars from the owner to the worker. We can achieve the same outcome by means of *progressive piece rates*. This is illustrated in Figure 4.5 with budget line ACD. The worker receives a basic salary of S. For (gross) profit levels less than R_C the worker is paid p dollars per unit of additional effort supplied. (The slope of the AC segment of the budget line is $-p$.) For profit above R_C the worker receives β dollars per unit of additional effort supplied. The contract would actually be written so that for output levels less than R_C the worker is paid p/β dollars per dollar of additional profit generated, and for output above R_C the worker receives the whole of each dollar of additional profit generated. The contract would not mention the unobservable e. This progressive piece rate system and the contract $y = R + F$ induce identical decisions. But the progressive piece rate system has a serious hidden action defect. Unless the quality of output can be easily verified – bushels of wheat, for example – the worker has an incentive to work quickly, sacrificing quality, to reach the output level R_C where the higher piece rate is available. There is no danger of this with the contract $y = R + F$ because the agent bears the full brunt of any production decision that affects profitability. Also, R_C must be less than the value of R at the effort level that maximizes N.

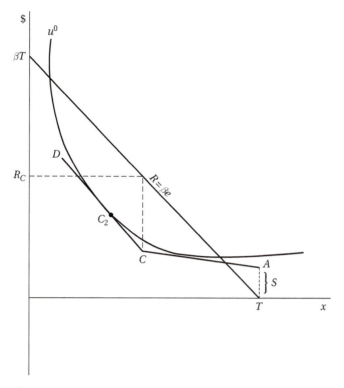

Figure 4.5

The Basic Agency Model

We assume that the owner of the firm is risk neutral. The manager contributes a level of effort e that is unobservable. Before making a payment to the manager the firm's profit is $R(e, \xi)$, a function of the effort e supplied by the manager and of a random variable ξ. The firm offers the manager a compensation package w that is a function $w(R)$ of the realized profit. Although R will depend in part on e, the effort level e is unobservable so the manager's contract will depend only on the actual, observable profit R. The manager can achieve a utility level u^0 by working elsewhere so the compensation schedule must allow the manager to achieve a level of expected utility at least as high as u^0. This is called the *participation constraint.*

DEFINITION: *The Participation Constraint*

    A manager will not accept a contract if it does not allow her to reach the highest expected utility level u^0 that can be attained by working elsewhere.

The manager's utility is $U(x, y)$, where x is leisure consumption and y is compensation – think of it as income. We let EU denote the manager's expected utility. We let T represent the initial endowment of time, a constant. Therefore, $x = T - e$. Note that y is a random variable, because it equals $w(R)$, and R depends on e and ξ. (Assume for convenience that the manager does not have an endowment of Y: that is, $y = 0$ before the manager goes to work.) The manager will maximize EU, the expected value of

$$U(x, y) = U(T - e, w[R(e, \xi)]),$$

subject to EU being at least u^0. The maximization exercise induces a dependence of effort on the compensation schedule, and the owner can use that relationship in designing a contract.

Suppose that $U(x, y) = B(x) + y$ and the compensation schedule is a member of the linear family $\theta R + F$, where θ and F are constants. (Think of θ as the commission rate paid to a salesperson, the share of taxi revenues going to the driver, or the royalty rate paid to a textbook author. In each case, the individual in question appears in our model as the manager.) The manager is risk neutral in this case, because x does not depend on the random variable ξ, so the manager's EU is $B(x) + E(y)$, where E is the expectation operator. Let $E(y) = E(\theta R + F) = \theta E(R) + F$. Now, maximize

$$EU = B(T - e) + \theta E[R(e, \xi)] + F.$$

This is a function of e, which the manager controls, given the owner's choice of θ and F. (The random variable ξ disappears when we take the expected value.)

DEFINITION: *The Agency Model*

Variables x, e, and y denote, respectively, the manager's leisure consumption, effort, and income. $R = \beta e + \xi$, where R is the firm's profit before deducting the manager's pay, β is a given positive constant, and ξ is a random variable. The time endowment is T, and thus $e = T - x$. If the manager's utility function $U(x, y)$ is quasi linear, with $U = B(x) + y$, then the manager is risk neutral. The manager's best alternative employment yields an expected utility of u^0. The manager will be offered a contract that determines his or her pay as a function $w(R)$ of profit. If $w(R) = \theta R + F$ then it is a member of the family of linear contracts.

Given θ, let e_θ be the value of e that maximizes EU. (The constant F does not influence the maximizing value of EU. But it does play a role via the participation constraint.) Then e_θ is the amount of effort supplied by the manager when facing the compensation schedule $\theta R + F$. If θ were increased then the manager's opportunity cost of leisure consumption increases because the manager now gets a larger fraction of an additional dollar of profit generated by increased effort. We would expect effort supply to increase.

Example 4.11 The Effort Supply Function

Let $U(x, y) = \alpha x - \frac{1}{2}x^2 + y$ and $R(e, \xi) = \beta e + \xi$. Assume also that $E(\xi) = 0$. Then $E[R(e, \xi)] = \beta e$. If $y = \theta R + F$ then $E(y) = \theta E[R(e, \xi)] + F$ and thus $E(y) = \theta\beta e + F$. Consequently

$$EU = \alpha x - \frac{1}{2}x^2 + \theta\beta e + F = \alpha(T - e) - \frac{1}{2}(T - e)^2 + \theta\beta e + F$$

because $x = T - e$. And $\alpha(T-e) - \frac{1}{2}(T-e)^2 = \alpha T - \alpha e - \frac{1}{2}T^2 + Te - \frac{1}{2}e^2$, so we have

$$EU = (\theta\beta - \alpha + T)e - \frac{1}{2}e^2 + [\alpha T - \frac{1}{2}T^2 + F].$$

The terms inside the square brackets are independent of e, and hence are treated as constants when maximizing EU to obtain the following effort supply function

$$e(\theta) = \theta\beta - \alpha + T.$$

(Because EU is a quadratic in e we can set its first derivative equal to zero or use the formula for maximizing a quadratic to obtain the maximizing value of e which will depend on θ. Note that $e(\theta)$ increases when θ increases.)

Note that when the manager is offered the contract $y = \theta R + F$, the parameters θ and F are constants from the manager's perspective. From the owner's standpoint, θ and F are variables, chosen by the owner to maximize the owner's net return subject to incentive compatibility (given the contract, the manager will choose e to maximize EU) and the participation constraint ($EU \geq u^0$). Therefore, F depends on θ because the maximization of the owner's net return requires $EU = u^0$ (as explained in the second paragraph of Section 4.5.3), and EU depends in part on y, and $E(y) = \theta R + F$.

We can now abandon the assumption that the manager's contract belongs to the linear family $y = \theta R + F$. It can be any function of R. What is the owner's objective? The owner is risk neutral and supplies no effort, so the owner simply wants to maximize the expected value of R net of the payment to the manager. In other words, the owner seeks to maximize the expected value of $N = R(e, \xi) - w[R(e, \xi)]$. We have seen that e depends on the compensation schedule w, so we let $e^*(w)$ denote the manager's effort supply when the manager is offered the contract w. Therefore, the owner chooses w to maximize the expected value of

$$R(e^*(w), \xi) - w(R(e^*(w), \xi))$$

subject to $EU \geq u^0$. How do we solve for e? Effort depends on the compensation schedule via the manager's optimization problem, but the owner's optimization problem causes the compensation schedule to depend on the manager's effort supply function. We'll start with an easy case, that of a risk-neutral manager.

4.5.3   Risk-Neutral Managers

The owner of the firm is risk neutral, and in this subsection we suppose that the manager is risk neutral as well. Then $U(x, y) = B(x) + y$ for some function B. We start by observing that $E(R)$ is a function of e. The random variable influences the value of the expected value $E(R)$, and $E(R)$ itself depends on e. The participation constraint is $E[B(x) + y] \geq u^0$. Note that $E[B(x) + y] = B(x) + E(y)$.

Profit maximization implies that the owner will choose a compensation schedule that equates the manager's EU with u^0. Why? We know that $EU \geq u^0$ must hold. If the manager's EU actually exceeded u^0 the owner could reduce her compensation by some fixed amount without violating the participation constraint $EU \geq u^0$. This would increase the owner's return. Therefore, at equilibrium we must have $EU = u^0$.

We assume temporarily that the owner can observe and mandate e. This allows us to find e^*, the level of effort that maximizes the owner's net return subject to the participation constraint (but without imposing the incentive compatibility constraint, which recognizes that the agent must have an incentive to set $e = e^*$). We are about to discover that there is a contract that induces the manager to choose e^* even though e is not observable and the manager knows it.

Profit maximization implies $EU = u^0$, so we have $B(x) + E(y) = u^0$. Therefore, $-E(y) = B(x) - u^0$. The owner then will maximize $E(N)$ subject to $-E(y) = B(x) - u^0$. Now, $E(N) = E(R) - E(y) = E(R) + B(x) - u^0$. Because $x = T - e$, this can be considered a function of e. The owner wants to maximize

$$f(e) = E(R) + B(T - e) - u^0.$$

If the manager receives the contract $y = R + F$, where F is a constant, then the manager will maximize $EU = E[B(x) + y] = B(x) + E(y) = B(x) + E(R + F) = B(x) + E(R) + E(F) = B(x) + E(R) + F$. That is, the manager will maximize

$$g(e) = B(x) + E(R) + F.$$

Again, $x = T - e$, so g really is a function of e.

Compare f and g. They differ by a constant: $g(e) = f(e) + F + u^0$. Therefore, e^* maximizes f if and only if e^* maximizes g. This means that the contract $y = R + F$ induces the manager to select the effort level that the owner would insist on if the owner could observe and enforce e. With effort supply determined, F is the solution to $B(T - e^*) + E[R(e^*, \xi)] + F = u^0$.

The effort supply e^* that maximizes both f and g satisfies the participation constraint because it is built into g. Therefore, the manager would accept the contract $y = R + F$. Having done so, the manager maximizes her expected utility by setting $e = e^*$. Even though e^* is the level of effort that would be mandated if the owner had full information, it is chosen by the manager even when effort is not observable. Let $M = -F$. Then $M = E[R(e^*, \xi)] - u^0 + B(T - e^*)$. The compensation schedule would give the manager the actual realized profit minus the constant M. To verify that it would be in the manager's interest to supply e^* *if* she accepted the contract let's compute the manager's EU for the compensation schedule $R - M$:

$$EU = B(T - e) + E[R(e, \xi)] - M.$$

Although the actual return R varies with ξ, the expected value is a number. Therefore, any value of e that maximizes $E(N) = f(e)$ also maximizes the manager's

EU. Therefore, it is in the manager's interest to set $e = e^*$ *if* her compensation is $R - M$ and she accepts that contract. But will she accept? By definition of M we have

$$B(T - e^*) + E[R(e^*, \xi)] - M = u^0,$$

so the compensation contract $w(R) = R - M$ does allow the manager to achieve the *EU* level u^0. Note that the profit-maximizing pay schedule is $y = \theta R + F$ for $F = -M$ and $\theta = 1$. In practice, the compensation contract would offer slightly more utility than u^0 to ensure that the manager will accept the contract in preference to the best alternative, which yields a utility level of u^0. We have proved the following:

Theorem: Optimal Contract for Risk-Neutral Managers

The manager pays a lump sum to the owner and keeps all remaining profit. In other words, the manager becomes the residual claimant. But the payment to the owner is set so that the manager's participation constraint is satisfied as an equality.

Here is a simple example that allows us to explicitly solve for the manager's choice of e as a function of w and then to solve for the profit-maximizing pay schedule w.

Example 4.12 Deriving the Optimal Contract

$U(x, y) = 20x - \frac{1}{2}x^2 + y$ is the utility function of Brendan, the manager. Then $B(x) = 20x - \frac{1}{2}x^2$. Brendan is endowed with 24 units of X and 0 units of Y. That means that $T = 24$. We assume that the manager's best alternative is to consume 24 units of X, so $u^0 = 20(24) - \frac{1}{2}(24)^2 = 192$. The production function is $R = 10e + \xi$, with $E(\xi) = 0$. Then $E(R) = 10e$. Assume for a moment that the owner can observe and mandate the effort level e. What e would he select? We know that the contract that maximizes the expected value of the owner's net return satisfies $EU = u^0$. In this case we have $EU = B(x) + E(y) = 192$. Then $E(N) = E(R) - E(y) = E(R) + B(x) - 192$. Therefore, the owner maximizes

$$f(e) = 10e + B(x) - 192 = 10e + 20(24 - e) - \frac{1}{2}(24 - e)^2 - 192 = 14e - \frac{1}{2}e^2.$$

Note that f is a quadratic, and when we apply the formula for maximizing a quadratic we get $e^* = 14$. (Alternatively, $f'(e) = 14 - e$, and $f''(e) < 0$. Therefore, we set $f'(e) = 0$ to maximize the owner's expected profit. This yields $e^* = 14$.)

Return to the case of unobservable effort. We show that the contract $y = R + F$ induces the manager Brendan to set $e = 14$: If $y = R + F$ then his *EU* is $B(x) + E(y)$, which equals

$$B(x) + 10e + F = 20(24 - e) - \frac{1}{2}(24 - e)^2 + 10e + F = 14e - \frac{1}{2}e^2 + 192 + F.$$

This function is maximized at $e^* = 14$. (We could have employed a shortcut. In Example 5.2 we derived the effort supply function. It is $e = 4 + 10\theta$ when $\alpha = 20$, $T = 24$, and $\beta = 10$. Therefore, when $\theta = 1$ the manager will supply the effort $e^* = 14$ that maximizes the owner's profit, even though the owner cannot observe or enforce e.)

Now, compute F under the profit-maximizing contract: $E(w) = 10e + F = 140 + F$ and $x = 24 - 14 = 10$. Therefore, the manager's EU is $20(10) - \frac{1}{2}(10)^2 + 140 + F = 192$. Then $F = -98$. The manager pays the owner a license fee of \$98 and then keeps the remaining profit.

The manager's contract is $y = R - 98$. We have $E(R) = 10e$, so the contract yields $\bar{y} = 10e - 98$, where $\bar{y}$ is the expected value of y. (The manager can observe her own effort supply of course.) If $\bar{y} = 10e - 98$ then $\bar{y} = 10(24 - x) - 98$. Therefore, $\bar{y} = 240 - 10x - 98$, and thus the contract that maximizes the owner's net return allows the manager to choose a consumption plan $(x, \bar{y})$ from the budget line $10x + \bar{y} = 142$. We can show that an individual with utility function $20x - \frac{1}{2}x^2 + \bar{y}$ and budget constraint $10x + \bar{y} = 142$ will choose the bundle $(x, \bar{y}) = (10, 42)$. Of course, if $x = 10$ then $e = 14$.

Note that for Example 4.12 we have proved that the contract $y = R - 98$ yields a higher expected profit to the owner than *any* other contract. This is much stronger than merely proving that $y = R - 98$ is profit maximizing within the family of linear contracts. Nevertheless, you might benefit from solving directly for the profit-maximizing values of θ and F within the linear family.

> **The \$1 club**: A number of prominent CEOs have restricted themselves to a single dollar in annual salary. Some of them are no longer even residual claimants, having waived bonuses and other financial incentives. The following corporate leaders receive only the \$1 salary, with no additional pay: Mark Zuckerberg, the founder and CEO of Google. Sergey Brin and Larry Page, founders of Google. David Filo, founder and former head of Yahoo. Jack Dorsey, CEO of Twitter. Elon Musk, CEO of Tesla Motors. Edward Lambert, CEO of Sears. (Rachel Gillet, *Business Insider*, August 14, 2015, at www.businessinsider.com/ceos-who-take-1-dollar-salary-or-less-2015-8.)

Example 4.13 Using the Effort Supply Function to Derive the Optimal Contract

Assume the setup of Example 4.12. The effort supply function is $e = 4 + 10\theta$ when $y = \theta R + F$. (Recall Example 4.11.) Profit maximization and the participation constraint imply $B(x) + E(y) = u^0 = 192$. Therefore, $E(y) = 192 - B(x) = 192 - 20x + \frac{1}{2}x^2 = 192 - 20(24-e) + \frac{1}{2}(24-e)^2$. We can use the effort supply function and substitute $4 + 10\theta$ for e, yielding

$$E(y) = 192 - 20(24 - 4 - 10\theta) + \frac{1}{2}(24 - 4 - 10\theta)^2 = -8 + 50\theta^2.$$

The owner wants to maximize $E(R) - E(y)$. Because $E(R) = 10e$ and $E(y) = -8 + 50\theta^2$ we have $E(R) - E(y) = 10e + 8 - 50\theta^2$. And the effort supply function gives us $e = 4 + 10\theta$, so the owner's objective function is $10e + 8 - 50\theta^2 = 10(4 + 10\theta) + 8 - 50\theta^2 = 48 + 100\theta - 50\theta^2$, a simple quadratic function of θ.

Using calculus or the formula for maximizing a quadratic, we achieve a maximum by setting $100 - 100\theta = 0$. Hence $\theta = 1$ maximizes the owner's expected profit. We solve for $F = -98$ as in Example 4.12.

If we think of the manager and the owner as a two-person "society" then the optimal contract leads to an efficient arrangement if the manager is risk neutral.

Efficiency Theorem
    The contract $y = R + F$ is efficient if the manager is risk neutral.

Proof:

We show that e^*, the equilibrium effort level, maximizes the *sum* of the expected utilities. (There may be other efficient outcomes, but anything that maximizes the sum of utilities will belong to the set of efficient outcomes.) The owner's *EU* is just the expected value of $y_1 = N$, the net return to the owner. The manager's *EU* is $B(x_2) + E(y_2)$, where y_2 is the payment from the owner to the manager, and $E(y_2)$ is its expected value. Therefore, we can find an efficient outcome by maximizing $E(y_1) + B(x_2) + E(y_2) = B(T - e) + E(y_2 + y_1)$. Now, $y_1 + y_2$ is $R(e, \xi)$, the gross return to effort. We get an efficient level of e when we maximize $B(T - e) + E(R)$. But this differs from f or g only by a constant, so all three functions are maximized by the same e^*. Hence, e^* is efficient.   ∎

Because θ is the fraction of an additional dollar of profit that goes to the manager, when $\theta = 1$ the social cost of leisure consumption, which is the change in $E(R)$ when the manager reduces e by one unit, equals the private cost of leisure consumption, which is the change in the managers EU when she reduces e by one unit. As a result, the optimal contract $y = R + F$ is efficient.

Alternative proof:

The optimal contract is obtained by maximizing the owner's utility subject to the manager's utility not falling below a specified level. In any context, any solution s^* to the problem "maximize U_1 subject to $U_h \geq u_h^0$ for all $h \neq 1$" is efficient. (Note that u_h^0 is a constant for each h.) If s^* were not efficient there would either be an alternative s such that $U_1(s) > U_1(s^*)$ and $U_h(s) \geq U_h(s^*)$ for all $h \neq 1$, contradicting the fact that s^* solves the constrained maximization problem, or else an alternative s such that $U_j(s) > U_j(s^*)$ for some $j \neq 1$ and $U_h(s) \geq U_h(s^*)$ for all $h \neq 1$. In the latter case, we could transfer a positive but sufficiently small amount of money from j to 1, resulting in an alternative s' such that $U_1(s') > U_1(s) \geq U_1(s^*)$ and $U_h(s') \geq U_h(s^*)$ for all $h \neq 1$, contradicting the fact that s^* solves the constrained maximization problem. Therefore, s^* is efficient.   ∎

We can drop the assumption that effort is one dimensional. Because the optimal contract makes the manager the residual claimant, the manager has an incentive to adopt any measure that will increase profit, and to modify any part of her decision strategy to that end.

4.5.4 Franchising

A franchise contract binds two legally independent firms and gives one of them, the *franchisee*, the right to use the products and trademarks of the other firm, called the *franchisor*. Currently, about one-third of all retail sales revenue in the US comes from stores that are part of a franchise arrangement.

Suppose that effort has two dimensions, quality and quantity. If the agent is not the residual claimant, giving a strong quantity incentive can result in severe shirking on quality. Consider this report from a worker in a Baltic firm producing television sets. It describes conditions – prior to the collapse of communism – toward the end of the month as the employees strive to earn bonuses: "We never use a screwdriver in the last week. We hammer the screws in. We slam solder on the connections, cannibalize parts from other televisions if we run out of the right ones, use glue or hammers to fix switches that were never meant for that model. All the time the management is pressing us to work faster, to make the target so we all get our bonuses" (Cook, 1990, quoted in Milgrom and Roberts, 1992, p. 14).

Franchising is not new. In the middle ages sovereigns granted franchises for the right to hold fairs or organize markets. The payment to the monarch by the franchisee, who was given a monopoly on the activity in question, was called a *royalty* when it took the form of a share of the revenue or profit. In the mid-1800s McCormack sold tractors and other farm machines through franchise agreements, and Singer sold sewing machines the same way. Each firm employed sales agents, the franchisees, who were given the exclusive right to sell the product in a specific region in the United States.

A present-day franchisor may have contracts with hundreds – or even tens of thousands – of franchisees. Fast-food chains such as McDonald's, which has over 30,000 restaurants worldwide, come to mind. Most franchisors have a relatively small number of franchises, however.

The simplest case is that of a barber shop with two chairs and one owner who gives haircuts in one of the chairs and contracts with another barber for the use of the other chair. The second barber, the franchisee, pays the owner, the franchisor, a fixed monthly fee for the use of the chair but keeps all the profit from his own chair, net of that franchise fee. This makes the second barber the residual claimant. Taxi fleets are often similarly organized. The owner of the fleet is the franchisor, to whom the taxi driver pays a fixed fee for the right to use one of the cabs. The driver's income is the sum of all the payments collected from passengers minus expenses, including the cost of gasoline and the fixed payment to the owner. The cab driver is the residual claimant. It is not unheard of for a waiter in an upscale restaurant to be required to pay the owner for the privilege of collecting tips (Reichl, 2005). In each of these three simple cases the franchisor employs the optimal contract, giving maximum incentive to the agent, the franchisee.

Apart from very small-scale franchises, only a fraction of the franchisor's return comes from the fixed fees. The franchisee typically pays a royalty rate, as a fraction of revenue or profit, and an advertising rate.

Example 4.14 A Royalty Contract

We employ the setup of Example 4.12: the optimal contact leads to $e^* = 14$, $E(R)^* = 140$, $N^* = 98$. $E(y)^* = 42$, and $EU^* = 198$. Consider the alternative contract $y = 0.6\,R - 20$. (The manager pays the owner a royalty of 40 percent of profit plus a fixed fee of 20.) The manager responds to that contract by maximizing

$$20x - \tfrac{1}{2}x^2 + 0.6E(R) - 20.$$

This is equivalent to maximizing $20x - \tfrac{1}{2}x^2 + 6e - 20$, or $20x - \tfrac{1}{2}x^2 - 6x + 124$ because $e = 24 - x$. This function is maximized at $x = 14$, and hence $e = 10$, $E(R) = 100$, $E(y) = 40$, and $E(N) = 60$. We have $EU = 20(14) - \tfrac{1}{2}(14)^2 + 40 = 222$ with the royalty contract. If $e = 14$, $y = 75$, and $N = 65$ we have a feasible outcome that leaves both the owner and manager with a higher level of expected utility than under the royalty arrangement.

Why don't franchisors typically employ the optimal contract, which has the franchisee simply paying a fixed annual fee, making that individual the residual claimant? The model used in Section 4.5.3 to derive the optimal contract does not have a time dimension. We can circumvent this difficulty by agreeing that each of the numbers involved was the discounted value of a stream of payments or receipts. This would require a huge initial lump-sum payment |F| by the franchisee. The value of a typical firm is many times greater than an executive's wealth. In most cases the manager would not have enough capital to make that payment and would have great trouble borrowing the money from a risk-averse lender. Moreover, future demand for the chain's product is uncertain and hence the present discounted value of the stream of a potential franchisee's profit is uncertain. Typically, the manager of a store gets the majority of his or her income from operating that store, and hence is risk averse. Our derivation of the optimal contract in the previous section depended critically on the assumption of risk neutrality. We consider the case of a risk-averse manager in the next section.

If the franchisee *did* pay a fixed lump sum to the franchisor then the latter would have little incentive to advertise the product or to regulate quality across the chain. That's another reason for a departure from a contract that makes the manager the residual claimant. It's obvious why the franchisee benefits from a national advertising campaign. The franchisee also benefits when the parent enforces standards across the board because the customer then comes to expect a uniform product at each of the franchise outlets. That clearly has a bearing on the demand for the franchisee's product.

On average 15 percent of a chain's outlets will be owned and directly operated by the franchisor. Motels and hotels are exceptional, and typically all of the units are franchised. At the other extreme, almost 30 percent of the McDonald's restaurants are owned and operated by the parent company. The demand for hotel and motel rooms depends on a wide range of factors, many of which are specific to local conditions. That makes it difficult for the owner of the chain to monitor a manager, and thus increases the benefit to that owner of franchising. The franchisee has a considerable stake in the success of the hotel. By franchising the owner of the chain can substitute motivation for monitoring.

4.5.5   Bad Guys and Residual Claimants

In the Middle Ages a monarch would sometimes award the job of collecting taxes in a remote region to a senior church official. This cleric would pay the monarch a fee for the privilege and keep all of the tax receipts, net of sovereign's fee (Thompson, 1971). This does not by itself make the tax collector a bad guy, but there are two obvious problems. The franchisee-collector has a strong incentive to extract more than the law requires. Moreover, laws and rules were not codified and publicized to the extent that they are today. It would have been difficult for an ordinary citizen to determine if the collector's demands were excessive. In addition to this moral hazard problem, there is the selection effect: individuals who know themselves to be good at pressuring their neighbors for money would have a strong incentive to apply for the job of tax collector. They might even compete for the job by offering to pay a higher fee to the monarch. Not only does the taxing authority have monopoly power – in any society – the "consumer" does not have the option of saying "No thanks. I'll go without." It is clearly in society's interest to have tax collectors who do not have an incentive to extract more than a citizen's legal obligation.

As peremptory and arbitrary as monarchs and dictators have been throughout history, their subjects typically preferred that form of autocracy to the anarchy that preceded it. Specifically, when a population is at the mercy of competing groups of roving bandits, the people are left with little or nothing above the subsistence level after the bandits depart – to terrorize other regions. The theft is devastating enough, but there is also the incentive effect. The incentive to invest time and other resources to increase the yield from the land is eroded when the fruits of innovation are regularly confiscated by one or other roving bandit. The problem is more than just the presence of multiple gangs; each gang will take the maximum possible, knowing that any surplus that it doesn't confiscate will be scooped up by the next gang. If one of the gangs succeeds in driving out the others, and settles in the region permanently, it can profit by protecting the locals from other thieves, thereby restoring the incentive to produce and innovate. This stationary bandit – who will call himself prince or monarch – will exact a reward for this protection in the form of tribute. The amount confiscated can be maximized by making his subjects the residual claimants, exacting a more-or-less *fixed* tribute (Olson, 2000).

The key is not so much having a fixed transfer from the subject to the monarch, but having a transfer that is independent of the subject's income, allowing the subject to retain close to 100 percent of any extra income earned thus providing incentive to work hard, invest, and innovate. This was played out in China in the 1920s when much of the country was under the control of competing warlords. When one of the warlords succeeded in driving rivals out of a region they taxed their subjects heavily. But the locals preferred that subjugation to their plight when they were at the mercy of two or more gangs (Olson, 2000).

The phenomenon is seen in modern democratic countries when a small region within the country – the inner city perhaps – is plagued by rival criminal gangs. If one of the gangs succeeds in driving out the others it typically takes advantage of this monopoly on criminal activity by protecting the residents from any crime not sponsored by the stationary gang, *and* limiting its own criminal activity to the sale of this protection. ("I'm not superstitious, but it's funny how often a store is destroyed by fire when the owner hasn't purchased our insurance policy.") Selling protection is far more profitable than widespread theft because the limitation on criminal activity by the monopoly gang leaves incentives for work and innovation. In general, theft is most profitable when the victims are residual claimants (Olson, 2000, p. 5, and Gambetta, 1993).

Widespread criminal activity is not always brought under the control of one ruling agency. A particularly egregious example of the effects of competitive criminal activity comes from Russia after the collapse of the Soviet Union in 1991. Russian firms had to deal with corruption from every quarter. Bribes had to be paid to state officials to lease a building, to import goods, to satisfy fire and safety inspectors, to win the blessing of the tax authorities, to install a telephone, to register the business, and so on. It was free-for-all corruption. The problem was so widespread that a corrupt official had little incentive to keep the graft on a modest scale, because any money that he or she left on the table would be scooped up by some other bureaucrat. It has been estimated that the total value of bribes collected by Russian government employees in the 1990s exceeded total government spending on education, science, and health care. Industries in which extortion was rife invested 40 percent less than firms in less vulnerable industries (McMillan, 2002).

Contrast the Russian experience with the massive corruption by the regime of General Suharto, which ruled Indonesia from 1968 to its overthrow in 1998. By awarding contracts to Suharto family members without competitive bidding, requiring foreign firms to take on a member of the family as a partner, and similar strategies the regime extracted billions of dollars, which were stashed in the foreign bank accounts of Suharto family members. The regime monopolized corruption and thus had ample incentive to ensure that theft was not so deep or extensive as to discourage business activity. They even adopted measures that promoted economic growth. (Their key advisors were Indonesian economists trained in the United States.) Government budgets were balanced and inflation was brought under control. Production enhancing reforms were introduced, particularly in agriculture. When Suharto took control in 1968 Indonesia was one of the poorest countries in the world. In 1992 income per capita was triple what it was in 1960 (McMillan, 2002). (Chapter 2 of Fisman and Miguel (2008) examines the Suharto case at length.)

4.5.6   Risk-Averse Managers and Binary Effort Supply

We turn to the case of a risk-averse manager of a large corporation. If you are unfamiliar with the elements of decision making under uncertainty you will need to read Section 2.6 of Chapter 2 before continuing.

To give us a point of comparison, suppose (temporarily) that e can be observed by the owner and verified by a court. This means that a contract can specify the effort level contributed by the manager. The owner can insist on a particular effort level e^*. Let $w(e^*,\xi)$ represent the compensation package offered to the manager. If this is not a constant, independent of ξ, let $C = E[w(e^*,\xi)]$, which is a constant. If the risk-averse manager had a choice between $w(e^*,\xi)$ and a constant salary that paid C whether profit was high or low then she would choose C because it has a higher expected utility. That follows from risk aversion and fact that the constant salary C has the same expected monetary value as w but C offers complete certainty. Therefore, for $\delta > 0$ sufficiently small, a constant income of $C - \delta$ would yield a higher expected utility than $w(e^*,\xi)$, and it would satisfy the participation constraint for δ sufficiently small, because $U(T - e^*, C)$ is higher than the expected utility yielded by the contract $w(e^*,\xi)$ which itself satisfies the participation constraint when effort is e^*. The return to the owner from $w(e^*,\xi)$ is $E[R(e^*,\xi)] - E[w(e^*,\xi)] = E[R(e^*,\xi)] - C$, and the return from $C - \delta$ is $E[R(e^*, \xi)] - C + \delta$. The constant salary $C - \delta$ would give the owner a higher expected profit than a variable schedule that gave the manager C in expectation. Therefore, the manager's compensation would be constant if monitoring were costless.

With observable and verifiable effort, incentives play no role because the profit-maximizing effort level can be mandated by the owner. Therefore, the manager receives a fixed payment (the constant salary), independent of random forces, and hence is fully insured. At the other extreme, with unobservable effort and risk-neutral management, the *owner's* return is fixed and the manager bears the full brunt of the vicissitudes of nature. This gives the manager the optimal incentive, from the standpoint of both society and the owner. We expect that if the manager were just a tiny bit risk averse then there would be a small constant element to the compensation, with the manager bearing almost all of the brunt of uncertainty.

We begin with a binary version of the model: the time endowment is $T = 1$, and the manager can either work $(e = 1)$ or shirk $(e = 0)$. We present an example in which the manager is risk averse and the contract that maximizes the owner's return does *not* make the manager the residual claimant. In fact, the optimal contract will pay the manager a fixed salary, to which the manager's best response is to set $e = 0$. After proving this we will go on to a richer model in which the optimal contract offers that manager a share θ of the profits strictly between 0 and 1.

Example 4.15 Binary Effort Supply

The manager can supply effort $e = 0$ or 1, but nothing in between. (Think of 0 as low effort and 1 as high effort.) Leisure consumption x is $2 - e$. $U(x,y) = 4x + \mu(y)$ and $u_0 = 28$. Seven points on the graph of μ are given in Table 4.1. Table 4.2 gives the probability distribution of the firm's profit R, depending on whether $e = 0$ or 1. In this case, when the manager puts in more effort the probability of the high return increases.

If the owner's expected net return is maximized by a contract that does *not* induce the manager to set $e = 1$ then that contract will offer a fixed salary S, with no dependence on the profit R. The contract will also drive the manager's expected utility down to u_0. Therefore, S must satisfy $4 \times 2 + \mu(S) = 28$. We solve this equation by checking the table to see that $\mu(y) = 20$ when $S = 70$. Because $e = 0$ the expected profit is $\frac{3}{4}(100) + \frac{1}{4}(200) = 125$. Hence, $E(N) = 125 - 70 = 55$, the owner's maximum expected net return when the contract offers no incentive to supply effort.

If the contract makes the manager the residual claimant it has the form $y = R + F$. The contract will also drive the manager's expected utility down to u_0, and hence it must satisfy $EU = u_0$. If the manager responds by setting $e = 1$ then $R = 100$ with probability $\frac{1}{4}$ and $R = 200$ with probability $\frac{3}{4}$, in which case $EU = 4 \times 1 + \frac{1}{4}\mu(100+F) + \frac{3}{4}\mu(200+F)$. When we set $EU = 28$ we get $\frac{1}{4}\mu(100+F) + \frac{3}{4}\mu(200+F) = 24$ and we can use Table 4.1 to solve for F. Thus, $F = -40$. The manager is the residual claimant in this case and hence $E(N) = 40$, the owner's maximum expected net return when manager supplies 1 unit of effort and is the residual claimant.

Table 4.1

Y	60	70	75	100	150	160	200
$\mu(y)$	12	20	25	26	27	28	29

Table 4.2

	Probability	
Effort → Profit ↓	$e = 0$	$e = 1$
$R = 100$	$\frac{3}{4}$	$\frac{1}{4}$
$R = 200$	$\frac{1}{4}$	$\frac{3}{4}$

The optimal contract does *not* have the form $y = R + F$ for the data of Example 4.15 because any such contract would result in the owner receiving a lower expected net return than the contract that pays the manager a fixed salary of 70. (Note that we haven't proved that there is some value of θ such that the contract $\theta R + F$ generates a higher value of $E(N)$ than a fixed salary of 70. But we have shown that $\theta = 1$ does not identify the contract that is optimal from the owner's standpoint.)

To confirm that the manager of Example 4.15 is risk averse fix e at some value and consider an asset that pays 60 with probability $\frac{1}{2}$ and 100 with probability $\frac{1}{2}$. The resulting expected utility is $4(2-e) + \frac{1}{2}\mu(60) + \frac{1}{2}\mu(100) = 4(2-e) + 19$, using Table 4.1. The expected monetary value of the asset is $\frac{1}{2}(60) + \frac{1}{2}(100) = 80$. Even a payoff of 75 with certainty yields a higher expected utility, $4(2-e) + 25$, than the asset.

The contract $y = 70$ of Example 4.15 is not efficient. It results in an expected return of 55 to the owner and an expected utility of 28 for the manager. *If* the manager were to choose $e = 1$ and receive a fixed payment of 100 the expected profit R would be $\frac{1}{4}(100) + \frac{3}{4}(200) = 175$. Then $E(N) = 75$ and the manager's $EU = 4 + \mu(100) = 30$ (Table 4.1), giving each agent a higher payoff than the contract $y = 70$. We have shown that $E(N) = 75$ and $EU = 30$ is *feasible*, but we do *not* claim that the manager can be motivated to set $e = 1$ when her pay is constant.

There is a trade-off between incentives and insurance. As the degree of risk aversion increases, the amount of insurance afforded to the manager by the optimal contract also increases. We return to Example 4.15 to investigate this, except we assume that we modify the manager's utility function. It is now $U(x,y) = 4x + \alpha\mu(y) + \lambda y$, where μ is consistent with Table 4.1 and α and λ are nonnegative constants. If $\alpha = 1$ and $\lambda = 0$ we have the manager of Example 4.15. If $\alpha = 0$ and $\lambda = 1$ the manager is risk neutral. If both α and λ are positive the manager is risk averse, but for a given value of λ the degree of risk aversion decreases as α decreases. The individual is "almost" risk averse if $\lambda = 1$ and $\alpha > 0$ is very small. Consider the risk-neutral manager, with $U = 4x + y$: We know that the optimal contract has the form $y = R + F$ and satisfies

$$EU = 4(2 - e) + E(R) + F = 28.$$

When $e = 1$ we have $E(R) = \frac{1}{4}(100) + \frac{3}{4}(200) = 175$, and hence $4 + 175 + F = 28$. Then $F = -151$ and thus $E(N) = 151$. When e = 0 we have $E(R) = \frac{3}{4}(100) + \frac{1}{4}(200) = 125$, and hence $4 \times 2 + 125 + F = 28$ which implies $F = -105$ in that case resulting in $E(N) = 105$. The contract $y = R - 151$ is optimal from the owner's standpoint. It allows the manager to reach the expected utility level 28, but only by setting $e = 1$. ($EU = 4 \times 2 + 125 - 151$ when $e = 0$.) When $U = 4x + \mu(y)$ the optimal contract has the form $y = \theta R + F$ for some $\theta < 1$, but when $U = 4x + y$ the optimal contract is $y = R - 151$. When the ratio λ/α increases the degree of risk aversion decreases, and it becomes more likely that the optimal contract will incorporate financial incentives.

4.5.7   Risk-Averse Managers and a Continuum of Effort Levels

We continue to assume that only linear contracts are practicable, but we now allow e to vary along a continuum.

We simplify the expression of the manager's expected utility, to make the model more amenable to the realistic case of costly monitoring of a risk-averse manager. If w is a compensation package let $E(w)$ denote its expected monetary value (EMV). This expected value depends on the effort supplied by the manager, because effort influences profit R, which has a bearing on the manager's pay. Now, instead of explicitly writing utility in terms of x (the amount of leisure consumption) and y (income from w and a particular realization of the random variable ξ), we write the manager's expected utility as

$$EU = E(w) - \theta^2 K - \frac{1}{2} e^2.$$

$E(w)$ is the EMV of the compensation contract, and that is affected by e. A contribution of e units of effort by the manager causes her utility to fall on that account, because leisure consumption falls by e. We subtract this loss of utility, $\frac{1}{2}e^2$, directly from the expected pay to determine the manager's net utility. (If $EU = B(x) + E(w) - \theta^2 K$ and $x = 24 - e$ then $EU = E(w) - \theta^2 K - \frac{1}{2}e^2$ if $B(x) = 24x - \frac{1}{2}x^2 - 288$.) The manager's exposure to risk also diminishes her utility, and the term $-\theta^2 K$ reflects the utility cost of this risk. The larger is K the more risk averse is the manager. (Here K is a nonnegative parameter and is constant for a particular manager.) We assume that the contract has the form $y = \theta R + F$, where $R = \beta e + \xi$. As usual, ξ is the random component and has an expected value of zero. The larger is θ the greater are the swings in the manager's realized pay as the random variable moves up and down. Therefore, the larger is θ the greater is the negative impact of risk on utility. Let's determine the contract that maximizes the owner's net return. (We do not specify the time endowment but simply assume that the solution value of e is feasible.)

Example 4.16 A Continuum of Effort Levels

Incentive compatibility is incorporated by maximizing the manager's EU. If $R = 10e + \xi$ and $y = \theta R + F$ then $E(y) = \theta 10e + F$, so

$$EU = 10\theta e + F - \theta^2 K - \tfrac{1}{2}e^2,$$

which is a function $V(e)$ of e. The parameter θ is determined by the owner. The manager responds by selecting e, the only variable that she can control. Therefore, from the manager's standpoint, $V(e)$ is a simple quadratic function of e. Calculus or the formula for maximizing a quadratic yields $e = 10\theta$, the effort supply function. Of course, e increases as θ increases. (In calculus terms, $V'(e) = 10\theta - e$. Obviously, $V'' < 0$ at every point, so we want to set $V'(e) = 0$, and this yields $e = 10\theta$.)

To calculate the owner's profit-maximizing values of F and θ we again recognize that profit maximization causes the participation constraint to be satisfied as a strict equality at equilibrium. (If $EU > u^0$ the owner can reduce F and that will reduce EU by the same amount for every value of e. Hence, the manager's choice of e will not be affected, but $E(N)$ will increase, and the participation constraint will still be satisfied if the reduction in F is sufficiently small.) Because $EU = E(y) - \theta^2 K - \tfrac{1}{2}e^2 = u^0$ we have

$$-E(y) = -\theta^2 K - \tfrac{1}{2}e^2 - u^0$$

Because $E(R) = 10e$, the owner's expected net return is

$$
\begin{aligned}
E(R) - E(y) &= 10e - \theta^2 K - \tfrac{1}{2}e^2 - u^0 \\
&= 10(10\theta) - \theta^2 K - \tfrac{1}{2}(10\theta)^2 - u^0 \\
&= 100\theta - (50 + K)\theta^2 - u^0,
\end{aligned}
$$

a quadratic function $G(\theta)$ of θ. By the formula for maximizing a quadratic, the function is maximized at

$$\theta^* = \frac{100}{100 + 2K}.$$

(Alternatively, $G'(\theta) = 100 - 2\theta K - 100\theta$ and $G''(\theta) < 0$ at every point. Therefore, we set $G'(\theta) = 0$.) If the manager is not risk averse then $K = 0$ and hence $\theta^* = 1$. But for all $K > 0$ we have $0 < \theta^* < 1$. Because G is a quadratic, profit rises as θ increases to θ^* and then falls as θ increases beyond that point (Figure 4.6). The expected return $E(R)$ is higher for θ greater than θ^* because more effort is supplied. But the manager is exposed to greater risk when θ is higher, and the participation constraint forces the owner to compensate the risk-averse manager for the increased risk. The expected return is higher but the manager's pay is higher still when $\theta > \theta^*$. We no longer have maximum incentive ($\theta = 1$) because the owner has to trade off insurance and incentive. Note that θ falls as K increases: The greater the degree of risk aversion

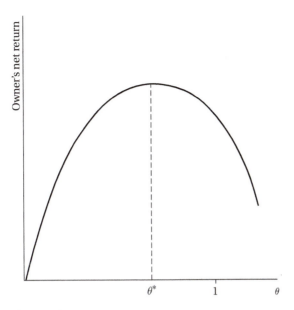

Figure 4.6

the lower is the profit-maximizing value of θ and the more insurance is provided to the manager by the profit-maximizing owner. To determine F we return to the participation constraint, $EU = E(y) - \theta^2 K - \frac{1}{2}e^2 = u^0$ and $E(y) = \theta^* E(R) + F$. Expected gross profit $E(R)$ depends on e, which in turn is a function of θ, which equals θ^*. Therefore, with θ^* and u^0 specified we can solve for F.

To summarize, when effort is unobservable the shareholders will have to provide the manager with an incentive to supply effort, and this means that the manager's compensation must be correlated with observed profit. Because profit is influenced by random forces as well as the manager's effort, the incentive prevents her from being fully insured against risk, even though the owners bear all the risk in the ideal case of costlessly observable effort. Because the manager is not fully insured, her expected pay must be higher than in the full information case to elicit her participation. Accordingly, the owner's expected return is lower. The manager is not fully insured but does not assume all risk – much of it falls on the shoulders of the owners. To the extent that the manager is insured, the contract diminishes the manager's incentive to maximize the owner's expected profit. The agent is no longer the sole residual claimant. Because she is insured against bad outcomes she will work less assiduously to avoid them. (This explains why managers are not paid solely in the form of stock options.) In short, there is a trade-off between insurance and incentives.

We saw in Section 4.5.3 that when the manager is the residual claimant she has an incentive to supply the efficient amount of effort in every dimension. When the manager is risk averse it is in the owner's interest to modify the managerial incentives to shelter the manager from risk, at least to a degree. That means that it cannot be taken for granted that the manager will do a reasonable job of looking out for shareholder welfare in every dimension.

Sources

The foundations of optimal incentive contracts were laid by Ross (1973), Mirlees (1974, 1976), Stiglitz (1975), and Holmström (1979a). Example 4.16 is from McMillan (1992, pp. 205-208). The progressive piece rate idea is due to Olson (1993). Much of the material on franchising is based on Blair and Lafontaine (2011).

Links

Hart (1995) is a seminal contribution to the theory of contracts, taking the subject well beyond the simple framework of this section. (Oliver Hart and Bengt Holmström shared the 2016 Nobel Prize in Economics.) The following parallel treatments of agency theory are listed in order of increasing difficulty: Chapters 8-10 in McMillan (1992); Sappington (1991); Chapter 1 in Tirole (1988); and Laffont and Martimort (2002). Baker (2002) and Baker et al. (2002) consider optimal contract design when *profit* is not verifiable. Their model and results are also presented in Dixit (2004), beginning on page 32. (Jean Tirole received the 2012 Nobel Prize in Economics.)

Problem Set

(1) A risk-neutral manager has utility function $U(x, y) = 20\ln(x + 1) + y$. Units have been chosen so that $T = 3$. (The individual is endowed with 3 units of X and 0 units of Y. We could have a positive endowment of Y but we assume that it has been netted out of both F and u_0.) The manager's best alternative opportunity is to consume 3 units of leisure and not work. If the manager supplies e units of effort then the firm's profit R will be $10e + \xi$, where ξ is a random variable with expected value zero. (R is profit before deducting the manager's pay.)

  (A) Suppose that the owner offers the manager the compensation contract $y = \theta R + F$. Determine the manager's effort supply function. Show that e increases when θ increases.

  (B) Solve for the contract that maximizes the owner's expected profit.

  (C) What is the owner's expected profit, the manager's expected utility, and the effort supplied by the manager under the contract that maximizes the owner's expected profit?

  (D) Is the outcome that maximizes the owner's expected profit efficient? Explain.

(2) A risk-neutral manager has utility function $U(x, y) = 2\sqrt{x} + y$. The time endowment is T. (The manager is endowed with T units of X and 0 units of Y.) The manager's best alternative opportunity provides a level of utility of $u^0 = 2\sqrt{T}$. If the manager supplies e units of effort then the firm's profit R will be $\beta e + \xi$, where ξ is a random variable with expected value zero and R is profit before deducting the manager's pay.

  (A) Suppose that the owner offers the manager the compensation contract $y = \theta R + F$. Determine the manager's effort supply function. Show that e increases when θ increases.

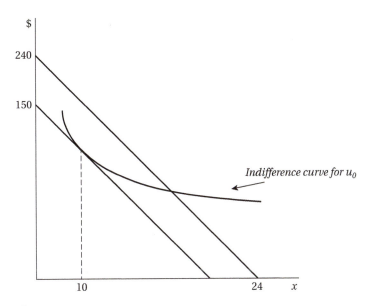

Figure 4.7

    (B) Solve for the contract that maximizes the owner's expected profit when the manager cannot be monitored.

    (C) What is the owner's expected profit, the manager's expected utility, and the effort supplied by the manager under the contract that maximizes the owner's expected profit?

(3) Figure 4.7 shows the indifference curve for a risk-neutral manager when the participation constraint is satisfied as an equality. (The two straight lines are parallel.) What is the output per unit of input coefficient β? Assuming that the manager is offered the contract that maximizes the owner's net return, determine the manager's effort supply, the firm's expected profit R, the manager's expected income, and the owner's expected net return, at the effort level of the manager that maximizes the owner's expected net return subject to the participation constraint. What is the form of the contract? Whose income is uncertain, the manager's, the owner's, or both?

(4) Figure 4.8 shows the indifference curve for a risk-neutral manager when the participation constraint is satisfied as an equality. Use the diagram to determine the manager's effort supply, the firm's expected profit, the manager's expected income, and the owner's expected net return, at the effort level of the manager that maximizes the owner's expected net return subject to the participation constraint. (*AB* is parallel to *FD*.) Now, write the contract represented by the budget line *ABCD*. Write it as it would appear in the real world with unobservable effort.

(5) A risk-neutral manager has utility function $U(x, y) = 2000 - 1690x^{-1} + y$. Set $T = 24$. The manager's best alternative opportunity provides a level of utility of $u^0 = 1910$. The firm's profit R is $10e + \xi$, where ξ is a random variable with expected value zero and R is profit before deducting the manager's pay.

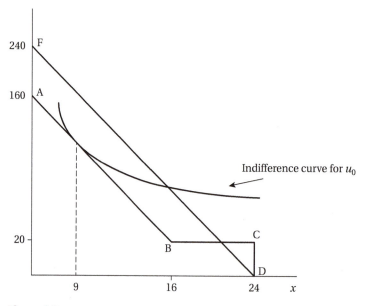

Figure 4.8

(A) Solve for the contract that maximizes the owner's expected profit, even though the manager cannot be monitored.

(B) Derive the manager's budget line, expressed in terms of x and y, that the optimal contract induces.

(6) A risk-neutral manager has utility function $U(x, y) = 10\ln(x + 1) + y$. Set $T = 2$. The manager's best alternative opportunity provides a level of utility of $u^0 = 9.93$. The firm's profit R is $5e + \zeta$, where ζ is a random variable with expected value zero and R is profit before deducting the manager's pay.

(A) Solve for the contract that maximizes the owner's expected profit, even though the manager cannot be monitored.

(B) Now derive the optimal contract by employing the manager's effort supply function.

(7) This question features a manager whose utility function is nonlinear in Y but there are no random variables affecting production. The manager's utility function is $U(x, y) = xy$, and the manager's best alternative yields $u^0 = 1$. Profit is $R = 4e$, where R is profit before deducting the manager's pay. $T = 2$: the manager has an endowment of 2 units of X and 0 units of Y. Find the contract that maximizes the owner's profit. What is the owner's net return, the manager's consumption of X and Y, the manager's utility, and the effort supplied by the manager under the contract that maximizes the owner's net return?

(8) Again we have a manager whose utility function is nonlinear in Y and no randomness in production. The manager's utility function is $U(x, y) = xy$, and the manager's best alternative yields $u^0 = 1$. Profit is $R = \beta e$, where β is a positive constant and R is profit before deducting the manager's pay. The manager's time endowment is T. Find the contract that maximizes the owner's net return. What is the owner's profit, the manager's consumption of X and Y, the manager's utility, and the effort supplied by the manager under the contract that maximizes the owner's net return?

(∂9) This question features a manager whose utility function is nonlinear in Y, but there are no random variables affecting production. Let $U(x, y)$ represent the manager's utility function. The manager's best alternative yields u^0. Profit is $R = \beta e$, where β is a positive constant and R is profit before deducting the manager's pay. The manager's time endowment is T. Initially, the manager has 0 units of Y. Show that the contract that maximizes the owner's profit has the form $y = R + F$, where F is fixed, independently of the profit R. *Hint:* use the implicit function theorem and the participation constraint to solve for dy/dx in terms of the partial derivatives of U. Then compare the first-order condition from the owner's maximization problem to the solution of

$$\text{maximize } U(x, y) \text{ subject to } p_1 x + p_2 y = C.$$

(10) Solve for the contract that maximizes the owner's net return in the model of Section 4.5.7 with $R = 4e + \xi$, $K = 8$, and $u^0 = 5$. Calculate F as well as θ. What is the owner's expected return?

(11) Solve for the contract that maximizes the owner's net return in the model of Section 4.5.7 when the manager's expected utility function is $EU = 24x - \frac{1}{2}x^2 + E(y) - 192\theta^2$ with $R = 16e + \xi$, and $u^0 = 320$. Calculate F as well as θ. What is the owner's expected return?

(12) The manager of a firm has the utility function $U = 50x - x^2 + y$. The manager will cease to work for the firm if her utility falls below 624. $T = 24$ and the manager's initial wealth is zero. The profit R realized by the owner, before deducting the manager's pay, is given by $R = 30e + \xi$, where e is effort supplied by the manager and ξ is a random variable with an expected value of zero. The owner cannot enforce a contract that mandates a specific input of effort. Show that the owner's net return is maximized if the owner offers the manager a contract that requires a payment of $196 from the manager to the owner with the manager keeping any additional profit realized by the firm.

5 Hidden Characteristics

This chapter and the next four investigate hidden characteristic problems, from voting to used-car markets to kidney exchanges. In some cases market forces have fostered contracts and other devices that induce agents to reveal their hidden characteristics. This does not mean that the equilibrium outcome is efficient in each case, however. There are incentive schemes that *do* induce truthful revelation of the hidden information while at the same time bringing the system close to efficiency – the Vickrey auction of Chapter 6 for instance.

Markets can be very creative in circumventing hidden information problems – for instance, warranties on consumer durables. The producer of a shoddy appliance cannot afford to offer a substantial warranty: the point of producing a low-quality item is to get more profit by keeping costs down, but if appliances are being returned for replacement or repair then costs will be high, not low. A producer who deliberately sets out to profit by misleading consumers about the quality of the product will not be able to offer the same kind of warranty as the producer of a high-quality product. The latter is credibly signaling high quality to the consumer by offering a substantial warranty. Reputable manufacturers often make good on a warranty even after it has expired, as long as the appliance is returned a month or less after the expiration date.

Although not always delivering an efficient outcome, the market system often goes a long way toward eliciting the hidden information. The next section begins with a standard example of the hidden characteristic phenomenon.

It can be in society's interest to have the hidden information remain hidden. It is often essential for communication about financial transactions to be encoded so that eavesdroppers cannot profit from the information. Electronic messages are encoded using an *asymmetric* form of encryption: the recipient R of the message publishes the key to encoding the text that R will receive. This key is the product of two very large prime numbers p and q. But only the product is published. To decode the message it is necessary to know both p and q, and only R knows these *prime factors*. If they are sufficiently large, it will be well beyond the ability of even a huge network of computers to determine them in anyone's lifetime, even though the product is known.

Links

See Mann and Wissink (1988, 1990a, 1990b) for a thorough discussion of warranties. For more on the technique of public key encryption see Singh (1999), which is a superb history and analysis of coding and decoding from ancient Egypt to the present, and Chapter 4 in MacCormick (2012).

5.1   PRICE DISCRIMINATION

Suppose that a firm's consumers can be divided into two categories, high-demand-elasticity (very price sensitive) and low-demand-elasticity (not very price sensitive) types. The firm's profit is maximized by charging a higher price to the latter group. Because of this, the low-elasticity customers cannot be expected to voluntarily disclose their (elasticity) characteristic. Consequently, suppliers will endeavor to find something that is both observable and correlated with the hidden demand characteristics. (Eurail passes cannot be purchased in Europe.)

Example 5.1 Haircuts

We can simplify the analysis by selecting a commodity for which no unit after the first has utility. A haircut, for instance. Suppose that everyone wants a haircut every thirty days but not more frequently. The community consists of A types who would be willing to pay $20 for a haircut, but no more, and B types who would pay a maximum of $9 for a haircut. There are n of each. There is only one barber in town, and the opportunity cost of the barber's time is $7 per haircut. If the barber has no way of distinguishing A types from Bs then the barber must charge one price P. If $P = 20$ then the barber's profit per haircut is $20 - 7$, and because only the A types will come to the shop, the profit will be $13n$. (The B types will get a friend or relative to do the job, or drive to another town.) If $P = 9$ then the profit per haircut would be $9 - 7 = 2$. Everyone would be a customer at $P = 9$, resulting in a total profit of $4n$. Clearly, if the barber can't distinguish A types from B types then the profit-maximizing price is $P = 20$.

Suppose, however, that all B types are sixty-five years of age or older. If the barber charges $9 per haircut to anyone older than sixty-four and $20 to everyone else the profit will be $2n + 13n$, which is 15 percent higher than the maximum profit of $13n$ obtainable without price discrimination. (It is essential to the story that a B type is not able to buy a $9 haircut and sell it to an A type for, say, $15.)

Consider plane travel: on average, business travelers have a lower demand elasticity than recreation travelers. The former pass their travel expenses on to their companies, who in turn pass on part of the cost to taxpayers. Moreover, business trips often have an urgency that nonbusiness travel seldom does. That makes the business traveler much less responsive to a price increase. Vacationers have lots of close substitutes for plane travel, and that makes their demand much more price sensitive. Most business trips do not extend through Saturday: a Saturday stayover is very costly to a business traveler because of the need to be back in the office promptly and the desire to spend the weekend with the family. In short, there is a relatively low elasticity of demand for plane tickets by business travelers. By charging a higher fare for travelers who don't stay over at least one Saturday night an airline can force most business travelers to pay the higher fare.

Xerox Corporation introduced the first push-button electrostatic copying machine in 1960 and for many years the company faced very little competition. Price discriminating profit maximization implies a higher charge for machines purchased by firms that intend to use them intensively. But these firms would not willingly admit that they are high-intensity users (and the machines can be resold anyway). The chief rival to Xerox in the 1960s was Electrofax, which produced a copier that required a special coated paper. Initially, Electrofax held a monopoly on the sale of the special paper. By charging a price for the paper that was significantly above marginal cost, the company in effect charged a higher price for copying machines purchased by high-intensity users. A similar principle applies to the charges for Polaroid film during the period when Polaroid Corporation had a monopoly on the production of self-developing film and the complementary camera. And again in the case of the early IBM computers, the punch cards sold by the company and used to enter input provided a way for IBM to meter the use of their machines. Initially, the firm had a monopoly on the sale of punch cards and they were priced above marginal cost to allow IBM to extract more revenue from the high-intensity users of its computers.

The Xerox copier did not require special paper, so the Xerox Corporation solved its hidden characteristic problem by refusing to sell the copiers; the machines had to be leased from Xerox. The rental fee was based on the number of copies made, so Xerox was able to meter its customers' usage and thus force high-intensity users to pay more for the use of the copier.

There is a tension between price discrimination and the extraction of consumer surplus. If all consumers had identical demand functions for the services generated by the machines and their variable input (paper, film, punch cards) then the monopolist would want to price the variable input at marginal cost to induce the buyer to use the equipment more intensively, which in turn allows a higher price to be charged for the equipment because of the larger consumer surplus. (One can show that profit is maximized when the price of the variable input is set at marginal cost and the price of the machine is set equal to the resulting consumer surplus. In this case there is only one demand curve to consider – the demand for the services of the machine.)

A firm will often make a high-quality, high-price product and at the same time offer a low-quality, low-price version of the same item. That, albeit imperfectly, allows the supplier to derive substantial profit from the high-demand, price-insensitive consumers while still squeezing some profit from the low-demand, price-sensitive buyers. Sometimes the low-quality version is more costly to manufacture: when the microprocessor – loosely speaking, a computer on a chip – was introduced by Intel the manufacturer took an extra step to disable some of the features of the product to create a low-quality, low-price version. IBM's Laser Writer has a sibling, the Laser Writer E, which is slower and less expensive. The economy model is manufactured by installing a chip in the upscale version to slow it down.

Nineteenth-century train travel in France provides an amusing example of the strategy of incurring additional costs to create a low-quality, low-price version of a product: when third-class carriages were made available – at a *very* low price – the railway simply removed the roof from a second-class carriage to create a product that the poor would be willing to pay for without also creating an incentive for travelers who had been buying second-class tickets to switch to third class (Harford, 2006, p. 50).

Sources

The copying machine details are from Phlips (1981). The Laser Writer E and microprocessor examples of price discrimination are drawn from Shapiro and Varian (1999, p. 59).

Links

To see why price discrimination can emerge in a competitive environment see Dana (1998) and Varian (2000).

Problem Set

Assume that all consumers are of the same type – they all have the same demand function. Prove that profit is maximized when the price of the variable input is set at marginal cost and the price of the machine required to turn this input into the desired product is set equal to the resulting consumer surplus.

5.2   TWO-PERSON EXCHANGE

A brother B and a sister S have jointly inherited a house. Each has a family, so they are not willing to share the house, which they suspect is worth more to B than to S. If it were worth, say, \$100,000 to B and only \$20,000 to S it doesn't seem fair for B to pay his sister only \$25,000 for her share. Moreover, S would not have an incentive to reveal her reservation value truthfully if the price will be 125 percent of the seller's value. However, the arbitration rule that has B paying half of what the house is worth to him gives B a strong incentive to understate his reservation value. But if the parties do not reveal their true reservation values we have no guarantee that the house will be used by the family that values it most – that is, gets the most benefit from it. The same problem arises when two business partners B and S have decided that they cannot continue working together. One of them will take over the business by buying the other's share. They have different abilities and different expectations about the future profitability of the enterprise. How should they dissolve the partnership?

Formally, there is a single asset, owned by individual S, and a potential buyer B. The asset is worth a minimum of V_S to S and a maximum of V_B to B. These are the respective reservation values. Think of V_S (resp., V_B) as the discounted stream of profits (*before* subtracting the cost of acquiring the asset) that S (resp., B) would realize by employing the asset in its production process.

DEFINITION: *The Two-Person Exchange Framework*
An asset is worth a minimum of V_S to the current owner S and a maximum of V_B to the potential buyer B. V_i is called the reservation value of agent i.

5.2.1   Dominant Strategy Equilibrium

We seek a recipe for deciding when the asset should be transferred from S to B and at what price. An *exchange mechanism* is a decision rule under which each party reports its reservation value and then determines whether B gets the asset.

The exchange mechanism also specifies a price paid by the buyer and an amount of money received by the seller. Both the decision and the price are functions of the reported reservation values.

DEFINITION: *Exchange Mechanism*

An exchange mechanism requires the seller S and the buyer B to report their respective reservation values and determines when the asset changes hands, as a function of the values R_B reported by B and R_S reported by S. If ownership passes from S to B the mechanism specifies the amount $P(R_B, R_S)$ paid by the buyer and the amount $Q(R_B, R_S)$ received by the seller.

We want to employ a mechanism that has three properties: *incentive compatibility*, which means that truthful revelation is a dominant strategy for each party; *asset efficiency*, which means that B gets the asset if it is worth more to B than to S, otherwise S keeps the asset; and the *participation constraint*, which means that neither B nor S winds up with less utility than he or she started with.

DEFINITION: *Incentive Compatibility, Asset Efficiency, and the Participation Constraint*

An exchange mechanism is incentive compatible if for each pair (V_B, V_S) (i) no reported value R_B gives the buyer B a higher payoff than reporting the true value V_B and (ii) no reported value R_S gives the seller S a higher payoff than reporting the true value V_S. The mechanism is asset efficient if B gets the asset when $V_B > V_S$ and S keeps the asset if $V_B \leq V_S$. The mechanism satisfies the participation constraint if neither S nor B pays anything when no trade takes place.

We prove that the *only* mechanism with these three properties requires the buyer to make a payment equal to the seller's reservation value, and the seller to receive an amount equal to the buyer's reservation value. When the seller's reservation value is at least as high as the buyer's then the asset stays with the seller, and no one pays any money or receives any money. This is called the *Groves bargaining mechanism* (GBM).

DEFINITION: *Groves Bargaining Mechanism (GBM)*

Let R_i denote the reservation values *reported* by agent i. When $R_B > R_S$ the asset is transferred from the seller to the buyer, with $P(R_B, R_S) = R_S$ and $Q(R_B, R_S) = R_B$. When $R_B \leq R_S$ the seller keeps the asset and $P(R_B, R_S) = 0 = Q(R_B, R_S)$.

Before proving that the *GBM* is the *only* one that satisfies asset efficiency, the participation constraint, and incentive compatibility, we demonstrate that the *GBM* actually does have our three properties.

Theorem

The GBM satisfies asset efficiency, the participation constraint, and incentive compatibility

---

Proof:

GBM satisfies asset efficiency and the participation constraint by definition.

Consider the buyer's incentive: suppose that $V_B < R_S$. Under truthful revelation there is no trade and no payment by B. Would it ever be to *B's* advantage to misrepresent V_B? What would happen if B reported a reservation value R_B greater than R_S? Agent B would get the asset and would be required to pay R_S, which exceeds the true worth V_B of the asset to B, resulting in a loss to B. Truthful revelation would have resulted in no gain or loss to B, and hence would be preferred by B to reporting $R_B > R_S$. Suppose B reported a reservation value R_B *less* than V_S. This yields the same outcome as V_B because both are below V_S. Therefore, when $V_B < R_S$ the buyer B can never profit by misrepresenting the true reservation value, but can lose by doing so. In other words, truthful revelation is a best response by B to any R_S for which $V_B < R_S$.

Now, consider the more interesting case of potential gains from trade: $V_B > R_S$. What would happen if B reported a reservation value R_B below V_S? B would not get the asset and would forego the profit of $V_B - R_S$ that would have resulted from truthful revelation. If B were to report any value $R_B > R_S$, then B would acquire the asset, just as in the case of truthful revelation. Moreover, the payment that B would have to make is the same for any $R_B > R_S$ because that payment is R_S, which is independent of R_B for any $R_B > R_S$. Therefore, the buyer cannot profit by deviating from truthful revelation when $V_B > R_S$ and would be hurt by any deviation that left R_B below R_S.

Consider the seller's strategy when $R_B < V_S$. Trade will take place if the seller reports R_S below R_B and S will receive R_B, which is less than his or her true value V_S, resulting in a loss of $V_S - R_B$ to the seller. Had S revealed the true value V_S there would have been no trade and no loss. When the seller reports V_S, or any other number R_S greater than R_B, there will be no trade and S will not take a loss.

Suppose that $R_B > V_S$ and the seller reports a reservation value R_S above R_B. Then no trade will take place, in which case the seller forfeits the profit of $R_B - V_S$ that would have accompanied truthful revelation. If the seller reports V_S or any other number R_S below R_B then trade will take place resulting in a profit of $R_B - V_S$ for S. (When $R_S < R_B$, the seller receives a payment R_B that is independent of R_S. If my house is worth \$300,000 to me but I tell you that it's worth \$1 the sale will take place if you have reported a reservation value of \$370,00. My profit will be \$370,000 − \$300,000, not \$370,000 − \$1.) When R_B is greater than V_S the *GBM* induces truthful revelation by both the buyer and the seller:

When V_B is less than V_S the *GBM* induces truthful revelation by both the buyer and the seller. That is, neither can benefit from deviating from the truth, but either can be hurt by doing so. Truthful revelation is a dominant strategy for each.   ∎

Proving that the *GBM* is the only mechanism with our three properties is more demanding.

To prove this we have to begin by examining the price and revenue functions of a mechanism that we know almost nothing about. All we know is that it satisfies asset efficiency, incentive compatibility, and the participation constraint. We show that the three properties imply that the price and revenue functions are precisely those of the *GBM*. We let $P(R_B, R_S)$ denote the price that our mystery mechanism requires the buyer to pay when the asset changes hands, and we let $Q(R_B, R_S)$ denote the amount received by the seller. If we can show that $P(R_B, R_S) = R_S$ and $Q(R_B, R_S) = R_B$ then we will have proved that this mechanism must be the *GBM*.

Before presenting the proof, we give an informal demonstration that our three properties force the price and revenue functions to be identical to the ones specified by *GBM*. Suppose that the asset is worth more to the buyer than the seller. Consider two different possible buyer reservation values V_B^1 and V_B^2, both of which are greater than V_S. (The seller can be relied on to report his or her true value because the mechanism in question satisfies incentive compatibility.) Asset efficiency implies that when B reports V_B^1 then B gets the asset for a price of $P(V_B^1, V_S)$, and when B reports V_B^2 then B gets the asset and pays $P(V_B^2, V_S)$. If $P(V_B^1, V_S) > P(V_B^2, V_S)$ then when B's true reservation value is V_B^1 the buyer is better off reporting V_B^2 and paying the smaller amount $P(V_B^2, V_S)$. Similarly, $P(V_B^1, V_S) < P(V_B^2, V_S)$ leads to a violation of incentive compatibility. Therefore, $P(V_B^1, V_S) = P(V_B^2, V_S)$ must hold for any two reservation values V_B^1 and V_B^2 that exceed V_S.

Why does the price have to equal V_S? The price can't be below V_S if $V_B > V_S$. Otherwise, there would be a situation ($V_S > B$'s true value $> P(V_B, V_S)$) in which the asset is worth more to the seller than the buyer, but the buyer could misrepresent and report V_B and get the asset for a price below B's true reservation value. Therefore, $P(V_B, V_S) \geq V_S$ if $V_B > V_S$. However, if $P(V_B, V_S) > V_S$ we can replace V_B with any V_B^1 above V_S. The price will still be $P(V_B, V_S)$ by the argument of the previous paragraph. Now bring V_B^1 closer and closer to V_S, but keep it above V_S. The price paid by the buyer will still not change, but it can't be above V_B^1 or else the participation constraint will be violated. And it can't be less than V_S. This rules out every possibility except $P(V_B, V_S) = V_S$. Similarly, one can show that $Q(V_B, V_S^1)$ must equal $Q(V_B, V_S^2)$ for any two seller reservation values V_S^1 and V_S^2 that are below V_B and then use that fact to establish $Q(V_B, V_S) = V_B$.

Theorem: Uniqueness of the GBM

The GBM is the only incentive-compatible mechanism satisfying asset efficiency and the participation constraint.

Proof:

We want to prove that if incentive compatibility is satisfied then the participation constraint and asset efficiency imply $P(V_B, V_S) = V_S$ and $Q(V_B, V_S) = V_B$. Incentive compatibility allows us to assume that $R_i = V_i$ for each agent i.

We begin by showing that the price paid by the buyer can never exceed the buyer's reservation value. That is, $P(V_B, V_S) \leq V_B$ must hold for every combination of V_B and V_S such that $V_B > V_S$. If we actually had $P(V_B, V_S) > V_B$ then truthful revelation would not be a dominant strategy for the buyer, who could report a reservation value of zero, resulting in no trade and no payment by the buyer. (If the buyer did not get the asset but still had to make a payment the participation constraint would be violated.) But when $P(V_B, V_S) > V_B$, truthful revelation would result in the buyer acquiring the asset worth V_B and having to pay a larger amount $P(V_B, V_S)$ for it. Therefore, incentive compatibility and the participation constraint imply $P(V_B, V_S) \leq V_B$. Similarly, if $Q(V_B, V_S) < V_S < V_B$ then the asset would change hands under asset efficiency and truthful revelation (because $V_B > V_S$), but the seller would be paid less than the minimum V_S that S would be willing to accept to part with the asset, resulting in a loss of $V_S - Q(V_B, V_S)$. The seller could avoid that loss by reporting a reservation value of $2 \times V_B$, in which case no exchange would take place. Therefore, if truthful revelation is a dominant strategy for the seller for all possible values of V_S we must have $Q(V_B, V_S) \geq V_S$ for arbitrary V_S and V_B such that $V_S < V_B$.

Suppose that $V_B > V_S$ but $P(V_B, V_S) < V_S$. In that case when the buyer's *true reservation* value is T_B, strictly between $P(V_B, V_S)$ and V_S, then asset efficiency requires that no trade take place, leaving no profit for the buyer with reservation value T_B. But if that buyer were to report a reservation value of V_B then trade would take place and the buyer would pay $P(V_B, V_S)$, which is less than T_B, leaving a positive profit of $T_B - P(V_B, V_S)$. Therefore, incentive compatibility requires $P(V_B, V_S) \geq V_S$ for every combination of V_B and V_S such that $V_B > V_S$.

To prove that $P(V_B, V_S)$ cannot actually be larger than V_S, we suppose the contrary and show that one or more of the required properties must be violated as a result. Suppose, then, that $P(V_B, V_S) > V_S$. When B's true reservation value is V_B the buyer B can report a value R_B *strictly* between V_S and $P(V_B, V_S)$. Agent B will still get the asset because $R_B > V_S$ but will pay some price $P(R_B, V_S) \leq R_B$. This price $P(R_B, V_S)$ must be less than $P(V_B, V_S)$ because $P(R_B, V_S)$ cannot exceed R_B, as the first paragraph demonstrated. The resulting profit to the buyer will be at least $V_B - R_B$ which is greater than the profit of $V_B - P(V_B, V_S)$ that results from truthful revelation. Therefore, incentive compatibility requires $P(V_B, V_S) \leq V_S$. Because we have also established $P(V_B, V_S) \geq V_S$, we have proved that $P(V_B, V_S) = V_S$ for all reservation values such that $V_B > V_S$. It remains to prove that $Q(V_B, V_S) = V_B$ when $V_B > V_S$.

Suppose that $Q(V_B, V_S) > V_B$ and $V_S < V_B$. In that case when the seller's *true* reservation value is T_S between V_B and $Q(V_B, V_S)$ then asset efficiency requires that no trade take place. But if the seller were to misrepresent and report V_S, then trade would take place and the seller would receive $Q(V_B, V_S)$, which is more than T_S, yielding a positive profit for the seller of $Q(V_B, V_S) - T_S$. Therefore, incentive compatibility requires $Q(V_B, V_S) \leq V_B$ for every combination of V_B and V_S such that $V_B > V_S$.

Finally, we show that $Q(V_B, V_S) < V_B$ cannot hold for any combination of V_B and V_S such that $V_B > V_S$. If we did have $Q(V_B, V_S) < V_B$, then when the seller's true reservation value is V_S individual S can report a value R_S between $Q(V_B, V_S)$ and V_B. There will still be a sale, but S will receive at least R_S, which is higher than $Q(V_B, V_S)$. (Recall the first paragraph showed that our three conditions require that the seller receives at least as much as his or her own reservation value.) Therefore, incentive compatibility implies $Q(V_B, V_S) \geq V_B$. But we have already ruled out $Q(V_B, V_S) > V_B$, so we have proved that $Q(V_B, V_S) = V_B$ holds for all reservation values such that $V_B > V_S$. Because we know that $P(V_B, V_S) = V_S$ also holds we have proved that the mechanism must be the *GBM* if it satisfies asset efficiency, incentive compatibility, and the participation constraint.   ∎

Applications

In the case of two heirs splitting an indivisible asset (such as a house) we begin by assuming that heir B will buy out the other heir, individual S. Then V_B is the value to B of S's share – specifically, the difference between the value to B of outright ownership of the asset and the value if it is shared with S. Then V_S is the value of the asset to S when ownership is shared. Assuming that the *GBM* is employed, if $V_B > V_S$ then B gets the asset and pays V_S with person S receiving V_B.

If players S and B are business partners dissolving their firm, with partner B buying out partner S – perhaps because the business would be more profitable under the stewardship of B – then V_B is the difference between the value to B of outright ownership of the firm and the value of continuing the partnership, and V_S is the value to S of continuing the partnership.

The Budget Imbalance Problem

When V_B is larger than V_S the *GBM* requires B to pay V_S for the asset but S receives the larger amount V_B. Is it possible that a third party would supply the difference $V_B - V_S$? Instead of using a mechanism such as the *GBM*, the two parties could battle each other in court and perhaps dissipate 50 percent of the value of the asset that is in dispute. Because that often happens, they should be willing to pay a modest fee to an arbiter – if they could be sure that the arbiter would settle the matter efficiently and fairly. That would certainly happen if the arbiter used the *GBM*. The arbiter could charge a fee that yielded a positive annual profit, although there would be a loss on some cases that could be covered by a profit from other cases. The fee could be set high enough so that the arbiter could supply the difference between $Q(V_B, V_S)$ and $P(V_B, V_S)$ in each case. The two parties would be willing to pay the fee because the alternative would be a costly legal battle.

This scheme has a fatal flaw: the two parties B and S would have a strong incentive to collude and have the buyer submit a very high (untruthful) R_B so that they could split $Q(R_B, V_S) - P(R_B, V_S) = R_B - V_S$.

Remark on the Participation Constraint

Suppose that the two parties did each pay a fee F to an arbiter who then applied the GBM. That would be equivalent to the following mechanism: $P(V_B, V_S) = V_S + F$ and $Q(V_B, V_S) = V_B - F$ when $V_B > V_S$, with $P(V_B, V_S) = F$ and $Q(V_B, V_S) = -F$ when $V_B \leq V_S$. In words, each pays a fee F, whatever happens, and then the GBM is applied. Truthful revelation is a dominant strategy for this mechanism: consider the buyer. Given V_S, *the difference* between $P(V_B^1, V_S)$ and $P(V_B^2, V_S)$ for any two reported reservation values V_B^1 and V_B^2 above V_S is the same for this mechanism as for the GBM. We've just added a constant to each of the GBM prices. Similarly, given V_B, the difference between $Q(V_B, V_S^1)$ and $Q(V_B, V_S^2)$) is the same for this mechanism as for the GBM, for any V_S^1 and V_S^2 below V_B. Of course this new mechanism does not satisfy the participation constraint but, problems of collusion aside, one can imagine individuals nevertheless being willing to participate anyway.

∂5.2.2 Nash Equilibrium

We now constrain the exchange mechanism by requiring the payment received by the seller to equal the amount paid by the buyer. Also, we now suppose that the buyer B is uncertain about the value of the asset, rather than assume a value V_B that is known to B. We also relax the incentive compatibility requirement and merely require the existence of a Nash equilibrium that is asset efficient. Because of the buyer's uncertainty, B's payoffs will be evaluated in terms of expected utility (EU).

A risk-neutral buyer and a risk-neutral seller must agree on the price at which the seller is to deliver a single asset to the buyer. The two agree that the asset is worth more to the buyer than the seller, but the buyer does not know the actual value of the asset. The value is known to the seller, though. We have a hidden characteristic problem. Even though the seller knows the value of the asset to himself before negotiation takes place, that value is a random variable from the buyer's perspective. (The seller cannot credibly signal the value to the buyer.) The asset may be a firm that the seller owns. The buyer is a better manager than the seller, so the firm would generate more profit if it were managed by the buyer. But the actual profit depends upon a technological innovation for which the seller is seeking a patent, and the seller knows much more about the discovery than the buyer.

DEFINITION: *Model with a Single Buyer and Single Seller*

The random variable v is the value of the asset to the *seller*, and from the buyer's perspective is uniformly distributed on the interval 0 to 1, inclusive. (This distribution is introduced in Section 2.6.5 of Chapter 2.) The value to the buyer is assumed to be $1.5v$. Although both people know that the value to the buyer is 50 percent higher than its value to the seller, the buyer does not know v itself until the sale is complete and the asset is in her hands.

Of course, the seller knows v before negotiations take place. Because $\int x dx = 0.5 x^2$, the expected value of v is

$$\int_0^1 v dv = \frac{1}{2}(1^2 - 0) = \frac{1}{2}.$$

Suppose that the following simple bargaining scheme is adopted. The buyer submits a bid for the asset, which the seller either accepts or rejects. If the buyer's bid of b is accepted by the seller then the asset changes hands at that price. The seller's payoff is the selling price minus the seller's value v, and the buyer's payoff is the difference between the value to the buyer and the price paid. However, the buyer's bid has to be determined before the asset changes hands and before the value is known to her. Therefore, the payoff used by the buyer to determine her optimal bid is the *expected value* of the difference between the value to her and the price that she pays, *conditional on acceptance of the offer by the seller*. If the buyer's offer is rejected there is no exchange and no further negotiation.

DEFINITION: *A Take-it-or-Leave-it Offer by the Buyer*
   The buyer bids b. If the seller accepts, his payoff is $b - v$, and the buyer's payoff is the expected value of $1.5v - b$, *conditional on acceptance*. If the offer is rejected there is no further negotiation, in which case the seller's payoff is zero and the buyer's is zero.

Surprisingly, whatever the buyer bids, her expected value will be negative. Even though the asset has more value to the buyer than the seller, and both agents know that, there is no price that the buyer would be willing to pay and the seller would accept. Because the asset stays with the individual who values it least, the outcome is inefficient.

Inefficiency Theorem for a Take-it-or-Leave-it Offer by the Buyer
   No trade will ever take place if the buyer makes a take-it-or-leave-it offer.

Proof:
The seller will accept b only if $v \leq b$. If $v > b$ then his payoff is higher if he keeps the asset. The buyer knows this, although she doesn't know v itself. Let's determine the expected value to the buyer resulting from a bid of b. If $v > b$ the buyer's payoff is 0. If $v \leq b$ the asset will change hands and the buyer's profit is $1.5v - b$. (Of course, a lower b means more profit to the buyer should the offer be accepted, but it also means a lower probability of acceptance.) Because $\int 1.5 x dx = 0.75x^2$ and $\int b dx = bx$ for any b, the *expected* payoff to the buyer is

$$\int_0^b (1.5v - b)dv = 0.75b^2 - b^2 = -0.25b^2.$$

Note that we have integrated over the subinterval $[0, b]$. That's because the seller keeps the asset when $v > b$, in which case the buyer's payoff is zero.   ■

The inefficiency of this mechanism is a direct consequence of asymmetric information. A bid of b is accepted by the seller only when v is below b, which means that the value to the buyer is $1.5b$ *at most*. However, the buyer pays b dollars for certain when an offer of b is accepted. She pays $b for something worth less on average – a losing proposition. Therefore, the buyer will bid 0 and the sale will never take place even though both parties are aware that the asset is worth 50 percent more to the buyer than the seller. This is surely inefficient. If *both* parties knew v they could split the profit – that is, trade at the price $1.25\ v$.

Consider another bargaining mechanism: the seller makes an offer s, which the buyer can either accept or reject. If the buyer accepts the seller's bid s then the asset changes hands at that price, in which case the seller's payoff is $s - v$ and the buyer's payoff is the expected difference between the value to the buyer and the price paid. If the offer is rejected there is no exchange and no further negotiation.

DEFINITION: *A Take-it-or-Leave-it Offer by the Seller*
The seller bids s, and if the buyer accepts she pays s to the seller in return for the asset. In that case the seller's payoff is $s - v$ and the buyer's payoff is the expected value of $1.5v - s$. If the offer is rejected there is no further negotiation, in which case the seller's payoff is 0 and the buyer's is 0.

Inefficiency Theorem for a Take-it-or-Leave-it Offer by the Seller
No trade will ever take place if the seller makes a take-it-or-leave-it offer.

Proof:
We know that $s \geq v$, and so does the buyer, although the buyer does not know v. If $v < s < 1.5v$ then both parties gain by a sale at s dollars because the asset is worth $1.5v$ to the buyer. The buyer does not know v but she knows that the seller knows that the asset is worth $1.5v$ to the buyer. Then the buyer should accept s, anticipating that the seller will set s between v and $1.5v$. But this cannot be an equilibrium strategy. The seller's best response is to charge a high s, even when v is very low, relying on the buyer to *assume* that $v > s/1.5$. But the buyer's best response to *that* is to reject the offer because the expected value of the asset to the buyer is

$$\int_0^1 1.5v\,dv = 0.75 \times (1^2 - 0^2) = 0.75.$$

There is no Nash equilibrium: the seller will set s above 0.75 and the buyer will only accept s when it is below 0.75. ■

Is there any bargaining mechanism that will permit the realization of the gains from trade, which both parties know to be positive for each? No! The most favorable scheme from the buyer's standpoint is the one where she makes a final offer that the seller has no authority to modify and can only accept or reject it. As we have seen, even that fails to leave the buyer with a positive expected profit.

Sources
Section 5.2.1 is based on Danilov and Sotskov (2002). Section 5.2.2 is based on Samuelson (1984, 1985).

Links
See Farrell (1987) and Maskin (1994) on laissez-faire and efficiency. See Osborne and Rubinstein (1990) for an analysis of sequential bargaining, with alternating offers.

Problem Set

(1) Section 5.2.1 doesn't acknowledge the possibility of a tie, in the sense that $V_B = V_S$. Show that truthful revelation is a dominant strategy for the *GBM*, whatever the tie-breaking rule – the asset goes to B in the case of a tie, or the asset goes to S in case of a tie, or a coin is flipped, and so forth – assuming that $P(V, V) = V = Q(V, V)$ for all V.

(2) By means of a numerical example demonstrate how profitable it is for B and S to collude if they pay a fee F to an arbiter who collects V_S from the buyer and pays V_B to the seller.

(3) Design a mechanism that is different from the *GBM* but satisfies asset efficiency and the participation constraint. Of course, truthful revelation will not be a dominant strategy for each agent.

(4) Design a mechanism, different from the *GBM*, that satisfies the participation constraint and such that truthful revelation is a dominant strategy for each agent. It will not satisfy asset efficiency of course.

(5) Prove the claim of the last paragraph of Section 5.2.1: truthful revelation is a dominant strategy for the mechanism that requires each agent to pay a fee F and then applies the *GBM*.

(6) Show that the *GBM* (of Section 5.2.1) is not the pivotal mechanism (of Section 8.2 of Chapter 8), although it is a Groves mechanism (of Section 8.3 of Chapter 8).

∂5.3   THE USED-CAR MARKET

The used-car market is one of the hidden characteristic problems for which the market system has not developed a completely satisfactory solution. Many used cars on the market are "lemons" – cars that frequently require expensive repair. Individuals who purchase new cars often try to sell them when they are discovered to be lemons, and hence the used-car market contains a disproportionately high number of low-quality cars. This depresses the price of used cars because the buyer can't tell which are lemons. There is asymmetric information. Many car owners who would otherwise put their good cars up for sale find that the selling price of their cars is too low. They are better off continuing to drive their high-quality automobiles than selling them for a low price that reflects the low *average* quality in the used-car market. This further lowers the average quality of used cars at equilibrium, resulting in an even lower equilibrium price. And so on. In terms of the economist's jargon, many car owners find that the *reservation value* of their cars is higher than the price that the car will fetch on the market.

DEFINITION: *Reservation Value*

The car owner's reservation value is the minimum that he or she would be willing to accept to part with the car. The buyer's reservation value is the maximum that he or she would be willing to pay.

Sellers' payoffs will increase if and only if they sell their cars for more than their reservation values. Buyers' payoffs will increase if and only if they buy their cars for less than their reservation values. These observations follow from the definition of "willing." (Read the definition of *reservation value* again.)

The used-car market exhibits a degree of market failure: there are owners of high-quality automobiles who would be willing to sell their cars at prices that buyers would be prepared to pay *if* they could be certain of the quality. However, one cannot distinguish high-quality cars from lemons *before* purchasing, so the price of high-quality used cars reflects the large fraction of lemons in the market. Consequently, there are buyers and sellers of the high-quality cars who are not able to strike a deal. The highest price that the seller could obtain is often below the seller's reservation price. The outcome is not efficient. To drive this point home – pun intended – consider what happens the day after you accept delivery of your new car. The car's value on the used-car market is already well below the price you paid on the previous day and is thus below your reservation value. (Why has the car's market price fallen so much in one day? This question has already been answered.)

The difference between the job-market example (Section 5.6) and the present model of the used-car market is that *signaling* occurs in the former and this can ensure that high-quality goods or services are credibly identified. (The outcome is not fully efficient in the job-market scenario because signaling consumes resources.) When it is possible for high-quality sellers to signal at a relatively low cost, the market can force low-quality sellers to reveal themselves.

We conclude with a numerical illustration of market failure when there is no signaling. Assume that there are many more buyers in the used-car market than sellers; competition among the latter will result in all sellers charging the same price if there is no possibility of signaling (no warranties, etc.).

Example 5.2 The Car is Worth 50 percent More to the Buyer than to the Seller

For a given quality level q the sellers' reservation value is q and the buyers' reservation value is $1.5q$. The buyers are risk neutral and they do not know q, and they do not expect owners of low-quality cars to truthfully reveal q. Quality is uniformly distributed over the interval from 0 to 1 (Section 2.6.5 of Chapter 2). Because $\int x dx = 0.5x^2$ the expected value of a car from the buyer's perspective is

$$\int_0^1 q dq = \frac{1}{2} \left(1^2 - 0\right) = \frac{1}{2}.$$

In the absence of signaling all cars sell for the same price p. Therefore, if $q < p$ a seller will put her car on the market, receiving a payoff of p, which is higher than the payoff of q from keeping the car. If $q > p$ the seller will not offer the car for sale. This enables us to determine the average quality of used cars on the market when buyers observe the price p: To do so we first compute the density function for the distribution of cars q satisfying $0 \le q \le p$. The density function for $0 \le q \le 1$ is $f(q) = 1$. Therefore, the density function for $0 \le q \le p$ is $f(q)$ divided by p, the probability that q falls between 0 and p. Hence, the relevant density function is $(1/p)f(q) = 1/p$. (See the next theorem.)

The average quality of cars on the market at a price of p is

$$\frac{1}{p} \int_0^p q dq = \frac{1}{p} \left(\frac{1}{2}p^2 - 0\right) = \frac{1}{2}p.$$

The risk-neutral buyer maximizes his expected payoff, and hence there will be no sale at any positive price p, because the expected payoff to a buyer would be $0.5p - p$, a negative number.

There are no trades, even though every agent knows that mutually beneficial trades are possible in principle: the value of any owner's car is two-thirds of what it is worth to any buyer. *If* quality could be costlessly discerned then competition among buyers would bid up the price of a car of quality q (from the buyer's perspective) to just about q and trade would take place.

Theorem: The Density Function for $0 \leq q \leq 1$

The quality q is uniformly distributed on the interval [0, 1]. But only cars with q ≤ p are on the market, so the used cars on the market are uniformly distributed on the interval [0, p], which has length p. The probability of a car on the market being somewhere in that interval must be 1. Therefore the density d must solve $d \times p = 1$. Note that

$$\frac{1}{p}\int_0^p f(q)dq = \frac{1}{p}\int_0^p dq = \frac{1}{p}(p-0) = 1.$$

We have calculated the density function for $0 \leq q \leq p$ in Example 5.2 *correctly.*

As Example 5.2 demonstrates, complete collapse of a market is a theoretical possibility when one side of the market has information that is hidden from the other side. In fact, the market will be active, but will function with less than complete efficiency. For instance, used-car dealers can inspect the cars that they sell and competition will force them to offer limited warranties on good-quality cars, mitigating the asymmetric information problem to some extent. But there will always be some information that the car owner can hide from the used car dealer. There will still be trades that could increase the utility of the buyer and seller but that will not take place because of the hidden information problem. For instance, someone who buys a new car one week and then finds the next week that he or she has to move two thousand miles away would sell the new car and buy another in the new locale if a potential buyer could verify that the car is not being sold because it is a lemon. As it is, the individual will spend the time and money required to drive it to the new home, because net of those expenses the reservation value of the car exceeds the price for which it could be sold. One of the many applications of Example 5.2 is the market for cars that are only a few weeks or months old but are owned by people who would like to sell, but *not* because they have discovered their cars to be of low quality.

Sources

Akerlof (1970), a seminal contribution to the theory of asymmetric information, is the basis of this section. In separate contributions, George Akerlof, Michael Spence, and Joseph Stiglitz showed that the presence of asymmetric information in real-world markets required a new way of modeling economic exchange and computing the welfare losses in such markets. They were awarded the Nobel Prize in Economics for 2001.

Links

Molho (1997) has an extensive discussion of the lemons problem. Hendel and Lizzeri (1999) analyze a model that incorporates interaction between new and used-car markets over time and manufacturers whose products differ with respect to reliability. That article includes many references to the literature.

Problem Set

Rework Example 5.2 with the buyer's reservation value set at λq instead of $1.5q$. (λ is some constant larger than 1.)

5.4   CREDIT RATIONING

The central paradigm of economic analysis is the notion that in any market operating under competitive conditions, the price will adjust until demand equals supply. This entails two principles: there will be a price P^* at which demand equals supply, and market forces will drive the price to P^* over time. How quickly the prevailing price moves close to its equilibrium value depends on the nature of the market, but in the case of financial markets we would expect fairly quick convergence to equilibrium.

In fact, credit markets are an important exception to the central paradigm because of a significant asymmetric information problem: the borrower knows considerably more about the riskiness of the project for which funding is sought than the lender does. (Borrowers also know a lot more about their willingness to work hard to bring the project to fruition.) This can prevent the lender from raising interest rates when the demand for loans exceeds the supply: an increase in the interest rate can induce an increase in the riskiness of the pool of applicants for loans, thereby *reducing* the lender's profit. If interest rates don't rise, and hence demand continues to exceed supply, the lender will screen applicants by investigating their background and examining in detail the business venture that will be financed by the loan. (The firm that sells me a stove doesn't care about my background.)

Asymmetric information by itself would not create problems were it not for the asymmetry in the return to the lender. On one hand, if the project flops then the lender will not be repaid at all or will only be paid a fraction of the amount borrowed. On the other hand, when the project is very successful, the lender's payoff is not proportionally high – it can never be more than the amount of the loan plus interest charges. Limited liability constrains the amount that the borrower repays when the project is a failure, but there is also a restriction on the amount to be repaid when the project is successful. Both limits are in the borrower's favor.

The asymmetry in the lender's payoff forces the lender to worry about the probability of default. By the same token, the possibility of default changes the pool of loan applications when the interest rate changes. There tend to be more very risky projects seeking funding when the interest rate is high, and hence a larger fraction of the projects would fail if all were to be funded. Assuming for the minute that that is true, it follows that when the demand for loanable funds exceeds the supply, an increase in the interest rate – which is possible, because of the excess demand at the current rate – will not necessarily increase the lender's profit. The higher interest rate brings the lender a higher payoff when a project is successful, but the higher interest rate also raises the number of loans that default. Therefore, beyond a certain point, the lender will stop raising the interest rate, even though there is excess demand, and will instead devote resources to investigating the project for which an applicant is seeking funding to try and weed out the very risky ones. We refer to this as *credit rationing*. (In the market for home loans, the lender can often require the borrower to put up collateral, but there is limited scope for collateral in business loans.)

DEFINITION: *Credit Rationing*

Credit rationing occurs at equilibrium if some borrowers' loan applications are turned down, even if they are willing to pay the market interest rate and fulfill all other requirements of the loan contract – putting up collateral, for instance.

As Figure 5.1 illustrates, credit rationing causes the supply of credit to diminish as the interest rate r increases beyond a certain level. Because the supply curve bends back at interest rates above r^0, the demand exceeds the supply at every interest rate. Consequently, the market rate of interest will settle at a level r^* at which demand exceeds supply. Even at equilibrium the total amount of money for which borrowers apply is greater than the amount that lenders are willing to part with. The lenders then have to ration, and they

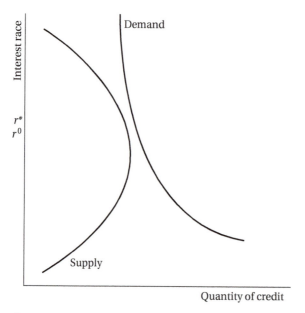

Figure 5.1

Table 5.1

	Tyler's Project		Samantha's Project	
Return	Probability	Payoff	Probability	Payoff
High	½	110	½	120
Low	½	100	½	90

typically use some measure of the degree of riskiness to screen out applications that they consider undesirable. But note that there is scope for pernicious screening devices, such as racial preferences.

The next subsection shows why there *will* be proportionally more risky projects seeking funding when the interest rate is high.

5.4.1 The Borrower's Point of View

We explore the credit market by means of simple examples. It is assumed throughout that both borrowers and lenders are risk neutral. That doesn't mean that lenders don't worry about risk. An increase in the riskiness of loans can reduce the lender's expected monetary payoff.

Example 5.3 Two Borrowers

Two individuals, Tyler and Samantha, each seek financing for their projects, which are specified by Table 5.1. Assume that in both cases the project requires $100 of capital to initiate, and each entrepreneur has applied for a $100 loan. Tyler is hoping to finance a project that will pay $110 with probability ½ and will return only $100 with probability ½. In Samantha's case, the project will yield more than Tyler's high payoff if it is successful but will yield less than Tyler's low payoff in case of failure. The return in the payoff column is the profit from a project, net of all economic costs except the cost of borrowing the necessary funds. Assume for simplicity that the money is only borrowed for one year – and that the project lasts only one year. (Alternatively, we could assume that the numbers are discounted to the end of the first year.)

Note that the two projects yield the same return on average. Confirm this by calculating the EMV (expected monetary value):

$$EMV \text{ for Tyler} = 0.5 \times 110 + 0.5 \times 100 = 105$$
$$EMV \text{ for Sam} = 0.5 \times 120 + 0.5 \times 90 = 105$$

Samantha's project is riskier, because the spread between the high and low payoffs is greater.

DEFINITION: *Degree of Risk*

If projects A and B have the same EMV and the same probability of success, we say that A is riskier than B if the high payoff from A is larger than the high payoff from B, but the low payoff from A is smaller than the low payoff from B.

Suppose that the current interest rate is 8%. Would Tyler be willing to borrow at that rate? The answer is "yes" if and only if the profit net of all costs, including borrowing costs, is positive. Let's calculate Tyler's EP (expected profit):

$$EP \text{ at } 8\% \text{ for Tyler} = 0.5(110 - 100 - 0.08 \times 100) + 0.5(100 - 100) = 1.$$

The borrowing cost is the principal ($100) plus the interest ($100 \times 8\%$), but when the project is unsuccessful Tyler can only pay back the principal. The entrepreneur's profit can never be lower than zero. The expected profit is positive, so Tyler would be one of the loan applicants at an interest rate of 8%. What if the rate were to rise to 11%? Even the high return of 110 is insufficient to cover the principal and the $11 interest charge on the loan. Tyler's payoff would be zero whether the project succeeded or failed. Tyler would not seek funding for his project at an interest rate of 11%. (Tyler's return would actually be negative if this project were one part of an ongoing concern and the interest had to be covered by profit from the firm's other activities.)

Now let's see what Samantha would decide at the two interest rates:

$$EP \text{ at } 8\% \text{ for Sam} = 0.5(120 - 100 - 0.08 \times 100) + 0.5(90 - 90) = 6.$$

When Samantha's project is unsuccessful she can only repay 90% of the principal and none of the interest. The expected profit is positive, so Samantha would apply for a loan at an interest rate of 8%.

$$EP \text{ at } 11\% \text{ for Sam} = 0.5(120 - 100 - 0.11 \times 100) + 0.5(90 - 90) = 4.5.$$

Profit is again positive, so Samantha would seek funding for her project at an interest rate of 11%. But Tyler would not, at that higher rate, illustrating our point that the riskiness of the loan applicant pool increases when the interest rate increases. Why does Samantha stay in the hunt for funding but Tyler does not when the interest rate rises? Because, even though the payoff *to the project* is lower for Samantha than for Tyler when their projects turn sour, the two *entrepreneurs* get the same payoff in that state – zero. But Samantha gets a higher payoff than Tyler when the projects succeed. Therefore, Samantha can make a profit for herself at a higher interest rate than Tyler can.

Let's find the watershed interest rate, above which Tyler will not apply for a loan: let r denote the interest rate expressed as a decimal fraction. (When the interest rate is 7% we have $r = 0.07$.) Then

$$EP \text{ at } 100r\% \text{ for Tyler} = 0.5(110 - 100 - 100r) + 0.5(100 - 100) = 0.5(10 - 100r).$$

This will be positive if and only if $10 - 100r > 0$, which is equivalent to $100r < 10$. At interest rates above 10% it will not be profitable for Tyler to undertake his project. Similarly,

$$EP \text{ at } 100r\% \text{ for Sam} = 0.5(120 - 100 - 100r) + 0.5(90 - 90) = 0.5(20 - 100r).$$

The EP for Samantha will be positive if and only if $20 - 100\,r > 0$, which is the same as saying that the interest rate is less than 20%. Therefore, at interest rates between 10% and 20%, Samantha will apply for a loan but Tyler will not. In that range, only the riskier of the two projects will attempt to get funding.

Now we consider a general version of our example. Again, let r denote the interest rate expressed as a decimal fraction.

Table 5.2

Return	Probability	Payoff
High	½	$105 + \alpha$
Low	½	$105 - \alpha$

Example 5.4 A Generic Version of Example 5.3

Each value of α identifies a different project (see Table 5.2). Assume again that a project requires $100 of capital, whatever the value of α. The interest rate is $100r\%$. Project α pays $105 + \alpha$ with probability ½ and only $105 - \alpha$ with probability ½. As before, the return is net of all economic costs except the cost of borrowing the necessary funds.

Note that all projects yield the same return on average:

$$EMV \text{ of project } \alpha = 0.5(105 + \alpha) + 0.5(105 - \alpha) = 105.$$

However, as α increases the riskiness of the project increases, because the spread between the high and low payoffs increases with α. To determine if an entrepreneur who is seeking funding for project α will actually apply for a loan when the interest rate is r, we have to consider two cases.

Case 1: Even when the project fails it yields enough to repay the loan and cover all the interest charges. In that case

EP of project α for the borrower

$$= 0.5(105 + \alpha - 100 - 100r) + 0.5(105 - \alpha - 100 - 100r) = 5 - 100r.$$

As we expect, the borrower's profit falls as the interest rate rises. Why is profit independent of α in this case? Because the entrepreneur (borrower) gains α with probability ½ but also loses α with probability ½.

Things are different when the borrower has to default on the loan if the project turns sour, because in that case the higher α imposes costs on the *lender*, who gets a smaller faction of the principal repaid on average as α increases. But when the project is successful, the higher the α the more the borrower gets to keep. That's why higher interest rates cause a reduction in the fraction of low-risk loans in the applicant pool.

Case 2: The borrower only pays back $105 - \alpha$ when the project fails, because $105 - \alpha$ is less than $100 + 100\ r$:

$$EP \text{ for project } \alpha \text{ at } r = 0.5(105 + \alpha - 100 - 100r) + 0.5(105 - \alpha - (105 - \alpha))$$
$$= 5 + \alpha - 100r.$$

For Case 2, when a project fails, the entrepreneur gets zero – but no less.

In either case the entrepreneur's expected profit at r is

$$0.5 \times (5 + \alpha - 100r) + 0.5 \times \max[(5 - \alpha - 100r),\ 0].$$

If $5 - \alpha - 100r$ is negative or zero expected profit is $0.5(5 + \alpha - 100r)$. If $5 - \alpha - 100r$ is positive then expected profit is $5 - 100r$. Note that expected profit is positive if and only if $5 + \alpha - 100r$ is positive. (If $5 - \alpha - 100r > 0$ then $5 + \alpha - 100r > 0$ as well. If $5 - \alpha - 100r < 0$ then the borrower gets zero, not $5 - \alpha - 100r$.) Therefore, the entrepreneur behind project α will apply for a loan if and only if $5 + \alpha - 100r > 0$. (If $5 + \alpha - 100r$ is negative then $5 - \alpha - 100r$ will certainly be negative.)

If $100r < 5$ then $5 + \alpha - 100r$ is positive for all α, so everyone will apply for a loan when the interest rate is less than 5%. When $100r \geq 5$ then the sponsors of α will apply for a loan if and only if $5 + \alpha - 100r > 0$ or $\alpha > 100r - 5$. The threshold value of α, which is $100r - 5$, increases with the interest rate. Entrepreneurs for whom α is below $100r - 5$ will not apply for a loan, but those for which α is above $100r - 5$ will seek funding. In short, the range of α values for which a loan is sought shrinks as the interest rate increases, with the sponsors of safer projects ($\alpha < 100r - 5$) withdrawing their loan applications. In other words, the riskier the project the more likely it is that the entrepreneur will apply for a loan at a given interest rate.

5.4.2 The Lender's Point of View

At a given interest rate r, a risky project will always be less profitable for the lender than a safer one for Example 5.4. That is because the lender's profit is $100r$ when the project is successful, whatever the value of α. But in the case of failure, the lender's loss increases with the riskiness of the project. The lender has advanced \$100 but only gets back $105 - \alpha$ when $100 + 100\ r > 105 - \alpha$, and $105 - \alpha$ is smaller the larger is α. Therefore, the lender has an interest in screening projects to estimate the riskiness of each application when $\alpha > 5 - 100\ r$.

There is more to the story. We have learned that the entrepreneurs backing less risky projects will not apply for a loan if the interest rate is sufficiently high. Therefore, the lender can't simply raise the interest rate and then accept only the safe applications: there may not be any. For Example 5.3, both Tyler and Samantha will apply for a loan when the interest rate is 8%, but only Samantha will apply at 11%.

Suppose that there are two applicants, Tyler and Samantha of Example 5.3, when the interest rate is 8%. What is the lender's profit? When a project succeeds the lender gets the principal back and an interest payment of \$8 from each borrower. When Tyler's project fails the lender gets the principal back but there is no interest payment. When Samantha's project fails then the lender only gets

$90. There is a loss of $10. Assuming that the two projects are statistically independent, the lender's expected profit is

$$\text{Lender's } EP \text{ per project at } 8\% = 0.5(8+0) + 0.5(8-10) = +3.$$

The lender's profit is $6 (= $3 \times 2)$ when the interest rate is 8%. At an interest rate of 6% we have

$$\text{Lender's } EP \text{ per project at } 6\% = 0.5(6+0) + 0.5(6-10) = +1,$$

or $2 from both projects. (Confirm that both Tyler and Samantha would apply for a loan when the interest rate is 6%.) The lender's profit is higher from the higher interest rate. Therefore, we know that there will be a range of interest rates at which profit increases as the interest rate increases. In other words, there is a range of interest rates in which the lender has an incentive to raise the rate if demand for credit exceeds supply. Hence, there will be an upward sloping segment of the supply of credit curve – the piece below r^0 in Figure 5.1.

Now consider the situation when the interest rate is 11%. Tyler will not apply for a loan! If Samantha's project were to succeed the lender gets the principal back and an interest payment of $11, but when it flops the lender loses $10. The lender's expected profit is

$$EP \text{ of lender at } 11\% = 0.5(11) + 0.5(-10) = +0.5$$

The lender's profit is lower at 11% than at 8% because of the change in the set of projects seeking credit. We refer to this as *adverse selection*. This accounts for the downward sloping part of the supply curve – that is, the piece above r^0 in Figure 5.1.

Return to Example 5.4. Suppose that if the project were to fail there would not be enough money to cover both the principal and the interest on the loan. When the interest rate is $100r\%$ and project α succeeds the lender gets the principal back along with an interest payment of $100r$. But when project α fails the lender only gets $105 - \alpha$. There is a loss of $100 - (105 - \alpha) = \alpha - 5$.

$$EP \text{ of lender from } \alpha = 0.5(100r) + 0.5(5 - \alpha) = 0.5(100r + 5 - \alpha).$$

This will be positive if and only if $100r + 5 - \alpha > 0$. That is equivalent to $\alpha < 100r + 5$.

In other words, given the interest rate r, only projects whose risk parameter α is below $100r + 5$ will be profitable for the lender, who will want to screen out projects for which α exceeds $100r + 5$.

Why is the lender's profit positive for *low* α? Because the lender's payoff doesn't rise with α when the project is successful. It remains at $100r$. But with failure, less is paid back when α is higher.

What about cases where the borrower can repay both principal and interest, even when the low payoff is realized? Could any of these projects have a risk parameter α that violated the inequality $\alpha < 100r + 5$? No. If $5 - \alpha - 100r \geq 0$ then $\alpha \leq 5 - 100r$, which certainly implies $\alpha \leq 5 + 100r$. Therefore, for *all* projects the entrepreneur backing the project will apply for a loan if and only if $\alpha < 100r + 5$. The higher the interest rate the higher the proportion of risky projects in the loan application pool.

Table 5.3

$\alpha = 5$ and $r = 0.04$	$\alpha = 5$ and $r = 0.08$	$\alpha = 5$ and $r = 0.10$
$\alpha = 9$ and $r = 0.04$	$\alpha = 9$ and $r = 0.08$	$\alpha = 9$ and $r = 0.10$
$\alpha = 12$ and $r = 0.04$	$\alpha = 12$ and $r = 0.08$	$\alpha = 12$ and $r = 0.10$

Source

Stiglitz and Weiss (1981) worked out the theory sketched in this section.

Links

Jaffee and Stiglitz (1990) and Chapter 1 of Freixas and Rochet (1997) provide comprehensive discussions of credit rationing.

Problem Set

(1) This question involves a set of entrepreneurs, each of whom is seeking funding for a project. Each project requires an initial $100 investment. To keep the calculations simple we assume that each project will be 100% loan financed *if* the entrepreneur decides to carry it out and *if* the loan is approved. Each entrepreneur is identified with a number α: Entrepreneur α's project will return $100 + \alpha$ with probability ⅔ and will return $100 - 0.5\alpha$ with probability ⅓.

    (A) For each combination of interest rate r (expressed as a decimal fraction) and α represented in Table 5.3, determine if entrepreneur α will apply for a loan to fund the project at the specified interest rate.

    (B) *As a function of* α, what is the threshold rate of interest, above which project α will not seek funding?

(2) Each member of a given set of projects returns $120 when successful and $60 otherwise. What makes one project riskier than another in this case is the fact that the probability π of success is lower for riskier projects. Each project requires an initial $100 bank loan. The bank charges an interest rate of $100r\%$ on loans. *As a function of* r, what is the value of π below which the bank will not make a profit by funding the project?

(3) What is the economic rationale for limited liability, which protects the borrower but not the lender?

(4) Why doesn't the lender insist on an equity stake in the project that would allow the lender to get a proportionally higher payoff when the project is proportionally more successful?

(5) Why does the lender usually insist that the borrowers put some of their own money into their projects?

∂5.5 BUNDLING AND PRODUCT QUALITY

The manufacturer of an appliance or car knows that some consumers have a high willingness to pay for a luxury model but would buy the economy version if the sticker price on the luxury model is too high. Because many consumers aren't prepared to buy a luxury model at any price that would be profitable for the manufacturer, the firm may have to supply two models – luxury and economy – to maximize profit. However, the existence of the economy version puts a constraint on the sticker price of the luxury model. This section demonstrates how to solve for the profit-maximizing menu of models and associated prices.

If the individual's willingness to pay for each model were actually known to the manufacturer, the firm could charge each consumer the maximum he or she would be willing to pay for the model – the one that is most profitable for the firm to sell to that individual – given the consumer's willingness to pay for each model. As it is, willingness to pay is hidden from the supplier. Moreover, cars can be resold. (An individual who is able to buy at the low price could purchase a car from the manufacturer and sell it to someone who would otherwise have to pay the manufacturer's high price. The transaction could take place at a price between the manufacturer's high and low prices and would thus provide a gain to both sides of the exchange.)

Assume that quality can be measured. We let x denote the amount of quality embedded in the model. Then higher values of x represent higher quality. Of course quality is really multidimensional, particularly in the case of a sophisticated product such as a car. But even a one-dimensional quality parameter gives us a framework from which we can draw much insight.

DEFINITION: *Quality*

We let x denote the level of quality in a particular unit of the good. A *package* (x, C) consists of a model embodying x units of quality that sells for C.

It is also possible to interpret x as the *quantity* of some good. We begin with that interpretation, and when the analysis is complete we reinterpret our findings in terms of quality choice by the firm.

A monopoly is attempting to price discriminate by offering its output in the form of sealed packages with fixed prices. A package containing more output bears a higher price tag, but the price is not a linear function of quantity. If package B has twice as much output as package A its price will be more than double that of A if the larger package is targeted for consumers who get more benefit from the good and are willing to pay proportionally more. This will generate more profit than a linear pricing schedule. (A linear schedule can be represented by a single number – the price. If Q units cost Q times as much as one unit let P denote the cost of one unit. For arbitrary Q the total cost is $P \times Q$.)

There are two potential problems for a monopolist attempting to impose a nonlinear, price-discriminating schedule. We illustrate the first with a simple example.

Example 5.5 Unbundling

Suppose package A contains ten units of output and sells for $10, and B contains twenty units of output and is priced at $30. Even if the manufacturer won't let a particular consumer buy two A packages, an arbitrageur can purchase two A packages and sell them for a total of $25 to someone who otherwise would have to buy a B package from the monopolist. Similarly, if there is a quantity discount, with A selling for $10 and B selling for $15, an entrepreneur might be able to buy a B package and divide it into two ten-unit packages and sell each for $9 to individuals who might otherwise have to pay $10 to the monopolist.

Note that *quality* cannot be unbundled. A garage cannot take apart a $50,000 automobile and use the parts to make two cars that sell for $30,000 each. When we apply the analysis of this section to *quantity* bundling we must confine our attention to goods that can't be resold. (Or goods such as airline travel for which resale can be blocked by the seller, in this case by checking the traveler's identity.) The case of a public utility producing electricity will provide the motivation. It is possible to store electricity for future resale but it is very costly to do so. We can assume that our public utility monopoly does not have to worry about resale.

The second difficulty arises from the fact that the monopolist cannot identify the consumers who are willing to pay more for electricity. Those individuals cannot be expected to voluntarily disclose their identity, knowing that they will be charged more when they do. In fact a consumer for whom the product provides a high level of benefit and for whom the B package is targeted can buy two "A packages." The monopolist can rule this out simply by offering this consumer an all-or-nothing proposition: "Either you buy one B package or we will not sell you anything." But there is a hidden characteristic problem. The firm cannot directly identify the individuals who derive a high level of benefit from the product. The best that the monopolist can do is to design the packages so that high-benefit consumers will not want to buy package A even though it costs less per unit than B. They will want to purchase B at the proportionally higher price because it provides more of the good. Of course they will not want B if the cost per unit is too high. Designing the packages and choosing the price tags is not a simple task. The trick is to design the packages and select the prices so that a high-benefit customer will *choose* to buy the package the monopolist designed for that person.

Our analysis applies only to cases for which the high-benefit consumer is unable to buy multiple A packages, and thereby get the same quantity as in a B package, but at a lower total cost. For instance, the monopoly public utility can control delivery and will offer a consumer an all-or-nothing choice between the two packages. When "quantity" actually refers to the "amount of quality" our assumption is satisfied because two low-quality appliances do not amount to the same thing as a single high-quality appliance. We begin the analysis by specifying production costs and consumer preferences.

Table 5.4

	Reservation Values		The Firm's Cost
	H	L	
Luxury model	100	60	30
Economy model	52	42	10

5.5.1 To Make a Long Story Short

An automobile manufacturer has two types of potential customers: H types, who get a high level of benefit from a car, particularly if it is luxurious, and L types, who would get more benefit from a luxury automobile than an economy model, but not enough to justify paying a very high price for the former. To simplify, assume that no customer wants more than one car. Then we can characterize individual preferences in terms of the reservation value – i.e., the maximum willingness to pay – of each individual for each car. These data are displayed in Table 5.4. An H type's reservation value is 100 for the luxury model and 52 for the economy model. An L's reservation values are 60 and 42 respectively. (These reservation values reflect the fact that automobiles are available from other manufacturers.) By definition of the word "maximum," if an individual has reservation value R for an item and the cost of purchasing it is C then her utility gain would be $R - C$ if she were to buy it. The manufacturer's cost of making the luxury model is 30 and the cost of making the economy model is 10. (The currency unit is $1,000, and thus 30 represents a cost of $30,000 and the maximum willingness to pay of an H type for a luxury car is $100,000.)

We now have enough information to work out the profit maximizing menu of models and sticker prices, *assuming that the supplier cannot directly distinguish an H type from an L type.* Suppose that there are n individuals of each type. Then we can identify the profit maximizing strategy by assuming one individual of each type. We'll call our two consumers H and L. (To get actual profit multiply the profit realized by each strategy by n.) Suppose the manufacturer offers two models with sticker prices 100 and 42 for the luxury and economy models, respectively. The aim is to charge H as much as possible for the luxury car and at the same time charge L as much as possible for the economy version. However, it will not then be in H's self-interest to buy the luxury car, as the following calculations reveal:

$$\Delta U_H(Lux) = 100 - 100 = 0 \text{ and}$$
$$\Delta U_H(Eco) = 52 - 42 = 10.$$

(In fact the price of the luxury item would be set a little below 100 to give H a positive gain in utility should she buy the car. Similarly, the economy model would be priced a little below 42.) Both H and L will buy the economy model, and thus profit is $2(42 - 10) = 64$.

To induce H to buy the luxury model the manufacturer will have to lower the sticker price. But suppose the economy model is withdrawn and the luxury car is priced at 100. Profit will then be $100 - 30$ which is greater than 64. But we have not yet found the profit maximizing pricing strategy. The economy model can be offered at a price of 42 with the luxury version also available at a sticker price that gives H an incentive to buy it. To make that work, we'll have to price the luxury car so that it yields more utility to H than the economy model. Recall that H will get a utility gain of 10 from the purchase of the economy car at a sticker price of 42. To provide H with at least as high a gain from the luxury car we'll have to bring the price down by 10, from 100 to 90. When 90 is the price of the luxury car and the economy model is priced at 30 individual H will buy the former and L will buy the latter. Profit equals $90 - 30 + 42 - 10$, or 92, which is certainly greater than 70. (This is known as *mixed bundling*.) We have found the profit maximizing pricing strategy. (In fact the luxury model would have to be priced slightly below 90 so that it would give an H a strictly greater utility gain than the economy car. The resulting profit would be a little less than 92 but still a lot greater than 70.)

5.5.2 The Model

The model has two commodities, X and Y. The former is the one that we're interested in, and we can interpret it as an automobile or electricity and so forth. In fact, X is anything that can't be unbundled. Y denotes money, or generalized purchasing power. In other words, Y is a composite commodity, representing expenditure on goods other than commodity X.

Customer i's utility function is $U_i = B_i(x_i) + y_i$ where x_i and y_i are the amounts of X and Y, respectively, consumed by individual i. The benefit that i derives from x_i units of X is $B_i(x_i)$. That is, B_i is a benefit function. We assume that the marginal benefit of X is positive for all x_i but that marginal benefit decreases and as x_i increases. Each individual is endowed with (begins with) θ_i units of Y.

DEFINITION: *The Bundling Model*

There are n individuals, and two goods, X and Y. $U_i = B_i(x_i) + y_i$ with $B_i{}'(x_i) > 0$ and $B_i{}''(x_i) < 0$ for each i and each x_i. Before purchasing any X individual i has θ_i units of Y. That is, $y_i = \theta_i$ initially. Each unit of X costs \$1 to manufacture.

If i pays a total of C_i dollars for x_i units of commodity X then i's utility will be $U_i = B_i(X_i) + \theta_i - C_i$. Because θ_i is constant we need only compute the change in utility, which is $\Delta U_i = B_i(x_i) - C_i$ assuming that $B_i(0) = 0$. If ΔU_i is positive then i will purchase the package (x_i, C_i) or some more attractive package if one is available, but if $\Delta U_i < 0$ then i will not purchase (x_i, C_i) because it would cause utility to decline. This takes us to the participation constraint.

DEFINITION: *The Participation Constraint*

If the monopolist's profit-maximizing strategy involves consumer i purchasing package (x_i, C_i) then $B_i(x_i) - C_i \geq 0$ must hold.

We have choosen units so that one unit of X costs \$1 to produce. (In other words, average cost is constant and fixed cost is zero.) If there are n individuals, and each individual i, purchases x_i units of X, the producer's cost will be $x_1 + x_2 + \cdots + x_n$. Its revenue is the total amount paid: $C_1 + C_2 + \cdots + C_n$. The profit-maximizing menu may contain many packages for which $x_i = 0 = C_i$.

DEFINITION: *The Firm's Profit*

There are n consumers. If the monopolist offers the menu of packages (x_1, C_1), $(x_2, C_2), \ldots, (x_n, C_n)$ and each consumer buys exactly one of the packages, then profit is

$$C_1 + C_2 + \cdots + C_n - x_1 - x_2 - \cdots - x_n$$

because one unit of X costs \$1 to produce.

There are n consumers, but there will typically be fewer than n types. For instance, individuals 1, 2, ..., m may be of one type, and the remaining $n - m$ individuals another type.

∂5.5.3 Full Information Equilibrium

To give us a point of comparison, begin with the full information assumption that the monopolist knows each person's benefit function B_i. What package should be offered to person i? Let x_i^0 be the value of x_i that maximizes $B_i(x_i) - x_i$, which is the consumer's benefit less the monopolist's cost of producing x_i. That is, x_i^0 solves $B_i'(x_i) = 1$. (Note that diminishing marginal benefit means that the second derivative of the function that we are maximizing is negative, and hence the first-order condition is sufficient for a global maximum.) Suppose the monopolist offers i the package $(x_i^0, B_i(x_i^0) - \varepsilon)$. The total cost to i of x_i^0 units of X is $C_i^0 = B_i(x_i^0) - \varepsilon$. Here ε is a small positive number, so the charge is just slightly less than the total benefit. Person i faces a take-it-or-leave-it proposition. Because $\Delta U_i = B_i(x_i^0) - C_i = B_i(x_i^0) - [B_i(x_i^0) - \varepsilon] = \varepsilon$, which is positive, the monopolist's offer will be accepted. This is the profit-maximizing strategy under the full information assumption that there is no hidden characteristic problem.

Why is it profit maximizing under full information? If $\Delta U_i < 0$ then i will not buy the package and the monopolist will receive zero profit from i. Therefore, the monopolist must respect the participation constraint $B_i(x_i) - C_i \geq 0$. As long as C_i is substantially below $B_i(x_i)$ the monopolist can raise C_i without violating $\Delta_i U_i > 0$ and sell the same x_i units at a higher price. Therefore, profit maximization requires C_i *almost* equal to $B_i(x_i)$. Let's approximate and set C_i *exactly* equal to $B_i(x_i)$. Because x_i^0 denotes the level of x_i that maximizes $B_i(x_i) - x_i$ and $C_i = B_i(x_i)$, the profit-maximizing set of take-it-or-leave-it offers has x_i^0 units of X offered to consumer i at the price $C_i = B_i(x_i^0)$.

Surprisingly, we have an efficient outcome even though the monopolist has succeeded in extracting all the benefit from each consumer. (Set $\varepsilon = 0$ for convenience.)

$$\Delta U_i = B_i(x_i^0) - C_i^0 = B_i(x_i^0) - B_i(x_i^0) = 0.$$

Therefore, each consumer pays a charge equal to the benefit the *consumer* derives from the quantity of X received and there is no net gain in utility. Nevertheless, the outcome is efficient if all the profits are returned to the community. (The company's shareholders are members of the community.) To prove this, we show that any outcome satisfying $x_i = x_i^0$ for all i actually maximizes total utility, $\sum_i U_i$, as long as $\sum y_i$, the total amount of Y consumed, equals the total amount left over after the required $\sum x_i^0$ units are used in the production of X. In other words, feasibility and efficiency require $\sum y_i = \sum \theta_i - \sum x_i^0$. ($\sum$ denotes summation over all individuals.)

$$\sum U_i = \sum [B_i(x_i) + y_i] = \sum B_i(x_i) + \sum y_i$$
$$= \sum B_i(x_i) + \sum \theta_i - \sum x_i,$$

and this is maximized by setting $B_i'(x_i) - 1 = 0$ for each i. We know that x_i^0 is the unique solution to this equation. (If $B_i'(x_i) - 1 = 0$ does not hold for some i, keep x_j fixed for all $j \neq i$. We can then increase $B_i(x_i) - x_i$ and hence increase total utility. Specifically, if $B_i'(x_i) > 1$ we can increase $B_i(x_i) - x_i$ by increasing x_i and if $B_i'(x_i) < 1$ we can increase $B_i(x_i) - x_i$ by reducing x_i, in either case without affecting the value of $B_j(x_j) - x_j$ for any $j \neq i$.)

Now set $\sum U_i = \sum [B_i(x_i^0) + y_i]$. Then $\sum U_i = \sum B_i(x_i^0) + \sum y_i$, and this total is preserved if we redistribute commodity Y among the consumers as long as the total $\sum y_i$ is unchanged. Therefore, an outcome maximizes total utility if $x_i = x_i^0$ for each i and $\sum y_i = \sum \theta_i - \sum x_i^0$. Any such outcome is efficient: if we could make one person's utility higher without lowering anyone else's we could make the sum higher, which is impossible. (See Section 2.5.1 of Chapter 2 on this point.)

In general, any outcome that has one of the agents extracting all of the surplus from the other agents is efficient. Once we specify formally what we mean by "extracting all the surplus" it is easy to prove efficiency. Suppose that each agent i has some initial level of utility μ_i. Agent 1 extracts all of the surplus from each of the other agents if, for all $i > 1$, the *final* level of utility is equal to μ_i, the starting level. In symbols, agent 1 chooses the outcome so as to maximize U_1 subject to the constraint $U_i \geq \mu_i$ for all $i > 1$. The solution s^* to this problem must be efficient: If s^* is *not* efficient then there is a feasible outcome t^* that gives one person more utility than s^* and gives everyone at least as much utility as s^*. If $U_1(t^*) > U_1(s^*)$ we contradict the fact that s^* maximizes U_1 subject to $U_i \geq \mu_i$ for all $i > 1$, because $U_i(t^*) \geq U_i(s^*) \geq \mu_i$ for $i > 1$. If $U_j(t^*) > U_j(s^*)$ for some $j > 1$ then we can extract some commodity Y from person j and still have $U_j > U_j(s^*)$, provided that we are careful to confiscate a sufficiently small amount of Y. If we then give this small amount of Y to person 1 we will have $U_1 > U_1(s^*)$, again contradicting the fact that s^* solves the constrained maximization problem, because $U_i(t^*) \geq U_i(s^*)$ for all $i > 1$.

Before determining the equilibrium outcome in the real-world interpretation of our model, with asymmetric information, we present the simple example to illustrate the theory.

Example 5.6 Two Preference Types

There are two types of consumers, H (high benefit) and L (low benefit) with

$$U_H = 4\sqrt{x_H} + y_H \text{ and } U_L = 2\sqrt{x_L} + y_L.$$

At the full information profit-maximizing equilibrium we have $C_i = B_i$ for $i = H$ and $i = L$. Therefore, the monopoly chooses x_H to maximize $4\sqrt{x_H} - x_H$. The first derivative of this function is $2/\sqrt{x_H} - 1$, and the second derivative is negative. We solve $2/\sqrt{x_H} - 1 = 0$ to get $x_H^* = 4$. Similarly, x_L^* maximizes $2\sqrt{x_L} - x_L$. The first derivative is $(1/\sqrt{x_L}) - 1$, and when we set that equal to zero we get $x_L^* = 1$. Then

$$C_H^* = B_H(x_H^*) = 4\sqrt{4} = 8 \text{ and } C_L^* = B_L(x_L^*) = 2\sqrt{1} = 2.$$

The full information equilibrium has the monopolist selling 4 units of X to each H type, on a take-it-or-leave-it basis, at a price of \$8 for all 4 units, and selling 1 unit of X to each L type at a price of \$2, also on a take-it-or-leave-it basis. If the number of H types and L types is n_H and n_L, respectively, then the firm's profit is

$$n_H \times (8 - 4) + n_L \times (2 - 1) = 4n_H + n_L.$$

Verify that $n_H \times U_H + n_L \times U_L$ (total utility) is maximized however the total profit is divided between the individuals. (If $n_H = 1 = n_L$ then profit is 5.)

Example 5.6 is the subject of our inquiry for the rest of Section 5.5.

∂5.5.4 Asymmetric Information Equilibrium

We continue our investigation of Example 5.6, but we now drop the full information assumption that the individual with utility function $B_H(x) + y$ can be identified. We do assume, however, that the monopolist knows the functional forms B_H and B_L. Of course, it does not know which person has which function. We also assume (for convenience) that there are exactly as many H types as L types. Consequently, total profit is maximized when the firm has maximized the profit from a pair of individuals consisting of one H and one L. When we use the word profit from now on we will be referring to the profit from sales to one H–L pair. If it helps, you can assume that the market consists of one H person and one L person.

DEFINITION: *The Participation Constraint for Example 5.6*

(x_H, C_H) must satisfy $4\sqrt{x_H} - C_H \geq 0$ and (x_L, C_L) must satisfy $2\sqrt{x_L} - C_L \geq 0$.

An offer (α, β) is a specification of the amount α of X in the package and the price β of the package. What is the profit-maximizing menu of offers? If the monopolist simply offers each person a choice of $(1, 2)$ and $(4, 8)$, the profit-maximizing strategy under full information, the H types will choose the former:

$$\Delta U_H(1,2) = 4\sqrt{1} - 2 = 2 \text{ but } \Delta U_H(4,8) = 4\sqrt{4} - 8 = 0.$$

The L types will choose $(1, 2)$ also:

$$\Delta U_L(1,2) = 2\sqrt{1} - 2 = 0 \text{ but } \Delta U_L(4,8) = 2\sqrt{4} - 8 = -4.$$

The monopolist's profit will be $2 + 2 - (1 + 1) = 2$, which is *not* a maximum even under the assumption that B_H and B_L cannot be identified by the monopolist. The monopolist can continue to offer $(1, 2)$, the contract that extracts all the surplus from the L types, but design a contract (x_H, C_H) such that the H types will not prefer $(1, 2)$, and it will otherwise extract as much surplus as possible. The first consideration requires

$$4\sqrt{x_H} - C_H \geq 4\sqrt{1} - 2.$$

This is called the *self-selection* (or *incentive compatibility*) constraint for type H.

DEFINITION: *Self-Selection Constraints in General*

If the producer wants the H type to choose x_H and the L type to choose x_L then the respective prices C_H and C_L must satisfy

$\Delta U_H (x_H, C_H) \geq \Delta U_H (x_L, C_L)$ (H's self-selection constraint), and

$\Delta U_L (x_L, C_L) \geq \Delta U_L (x_H, C_H)$ (L's self-selection constraint).

Return to the examination of Example 5.6 for the asymmetric information case: H's self-selection constraint is $4\sqrt{x_H} - C_H \geq 4\sqrt{x_L} - C_L$. Assume that in computing the profit-maximizing strategy, we don't have to worry about the L types buying the package designed for the H types. (We'll justify this assumption later.) If $(1,2)$ is offered the monopolist will maximize $C_H - x_H$ subject to $4\sqrt{x_H} - C_H \geq 2$. If $4\sqrt{x_H} - C_H > 2$ then C_H can be increased without violating H's self-selection constraint and without changing x_H. This will increase profit, so profit maximization requires $4\sqrt{x_H} - C_H = 2$, or $C_H = 4\sqrt{x_H} - 2$. Then the monopolist maximizes $4\sqrt{x_H} - 2 - x_H$. Setting the first derivative equal to zero gives us $2/\sqrt{x_H} = 1$ and thus $x_H = 4$. (This does yield a maximum because the second derivative is negative.) The same level of service is provided as at the full information equilibrium (a consequence of our simple utility functions) but this time at a charge of $C_H = 4\sqrt{x_H} - 2 = 6$. The monopolist's profit is $6 + 2 - (4 + 1) = 3$, which is lower than the full information profit of 5 but higher than 2, the profit that results when the "full information" solutions are packaged and the consumers are allowed to choose between them.

The strategy of placing packages (1, 2) and (4, 6) on the market and letting the individual choose results in an efficient outcome: We have already shown that $x_L = 1$ and $x_H = 4$ maximizes $U_L + U_H$. We still haven't reached the maximum profit, however. Suppose the monopolist offers only one package, (4, 8). Four units of X at a total cost of $8, take it or leave it:

$$\Delta U_L(4, 8) = 2\sqrt{4} - 8 = -4 \text{ and } \Delta U_H(4, 8) = 4\sqrt{4} - 8 = 0.$$

Consumer L will be better off not buying the package and would not buy even if the cost were reduced slightly. Consumer H would buy the package because it satisfies H's participation constraint – with no room to spare: $\Delta U_H(4, 8) = 0$. The firm sells one package – to consumer H – and its profit is $8 - 4 = 4$. This is the highest profit yet, apart from the full information solution. (In fact, to induce the H type to buy, the cost of $8 would be reduced slightly, and the resulting profit would be slightly less than $4, say $3.99.) We have actually found the firm's profit maximizing strategy under asymmetric information. Before proving that the equilibrium for our current example has the firm offering only the luxury model we prove that, in general, H's participation constraint is satisfied whenever both the H's self-selection constraint and the L's participation constraint are satisfied, regardless of how many individuals of each type there are.

Lemma

If $B_H(x) \geq B_L(x)$ holds for all $x \geq 0$ then an H's participation constraint is satisfied by any pricing and output strategy that satisfies both an H's self-selection constraint and an L's participation constraint.

Proof:

The hypothesis implies that

$$B_H(x_H) - C_H \geq B_H(x_L) - C_L \geq B_L(x_L) - C_L \geq 0.$$

The first inequality is H's self-selection constraint. The second is a consequence of the fact that $B_H(x) \geq B_L(x)$ for all $x \geq 0$. The third is L's participation constraint. The string of inequalities implies $B_H(x_H) - C_H \geq 0$, which is H's participation constraint. ∎

Intuition suggest that we can ignore L's self-selection constraint: the individuals for whom $B_L(x)$ is low will not be motivated to purchase the luxury model with the high sticker price. We will, however, confirm that L's self-selection constraint *is* satisfied by our candidate for the asymmetric information profit maximizing quality and pricing strategy. We certainly need to impose H's self-selection constraint: we have seen that given the choice between the two models that would be profit maximizing under full information an H type will choose the economy model with lower quality and a lower price.

Theorem: Asymmetric Information Profit Maximization for Example 5.6
The strategy of offering only the package (4, 8) maximizes profit, subject to the participation and self-selection constraints. Specifically, $x_H = 4$, $C_H = 8$, and $x_L = 0 = C_L$. Profit is $8 - 4 = 4$.

Proof:

Maximize $C_H + C_H - x_L - x_H$ subject to H's self-selection constraint

$$4\sqrt{x_H} - C_H \geq 4\sqrt{x_L} - C_L$$

and L's participation constraint $2\sqrt{x_L} - C_H \geq 0$. (Recall that the Lemma establishes that these two inequalities imply the satisfaction of H's participation constraint.)

The first step is to show that profit maximization implies $C_L = 2\sqrt{x_L}$. If $2\sqrt{x_L} - C_L > 0$ then we can increase C_L without violating $2\sqrt{x_L} - C_L \geq 0$. If we don't change any of the other variables we will have increased profit, and H's self-selection constraint will still hold as a consequence of increasing C_L alone. Therefore, profit maximization requires $2\sqrt{x_L} - C_L = 0$, and hence $C_L = 2\sqrt{x_L}$. In that case, H's self-selection constraint reduces to

$$4\sqrt{x_H} - C_H \geq 4\sqrt{x_L} - 2\sqrt{x_L} = 2\sqrt{x_L}.$$

It follows from $4\sqrt{x_H} - C_H \geq 2\sqrt{x_L}$ that H's self-selection constraint must hold as an equality, and hence $C_H = 4\sqrt{x_H} - 2\sqrt{x_L}$. If, to the contrary, $4\sqrt{x_H} - C_H > 2\sqrt{x_L}$ holds then profit could be increased by increasing C_H without changing x_H or x_L, and this could be done without violating H's self-selection constraint. (Note that H's participation constraint $4\sqrt{x_H} - C_H \geq 0$ will automatically hold if $2\sqrt{x_L} - C_L \geq 0$ and H's self-selection constraint is satisfied.) Now that we have $C_H = 4\sqrt{x_H} - 2\sqrt{x_L}$ we can express profit as

$$C_H + C_L - x_H - x_L = 4\sqrt{x_H} - 2\sqrt{x_L} + 2\sqrt{x_L} - x_H - x_L$$
$$= 4\sqrt{x_H} - x_H - x_L.$$

H's self-selection constraint and L's participation constraint have been embodied in the objective function $4\sqrt{x_H} - x_H - x_L$. Obviously, maximization of this expression requires $x_L = 0$, and hence the participation constraint implies $C_L = 0$. Then we want to maximize $4\sqrt{x_H} - x_H$. The first derivative is $2/\sqrt{x_H} - 1$. When we set that equal to zero we get $x_H = 4$. Then $C_H = 4\sqrt{x_H} - 2\sqrt{x_L} = 4\sqrt{4} - 2\sqrt{0} = 8$. ∎

The proof employed only three of the constraints that must hold at an asymmetric information equilibrium. Because $U_L(x_L=0=C_L) = 0 > 4 - 8 = U_L(x_H = 4, C_L=8)$, our candidate equilibrium, $x_H = 4$, $C_H = 8$, $x_L = 0 = C_L$, also satisfies L's self-selection constraint. Therefore, we can say that our candidate maximizes profit subject to all four constraints. It *is* the equilibrium.

Interpret x_i as the model designed for the consumers in market group i, with the model identified by the "amount" of quality that it provides. We can see why profit-maximizing firms sometimes discontinue production of a popular model if it is at the low-quality end of the spectrum. Doing so relaxes the constraint on the price of the luxury model. This gives a new interpretation to the automobile manufacturer's boast that features that used to be optional are now standard. (In this case, low quality does not mean unreliable; it simply means less luxurious.)

Does the material in this section shed any light on why publishers of textbooks stop selling the first edition of a book after the second edition appears, even when they have a stock of first editions that could be sold at a discounted price?

When x_L is positive at the asymmetric information equilibrium C_H will be lower than at the full information equilibrium because of H's self-selection constraint. But x_H is the same in the two cases.

Asymmetric Information Equilibrium Short Cut

The value of x_H is the same at the asymmetric and full information equilibria whether x_L is positive or zero. If $B_H(x) > 2B_L(x)$ for all $x > 0$ then $x_L = 0$ at the asymmetric information equilibrium.

Proof:

At the asymmetric and full information equilibrium $C_L = B_L(x_L)$ because L's participation constraint is satisfied as a strict equality. And $B_H(x_H) - C_H = B_H(x_L) - C_L$ because H's self-selection constraint is satisfied as a strict equality. Therefore,

$$B_H(x_H) - C_H = B_H(x_L) - B_L(x_L) \text{ and hence}$$
$$C_H = B_H(x_H) - B_H(x_L) + B_L(x_L).$$

The firm's profit is $C_H - x_H + C_L - x_L$ which equals

$$B_H(x_H) - B_H(x_L) + B_L(x_L) - x_H + B_L(x_L) - x_L \text{ which equals}$$
$$B_H(x_H) - x_H + 2B_L(x_L) - B_H(x_L) - x_L.$$

For *any* value of x_L we can increase profit if we can increase $B_H(x_H) - x_H$. Therefore, maximization of profit requires maximization of $B_H(x_H) - x_H$, which is achieved at the full information value of x_H.

Profit maximization also implies maximization of $2B_L(x_L) - B_H(x_L) - x_L$. (For *any* value of x_H we can increase profit if we can increase $2B_L(x_L) - B_H(x_L) - x_L$.) If $B_H(x) > 2B_L(x)$ for all x we must set $x_L = 0$ to maximize $2B_L(x_L) - B_H(x_L) - x_L$. ∎

The profit-maximizing solution for Example 5.6 is not efficient. We don't know the utility level of each individual because we don't know the share of profit received by each. But we can compute the change in utility for each as a result of an increase in the production of X by one unit, if that unit is delivered to person L and at the same time L's consumption of Y is reduced by one unit. If we do not change x_H or y_H we have a feasible outcome. Certainly, H's utility will not change. The change in L's utility is $2\sqrt{1} - 1 = 1$, so L is better off and H's utility is unchanged. Note that profit is unchanged: the unit of Y needed to finance the production of the additional unit of X is contributed by L, who also receives the extra unit of X. Because profit is unchanged, there is no change in the income of the firm's shareholders, and hence no change in the utility of anyone in society, other than L.

This is a special case of a general phenomenon. The strategy that maximizes profit subject to self-selection constraints typically results in inefficiency. If we ignore the self-selection constraints and simply maximize profit subject to the participation constraints then we get an efficient outcome because we are maximizing one agent's payoff subject to preventing the payoff of everyone else from falling below a given level. (See the argument just prior to Example 5.6.) However, in the real (asymmetric information) world, we must add self-selection constraints, and hence the resulting profit-maximizing solution is constrained away from an efficient one. Nevertheless, it is not necessarily the case that the asymmetric information equilibrium could be modified to increase one person's utility without diminishing anyone else's utility. If the government or some other agency could identify the consumer with utility function U_L then the firm can do so as well, and it will impose the full information profit-maximizing outcome, and that *is* efficient. (The identity of H is known *after* the individual choices are made, but if H knows in advance that this disclosure will be used to modify the outcome then H would have behaved differently in the first place.)

Source
The example of this section is based on Arrow (1984).

Problem Set

(1) $U_H = 8\sqrt{x_H} + y_H$ and $U_L = 6\sqrt{x_L} + y_L$. The monopolist offers two packages on a take-it-or-leave-it basis. Package M_L is designed for consumer L and offers 9 units of X at a total cost of \$18. Package M_H is designed so that consumer H will not prefer M_L, and M_H maximizes profit subject to that that self-selection constraint. Derive M_H.

(2) Electricity is provided by a monopoly. There are two consumers, H and L, with utility functions $U_H = 6\ln(x_H + 1) + y_H$ and $U_L = 4\ln(x_L + 1) + y_L$. Each unit of X costs \$1 to produce.

   (A) Compute the full information equilibrium. Determine the monopolist's profit.

   (B) Assume that the monopolist continues to offer the package designed for consumer L in your solution to A. Then what is the profit-maximizing package associated with consumer H, assuming that the monopolist cannot determine who H is or who L is? What is the associated profit?

   (C) Determine the asymmetric information equilibrium and the monopolist's profit.

   (D) Rank the three profit levels.

(3) Rework question 2 when each unit of X costs \$2 to produce, leaving all other features of the model unchanged.

(4) There are two consumers, H and L, with utility functions $U_H = 4\sqrt{x_H} + y_H$ and $U_L = 3\sqrt{x_L} + y_L$. It costs x dollars to produce x units of commodity X. Show that $x_L > 0$ at the asymmetric information equilibrium, even though the presence of L causes C_H to be \$1 lower than it would be if there were no L-type. Show that the profit that is gleaned from L more than compensates for the reduction in C_H.

(5) Extend the Lemma of Section 5.5.4 to the case $n_H \neq n_L$. In other words, find the value of λ (as a function of n_H and n_L) such that the asymmetric information equilibrium must separate the H's from the L's if $B_H(x) \geq \lambda B_L(x)$ holds for all $x \geq 0$.

5.6   JOB-MARKET SIGNALING

When the hidden characteristic is a quality variable, and quality can be either good or bad, producers of the high-quality version have an incentive to *signal* their quality. But would the signal be credible? Only if the low-quality supplier cannot gain by transmitting the same signal. When would this be possible? Typically signaling consumes resources, and it is substantially more costly for the supplier of the low-quality commodity to transmit the same signal as the supplier of the high-quality commodity. Under the right conditions, the additional cost to those who have only low-quality items to sell motivates them to provide a weaker signal and hence reveal their type. However, because the signal imposes real costs on the individual and on society, truthful revelation comes at a price: the resources consumed in signaling do not provide enough direct utility to compensate for the lost consumer benefit due to these resources being diverted away from the production of other commodities. We show that there is a range of signals consistent with equilibrium, and often the same result could have been obtained with a lower investment in signaling. There are even cases for which everyone invests in signaling but the signaling doesn't distinguish the high-quality from the low-quality producers.

We use the labor market to illustrate. The signal is the amount of higher education that an individual has undergone. Education is costly and individuals who know themselves to be innately intelligent and hard working (relatively speaking) are more likely to graduate and be certified. Therefore, the population of graduates contains a disproportionately high number of individuals who are innately productive – that is, intelligent and hard working. In other words, education can be used to sort workers into H types, who have relatively high ability and productivity, and L types, who have relatively low ability and productivity. A simple model makes the point.

5.6.1   To Make a Long Story Short

High-quality (H type) workers generate substantially more profit for the firm than low-quality workers (L types) because H types are more productive. Although individuals (and their parents) make choices during the formative years that help to determine a person's type, at the time an employer makes a hiring decision the worker's type has been determined. Therefore, the employer faces a hidden characteristic problem. To attract H types a firm can offer a higher wage: $W_H > W_L$, where W_H is the wage paid to H types and W_L is the wage paid to L types. (We refer to the payment to the worker as a wage, but it is in fact the present value of the expected compensation – including benefits – over the lifetime of the job.) But the L types cannot be expected to truthfully identify themselves, and claim the lower wage W_L. If we suppose that production takes place in teams in a setting that makes it very costly to identify the contribution of individuals in the short run, then employers can't directly separate the L types from the H types when they are hired.

Suppose, however, it costs H types C_H dollars to graduate from college and it costs L types a higher amount, C_L. The L types may take one or two extra semesters to graduate. They will also have to work much harder in high school to get admitted to a good college. Then it is possible to induce the L types to reveal themselves in spite of their preference for anonymity. The firm simply pays a salary W_H to anyone who has a graduation certificate and a salary W_L to workers without a certificate. If $W_H - C_L < W_L$ the L types will not pay the cost C_L necessary to obtain a certificate; it is more advantageous to obtain the lower salary W_L without the additional education required to qualify for the higher wage. (To simplify, we initially assume that education is not productive; it serves only to sort the two types.) If $W_H - C_H > W_L$ then H types *will* incur the cost C_H of obtaining a graduate certificate, obtaining the higher net salary $W_H - C_H$. Note that both conditions hold if $C_H < W_H - W_L < C_L$. (All monetary amounts are discounted present values.) If $W_H = 1000$ and $W_L = 600$ then $C_H < 400 < C_L$ is required for signaling to reveal a worker's characteristic. This gives a *range* of equilibria, many of which will be inefficient because the signaling could be done at lower cost to society. This phenomenon will be encountered in the more sophisticated model to follow.

> A firm will pay a huge sum for a celebrity to advertise its product, even when consumers know that the testimony has been paid for and probably does not represent the celebrity's true opinion. The point is to signal the firm's confidence in the quality of its product. The producer cannot recover its advertising expenditure if consumers find that its product is inferior and hence stop buying it. Introductory offers at very low prices have the same effect, but in that case there is a danger that the consumer will interpret the low price as evidence of low quality.

We have shown that workers can pay for and receive training in equilibrium, even when that education does not enhance productivity. What's missing from the story is a discussion of employer profit maximization, which will depend in part on employer beliefs about the relationship between the amount of training attained and the worker's ability. We now consider a more elaborate model with an explicit role for firms. The amount of education (measured in years) can have more than two values, and education can contribute directly to productivity. The richer model will also exhibit different kinds of equilibria, and equilibria with different levels of educational attainment.

5.6.2 A General Model

There are two types of workers, H types and L types. It is common knowledge that the fraction ρ of the population is type H. Worker i ($= H$ or L) has the utility function

$$U_i(x, y) = B_i(x) + y$$

where x is leisure consumption and y the total market value of all other goods and services. Although x and y will typically be different for H and L, we do not often use subscripts on x or y. The identity of the worker will be clear from the context. We assume that the marginal utility of leisure consumption is positive for all x, but if $x'' > x'$ then the marginal utility of leisure is lower at x'' than at x'. (You can follow this section without knowing any calculus, but if you do know calculus a few shortcuts are available. We assume $B_i'(x) > 0$ and $B_i''(x) < 0$ for all $x > 0$.)

We let T denote the individual's time endowment. For instance, if the basic period is a day and we measure time in hours, then $T = 24$. If e is the amount of time it takes (per day, say) for the individual to acquire an education, then $x = T - e$. If $e'' > e'$ then the marginal utility of leisure is higher at e'' than at e' because leisure consumption is lower at e''. That is, the marginal cost of education is positive, and the marginal cost increases as education increases. The cost of acquiring an education will play a central role, so we simplify and write

$$U_i = w(e) - c_i(e)$$

where w is income, as a function of years of education e, and $c_i(e)$ is the amount of leisure sacrificed when e years of education are attained. The function $w(e)$ is the compensation schedule posted by firms.

Example 5.7 A Simple Utility Function

Let $U = 3\sqrt{x} + y$. That is, $B(x) = 3\sqrt{x}$. We have $B(0) = 0$ and $B(4) = 6$. Then $\Delta B = 6$, and $\Delta B/\Delta x = 6/4 = 1.5$. And $B(9) = 9$, so when we increase x from 4 to 9 we have $\Delta B/\Delta x = 3/5 = 0.6$. The marginal utility of leisure is lower at higher values of x. If $T = 24$ then $c(8) = B(24) - B(16) = 14.7 - 12 = 2.7$. And $c(10) = B(24) - B(14) = 3.47$. Consequently, $\Delta c/\Delta e = 0.76/2 = 0.38$. However, when $e = 12$ we have $c(12) = B(24) - B(12) = 4.30$. When e increases from 10 to 12 we have $\Delta c/\Delta e = 0.83/2 = 0.415$. The marginal cost of acquiring an education has increased.

A key assumption is that it is more costly for an L type to achieve a given education level because an L type has to put in more hours studying (over more semesters, perhaps) than an H type. Let $m_i(e)$ be the value of the marginal product of individual i. We assume that m_i increases with e, to reflect the fact that productivity increases with education. By definition, for any level of education e, the high-ability (H) type has a higher marginal product than the low-ability (L) type.

DEFINITION: *The Basic Model*

Type i's utility function is $U_i = w(e) - c_i(e)$ where $w(e)$ is the pay offered by the employer as a function of e, the level of education attained, and $c_i(e)$ is the cost of acquiring e. We assume that for any education level e we have $c_H(e) < c_L(e)$ and $m_H(e) > m_L(e)$, where $m_i(e)$ is the value of the marginal product of type i.

Example 5.8 Two Simple Cost Functions

We use the following cost functions for the rest of Section 5.6:

$$c_H(e) = \tfrac{1}{2}e^2 \text{ and } c_L(e) = \tfrac{3}{4}e^2.$$

We can derive these cost functions from the function $B(x)$. For instance, suppose that $B_H = xT - \tfrac{1}{2}x^2$, where T is the time endowment. Then

$$c_H(e) = B(T) - B(T - e) = T^2 - \tfrac{1}{2}T^2 - \left[(T - e)T - \tfrac{1}{2}(T - e)^2\right] = \tfrac{1}{2}e^2.$$

Of course, education is more than a signal; it also enhances productivity. However, to get some quick insight we temporarily assume that each type's value of the marginal product is independent of the highest level of education reached. This assumption is dropped in Section 5.6.3.

Example 5.9 Education is Not Productive

Let $m_L = m$ and $m_H = 2m$, where m is some positive constant.

What happens at equilibrium? There are many equilibria. In fact there are two *types* of equilibria, pooling and separating, as we are about to see.

DEFINITION: *The Two Kinds of Equilibria*

At a *pooling* equilibrium the two types of workers get the same amount of education, and each receives the same pay, namely the weighted average marginal product, weighted by the proportion of each type in the work force. At a *separating* equilibrium, the H types get more education than the L types, and the firms pay more to the workers with the higher level of education.

Pooling Equilibria

All workers obtain the same number of years of schooling and are paid the same wage. What values of the wage and of e are consistent with worker utility maximization and firm profit maximization?

Recall that the proportion ρ of the population is H type, so the expected (or mean) productivity is $\rho \times 2m + (1 - \rho) \times m = m\rho + m$. At this point we import a classical result from the theory of competitive labor markets: the workers are paid the value of their marginal product. Therefore, in this model $m\rho + m$ is paid to each worker at equilibrium *if* the same wage is paid to all.

Pooling Equilibrium Wage Schedule Offered by Each Firm, Based on a Given Critical Level g of Education

- If $e < g$ assume that the worker is L type and pay that individual m.
- If $e \geq g$, assume that the worker is H type with probability ρ and L type with probability $1 - \rho$ and offer the wage $m\rho + m$.

What we have here is an equilibrium system of *beliefs* in addition to the usual market clearance property of equilibrium. The employers' demand schedules for workers are functions of their beliefs. At equilibrium, employers' beliefs must be confirmed by observation – of the amount of output produced, which in turn is a function of the wage schedule, via worker's decisions about how much education to acquire. At equilibrium, we have a completed circle.

What decision will an individual make when confronted with this wage schedule? There is no point in choosing $e > g$ because that would increase education costs without bringing any increase in pay. There is no point in choosing a value of e satisfying $0 < e < g$ because compensation would not change if e were reduced to zero, and the cost of education would certainly fall. Therefore, H will set $e = g$ if $m\rho + m - 0.5g^2 > m$ and L will set $e = g$ if $m\rho + m - 0.75g^2 > m$. The following conditions hold for H and L respectively:

$$m\rho + m - 0.5g^2 > m \text{ and } m\rho + m - 0.75g^2 > m.$$

Both inequalities will hold if $m\rho + m - 0.75g^2 > m$.

Example 5.10 A Third of the Labor Force is *H* Type

We continue with the basic example but explicitly examine the case $\rho = \frac{1}{3}$. Then L types will acquire g units of education if $\frac{1}{3}m + m - \frac{3}{4}g^2 > m$, or $g^2 < 4m/9$, which is equivalent to

$$g < \frac{2}{3}\sqrt{m}.$$

H types will also set $e = g$ if this inequality holds.

Suppose that $m = 9$. Then we have a pooling equilibrium for any value of g satisfying $0 \leq g < 2$, with a wage of 12 to each worker. Each worker will be optimizing by setting $e = g$ and taking a wage of 12 instead of 9. (Verify: If H chooses $e < g$ then he or she will be paid 9, resulting in $U_H \le 9 - \frac{1}{2}(0)^2$. But if H sets $e = g$ then the pay will be 12 and $U_H > 12 - \frac{1}{2}(2)^2 = 10$. If L chooses $e < g$ then the pay will be paid 9 and $U_H \le 9 - \frac{3}{4}(0)^2$, and if L sets $e = g$ then the pay is 12 and $U_L > 12 - \frac{3}{4}(2)^2 = 9$.) Under competitive conditions each firm pays a wage of 12, the expected value of the per capita marginal product. The firm's subsequent observations confirm this expectation. Everyone obtains g years of schooling, so the productivity of the group with g years of schooling will be observed to be 12 per capita. We are at equilibrium. This corresponds to a cohort of individuals with the same undergraduate degree earning the same pay in spite of their different abilities.

With full information, every worker would be required to set $e = 0$ for efficiency, if education makes no contribution to productivity. With asymmetric information we can have an equilibrium with each worker spending a substantial amount of time in higher education. (If average productivity per worker is 12, then even $g = 1$ is a substantial investment in education.) But we're not finished with the analysis. Continue to assume that education is not productive.

Separating Equilibria

Suppose H types obtain more education in equilibrium than L types. Let e_H and e_L denote the equilibrium education levels of H types and L types, respectively.

> **Separating Equilibrium Wage Schedule Offered by Each Firm, Based on a Given Critical Level g of Education**
>
> - If $e < g$ assume that the worker is L type with probability 1 and pay m.
> - If $e \ge g$, assume that the worker is H type with probability 1 and pay $2m$.

What is the worker's response? Setting $e > g$ just increases the worker's costs without any reward in terms of higher salary, so no worker will choose more than g years of schooling. Similarly, if $0 < e < g$ then the worker will receive the same wage as someone who sets $e = 0$. Therefore, regardless of type, the worker will set $e = 0$ or $e = g$. Table 5.5 displays the relevant data.

A separating equilibrium must satisfy the *self-selection constraints*: Each type must find it advantageous to send a signal that is different from the one transmitted by the other type.

Table 5.5

e	U_H	U_L
0	m	m
g	$2m - 0.5g^2$	$2m - 0.75g^2$

DEFINITION: *Self-Selection (or Incentive Compatibility) Constraints*
At a separating equilibrium the H types do not get higher utility from $e = 0$ than from $e = g$, and the L types do not get higher utility from $e = g$ than from $e = 0$.

A separating equilibrium must be incentive compatible: an H type must get higher utility with $e = g$ than with $e = 0$, and the L type must get higher utility with $e = 0$ than with $e = g$. Therefore

$$2m - 0.5g^2 > m \quad [H\text{'s self-selection constraint}] \text{ and}$$
$$m > 2m - 0.75g^2 \quad [L\text{'s self-selection constraint}].$$

The two inequalities reduce to

$$0.75g^2 > m > 0.5g^2.$$

Example 5.11 The L Type's Value of Marginal Product is 9

If $m = 9$ then $0.75g^2 > m > 0.5g^2$ implies $\sqrt{12} < g < \sqrt{18}$. If g is between 3.464 and 4.243 then H types will set $e = g$, and the L types will set $e = 0$. Each H is paid 18 and each L is paid 9.

The critical g has to be large, to discourage L types from setting $e = g$, but not so large as to induce H types to forego higher education. Specifically, if $\frac{3}{4}g^2 > m > \frac{1}{2}g^2$ then only H types will obtain higher education (i.e., will set $e = g$) and firms' expectations will be confirmed. Again we have a range of equilibria in which there is investment in education even though education does not enhance productivity. In a model in which education *does* contribute to productivity, one would expect to find investment beyond the point justified by considerations of productive efficiency. This is what we encounter in the next section.

5.6.3 Education is Productive

For both the H types and the L types value added increases with e, but an additional unit of higher education adds more to the productivity of an H type than it does to the productivity of an L type.

Example 5.12 Marginal Product is a Function of Education

We work out the equilibria for the case $m_H(e) = 6e$ and $m_L(e) = 3e$. We continue to assume that the cost functions are $c_H(e) = \frac{1}{2}e^2$ and $c_L(e) = \frac{3}{4}e^2$.

Table 5.6

e	Pay	U_H	U_L
6	36	18	9
2	6	4	3

The gap between the average earnings of high school and college graduates almost doubled between 1979 and 1991 (Mishel and Bernstein, 1992). Much of this increase in the rate of return to education is attributable to training in the use of computers. The proliferation of computers accounts for at least one-third, and perhaps as much as one-half, of the increase in the rate of return to education (Krueger, 1993). See also Autor et al. (1998).

To establish a benchmark case, assume temporarily that the worker's type (ability) is directly observable.

Full Information Equilibrium

Each worker i will be confronted with the wage schedule $m_i(e)$, because the worker's type is known and competition ensures that the wage will equal the value of the *individual's* marginal product. If workers' utility is not maximized at e then we can't be at equilibrium. Another firm will offer the worker a contract that requires the utility-maximizing value of e. This can be done in a way that increases the worker's utility and also the profit of that firm attempting to attract the worker.

The H-type worker's utility-maximizing level of e is obtained by maximizing $w - c = 6e - \frac{1}{2}e^2$.

To maximize this quadratic we set $e = 6/(2 \times \frac{1}{2}) = 6$. (The first derivative is $6 - e$. Because the second derivative is negative, utility maximization requires $e = 6$.) Then W_H, the H type's pay, is 36 because $m_H(6)=36$. Similarly, at equilibrium the L-type worker's education level will maximize $w - c = 3e - \frac{3}{4}e^2$ and hence $e = 3/(2 \times \frac{3}{4}) = 2$. (The first derivative of the objective function is $3 - 1.5e$, so $e = 2$ at the maximum.) Then $w_L = 6$ because $m_L(2) = 3 \times 2$. Table 5.6 summarizes.

Note that if we drop the full information assumption, L types would masquerade as H types because they prefer a wage of 36, even though it would cost $\frac{3}{4} \times 6 \times 6 = 27$ to obtain the 6 years of education necessary to pass as H types ($36 - 27 = 9$, which is greater than $6 - \frac{3}{4} \times 2 \times 2 = 3$). Therefore, the full information outcome is not an equilibrium in an asymmetric information world. The firms could not pay a wage of 36 to *everyone* with 6 years of higher education because, when $\rho = \frac{1}{3}$, the average value of marginal product is only $\frac{1}{3} \times 36 + \frac{2}{3} \times 18 = 24$. Firms would be taking a loss so the industry can't be at equilibrium. We need to work out the asymmetric information equilibria.

Asymmetric Information Pooling Equilibria

Both H and L types choose g years of education, with g to be determined. Because education is the only observable variable that depends on ability, each worker is paid the same wage, the expected value of marginal product when everyone sets $e = g$. We need to work out the implications of worker utility maximization and firm profit maximization. (The formula for maximizing a quadratic is used repeatedly. See Section 2.1 of Chapter 2).

The fraction ρ of the entire population is H type, so the expected productivity when everyone sets $e = g$ is

$$\rho m_H(g) + (1 - \rho)m_L(g) = \tfrac{1}{3}(6g) + \tfrac{2}{3}(3g) = 4g.$$

When the wage is same for each worker then each is paid $4g$ at equilibrium as a consequence of competition among firms for workers.

> **Pooling Equilibrium Wage Schedule Offered by Each Firm, Based on a Given Critical Level g of Education**
>
> If $e < g$ assume that the worker is L type, and pay $3e$.
> If $e \geq g$ assume that the worker is H type with probability $\tfrac{1}{3}$ and pay $4g$.
> (Recall that $\rho = \tfrac{1}{3}$.)

There is a pooling equilibrium if each type is motivated to set $e = g$. What does that imply about the value of g?

Pooling Equilibrium Condition

There is a pooling equilibrium for each $g \leq 4.43$.

Proof:

Will the H type choose the wage $4g$ or the wage $3e$ for some $e < g$? Because $4e - \tfrac{1}{2}e^2$ is maximized at $e = 4$, and hence the graph of $4e - \tfrac{1}{2}e^2$ is a hill with peak at 4, if $e < g \leq 4$ then

$$3e - \tfrac{1}{2}e^2 < 4e - \tfrac{1}{2}e^2 < 4g - \tfrac{1}{2}g^2.$$

Therefore, the H type sets $e = g$ and receives a wage of $4g$ when $g \leq 4$.

Consider L's decision: $4e - \tfrac{3}{4}e^2$ is maximized at $e = 4/(2 \times \tfrac{3}{4}) = 2\tfrac{2}{3}$ (Figure 5.2). Hence $e < g \leq 2\tfrac{2}{3}$ implies

$$3e - \tfrac{3}{4}e^2 < 4e - \tfrac{3}{4}e^2 < 4g - \tfrac{3}{4}g^2.$$

Therefore, L sets $e = g$ and receives a wage of $4g$ when $g \leq 2\tfrac{2}{3}$.

What about L's decision at $g > 2\tfrac{2}{3}$? The function $3e - \tfrac{3}{4}e^2$ is maximized at $e = 2$, where $U_L = 3$. Consequently, $g > 2\tfrac{2}{3}$ and $4g - \tfrac{3}{4}g^2 > 3$ implies that L will set $e = g$. Now, $4e - \tfrac{3}{4}e^2 - 3 = 0$ implies $g = 0.9$ or 4.43 (Figure 5.2 again). Because the graph of $4e - \tfrac{3}{4}e^2 - 3$ is a hill that reaches its peak at $g = 2\tfrac{2}{3}$, if $0.9 \leq g \leq 4.43$, and $e = g$ we have $U_L \geq 3$, and hence L sets $e = g$ and receives a wage of $4g$. Therefore, if $g > 2\tfrac{2}{3}$ we can have a pooling equilibrium only if $g \leq 4.43$ also holds, otherwise U_L will be less than its value when $e = 2$.

Will H set $e = g$ if $g \leq 4.43$? We have already demonstrated that H sets $e = g$ if $g \leq 4$. Can we have $3e - \tfrac{1}{2}e^2 > 4g - \tfrac{1}{2}g^2$ if $e < g$ and $4 \leq g \leq 4.43$? The maximum value of $3e - \tfrac{1}{2}e^2$ is 4.5, which occurs at $e = 3$. But for $g = 4.43$ we have $4g - \tfrac{1}{2}g^2 > 7.9$, and that's the lowest value of $4g - \tfrac{1}{2}g^2$ over all g satisfying $4 \leq g \leq 4.43$. (See Figure 5.3: Note that $4g - \tfrac{1}{2}g^2 = 4.5$ if $g = 1.35$ or $g = 6.65$.) Therefore, H will choose g and receive a wage of $4g$ if $g \leq 4.43$. ∎

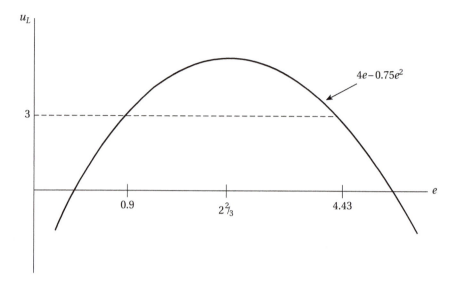

Figure 5.2

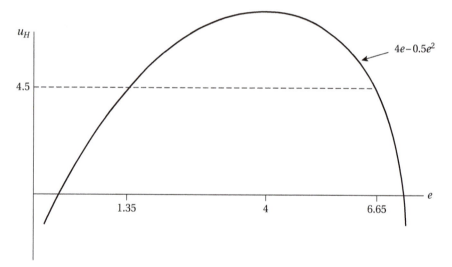

Figure 5.3

Whatever value of g emerges at equilibrium, we don't have the full information choices $e_L = 2$ and $e_H = 6$ that would be mandated by efficiency considerations alone.

Asymmetric Information Separating Equilibria

Suppose H types obtain more education in equilibrium than L types. Could we have $e_H = 6$ and $e_L = 2$ (the full information equilibrium choices from Table 5.6) at equilibrium? No. An L type would prefer setting $e = 6$ and a having a wage of 36, on the one hand, to $e = 2$ with a wage of 6, on the other hand. Everyone would choose $e = 6$. This cannot be sustained as an equilibrium because the average product is

⅓ × 36 + ⅔ × 3 × 6 = 24 : cost per worker (to the firm) is 36 and revenue per worker is 24. What *are* the possible equilibrium values of e_H and e_L?

Separation requires that the workers' choices reveal their types. Hence, a worker choosing e_L will receive a wage of $3e_L$, and a worker choosing e_H will receive a wage of $6e_H$. Both are consequences of competition among producers for workers. The equilibrium will then have to satisfy the self-selection constraints – also called the incentive compatibility constraints. The following are the self-selection conditions for H and L respectively:

$$6e_H - \tfrac{1}{2}e_H^2 \geq 3e_L - \tfrac{1}{2}e_L^2, \qquad\qquad [1]$$

$$3e_L - \tfrac{3}{4}e_L^2 \geq 6e_H - \tfrac{3}{4}e_H^2. \qquad\qquad [2]$$

Statement [1] says that an H type prefers obtaining e_H years of education and a wage of $6e_H$ to a wage of $3e_L$ with e_L years of education. Note that both sides of [1] use H's cost function. And [2] says that L prefers obtaining e_L years of education and a subsequent wage of $3e_L$ to e_H years of education with a wage of $6e_H$. Both sides of [2] use L's cost function. In short, if [1] and [2] hold then no worker will have an incentive to conceal his or her true type. We already know that the maximum value of the left-hand side of [2] is 3, occurring when $e_L = 2$.

If L-types do not get individual utility of at least 3 at equilibrium they could set up their own firm. They could each set $e_L = 2$ in this new firm and could pay themselves a wage of 6, yielding $U_L = 3$. If they received applications from H-types wanting to work for a wage of 6 the L-type owners of the firm would gladly welcome them aboard, realizing a profit of $6 \times 2 - 6 = 6$ per H-type worker. (This argument will not work for H types. If they form their own firm they will face the same problem as existing employers: L types will attempt to masquerade as high-productivity workers. In that case, a wage that would be viable if the firm were staffed by H types alone would not be viable if L types joined the firm and received the same wage.) Therefore, $U_L \geq 3$ at a separating equilibrium. The only way that an employer could provide $U_L \geq 3$ would be to offer a wage of 6 and insist on 2 years of education. (That's because $3e_L - \tfrac{3}{4}e_L^2$ is maximized at $e_L = 2$.) Therefore, $e_L = 2$ at the equilibrium. When we substitute 2 for e_L in [1] and [2] we get

$$6e_H - \tfrac{1}{2}e_H^2 \geq 3 \times 2 - \tfrac{1}{2} \times 2 \times 2 = 4 \text{ and } 3 \geq 6e_H - \tfrac{3}{4}e_H^2. \qquad [3]$$

Now, maximize U_H subject to [3]. Consider the second part of [3]. The function $6e_H - \tfrac{3}{4}e_H^2$ is maximized at $e_H = 4$. Starting at $e_H = 4$, the value of the function decreases as e_H increases *or* decreases (Figure 5.4). Now, $e_H = 0.54$ and $e_H = 7.46$ are the solutions to the equation $6e_H - \tfrac{3}{4}e_H^2 = 3$. Therefore, the second part of [3] will be violated if $0.54 < e_H < 7.46$, and it will be satisfied otherwise. Therefore, [3] can be replaced by

$$6e_H - \tfrac{1}{2}e_H^2 \geq 4 \text{ and either } e_H \leq 0.54 \text{ or } e_H \geq 7.46. \qquad [4]$$

The function $6e_H - \tfrac{1}{2}e_H^2$ is maximized at $e_H = 6$, and so U_H falls as e_H increases beyond 7.46 or falls below 0.54. Therefore, if we maximize U_H subject to [4] we will have either $e_H = 0.54$ or $e_H = 7.46$. It is easy to see that 7.46 gives the higher value

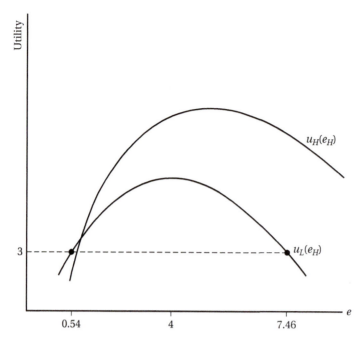

Figure 5.4

of U_H. (Besides, $0.54 < e_L = 2$.) We get $U_H = 6 \times 7.46 - \frac{1}{2} \times (7.46)^2 = 16.9$, so [4] is satisfied. We have a separating equilibrium.

Separating Equilibrium Condition

At a separating equilibrium $e_H = 7.46$ and $e_L = 2$. Firms pay a wage of $3e$ if $e < 7.46$ and pay $6e$ if $e \geq 7.46$. H types respond by setting $e_H = 7.46$ and Ls respond by setting $e_L = 2$.

Proof:

Confirm that we have an equilibrium by computing the worker's response: consider an L type's decision. Because $6e - \frac{3}{4}e^2$ is maximized at $e = 6/(2 \times \frac{3}{4}) = 4$, when $e > 4$ the value of the function declines as e increases. Therefore, an L type would never set $e > 7.46$. Similarly, $6e - \frac{1}{2}e^2$ is maximized at $e = 6/(2 \times \frac{1}{2}) = 6$, so that function decreases as e increases, if $e > 6$ initially. Consequently, an H type would not set $e > 7.46$. An L type's decision reduces to a choice between $e_L = 2$ (which provides the maximum utility available with the wage schedule $3e$) and $e_L = 7.46$. Now, $U_L(7.46) = 6 \times 7.46 - \frac{3}{4}(7.46)^2 = 3$, which does not exceed the utility of 3 realized by L when $e_L = 2$ and the wage is 3×2.

An H type will set $e_H = 7.46$ because $U_H = 6 \times 7.46 - \frac{1}{2}(7.46)^2 = 16.9$, which is larger than $3 \times 3 - \frac{1}{2}(3)^2 = 4.5$, the highest level of utility attainable by H with the schedule $3e$.

We have confirmed that each H type maximizes utility by setting $e_H = 7.46$, and each L type maximizes utility by setting $e_L = 2$. If no firm wants to depart from the wage schedule "pay $3e$ if $e < 7.46$ and $6e$ if $e \geq 7.46$" then we are indeed at equilibrium. Each firm expects that a worker presenting a certificate for 2 years of education is an L type and that each worker with a certificate for 7.46 years of education is an H type. If the firm hires n_L of the former and n_H of the latter it will expect its output to be $3 \times 2 \times n_L + 6 \times 7.46 \times n_H$ and that is exactly what it will be. Employers' expectations are confirmed, and they have no reason to modify the wage schedule.   ■

Note that L types make the same investment in education as in the full information efficient outcome, but H types invest more than they would in full information. Surprisingly, the proportion ρ of H types plays no role in the computation of a separating equilibrium. Asymmetric information results in more investment in education than can be justified by considerations of the return to society from enhanced productivity, even if the fraction of L types is small. (Given that workers in industrialized economies do not have a uniform educational background we conclude that the separating equilibrium is the applicable one.)

Sources

Spence (1973) was the first to show how signaling could emerge as a solution to the asymmetric information (hidden characteristic) problem introduced into the literature by Akerlof (1970). In separate contributions, George Akerlof, Michael Spence, and Joseph Stiglitz showed that the presence of asymmetric information in real-world markets required a new way of modeling economic exchange. They were awarded the Nobel Prize in Economics for the year 2001.

Links

Heckman (2013) cites mounting evidence that an individual's "type" is often determined at a *very* early age. He finds that the accident of birth is the greatest source of inequality in the United States, and offers a plan to circumvent the problem. Cameron and Heckman (1993) find that workers who enter the labor market with a high school equivalency degree are paid 10 percent less on average than workers who enter with a conventional high school diploma. Riley (2000) and Chapter 13 of McAfee (2002) give an overview of the economics of signaling. The latter is decidedly nontechnical, and the former is intended for readers with a good economics background. Riley (1989) fits between the two.

Problem Set

(1) Use the technique of Example 5.8 to derive the cost function $c_L(e) = \frac{3}{4}e^2$ from a utility function of the form $U_L = B_L(x) + y$. That is, specify B_L so that $c_L(e) = \frac{3}{4}e^2$.

(2) For the model of Section 5.6.3, show explicitly that there is a pooling equilibrium for $g = 1.5$ and also for $g = 3.5$.

(3) There are two types of workers, H and L. The value of the marginal product of an H type is $30e$ and the value of the marginal product of an L type is $12e$, where e is the level of education attained. One-third of the workers are H types, but an employer cannot directly distinguish an H from an L. The cost to an H type of e units of education is $\frac{1}{2}e^2$, and the cost to an L type of e units of education is e^2.

    (A) Find a separating equilibrium, and characterize it.

    (B) For what range of values of g would a pooling equilibrium exist? Describe a pooling equilibrium.

(4) There are two types of workers, H and L. The value of the marginal product of an H type is $25e$, and the value of the marginal product of an L type is $10e$. Half of the workers are H types, but an employer cannot directly distinguish an H from an L. The cost to an H type of e units of education is $0.6e^2$, and the cost to an L type of e units of education is $0.8e^2$.

    (A) Find a separating equilibrium, and characterize it.

    (B) For what range of values of g would a pooling equilibrium exist? Describe a pooling equilibrium.

(5) When will the producer of a high-quality product be able to use a warranty to signal that its output is superior to that of its low-quality rival even though consumers cannot directly determine quality?

5.7   COMPETITIVE INSURANCE MARKETS

This section highlights the difficulties of eliciting hidden information when agents differ with respect to their information about the likelihood of events. The hidden characteristic in this case is the probability that an individual will suffer a mishap – have a car accident, be burglarized, be hospitalized, and so forth. We assume that the individual knows the probability of this happening, but no one else does. Moreover, this person cannot be expected to willingly disclose this hidden characteristic, especially if those who report a higher probability of accident are charged higher insurance premiums. We embed these facts in a model of a competitive insurance market in a mature capitalist economy. We see that there exists no competitive equilibrium for some values of the parameters. When an equilibrium *does* exist, individuals will reveal their accident probability by their choice of insurance contract. Nevertheless, the competitive equilibrium may not be efficient when it does exist, although it is not easy to determine when government regulation can improve on the market outcome.

5.7.1   The Model

Harry knows more about the likelihood of his having an accident in a certain situation than others do. This means that some of the information about the probability of an accident is hidden from the company offering him an insurance contract. In the case of automobile insurance, there is a lot of information about our driving habits that is available to insurance companies. Young men are more likely to be risky drivers than young women, and this observation is used by companies in determining rates. The correlation is far from perfect, however, but to the extent that a riskier driver is identified and charged a higher premium we can say that prices reflect costs to society – part of the cost in this case is the possibility of you or I being the dangerous driver's victim. Information about speeding tickets and prior accidents are also used in determining automobile insurance premiums. This is called experience rating.

I was driving home one day, correcting the manuscript for this section, trying to think of a good example of private information in this context. Then I realized that my practice of correcting manuscripts while driving is the perfect illustration. My insurance company would love to know about this dangerous habit.

Suppose that an insurance company has already used all available information to categorize drivers by risk and has determined that Harry and Dana are in the same risk category. There is additional private information that Harry has about his driving habits and Dana has about hers that is hidden from the insurance provider. Given the evidence available to insurance companies, there will still be differences in risk that cannot be directly observed, and it is these additional, private characteristics that are the subject of this section.

To abstract from most of the other issues, assume that there is only one basic commodity, which we call wealth. Uncertainty concerns the status of an individual's wealth, which is either partly destroyed – by accident or fire, say – or remains intact. We let a represent the value of an individual's wealth after an accident when no insurance is purchased and let z represent the value of the same individual's wealth without insurance and also without an accident. The actual wealth level may be different from both a and z. If the individual buys insurance and does not have an accident, then his or her wealth will be lower than z by the amount of the premium. If the individual has an accident after buying insurance then his or her wealth will be higher than a after receiving a claim check from the insurance company to partly compensate for the loss $z - a$.

Let x denote the amount of wealth available to finance consumption when the individual suffers an accident, and let y denote the amount of wealth available for consumption when there is no accident. An insurance contract or policy P requires the purchaser to pay a stipulated fee (the premium) of f dollars before the resolution of uncertainty. If the person does not have an accident then no further exchange takes place, but if he or she is involved in an accident then the insurance company pays c dollars net. The amount of the claim check is actually $c + f$, but the net claim is c because the individual must pay the annual premium whether there is an accident or not. Therefore, if the individual purchases a policy charging a premium f and paying the net claim c we have

$$x = a + c \text{ and } y = z - f.$$

We allow $f = 0 = c$, which holds when no insurance is purchased.

The number π is the probability that the individual has a car accident (or the house catches fire, etc.). To make the model extremely simple, we assume there are only two possible values of π and hence only two types of individuals: low risk, L, and high risk, H, so we write π_L and π_H, respectively. The hidden characteristic is the value of π. Of course, $\pi_H > \pi_L$, and $1 - \pi_L$ is the probability that an L type does not have an accident. Similarly, $1 - \pi_H$ is the probability that an H type does not have an accident. (The event "Harry has an accident" is statistically independent of the event "Dana has an accident." Don't jump to the conclusion that they have accidents simultaneously.)

For analytical convenience all individuals are assumed to have the same utility-of-wealth function $U(w)$. They are risk averse: the marginal utility of wealth is positive, but it diminishes as wealth increases. (In terms of calculus, $U'(w) > 0$ and $U''(w) < 0$, for all $w > 0$.) Each individual has the same endowment allocation: a if there is an accident, and z if there is no accident. And $z > a$ because an accident destroys wealth. We are assuming that individuals are identical, except for the value of π. There are n_L low-risk individuals and n_H high-risk individuals. Although $U(w)$ is the same for each individual, it is not the case that expected utility is the same for an L type and an H type because the probabilities differ. Expected utility for L and H respectively is

$$u_L(x, y) = \pi_L U(x) + (1 - \pi_L)U(y),$$
$$u_H(x, y) = \pi_H U(x) + (1 - \pi_H)U(y).$$

We assume that U is monotonic: if $v > w$ then $U(v) > U(w)$. Therefore, u_L will increase if x increases and y does not decrease, or if y increases and x does not decrease. The same can be said of u_H. (The utility derived from leisure is not needed for this model because we assume that there is no opportunity for the individual to affect the probability of an accident by sacrificing leisure to devote effort to preventive care.)

Theorem

Risk aversion implies diminishing marginal rate of substitution (MRS) along an indifference curve.

Proof:

To confirm that the indifference curve has the shape of the one in Figure 5.5, note that the MRS at (x, y) for type i ($i = L$ or H) is

$$\frac{\pi_i U'(x)}{(1 - \pi_i)U'(y)}$$

where $U'(x)$ and $U'(y)$ denote the marginal utility of wealth at x and y respectively. As we move down the indifference curve, increasing x and decreasing y, $U'(x)$ will fall and $U'(y)$ will increase because marginal utility diminishes with wealth as a consequence of risk aversion. (See Sections 2.6.2 and 2.6.3 of Chapter 2.) Therefore, we have diminishing MRS. ∎

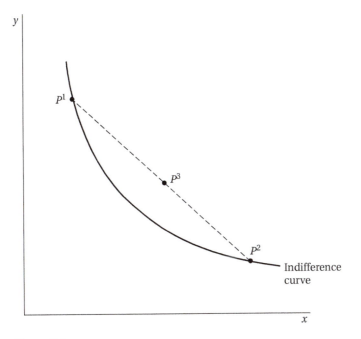

Figure 5.5

The crucial assumption is that insurance companies cannot identify L types and H types directly. They can distinguish them only by observing their choices, and then only if the H types have no incentive to purchase the contract designed for the L types and vice versa. Consequently, even within our very abstract framework, in which individuals are identical in all but one respect and only wealth available for consumption affects well-being, there are potential difficulties in terms of the satisfactory performance of competitive markets.

DEFINITION: *The Individual Variables and Parameters*

Without insurance, an individual's wealth is a if he or she has an accident and z otherwise. With insurance, the individual's wealth is x if he or she has an accident and y otherwise. If the insurance premium is f then $y = z - f$, and $x = a - f + v$, where v is the value of the claim check and $c = x - a$ is the net claim The number of L types is n_L, and the number of H types is n_H. The probabilities of an accident for L types and H types are π_L and π_H respectively.

Assume that n_L and n_H are both large in absolute value, although one number might be small relative to the other. For $J = H$ or L, if n_J is large, then the total number of accidents suffered by J types will be very close to the expected number, $\pi_J n_J$. This is the *law of large numbers*. (See Section 2.6.8 of Chapter 2.)

We assume that the total number of accidents is always exactly equal to the expected number to avoid having to say repeatedly that the results hold only approximately but with high probability.

DEFINITION: *The Number of Accidents*

We assume that n_H is large, and use the law of large numbers to assume that the total number of accidents suffered by H types is exactly $\pi_H n_H$. Similarly, we assume that n_L is large, and that the total number of accidents suffered by L types is exactly $\pi_L n_L$.

Let's also assume, for simplicity, that administration costs are constant and relatively small. This permits us to assume zero administrative costs without affecting the results. (When administrative costs are constant – i.e., independent of x and y – we can assume that they have been incorporated in the values of a and z.) In that case, competition among insurance companies will ensure that the value of premiums taken in at equilibrium equals the value of gross claims paid out at equilibrium. (This is derived with care in Section 2.7.4 of Chapter 2.)

5.7.2 The Number of Contracts in Equilibrium

The H types are identical, so they will make the same choices at equilibrium, and hence will have identical policies. Similarly, the L types will wind up with the same policies. If the policy purchased by the Ls is the same as the one purchased by the Hs then there will be one policy with $n_L + n_H$ buyers. Otherwise there will be one policy with n_L buyers and another with n_H buyers.

Equilibrium Theorem

At equilibrium, a contract will have n_H, or n_L, or $n_H + n_L$ buyers.

Proof:

Suppose to the contrary that some H types choose policy P^1 and some choose P^2, different from P^1. If one yields a higher value of u_H than the other, we can't be at equilibrium. Some H types will switch from the low-utility policy to the high-utility policy. Therefore $u_H(P^1) = u_H(P^2)$ at equilibrium. Further, P^1 and P^2 yield the same expected profit to the insurance company. If, say, P^1 provided higher expected profit per policy than P^2 then insurance companies would all offer P^1 and withdraw P^2. Their customers wouldn't object because $u_H(P^1) = u_H(P^2)$.

Suppose that P^1 is purchased by k_1 of the Hs and P^2 is purchased by k_2 of them. At equilibrium they yield the same utility and the same profit. Let f^1 and f^2 denote the premiums of the respective policies and let c^1 and c^2 represent the respective net claims. The insurance company's profit from P^1 is

$$k_1 \times f^1 - k_1 \pi_H \times (c^1 + f^1).$$

(Each policy holder pays a premium of f^1 and each accident results in a claim check of $c^1 + f^1$ being issued. There will be $k_1 \pi_H$ accidents.) The profit from P^2 is

$$k_2 \times f^2 - k_2 \pi_H \times (c^2 + f^2).$$

The two policies yield the same profit at equilibrium:

$$k_1 f^1 - k_1 \pi_H (c^1 + f^1) = k_2 f^2 - k_2 \pi_H (c^2 + f^2).$$

Suppose $P^1 \neq P^2$. Consider policy P^3 constructed by averaging P^1 and P^2. That is, P^3 charges the premium $f^3 = \frac{1}{2} f^1 + \frac{1}{2} f^2$ and pays the net claim $c^3 = \frac{1}{2} c^1 + \frac{1}{2} c^2$. If all the Hs who purchased P^1 or P^2 would purchase P^3 the resulting profit would be

$$k_1 (\tfrac{1}{2} f^1 + \tfrac{1}{2} f^2) + k_2 (\tfrac{1}{2} f^1 + \tfrac{1}{2} f^2) - k_1 \pi_H (\tfrac{1}{2} c^1 + \tfrac{1}{2} c^2) - k_2 \pi_H (\tfrac{1}{2} c^1 + \tfrac{1}{2} c^2)$$
$$= \tfrac{1}{2} [k_1 f^1 - k_1 \pi_H (c^1 + f^1)] + \tfrac{1}{2} [k_2 f^2 - k_2 \pi_H (c^2 + f^2)],$$

the average of the expected profits from P^1 and P^2.

At equilibrium, P^1 and P^2 yield the same per capita expected profit. Then P^3 must generate the same profit as P^1 and P^2 because the profit from P^3 is the average of the profit from P^1 and P^2. The three policies yield the same profit. But P^3 *affords higher expected utility!* A glance at Figure 5.5 makes this evident. P^3 is on the straight line between P^1 and P^2, which are on the same indifference curve, and hence P^3 is on a higher indifference curve. Because P^3 will yield the same profit as P^1 and P^2 but will afford more utility the insurance company could modify P^3 slightly, raising the premium and providing the same claim, c^3. This new policy will certainly bring in more profit than P^1 or P^2 and H types will prefer it to either P^1 or P^2 – as long as the increase in premium is not too large. Both insurance companies and their clients will prefer this new outcome to the one in which only P^1 and P^2 were available, so the original situation cannot be an equilibrium. We have proved that there is only one contract offered to the H types in equilibrium. Obviously, the same kind of argument will establish that the L types will all choose the same contract at equilibrium. ∎

Now, let π denote the probability that an individual randomly selected from the entire population has an accident. Then π is the expected number of accidents divided by the total population. Therefore

$$\pi = \frac{\pi_H \times n_H + \pi_L \times n_L}{n_H + n_L}.$$

Recall that $x = a + c$ and $y = z - f$ when an individual purchases policy P with premium f and net claim c. Because the individual ultimately cares only about x and y, we think of an insurance contract as a specification of x and y. If we need to, we can recover the premium and net claim by setting $f = z - y$ and $c = x - a$. (Of course the value of the claim check is $x - a + f = x - a + z - y$.)

DEFINITION: *An Insurance Policy*

An insurance policy specifies the values of x and y. Given those values we can recover the actual premium f and net claim c, because $f = z - y$ and $c = x - a$.

At a competitive insurance market equilibrium the total value of premiums collected from policy holders will be exactly equal to the total amount paid out in the form of claim checks. (See Section 2.7.4 of Chapter 2 for proof.) Let ρ denote the probability of an accident for a particular group of policy holders. We can derive a simple linear equation that restricts the values of x and y at equilibrium: if $\rho x + (1-\rho)y > \rho a + (1-\rho)z$ then more money is paid out in the form of claim checks than is collected from policy holders, and the insurance industry is sustaining losses. This is not consistent with equilibrium because insurance carriers will respond to the losses by making changes. If $\rho x + (1-\rho)y < \rho a + (1-\rho)z$ then more money is collected from policy holders than is paid out in the form of claim checks. We are not at equilibrium in that case because the insurance industry is making positive economic profit, leading to capital inflow and hence changes in supply and price.

Theorem: Competitive Equilibrium Generates Fair Odds

$\rho x + (1-\rho)y = \rho a + (1-\rho)z$, where ρ is the probability that an individual policy holder has an accident. That is, $\rho = \pi_H$ and the number of policy holders is n_H, or $\rho = \pi_L$ and the number of policy holders is n_L, or $\rho = \pi$ and the number of policy holders is $n_H + n_L$.

Proof:

The condition that all money taken in from a contract is paid out in the form of claim checks is

$$n(z - y) = \rho n(x - a + z - y) \tag{5}$$

where $n = n_H$ (in which case $\rho = \pi_H$), or $n = n_L$ and $\rho = \pi_L$, or $n = n_H + n_L$ and $\rho = \pi$. The term on the left-hand side of equation [5] is the total amount of money collected in premiums from policyholders, and the term on the right is the amount of the claim check (the net claim $x - a$ plus the premium $z - y$) sent to each policyholder having an accident multiplied by ρn, the number of accidents. We can divide both sides of [5] by n and rewrite the zero-profit conditions as

$$\pi_L x + (1 - \pi_L)y = \pi_L a + (1 - \pi_L)z, \tag{6}$$
$$\pi_H x + (1 - \pi_H)y = \pi_H a + (1 - \pi_H)z, \tag{7}$$
$$\pi x + (1 - \pi)y = \pi a + (1 - \pi)z. \tag{8}$$

Equation [6] is the zero-profit condition for a group composed exclusively of L types. It equates the expected market value (*EMV*) of wealth with insurance to

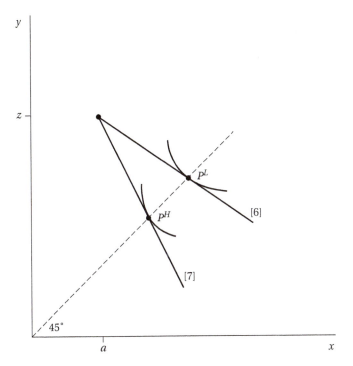

Figure 5.6

the EMV of wealth without insurance. Why bother buying insurance then? Because *(x, y)* delivers higher expected utility than *(a, z)*. Equation [7] is the zero-profit condition for a group composed exclusively of *H* types, and [8] is the zero-profit condition when the two types buy the same policy. Consider Figure 5.6. If the *L* types had a contract that left them above line [6] then it would not generate enough premium income to pay all the claims. If they had a contract below line [6] then it would yield a positive profit because it takes in more premium income than required to honor the claims, and that is not consistent with equilibrium. The analogous statement holds for [7] with respect to *H*, of course.   ∎

∂5.7.3 Full Information Equilibrium

To establish a benchmark case, suppose that insurance companies *are* able to distinguish *H* types from *L* types. Perhaps individuals can be relied on to answer truthfully when asked to which risk group they belong or, more realistically, the *L* types all belong to a particular age group which can be verified by consulting driving licenses. Then the competitive equilibrium separates the types, with each obtaining a policy that maximizes individual expected utility subject to the policy putting the individual on the fairs odds constraint for the type.

Theorem: Full Information Equilibrium

At the full information equilibrium the L types obtain $x = y = \pi_L a + (1 - \pi_L)z$, and the H types get $x = y = \pi_H a + (1 - \pi_H)z$.

Proof:

There will be no cross-subsidization at equilibrium: all claims made by H types are paid out of premiums contributed by H types, and all claims made by L types are paid out of premiums contributed by L types. Here's why: we can't have L above [6] and H above [7] in Figure 5.6 because neither policies would collect enough revenue to pay the claims presented.

What about a cross subsidy? Could the L types wind up below [6] with the Hs above [7]? This means that the policy obtained by L types collects more premium income than is required to finance claims by L types. The surplus is used to finance the deficit from the H policy. But this is inconsistent with equilibrium. A company could offer a policy to Ls that cut the surplus in half. This would be preferred by the Ls, and it would be profitable for the company offering it. (The company would not have to worry that H types would buy it as well. We are temporarily assuming that insurance companies know who the Hs are: They would not be allowed to purchase the contract designed for the Ls.) The original policy would quickly be driven off the market. A similar argument will show that the H types will not subsidize the L types at equilibrium. There is no cross subsidy at equilibrium. (Group insurance is discussed at the end of this section.)

Because there is no cross-subsidization, H types and L types will buy different contracts at equilibrium because equation [6] must hold for P^L, the contract obtained by L types at equilibrium, and [7] must hold for the H types' contract P^H. If the left-hand side of equation [6] exceeds the right-hand side, the contract is not consistent with equilibrium because the value of gross claims paid out will exceed the value of premiums collected. If the right-hand side exceeds the left-hand side, then insurance companies are earning excess profits and competition will force premiums to fall, and hence the original state was not in equilibrium. Similarly for [7]. Therefore, we can apply the complete insurance theorem of Section 2.7.4 of Chapter 2 to each risk type: the policy P^L obtained by the L types solves [6] with $x = y$. The H types will get the policy P^H that solves [7] with $x = y$, as shown in Figure 5.6.   ■

The full information equilibrium is efficient: as we demonstrated in Section 2.7.5 of Chapter 2, the outcome $x = y = \pi_L a + (1 - \pi_L)z$ would be efficient if the economy consisted only of L types. And the outcome $x = y = \pi_H a + (1 - \pi_H)z$ would be efficient if the economy consisted only of H types. Therefore, we can't increase anyone's expected utility without harming someone else if we are limited to rearrangements within the L group or within the H group, or both. If we shifted some wealth from one group to another we would obviously have to reduce the expected utility of someone within the former group. Hence, it is not possible to increase one person's expected utility without diminishing someone else's.

Example 5.13 Full Information Equilibrium in a Special Case

The probability that L has an accident is 0.25 and 0.75 is the probability that an L type does not have an accident. The probability that H has an accident 0.5 which is also the probability that an H type does not have an accident. Each individual has the utility-of-wealth function

$$U(w) = \ln(w+1).$$

Then $U'(w) = (w+1)^{-1}$, and hence $U''(w) = -(w+1)^{-2} < 0$ for all $w \geq 0$,: the individuals are risk averse. Each person's endowment is $a = 4$ if there is an accident and $z = 12$ when there is no accident. The expected utility functions are

$$u_L(x,y) = 0.25 \ln(x+1) + 0.75 \ln(y+1), \text{ and}$$
$$u_H(x,y) = 0.5 \ln(x+1) + 0.5 \ln (y+1).$$

Let's determine the policy $P^L = (x, y)$ that would be chosen by L types if the amount of money they paid into insurance companies in premiums were paid out in claims. The premium per capita is $12 - y$ and the claim check per capita is $x - 4 + 12 - y$, the net claim plus the premium. Assuming that n_L is large, the total number of accidents suffered by L types will be close to the expected number, $0.25n_L$. For convenience, assume that it is exactly equal to $0.25n_L$. Then we have $n_L(12 - y) = 0.25n_L(x - 4 + 12 - y)$ and thus

$$0.25x + 0.75y = 10 \qquad [9]$$

after dividing both sides by n_L and rearranging. Note that equation [9] says that the EMV of wealth with insurance equals the EMV of wealth without insurance, namely $1/4 \times 4 + 3/4 \times 12$. That is what we would expect to see if all premium money received by insurance carriers were paid out as claims. Now, to find P^L we maximize u_L subject to [9]. (If you prefer a shortcut, use the complete insurance theorem of Section 2.7.4 of Chapter 2.) We have $y = 40/3 - x/3$ from [9], and substituting this into u_L yields

$$V(x) = 0.25 \ln(x+1) + 0.75 \ln(40/3 - x/3 + 1),$$

which we want to maximize.

$$V'(x) = \tfrac{1}{4}(x+1)^{-1} + \tfrac{3}{4}(y+1)^{-1} \times -\tfrac{1}{3} = \tfrac{1}{4}(x+1)^{-1} - \tfrac{1}{4}(y+1)^{-1}.$$

Note that $V'' < 0$ at all points. Therefore, if $V'(x) = 0$ yields nonnegative values of x and y the equation $V'(x) = 0$ will characterize the solution to our problem. But $V'(x) = 0$ implies $x = y$, and substituting this into [9] yields $x = y = 10$. Therefore, $P^L = (10, 10)$, and $u_L(P^L) = 2.40$. This means that, subject to constraint [9], L would want a policy with a premium of $2 = 12 - 10$ and a net claim of $6 = 10 - 4$ in case of an accident. Note that the value of the claim check is $8 when L suffers an accident, but L still has to pay the premium in a year when L makes a claim, so the net addition to consumption is $6.

Similarly, to find P^H, the choice of H types when the amount of money paid in as premiums by H types is paid out in claims to H types, we maximize u_H subject to

$$0.5x + 0.5y = 0.5 \times 4 + 0.5 \times 12 = 8 \qquad [10]$$

We know we will have $x = y$ (the individuals are risk averse and [10] exhibits fair odds), in which case [10] implies $x = y = 8$. Therefore, $P^H = (8, 8)$, with $u_H(P^H) = 2.20$. The premium per capita is $12 - 8 = 4$ and the net payment in case of accident is $8 - 4 = 4$. Note that in the full information world, the H types pay a higher premium and get less coverage than L types.

Even though H's net claim equals the premium, it would not be true to say that the insurance contract provides nothing of value. The expected utility of an H type without insurance is $u_H(4, 12) = 2.087$, and expected utility with insurance is $u_H(8, 8) = 2.20$, which is significantly higher.

The competitive equilibrium is efficient if all individuals disclose their risk category truthfully. A problem arises only when there are two risk categories and the insurer does not know to which group a client belongs. This is the situation that insurers actually face. H types have no incentive to reveal their true characteristic because they prefer the policy P^L intended for L types to policy P^H. The former provides more of each good: the H types will have much more wealth if they masquerade as L types. Everyone will declare himself or herself to be in risk category L and will purchase P^L. This outcome is not feasible, however, because P^L yields zero profit only when H types are excluded. If P^L is purchased by some H types, who file more claims per dollar of premium than L types, there will not be enough premium income to honor each claim.

> Life insurance policies have a suicide clause that exempts the insurance company from its obligation to pay off if death is self-inflicted and occurs 365 days or less from the date of issue of the policy. (Some contracts have a two-year limit.) The suicide rate is lowest in the twelfth month of the life of the policy and highest in the thirteenth month – the twenty-fourth and twenty-fifth months, respectively, for polices with a two-year limit (Milgrom and Roberts, 1992, p. 178). Evidently, some people insure their lives knowing that suicide is a serious possibility. (There is undoubtedly a moral hazard element as well. Some insured individuals commit suicide in the thirteenth month who would not end their lives at all if their heirs weren't going to collect on a life insurance policy. See Choi et al., 2015.)

∂5.7.4   Asymmetric Information Equilibrium

Assume from now on that high-risk individuals will not directly reveal their identity and only individual i knows his or her own risk parameter π_i. There are only two possible equilibria, one in which everyone has the same policy and one in which the different types make different decisions.

A pooling equilibrium is one in which the same contract is obtained by both risk categories.

A separating equilibrium is one in which the H types are separated out by providing the L types with a contract that is less desirable to the H types than the contract designed for them.

The constraint that incorporates feasibility and the zero-profit condition for a pooling equilibrium is obtained from [5] for ρ equal to π, the probability that an individual randomly selected from the entire population has an accident. That probability is

$$\pi = \frac{\pi_H \times n_H + \pi_L \times n_L}{n_H + n_L} \qquad [11]$$

Let MRS_H and MRS_L denote the MRS of an H type and an L type, respectively:

$$MRS_H = \frac{\pi_H U'(x)}{(1 - \pi_H) U'(y)},$$

$$MRS_L = \frac{\pi_L U'(x)}{(1 - \pi_L) U'(y)}.$$

Now, $MRS_L < MRS_H$ at any point because $\pi_L < \pi_H$ and $1 - \pi_L > 1 - \pi_H$ (Figure 5.7). (We're computing the MRS at the same values of x and y for the two individuals.) The high-risk types are willing to sacrifice more y (consumption in the "no accident" state) to get an additional unit of x (consumption in case of an accident) because they have a higher probability of an accident.

Theorem

No pooling equilibrium exists.

Proof:

$MRS_L < MRS_H$ holds for any (x, y). Therefore, at the exchange rate $\xi = \frac{1}{2} MRS_L + \frac{1}{2} MRS_H$ there is a number δ small enough in absolute value so that

$$u_L(x - \delta, y + \xi\delta) > u_L(x, y) \text{ and } u_H(x - \delta, y + \xi\delta) < u_H(x, y).$$

Suppose that we claim to have a *pooling equilibrium* with each consumer, regardless of type, obtaining the policy (x, y). If an insurance company offered a different contract P giving rise to $(x - \delta, y + \xi\delta)$ it would be preferred to (x, y) by L types but not by H types (Figure 5.7). The insurance company could offer P and be sure that L types would purchase it in preference to (x, y) but that H types would not. Even though the company would not be able to distinguish an L-type individual from an

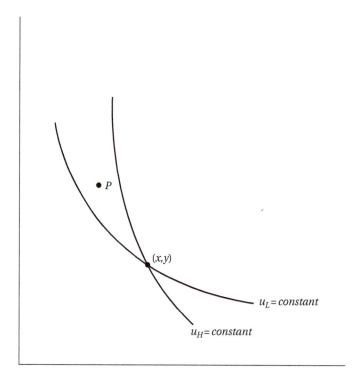

Figure 5.7

H type, by judicious contract design a company could rely on the H types to reveal themselves by their choice.

An insurance company that catered exclusively to L-type risks would have to pay claims to the fraction π_L of its policyholders. Before P was available, both types purchased (x, y) and the fraction π of policyholders filed claims. If $\delta > 0$ is small, then (x, y) and P are almost the same, but $\pi_L < \pi_H$, and a company offering P will pay a smaller fraction of its premium receipts in claims, though the premium and net claim per person will be almost the same as for (x, y). Therefore, P will yield more profit to the insurance companies offering it, and this means that the original situation in which each person purchased (x, y) is not in equilibrium. Companies would have incentive to offer a new contract P, and it would be more profitable if the individuals who preferred it in preference to (x, y) purchased it. (We still won't have equilibrium when P is introduced because the viability of (x, y) depends, through equation [8], on its being purchased by L types as well as by H types, but the former will defect to P as soon as it is offered. The companies that continue to offer (x, y) will take a loss, and that is not consistent with equilibrium.) We have established that an equilibrium must separate H types from L types by offering different contracts such that neither type would want to buy the contract intended for the other. ∎

There must be separate contracts at equilibrium, and hence the contract designed for L types must satisfy equation [6], and the contract designed for H types must satisfy equation [7]. Moreover, individuals of the same risk type will buy the same contract. Therefore, only two contracts will be offered at equilibrium because there are two risk categories. And each type must have an *incentive* to purchase the contract designed for it by the insurance company. This *incentive compatibility, or self-selection* condition, is a constraint on a firm's profit-maximization calculation: if the firm makes high profit when the H types purchase policy B^H but the H types get higher expected utility from the policy B^L intended for the L types, then the firm has not maximized profit because the H types won't buy B^H.

DEFINITION: *Self-Selection Constraints*

If L types purchase B^L at equilibrium, and H types purchase B^H, then

$$u_L(B^L) \geq u_L(B^H) \text{ and } u_H(B^H) \geq u_H(B^L).$$

We are now in a position to characterize the competitive equilibrium.

Asymmetric Information Equilibrium Theorem

The equilibrium provides the H types with the contract P^H that they would obtain in a full information world, but the L types get less utility than they would in the full information equilibrium. The L types get their most-preferred contract subject to the zero-profit condition and the constraint that it is not preferred to P^H by the H types.

Proof:

If the contract B^L available to L types is below the line representing equation [6], then the L types are subsidizing the H types. But this is inconsistent with equilibrium, because a new firm could enter and obtain a positive profit by offering a contract close to B^L but below the line representing [6]. This could be done in such a way that L types prefer the new contract and H types still prefer their original choice. Therefore, equation [6] must be satisfied at equilibrium by the contract designed for L types. (The new contract might not be more profitable to an incumbent insurer than B^L, but it would provide a positive economic profit and hence would be offered by a new entrant to the industry.)

If H types wind up below the line representing [7] an entrepreneur could enter the market and offer a contract that yields higher x and higher y, but still yielding the entrant a positive profit – that is, the new value of x and y would also be below [7]. It would be profitable even if it were purchased only by H types. Therefore, at equilibrium, the contract purchased by H types must satisfy [7] and, as the previous paragraph established, the contract purchased by L types must satisfy [6].

Conditions [6] and [7] are represented geometrically as straight lines in Figure 5.8. Because (a, z) satisfies both equations, it is on both lines. Because the individuals are

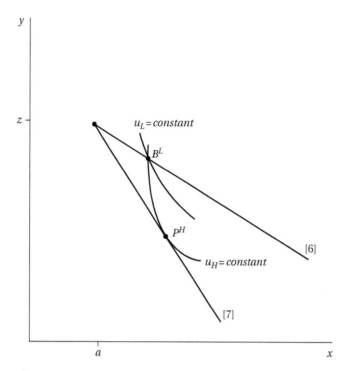

Figure 5.8

risk averse, we need not be concerned with any (x, y) for which $x < a$. (Why?) Is there any reason why the H types can't have their most-preferred contract subject to [7]? No. If any other contract B^H were offered, a company would have incentive to offer the most-preferred contract P^H consistent with [7], and this would be purchased by H types in preference to B^H. Both would give rise to the same profit (zero), but because P_H is preferred, a company could actually raise the premium slightly and make more profit (even if purchased only by H types) than with B^H, and H types would still prefer the new contract to B^H. Therefore, P^H, depicted in Figure 5.8, is offered to H types and chosen by them at equilibrium: $B^H = P^H$.

Now, P^H imposes a constraint on B^L, the contract offered to L types. B^L must satisfy

$$u_H(P^H) \geq u_H(B^L), \tag{12}$$

the self-selection constraint for an H type. At equilibrium B^L will maximize u_L subject to conditions [6] and [12]. This means that the L types will not be offered their most-preferred contract P^L subject to [6], because that would be preferred by H types to P^H, and P^L is feasible if and only if it is purchased exclusively by L types. (The policy P^L offers more of both goods than P^H, as is demonstrated by Figure 5.6.) ∎

Note that the equilibrium pair of contracts is determined independently of n_H and n_L, the number of H types and L types respectively. The contract B^L offered to

L types at equilibrium is depicted in Figure 5.8. The H types are exactly as well off as they would be if the L types did not exist, but the L types are worse off as result of the presence of individuals with a higher accident probability! Without the H types the L types would have P^L at equilibrium (Figure 5.6), but as it is, they wind up with B^L. The existence of a tiny group of H types can have a strong negative impact on the welfare of the L types, but the loss in welfare to the latter is not balanced by any gain in welfare to the former group.

Example 5.14 Asymmetric Equilibrium in the Market of Example 5.13

We know that there will be a separating equilibrium, and H types will get the bundle (8, 8) at equilibrium. To find B^L, the bundle obtained by L types at equilibrium, we solve [9] and $u_H(x, y) = u_H(8, 8)$. That is

$$\tfrac{1}{4}x + \tfrac{3}{4}y = 10 \text{ and } \tfrac{1}{2}\ln(x+1) + \tfrac{1}{2}\ln(y+1) = \tfrac{1}{2}\ln(8+1) + \tfrac{1}{2}\ln(8+1).$$

The first equation yields $x = 40 - 3y$. Multiply both sides of the second equation by 2. We get $\ln(x+1) + \ln(y+1) = \ln(8+1) + \ln(8+1)$, and hence $\ln(x+1)(y+1) = \ln(9 \times 9)$. (The logarithm of a product is the sum of the logarithms.) We have $(x+1)(y+1) = 81$. Now substitute $40 - 3y$ for x:

$$(40 - 3y + 1)(y+1) = 81.$$

Then $3y^2 - 38y + 40 = 0$ and hence $y = (38 \pm 31.048)/6$. The smaller value won't do (why?) so we must have $y = 11.51$, and thus $x = 5.47$. Then $B^L = (5.47, 11.51)$. (We have rounded off.) And $u_L(B^L) = 2.36 < 2.40 = u_L(P^L)$. Finally, $u_H(B^L) = 2.19685 < 2.1972 = u_H(P^H)$. Therefore, H would choose P^H in preference to B^L.

The pair consisting of P^H and B^L of Figure 5.8 is the only candidate for equilibrium, but even this may not *be* an equilibrium.

Nonexistence Theorem

If $\pi_H > \pi_L$ and n_H/n_L is sufficiently small, then there does not exist a competitive insurance market equilibrium.

Proof:

Suppose that n_H is relatively small. Then the line corresponding to equation [8] is close to the line depicting equation [6] as shown in Figure 5.9. Then there is a profitable contract C that the H types prefer to P^H and the L types prefer to B^L. (Contract C in Figure 5.9 is profitable because it provides the same net claim as C^0 but requires a larger premium than C^0, which is on the zero-profit line.) Therefore, (P^H, B^L) is not an equilibrium. But we have just established that it is the only candidate for equilibrium. (We haven't got the *wrong* equilibrium; we've discovered that there is no equilibrium.) ∎

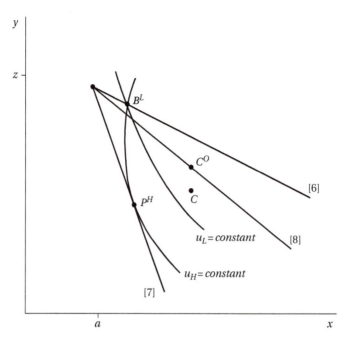

Figure 5.9

How small is small? The next example shows that the ratio does not have to be tiny for equilibrium to be ruled out.

Example 5.15 Nonexistence of Equilibrium for a Special Case of Example 5.14

We show that both H and L prefer the bundle $C = (9.8, 9.8)$ to P^H and B^L, respectively. We then determine the values of n_H and n_L that would allow each person to have bundle C. Certainly, H prefers C to P^H because $C = (9.8,9.8)$ provides more of each good than $P^H = (8, 8)$. And $u_L(9.8, 9.8) = \frac{1}{4}\ln 10.8 + \frac{3}{4}\ln 10.8 = \ln 10.8 = 2.3795 > 2.3617 = u_L(B_L)$. If there is a competitive equilibrium, then H will get P^H and L will get B^L, but both prefer C to their own equilibrium bundle. If the outcome that gives each person the bundle C is *feasible* it will satisfy

$$\pi n \times (9.8 - 4 + 12 - 9.8) \le n \times (12 - 9.8),$$

which is equivalent to

$$\pi \le 0.275. \tag{13}$$

(As usual π is the probability that an individual chosen at random from the entire population has an accident, and $n = n_H + n_L$ is the total population. Note that [13] is equivalent to $\pi x + (1 - \pi)y \le \pi 4 + (1 - \pi)12$ for $x = 9.8 = y$. In words, the expected consumption per individual cannot exceed an individual's expected wealth,

$\pi 4 + (1- \pi)12$, a condition that must hold if everyone winds up with the same bundle.) Recall that

$$\pi = \frac{\frac{1}{2} \times n_H + \frac{1}{4} \times n_L}{n_H + n_L}.$$

Therefore, statement [13] becomes:

$$\frac{1}{2}n_H + \frac{1}{4}n_L \leq 0.275(n_H + n_L), \text{ or } 2n_H + n_L \leq 1.1n_H + 1.1n_L, \text{ or } n_H \leq \frac{n_L}{9}.$$

A small group of H types (10 percent or less of the population in this case) can spoil the possibilities for a competitive equilibrium in the insurance market.

What condition would ensure the existence of equilibrium for Example 5.14? We need an L-type indifference curve through B_L that lies above the line [8], which is $\pi x + (1- \pi)y = \pi 4 + (1- \pi)12 = 12 - 8\pi$. This would mean that no feasible pooling contract is preferred by L types to B^L.

Example 5.16 Existence of Equilibrium for a Special Case of Example 5.14

We find the bundle on $\pi x + (1- \pi)y = 12 - 8\pi$ that maximizes u_L. Solving this equation for y yields $y = (12-8\pi)/(1- \pi) - \pi x/(1 - \pi)$. Then $dy/dx = -\pi/(1 - \pi)$. Set

$$V(x) = \frac{1}{4}\ln(x+1) + \frac{3}{4}\ln(y+1)$$

with y treated as a function of x.

We want to maximize $V(x)$. If this yields less expected utility than $u_L(B_L)$ we will know that no bundle on [8] is preferred by L to B_L We have

$$V'(x) = \frac{1}{4(x+1)} + \frac{3}{4(y+1)} \times \frac{dy}{dx}$$

$$= \frac{1}{4(x+1)} + \frac{3}{4(y+1)} \times -\frac{\pi}{1 - \pi}$$

Confirm that $V''(x) < 0$ for all $x \geq 0$. If we set $V'(x) = 0$ we have

$$3\pi(x+1) = (y+1)(1 - \pi).$$

Now substitute $y = (12- 8\pi)/(1 - \pi) -\pi x/(1 -\pi)$ into this equation and solve for x. We get $x = 3.25/\pi - 3$, and hence $y = (12- 8\pi)/(1 - \pi) - [3.25/\pi - 3] \times \pi/(1 - \pi) = (8.75 - 5\pi)/(1 - \pi)$. These two values are functions of π, so we can state

$$x(\pi) = \frac{3.25}{\pi} - 3 \text{ and } y(\pi) = \frac{8.75 - 5\pi}{1 - \pi}.$$

Recall that $u_L(B_L) = 2.36169$. We want $\frac{1}{4}\ln(x(\pi)+1) + \frac{3}{4}\ln(y(\pi)+1) < 2.36169$. Try $\pi = 0.4$, which is close to $\pi_H = 0.5$. Confirm that

$$x(0.4) = 5.125 \text{ and } y(0.4) = 11.25.$$

But $u_L(5.125, 11.25) = \frac{1}{4}\ln(6.125) + \frac{3}{4}\ln(12.25) = 2.3322$, which is less than $u_L(B^L)$, as desired. Now, $\pi \geq 0.4$ implies

$$\frac{2n_H + n_L}{4n_H + 4n_L} \geq 0.4,$$

and hence $n_H \geq 1.5n_L$ is *sufficient* for existence of equilibrium. If, for example, $n_L = k$ and $n_H = 2k$, an equilibrium exists, and it will be the one that gives each H the bundle P^H and each L the bundle B^L.

When a competitive equilibrium exists is the assignment of P^H to H and B^L to L efficient? *Assuming* knowledge of each individual's accident probability it is not difficult to find a feasible outcome that would make everyone better off. If L types consume P^L and H types continue to consume P^H then we have a feasible allocation that makes the former better off without affecting the utility of the latter. (Of course, we can modify this outcome slightly so that *everyone* is better off.) But how would a planner or government offer P^L to low-risk individuals without the high-risk individuals claiming to be low-risk and also lining up for P^L? Even though (P^H, P^L) is feasible and each L prefers it to (P^H, B^L) and each H is indifferent, it would be impossible to implement the former. Is there a superior feasible allocation that *could* be implemented? Such an allocation exists if n_H/n_L is not too large.

An example, giving S^H to the H types and S^L to the L types, is depicted in Figure 5.10. First, note that H types prefer S^H to P^H, but they also prefer S^H to S^L, so they would choose S^H if the government offered S^H and S^L. They would not choose to masquerade as low-risk individuals. Second, the low-risk individuals themselves prefer S^L to B^L and to S^H. Third, S^L yields a positive profit because it requires a higher premium than A, which pays the same net claim and yields a zero profit. (See Section 2.7.4 of Chapter 2 for a full explanation of the relation between profit and the fair odds line.) Finally, S^H entails a loss because it requires a lower premium than Q while paying the same net claim as Q, which breaks even. But the government could use the profit from S^L to cover the loss from S^H as long as

$$n_L \times [\text{value of } y \text{ at } A - \text{value of } y \text{ at } S^L] \geq n_H \times [\text{value of } y \text{ at } S^H - \text{value of } y \text{ at } Q].$$

This will be possible if n_H/n_L is not too large. (Note that the value of y at A less the value of y at S^L will be very small, because S^L must be near B^L to ensure that $u_H(S^H) > u_H(S^L)$.)

The pair (S^H, S^L) is not consistent with equilibrium in competitive markets because it involves cross-subsidization. But (S^H, S^L) could be implemented by the government if n_H/n_L is not too large. (Given n_L, the larger is n_H the more high-risk individuals there are to be subsidized by the low-risk group.) The plan (S^H, S^L) is feasible if the H types chose S^H and the L types chose S^L. As we have seen, the individuals do have an incentive to make those choices. Therefore, the competitive equilibrium is not efficient.

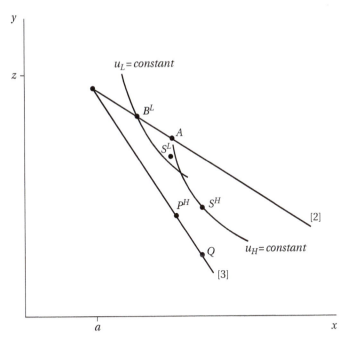

Figure 5.10

Inefficiency Theorem

If $\pi_H > \pi_L$ and n_H/n_L is sufficiently small, then the competitive insurance market equilibrium is not efficient even if it exists.

Example 5.17 Inefficiency of Equilibrium in the Market of Example 5.14

Let's see if we can find conditions under which the competitive equilibrium, with $B^L = (5.47, 11.51)$ and $P^L = (8, 8)$, is inefficient. Set $S^L = (7, 10.8)$: the government offers a contract that results in $x = 7$ and $y = 10.8$. If we set $x = 7$ in equation [6] and then solve for y we get $y = 11$. That is, $x = 7$ and $y = 11$ satisfies the zero-profit condition for L types. Therefore, if L types consume $x = 7$ and $y = 10.8$ they generate a surplus that can be used to subsidize the H types. The L types are better off with S^L than with B^L because $u_L(B^L) = 2.36169$ and $u_L(S^L) = 2.37$. What would it take to make the H types better off than they would be with P^H? If we set $S^H = (8, 10)$ then we certainly have $u_H(P^H) < u_H(S^H)$ because S^L provides the same amount of x as P^L and provides 2 more units of y. But that also means that S^H is above the line representing equation [7]. In other words, S^H operates at a loss, and that will have to be covered by the surplus from S^L. If n_H is sufficiently small relative to n_L then no matter how small the per capita surplus from S^L it will cover the deficit from S^H. Finally, Table 5.7 shows that the self-selection constraints are satisfied. We have $u_L(S^L) > u_L(S^H)$ and $u_H(S^H) > u_H(S^L)$.

Table 5.7

Policy	U_L	U_H
$S^L = (7, 10.8)$	2.3709	2.2738
$S^H = (8, 10)$	2.3477	2.2976

In determining whether the market outcome can be improved we have been careful to impose the same informational constraint on the government that private insurance companies face. What additional information would the government have to possess to verify that (S^H, S^L) is feasible? It would have to know n_H and n_L to be sure that the surplus collected from the L types is sufficient to cover the subsidy to the H types. But how could it know the number of H types without being able to identify the H types? One answer is that the H types reveal themselves by their choice of P^H at equilibrium. But suppose that insurance is provided initially by the government and not private insurance companies. The numbers n_H and n_L can actually be determined from data that are available to the government. Recall the definition of π from [11]. If we let n denote the total population, $n_H + n_L$, then the expected number of accidents for the population as a whole is πn. This will be very close to ω, the actual number of accidents. Then $\omega = \pi_H n_H + \pi_L n_L = \pi_H n_H + \pi_L (n - n_H)$. Because ω is known, if π_H and π_L are known we can solve for n_H, which will then also give us n_L. However, U will also have to be known, to ensure that the H types will choose S^H in preference to S^L and to ensure that each group is better off than it would be under a competitive equilibrium. It's not clear that the government can obtain the relevant information, but it is also not clear that the market outcome is the best that can be achieved, given the hidden information problem.

Group health insurance is common in many countries. It usually takes the form of an employer with a large number of employees contracting with an insurance carrier to provide insurance to the employees at a specified price per person — typically, the same price to each individual regardless of age or health status. Because of the lower administration and claims costs under the group arrangement the provider is willing to offer coverage at a premium that is below the average charged to individuals who purchase coverage directly. When the group insurance is compulsory, as it often is, the adverse selection problem is eliminated. (The insurance is compulsory when an employee cannot opt out.)

Sources

Rothschild and Stiglitz (1976) found some limitations in the Spence (1973) notion of asymmetric information equilibrium and used competitive insurance markets to illustrate. This section is based on the Rothschild-Stiglitz analysis. In separate contributions, George Akerlof, Michael Spence, and Joseph Stiglitz showed that the presence of asymmetric information in real-world markets required a new way of modeling economic exchange. They were awarded the Nobel Prize in Economics for the year 2001.

Links

Molho (1997) and Hirshleifer and Riley (1992) are similar to this section's treatment of competitive insurance markets, but different issues are highlighted. The latter is the more technical of the two. Riley (2012) is a superb graduate-level text that covers most of the asymmetric information problems featured in the present book. Riley's book not only presents theorems and proofs, but explains *why* a theorem is true, usually with the aid of a clear and simple diagram.

Problem Set

(1) In Section 5.7.2 we proved that a particular type will not purchase two distinct contracts in equilibrium. Prove that for any positive integer K, if each of the policies P^1, P^2, ..., P^K is purchased by at least one member of a particular risk group in equilibrium, then $P^1 = P^2 = \cdots = P^K$.

(2) Prove that policies P^1 and P^2 generate the same profit then the policy $\frac{3}{4}P^1 + \frac{1}{4}P^2$ would yield the same profit as P^1 or P^2 if everyone buying P^1 or P^2 switched to $\frac{3}{4}P^1 + \frac{1}{4}P^2$.

(3) Explain why $(\pi_H \times n_H + \pi_L \times n_L)/(n_H + n_L)$ is the probability that an individual randomly selected from the entire population will have an accident.

(4) In uncovering the properties of a competitive equilibrium, why didn't we have to worry about the possibility that the insurance contract would make an individual worse off, and hence the individual would not buy a policy at all? (*Hint:* show that L's expected utility increases as we move along [6] and away from the endowment point, and similarly for H and [7].)

(5) Show that at the separating equilibrium u_L increases as π_H falls.

(6) Using the definitions of $x(\pi)$ and $y(\pi)$ from Example 5.16, find a necessary and sufficient condition on π such that $U_L(B^L)$ is at least as high as $U_L(x, y)$ for any (x, y) on [8].

(7) For the setup of Example 5.17, find values of n_H and n_L such that an asymmetric information equilibrium exists, *and* there exist S^H and S^L such that

$$U_H(S^H) > U_H(P^H) > U_L(S^L) > U_L(B^L),$$

and any loss from S^H is covered by a surplus from S^L.

(8) Find the point in the derivation of the competitive equilibrium at which we use the assumption that the two types have the same utility-of-wealth function. How would the argument be modified to handle the general case?

(9) There are two types of individuals, and there is the same number of each type. The probability that one type has an accident is 0.10, and the probability is 0.40 for the other type. Each individual has the utility-of-wealth function $\sqrt{w}$, where w is wealth. If an individual has an accident his or her wealth is 1,000, but if there is no accident wealth is 2,000. This is true of either type.

    (A) What is each type's expected utility function? Write down the competitive insurance market's zero-profit condition for a society consisting only of individuals with the probability of accident of 0.10. Write down the zero-profit condition for a society consisting only of individuals with the probability of accident of 0.40. Now, give the zero-profit condition for a competitive insurance market that offers everyone, regardless of type, the same contract.

(B) Find the full information competitive equilibrium. (You may use the complete insurance theorem.) State the expected utility of each individual at equilibrium and the expected profit of the insurance companies.

(C) Determine the pooling contract P^0 for which $x = y$. Now find a new contract P that would provide positive expected profit for any firm offering it if only P^0 were initially available. Show that the individuals purchasing P would have more utility than with P^0. Calculate the expected profit for the firm selling P.

(D) Identify the asymmetric information competitive equilibrium. Calculate the expected utility of an individual of each type, and calculate a firm's expected profit. Explain why the equilibrium really is an equilibrium. (*Hint:* compare the expected utility at the endowment point with expected utility at equilibrium for the relevant type. Now, starting at the endowment point, show that this type's expected utility falls as y increases. If you have to solve an equation of the form $ay + b\sqrt{y} + c = 0$, set $q = \sqrt{y}$ and $q^2 = y$ and use the formula for solving a quadratic equation: $q = \frac{-b \pm \sqrt{b^2 - 4ac}}{2a}$.)

(10) Each of n individuals has utility-of-wealth function $U(w) = 50w - w^2$. Let x represent wealth if there is an accident and let y denote wealth if there is no accident. If the individual buys no insurance then $x = 10$ and $y = 20$.

(A) Is the individual risk averse? Explain.

(B) Show that when the odds are fair and the individual is risk averse he or she will set $x = y$. You may use a general argument, or the utility-of-wealth function $U(w) = 50w - w^2$.

(C) Find the competitive equilibrium insurance contract assuming that everyone has a probability of accident of 0.10.

(D) Find the competitive equilibrium insurance contract assuming that everyone has a probability of accident of 0.20.

(E) By means of a diagram, identify the full information competitive equilibrium and also the asymmetric information competitive equilibrium when some individuals have a probability of accident of 0.10 and some have a probability of accident of 0.20.

6

Auctions

Auctions have been used for more than 2,500 years to allocate a single indivisible asset. They are also used to sell multiple units of some commodities, such as rare wine or a new crop of tulip bulbs. There are many different types of auctions in use, and far more that have never been tried but could be employed if we felt that they served some purpose. The aim of this chapter is to determine which type of auction should be used in a particular situation. Accordingly, we need to determine which bidder would get the asset that is up for sale and then how much would be paid for it.

6.1   INTRODUCTION

When the government sells things at auction – treasury bills, oil-drilling rights, or a TV broadcast frequency, for instance – the appropriate criterion for determining which type of auction should be used is the maximization of general consumer welfare. Because the bidders are usually firms, we recommend the auction type that would put the asset in the hands of the firm that would use it to produce the highest level of consumer welfare. Fortunately, this is correlated with the value of the asset to a bidder: the more valuable the asset is to consumers when it is used by firm X, the more profit X anticipates from owning the asset, and thus the higher the value that X itself places on the asset. (Section 6.1.2 explains why revenue net of cost is a good measure of the benefit that consumers derive from a firm's activities.) The discounted stream of profits that would flow from the asset is the individual firm's *reservation value*, and it is a hidden characteristic. If the government were to ask each firm to report its reservation value and awarded the asset to the high-value firm it would get nothing resembling truthful revelation. Each would have a strong incentive to overstate the value it places on the asset in an attempt to increase the probability of being awarded the asset. If, however, each firm is asked to report its reservation value and then the asset is awarded to the high-value firm at a

A sample of things that are auctioned: estates, wine, art, jewelry, memorabilia, estate furniture, used cars to dealers, foreclosed houses, repossessed goods, import quotas in Australia and New Zealand, oil-drilling rights, assets from failed banks, carbon permits, confirmed seats on overbooked flights, contract jobs, government surplus goods, tulip bulbs, racehorses, fishing quotas, and tobacco.

price that is proportional to its reported value, a firm can be expected to understate the maximum that it would be willing to pay. In either case it would be sheer coincidence if the asset were assigned to the high-value firm. One of the many goals of this chapter is the identification of the auction mechanism that gives bidders an incentive to reveal their precise reservation values truthfully.

Private individuals and firms also use auctions to sell things, of course, and in those cases the seller's objective is to maximize its revenue. The private seller also has a hidden characteristic problem because the potential buyers have no incentive to truthfully reveal the maximum they would be willing to pay. Otherwise, the seller could simply select the buyer with the highest reservation value and charge that buyer a price a little below that value on a take-it-or-leave-it basis. We will identify the auction formula that maximizes the seller's revenue under asymmetric information.

6.1.1 Eleven Significant Auctions

T-Rex skeleton: in October 1997, a Tyrannosaurus Rex skeleton that was 90 percent complete was sold for $8.36 million at an auction conducted by Sotheby's. The winning bidder was the Field Museum of Natural History in Chicago. Paleontologists had worried about the sale, fearing that the winner would not make the skeleton available for research. (Someone with enormous inherited wealth could outbid the museums and then allow children to use the skeleton as a climbing apparatus.) In fact, the highest 50 percent of the bids were from institutions. The Field Museum's supporters had raised more than $7 million from private (anonymous) donors specifically for the T-Rex auction.

Radio spectrum: since the mid 1990s previously unallocated portions of the radio spectrum have been sold in auctions around the world. More than $100 billion flowed into government treasuries. Academic economists played a leading role in designing these auctions, which were considered a big success, particularly in Britain and America. The initial US auctions allocated narrowbands, used for pagers, and the later ones involved broadbands, for voice and data transmission. In 2000 the British government sold airwaves licenses for a total of $34 billion or 2.5 percent of the British GDP. Similar sales were conducted in other European countries. The European licenses were for frequencies to be used by third-generation mobile phones, which allowed high-speed access to the internet. Other European countries also sold portions of the radio spectrum, with varying degrees of success. In terms of the money raised per capita, the Swiss auction realized only 20 Euros whereas the German and UK auctions yielded 615 and 650 Euros, respectively. Poor auction design accounts for the low yield in Switzerland and some other countries. Surprisingly, Spain and Sweden used the traditional "beauty contest" method to allocate licenses. This means that a jury of experts appointed by the government looked over the applications and selected the ones that they deemed best. Not only does this not solve the hidden information problem, it is susceptible to favoritism and corruption. (The vast sums that would have been paid had an auction been used are available to bribe the members of the selection committee.)

Pollution permits: since 1990 the US Environmental Protection Agency (EPA) has been auctioning permits for dumping sulphur dioxide (SO_2) into the air, resulting in a 50 percent reduction in the amount of SO_2 released into the air. This is significant because SO_2 is a prime ingredient in acid rain. The buyers of the pollution permits are firms that produce electricity by burning fossil fuel. An electric utility must surrender one permit to the EPA for each ton of SO_2 released. More recently, many countries have introduced carbon permits, which require firms that emit CO_2 as a byproduct of the production process to surrender to the regulatory authority one permit for each ton of CO_2 dumped into the air. China is the latest country to announce its intention to use these devices. Pollution permits have a high opportunity cost because they can be sold at auction to other polluters. This gives the firm an incentive to invest in cleaner production processes. If fewer permits are issued the total amount of CO_2 or SO_2 released will fall. By allowing the permits to be traded, the reduction in emissions is obtained at the lowest cost: firms that can find a low-cost way of modifying the production process to reduce emissions will sell pollution permits to firms that can reduce emissions only by switching to high-cost techniques. The additional permits allow the purchasing firm to escape some of the costly adjustments that would otherwise be required. The auction of pollution permits in the US was initially run by the EPA, but private markets have taken over. (The EPA auction now handles only 3 percent of the transactions.) Auctioning pollution permits solves the hidden characteristic problem: a firm would not willingly disclose the cost of reducing its emissions if it were required to modify its production processes on the basis of that information. (See Section 3.2 of Chapter 3 for an extended discussion.)

Search engine ad auctions: when Google or Yahoo presents you with the results of your search request the relative positions of the ads that you see are determined by an auction that takes place instantly. The higher an advertiser bids, the more prominently its ad will be placed. (See Section 6.2.4 of this chapter for details.)

Offshore oil: the US federal government raised $560 million in 1990 by auctioning licenses to drill for oil in the Gulf of Mexico.

Bank assets: in the 1980s and 1990s, the federal government auctioned off the assets of hundreds of failed banks and savings and loan institutions. These financial firms failed because the value of their assets was far below the value of their obligations to depositors. The assets were claimed by the government because it had to honor the deposit liabilities of the failed lending institutions. It could at least sell their assets to the private sector for whatever they would fetch. The auctions were not a great success because the government was too anxious and typically did not wait until more than a few bidders participated.

Kidneys: each year about 100,000 people around the world are told that they will have to continue to wait for a kidney transplant. Each year, about 6 percent of those on the waiting list will die, and almost 2 percent of the others will become too ill to qualify for a transplant. In 1999 a citizen of the United States attempted to auction one of his kidneys on the internet. Such a transaction is illegal in most countries, and it was annulled by the firm operating the auction, but by that point the bidding had reached $5.7 million.

Privatization: since 1961 when the German government sold a majority ownership of Volkswagen to the public, removing it from state control, a large number of state-owned enterprises have been transferred to public ownership in Europe and Japan. In Britain, the value of state-owned enterprises decreased from about 10 percent of GDP to virtually zero in the 1980s. Transition economies – primarily, the former Soviet Union countries and Eastern European satellites – have privatized much of the production sector. In some of these transition economies, the assets have been sold at auction. In the case of the Czech Republic and Russia, some of these auctions involved the use of vouchers that were fairly evenly distributed to the public. The shares in each firm would have a voucher price, and each bidder would have to allocate a limited number of vouchers across the available shares. The voucher auctions typically did not lead to a high level of performance for the firms involved, primarily because the insiders managed to retain control of a firm's operations.

Electricity: for almost all of the twentieth century, the production of electricity in the United States was largely undertaken by local monopolies that were regulated by state governments. Most of the European producers were state enterprises. There was a wave of deregulation of electricity markets in the European Union and the United States at the end of the century, with Britain leading the way in 1990 when it substituted an electricity auction for state management. In country after country, the new industrial structure featured competition between private suppliers of electric power, with an auction mechanism used to allocate electricity among consumers of electric power. In Britain, France, the United States, and other countries the auction rules were designed by leading economists, and they are revised when defects are detected.

Google's initial public offering: the term initial public offering (IPO) refers to the offer of shares to the general public by a firm owned by a handful of individuals – usually the founders – whose ownership shares were not previously traded on a stock exchange. The buyers become shareholders in the firm and the money they pay goes into the bank accounts of the original owners. An IPO is traditionally marketed by one of a handful of select investment banks, which charge a fee of 7 percent of the proceeds of the sale. In return for this substantial fee, the investment bank guarantees that the shares will be sold at the asking price. The fees and asking prices are not competitively determined – the

Online auctions: In September 1995 the web site eBay began life as one of the three pages on its founder Pierre Omidyar's home page. Omidyar did not expect it would become the great success that it is today. He felt that because people are basically good and honest, any conflict that arose between buyer and seller could be policed by the "Feedback Forum" at which people could report their good and bad experiences with sellers. The reports were mostly favorable. However, as the site rapidly grew in popularity it attracted sellers intent on profiting through fraud – the adverse selection problem. (At that point eBay had grown faster than any company in the history of the world.) There was a serious Rolex scam in the spring on 1999. The sale of sports memorabilia was especially rife with fraud. The company now has more than eight hundred people on its full-time security staff – including many former law enforcement officials from around the world. Some internet auction sites advise the use of an escrow service. The buyer sends the payment to the escrow firm which transfers the money to the sellers only after being informed by the buyer that the goods arrived and are as advertised.

banks act like a cartel. Google, which runs one of the leading internet search engines, broke tradition by offering its initial shares by auction over the internet. A Dutch auction (see Section 6.3.1) collected more than $1.6 billion for the shares in August 2004. The advantage of the auction over the traditional method is that the latter is too vulnerable to manipulation. The investment bank handling the IPO can price the shares below their market value, in return for some form of (implicit) future compensation from the firms purchasing large blocks of the shares. Google used the online auction created by WR Hambrecht & Co.

6.1.2 Auctions and Efficiency

When the government sells assets to the public it should strive to see that the asset goes to the agent with the highest reservation value, not to maximize revenue from the sale. Let's see why.

Suppose that no production is involved. An antique of some sort – say a painting – is being allocated. Suppose also that individual preferences are quasilinear. Thus the individual's utility function has the form $U(x, y) = B(x) + y$, where commodity X is the good being auctioned and Y is generalized purchasing power – dollars of expenditure on everything but X. Assume for convenience that $B(0) = 0$. Then one unit of X obtained without cost would cause the individual's utility to increase from zero to $B(1)$. If the individual actually paid P for the unit of X then the change in utility would be $\Delta U = B(1) + \Delta y = B(1) - P$. If $P < B(1)$ then ΔU is positive. The individual would be willing to pay any price P less than $B(1)$ for one unit of X because that would increase utility. (A lower price is preferred to a higher price, of course.) But any price above $B(1)$ would cause utility to fall. ($\Delta U = B(1) - P < 0$ when $P > B(1)$.) Therefore, $B(1)$ is the *maximum* that the individual would pay for one unit of X, and is called the individual's reservation value for one unit of X.

DEFINITION: *Reservation Value*

A bidder's reservation value is the maximum that the bidder would be willing to pay for the asset. We let V_i denote the reservation value of bidder i.

If the individual already has x units of X then the reservation value for the next unit is $B(x + 1) - B(x)$. One of the factors influencing the reservation value is the degree to which close substitutes are available. The function B is different for different individuals, so we need one reservation value $B_i(1)$ for each individual i. To simplify the notation, we'll let V_i denote that value. Efficiency requires that the asset be awarded to the individual with the highest reservation value.

Efficiency Theorem

If V_H is the highest reservation value, and every bidder has at least V_H units of commodity Y, then efficiency requires that the asset be held by an individual whose reservation value is V_H.

Proof:

Suppose to the contrary that $V_i < V_j$ and i has the asset. There exists a positive number T such that $V_i < T < V_j$. Then U_i and U_j will both increase if i transfers the asset to j in return for T units of money. The change in i's utility is $\Delta U_i = -V_i + T$, which is positive because $T > V_i$. And the change in j's utility is $\Delta U_j = + V_j - T$, and that is obviously positive. The transfer is feasible because $V_i < V_j \leq V_H$. (Assume that individual j *has* T units of money.) We have increased the utility of both i and j, without affecting the utility of anyone else. ∎

The *sum* of utilities is maximized when the asset is in possession of the agent with the highest reservation value, provided that the total consumption of Y is not affected. That's because there is a single indivisible asset, and hence the sum of utilities is

$$\alpha_1 V_1 + y_1 + \alpha_2 V_2 + y_2 + \alpha_3 V_3 + y_3 \ldots + \alpha_n V_n + y_n$$
$$= \alpha_1 V_1 + \alpha_2 V_2 + \alpha_3 V_3 + \ldots + \alpha_n V_n + y_1 + y_2 + y_3 + \ldots + y_n$$

where $\alpha_i = 1$ if individual i gets the asset and $\alpha_i = 0$ if i does not receive the asset. If $y_1 + y_2 + y_3 + \ldots + y_n$ does not change then this sum is obviously maximized by setting $\alpha_i = 1$ for the individual i with the highest V_i.

The outcome that assigns the asset to the individual with the highest V_i is efficient whether or not money changes hands, as long as $y_1 + y_2 + y_3 + \ldots + y_n$ is unaffected. That's because any outcome that maximizes total utility is efficient. (See Section 2.5.1 of Chapter 2.) In the interest of *fairness* we might require that the individual acquiring the asset make a payment that is some function of the reservation values of the individuals in the community. In Section 6.2.3, we demonstrate that because the individual reservation values are hidden information, *efficiency* considerations require that a payment be made by the individual receiving the asset. Moreover, we determine precisely how that payment must be related to the reservation values of the other members of the community.

We have assumed away the possibility of a trade after the auction. But does it really matter who gets the asset initially? If Olivia gets the asset and her reservation value is 600 but Philip's reservation value is 1,000, can't they strike a mutually profitable trade, resulting in an efficient outcome? That assumes that both would disclose their reservation values willingly. Philip has an incentive to understate his, to keep the negotiated price down. But because he does not know Olivia's reservation value there is a possibility that he will claim that his value is, say, 500. But there is no price below $600 at which Olivia is willing to trade. The negotiations might break down at this point. Note also that Olivia has an interest in overstating her reservation value. The efficient post-auction trade might not take place.

We are back to the original hidden characteristic problem. Heirs have been known to squander the majority of a disputed legacy by battling each other in court. A more common instance is that of a firm's owners and workers enduring a lengthy strike that does considerable harm to both, as management tries to convince workers that the owners' reservation value is too low to permit it accept their demands, and the workers try to convince management that their reservation value is too high to permit them to accept the owners' offer. Incentives are needed to ensure that an efficient outcome emerges when individuals are motivated by self-interest. We cannot rely on self-interest to lead to an efficient outcome without a framework of appropriate incentives.

Example 6.1 A Bargaining Breakdown

Individual J owns an asset that he wishes to sell to individual K. Agent J's reservation value is 2, but J does not know K's reservation value. As far as J is concerned, K's value is drawn from the uniform probability distribution on $[0, 5]$, the interval from 0 to 5 inclusive. By definition, this distribution is such that the probability that her reservation value is less than the number P is equal to the fraction of the interval $[0, 5]$ that is covered by the subinterval $[0, P]$. (See Section 2.6.5 of Chapter 2.) In other words, the probability that the random value is less than P is $P/5$. Now, J offers to sell the asset to K at price P. This is a take-it-or-leave-it offer, so K will accept the offer if and only if her reservation value V_K is greater than P. The probability of $V_K > P$ is 1 minus the probability of $V_K < P$. Hence, the probability of $V_K > P$ is $1 - P/5$. The payoff (i.e., expected profit) to the seller J is $P - V_J$, the profit realized by J in case of acceptance, multiplied by the probability that the offer will be accepted. Therefore, J's payoff is

$$\left(1 - \frac{P}{5}\right) \times (P - 2) = \left(1 + \frac{2}{5}\right)P - \frac{1}{5}P^2 - 2.$$

This is a quadratic, which we wish to maximize. The value of P that maximizes J's payoff is

$$P^* = \frac{1 + \dfrac{2}{5}}{\dfrac{2}{5}}.$$

Therefore, J will offer to sell the asset to K at a price of 3.5. However, if $V_K < 3.5$ the offer will be rejected by K. But if $V_K > 2 = V_J$ efficiency requires that the asset be held by K. Therefore, if J owns the asset and $2 < V_K < 3.5$, the outcome will not be efficient, and the inefficiency will not be corrected by a voluntary exchange between J and K.

Suppose that the asset is up for auction because it is used in a production process. The bidders are firms, and V_i is the firm i's *economic* profit: if the firm were to use the asset in combination with other inputs it would be able to earn enough revenue to cover all the production costs, including a normal return on capital, and have V_i dollars left over. (Specifically, V_i is the present value of the stream of profits.) If firm i were to obtain the asset at any price P less than V_i it would still obtain a positive economic profit, and hence would be willing to pay any price less than V_i. (Of course, lower prices are more profitable than higher prices.) However, if it paid more than V_i, ownership of the asset would not yield enough revenue to cover all production costs and provide a normal return on capital. Therefore, V_i is the maximum that firm i would be prepared to pay for the asset, and hence is the firm's reservation value. It follows that a firm suffers a loss if it pays more than its reservation value to acquire an asset, and earns a positive economic profit if it pays less than its reservation value.

We establish that it is in consumers' interest to have the asset awarded to the firm with the highest reservation value by showing that V_i is the net benefit that firm i would provide to consumers by employing the asset in production. V_i is economic profit, which in turn equals revenue minus cost. Revenue is a measure of consumers' willingness to pay for the firm's output. Consumers wouldn't pay a lot for the good if it didn't deliver a correspondingly high level of benefit. Therefore, the revenue that a firm takes in can be used as a measure of the gross benefit that consumers derive from the firm's activities. However, a commodity may provide a high level of benefit only at a very high cost in terms of foregone output of other goods and services. A yacht, for example uses a lot of scarce resources – skilled labor and highly productive equipment – so the resources employed in producing the yacht could have been employed in producing other goods and services that generate a lot of consumer benefit. The more productive firm i's inputs would be if employed somewhere else in the economy, the higher the demand for those inputs and hence the higher their market value – as a result of competition by all firms for their use. Therefore, the cost of inputs used by firm i is a measure of the value of the goods and services that could be produced if the inputs were employed elsewhere. This

Negotiations don't always break down, particularly when the difference in reservation values is extreme. Spectrum licenses were allocated by lottery in the United States from 1982 to 1993. In 1991 the lucky winner of a cellular telephone license subsequently sold it to Southwestern Bell for $41.5 million (*New York Times*, May 30, 1991, p. A1). However, the lotteries spawned serious inefficiencies that were not quickly rectified by the market. The individual communications provider served a relatively small territory, significantly delaying the creation of a nationwide network that would allow cell phone users to "roam" (Milgrom, 2004, pp. 3, 20).

means that the market value (i.e., cost) of the inputs used by firm i are a measure of the value of consumer goods and services lost to the economy by employing the inputs in firm i. The firm's cost is a measure of the cost of the firm's activities to consumers. Therefore, "revenue minus cost" equals "gross benefit to consumers of firm i's activities minus the cost to consumers of those activities." That is, revenue − cost = net benefit to consumers.

We want the asset to be awarded to the firm that delivers the highest net benefit to consumers. We refer to this as asset efficiency. Therefore, we want to employ an auction mechanism that always allocates an asset to the firm with the highest reservation value, even when the firms bid strategically. We reached the same conclusion for assets that are not involved in production and the bidders are households.

DEFINITION: *Asset Efficiency*
We say that the asset is allocated efficiently if it is assigned to the agent with the highest reservation value.

If the government simply asked each firm to report its reservation value, on the understanding that the asset would go to the firm with the highest value, it wouldn't get anything resembling truthful revelation. Every firm would have a strong incentive to vastly overstate its value, to increase its chance of obtaining the asset. But perhaps there is an auction that would give each firm an incentive to reveal its value truthfully. There is, and it is the subject of the next section.

Sources

The T-Rex auction is reported in *Science News*, December 13, 1997, vol. 152, pp. 382–383. The discussion of the European airwaves auctions is based on Binmore and Klemperer (2002) and Klemperer (2002b). The data on the kidney transplant waiting list are from Roth et al. (2004). The brief sketch of privatization is based on Megginson and Netter (2001). The discussion of online auctions is based on Goldsmith and Wu, 2006, p. 132 and Bichler, 2001, p. 135. Example 6.1 is from Maskin (2003). Eric Maskin was awarded the Nobel Prize in 2007 for his contributions to auction theory and many other branches of economic theory. Support for the claim that investment banks exploit their substantial market power can be found in *The Economist*, May 8, 2004, p. 14: "Acting like a cartel, these banks rarely compete on price." See also Nalebuff and Ayres (2003, p. 198): in effect they give gifts to "favored clients and executives whose business they are courting" in return for (implicit) future considerations.

Links

McMillan (1994, 2002) gives good accounts of the auctioning of radio frequencies. Demsetz (1968) suggested that the government auction the right to be the sole supplier of a particular good in the case of a natural monopoly. The winner would be the firm proposing the lowest output price. Laffont and Tirole (1987) extend this to the auctioning of the right to complete a government project. (Alternatively, see Chapter 7 of Laffont and Tirole, 1993.) Arrow (1979) and d'Aspremont and Gerard-Varet (1979) extend the analysis of resource allocation under uncertainty well beyond the single indivisible asset case.

Problem Set

(1) The proof that an outcome is efficient only if the asset has been awarded to the individual with the highest reservation value implicitly assumed that individual j has a sufficient amount of money. Show that the outcome in which the individual with the lowest reservation value has both the asset and all of the commodity Y is in fact efficient.

(2) Example 6.1 assumed that $V_J = 2$. Rework Example 6.1 with the individual J's reservation value represented as a variable V_J, known to J of course. For what values of V_J and V_K will there be an inefficient outcome?

6.2 THE VICKREY AUCTION AND SEARCH ENGINE AD AUCTIONS

Assume that a piece of physical capital – an asset – is to be sold, and there are several potential buyers. Each buyer attaches a different value to the asset because the bidders have different opportunities for combining it with other real assets that they own. This *reservation value* is the maximum sum of money that the individual or institution would be willing to pay for the asset. The reservation values are unknown to the seller. If they were known, the seller would simply sell the asset to the party with the highest reservation value for a price just below that reservation value. And because of that, buyers would not willingly and truthfully disclose those values. The seller faces a hidden characteristic problem. Is there a scheme by which the seller could discover the individual reservation values and thereby sell the asset to the individual (or company) with the highest reservation value?

In the language of auction theory, we are assuming *private values.* At the other extreme is the *common value* case in which the asset has one specific value – its equilibrium market price – and every bidder accepts this, but they have different estimates of that market value. The common value case is discussed in Section 6.6.

DEFINITION: *Private Versus Common Values*

Reservation values are private if each bidder's value is independent of the others'. In a common values auction, each bidder knows that the asset is worth exactly the same to others, but each has a different estimate of what that common value is.

Everyone is familiar with the oral auction with ascending bids. The auctioneer calls out a price until someone accepts that price, whereupon the auctioneer

Until very recently it was widely believed by economists that the second-price, sealed-bid auction was invented by William Vickrey in 1961. In fact, this auction has been used to sell stamps to collectors since at least 1893 (Lucking-Reiley, 2000a).

raises the price again. He then asks for a new bid – that is, acceptance of the new price – and so on until no one is willing to accept the price, at which point the article is sold to the bidder who accepted the last price, which will be the amount actually paid by the winner. This is the standard *English auction*. However, we begin by investigating a close relative, the *second-price* auction, and show that it induces truthful revelation of an individual's reservation value: the asset goes to the highest bidder who then pays a fee equal to the second-highest bid.

DEFINITION: *The Vickrey or Second-Price Auction*

Each individual submits one bid, usually without knowing what anyone else has bid. The asset is awarded to the high bidder at a price equal to the second-highest bid. If there are two or more individuals with the same high bid, the tie can be broken in any fashion, perhaps randomly.

6.2.1   Equilibrium Bids

If the Vickrey auction is used it is in a person's self-interest to enter a bid equal to his or her true reservation value. Let's prove this. First, consider a simple example.

Example 6.2   Four Bidders

The reservation values of bidders A, B, C, and D are displayed in Table 6.1. What should individual B bid if the Vickrey auction is used? Will it depend on what the others bid? Suppose B bids 125. If that were the highest bid and the next highest bid is 100 then B would be awarded the asset at a price of 100. With any bid over $100, B$ would wind up paying $100 for something worth only $70 to him. Submitting a bid above one's reservation value can be very unprofitable. What if B bids below 70, and the highest bid is 100? From the standpoint of B, the outcome would be the same as if B bid 70, or anything below 100: the asset would go to someone else. But B will not know what others will bid. The highest amount bid by anyone else could be 60, in which case a bid of 50 by B would deprive him of the profit he would have obtained by bidding 70. A bid below 70 couldn't benefit B but it could hurt him. The same reasoning will show that neither C nor D could benefit from submitting a bid different from their own reservation values but could be made worse off as a result. Now, consider A's bid. If A bids 100, or anything above 70, and the highest bid submitted by anyone else is 70 then A gets the asset at a price of $70, leaving A with a profit of $100 - 70 = 30$. If A's bid is below 70, and someone else has submitted a bid of 70, then A will not be awarded the asset and will sacrifice the profit of 30. A bid different from A's reservation value cannot benefit but could harm that agent.

Table 6.1

Bidder	*A*	*B*	*C*	*D*
Reservation value	100	70	40	20

Now, we prove that for any number of bidders, and any set of reservation values, no individual can profit from submitting a bid different from that person's reservation value if the Vickrey auction is used. In other words, bidding one's reservation value is a dominant strategy, regardless of what anyone else bids.

DEFINITION: *Incentive Compatibility*

An auction mechanism is incentive compatible if for each participant, submitting a bid equal to the individual's reservation value is a dominant strategy.

Theorem

The Vickrey auction is incentive compatible.

Proof:

Consider a situation in which bidder 1 would be the high bidder if its bid equalled its reservation value V_1. Let R_2 denote the highest of all bids other than 1's. Then $V_1 > R_2$. Under truthful revelation agent 1 would bid V_1 and be awarded the asset at price R_2, for a positive profit of $V_1 - R_2$. Let R_1 denote 1's actual bid and suppose that $R_1 < R_2$. Then the asset would go to agent 2, and agent 1 forgoes the positive profit that can be had by bidding V_1. In fact, with any bid above R_2 bidder 1 gets the asset for $\$R_2$ yielding a profit of $V_1 - R_2$, as in the case of truthful revelation. Bidder 1 can't gain by bidding something other than V_1, but can lose by doing so. (If 1 bids R_2 there would be a tie. The asset might go to bidder 2, but if it goes to agent 1 the profit would be $V_1 - R_2$, the same as under truthful revelation because R_2 would be the second highest bid. Even in the case of a tie, agent 1 can't do better than submitting a bid other than V_1, but can lose by doing so.)

Suppose that bidder 1 would *not* be the high bidder if its bid equalled its reservation value. Again, let R_2 denote the highest of all bids other than 1's. Then $V_1 < R_2$. Under truthful revelation agent 1 bids V_1 and receives nothing and pays nothing. Let R_1 denote 1's actual bid, and suppose that $R_1 > R_2$. Then 1 does get the asset and pays $\$R_2$ for it. But $R_2 > V_1$ and thus agent 1 incurs the loss of $R_2 - V_1$ that would be avoided by bidding V_1. (Agent 1 avoids a loss with any bid below R_2.) Bidder 1 can't gain by bidding something other than V_1, but can lose by doing so. (In the case of a tie we have $R_1 = R_2$ in which case the asset *could* go to agent 1 who would then incur a loss of $R_2 - V_1$.)

We have shown that for any configuarion of bids by rival participants an agent can do no better than submitting a bid different from his or her reservation value, but can be hurt by doing so.   ∎

We have demonstrated that submitting a bid equal to your reservation value is a dominant strategy for the Vickrey auction. The argument appeared to assume that individual X knew what the others would bid. To the contrary, we showed that even if X *could* read everyone else's mind, X could never profit by deviating from truthful revelation. And this holds true whether others bid wisely or not. (The proof didn't require us to make any assumption about the soundness of the other bidders' strategies.) Whatever the other bids are, and however they were arrived at, you can't do better than bidding your own reservation value in a Vickrey auction, whatever you know about the bids of others.

Our proof pointed out that if V_1 exceeds all other bids then agent 1 could realize the same profit as truthful revelation by bidding more than V_1. Why not bid more than your reservation value V to increase your chances of winning? Because you can never do better than bidding your true value V, and you could be hurt by doing so. You won't know what the others will bid, and by bidding more than V you could win the asset but pay more than V for it.

Because all individuals' bids equal their true reservation values, the asset will in fact be awarded to the individual with the highest value. Therefore, the Vickrey auction is asset efficient.

In terms of Example 6.2, A will bid 100, B will bid 70, C will bid 40, and D will bid 20. A will get the asset and pay 70 for it. But our argument was completely general. It applies to the auctioning of any object among any number of individuals. And once the object is allocated it is not possible for two individuals to engage in a mutually beneficial trade because the object has gone to the person who values it most.

6.2.2 Social Cost Pricing

A mechanism uses *social cost pricing* if the individual taking an action incurs a cost equal to the cost that the action imposes on the rest of society. For the special case of the allocation of a single indivisible asset, if the asset is awarded to individual A, then the cost of this allocation to the rest of society is the highest payoff that would be realized if the asset were to go to someone else.

DEFINITION: *Social Cost*

If the asset is awarded to agent J then the cost to the rest of society is the highest payoff that could be generated by giving the asset to someone else.

In determining the cost of giving the asset to individual J we calculate the payoff that would be realized by giving the asset to, say, individual K *without* deducting any payment that K might have to make. That is because the payment is a transfer from one person to another and thus is not a net loss to the group of individuals as a whole. However, if K's reservation value is $800 and J's is $500 then there is a net loss to the "economy" in giving the asset to J: the society as a whole loses $300 of benefit. We say that the cost of giving the asset to J is $800, so the net gain to society is $+500 - 800 = -300$.

We consider seven different mechanisms in which social cost pricing plays a central role, beginning with the Vickrey auction.

The Vickrey Auction

The asset is awarded to the high bidder at a price equal to the second-highest bid. Because truthful revelation of the individual's reservation value is a dominant strategy, the second-highest bid will be the second-highest reservation value. Therefore, the price that the winner pays is equal to the second-highest reservation value, which is the cost to the rest of society of giving the asset to the winner of the Vickrey auction. In other words, the Vickrey auction uses social cost pricing.

Example 6.3 Four Bidders Again

A's reservation value is 100, B's is 70, C's is 40, and D's is 30. If the asset were given to individual A then the cost to the rest of society is 70, because that is the highest payoff that could be generated by giving it to someone other than A. If the asset were given to B or C or D then the cost to the rest of society would be 100.

Before presenting the other six mechanisms we recall that social cost pricing in general involves charging an individual a fee equal to the cost that the individual's action has imposed on the rest of society.

Resource Allocation

A general equilibrium is a configuration of prices at which every market simultaneously clears. A general *competitive* equilibrium is a general equilibrium in an economy in which each industry is competitive. Consider a private ownership market economy. At equilibrium, each consumer chooses a consumption plan at which the marginal rate of substitution between goods X and Y is equal to the ratio P_X/P_Y of the respective prices. This holds for any two goods X and Y that are consumed. The opportunity cost incurred by Jordan when he orders a unit of X is P_X/P_Y. It costs P_X dollars to buy a unit of X; each dollar will buy $1/P_Y$ units of Y so P_X dollars spent on X could have been used to purchase $P_X \times (1/P_Y)$ units of commodity Y. Jordan takes the opportunity cost P_X/P_Y of X into consideration in determining his utility-maximizing consumption plan. Because the ratio P_X/P_Y also equals Leo's marginal rate of substitution (MRS_L), Jordan must take the preferences of Leo into consideration when he formulates his consumption plan. Every unit of X consumed by Jordan is worth MRS_L to Leo, in the sense that $MRS_L = P_X/P_Y$ is the minimum amount of Y that would compensate Leo for

Rice, a very thirsty crop, is grown profitably in the California desert thanks to lavish water subsidization. Urban dwellers pay a thousand times more per gallon of water than farmers (Segerfeldt, 2003, p. 48). Oil prices soared between 1972 and 1987, and demand adjusted. The rate increase of increase of CO_2 emissions slowed worldwide, and it stopped completely in the US over those fifteen years (Stoft, 2008).

the loss of a unit of X. We can say that MRS_L is the cost to society of Jordan taking a unit of good X for himself. In other words, P_X/P_Y is the cost that one imposes on society by consuming a unit of good X.

The ratio P_X/P_Y is also the amount of Y that could have been produced, given available technology, with the resources required to provide one more unit of X to consumers. This is another sense in which P_X/P_Y can be viewed as the cost individuals impose on society by ordering a unit of commodity X for their own use.

∂Constrained Optimization

Mathematical programming entails social cost pricing. Consider the problem

$$\text{maximize } f(x,y), \quad \text{subject to } g(x,y) \le a \text{ and } h(x,y) \le b.$$

The function f represents the goal or objective, and we want to pick the values of x and y that maximize f. But there are constraints g and h, and they restrict the values of x and y that we can select.

The function f expresses the goals of society. The society could be the set of shareholders of a particular firm, with $f(x, y)$ denoting the profit from the production of x units of commodity X and y units of commodity Y. The constraints represent limitations such as warehouse and transportation capacity. The example has a wide range of interpretations. If f is the value to society of the plan (x, y) then g and h reflect resource utilization by the plan of two inputs A and B – labor and capital, say – with a and b denoting the total amount available of A and B, respectively. The plan (x, y) uses $g(x, y)$ units of labor, and that cannot exceed the total amount of labor, a, in the economy. Similarly, the plan (x, y) uses $h(x, y)$ units of capital, and the economy has only b units of capital.

The solution of the constrained optimization program can be characterized by means of two *Lagrangian* (or *Karush-Kuhn-Tucker*) variables, α and β associated with the respective constraints g and h. If x^0 and y^0 constitute a solution to the problem then there exist $\alpha \ge 0$ and $\beta \ge 0$ such that

$$\frac{\partial f(x^0,y^0)}{\partial x} - \alpha\frac{\partial g(x^0,y^0)}{\partial x} - \beta\frac{\partial h(x^0,y^0)}{\partial x} = 0, \tag{1}$$

$$\frac{\partial f(x^0,y^0)}{\partial y} - \alpha\frac{\partial g(x^0,y^0)}{\partial y} - \beta\frac{\partial h(x^0,y^0)}{\partial y} = 0, \tag{2}$$

The variable α is a price in the sense that it is the value of the resource A underlying constraint g: if additional units of A can be obtained then α is the rate at which f will increase per unit of A added. And $\partial g(x^0 y^0)/\partial x$ is the rate at which A is consumed at the margin. We interpret B and β similarly.

Notice that we arrive at the same optimal plan (x^0, y^0) if we maximize

$$f(x,y) - \alpha g(x,y) - \beta h(x,y)$$

treating α and β as given prices of A and B respectively. Therefore, α and β are social cost prices. (See Section 2.3 of Chapter 2 for an extensive treatment.)

A Computer Network

Suppose that the society that we are studying is actually a network of computers. Each computer is capable of carrying out a variety of tasks, but some agent must assign tasks to the individual computers. Computer scientist C. A. Waldspurger and colleagues at the Palo Alto Research Center (owned by Xerox) have programmed another computer to assign the tasks. One *could* program the central computer to gather data on the computational burden that each computer is currently carrying and then do the complex job of computing the optimal assignment of new jobs. Instead, the Xerox technicians have the central computer auction computer time. An individual computer can bid for time on other computers – each computer is given a "budget." Computational capacity is transferred from computers that "have time on their hands" to computers that currently do not have enough capacity to complete their assigned tasks. The price at which the transaction takes place is adjusted by the center in response to demand and supply.

Tort Damages

A *tort* is an instance of unintentional harm to person A as a result of the action of individual B. If the injury occurred because B did not exercise reasonable care then B can be held liable for the damages to A according to the law of many countries.

Millions of automobiles have been recalled as a result of safety defects that are then repaired at the manufacturer's expense. If one car maker does this the others have to follow suit to protect their reputations. But why would one manufacturer make the first move? To forestall civil suits by injured customers.

Frequently, the potential harm to B can be avoided by means of a contract between A and B. In such cases government intervention is not required, except to enforce the contract. For example, the contract signed by professional athletes and their employer can specify penalties in the event an athlete fails to show up for a game or even a practice. But in many cases, it would be too costly to arrange all the contracts necessary for efficiency. You can't enter into a contract with every motorist who could possibly injure you as you walk down the sidewalk. By allowing you to collect for damages in civil court, tort liability implicitly imposes costs on anyone who unintentionally injures another. The closer the tort liability is to the amount of harm inflicted the greater the incentive an individual has to take decisions that reflect the potential harm to others as a result of personal negligence.

The Pivotal Mechanism

The pivotal mechanism discussed in Section 8.2 of Chapter 8 induces truthful revelation of the net benefit that an individual derives from a public project. It does so by imposing a tax surcharge on person A that is equal to the total loss in utility suffered by everyone else as a result of A's participation. If that has no effect on the outcome then there is no loss suffered by others and hence no surcharge paid by A. But if the outcome would have been F without A's participation and the inclusion of A's benefit function leads to G, then A's tax surcharge is the difference between the total utility that everyone but A would have derived from F and the total utility that everyone but A will derive from G. This makes the tax surcharge equal to the cost that A's action (participation) imposes on the rest of society. (Chapter 8 shows that the surcharges will typically be zero, but the *threat* of a surtax motivates an individual to report truthfully.)

Taxi Fleets

What payment schedule should the owner of a fleet of taxi cabs offer to the drivers to maximize the owner's income from the taxi company? The pure franchise solution gives each driver the incentive maximize the owner's income, even though the driver's goal is the maximization of her own income. The pure franchise solution *gives all of the profit to the driver* – all of the profit, that is, except a fixed payment (the *franchise fee*) to the owner by the cab driver. The driver becomes the residual claimant: after the fixed payment (franchise fee) is made, every dollar of profit from operating the cab goes into the driver's pocket. This is an example of social cost pricing because the cost to the team – driver-owner pair in this case – of shirking by the driver is exactly equal to the cost borne by the driver. Even though the driver is not the fleet's owner, the owner's return is maximized because the high degree of incentive under which the manager operates leads to high profits, and hence a high franchise fee can be set.

6.2.3 Incentives, Efficiency, and Social Cost Pricing

We have shown that the Vickrey auction satisfies incentive compatibility and asset efficiency (defined in Sections 6.2.1 and 6.1.2, respectively). Now we show that it is the only auction mechanism satisfying those two properties plus the requirement that an individual who doesn't get the asset doesn't have to pay anything. This new criterion is called the participation constraint.

DEFINITION: *Participation Constraint*
An individual who is not awarded the asset doesn't make or receive a payment.

Consequently, participating in the auction cannot make you worse off. At the very least this means that the winner cannot be charged more for the asset than the winner's reservation value. How can that constraint be put into practice if an agent's reservation value is unknown to anyone else? Only by giving the bidders the appropriate incentive.

We begin by confining attention to *direct* auction mechanisms, which simply ask all individuals to report their reservation values. Two simple rules identify a specific direct mechanism: selection of the individual who receives the asset as a function of the reported reservation values and specification of how much that individual pays, as a function of the reported reservation values.

DEFINITION: *Direct Auction Mechanism*

Agents are asked to report their reservation values, and the asset is awarded to one of these, depending on the reported values $R_1, R_2, \ldots, R_n$ of the n agents. $P(R_1, R_2, \ldots, R_n)$ is the price paid by the winner of the asset, as a function of the reported values.

The Vickrey auction satisfies the participation constraint and asset efficiency by definition. Section 6.2.1 demonstrated that it is incentive compatible. We prove that it is the *only* direct mechanism that has all three properties, but first we sketch the argument: suppose that $R_1 > R_2$ and R_2 is the second highest reported reservation value. If $R_1 = 300 = V_1$ but $P(R_1, R_2, \ldots, R_n) = 225 > 175 = R_2$ then bidder 1 can get the asset for 180 or less by reporting a reservation value of 180. (The participation constraint implies that the price cannot be higher than the winner's reported value, which would be 180 when bidder 1 reports a value of 180.) Under truthful revelation bidder 1 would report a value of 300 and get the asset for 225. Bidding V_1 is not a payoff maximizing strategy when $P(V_1, R_2, \ldots, R_n) > R_2, R_1 > R_2,$ and R_2 is the second largest reported reservation value. Therefore, $P(R_1, R_2, \ldots, R_n) \leq R_2$ must hold. Suppose that $P(R_1, R_2, \ldots, R_n) = 100 < 175 = R_2 < R_1$. If 1's true reservation value is 150 then truthful revelation would see the asset going to person 2, but a report of R_1 would give agent 1 the asset at a price of 100 for a profit of 50, exceeding the profit of zero that results from truthful revelation. The price paid by the winner can't be higher or lower than the second highest reported reservation value. It must use the Vickrey auction pricing formula.

Theorem: Uniqueness of the Vickrey Auction

The Vickrey auction is the only direct auction mechanism satisfying incentive compatibility, asset efficiency, and the participation constraint.

Proof:

We work out the properties of a given auction mechanism about which we know nothing except that it satisfies incentive compatibility, asset efficiency, and the participation constraint.

Incentive compatibility means that each agent i reports his or her true reservation value. In symbols, we have $R_i = V_i$, for each individual i, where V_i denotes i's true reservation value, known only to i, and R_i is i's reported reservation value. Incentive compatibility and asset efficiency together imply that the asset is awarded to the individual with the highest R_i. Therefore, the only property of the auction mechanism that remains to be determined is the payment function

$P(R_1, R_2, \ldots, R_n)$. We show that our three criteria imply that it has to be the Vickrey payment function. That is, $P(R_1, R_2, \ldots, R_n)$ will equal the second-highest R_i.

Step 1: $P(R_1, R_2, \ldots, R_n)$ can't exceed the highest R_i.

Consider an individual acting alone, as opposed to someone representing a firm. That person's payoff is captured by the quasi-linear utility function $U(x, y) = B(x) + y$. An individual who is not awarded the asset pays nothing (because the participation constraint is satisfied): the individual's consumption of X is unchanged, and consumption of Y does not go down. Therefore, the change in utility of an individual who does not receive the asset cannot be negative. If, say, person 1 does get the asset then her change in utility is

$$\Delta U_1 = B_1(1) + \Delta y_1 = B_1(1) - P(R_1, R_2, \ldots, R_n)$$
$$= V_1 - P(R_1, R_2, \ldots, R_n),$$

which is the net benefit from acquiring the asset, the value of the asset minus what she pays for it. If $\Delta U_1 < 0$ then bidder 1 has an incentive to report a reservation value of zero, ensuring that the asset goes to someone else. That would violate incentive compatibility because the participation constraint implies $\Delta U_1 = 0$ when bidder 1 does not get the asset.

If the winning bidder is a firm, its payoff is the effect of the auction on its profit, which equals its reservation value minus the price paid. Therefore, whether agent H is a firm or an individual the change in its payoff is $V_H - P(R_1, R_2, \ldots, R_n)$ if $R_H = V_H$ and H wins the asset. If that change is negative then either incentive compatibility or the participation constraint is violated. Whether the bidders are firms or individuals, $P(R_1, R_2, \ldots, R_n)$ cannot exceed the highest R_i. Formally, for all $R_1, R_2, \ldots, R_n$ we have

$$R_1 - P(R_1, R_2, \ldots, R_n) \geq 0 \text{ if } R_1 > R_2 \geq R_i \text{ for all } i > 2. \qquad [3]$$

In words, the price paid by the winner can never exceed the reservation value reported by the winner. For the rest of this section we refer to a bidder as an *agent*.

Step 2: $P(R_1, R_2, \ldots, R_n)$ cannot exceed the second highest reported reservation value.

Suppose that $P(R_1, R_2, \ldots, R_n) > R_2$ does hold, and $R_1 > R_2 \geq R_i$ for all $i > 2$. Let T_1 be the average of $P(R_1, R_2, \ldots, R_n)$ and R_2. That is, $T_1 = \frac{1}{2}P(R_1, R_2, \ldots, R_n) + \frac{1}{2}R_2$. This means that T_1 will be less than $P(R_1, R_2, \ldots, R_n)$ but more than R_2:

$$P(R_1, R_2, \ldots, R_n) > T_l > R_2. \qquad [4]$$

Therefore, [3] implies $P(R_1, R_2, \ldots, R_n) > T_1 \geq P(T_1, R_2, \ldots, R_n)$ and hence

$$P(R_1, R_2, \ldots, R_n) > P(T_1, R_2, \ldots, R_n).$$

But we also have $T_1 > R_2$. Therefore, the strategy T_1 results in agent 1 getting the asset but at a lower price than when she bids R_1. Apply this to the case $R_1 = V_1$: agent 1 gets a higher payoff by reporting T_1 than by truthfully reporting $R_1 = V_1$. Incentive compatibility and the participation constraint therefore require

$$P(R_1, R_2, \ldots, R_n) \leq R_2 \text{ whenever } R_1 > R_2 \geq R_i \text{ for all } i > 2.$$

Step 3: $P(R_1, R_2, \ldots, R_n)$ cannot be less than the second highest reported reservation value.

Suppose that we actually have $P(R_1, R_2, \ldots, R_n) < R_2$ and $R_1 > R_2 \geq R_i$ for all $i > 2$. Set $V_1 = \frac{1}{2}P(R_1, R_2, \ldots, R_n) + \frac{1}{2}R_2$. That is, suppose that agent 1's true reservation value is halfway between $P(R_1, R_2, \ldots, R_n)$ and R_2. We have $P(R_1, R_2, \ldots, R_n) < V_1 < R_2$. When agent 1 (untruthfully) reports R_1 she gets the asset, and her payoff is $V_1 - P(R_1, R_2, \ldots, R_n) > 0$, which is greater than the payoff of zero that she gets by truthfully reporting V_1. (When $V_1 < R_2$ she does not get the asset and she does not receive any money if her bid is V_1.) Therefore, incentive compatibility rules out $P(R_1, R_2, \ldots, R_n) < R_2$ when $R_1 > R_2 \geq R_i$ for all $i > 2$. (We are allowed to "choose" agent 1's reservation value because the mechanism is required to work for all possible combinations of individual reservation values. Hence, it has to satisfy the three criteria when 1's true value is between $P(R_1, R_2, \ldots, R_n)$ and R_2.)

There is only one possibility left: we have to have $P(R_1, R_2, \ldots, R_n) = R_2$ whenever $R_1 > R_2 \geq R_i$ for all $i > 2$. The mechanism must be the Vickrey auction. ∎

We started with an unknown mechanism. All we knew was that it had our three properties. We proved that these properties imply that it must actually be the Vickrey auction. We know that this scheme induces truthful revelation, so we must have $R_2 = V_2$ and $P(V_1, V_2, \ldots, V_n) = V_2$, which is the cost to society of giving the asset to agent 1. In general, if V_H is the highest reservation value and V_J is second highest, then we must have $P(V_1, V_2, \ldots, V_n) = V_J$ with the asset going to H.

With the Vickrey auction the agent who gets the asset must pay a price equal to the cost the agent imposes on the rest of society by making the asset unavailable for use by anyone else. Moreover, this social cost pricing scheme has been *derived from* considerations of efficiency and incentive compatibility.

We can extend our result to a much wider family of auction mechanisms. A *general auction mechanism* specifies for each agent i a set M_i of reports from which that agent is able to choose. The mechanism also specifies for each agent i a function σ_i that tells the agent what to report as a function of the agent's true reservation value. That is, if agent i's true value is V_i then i is expected to report $\sigma_i(V_i)$, a member of M_i. If the mechanism is a direct one then $\sigma_i(V_i) = V_i$.

Example 6.4 Reporting a Fraction of One's Reservation Value

There are n bidders, and all are asked to report the fraction $(n - 1)/n$ of their reservation values. In symbols, $\sigma_i(V_i) = [(n - 1)/n]V_i$. The high bidder gets the asset at a price equal to the bid. Asset efficiency is satisfied by this mechanism. (Why?) Incentive compatibility is not, however. For instance, if $n = 3$, $V_1 = 300$, $V_2 = 150$, and $V_3 = 120$, then under truthful revelation agent 1 will bid 200, agent 2 will bid 100, and 3 will bid 80. However, 1's payoff would be higher with a bid of 101.

Example 6.4 may make you wonder if there is any point to considering more general auction mechanisms. By allowing a more detailed report by a bidder - say the reservation value plus additional information – the additional information may be used to arrive at an asset-efficient outcome in a way that satisfies some properties that the Vickrey mechanism lacks. Because the true payoff functions are still hidden information, the individual must have an *incentive* to behave according to σ_i. We say that truthful revelation is a dominant strategy if, for each individual i, each V_i, and each configuration of messages by others, there is no message m_i in M_i such that i's payoff is higher when i reports m_i than when i reports $\sigma_i(V_i)$.

Theorem: Uniqueness of Social Cost Pricing

If a general auction mechanism satisfies incentive compatibility, asset efficiency, and the participation constraint then the winner of the auction must be charged a price equal to the second-highest reservation value.

Proof:

Construct a direct auction mechanism from a given general mechanism satisfying asset efficiency and the participation constraint, and for which truthful revelation is a dominant strategy. Given the general mechanism G, construct a direct auction mechanism D by having each agent i report his or her reservation value V_i, awarding the asset to the agent with the highest V_i (as G must do, by asset efficiency), and then charging the winner the price $P(\sigma_1(V_1), \sigma_2(V_2), \ldots, \sigma_n(V_n))$, where n is the number of bidders and P is the pricing formula used by G. By the uniqueness theorem for *direct* mechanisms, $P(\sigma_1(V_1), \sigma_2(V_2), \ldots, \sigma_n(V_n))$ must equal the second-highest V_i. Therefore, at equilibrium, G must charge the winner a price equal to the second-highest reported reservation value. ∎

We could modify the Vickrey auction's pricing rule so that individuals who don't receive the asset still have to pay a fee. But that would violate the *participation constraint*. We could have payments made *to* individuals who do not receive the asset. But who would make the payment? It can't be the person who is awarded the asset because that would increase the price that that person would have to pay. But any higher price than the second-highest bid would spoil the incentive to report truthfully, as we have seen. The payment can't come from one of the losers if the participation constraint is to be respected. Therefore, charging the losers precisely nothing and having the winner pay a price equal to the second-highest bid – and hence equal to the cost imposed on society by the winner's participation – is the only pricing scheme that satisfies asset efficiency, incentive compatibility, and the participation constraint.

But do we have *full* efficiency? Who *gets* the payment made by the winner? It can't be one of the bidders. Otherwise, that agent would have an incentive to submit a high bid, just under the winner's reservation value, to increase the fee paid by the winner and hence the amount of money going to the one who gets the winner's payment. The problem with that is that individuals no longer have an incentive to submit bids equal to their respective reservation values. Therefore, the payment by the winner can't go to anyone. This represents waste and destroys the efficiency of the system. In this setting, efficiency is equivalent to the maximization of $\sum_{t=1}^{n} U_t$ subject to $x_t = 1$ for one and only one individual, and $y_t \geq 0$ for all t, and $\sum_{t=1}^{n} y_t = \theta$ where θ is the total initial amount of Y available. However, if the winner of the asset makes a payment that doesn't go to anyone else in the society, then we have $\sum_{t=1}^{n} y_t < \theta$ and hence an inefficient outcome.

Why don't we give the payment to the person who owned the asset initially? There are two objections to this. If we want to *derive* the efficient and incentive-compatible pricing schedule, private ownership should emerge as part of the solution; it shouldn't be assumed at the outset. Moreover, as soon as we put an original owner in the model and have the winner's payment go to the owner we again spoil the incentive for truthful revelation. Consider: let agent 0 be the seller, whose reservation value is V_0. Suppose that the seller's bid B_0 is used when determining the second-highest bid and hence the price to charge the winner. If the winner's payment goes to the seller then the seller has an incentive to overstate the reservation value to increase the payment that he or she will receive. Suppose, however, that B_0 is not taken into consideration when determining the price that the winner of the asset will pay. We just use B_0 to determine if the seller should keep the asset. Efficiency still demands that the asset go to the agent with the highest reservation value. If V_0 is higher than every other reservation value, efficiency requires that agent 0 keep the asset. Suppose, however, that $B_1 > V_0 > B_2 > B_i$ for all $i > 2$. The asset will go to agent 1 at price B_2. If $B_0 = V_0$ the seller has to part with the asset but receives less than it's worth to him. In this case the seller would have an incentive to misrepresent his reservation value and report $B_0 > B_1$.

If there is an initial owner of the asset we can't "close the system" so that the winner's payment goes to the seller without destroying the incentive for truthful revelation. If, however, we have a large number of agents then there will be a very low probability that one and only one person has a reservation value above or close to that of a seller. In other words, the probability that $B_1 > V_0 > B_i$ for all $i > 1$ is very small if there is a large number of bidders. With social cost pricing the probability that there is a significant efficiency loss will be very low if the winner's payment goes to the original owner – i.e., the seller.

6.2.4 Search Engine Ad Auctions

Google and Yahoo are the most frequently used search engines. A search for a particular web site elicits a list of possibilities, with the best fit cited first, followed by the next best fit, and so on. The list will be accompanied by a number of ads. In almost every case the position of each ad is determined by an auction – one that generalizes the second-price, or Vickrey, auction. Here's what happens: each advertising firm submits a bid that is interpreted as the amount that the firm is willing to pay *per click* for a spot on the web page in question. (In fact the advertiser must also submit keywords, which are used by the search engine to determine the web sites at which the advertiser wants its ad placed.) A click is recorded when a visitor to the web site clicks on the ad. The most prominent position on the page is awarded to the firm submitting the highest bid at a price *per click* equal to the second highest bid. The second best spot is given to the advertiser submitting the second highest bid at a *per click* equal to the third highest bid. In general the kth best position is awarded to the advertiser with the kth highest bid, at a price per click equal to the next highest bid. The advertiser is charged a fee equal to the price per click multiplied by the number of recorded clicks. Of course, the more prominent the ad the more visits to the ad there will be, whichever firm's ad occupies that position. The *value* of a single click is specific to the individual advertiser. (The advertiser submits a bid only once. The search engine software runs the auction in a fraction of a second when you summon a particular web site.)

Let v_i denote the value per click of advertiser i's ad. Let x_j be the number of clicks that an ad in position j is expected to yield. (Position 1 is the best spot, 2 denotes the second best spot, and so on). Let m denote the number of available ad positions. We assume that $x_1 > x_2 > \ldots x_{m-1} > x_m$. In fact, the number of available ad positions is unlimited, but we fix the number at m on the understanding that position $m+1$ is not profitable for any potential advertiser. Therefore, we set $x_{m+1} = 0$. If p_j is the price paid per click for an ad in position j then $(v_i - p_j)x_j$ is the profit to firm i of an ad in position j. As a convenience we'll label the advertisers so that the auction results in firm 1's ad being placed in position 1, firm 2's ad in position 2, and so on. In general, firm i's ad winds up in position i and hence i's payoff is $(v_i - p_i)x_i$.

The General Position Auction Model

An ad in position j will attract x_j clicks, and the value of a single click to firm i is v_i. Firm i's revenue from an ad in position j is $v_i x_j$, and hence its profit is $x_j(v_i - p_j)$, where p_j is the price per click of an ad in position j.

For any position auction p_j, the price per click of an ad in position j, is a function of all the bids. We let b_i denote the bid of advertiser i, and for notational convenience we choose subscripts so that at equilibrium firm i's ad is placed in position i. Consequently, in the case of the general position auction p_j equals the bid of the firm whose ad occupies position $j+1$. The ad positions are determined by the bids, with firm i receiving a better position than j if and only if $b_i > b_j$.

The Generalized Vickrey Auction

At equilibrium we have $b_1 > b_2 > b_3 > \ldots b_{m-1} > b_m > 0 = b_{m+1}$, where i is the name of the advertiser in position i. For each $i \le m$, $p_i = b_{i+1}$, with p_m, the price paid by the firm occupying the last and lowest position, equal to zero.

At a Nash equilibrium configuration of bids no firm could increase its payoff by paying more for a better spot or paying less for a less prominent spot. Given the bids $b_1, b_2, \ldots, b_{m-1}, b_m$ what would be the payoff to firm i in position i if it changed its bid to move to a higher position j while the other bids remained the same?

Example 6.5 Moving to a Higher Spot

There are three advertisers with $b_1 = 5$, $b_2 = 3$, and $b_3 = 1$. Firm 2 occupies the second position and pays \$1 per click. If firm 2 wanted the highest position it would have to outbid firm 1, in which case the second highest bid would be \$5, the price paid per click by firm 2 for the best spot when $b_1 = 5$ and $b_3 = 1$.

In general, if $i > j$ and i were to displace firm j and occupy position j, the price that i would have to pay for that higher position is b_j, although b_{j+1} is the price paid by j for position j when i stays in position i.

How would a move to a lower position affect an advertiser's payoff? Suppose that $i < j$. What price would i pay if it wanted to change its bid and replace j in the jth position? It would be b_{j+1}, the price that would be paid for position j by firm j if i were to remain in position i. When i displaces j there will be exactly $j-1$ advertisers with higher bids and hence the next lowest after i's new bid is b_{j+1}, the price that would be paid by i for an ad in position $j+1$ when each firm $h \neq i$ bids its original b_h.

Example 6.6 Moving to a Lower Spot

There are three advertisers with $b_1 = 5$, $b_2 = 3$, and $b_3 = 1$. Firm 1 occupies the highest position and pays \$3 per click. If firm 1 wanted to move to second position it would have to bid an amount between 1 and 3, in which case \$1 would be the next highest bid and thus the price paid for second position by firm 1, when $b_2 = 3$ and $b_3 = 1$.

At a Nash equilibrium $b_1, b_2, \ldots, b_{m-1}, b_m$ arbitrary firm i in position i must find that spot at least as profitable as any other.

Nash Equilibrium of the Position Auction

$(v_i - b_{i+1})x_i \geq (v_i - b_j)x_j$ for all i and j such that $i > j$, and

$(v_i - b_{i+1})x_i \geq (v_i - b_{j+1})x_j$ for all i and j such that $i < j$.

The first inequality states that moving to a higher spot cannot be more profitable for arbitrary advertiser i in position i. The second states that moving to a lower spot cannot be more profitable for i in position i.

Example 6.7 Equilibrium with Three Advertisers

The three reservation values are $v_1 = 20$, $v_2 = 14$, and $v_3 = 5$. The three position values are $x_1 = 10$, $x_2 = 5$, and $x_3 = 2$. We show that $b_1 = 8$, $b_2 = 4$, and $b_3 = 1$ constitutes a Nash equilibrium. We begin by computing the resulting payoffs. With the given bids the prices are $p_1 = 4$, $p_2 = 1$, and $p_3 = 0$ for the respective positions 1, 2, and 3.

Advertiser 1's payoff is $(20 - 4)10 = 160$.
Advertiser 2's payoff is $(14 - 1)5 = 65$.
Advertiser 3's payoff is $(5 - 0)2 = 10$.

Consider 1's strategy: if it were to submit a bid between b_2 and b_3 it would pay $1 per click for a payoff of $(20 - 1)5$ which is obviously less than 160. If it were to submit a bid below $1, putting it in position 3, its payoff would be $(20 - 0)2$. Therefore, $b_1 = 8$ is a best response to $b_2 = 4$ and $b_3 = 1$. (Any bid higher than 8 gives 1 the same payoff as a bid of 8.) Consider 2's strategy: a bid that put it in first position would result in a payoff of $(14 - 8)10 = 60$ because $8 would be the second highest bid. A bid to put it in third position would yield a payoff of $(14 - 0)2 = 28$. Therefore, $b_2 = 4$ is a best response to $b_1 = 8$ and $b_3 = 1$, as is any bid strictly between 4 and 8. Consider 3's strategy: because $b_2 = 4$, if advertiser 3 were bid enough to move to position 1 or 2 it would pay at least $4 per click resulting in a profit of no more than $(5 - 4)5$, which is less than its profit in position 3, given $b_1 = 8$ and $b_2 = 4$. Therefore, $b_3 = 1$ is a best response to $b_1 = 8$ and $b_2 = 4$, as is any bid less than 4.

Example 6.7 shows that bidding one's reservation value is *not* a dominant strategy in the case of the position (or general Vickrey) auction if $m > 1$. Bidding one's reservation value *is* a dominant strategy in the case of the Vickrey auction of a single indivisible asset. Why the difference? In the case of the position auction, the location of a firm's ad is a function of all the bids, and thus the value of the asset that is secured by a particular bid is a function of all the bids. There can be no dominant strategy for the position auction. With the Vickrey auction of a single indivisible asset the bidder knows in advance the value to her of the item on sale.

A *symmetric* Nash equilibrium for the generalized Vickrey auction is one for which no firm i could increase its payoff by paying more for a better spot or paying less for an inferior spot, even if moving to a different position would result in the same price being paid for that spot as would be paid by the current occupant of that position. Recall that if $i > j$ and i were to displace firm j and occupy position j, the price that i would have to pay for that higher position is b_j, not b_{j+1}, the price paid by j for position j when i remains in position i.

Symmetric Nash Equilibrium of the Generalized Vickrey Auction
$(v_i - b_{i+1})x_i \geq (v_i - b_{j+1})x_j$ holds for all i and j.

At a *symmetric Nash* equilibrium a firm will not suffer a loss by participating in the auction and the more prominent positions go to firms with higher values v_i. Moreover, better ad positions command higher prices and the total cost of an ad position is higher for a better spot. Because we want the price paid by i if it were to displace firm j to be the same as the price paid by j if i were to remain in position i we can let p_j denote the price paid by the firm occupying position j. We have a symmetric Nash equilibrium if

$$(v_i - p_i)x_i \geq (v_i - p_j)x_j \quad \text{holds for all } i \text{ and } j. \tag{5}$$

Properties of the Symmetric Equilibrium of the Generalized Vickrey Auction
(i) $v_i \geq p_i$, (ii) $v_i \geq v_{i+1}$, (iii) $p_i x_i > p_{i+1} x_{i+1}$, and (iv) $p_i \geq p_{i+1}$ hold for all i.

Proof:

To establish that $v_i \geq p_i$ holds for all i we set $j = m+1$ in [5], the inequality characterizing a symmetric Nash equilibrium. We get $(v_i - p_i)x_i \geq (v_i - p_{m+1})x_{m+1} = 0$. (Recall that $x_{m+1} = 0$ by definition of m.) It follows that $(v_i - p_i)x_i \geq 0$, and hence $v_i - p_i \geq 0$ because $x_i > 0$ if $i \leq m$.

To prove that $v_i \geq v_{i+1}$ holds for all i we add $p_i x_i - v_i x_j$ to both sides of the equilibrium inequality [5]. We get $v_i(x_i - x_j)$ on the left and $p_i x_i - p_j x_j$ on the right:

$$v_i(x_i - x_j) \geq p_i x_i - p_j x_j \quad \text{for all } i \text{ and } j \tag{6}$$

Now we rewrite [6] for two special cases: $i = k$ and $j = k+1$ on the one hand and $i = k+1$ and $j = k$ on the other, yielding the inequalities [7] and [8] respectively for arbitrary k:

$$v_k(x_k - x_{k+1}) \geq p_k x_k - p_{k+1} x_{k+1} \tag{7}$$

$$v_{k+1}(x_{k+1} - x_k) \geq p_{k+1} x_{k+1} - p_k x_k. \tag{8}$$

If we sum the left-hand sides of [3] and [4] and then sum the right-hand sides the direction of the inequality is preserved. We get

$$(v_k - v_{k+1})(x_k - x_{k+1}) \geq 0 \quad \text{for arbitrary } k. \tag{9}$$

We know that $x_{k+1} < x_k$ holds for all k, and thus [9] implies that $v_{k+1} > v_k$ cannot hold. In words, the more prominent the ad position the higher is the value v_i of the firm whose ad occupies that position at equilibrium.

To prove (iii) and (iv) we restate the Nash equilibrium condition for the special case $j = k$ and $i = k+1$:

$$(v_{k+1} - p_{k+1})x_{k+1} \geq (v_{k+1} - p_k)x_k \quad \text{for arbitrary } k. \tag{10}$$

Now add $p_k x_k - (v_{k+1} - p_{k+1})x_{k+1}$ to both sides of [10], yielding

$$p_k x_k \geq p_{k+1} x_{k+1} + v_{k+1}(x_k - x_{k+1}) \quad \text{for arbitrary } k. \tag{11}$$

We know that $v_{k+1} > 0$ and $x_k - x_{k+1} > 0$, which implies that $p_{k+1} x_{k+1} + v_{k+1}(x_k - x_{k+1}) > p_{k+1} x_{k+1}$. Therefore, [11] yields $p_k x_k > p_{k+1} x_{k+1}$ which is (iii).

Note that [11] and property (i) imply

$$p_k x_k \geq p_{k+1} x_{k+1} + p_{k+1}(x_k - x_{k+1}) \quad \text{for arbitrary } k.$$

Because $p_{k+1} x_{k+1} + p_{k+1}(x_k - x_{k+1}) = p_{k+1} x_k$ we have $p_k x_k \geq p_{k+1} x_k$. Dividing both sides of that inequality by x_k, which is positive, yields $p_k \geq p_{k+1}$, which is (iv). If v_{k+1} is strictly greater than p_{k+1} we have $p_k > p_{k+1}$. ∎

Example 6.8 Symmetric Equilibrium with Three Advertisers

The three reservation values are $v_1 = 20$, $v_2 = 14$, and $v_3 = 5$ and the three position values are $x_1 = 10$, $x_2 = 5$, and $x_3 = 2$, as in Example 6.7. We show that $b_1 = 15$, $b_2 = 10$, and $b_3 = 3.5$ constitutes a symmetric Nash equilibrium. With the given bids the prices are $p_1 = 10$, $p_2 = 3.5$, and $p_3 = 0$ for the respective positions 1, 2, and 3.

Advertiser 1's payoff is $(20 - 10)10 = 100$.
Advertiser 2's payoff is $(14 - 3.5)5 = 52.5$.
Advertiser 3's payoff is $(5 - 0)2 = 10$.

Do we have $(v_1 - p_1)x_1 > (v_1 - p_j)x_j$ for $j = 2$ and 3? Yes: $(20 - 3.5)5 = 82.5$ and $(20 - 0)2 = 40$. Do we have $(v_2 - p_2)x_2 > (v_2 - p_j)x_j$ for $j = 1$ and 3? Yes: $(14 - 10)10 = 40$ and $(14 - 0)2 = 28$. Do we have $(v_3 - p_3)x_3 > (v_3 - p_j)x_j$ for $j = 1$ and 2? Yes: $(5 - 10)10$ is negative and $(5 - 3.5)5 = 7.5$. We do indeed have a symmetric Nash equilibrium.

Sources

Vickrey (1961) pioneered the study of auctions in economic theory and his seminal article anticipated important discoveries in the theory of public goods in addition to the contemporary literature on auctions and bidding. In 1996 Vickrey was awarded the Nobel Prize in economics, along with James Mirlees, another seminal contributor to the theory of incentives. The "computer network" paragraph of Section 6.2.2 is based on Waldspurger et al. (1992). Section 6.2.4 is based on Varian (2007).

Links

Milgrom (1987, 1989) provides introductions to the theory of auctions and bidding. Ashenfelter (1989) discusses the particular cases of wine (excuse the pun) and art. Lucking-Reiley (2000b) is a survey of online auctions. Levin (2013) discusses internet markets in general. Makowski and Ostroy (1987) arrive at social cost pricing by a different route. (See also Roberts, 1979, and Makowski and Ostroy, 1991, 1993). Sternberg (1991) analyses the sale of the assets of failed banks under both the private values and the common values assumptions. Green and Laffont (1979) derive incentive-compatible mechanisms for allocating pure public goods. A more general result is presented in Walker (1978). Holmström (1979b) treats divisible private goods. He was awarded the Nobel Prize in Economics in 2016. Kirby et al. (2003) use the Vickrey auction in an experiment designed to determine if students who are more patient perform better. There are artificial intelligence models that use market-like evaluation to direct the transition of a computer from one state to another. See, for example, Waldrup (1992, pp. 181–189). See Chapter 8 in Cooter and Ullen (1994) or Ullen (1994) for an extended discussion of the economics of tort damage awards. Hurwicz and Walker (1990) prove that the inefficiency due to the inequality between the initial and final total Y consumption is almost inevitable. Their argument applies to a wide variety of models of resource allocation. Auctions for assigning students to courses are analyzed in Sönmez and Ünver (2010) and Budish and Kessler (2016). The subject is discussed briefly in Section 11.3 of Chapter 11.

Problem Set

(1) Suppose that when the Vickrey auction is used each bidder other than number 1 always (mistakenly) reports a reservation value equal to half his or her true reservation value. Suppose also that bidder 1 knows that. Is truthful revelation still a dominant strategy for bidder number 1? Explain.

(2) Ten different direct auction mechanisms are described. Each participant i submits a bid S_i. Any money paid by the individual who gets the asset does not go to the other participants, unless there is an explicit statement to the contrary. In each case determine if the mechanism would satisfy (i) asset efficiency if the individuals reported truthfully, (ii) the participation constraint if the individuals reported truthfully, and (iii) incentive compatibility. If a criterion is not satisfied you have to give a numerical example to show that. If the criterion is satisfied then you have to prove that it is.

(A) The asset goes to the individual i submitting the highest S_i at a price equal to that S_i. No one else pays anything or receives any money.

(B) The asset goes to the individual submitting the highest S_i at a price equal to the second-highest S_i. The other individuals each receive $5.

(C) The Vickrey auction is used but there is an entry fee of $100. This fee must be paid by each participant before the bidding starts.

(D) The asset goes to the individual submitting the *second-highest* S_i at a price equal to the *third-highest* S_i. No one else pays anything or receives any money.

(E) The asset is always given to individual 1 *free of charge*. No one else pays anything or receives any money.

(F) The asset is always given to individual 1, who is then taxed $100. No one else pays anything or receives any money.

(G) The asset goes to the individual submitting the highest S_i at a price equal to the *average* of the second-highest bid and the lowest bid. No one else pays anything or receives any money.

(H) The asset goes to the individual i submitting the highest bid at a price equal to the *average* of the second-highest bid and the high bid itself. No one else pays anything or receives any money.

(I) For this part only, assume that there are three individuals ($n = 3$). The asset goes to the individual submitting the highest bid at a price P equal to second-highest bid. The other two individuals each receive ½P.

(J) For this part only, assume that there are two individuals ($n = 2$). A fair coin is tossed, and the asset goes to person 1 if it turns up heads and to person 2 if it turns up tails. Neither person pays any money or receives any money.

(3) A government agency is accepting tenders for the construction of a public building. There are n firms with an interest in undertaking the project. Each firm i has a minimum cost C_i that it would incur in construction. (C_i includes the opportunity cost of capital.) The contract will be awarded by having the firms submit sealed bids. Firm i's bid B_i is the amount of money that it requires to undertake the project. The contract will be awarded to the firm submitting the lowest bid and that firm will be paid an amount of money equal to the second-lowest bid. Prove that a bid of C_i is a dominant strategy for arbitrary firm i.

(4) The Vickrey auction is used, but ties are broken as follows: if 1 and 2 submit the highest bids and those bids are identical, then the asset goes to bidder 1 at a price equal to 2's bid. Can 1 ever benefit by deviating from truthful revelation? Can 2 ever benefit by deviating from truthful revelation? Can any other bidder ever benefit by deviating from truthful revelation? In each case, if your answer is "no" prove that truthful revelation is a dominant strategy for the bidder in question. If your answer is "yes" provide proof by means of an example.

(5) The Vickrey auction is used, but ties are broken as follows: if 1 and 2 submit the highest bids and those bids are identical, then the asset goes to bidder 1 at a price equal to the next highest bid. (If $b_1 = b_2 = 100$, $b_3 = 80$, and every other bid is below 80 then 1 gets the asset for $80.) Can 1 ever benefit by deviating from truthful revelation? Can 2 ever benefit by deviating from truthful revelation? Can any other bidder ever benefit by deviating from truthful revelation? In each case, if your answer is "no" prove that truthful revelation is a dominant strategy for the bidder in question. If your answer is "yes" provide proof by means of an example.

(6) This question pertains to the Vickrey auction when the asset to be auctioned is owned by one of the participants, individual 0, whose true reservation value is V_0. Answer the following two questions by means of specific numerical examples, one for A and one for B.

(A) Show that if the owner's bid B_0 is used when determining the second-highest bid (and hence the price to charge the winner) then the incentive for truthful revelation is spoiled if the buyer's payment goes to individual 0.

(B) Now, suppose that B_0 is not taken into consideration when determining the price that the winner of the asset will pay. We just use B_0 to determine if agent 0 gets to keep the asset. Show that efficiency may be sacrificed.

(7) Prove the uniqueness of the Vickrey auction when we weaken the participation constraint to the following *normalization rule*: an individual whose reservation value is zero will not see his or her utility change as a result of participating in the auction. (Hint: all you have to do is show that asset efficiency, incentive compatibility, and the normalization rule imply the participation constraint.)

6.3 FOUR BASIC AUCTION MECHANISMS

We have encountered the Vickrey auction. This section considers three other auction formulas. Each of them is frequently employed. We compare them and work out the equilibria for two of them. (The other two have equilibria that are easy to identify.)

6.3.1 Vickrey, English, Dutch, and First-Price Auctions

The Vickrey auction was introduced in Section 6.2. It is a sealed-bid auction, as is the *first-price auction*, which awards the asset to the highest bidder but at a price equal to the winner's bid.

DEFINITION: *First-Price, Sealed-Bid Auction*

Each individual submits a bid. The high bidder receives the asset at a price equal to that high bid.

For both the Vickrey and first-price auctions there is only one round of bidding in which each agent submits his or her bid in a sealed envelope – that is, without disclosing the bid to anyone else. At the deadline for submission the envelopes are opened and the winner is announced. Don't jump to the conclusion that the winner pays less in a Vickrey auction than in a first-price auction. If Nan's reservation value is $1,000, Diane's is $650, and everyone else's is below that, then in a Vickrey auction Nan will bid $1,000, Diane will bid $650, and Nan will win the asset at a price of $650. With a first-price auction Nan would not bid $1,000 because she would not gain anything by paying $1,000 for something worth a maximum of $1,000 to her. She would bid considerably less than $1,000 in a first-price auction. How much less? Sections 6.3.3 and 6.3.4 address that question.

The *English oral auction* is the one that we see in the movies. It has been used by the English auction house Sotheby's since 1744 and by Christie's since 1766. There are many quick rounds of bidding, and each round ends when someone shouts out a bid that is above the previous high. This continues until no one is willing to pay more for the asset than the previous high bid. It is then sold to the individual who made the last bid at a price equal to that bid. Of course, when this auction is used on the internet – by eBay for instance – it is submitted electronically.

DEFINITION: *The English Oral Auction*

The bidders interact directly with each other, in stages. Someone makes an initial bid, and anyone can raise it. This process continues until no one is willing to raise the bid. The asset goes to the last bidder at a price equal to his or her bid.

The *Dutch auction* has been used for centuries to allocate tulip bulbs in the Netherlands. It is the English auction turned upside down: the Dutch auction begins with the auctioneer announcing a ridiculously high price. No one will want the asset at that price, so it is lowered. And the price is lowered again and again, until someone shouts "I'll take it." The asset is then sold to that individual at that price.

DEFINITION: *The Dutch Auction*

The auctioneer announces a very high price and then lowers it in small increments until one of the bidders declares that he or she will buy the asset at the current price. It is then sold to that agent at that price.

6.3.2   Outcome Equivalence

Two auction mechanisms that look quite different, with different rules, can have the same outcome in the sense that the winner would pay the same price in either case. We say that the mechanisms are *outcome equivalent* if that would be true whatever the individual reservation values.

DEFINITION: *Outcome Equivalence*

Two auction mechanisms are outcome equivalent if, however many bidders there are and whatever their reservation values, the same individual would be awarded the asset with either mechanism, and at the same price. Moreover, if the non-winners have to make a payment it would be the same in the two auctions for a given specification of the individual reservation values.

Example 6.9 The Vickrey and English Auctions

We use the reservation values of Table 6.1 of Example 6.2: A's reservation value is 100, B's is 70, C's is 40, and D's is 30. If the Vickrey auction were used then A would win at a price of $70. If the English auction were used, the bidding would not stop at a price below $70 because either A or B would be willing to raise the bid. For either agent, there would be a new higher bid that is still below that agent's reservation value. If that new bid won, there would be a positive profit for the bidder and that would be preferred to the profit of zero that results when someone else gets the asset. Therefore, the bidding won't stop below $70. If A raised the bid to $70 then B would not be willing to bid more, because B's reservation value is only $70. Then A would get the asset for a price of $70. The bidding would not stop below $70, and it would not go above $70. Therefore, the asset would go to A at a price of $70. This is the same outcome as the Vickrey auction.

Theorem
The Vickrey and English auctions are outcome equivalent.

Proof:
It is clear that the argument of Example 6.9 goes through with any number of bidders and any assignment of reservation values.   ∎

We have ignored one possibility. Suppose that B opens the bidding at $50. Then A will raise the bid, but A won't know B's reservation value. If A bids $60 then B might respond with $65. Then A will raise again, but A's second bid might be $72 or $75. Strictly speaking, the best that we can do is claim that the winner of an English auction will pay something very close to the second-highest reservation value but not necessarily precisely that value. For practical purposes the outcomes of the Vickrey and English auctions are essentially the same. We will speak as if they are always identical. In fact, most internet auction sites now use a technique that essentially turns their English auction into a Vickrey auction. To obviate the need for a bidder to sit at a computer terminal for hours, or even days, the software running the auction now allows a bidder to enter the maximum that he or she is willing to pay. The algorithm then raises the bids. submitted by others as long as the maximum has not been reached. This is called proxy bidding.

One advantage of the Vickrey auction over its English twin is the fact that the former does not require the bidders to assemble in the same place or even submit their bids at the same time. This is a consequence of the fact that truthful revelation is a dominant strategy for the Vickrey auction. Even if you knew the bids of every other participant you could not do better than bidding your own reservation value. Consequently, information about the bidding of anyone else is of no value to a bidder in a Vickrey auction, and thus a bidder can submit a sealed bid at any time.

One defect of the Vickrey auction is that bidders may fear that the auctioneer will cheat and announce a second-highest bid that is substantially above the one that was actually submitted. This raises the selling price, of course, and thus the auctioneer's commission. This danger is even more acute if the auctioneer is also the seller. This sort of overstatement is not possible with the English auction because the bids come directly from the lips of the bidders. In addition, with a Vickrey auction the bidders may fear that a very high bid will tip the seller off to the asset's true value, resulting in the item being withdrawn. In the case of an English auction, neither the seller nor the auctioneer will find out how high the winner was prepared to go. However, because the two auctions are outcome equivalent, and the Vickrey auction is easier to analyze, we continue to give it serious consideration.

Surprisingly, the Dutch and the first-price auctions always lead to the same outcome.

Example 6.10 The Dutch and First-Price Auctions

A's reservation value is 100, B's is 70, C's is 40, and D's is 30. Suppose that the first-price, sealed-bid auction is used. We'll put ourselves in the shoes of agent A. He wants to outbid the other three, but at the same time wants to get the asset at a low price. He doesn't know the reservation values of the other three bidders, and even if he did he wouldn't know how much each would bid. Agents have to determine their bids as a function of their own reservation values *and* as a function the bids they expect the others to make, knowing that their bidding strategies will be based in part on what they think that others will bid. Suppose that A decides that a bid of $75 maximizes his expected payoff when the first-price auction is used. It follows that if a Dutch auction is used instead, A would claim the asset when the price got down to $75, provided that no one else claimed it at a higher price. Here's why: in a Dutch auction bidder A is in precisely the situation that he faces in deciding what to bid in a first-price auction. In either case he doesn't know what the others will bid, so he has to decide how much he will pay if no one else outbids him. Granted, in a Dutch auction the bidders get some information about what the others are prepared to bid. As the auctioneer brings the price down from $200 to $175 to $150 they learn that the maximum anyone is prepared to pay is below $150. But that is no longer useful information to anyone who has decided that he or she will not claim the asset at a price above $75. It would be valuable information to someone who decided to claim the asset at a price of $175. If that bidder knew in advance that no one else would pay more than $150 then that bidder wouldn't have to pay $175. But the only way to find that out in a Dutch auction is to let the price fall below $175, and then the bidder might lose the asset to someone else, although he or she would have been prepared to pay $175. In short, the bidders have more information in a Dutch auction than in a first-price auction, but by the time they get that information it is no longer of value. With either auction, the bidder has to decide the price at which he or she will buy the asset, should that be the high bid, and he or she has to do it before the bidding starts.

Given the individual reservation values, the amount that each decides to bid in a first-price auction will be the same as in a Dutch auction. Therefore, the same individual will win in both cases, and the price will be the same.

Theorem
The Dutch and First-Price Auctions are Outcome Equivalent

A good way to show that the Dutch and first-price auctions are outcome equivalent is to turn one into the other. Imagine that n bidders have assembled to participate in a first-price auction. The auctioneer begins by saying, "I'm feeling too lazy to open a bunch of envelopes. I'll call out numbers, starting very high, and then lower them in small increments. Shout when I call the number that you have placed in your envelope. The first one to shout will be the high bidder, and hence the winner of the first-price auction. I'll check your envelope to make sure that the price at which you claimed the asset is in fact the bid in your envelope."

Suppose that the auctioneer omits the last sentence. No one is going to check to see if the price at which you claim the asset is the same as the bid that you decided on when you thought it would be a conventional first-price auction. That means that you can claim the asset at any price you like, provided that no one else has claimed it first. Would you claim the asset at a price that is different from the bid that you decided on before you knew about the rule change? In other words, is the information that you get when the price falls, and you discover that no one was willing to claim the asset at a higher price, of use to you in revising your bid? No. The same number of bidders remain – no one has claimed the asset – and you don't know what their bids are. As soon as someone does claim the asset you learn something, but it's too late to be of use.

We've just shown that we can turn a first-price auction into a Dutch auction, and that the equilibrium bids will not change. Whatever bid is optimal for someone in the former will be optimal in the latter. Now, imagine that n bidders have assembled to participate in a Dutch auction. Before it gets under way the auctioneer circulates the following memo: "I have laryngitis. Instead of calling out prices, starting high and then slowly lower the price, I'm asking you to write down the price at which you've decided to claim the asset – assuming that no one has beaten you to it – and seal it in an envelope and hand it to me. I will then open the envelopes to see who would have won the Dutch auction if I had conducted it in the usual fashion." Would this change in procedure cause you to submit a price that is different from the one at which you had decided to claim the asset when you thought it would be a conventional Dutch auction? No, because you are in the same position in either case. A Dutch auction can be turned into a first-price auction. The price at which an individual decides to claim the asset with the Dutch auction will be the bid that the individual submits in the first-price version. The two schemes are outcome equivalent.

We know that for both the Vickrey and English auctions the price paid by the winner will be equal to the second-highest reservation value. The seller won't know what that value is, so the seller won't know how much revenue to expect if either of those auctions is used. However, we do at least have a useful starting point. But for the Dutch and first-price auctions we need to work out the price paid by the winner as a function of the individual reservation values.

6.3.3 Equilibrium Bids in a First-Price, Sealed-Bid Auction

Suppose that you are one of the bidders in a first-price, sealed-bid auction of a single asset. You know that your reservation value is v_1, but you don't know anyone else's. How should you bid? You don't want to bid v_1 because if you won then you would be paying v_1 dollars for an asset that is worth no more than v_1 to you. Your payoff-maximizing strategy is to bid something less than v_1. But how much less? To simplify our calculations, we'll assume that there is only one other bidder. We'll also assume that bidder 2's value v_2 is somewhere between 0 and 1, and that from your point of view any value in that interval is just as likely to be the actual v_2 as is any other value in the interval. (We are really supposing that both bidders agree that the asset has a maximum possible value of, say, $10 million to anyone, and the value placed on the asset by bidder i is the fraction v_i of that number. Hence, if $v_2 = 0.72$ we're saying that bidder 2's reservation value is $7.2 million.)

In assuming that bidder 2's value is a random draw from the interval from 0 to 1, with each value being as likely as any other, we are employing the *uniform probability distribution* for v_2. (See Section 2.6.5 of Chapter 2.) In short, this means that the probability that v_2 is less than a given number β is β itself. This holds for any value β in the interval. So, the probability that bidder 2's value is less than 0.8 is 0.8, the probability that bidder 2's value is less than 0.35 is 0.35, and so on. The probability that your reservation value v_1 is higher than bidder 2's value is v_1, because that's the probability that v_2 is less than v_1. But you need to know the probability that b_2 is less than b_1, where b_1 and b_2 are, respectively, the bids of individuals 1 and 2.

Suppose that the optimal strategy is to submit a bid equal to the fraction λ of one's reservation value. Then b_2 will equal λv_2, but you still don't know the value of v_2. But now you know that b_2 will never exceed λ, because v_2 cannot be larger than 1, so λv_2 cannot be larger than λ. That means that it is not payoff maximizing for you to submit a bid greater than λ. Of course a bid of $\beta > \lambda$ would win for sure, because $b_2 \le \lambda$. But a bid halfway between λ and β would also win for sure, for the same reason. You'd still get the asset, but you'd pay less for it than if you had bid β. In general, no bid greater than λ can be payoff maximizing for you. Therefore, you can restrict your attention to bids $b_1 \le \lambda$. Because v_2 is uniformly distributed on the interval 0 to 1, we can think of $b_2 = \lambda v_2$ as being uniformly distributed on the interval 0 to λ.

What's the probability that a random draw from the uniform distribution on the interval 0 to λ is less than b_1? It's just b_1 / λ, the distance from 0 to b_1 as a fraction of the length of the interval 0 to λ itself.

Here is an alternative derivation of the probability of winning with a bid of b_1 when $b_2 = \lambda v_2$:

$$\text{Prob}(b_1 > b_2) = \text{Prob}(b_1 > \lambda v_2) = \text{Prob}(\lambda v_2 < b_1) = \text{Prob}(v_2 < b_1/\lambda) = b_1/\lambda.$$

Example 6.11 The Probability that Your Bid is Highest

If $\lambda = \frac{3}{4}$ and $b_1 = \frac{3}{8}$ then λv_2 will be less than b_1 for half of the values of λv_2 in the interval from 0 to $\frac{3}{4}$. If $\lambda = \frac{3}{4}$ and $b_1 = \frac{1}{4}$ then $\lambda v_2 < b_1$ for one-third of the values of λv_2 in the interval from 0 to $\frac{3}{4}$. Suppose that $\lambda = \frac{1}{2}$. Then for $b_1 = \frac{3}{8}$ (respectively, $b_1 = \frac{1}{4}$) we have $\lambda v_2 < b_1$ for three-quarters (respectively, one-half) of the values of λv_2 in the interval from 0 to $\frac{1}{2}$.

In general, the probability that λv_2 is less than a given b_1 is b_1/λ. That's the probability that bidder 1's bid is higher than bidder 2's bid.

We use the word profit for the gain that bidder J realizes, *given* that J acquires the asset. If the asset is worth v_1 to you, but you paid b_1 your *profit* is $v_1 - b_1$. Your *payoff* from a bid of b_1 is the probability of winning with b_1 multiplied by the profit you get when you do win.

DEFINITION: *Profit and Payoff*

Given that bidder J has acquired the asset, J's profit is $v_J - p$, the value of the asset to J minus the price p paid. J's payoff is J's profit multiplied by the probability of winning the asset.

We want to find the bidding strategy that maximizes your payoff because you (bidder 1) have to decide what to bid before knowing if you will get the asset. Your payoff from a bid of b_1 is

$$\frac{b_1}{\lambda} \times (v_1 - b_1)$$

because b_1/λ is the probability of winning with a bid of b_1. Note that we are assuming that the individual is risk neutral. (See Section 2.6.2 of Chapter 2.)

Theorem: Nash Equilibrium with Two Bidders in a First-Price Auction

If the bidders are risk neutral and each models the other's reservation value as a random draw from the uniform probability distribution from 0 to some given positive K, then at a symmetric Nash equilibrium both will submit bids equal to half of their respective reservation values.

Proof:

To find your payoff-maximizing bid we have to determine the value of b_1 that maximizes

$$(b_1/\lambda) \times (v_1 - b_1) = (v_1/\lambda)b_1 - (1/\lambda)b_1^2,$$

a simple quadratic. Employ the formula for maximizing a quadratic or use elementary calculus. We get

$$b_1 = \frac{v_1/\lambda}{2/\lambda} = \frac{v_1}{2}.$$

Therefore, if you expect bidder 2 to submit a bid equal to some fraction of her reservation value, then you maximize your payoff by sending in a bid equal to *half* your reservation value. Of course, because your bid is a fraction of your reservation value, bidder 2 maximizes her payoff by setting her bid equal to half her reservation value. (We're assuming that bidder 2 is clever enough to deduce that you will set $b_1 = \frac{1}{2}v_1$.) We have a Nash equilibrium: each person is playing a best response to the other's strategy. ∎

We proved that for any λ, if bidder j sets $b_j = \lambda v_j$ then bidder i's payoff will be maximized by setting $b_i = \frac{1}{2}v_i$. But it is possible that $\frac{1}{2}v_i > \lambda$. We know that *that* does not maximize i's payoff. A slightly smaller bid will guarantee that i wins, and the price paid will be slightly lower. Now, i's payoff as a function of b_i is a hill-shaped quadratic, and thus if we maximize that payoff subject to $b_i \leq \lambda$ we get $b_i = \frac{1}{2}v_i$ if $\frac{1}{2}v_i \leq \lambda$ but if $\frac{1}{2}v_i > \lambda$ the solution must be $b_i = \lambda$. However, if $\lambda = \frac{1}{2}$ then we will certainly have $\frac{1}{2}v_i \leq \frac{1}{2}$ because $v_i \leq 1$. Therefore, we really do have a Nash equilibrium with two bidders when both submit bids equal to half their respective reservation values.

We have discovered that if there are two bidders in a first-price auction then the seller's revenue will be exactly half of the larger of the two reservation values because that is the price paid by the winner. Because the Dutch and first-price auctions are outcome equivalent we have also shown that the seller's revenue from a Dutch auction will be exactly half of the larger of the two reservation values.

Now, suppose that there are more than two bidders. The larger the number of bidders, the greater the probability that someone else has a high reservation value and hence is prepared to submit a high bid. Therefore, the more bidders there are, the greater the probability that the high bid among all the others is close to the maximum that you would be prepared to bid. That means that the greater the number of bidders, the higher you will have to bid to maximize your payoff. With n bidders we have an equilibrium in which each individual i sets

$$b_i = \frac{n-1}{n} \times v_i.$$

Theorem: Nash Equilibrium with n Bidders in a First-Price Auction

If the bidders are risk neutral and each models the others' reservation values as random draws from the uniform probability distribution from 0 to some given positive K, then at a symmetric Nash equilibrium each will submit a bid equal to the fraction $(n-1)/n$ of his or her reservation value.

If you know a little calculus you can prove this with ease, as we do in the next subsection.

It follows that if there are n bidders in a first-price or a Dutch auction then the seller's revenue will be the fraction $(n-1)/n$ of the largest reservation value.

∂6.3.4 The Case of n Bidders

Suppose that you, bidder 1, are in competition with $n-1$ other risk-neutral bidders in a first-price, sealed-bid auction. As in Section 6.3.3, the probability that your bid is higher than individual i's, when $b_i = \lambda v_i$, is b_1/λ. The probability that b_1 is higher than *everyone else's* bid is the probability that b_1 is higher than b_2, *and b_1 is* higher than b_3, *and b_1 is higher than $b_4, \ldots, and b_1$ is higher than b_n. The probability that b_1 is higher than each other b_i is

$$\frac{b_1}{\lambda} \times \frac{b_1}{\lambda} \times \frac{b_1}{\lambda} \times \ldots \times \frac{b_1}{\lambda} = \frac{b_1^{n-1}}{\lambda^{n-1}}.$$

Therefore, your payoff from a bid of b_1 is

$$\frac{b_1^{n-1}}{\lambda^{n-1}} \times (v_1 - b_1) = \frac{v_1}{\lambda^{n-1}} b_1^{n-1} - \frac{b_1^n}{\lambda^{n-1}}.$$

Maximize this function: the first derivative (with respect to b_1) must be zero at the maximum, because $b_1 = 0$ can't be the solution. (With a bid of zero the probability if winning is zero, and hence the payoff is zero. But with $v_1 > 0$ and a bid of even $0.1 v_1$ there is a positive, but very small, probability of winning and getting a positive profit of $0.9 v_1$.) When we take the first derivative of bidder 1's payoff function and set it equal to zero we get

$$(n - 1) \frac{v_1}{\lambda^{n-1}} b_1^{n-2} - n \frac{b_1^{n-1}}{\lambda^{n-1}} = 0.$$

Because λ is positive (no one will bid zero at equilibrium) and b_1 is positive we can multiply both sides by λ^{n-1}/b_1^{n-2} to obtain $(n-1)v_1 - nb_1 = 0$, the solution of which is

$$b_1 = \frac{n - 1}{n} v_1.$$

With n bidders we have an equilibrium when all individuals submit a bid equal to the fraction $(n-1)/n$ of their reservation values. (Note that if every $i > 1$ sets $b_i = (n - 1)v_i/n$ then $(n - 1)v_1/n$ does not exceed $\lambda = (n - 1)/n$. Therefore, for each bidder j setting $b_j = (n - 1)v_j/n$ clearly is a best response by j to the strategy $b_i = (n - 1)v_i/n$ for all $i \neq j$.)

Source
The paragraph on proxy bidding is based on Lucking-Reiley (2000).

Link
Krishna (2002) is a very technical, but insightful, presentation of auction theory.

Problem Set

(1) Explain why the first-price, sealed-bid auction is *not* outcome equivalent to the Vickrey auction.

(2) Explain why the English auction is *not* outcome equivalent to the Dutch auction.

(3) There are two bidders in a first-price, sealed-bid auction. Bidder 1 has learned that bidder 2 plans to bid $50. What is bidder 1's payoff-maximizing response as a function of his or her reservation value? Each bid must be an integer and a tie goes to bidder 2.

(4) There are two bidders in a first-price, sealed-bid auction. Bidder 1 knows that individual 2 will submit a bid of $19 with probability ½ and $49 with

probability ½. Under each of the following four assumptions, calculate individual 1's payoff-maximizing bid, determine the probability of person 1 winning the asset, and calculate bidder 1's payoff. Each bid must be an integer and a tie goes to bidder 2.

(A) Bidder 1's reservation value is $100.

(B) Bidder 1's reservation value is $60.

(C) Bidder 1's reservation value is $30.

(D) Bidder 1's reservation value is $15.

(5) There are two bidders in a first-price, sealed-bid auction. Bidder 1 knows that individual 2 will submit a bid of $29 with probability ⅔ and $59 with probability ⅓. Under each of the following four assumptions, calculate individual 1's payoff-maximizing bid, determine the probability of person 1 winning the asset, and calculate bidder 1's payoff. Each bid must be an integer and a tie goes to bidder 2.

(A) Bidder 1's reservation value is $99.

(B) Bidder 1's reservation value is $60.

(C) Bidder 1's reservation value is $42.

(D) Bidder 1's reservation value is $15.

(6) There are two bidders in an English auction. Bidder 1's reservation value is $75. Determine bidder 1's payoff-maximizing bid, the winner of the asset, the price paid, and person 1's payoff, under each of the following four assumptions:

(A) Bidder 2's reservation value is $100.

(B) Bidder 2's reservation value is $60.

(C) Bidder 2's reservation value is $30.

(D) Bidder 2's reservation value is $15.

(7) Determine an individual's payoff-maximizing bidding strategy at equilibrium in a first-price, sealed-bid auction for the following four cases:

(A) There are two bidders and each reservation value is drawn from the uniform probability distribution on the interval from 0 to 5.

(B) There are two bidders and each reservation value is drawn from the uniform probability distribution on the interval from 2 to 5.

(∂C) There are four bidders and each reservation value is drawn from the uniform probability distribution on the interval 0 to 1.

(∂D) There are four bidders and each reservation value is drawn from the uniform probability distribution on the interval 1 to 11.

(8) There are two bidders, A and B. Each bidder's value is drawn from the uniform probability distribution, with values between zero and unity, inclusive. Will the first-price, sealed-bid auction and the Vickrey auction yield the same revenue when $V_A = $ ¾ and $V_B = $ ¼, where V_i is the value that i places on the asset? (The two auctions will generate the same revenue on average, but this question asks you for the revenues in the specific situation $V_A = ¾$ and $V_B = ¼$.)

(9) There are two bidders, A and B. Each bidder's value is drawn from the uniform probability distribution, with values between zero and unity, inclusive. Will the English auction and the first-price, sealed-bid auction yield the same revenue when $V_A = ¾$ and $V_B = ¼$, where V_i is the value that i places on the asset?

6.4   REVENUE EQUIVALENCE

The seller of an item at auction wants as much revenue as possible. Therefore, many different types of auctions have to be considered to see which would be most profitable from the seller's point of view. This is problematic because auction A might be optimal for one range of buyer reservation values, whereas auction B is best for a different range of values. The buyers know their own reservation values, but these are unknown to the seller. From the seller's point of view, we can think of the buyer reservation values as random variables drawn from some probability distribution. The seller will want to employ the auction that maximizes the *seller's expected revenue*. We assume in this section that buyers and seller are risk neutral.

The surprise is that there is a large family of auctions that generate the same expected revenue. Each has its own set of formulas to determine who wins and how much each bidder pays. Astonishingly, the expected revenue is the same for each auction in the family, which we refer to as the set of standard auctions.

DEFINITION: *Standard Auction Mechanism*

If an agent with a reservation value of zero gets a payoff of zero at equilibrium and the agent with the highest reservation value always gets the asset at equilibrium we say that the auction mechanism is a standard one.

A standard auction is not necessarily a direct mechanism. The first-price, sealed bid auction is obviously standard: no one who places a zero value on the asset will submit a positive bid, and the higher the reservation value the higher is the individual's optimal bid at equilibrium. Therefore, the high-value agent will win the asset at an equilibrium of a first-price, sealed-bid auction. But it is not a direct mechanism because individuals are not asked to report their reservation values. At equilibrium, all individuals bid amounts equal to a fraction of their respective reservation values. Fortunately, in proving the revenue equivalence theorem, we do not have to go into detail as far as the bidding is concerned. We map individuals' reservation values into their payoffs at equilibrium, embedding all the details in this mapping.

In general, the agent with the highest reservation value may not submit a bid equal to his or her reservation value. But as long as the *equilibrium* strategies result in the asset going to the agent with the highest reservation value, the second defining condition of a standard auction will be satisfied.

The Revenue Equivalence Theorem

If each of the n agents is risk neutral and each has a privately known value independently drawn from a common probability distribution, then all standard auctions have the bidders making the same expected payments at equilibrium, given their respective values, and thus the seller's expected revenue is the same for all standard auctions.

To see what's behind the revenue equivalence theorem, compare the first-price, sealed-bid auction with the all-pay auction. The all-pay auction requires each participant to submit a sealed bid, and the high bidder gets the asset at a price equal to his or her bid. However, *all* participants have to pay the seller the amount of their bids. The fact that you pay whether you win or not depresses your bid – for two reasons. First, you know that you will have to pay even if you lose, so every dollar you bid has a higher expected cost than it would in a first-price auction. Second, you know that others are in the same situation and hence will be submitting low bids, so the benefit of adding a dollar to your bid is also lower – it's not as likely to be key to winning. So, everyone will be paying the seller a small amount of money in an all-pay auction, and the seller's expected revenue turns out to be the same as in a first-price auction. Before proving the general theorem we'll illustrate what revenue equivalence *is* with an elementary situation.

Example 6.12 Two Bidders and Two Pairs of Reservation Values

There are two bidders and only two possible scenarios: case A, in which v_1 is 240 and v_2 is 200. For Case B, $v_1 = 70$ and $v_2 = 300$. With the Vickrey auction all individuals' bids are equal to their reservation values. Hence, in Case A if the Vickrey auction were employed the asset would go to agent 1 at a price of 200. However, if the first-price, sealed-bid auction were used and agent 1 bids 120 and agent 2 bids 100 – half their respective reservation values – agent 1 would get the asset for 120. If the Vickrey auction were employed in Case B, the asset would go to individual 2 at a price of 70, but if the first-price, sealed-bid auction were used instead, agent 2 would get the asset for 150 if agent 1 bids 35 and agent 2 bids 150.

Now, suppose that Case A occurs with probability ½, and so does Case B. Then the expected revenue from the Vickrey auction is $½ \times 200 + ½ \times 70 = 135$, and expected revenue from the first-price auction is $½ \times 120 + ½ \times 150 = 135$ also, as shown in Table 6.2.

The two auctions provide the same expected revenue in Example 6.12. This is not true in general when there are only two possible scenarios. The purpose of the example is to show what revenue equivalence means: it's weaker than outcome

Table 6.2

	Seller's Revenue		
Auction	Case A	Case B	Average
Vickrey	200	70	135
First-price	120	150	135

equivalence because we're only claiming that revenue will be the same *on average* for any two standard auctions. To prove this we need to assume that the possible reservation values stretch over a wide range.

6.4.1 Revenue Equivalence for the Four Basic Auctions

This subsection gives an intuitive explanation of revenue equivalence for a narrow but important family of cases. (The formal proof is in Sections 6.4.5 and 6.4.6. The latter is shorter, but it employs integral calculus.)

Assume that all reservation values are drawn from the uniform distribution. We show that the Vickrey and first-price auctions are revenue equivalent.

Theorem: Expected Revenue from the Vickrey and First-Price Auctions

If there are n bidders and each views the other reservation values as random draws from the uniform probability distribution on the interval [0,1] then the expected revenue from both auctions is $(n-1)/(n+1)$. If $n = 2$ then the expected revenue is ⅓ with either auction.

We begin with the case of two bidders. Because the values are uniformly distributed in the interval 0 to 1, the average high bid V_H and the average low bid V_L divide the interval into three segments of equal length (Figure 6.1). The average second highest reservation value is ⅓, and hence average price paid by the winner ⅓, which is the expected revenue from the Vickrey auction.

Because bidders in a first-price auction submit bids equal to half their reservation values, the average reservation value of the winner is ⅔ with a bid of half that, or ⅓. Therefore, the expected revenue from the first-price auction is ⅓, the same as for the Vickrey auction. (The next Section, 6.4.2, rigorously proves that the average low reservation value is ⅓ and the average high is ⅔, but integral calculus is used.)

Now, let's do the general case, with n bidders. Again, we assume that the reservation values are uniformly distributed in the interval 0 to 1, but there are n

Figure 6.1

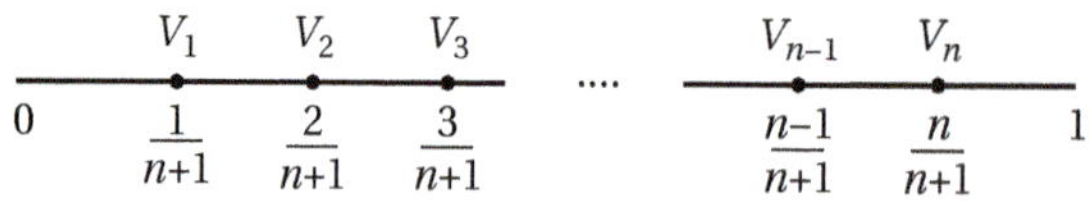

Figure 6.2

of them this time. They will divide the interval into $n + 1$ segments of equal length, as shown in Figure 6.2. The average second-highest bid is $(n − 1)/(n+1)$, and hence the expected revenue from the Vickrey auction is $(n − 1)/(n+ 1)$.

In a first-price auction with n bidders, payoff maximization requires the individuals to submit bids equal to the fraction $(n − 1)/n$ of their reservation values. The average high value is $n/(n + 1)$, and thus the average price paid by the winner is $[(n − 1)/n] \times [n/(n + 1)] = (n − 1)/(n + 1)$, which is then the seller's expected revenue from the first-price auction, the same as it is for the Vickrey auction.

Finally, because the first-price auction is outcome equivalent to the Dutch auction, and the Vickrey auction is outcome equivalent to the English auction, we have established the revenue equivalence of all four auctions when the reservation values are drawn from the uniform distribution. (If two auction mechanisms are outcome equivalent, then for *any* specification of the individual reservation values, the price paid by each agent will be the same for either auction, and thus the seller's actual revenue will be the same.) The next subsection uses integral calculus to prove the revenue equivalence of the four basic auctions when the reservation values have the uniform probability distribution.

∂6.4.2 Expected Revenue is Equal for the Vickrey and First-Price Auctions

We again assume that there are two bidders, and that each treats the other's reservation value as a random draw from the interval 0 to 1. We begin by calculating expected revenue for the Vickrey auction.

We know that all individuals will submit bids equal to their reservation values. Let r denote the value of one of the bidders and let s denote the value of the other. Then one person will bid r, and the other will bid s. Consider a particular value of r. When s is less than r, the bidder who submitted r will win the asset and will pay s, the second-highest bid. When s is more than r the second-highest bid will be r, and that will be the price paid for that range of values of s. Therefore, given r, the seller's expected revenue from the Vickrey auction is

$$\int_0^r s\, ds + \int_r^1 r\, ds = 0.5r^2 + r(1 − r) = r − 0.5r^2.$$

This is obviously a function of r, which is not fixed – it's a random variable. Therefore, the seller's expected revenue (ER) is

$$ER = \int_0^1 (r − 0.5r^2)\, dr.$$

Because $\int r \, dr - \int \frac{1}{2} r^2 dr = r^2/2 - r^3/6$ we have $ER = 1^2/2 - 1^3/6 - (0^2/2 - 0^3/6) = \frac{1}{2} - \frac{1}{6} = \frac{1}{3}$, as we claimed in the previous subsection. Note that this calculation also proves that the average low reservation value is $\frac{1}{3}$.

Now calculate ER for the first-price auction for which all individuals will submit bids equal to half their reservation values. When r and s are the values then the bids will be $\frac{1}{2}r$ and $\frac{1}{2}s$, respectively. For a particular value of r, when s is less than r the winner (the one bidding r) will pay $\frac{1}{2}r$. When s is more than r the winner (the one bidding s) will pay $\frac{1}{2}s$. Therefore, given r, the seller's expected revenue from the first-price auction is

$$\int_0^r 0.5r \, ds + \int_r^1 0.5s \, ds.$$

Because $\int \frac{1}{2}r \, ds = \frac{1}{2}rs$ and $\int \frac{1}{2}s \, ds = \frac{1}{4}s^2$ we have

$$\int_0^r 0.5r \, ds + \int_r^1 0.5s \, ds = (0.5r \times r - 0.5r \times 0) + (0.25 \times 1^2 - 0.25 \times r^2)$$

$$= 0.25r^2 + 0.25.$$

This is obviously a function of the random variable r. Therefore, the seller's expected revenue is

$$ER = \int_0^1 (0.25r^2 + 0.25) \, dr.$$

Because $\int \frac{1}{4}r^2 \, dr = r^3/12$ and $\int \frac{1}{4} dr = \frac{1}{4}r$, we have

$$ER = \frac{1^3}{12} - \frac{0^3}{12} + \frac{1}{4} - \frac{0}{4} = \frac{1}{12} + \frac{1}{4} = \frac{1}{3}$$

the same as the expected revenue for the Vickrey auction.

We can use a similar derivation to show that the average high reservation value is $\frac{2}{3}$. When $r < s$ the high is s and when $r > s$ the high is r. Therefore, given s the average high is

$$\int_0^s s \, dr + \int_s^1 r \, dr = s^2 + 0.5(1 - s^2) = 0.5s^2 + 0.5.$$

Because s itself is a random variable the average high is

$$\int_0^1 (0.5s^2 + 0.5) \, ds = 1/6 + 1/2 = \frac{2}{3}.$$

6.4.3 Other Probability Distributions

Let's assume that the reservation values are drawn from a distribution that is not uniform. After all, we would expect relatively small probabilities for values that are extremely high or extremely low. We won't actually specify the distribution in this section. Therefore, we can't calculate the equilibrium configuration of strategies for the first-price auction. We do assume that the distribution is known by all n bidders. The best that we can do is to let $\sigma(v_i)$ denote the optimal bid for an individual with reservation value v_i. Of course, $\sigma(v_i)$ will be higher as v_i is higher. Therefore, the asset will be won by the individual with the highest reservation value for a price of $\sigma(v_H)$, where H denotes the individual with the highest v_i.

Now, consider a sealed-bid auction in which the asset goes to the high bidder for a price that is *four times* that bid. It is not hard to see that the optimal strategy for someone participating in this auction is to bid $\frac{1}{4}\sigma(v_i)$. Therefore, the winner will pay $4 \times \frac{1}{4} \times \sigma(v_H)$, which is the same as the price paid with the first-price auction. Therefore, the two auctions are outcome equivalent, and hence they generate the same revenue. We will see that even standard auctions that are not outcome equivalent are revenue equivalent. *On average*, the expected payments by a given bidder will be the same in the two auctions. To prove this we have to track the payments made by a bidder in equilibrium.

6.4.4   Equilibrium Payoffs

We begin by reducing an auction to its bare essentials, assuming a given number n of bidders and a given probability distribution for an individual's reservation value. To see what the seller will gain, we have to spend some time figuring out what the buyers will do. We are going to highlight the strategy and the profit of a generic agent whose value for the asset to be auctioned is represented by v. From the point of view of the seller, v is a random variable drawn from a particular probability distribution: the agent's reservation value v is known precisely to the agent, but because v is unknown to the seller, the seller will calculate his expected revenue as though the individual reservation values were random variables.

Assume a particular auction mechanism, and let $\mu(v)$ denote the expected payoff at equilibrium of our bidder when his or her reservation value is v. If the agent is a business then $\mu(v)$ is expected profit in the usual sense. If the agent is a household, bidding on a painting say, then $\mu(v)$ will denote expected utility net of the purchase price. We assume that all bidders are risk neutral, which simply means that they seek to maximize $\mu(v)$.

Let $p(v)$ be the probability that an agent with reservation value v gets the asset. Given that the agent knows his or her own v, and that the agent assumes that the reservation values of the other agents are drawn from the given probability distribution, the agent can calculate the probability $p(v)$ of getting the asset after submitting the bid that is optimal at equilibrium, given what the agent knows. Therefore, the expected value of the asset is $v \times p(v)$. In words, it is the value the agent places on the asset multiplied by the probability of getting it. But if the agent wins the asset then he or she will have to make a payment to the seller, and we let $e(v)$ denote the expected value of the payment at equilibrium. In some auctions, one or more losers have to make a payment. In general, $e(v)$ is the expected value of the payment at equilibrium made by a bidder with reservation value v, whether or not that bidder wins.

DEFINITION: *Equilibrium Quantities*

For a bidder with reservation value v, we let $p(v)$ denote the probability of winning the auction and receiving the asset and $e(v)$ is the expected payment. We allow for the possibility that the winner is not the only one who makes a payment. A bidder's payoff (expected profit) is $\mu(v)$.

By definition, a bidder's *expected* profit is value of the asset to that bidder multiplied by the probability of winning it, net of the expected payment that has to be made. In symbols,

$$\mu(v) = vp(v) - e(v).$$

This is the basic identity on which everything else hinges. It is comparable to saying that a manufacturing firm's profit is revenue minus cost.

Example 6.13 $\mu(v)$ and $e(v)$ for a First-Price Auction with Two Bidders

There are two bidders. Diane's reservation value is \$120, and the probability of winning is ⅓ with the bid that is payoff maximizing at equilibrium for someone with $v = 120$. At equilibrium, a bid of ½ × 120 = 60 is payoff maximizing for Diane. When she wins, the profit is 120 − 60 = 60, and that happens ⅓ of the time. Hence $\mu(120) = $ ⅓ × 60 = 20. Now let's calculate $\mu(120)$ by using $\mu(v) = vp(v) - e(v)$: We have $p(120) = $ ⅓ by assumption. Diane's payment when she wins is 60, so $e(120) = $ ⅓ × 60 = 20. Then $\mu(120) = 120 \times $ ⅓ $ - 20 = 20$.

There are auctions in which even the losers have to pay. An all-pay auction requires each participant to submit a bid. The winner is the high bidder, and the price is the amount that the winner bid. But all losers also pay the amounts that they bid. In that case, all bids will be depressed relative to a first-price auction. The fact that your bid is lower in an all-pay auction than it would have been in a first-price auction is due to the fact that you have to pay your bid even if you lose, *and* you know that the other bidders will be in the same position and hence will bid relatively low. According to the revenue equivalence theorem, the total amount taken in by the seller on average will be the same in an all-pay auction as in a first-price auction.

Example 6.14 The Winner Has to Pay Four Times the Bid

Suppose that there are n bidders in an auction that awards the asset to the high bidder at a price equal to *four times* the winner's bid. No one else pays anything. It is easy to see why this auction will yield the same revenue as the first-price, sealed-bid auction. (We do not necessarily assume the uniform probability distribution.) Let b_1, b_2, b_3, ..., b_n denote the equilibrium bids in a conventional first-price auction. Then ¼b_1, ¼b_2, ¼b_3, ..., ¼b_n will be the equilibrium bids in the new auction. Here's why: an individual's probability of winning will be the same with both auctions: the probability that $b_i > b_j$ is the same as the probability that $\frac{1}{4}b_i > \frac{1}{4}b_j$. Moreover, the profit *if* you win is the same, because $v_i - b_i = v_i - 4 \times \frac{1}{4}b_i$. Therefore, $\frac{1}{4}b_i$ maximizes i's expected payoff in the new auction if b_i, maximizes i's payoff in the first-price auction.

6.4.5 Proof of the Revenue Equivalence Theorem

Assume a particular auction mechanism. We put the spotlight on a particular bidder, and begin by proving that for a given reservation value the bidder's expected payoff is the same in any two standard auctions. We do this by showing that expected payoff depends only on the individual's reservation value and on the details of the probability distribution from which the reservation values are drawn, not on anything specific to the auction mechanism itself.

We can solve the identity $\mu(v) = vp(v) - e(v)$ for $e(v)$: we obtain

$$e(v) = vp(v) - \mu(v).$$

In words, the difference between the expected value of the asset and the expected payoff from owning the asset must be the expected payment that one must make to have a chance of acquiring the asset.

So far we haven't said much, but we begin to make progress by considering the possibility that the agents can misrepresent their reservation values to increase their expected payoff. But if $\mu(v)$ is an agent's expected payoff *at equilibrium*, it must be the highest payoff that the agent can get, given what this agent knows about others. This agent may be misrepresenting his or her reservation value, but at equilibrium the agent does so in a way that maximizes the return. Consider a different strategy s, by which we mean adopting the strategy that would be optimal for someone with reservation value s. Let $\mu(v \mid s)$ denote the expected payoff to an agent with reservation value v when that agent masquerades as someone with reservation value s. We have

$$\mu(v|s) = v \times p(s) - e(s).$$

Let's explain this: the agent is behaving as an s type, so he or she has to pay the amount $e(s)$ that an s type would be required to pay. And the agent will win the asset with probability $p(s)$. However, the agent's true reservation value is v, so her expected revenue is $v \times p(s)$. Consequently, $\mu(v \mid s) = v \times p(s) - e(s)$.

Example 6.15 Misrepresentation in a First-Price Auction with Two Bidders

Each bidder views the other's reservation value as a random draw from the uniform probability distribution. Diane's reservation value is $120, in which case a bid of $\frac{1}{2} \times 120 = 60$ is payoff maximizing for her at equilibrium. If she were to bid 50 she would be masquerading as an individual whose reservation value is $s = 100$. Therefore, $\mu(120|100) = 120 \times p(100) - e(100)$.

We know that $e(s) = sp(s) - \mu(s)$. Therefore, for any v and s,

$$\mu(v|s) = vp(s) - e(s) = vp(s) - sp(s) + \mu(s)$$

which can be written
$$\mu(v|s) = \mu(s) + (v - s)p(s).$$

In words, the expected payoff to a v type from employing the strategy that would be payoff maximizing for an s type is the payoff $\mu(s)$ that an s type would get plus $v - s$, the difference in the actual value of the asset to a v type, weighted by the probability that the individual would get the asset by employing the strategy of an s type.

Because $\mu(v)$ is the best that a type-v agent can do, we must have $\mu(v) \geq \mu(v \mid s)$. If we had $\mu(v \mid s) > \mu(v)$ then the agent would do better masquerading as a type-s agent than the agent does at equilibrium, contradicting the fact that $\mu(v)$ is her expected return at equilibrium, where each agent maximizes her expected payoff. (If the agent can do better, we can't be at equilibrium.) Therefore, $\mu(v) \geq \mu(v \mid s)$. Because $\mu(v \mid s) = \mu(s) + (v - s)p(s)$, we have

$$\mu(v) \geq \mu(s) + (v - s)p(s). \tag{12}$$

Given v, this is true for all s. Hence [12] is true for all v and s.

Before returning to the formal argument, we pause to highlight the intuition behind our theorem: *if* we could establish

$$\mu(s+1) = \mu(s) + p(s) \quad \text{for all } s \tag{13}$$

revenue equivalence could be established easily. (Equation [13] is obtained from inequality [12] by setting $v = s+1$ and replacing $\geq$ with an equal sign.) Setting $s = 0$ in [13] yields

$$\mu(1) = \mu(0) + p(0)$$

and because $\mu(2) = \mu(1) + p(1)$ from [13] we can state that

$$\mu(2) = \mu(0) + p(0) + p(1)$$

after replacing $\mu(1)$ with $\mu(0) + p(0)$. And [13] implies $\mu(3) = \mu(2) + p(2)$. Therefore we have

$$\mu(3) = \mu(0) + p(0) + p(1) + p(2).$$

Continuing in this manner, we find that for any reservation value v we have

$$\mu(v) = \mu(0) + p(0) + p(1) + p(2) + \ldots + p(v - 2) + p(v - 1).$$

This gives us *payoff* equivalence because $\mu(0)$ is zero for all standard auctions, and for any s the probability $p(s)$ is the same for all standard auctions: the probability of winning if your reservation value is s is just the probability that s is higher than any other bidder's reservation value. But why does payoff equivalence imply revenue equivalence? Recall the identity $e(v) = vp(v) - \mu(v)$. Clearly, v is the same across all auctions. (The *net gain* from acquiring an asset depends on its value and the price paid to get it, but the *value* v of the asset itself is independent of how the asset is acquired.) By definition, $p(v)$ is the same across all standard auctions because the high-value bidder obtains the asset at equilibrium. Then if $\mu(v)$ is the same across all standard auctions, the expected payment $e(v)$ of a bidder with reservation value v is the difference between two numbers, $vp(v)$ and $\mu(v)$, that are the same across all standard auctions. The winning bidder's payment is the seller's revenue. We can't actually establish [13] but we are about to show that $\mu(s+1)$ is extremely close to $\mu(s) + p(s)$.

Return to the formal argument. Suppose $v = s + 1$. In other words, suppose that agent $s + 1$ masquerades as an agent whose reservation value is s. Then [12] becomes

$$\mu(s+1) \geq \mu(s) + p(s).$$ [14]

When $s = 0$ we have

$$\mu(1) \geq \mu(0) + p(0)$$ [15]

When $s = 1$ statement [14] yields

$$\mu(2) \geq \mu(1) + p(1)$$ [16]

and because we already have inequality [15], we can replace $\mu(1)$ in [16] with $\mu(0) + p(0)$, which cannot be larger than $\mu(1)$, giving us

$$\mu(2) \geq \mu(0) + p(0) + p(1)$$ [17]

(If $\mu(2)$ is at least as large as $\mu(1) + p(1)$, and $\mu(1)$ is at least as large as $\mu(0) + p(0)$, then $\mu(2)$ is at least as large as $\mu(0) + p(0) + p(1)$.)

Now suppose that $s = 2$. In that case inequality [14] reduces to $\mu(3) \geq \mu(2) + p(2)$ and we can replace $\mu(2)$ by the right-hand side of [17] without invalidating the inequality. Therefore

$$\mu(3) \geq \mu(0) + p(0) + p(1) + p(2).$$

In general, for any reservation value v we will have

$$\mu(v) \geq \mu(0) + p(0) + p(1) + p(2) + p(3) + \ldots + p(v-2) + p(v-1).$$ [18]

Proof of Statement [18]

Having established [15], we know that [18] is true when $v = 1$. Suppose that [18] is true for all reservation values up to and including $v = t$. We want to show that it is also true for $v = t + 1$. From [14] we have

$$\mu(t+1) \geq \mu(t) + p(t).$$ [19]

By hypothesis, [18] is true for t so we also have

$$\mu(t) \geq \mu(0) + p(0) + p(1) + \ldots + p(t-2) + p(t-1).$$ [20]

Now, substitute the right-hand side of [20] for $\mu(t)$ in statement [19]. We then get

$$\mu(t+1) \geq \mu(0) + p(0) + p(1) + \ldots + p(t-2) + p(t-1) + p(t),$$

which is statement [18] when $v = t + 1$. We have established that [18] is true for $t = 1$, and that if [18] is true for arbitrary reservation value v then it is true for $v + 1$. This tells us that [18] is true for all values of v.   ∎

We are trying to show that $\mu(v)$ depends only on $\mu(0)$ and on the probabilities $p(0), p(1), \ldots, p(v-2), p(v-1), p(v)$. We are halfway there by virtue of [18]. What we need is a statement that puts an *upper* limit on the magnitude of $\mu(v)$. Go back to [12] and suppose this time that $v = s - 1$. From [12] we get

$$\mu(s) \leq \mu(s-1) + p(s).$$ [21]

If $s = 1$ for example, [21] tells us that

$$\mu(1) \leq \mu(0) + p(1)$$ [22]

and for $s = 2$ we get

$$\mu(2) \leq \mu(1) + p(2).$$ [23]

Now substitute the right-hand side of [22] for $\mu(1)$ in [23] to get

$$\mu(2) \leq \mu(0) + p(1) + p(2).$$ [24]

For $s = 3$ we get $\mu(3) \leq \mu(2) + p(3)$, and when we substitute the right-hand side of [24] for $\mu(2)$ we get

$$\mu(3) \leq \mu(0) + p(1) + p(2) + p(3).$$

In general, we have

$$\mu(v) \leq \mu(0) + p(1) + p(2) + p(3) + \ldots + p(v-1) + p(v)$$ [25]

It is left to you to prove [25] in the same way that we established [18]: we know that [25] is true when $v = 1$, and thus proving that [25] is true for $v + 1$ if it is true for v gives us the general result.

Statement [18] gives us a lower bound on $\mu(v)$ and [25] gives an upper bound. Combining the two yields

$$\mu(0) + p(0) + p(1) + p(2) + \ldots + p(v-2) + p(v-1) \leq \mu(v) \leq$$
$$\mu(0) + p(1) + p(2) + \ldots + p(v-1) + p(v)$$ [26]

The left-hand side of [26] is almost identical to the right-hand side. To get the latter from the former we add $p(v)$ and subtract $p(0)$. But $p(0)$ is the probability of winning when your reservation value is zero. That probability will be zero, so the difference between the lower bound and the upper bound is the presence of $p(v)$ in the latter. But that is not a big number at all – not relative to the sum of the other probabilities. Suppose that your reservation value is exactly \$1 million. Then $p(1,000,000)$ is the probability of your winning when your reservation value is exactly 1 million. Even if that number is not close to zero, each of the terms in the sum $p(900,000) + p(900,001) + p(900,002) + \ldots + p(999,998) + p(999,999)$ will be fairly close to $p(1,000,000)$. The sum of 100,000 positive numbers that are significantly greater than zero will be rather large. In other words, $p(v)$ will be tiny compared to the sum of the numbers that precede it. Therefore, the difference between the right-hand and the left-hand sides of [26] is very tiny. (If v is small then $p(v)$ will be exceedingly small.)

Example 6.16 A Simple Illustration

Suppose that $p(1,000,000) = \frac{1}{2}$ but $p(900,000) = \frac{1}{4}$. Then the sum of the probabilities for reservation values between 900,000 and 999,999 inclusive cannot be smaller than $\frac{1}{4} \times 100,000 = 25,000$, and this is extremely large compared to $p(1,000,000)$. (These probabilities do not have to sum to 1. Why?)

We are justified in ignoring the difference between the left-hand and the right-hand sides of [21], and can say that the lower bound on $\mu(v)$ is "equal" to

$$\mu(0) + p(0) + p(1) + p(2) + p(3) + \ldots + p(v-1) + p(v).$$

Formally,

$$\mu(v) = \mu(0) + p(0) + p(1) + p(2) + p(3) + \ldots + p(v-1) + p(v). \qquad [27]$$

We have proved that [27] is true – well, approximately true – for every value of v. Therefore, it is true for every bidder, whatever his or her reservation value v.

Equation [27] takes us to the threshold of the revenue equivalence theorem. Compare two standard auctions A and B that each award the asset to the buyer with the highest reservation value at equilibrium. It follows that for any reservation value v, the probability $p(v)$ of winning is the same for the two auctions: If there are n bidders, $p(v)$ is just the probability that v is higher than the other $n-1$ randomly drawn reservation values. That means that every term in the right-hand side of [27] will be the same for the two auctions, except perhaps for $\mu(0)$. But if $\mu(0) = 0$ in both auctions, then that term will also be the same for A and B. Therefore, for any reservation value v the payoff $\mu(v)$ will be the same for each auction. This tells us that a buyer's expected payoff is the same in the two auctions, given his or her reservation value.

Recall our starting point: the identity $\mu(v) = v \times p(v) - e(v)$. We have proved that $\mu(v)$ is identical for the two auctions, given v. Because, by assumption, v and $p(v)$ are the same for the two auctions, it follows that $e(v)$ must be the same for the two auctions. For a given bidder, for each possible value v of that bidder, the expected payment $e(v)$ is the same for any two standard auctions. Therefore, that bidder's expected payment averaged over all possible reservation values must be the same for any two standard auctions. If every bidder's expected payment is the same for any two standard auctions, then the total of those expected payments over all bidders must be the same for the two auctions. But the total of the bidders' payments is the seller's revenue. We have proved that standard auctions A and B yield the same expected revenue.

Integral Calculus Proof of the Revenue Equivalence Theorem

We begin with inequality [12] from the previous section:

$$\mu(v) \geq \mu(s) + (v - s)p(s).$$

This holds for all v and s. Let $v = s + ds$. Then $v - s = ds$, and we have $\mu(s + ds) \geq \mu(s) + ds \times p(s)$; hence

$$\mu(s + ds) - \mu(s) \geq ds \times p(s).$$

If $ds > 0$ we can divide both sides of this inequality by ds without changing the direction of the inequality: we get

$$\frac{\mu(s + ds) - \mu(s)}{ds} \geq p(s).$$

As $ds > 0$ approaches zero, the left-hand side of this inequality approaches the derivative $\mu'(s)$. This establishes that $\mu'(s) \geq p(s)$ holds for all s.

If $ds < 0$ then we do change the direction of the inequality when we divide ds into both sides of $\mu(s + ds) - \mu(s) \geq ds \times p(s)$. This yields

$$\frac{\mu(s + ds) - \mu(s)}{ds} \leq p(s).$$

As $ds < 0$ approaches zero through negative values, the left-hand side of this last inequality also approaches the derivative $\mu'(s)$, and thus $\mu'(s) \leq p(s)$ for all s.

We have shown that $p(s) \leq \mu'(s) \leq p(s)$ for all s, and thus we must have $\mu'(s) = p(s)$ for all s. By the fundamental theorem of calculus $\int \mu'(s)ds = \mu(s)$. Therefore, $\mu(s) = \int \mu'(s)ds = \int p(s)ds$. It follows that

$$\mu(v) = \int_0^v p(s)ds + C. \tag{28}$$

C is a constant, which must be equal to $\mu(0)$ because, by [28], $\mu(0) = \int_0^0 p(s)ds + C = 0 + C$. Therefore,

$$\mu(v) = \int_0^v p(s)ds + \mu(0). \tag{29}$$

By assumption $\mu(0)$ is zero for any standard auction. And because any two standard auctions award the asset to the buyer with the highest reservation value at equilibrium, the probability $p(s)$ of winning is the same for the two auctions, for any value of s. It's simply the probability that s is higher than the reservation value of any other bidder. Therefore, $\mu(v)$ is the same for all standard auctions.

By definition, $\mu(v) = v \times p(v) - e(v)$, and we now know that $\mu(v)$ is identical for any two standard auctions. And because v and $p(v)$ are the same for any two such auctions, it follows that $e(v)$ is the same. Finally, if for each reservation value v, a bidder's expected payment $e(v)$ is the same for the two auctions, then the total of those payments over all bidders must be the same for the two auctions. But the total

of the bidders' payments is the seller's revenue. We have proved that any two
standard auctions will yield the same expected revenue.

∂6.4.7 The All-Pay Auction

The asset is awarded to the high bidder but each agent has to pay the amount that
he or she bid. That will obviously result in lower bids at equilibrium than in a first-
price auction. We can employ the revenue equivalence theorem to determine how
much an agent will bid in an all-pay auction. Specifically, we exploit the fact that,
given the probability distribution and the number of bidders, $e(v)$ is the same for all
standard auctions regardless of whether a loser has to pay anything. (In proving
that we didn't have to assume that only the winner pays.)

Suppose that there are two bidders and each views the other's reservation value
as a random draw from the uniform probability distribution on the interval 0 through
1. At equilibrium each agent bids half her reservation value, or $\frac{1}{2}v$, in a first-price
auction. The probability of winning with a reservation value of v is v. Therefore,

$$e(v) = \tfrac{1}{2}v^2$$

in a first-price auction. Therefore, $e(v) = \frac{1}{2}v^2$ in an all-pay auction as well. In an all-
pay auction an agent must pay her bid with certainty, so $\frac{1}{2}v^2$ is also the actual bid,
not just the expected payment. Let's confirm that we have an equilibrium in an all-
pay auction when each agent bids half of the square of her reservation value.

Theorem: Equilibrium for a Two-Person, All-Pay Auction
*If each views the other's reservation value as a random draw from the
uniform probability distribution on the interval 0 through 1 then each will
bid $\frac{1}{2}v^2$ as a function of the individual reservation value v, and the seller's
expected revenue is $\frac{1}{3}$.*

Proof:

To simplify the notation, let b denote the bid of one of the agents, with c representing the other's bid. The reservation values will be v and w, respectively. Let $\text{Prob}(b)$
be the probability of winning with a bid of b. Then

$$\mu(v) = v \times \text{Prob}(b) - b$$

because the bid must be paid whether the agent wins or not. The agent knows her
own reservation value v, so we hold that fixed, and choose b to maximize

$$\mu(b) = v \times \text{Prob}(b) - b,$$

assuming that the rival bidder will set $c = \frac{1}{2}w^2$.

$$\text{Prob}(b) = \text{Prob}\left(b > \tfrac{1}{2}w^2\right) = \text{Prob}\left(w^2 < 2b\right) = \text{Prob}(w < \sqrt{2b}) = \sqrt{2b}.$$

Therefore, we maximize

$$\mu(b) = v(2b)^{\frac{1}{2}} - b.$$

We have $\mu'(b) = \frac{1}{2}v(2b)^{-\frac{1}{2}}(2) - 1 = v(2b)^{-\frac{1}{2}} - 1$. Note that $\mu''(b) < 0$ for all $b > 0$, and thus we set $\mu'(b) = 0$. We get $v(2b)^{-\frac{1}{2}} = 1$, or $\sqrt{2b} = v$, and hence $b = \frac{1}{2}v^2$.

This argument also establishes that a bid of $c = \frac{1}{2}w^2$ is a best response to $b = \frac{1}{2}v^2$ (just make a notation substitution) and hence we have identified a Nash equilibrium.   ∎

The proof employed the revenue equivalence theorem, so we don't need a direct proof that the expected revenue from the all-pay auction (for the framework of this section) is $\frac{1}{3}$. But it might be comforting to have one: the two bidders employ identical strategies, and thus the sellers revenue is twice the expected payment of one bidder. The bid is $\frac{1}{2}v^2$ and thus the expected payment by the bidder is $\int_0^1 0.5v^2$ dv. Because $\int 0.5v^2 dv = v^3/6$ we have

$$\int_0^1 0.5v^2 \, dv = 1/6.$$

It follows that each bidder's expected payment is one-sixth and hence the seller's expected revenue is $\frac{1}{3}$.

Sources
Section 4.6 is based on Klemperer (1999). The revenue equivalence theorem was discovered (as a special case) by Vickrey (1961), where a proof was also given. The general version first appeared simultaneously in Myerson (1981) and Riley and Samuelson (1981).

Links
Klemperer (2004) and Illing and Klüh (2003) take you deeper into auction theory and practice. The first book is a general treatment, and the second one is specifically devoted to the recent auctions of the radio spectrum in Europe.

Problem Set
(1) Determine the seller's expected revenue in a first-price, sealed-bid auction for the following four cases:

(A) There are two bidders and each reservation value is drawn from the uniform probability distribution on the interval from 0 to 5.

(B) There are two bidders and each reservation value is drawn from the uniform probability distribution on the interval from 2 to 5.

(C) There are four bidders and each reservation value is drawn from the uniform probability distribution on the interval 0 to 1.

(D) There are four bidders and each reservation value is drawn from the uniform probability distribution on the interval 1 to 11.

(2) There are n bidders in an auction that awards the asset to the high bidder at a price equal to 20 percent of the winner's bid. No one else pays anything. Without using mathematics, and without appealing to the revenue equivalence theorem, explain why this auction yields the same revenue as the first-price, sealed-bid auction. (You should be able to do this without assuming the uniform probability distribution.)

(3) The following questions pertain to a first-price, sealed-bid auction with exactly two bidders. Each individual's reservation value is drawn from the uniform probability distribution on the interval 0 to 1. Calculate the three quantities $e(v)$, $v \times p(v)$, and $\mu(v)$ for each of the five values of v listed. Calculate $\mu(v)$ in two different ways:

$$\mu(v) = v \times p(v) - e(v)$$

and $\mu(v) = (v \text{ minus this individual's bid}) \times p(v)$.

   A. $v = 1$. B. $v = 0$. C. $v = \frac{2}{3}$. D. $v = \frac{1}{4}$.

   E. Generic v. That is, leave the reservation value as v, so your answers will be functions of v.

(4) Why does the expected (i.e., average) revenue of the first-price, sealed-bid auction increase when the number of bidders increases?

(5) What is the expected (i.e., average) revenue from the first-price, sealed-bid auction when there are four bidders and each reservation value is drawn from the uniform probability distribution on the interval 0 to 1?

(6) What is the expected (i.e., average) revenue from the Vickrey auction when there are four bidders and each reservation value is drawn from the uniform probability distribution on the interval 0 to 5?

(7) Why does the expected (i.e., average) revenue of the second-price (Vickrey) auction increase when the number of bidders increases?

(8) What is the expected (i.e., average) revenue from the Dutch auction when there are two bidders and each reservation value is drawn from the uniform probability distribution on the interval 0 to 1?

(9) There are n bidders. What is the expected (i.e., average) revenue of the first-price, sealed-bid auction, assuming that the reservation values are drawn from the uniform probability distribution (with values between zero and unity, inclusive)? Explain briefly.

(10) Prove statement [25] in Section 6.4.5.

(11) Assuming exactly two bidders, construct a simple example of revenue equivalence between the first-price, sealed-bid auction and English auction when there are two possible pairs of reservation values – case 1 and case 2 – and they are equally likely.

(12) Assuming exactly two bidders, construct a simple example of a *failure* of revenue equivalence between the first-price, sealed-bid and English auctions

when there are only two possible pairs of reservation values – case 1 and case 2 – and they are equally likely.

(13) Consider the following new auction mechanism: after the bidders have gathered, the auctioneer flips a coin. If it turns up heads then the (English) ascending auction is used, but if tails turns up then the (Dutch) descending auction is used. Will this new auction be revenue equivalent to the first-price, sealed-bid auction? Explain.

6.5 APPLICATIONS OF THE REVENUE EQUIVALENCE THEOREM

The US government (through the Resolution Trust Corporation) sold the assets of almost 1,000 failed banks and savings and loan institutions in the 1980s and early 1990s. It solicited sealed bids but conducted the auctions prematurely, hence there were few bidders, and the auctions yielded far less than their potential (Sternberg, 1991).

A 1999 spectrum auction in Germany used the ascending bid format, but required a new bid to be at least 10 percent more than its predecessor. Mannesman opened by bidding 18.18 million deutschmarks on licenses 1 through 5, and 20 million deutschmarks on licenses 6 through 10. The only other credible bidder was T-Mobile, and its opening bids were lower. One of the T-Mobile managers reported that there was no explicit agreement with Mannesman, but the T-Mobile team understood that if it did not raise the bid on lots 6–10 then T-Mobile could have lots 1–5 for 20 million, which is slightly more than 110 percent of 18.18 million. That is in fact what happened: the auction ended after two rounds of bidding (Klemperer, 2004, pp. 104–105). A 1997 spectrum auction in the United States was expected to raise $1.8 billion but realized only $14 million. Bidders used the final three digits of bids to signal the market code of the area that they intended to go after (Cramton and Schwartz, 2000).

If any two standard auctions yield the same expected revenue, should the seller devote any effort to choosing or designing an auction mechanism? Yes. Many practical issues do not arise within the abstract framework employed in the previous section. In particular, the revenue equivalence theorem takes the number of bidders and the absence of collusion for granted. In any particular sale, both issues should receive careful consideration. We deal with them in turn.

We expect the seller's revenue to increase with the number of bidders. All other things being equal, the seller should employ the auction mechanism that attracts the most bidders. An English auction can discourage entry, particularly if it is known that one or two bidders have very high reservation values. The weaker bidders know that they will be outbid and thus will not even compete. This leaves only two or three bidders, who will then be tempted to collude. However, a first-price, sealed-bid auction gives weak bidders at least a chance of winning, because everyone knows that every firm will submit a bid below its reservation value. A sealed-bid auction might even attract firms who have no intention of using the asset but simply hope to sell the asset for a profit after the auction. (It's hard to profit from resale in the case of an English auction. The winner will be the high-value agent, and so no one else would be willing to pay more than the asset is worth to the winner of the auction.)

The very advantage of sealed-bid auctions from the standpoint of encouraging entry – low-value agents have a chance of winning – is a disadvantage from an efficiency standpoint.

Paul Klemperer has proposed a middle ground, the *Anglo-Dutch auction*. The first stage is an English auction, which is allowed to run its course until only two bidders remain. These two then enter sealed bids, which must not be less than the last bid from the English stage. The asset is sold to the high bidder in stage two for a price equal to that bid. (The sealed-bid stage is "Dutch" because the Dutch auction is outcome equivalent to the first-price, sealed-bid auction.)

Collusion by the bidders can significantly depress the seller's revenue. The English auction is vulnerable to bidder collusion for two reasons: first, there are several rounds of bidding, so members of a cartel have a chance to punish a member who deviates from the cartel strategy. Second, the bids are not sealed and thus can be used to signal information to other bidders.

The analysis of Section 6.4 applies even to mechanisms that are not auctions in the conventional sense of the word. The revenue equivalence theorem is valid for any two mechanisms that use a formula for allocating a single asset – or something of value – provided that an agent with a reservation value of zero gets zero profit on average, and the agent with the highest reservation value always gets the asset at equilibrium. The mechanism can even allocate the asset randomly, as a function of the bids or messages submitted by the agents. Moreover, if you go back and check the proof, you'll see that we can weaken the assumption that an agent with a reservation value of zero gets zero profit on average. As long as the expected profit of an agent with the lowest possible reservation value is the same across two auction mechanisms, then they will generate the same expected revenue (provided that the agent with the highest reservation value always wins). The following are five significant applications of the theorem.

6.5.1   Multistage Auctions

The US and British airwaves auctions were designed by academic economists to allocate radio frequencies to companies selling personal communication devices and broadcast licenses. Bidding takes place in several rounds, and bidders can revise their bids after observing what happened on the previous round. The revenue equivalence theorem doesn't say anything, one way or another, about how many stages an auction can take, so it applies to multistage auctions. All that we need to know about an auction is the probability of winning, as a function of the reservation value, and the expected payoff of an agent whose reservation value is zero.

6.5.2   Adoption of a Standard

There are auctions in which the losers have to make a payment, in addition to the winner. This is true of a "war of attrition," a term that covers a family of allocation problems not normally thought of as auctions. When two or more candidates compete for a seat in the legislature, each will spend a considerable amount of money wooing voters. Only one candidate will be victorious, but the losers will not get their money back. When competing firms lobby the government, each aiming to have its own technology adopted as the industry standard, only one technology will be adopted. The losing firms don't get their money back. In both cases, the higher the value of the prize to an individual candidate or firm, the greater the incentive to spend money to get it. In both cases, an increase in expenditure by a competitor raises the probability of success, but we can't say that the prize goes to the biggest spender with certainty. Therefore, we can't say that the agent with the highest reservation value will win the prize at equilibrium. But to establish a benchmark, let's assume that such *is* the case. A safer assumption is that an agent with reservation value zero will get a payoff of zero at equilibrium. (If the prize isn't worth anything to me I won't spend any money to get it, and hence I am sure not to get it.) We have a standard auction. We can invoke the revenue equivalence theorem: the expected payment (summed over all firms) is equal to the expected payment by the winner in a Vickrey auction. The latter will be much easier to compute.

6.5.3 Civil Litigation

Currently, the laws governing civil suits in the United States require all contestants to pay their own expenses. If the law were changed so that the loser were also required to pay the winner an additional amount equal to the loser's expenses, would expenditures on lawsuits be reduced? A party would have to pay more if it lost, but every additional dollar paid by the loser is an additional dollar gained by the winner, so the expected value of a lawsuit might not change. In fact, even under the new rule, if a party spent nothing it would not win and thus would gain nothing. So the first part of the definition of a standard auction is confirmed. If we assume that the party that spends the most wins the suit, then we also have the second part. Therefore, the two systems result in the same total expenditure on civil suits. Because the expected profit from a lawsuit is the same for the two systems, the incentive to bring an action is the same. Hence the same number of lawsuits are contested in the two systems, so total expenditure really would be the same.

6.5.4 Procurement

When a government or a firm puts a contract up for bids, the winning bidder will have to deliver an asset (i.e., it will have to construct a hospital, road, or office building, etc.), and in return the winner is *paid* an amount of money. This is an auction in reverse. The bidder's reservation value v is a cost (the cost of construction) and thus it is a negative number. The winner's payment is negative (it is a receipt) so $e(v)$ is negative. If we let c denote cost and $r(c)$ denote the *bidder's* expected revenue as a function of the bidder's cost c we have

$$\mu(c) = r(c) - c \times p(c),$$

which says that expected payoff is equal to the bidder's expected revenue minus expected cost.

Now, let $c = -v$ and $r(v) = -e(c)$. Then $\mu(c) = r(c) - c \times p(c)$ becomes

$$\mu(v) = v \times p(v) - e(v),$$

which was the starting point for the revenue equivalence theorem, which now tells us that the winner's expected profit will be the same and the government's expected expenditure will be the same in any two procurement auctions in which the low-cost supplier always wins the contract at equilibrium, and the highest cost supplier will get zero profit at equilibrium.

6.5.5 Car Sales

There is great enthusiasm in Europe for internet sales of automobiles as a substitute for dealer sales. They are gaining popularity in the United States. Prices are more transparent on the internet, and the assumption is that consumers benefit from this because of the reduction in search costs. The assumption may be wrong. Certainly there are many more sellers competing for a given customer's favor in an internet sale. This means that internet sales approximate the standard English, oral ascending auction. Purchase at a dealership is similar to a first-price, sealed-bid auction because the buyer has no way of credibly reporting one dealer's offer to another, particularly when dealers so rarely put an offer in writing. The offers are, in effect, sealed.

An internet sale to one customer can be treated as a separate auction. The bidders are sellers, not buyers, and the bids are lowered until only one seller remains – the car is then sold at that survivor's bid. So it is a procurement auction and, after inserting minus signs, equivalent to an ascending auction. The revenue equivalence theorem tells us that the expected outcome is the same in the two situations. However, that theorem assumes away *collusion* on the part of the bidders. Collusion among automobile sellers is much easier to orchestrate in the case of internet sales. Early rounds can be used to signal information from one seller to another. Finally, sealed-bid procurement auctions typically generate lower prices for the buyer.

Source

These examples are drawn from Klemperer (2003). Klemperer (1998) proposed the *Anglo-Dutch auction.*

Links

Chapters 3 and 4 of Klemperer (2004) provide insight into the practical side of designing an auction. The former is also available as Klemperer (2002a). Paul Klemperer played a central role in the design of the British spectrum auctions. John McMillan and Paul Milgrom played a key role in designing the US spectrum auction. Milgrom (2004, Chapter 1) discusses the practical side of auction design, and McMillan (2002, Chapter 7) is a superb account of modern auctions.

6.6 INTERDEPENDENT VALUES

Up to this point we have assumed that the auctions in question apply to private values cases, by which we mean each agent has a reservation value that is statistically independent of the reservation value of any other agent. The pure common values case is the opposite: the asset has a market value that is the same for all bidders, but no bidder knows the true value. Each has some information about the true value, but the information is different for different agents. The intermediate case is encountered most often: the asset is worth more to some firms than to

The value of a TV license could be higher for bidder A than bidder B because A owns a baseball franchise and can use the TV station to hide some of the profit from baseball operations, say by buying broadcast rights from the baseball team at below market value. This would allow the owners of the baseball team to tell the players that they can't have a salary increase because there is no profit (Chapter 4 of Zimbalist, 2004).

others – perhaps because the former have other resources that combine well with the asset that is up for sale – but the values of the different bidders are closely related, perhaps because the asset would be used to serve a particular consumer group, such as smart phone users.

The standard example of the pure common value situation is the competition between oil-drilling firms for the right to extract crude oil from a presently undeveloped tract of land. Each firm will employ experts to estimate the size of the underground reserve and the cost of extracting it. The estimates won't agree, and the data will not be made public until the bidding is over – if then. Each firm keeps its estimate to itself. There will be *some* publicly available information – perhaps the amount of oil pumped from nearby land. Hence, each firm has a *signal* (i.e., estimate) of the value of the tract, based on the public information and its own private information, and the signals are different for different firms.

DEFINITION: *Bidder Signal*

Firm i's signal σ_i is its estimate of the asset's worth to i itself.

In a private values auction a firm's signal is just its own reservation value. Even if the firm knew the reservation values of the other firms, its own estimate of the asset's value would be unaffected. (But the information would be useful in guessing how much the other agents would bid.) In a pure common value auction the firm's signal is its own particular estimate of the value of the asset. The asset is worth the same amount to each bidder – the common value – but that number is not precisely known by any bidder. Each knows that the average of all the estimates would be a much more reliable indicator of the value of the asset, but no firm will know any other firm's estimate before bidding begins.

The techniques for estimating the oil reserves trapped in a geological formation are significantly more reliable than a hundred years ago, but geologists can still disagree about a particular tract. Thousands of licenses for drilling oil off the coasts of Louisiana and Texas have been auctioned by the US Department of the Interior, but many of the sales attracted only one bid (McAfee, 2002, pp. 307-308).

In this last section we abandon the private values assumption and reconsider auctions when one agent's signal embodies information that is relevant to the value of the asset to other agents. Happily, much of what we learned in the private values case can be adapted to the general framework.

For the pure common value case, in which the asset has precisely the same (unknown) value to all the bidders, asset efficiency is satisfied by *any* assignment of the asset! This suggests that an auction is unnecessary; just allocate the asset by lottery. On the contrary, there are two reasons why an auction should be used. The first is a fairness argument. If the asset (e.g., off-shore oil reserves) belongs to all citizens, it shouldn't be given free to any of them. A competitive auction would eliminate much (sometimes all) of the excess profit from asset ownership. Second, even if the asset has the same value to all *bidders*, this won't be the case for all firms in the economy. Firms that have no expertise in exploiting the asset would not be able to realize the "common" value. An auction attracts only firms that can hope to realize the asset's potential. But if the value is the same for all *bidders*, then asset efficiency is satisfied, regardless of the outcome. For situations that are intermediate between the pure private values and the pure common value case, asset efficiency can be problematic, as the next example demonstrates.

Example 6.17 The Intermediate Case

There are three bidders, 1, 2, and 3. Their respective signals are σ_1, σ_2, and σ_3. The values v_1 and v_2 of the first two bidders each depend on all three signals, but the value v_3 of the asset to agent 3 is a function of 3's signal only. Specifically:

$$v_1 = \alpha + \tfrac{2}{3}\sigma_2 + \tfrac{1}{3}\sigma_3, \quad v_2 = \alpha + \tfrac{1}{3}\sigma_1 + \tfrac{2}{3}\sigma_3, \quad \text{and} \quad v_3 = \sigma_3.$$

The asset is to be auctioned, and each firm has to submit a bid before knowing the signal received by the other two. Suppose that $\sigma_1 = \alpha = \sigma_2$ and $\sigma_3 = \alpha + \xi$, where α is positive, although the random variable ξ can be positive or negative. We have

$$v_1 = 2\alpha + \tfrac{1}{3}\xi, \quad v_2 = 2\alpha + \tfrac{2}{3}\xi, \quad \text{and} \quad v_3 = \alpha + \xi.$$

If $\xi < 0$ then $v_1 > v_2 > v_3$, in which case asset efficiency requires that agent 1 is the winning bidder. If $0 < \xi < 1.5\alpha$ then $v_2 > v_1 > v_3$, and asset efficiency is satisfied only if agent 2 is the winning bidder. Suppose that an agent's bid can depend only on his or her own signal. (That would be the case in any sealed-bid auction.) When $\sigma_1 = \alpha = \sigma_2$ neither the bid of 1 or 2 will be influenced by the sign of ξ. If agent 1 is the winning bidder then asset efficiency is violated when $1.5\alpha > \xi > 0$, and if agent 2 is the winning bidder then $\xi < 0$ is inconsistent with asset efficiency, whatever sealed-bid auction is used.

The rest of this section treats the pure common value case. The asset has the same value to each bidder, but the common value is unknown to each.

6.6.1 Revenue Equivalence

For the family of *sealed-bid* auctions, the revenue equivalence theorem is valid for the common value case. All we have to do to prove this is replace the agent's reservation value v in the proof of Section 6.4.5 (or 6.4.6) with the agent's signal σ. (In the case of an open auction, a bidder can make inferences about the signals received by others when they hear their bids. In that case replacing the reservation value by the signal is invalid.) The bidder's behavior is now based on σ instead of v, but the mathematics is otherwise unchanged – after replacing v with σ (or even better, interpreting v as the agent's signal). It needs to be emphasized, though, that the assumption that each bidder's signal is statistically independent of any other agent's signal is crucial. This rules out Example 6.17 and similar cases.

The Common Value Version of the Revenue Equivalence Theorem

If each of the n agents is risk neutral, and each has a privately known signal independently drawn from a common probability distribution, then all standard sealed-bid auctions have each bidder making the same expected payment at equilibrium, given his or her value, and thus the seller's expected revenue is the same for all standard auctions.

6.6.2 The Winner's Curse

Before bidding, each potential buyer hires a team of experts. In the case of oil drilling, the bidder will employ a team of geologists to determine how much oil is under the tract of land up for auction and how difficult it will be to extract the oil. Economists will be called on to estimate the future market value of oil. Each bidder hires a different team of experts, and the estimates of the asset's market value will disagree. There are three reasons why the potential buyers will *not* exchange their information before the auction is run. First, if they did then each buyer would have little incentive to fund research because it would get the results of others' estimates for free. Second, bidder A's estimate would help bidder B, but A's goal is to profit at the expense of B. Third, each bidder would have an incentive to mislead the others.

Each bidder has an estimate of the common value – the value of the asset – and no bidder will know the estimates obtained by the others. Some of the estimates will be on the high side and some will be on the low side. The average of all the estimates will be a good approximation to the common value, but the highest estimate will not. Because each agent's bid will be proportional to its own estimate, the high bidder will be the one with the highest estimate. As soon as that agent learns that he has won, he knows that he has paid too much: he had the extreme estimate (on the high side) of the value of the asset.

Example 6.18 Three Hats

The asset is a hat containing five pieces of paper. Each of the five slips has a number on it, and if you obtain the asset by outbidding your rival you will be paid an amount of money equal to 100 times the average of the five numbers. You are allowed to sample before deciding how much to bid. Specifically, you can draw one piece of paper at random from the hat and look at it. You have to replace it before your rival, who cannot see what number you drew, takes a sample. And you won't know what number your rival drew before entering your bid. Moreover, neither of you knows which of three hats you are bidding for: hat A contains the numbers 1, 2, 3, 4, and 5, so that asset is worth \$300. Hat B contains 2, 3, 4, 5, and 6, so it is worth

$400. Hat C is worth $500 because it contains the numbers 3, 4, 5, 6, and 7. You draw a 4. How much should you bid? Four hundred dollars is the value of asset B, so it might be smart to suppose that you are bidding for B. Much more useful information would be obtained by averaging your sample with the other person's. (If the average of the two draws is 6.5 then the asset is certainly C. If the average is 5.5 then it is certainly not A.) But comparing sample values is against the rules. Now, you submit your sealed bid, based solely on the information you possess, and you are told that you won the asset because you are the high bidder. That means that your rival drew a lower number than you and submitted a lower bid. Drawing a number smaller than 4 is much more likely to happen when sampling from A than from C. It is 50 percent more likely with A than with B. *Conditional on winning the first-price, sealed-bid auction* a draw of 4 should lead to a bid below $300 because the chances are good that you are competing for asset A. If you draw the number 4 and bid, say, $325 on the supposition that the asset is more likely to be B than A or C you have a good chance of experiencing the winner's curse. (When two samples are taken from A the average low draw is 2.28 and the average high is 3.8. When two samples are taken from B, the average high is 4.8, although the mean of the numbers in hat B is 4.)

Oil companies appear to have fallen victim to the winner's curse during the auctions for offshore oil-drilling rights. Book publishers often feel that by outbidding rivals for the right to publish a book they have paid more than they will ever recoup in profits from book sales. Baseball teams have outbid other teams for a free agent only to find that they have paid too much for the player's services. The phenomenon also occurs in corporate takeover battles (Thaler, 1992, pp. 57–58, and Dyer and Kagel, 2002, p. 349).

Any mechanism in which firms or individuals compete with each other for a single asset, or a handful of assets, can be viewed as an auction. Accordingly, the winner's curse can emerge in a wide variety of market contexts.

If the bidders *did* exchange their information before the auction they could produce a common estimate of the asset's market value. The average of all the estimates can be expected to be as close as anyone could forecast to the actual market value of the asset. The buyer whose team produced the highest estimate of the asset's value would know that its team overestimated. But that buyer would be the one with the highest reservation value going into the auction and hence would be the winning bidder. Without an exchange of information, the appropriate strategy is to adjust one's estimate, and hence one's bid, to avoid falling victim to the winner's curse.

Note that the winner's curse becomes more pernicious as the number of bidders increases: as the number of bidders increases, so does the probability of someone drawing an extremely high sample estimate. In the case of Example 6.19 the probability of someone drawing either $\mu + 100$ or $\mu + 200$ when there are only two agents is 1 minus the probability that both individuals draw one of the other three numbers. The probability of a single individual drawing one of the three lowest numbers is $0.1 + 0.2 + 0.4 = 0.7$. Therefore the probability of one of the two bidders drawing an estimate greater than μ is $1 - 0.7 \times 0.7 = 0.51$. (Alternatively,

Example 6.19 Correcting for the Overestimate

There are two bidders (to keep the calculations simple), and each draws a single sample from a probability distribution. Each knows everything about the distribution except the mean μ, which is also the common value of the asset. An individual will draw $\mu + 0$ with probability 0.4, $\mu + 100$ with probability 0.2, $\mu - 100$ with probability 0.2, $\mu + 200$ with probability 0.1, and $\mu - 200$ with probability 0.1 as summarized by Table 6.3. The average draw is μ, but typically one of the bidders will have an above-average draw and the other will have a below-average estimate. Because neither knows the value of μ, or the other's estimate, neither will know if his or her own estimate is too high or too low. Let's calculate the average high estimate. Table 6.4 displays the probability of every pair of draws. For instance, A will draw $\mu - 100$ with probability 0.2 and B will draw $\mu + 200$ with probability 0.1. The probability of both happening is $0.2 \times 0.1 = 0.02$, and when it does the high estimate is $\mu + 200$. You can use Table 6.4 to calculate the average high estimate, which is $\mu + 60$. Therefore, bidders should offset the winner's curse by subtracting $60 from their estimates.

Table 6.3

Draw	Probability
$\mu - 200$	0.1
$\mu - 100$	0.2
μ	0.4
$\mu + 100$	0.2
$\mu + 200$	0.1

eliminate the last two columns and the last two rows of Table 6.4, add the remaining numbers, and then subtract the result from 1.) If there are three agents, the probability of someone drawing $\mu + 100$ or $\mu + 200$ is $1 - 0.7 \times 0.7 \times 0.7 = 0.657$. With four bidders the probability increases to 0.7599.

Is the winner's curse more dangerous with the first-price, sealed-bid auction or with the English auction? The former. If you seriously overestimate the asset's value in an English auction, you won't pay too much if you are the only one to overestimate, because you won't have to pay more than the second-highest estimate of its value. Moreover, as the auction proceeds you acquire information about some of the other estimates. As bidders drop out, you get an upper bound on their estimates of the asset's value.

Table 6.4

			B's estimate		
A's estimate	$\mu - 200$	$\mu - 100$	μ	$\mu + 100$	$\mu + 200$
$\mu - 200$	0.01	0.02	0.04	0.02	0.01
$\mu - 100$	0.02	0.04	0.08	0.04	0.02
μ	0.04	0.08	0.16	0.08	0.04
$\mu + 100$	0.02	0.04	0.08	0.04	0.02
$\mu + 200$	0.01	0.02	0.04	0.02	0.01

Source

Example 6.17 is from Maskin (2003).

Links

Thaler (1992) is a rich and wonderful book on the winner's curse and related phenomenon. Richard Thaler won the Nobel Prize for Economics in 2017. McAfee (2002, pp. 307–311) has some valuable observations on the winner's curse. The winner's curse emerges in laboratory experiments, but with experience the subjects learn to mitigate its effects, so that the winner realizes some profit while still bidding too high. Experimental subjects submit bids that are closer to the Nash equilibrium levels in English auctions than in first-price, sealed-bid auctions. See Kagel and Levin (2002b).

Voting and Preference Revelation

This chapter examines decision making by a *community* (or any group) in a simple model: the community must choose from a finite set of mutually exclusive alternatives. (The next chapter endows the model with much more structure by specifying individual utility functions and a production function – and resource constraints. The utility functions will have classical economic properties.)

We look at situations in which a group must make a decision that will be binding on all of its members. For example, a class has to determine a time for a review session, a town has to decide whether to build a new school, a nation has to elect a legislature. The resulting choice will have no other implications for personal consumption – in this chapter. Suppose for instance that X, Y, Z, etc. denote alternative ways of spending a fixed amount of government revenue, with the same individual tax burdens in each case. In this setting we can't rule out any ranking of the available options as a possible preference scheme for a member of the group. This makes it very difficult to induce truthful revelation of the hidden characteristic, which in this chapter and the next is the individual's true preference scheme. We want the individuals to reveal enough information about their preferences to enable the system to select the outcome that best reflects those individual preferences.

Clearly, one could write an entire book on the criteria for determining the alternative that "best" reflects individual preferences. Indeed, hundreds of volumes have been written on that theme. In this chapter we set that issue aside and simply determine which selection rules elicit truthful information about individual preferences. A selection rule is essentially a mapping from individual preferences into a social choice, and it must be defined for each possible specification of individual preferences.

7.1   VOTING RULES

Although this section examines voting procedures, you are encouraged to think of the candidates standing for election not as individuals seeking careers in government but as alternative packages of public projects. Candidate (or alternative) X may, for example, be a proposal to reduce expenditure on space exploration by a specific amount and to use the proceeds to fund research on the production of energy by nuclear fusion. Alternative Y may be a proposal to maintain the level of expenditure on space exploration while increasing federal expenditure on health care at the expense of grants to university professors. Other candidates or alternatives may present mixtures of X and Y, and each would be identified by its own label, W, Z, and so forth. The voters may be the members of the legislature or even the citizens themselves who are asked to vote directly for public projects.

DEFINITION: *Voting Rule*

Given a set of voters, 1, 2, . . ., n and a set of alternatives, X, Y,. . ., Z, a voting rule specifies a single one of those alternatives as a function of individual preferences.

The fact that citizens do not presently vote directly on public projects should not stand in our way. A particular voting scheme may not be widely used, but it deserves consideration if it would serve society better than the methods presently in use. When examining alternative voting systems our main concern is the extent to which a voting procedure embodies incentives that induce individuals to mark their ballots to reflect their preferences in the way prescribed by the systems rules. (Other criteria are important, of course, but this book examines incentives.)

7.1.1 Majority Rule

Our aim is to employ a voting scheme that induces individuals to reveal their preferences truthfully. Majority rule meets the case *when there are only two alternatives on the agenda.* (Some tie-breaking rule is employed when necessary.)

Majority Rule Theorem for Two Alternatives
   Majority rule induces truthful preference revelation – even by coalitions – if there are only two feasible alternatives.

Proof:

If X wins but Vince voted for Y because he prefers Y to X then Vince cannot precipitate an outcome that he prefers to X by changing his vote. With only two alternatives Vince can only change his vote to X, but X already wins even when he votes for Y. Note that we can apply this argument to a coalition of individuals: if everyone in group G prefers Y to X but X wins the election when the members of G vote for Y over X, then there is nothing they can do individually or as a group to secure the election of Y. If there are only two alternatives, then majority rule always renders a decision that is invulnerable to manipulation by misrepresentation of preference.   ∎

When the feasible set has only two alternatives, X and Y, the majority winner is efficient: if alternative X is not efficient then no one strictly prefers X to Y and at least one person strictly prefers Y to X. But then Y would defeat X in the election.

Even if there is a large number of alternatives we can induce truthful revelation by selecting two alternatives, X^* and Y^*, and have the rule select the majority winner between X^* and Y^*. According to this decision scheme, the other alternatives (Z, A, B, etc.) don't have a chance, even if everyone ranks Z at the top and X^* and Y^* either last or second last. Disqualifying all but two of the alternatives from ever receiving consideration, whatever the individual preferences, is an extremely poor way to solve the hidden information problem .

The majority rule theorem is of no comfort in an economic context because there are always more than two alternatives. For one thing, a given amount of tax revenue can finance an astronomically large number assortments of public policies. To see how this affects our evaluation of majority rule we revisit the case of two alternatives but use utility functions to express individual preferences.

We have uncovered a general principle: if we are using majority rule in an economic context, and we restrict the agenda to two alternatives to ensure truthful revelation of individual preference, then we could wind up with an inefficient

Table 7.1

Utility	Soren	Rosie	Edie
$U_i(F)$	5000	100	150
$U_i(G)$	3000	105	160

Table 7.2

Utility	Soren	Rosie	Edie
$U_i(F)$	5000	100	150
$U_i(G)$	3000	105	160
$U_i(H)$	4800	200	250

Example 7.1 Two Projects F and G and Three Individuals

Table 7.1 represents individual preferences by means of the utility levels U_i (net of any taxes paid). If the two projects come up for election then G will win because Rosie and Edie both prefer G to F. (If you like, you can suppose there are 3 million individuals, with each voter of the table belonging to a group of 1 million individuals with identical preferences.) Outcome G is inefficient *if* we expand the feasible set by allowing side payments. If Soren were to compensate the other two individuals by paying them each $100 for throwing their support to F we have a new outcome H, which everyone prefers to G, as illustrated by Table 7.2. That is, we create H from F by reducing Soren's consumption of the private good by 200 and increasing the private good consumption of Rosie and Edie by 100 each. (There is an implicit assumption here of quasi-linear preferences that justifies the claim that $100 would be sufficient compensation. See Section 2.5.1 of Chapter 2)

outcome. Note that we could modify Example 7.1 so that the difference between total utility from F and the total utility from G is as large as we like.

Majority voting with a two-alternative agenda can select an inefficient outcome because an individual who cares very little about the choice between two projects is given the same number of votes as an individual who has a great deal at stake. The intensity of an individual's preference is not recorded, and therefore there is no way to ensure that the majority's gain outweighs the minority's loss. We attempt to correct this defect by considering a voting scheme that allows an individual to cast a variable number of votes.

Example 7.2 A Variable Number of Votes

Each individual i is required to report the net benefit $U_i(A)$ that i receives from each feasible project A. We can interpret $U_i(A)$ as the number of votes cast by i for A. The project that receives the largest total vote is adopted.

If individuals report truthfully then an inefficient outcome will not survive the voting process of Example 7.2: suppose that C is feasible, but so is D which gives at least one person higher utility than C and no one less utility than at C. Then total utility is higher at D than at C.

Of course individuals have a strong incentive *not* to report truthfully. Suppose that Table 7.1 of Example 7.1 gives the true utility levels for F and G, the only feasible

Table 7.3

Utility	Soren	Rosie	Edie
$U_i(F)$	5000	100	150
$U_i(G)$	3000	5105	160

projects. If Rosie declares that her net utility from G is 5105 (i.e., casts 5,105 votes for G) and in all other cases each individual reports truthfully, the result is displayed in Table 7.3. Project G will receive the most votes and will be adopted. Of course this voting pattern does not constitute an equilibrium. All individuals have an incentive to overstate their preference for the project they prefer, however slight their intensity of preference for one option over the other, and there is no limit to the number of votes individuals would be willing to cast for their preferred outcome if this voting mechanism is used.

Suppose that we modify Example 7.2 by imposing an upper limit. Let's consider the implications of a cap of 10,000 on the number of votes that one can cast for an outcome. An individual is asked to cast a number of votes for an alternative in accord with the net utility that the individual would receive from that alternative, but in no case can he or she exceed 10,000 votes. All individuals will cast exactly 10,000 votes for the option that they prefer and 0 votes for the other project, so the mechanism imitates majority rule. (The number of votes cast has no effect on the tax formula used to finance the winning project – the financing formula is part of the definition of a project.) Each alternative will now receive 10,000 times as many votes as under majority rule, so the two mechanisms yield the same decision. The problem with this new scheme is that there is still insufficient restraint on individuals' desire to overstate the benefit derived from their preferred alternative, even if it gives only slightly more utility than the other. Therefore, we want to consider a modification of the variable number of votes model in which there is a built-in incentive not to exaggerate. We don't investigate this until Chapter 8.

To forestall the potential inefficiency of majority rule let's have all of the feasible alternatives on the ballot. From now on we assume that there are three or more feasible alternatives. It is certain that a majority winner will be efficient if *every* feasible alternative is on the ballot: if X defeats every other alternative by a majority then there is no other feasible alternative Y that everyone prefers to X. If there were such an alternative then it would have defeated X by a majority – an overwhelming majority. For the same reason, there can be no other feasible alternative Y such that some people prefer it to X and the rest are indifferent between the two alternatives.

Efficiency of Majority Rule

If every feasible alternative is on the ballot and *if* there is an alternative that defeats every other by a majority then that alternative is efficient.

The winner from Example 7.1 was not efficient because there were feasible alternatives not on the ballot, which listed only two outcomes, F and G. However, even with only three alternatives, majority rule can fail to deliver a clear winner, as we are about to see. For the rest of this chapter, we represent individual preference as a ranking of the feasible alternatives.

DEFINITION: *Individual Preference Ordering*

We represent an individual's preference scheme as a ranking of the alternatives in order of preference: most preferred, second most preferred, and so on. We refer to it as an *ordering* (or ranking) and display it as a column, with the most preferred alternative at the top and the other alternatives (or outcomes) arranged below in order of preference.

Example 7.3 A Majority Rule Cycle with Three Feasible Alternatives

Table 7.4 illustrates how we use an ordering to represent individual preferences. There are three voters. Person 1 prefers X to Y and Y to Z (and hence X to Z). Person 2 prefers Y to the other two policy options and so on. There is such diversity of individual preference here that it is far from obvious how one of these policies can be selected as the best for this three-person group. Each person has a different most-preferred alternative, and any individual's first choice is someone's last choice. The alternative that defeats the other two by a clear majority is the one that will be selected. Consider first the contest between Y and Z. Persons 1 and 2 will vote for Y over Z. (You can imagine three groups of roughly equal size if you think the case of three individuals is too unrealistic.) But Y will not defeat *both* of the other two alternatives by a majority. Persons 1 and 3 will vote for X over Y. This seems to leave us with X as the group choice. But alternative Z defeats X by a clear majority, with persons 2 and 3 both voting for Z in preference to X. We say that there is a majority rule cycle: X beats Y, Y beats Z, and Z beats X.

In 1956 the US House of Representatives voted on a program of grants for school construction – option G. An amendment was introduced to deny aid to any state with segregated public schools – option A. The third alternative was the status quo, S. Southern Democrats preferred G to the other two but also preferred S to A. A second group, mostly northern Democrats, preferred A to G and G to S. The remaining representatives, mostly Republicans, preferred S to either of the other alternatives but preferred A to G. The three groups were roughly equal in size; hence a voting cycle. The House voting rules precipitated S as the outcome in this case (Brams, 1976, p. 44).

We can fix the indecisiveness problem by augmenting majority voting to include by a rule for selecting one of the alternatives in case of a cycle. However, there is no way of doing this without creating opportunities for someone to profit by misrepresenting his or her individual preference, as illustrated by the next example.

With the preferences of Table 7.4, whatever alternative is selected will be the bottom ranked alternative for someone. That's the source of the incentive to misrepresent. If the majority winner is adopted whenever there is one, the individual whose bottom-ranked alternative is selected can benefit by reporting an ordering for which the top-ranked alternative is the one that ranks second in his *true* ordering. There will then be two individuals reporting the same top alternative, and that will be selected as the majority winner. Note that the individual who misrepresents precipitates the

Example 7.4 The Status Quo Receives Special Treatment

If there is an overall majority winner that will be the outcome. If there is a cycle and hence no overall winner, as with Example 7.3, the outcome will be X, which we take to be the status quo. On one hand, suppose Table 7.5 gives the true individual preferences. Then the outcome is Z because Z defeats X by two votes to one (persons 2 and 3 prefer Z to X) and Z defeats Y by two votes to one (persons 1 and 3 prefer Z to Y). If individual 1 does *not* report truthfully and declares a preference for X over Y and Y over Z then the reported preference pattern is the one of Table 7.4: there will be no overall majority winner. Alternative Y defeats Z by two votes to one, X defeats Y by two votes to one, and Z defeats X by two votes to one. According to the definition of our new decision rule the outcome will be X. Because person 1 actually prefers X to Z person 1 has profited by misrepresenting his or her preference scheme. (Note that the preferences of persons 2 and 3 are identical in the two situations.) On the other hand, suppose that Table 7.4 gives the true individual preferences. Then the outcome is X if everyone reports truthfully. However, if person 2 reports an ordering with Z on top then Z will be the majority winner because Z will be the top alternative for 2 and 3. Then Z, the overall majority winner, will be selected and person 2 prefers Z to X according to his or her true preferences and thus has benefitted by misrepresentation.

selection of an outcome that he prefers, *according to his true preference ordering*, to the one that is adopted when he reports truthfully.

We can extend the example to any odd number $n > 3$ by adding $(n - 3)/2$ individuals with the same preference as person 1 in Table 7.4 and $(n - 3)/2$ individuals with the preference of person 1 turned upside down. The preferences of these added voters will offset each other. There will again be a majority cycle. The individual $i < 4$ whose bottom-ranked alternative is selected can benefit by misrepresenting his prefence ordering as in the previous paragraph.

The case of an even number of individuals presents additional problems: suppose that half the voters have the preference ordering of person 1 of Table 7.4 and the others have that ordering turned upside down. Every alternative will tie every other in a head-to-head contest. The fact that this indeterminacy cannot be fixed without creating opportunities for individuals to profit by misrepresenting preference is a consequence of the theorem presented in Sections 7.2 and 7.3. (Section 7.3 has the more general version.)

Table 7.4

Person 1	Person 2	Person 3
X	Y	Z
Y	Z	X
Z	X	Y

Table 7.5

(a) Person 1	Person 2	Person 3
X	Y	Z
Z	Z	X
Y	X	Y

When an individual precipitates the election of a different alternative by deviating from truthful revelation we say that the person has *manipulated* if he or she prefers that alternative to the one that would have been selected had that person reported truthfully.

DEFINITION: *Manipulation*

We say that individual i can *manipulate* the voting rule if there is some assignment p of individual preferences at which individual i can profit by reporting a preference scheme that is not i's true preference. That is, individual i can manipulate at p if, given i's preferences at p, i prefers the outcome that is precipitated when i reports a different preference to the one that is selected when i truthfully reports his or her actual preference at p and everyone else continues to report their preferences at p. If no one can manipulate at any p we say that truthful revelation is a dominant strategy.

How do we know that the individual preference pattern of Table 7.4 will arise? We don't, because an individual's preference ordering is private information. That requires us to define a rule that can handle any preference input because we don't know what people's preferences might be. Note that even if we are committed to using majority rule, different specifications of the rule for selecting an outcome when there is a voting cycle define different voting schemes. Moreover, we do *not* assume that public decisions have to be made via a process that is based on majority rule. We *do* assume that the process is fundamentally democratic, but we're not sure at this stage exactly what that means.

7.1.2   Other Voting Schemes

The Gibbard-Satterthwaite Theorem of Section 7.2 establishes that if there are three or more alternatives, then every nondictatorial voting scheme can be manipulated. (A dictatorial scheme specifies an individual in advance, say person J, and always selects the alternative that is at the top of J's reported preference scheme.) In spite of the theorem, there is much that we can learn about preference revelation by attempting to find a scheme that is invulnerable to manipulation. First, even if invulnerability to manipulation implies that one individual has considerable power, why can't that power ever be mitigated? The next example shows what can go wrong.

Table 7.6

True		Reported	
Person 1	**Person 2**	**Person 1**	**Person 2**
X	Y	X	Y
Y	X	Y	Z
Z	Z	Z	X

Example 7.5 Sharing the Power

There are two voters. Suppose that we let the mechanism select person 1's top alternative, unless it is ranked at the bottom by person 2, in which case person 2's top alternative is selected. Consider the situation of Table 7.6. The "True" cell gives the respective true preferences of the individuals. Under truthful revelation, alternative X is top ranked by person 1 but is not bottom ranked by person 2. Thus the rule requires that X be selected. But if individual 2 changes her reported preference ordering to the one represented as the second column in the "Reported" half of the table, then X will not be selected because it is bottom ranked by person 2, and according to the rule, alternative Y will be selected. Note that person 2 does not require 1's cooperation. Person 1's reported ordering is the same in the two situations. Person 2 can do better than reporting her true preference by reporting a different ordering. When person 2 does this she precipitates the selection of an alternative that she prefers, according to her true preference scheme, to the alternative that is selected when she reports truthfully.

We run into the same difficulty if we seek a compromise.

Example 7.6 Compromise

There are two individuals and three alternatives. If the individuals have the same top-ranked alternative then that is selected. Suppose that they have different top alternatives. If each person's top is the other's second-ranked alternative, or each person's top is the other's third-ranked alternative, then select whichever of the tops precedes the other in the alphabet. Otherwise, one person's top will be the other's second-ranked alternative and one person's top is the other's third-ranked alternative, in which case select the alternative that ranks first for one person and second for the other. Consider the situation of Table 7.6. Alternative X is selected under truthful revelation, but if person 2 reports the ranking in column 2 of the "Reported" table instead then Y will be selected. Again, person 2 can misrepresent in a way that precipitates the selection of an alternative that she prefers, according to her true preference scheme, to the alternative that is selected when she reports truthfully.

The voting rule of Example 7.5 treats alternatives symmetrically but treats individuals asymmetrically. Example 7.6 and the next one treat individuals symmetrically but alternatives asymmetrically.

Note that the voting rule of Example 7.7 is well defined even if there are only two individuals. If there are more than three individuals we can extend the example by adding $n-3$ voters with preferences identical to persons 2 and 3. We will still have Y selected under truthful revelation, but X is adopted when person 1 claims that X is his most-preferred alternative. And this constitutes a Nash equilibrium. There is

Example 7.7 Everyone has Veto Power

There are three feasible alternatives, and all voters are asked to name the one they most prefer. If at least one person names X then X is adopted; otherwise Y is selected, unless everyone nominates Z, in which case Z is adopted. In other words, any individual can veto Z by naming either X or Y, and any individual can veto both Y and Z by naming X. Suppose that there are three voters 1, 2, and 3 with the true preference orderings given in Table 7.7. If each reports truthfully then the outcome is Y. However, person 1 can profit from misrepresentation. If person 1 nominates X then X will be selected, and person 1 prefers that alternative to Y according to his true preference ordering.

Table 7.7

Person 1	Person 2	Person 3
Z	Y	Y
X	Z	Z
Y	X	X

nothing that any $j > 1$ can do to change the outcome to Y or Z, and there is nothing that person 1 can do to precipitate the selection of Z. Not only is X the only outcome to emerge at a Nash equilibrium, it is inefficient: everyone prefers Z to X according to his or her true preference ordering.

What about plurality rule, for which voters simply declare their most-preferred alternative. The one receiving the most votes is the outcome. It is well known that this rule is not guaranteed to induce truthful revelation. Before looking at an example, we specify a tie-breaking rule, because we want the decision scheme to always select one and only one alternative. Let's agree that in case of a tie the alternative coming first in the alphabet is selected from the tied alternatives receiving the most votes.

Example 7.8 Plurality Rule

There are three individuals and three alternatives. Again, think of the left-hand cell of Table 7.8 as the true preferences of the respective individuals. The three alternatives are tied, with one vote each, so X is selected. But if person 2 reports the preference scheme of the middle column of the "Reported" table the winner will be Z with two votes, assuming that the other two report truthfully. By misrepresenting her preference and claiming that she prefers Z to the other alternatives, person 2 precipitates the selection of an outcome that she prefers according to her true preference – the middle column of the "true" table – which ranks Z above X. This is a case of voting for your second choice instead of your first choice, because your favorite candidate doesn't have much chance of victory.

Table 7.8

	True			Reported	
Person 1	**Person 2**	**Person 3**	**Person 1**	**Person 2**	**Person 3**
X	Y	Z	X	Z	Z
Y	Z	X	Y	Y	X
Z	X	Y	Z	X	Y

Suppose that we use plurality rule, but if there is a tie then we have a second election involving only the first-round winners. The next example shows how easily this scheme can be manipulated.

Example 7.9 Plurality Rule with Runoff

There are five individuals and four alternatives. The true preferences of each person are given in the top half of Table 7.9. If everyone reports his or her most-preferred alternative truthfully then X will receive two votes and Y, Z, and W will receive one vote each. Then the outcome will be X, which is the alternative preferred least by person 5. If 5 deviates from the truth and claims Y as his most preferred alternative – see the last column in the bottom half – then there will be a tie between X and Y. Alternative Y will win the runoff, receiving votes from 3, 4, and 5, each of whom prefers Y to X. Individual 5 obviously prefers Y to X according to his true preference ordering.

Table 7.9

		True		
Person 1	**Person 2**	**Person 3**	**Person 4**	**Person 5**
X	X	Y	Z	W
Y	Y	Z	Y	Z
Z	Z	X	X	Y
W	W	W	W	X

		Reported		
Person 1	**Person 2**	**Person 3**	**Person 4**	**Person 5**
X	X	Y	Z	Y
Y	Y	Z	Y	W
Z	Z	X	X	Z
W	W	W	W	X

Consider now conventional rank order voting – also called the *Borda rule* after the eighteenth-century French mathematician Jean-Charles de Borda. If there are four alternatives an individual casts four votes for the alternative that ranks at the top of his or her preference ordering, three votes for the alternative that ranks second, two votes for the alternative that ranks third, and one vote for the last-placed alternative.

DEFINITION: *The Borda (or Rank Order) Rule*

If there are m alternatives, each individual casts m votes for the alternative that ranks at the top of his or her preference ordering, $m-1$ votes for the alternative that ranks second, and so on. Then the alternative selected is the one with the most total votes.

Example 7.10 Borda or Rank Order Voting with Four Alternatives

There are three individuals and four alternatives (Table 7.10). The left half displays the true preferences of each person. For the true preference pattern alternative X receives nine votes, Y receives eight, and Z and W get seven and six votes respectively. Therefore, X would be selected by the Borda rule in this situation. The right half displays the reported preferences resulting from a change in person 3's reported preference ordering: this time Y receives nine votes, X and Z each receive eight, and W gets five votes. Then Y would be selected. Person 1's ranking is the same in the two tables, and so is 2's. If, instead of reporting truthfully (the third column of the "True" cell), person 3 reports the ranking in the third column of the "Reported" cell then the outcome will be Y, which individual 3 prefers to X according to his true preference ordering.

Table 7.10

	True			Reported	
Person 1	Person 2	Person 3	Person 1	Person 2	Person 3
X	Z	W	X	Z	Y
Y	X	Y	Y	X	W
Z	Y	X	Z	Y	Z
W	W	Z	W	W	X

We could investigate many more voting rules, but our search is destined to fail. The Gibbard-Satterthwaite Theorem of Section 7.2 implies that any voting rule can be manipulated unless it is sensitive to the preferences of only one individual or all but two of the feasible alternatives are arbitrarily eliminated from consideration at the outset. Suppose, however, that one of the three orderings of Table 7.4 could not possibly represent an individual's preferences for the chosen application. Perhaps the remaining preference orderings could never give rise to a voting cycle. The next section considers the possibility that majority rule is free of cycles and invulnerable to manipulation when some individual preference orderings can be eliminated from consideration.

7.1.3 Value-Restricted Preferences

Suppose that the feasible alternatives can be arranged in some intrinsic order that has significance for individual preferences. For instance, the three alternatives are L (left), M (middle), and R (right), as illustrated in Figure 7.1. They may represent three different levels of expenditure on a public fireworks display, with L requiring the smallest amount of money and R the largest. Similarly, the alternatives could be three different regulatory policies for a particular industry, with L requiring the greatest amount of government regulation and R the least. In some contexts we know in advance that anyone who prefers L to the other two alternatives would never prefer R to M. Similarly, anyone who prefers R to the other two could not conceivably have a preference for L over M. That means that we can rule out any preference scheme that has M as the least-preferred alternative. (If neither L or R is the most-preferred alternative then M must be preferred to the other two.) If we restrict the true *and* the reported preferences to the set of all logically possible orderings except the ones that have M ranked last then we can be sure of two things:

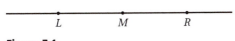

Figure 7.1

[1] There will be an alternative that would not be defeated by any other alternative under majority rule.

[2] If a majority winner were selected as the outcome then no individual can manipulate.

When the alternatives can be naturally ordered on a line, and an alternative is never ranked below one to its right *and* one to its left we say that individual preferences are *single peaked*. However, we can prove statements [1] and [2] under a much weaker restriction on individual preference. A set of preference orderings is *value restricted* if we *cannot* find three preference orderings in that set and three alternatives that generate the preference pattern of Table 7.4.

DEFINITION: *Value-Restricted Preferences*

Given three alternatives x, y, and z, a set of preference orderings is x restricted if alternative x does not rank above *both* y and z for any of the orderings in the set, *or x* does not rank below both y and z for any of the orderings in the set, *or x* does not rank in between y and z for any of the orderings in the set. We say that the set of preference orderings is *value restricted* if for any three alternatives, x, y, and z, the set is either x restricted, y restricted, or z restricted.

The three preferences of Table 7.4 are not value restricted because each of the three alternatives is first for one individual preference, last for one individual, and ranked in between the other two for the remaining individual.

For the rest of this section we assume an odd number of voters. The results go through with an even number of voters and some rule to select a winner in case of a tie, but by restricting attention to an odd number of individuals we are able to greatly simplify the argument. Up to this point we have implicitly assumed away ties at an individual level. That is, an individual is never indifferent between distinct alternatives. We maintain this assumption – for convenience. With an odd number of individuals and the absence of individual indifference, then for any two alternatives x and y, either a majority of individuals prefers x to y or a majority prefers y to x.

Theorem on Majority Cycles and Value Restriction

If individual indifference is ruled out and individual preferences are value-restricted there are no three-alternative majority rule cycles. If the number of voters is odd and preferences are value restricted there are no majority rule cycles of any length.

Proof:

We begin by showing that preferences cannot be value restricted if there exists a majority rule cycle involving only three alternatives: suppose that x defeats y by a majority, y defeats z by a majority, and z defeats x by a majority. Let J be the set of individuals who prefer x to y, and let K be the set of individuals who prefer y to z. Then J contains more than half of the individuals, and so does K. Therefore, J and K must have at least one individual in common. (If J is a majority, then the individuals *not* in J constitute a minority. If no one in J belongs to K then K cannot constitute a majority.) Therefore, there is at least one individual who prefers x to y *and* y to z. Now, let H be the set of individuals who prefer z to x. We know that H is a majority. The individuals in K prefer y to z, and the individuals in H prefer z to x. Because K and H each contain a majority of voters, the two sets must have at least one individual in common. Therefore, there is someone who prefers y to z and z to x. Similarly, because H and J are both majorities there is at least one individual who prefers z to x *and* x to y. But now we have the three preference orderings of Table 7.4 and value restriction does not hold.

Suppose that n is odd and $x^1 x^2 \ldots x^m x^1$ is a majority cycle. That is, x^t defeats x^{t+1} by a majority for $t = 1, 2, \ldots, m-1$, and x^m defeats x^1 by a majority. We show that preferences cannot be value restricted, even if $m > 3$. Because the number of voters is odd and individual indifference is assumed away either x^3 defeats x^1 by a majority or x^1 defeats x^3 by a majority. In the former case we have the cycle $x^1 x^2 x^3 x^1$, violating value restriction by the argument of the previous paragraph. In the latter case we have the cycle $x^1 x^3 x^4 \ldots x^m x^1$ which is shorter than the original cycle. Given any majority cycle of more that three alternatives we can find a shorter one, and hence we will eventually find a cycle involving just three alternatives, a violation of value restriction. ∎

Existence and Uniqueness Theorem for Majority Rule

Suppose that the number of alternatives is finite. If there exists no majority cycle of any length then there exists a majority winner – i.e., an alternative x^* such that no alternative defeats x^* by a majority. If preferences are value restricted and the number of voters is odd then there exists an alternative x^* that defeats every other by a majority – i.e., there is a majority winner and it is unique.

Proof:

Suppose that there are no majority cycles of any length. Choose any alternative x^1. If no alternative defeats x^1 by a majority then x^1 is a majority winner. If we can find some alternative, call it x^2, that defeats x^1 by a majority and no alternative defeats x^2 by a majority then x^2 is a majority winner. Suppose that x^{t+1} defeats x^t by a majority for $t = 1, 2, 3, \ldots, m$. If x^j defeats x^k by a majority for $j < k \le m$ then $x^j x^k x^{k-1} \ldots x^{j+1} x^j$ is a cycle, contrary to our hypothesis. In particular, x^j does not defeat x^m for any $j < m$. Because the number of alternatives is finite we will reach a stage T such that no alternative in the sequence $x^1 x^2 \ldots x^{T-2} x^{T-1}$ defeats x^T by a majority *and* no alternative not belonging to the sequence defeats x^T by a majority.

If the number of voters is odd and preferences are value restricted then there is no majority cycle of any length (by the previous theorem) and hence there is a majority winner x^* (by the previous paragraph). For any other alternative y either x^* defeats y by a majority or y defeats x^* by a majority because there is an odd number of voters and individual indifference has been assumed away. Clearly, x^* defeats every other alternative. ∎

Now that we know that there is always a unique majority winner whenever the individual preferences belong to the value-restricted family and the number of voters is odd we are ready to show that no individual or group can profit by deviating from truthful revelation, provided that the reported preferences must also belong to this family. First we extend the definition of manipulability to groups of individuals. They can manipulate if they can jointly deviate from truthful revelation in a way that leaves all members of the group better off according to their true preferences.

DEFINITION: *Manipulation by a Group*

We say that the individuals in group C can *manipulate* the voting rule if there are two different assignments p and q of individual preferences such that, for any individual i not belonging to C, p and q assign the same preference ordering to i and, according to the individual preferences at p, everyone in C prefers the outcome that emerges when she reports the preference assigned to her at q to the alternative that is selected when all members of C truthfully report their actual preferences at p.

Group C could consist of a single individual, so the definition covers manipulation by an individual. We think of the preferences assigned by p as the true preferences of the respective individuals. The members of C can manipulate if they can coordinate their strategies by reporting the preferences assigned to them at some q, *and* each member of C prefers the resulting outcome to the one that emerges when each reports truthfully, *and* each individual not in C has the same preference at q as at p. The individuals not in C cannot be expected to assist the coalition, hence the assumption that no one outside of C reports a different preference at q than the one reported at p.

Suppose that some family F of value-restricted preferences is known to contain the true preference ordering of each individual in the community, although the actual preference of an individual is still hidden information. If the reported preference of each individual must also belong to F then majority rule cannot be manipulated by any individual or group, as we now prove.

Theorem: Nonmanipulability of Majority Rule for Value-Restricted Preferences

Suppose that the number of individuals is odd, the number of alternatives is finite, individual indifference is ruled out, and both the true and reported individual preferences belong to some set F that is value restricted. Then majority rule cannot be manipulated by any individual or coalition.

In other words, truthful revelation is a dominant strategy for groups as well as individuals.

Proof:

Suppose that under truthful revelation alternative x is the unique majority winner but everyone in group C prefers y to x. If no one outside of C changes his or her reported preference ordering then there is nothing the members of C can do to precipitate the selection of y, because x defeats y by a clear majority even when everyone in C truthfully declares a preference of y over x. Whatever preferences are reported by the members of C, they must belong to F, so there will be a unique majority winner by the existence and uniqueness theorem. But that winner cannot be y, as we have just demonstrated. ∎

The assumption that the reported preferences must also belong to the family F is essential. Otherwise a voting cycle could be precipitated, in which case the definition of majority rule would have to be augmented to specify the alternative selected when there is a cycle, and that opens the door to manipulation by an individual. That fact is a consequence of the striking theorem introduced and proved in the next section for a special case. Section 7.3 provides the general result.

Sources

The possibility of a majority voting cycle appears to have been noticed first in Condorcet (1785). The rank order method of voting was advocated in Borda (1781). Sen (1966) introduced the notion of value-restricted preferences and proved that they imply the existence of a unique majority winner if the number of individuals is odd. For this and his many contributions to other branches of economics, including development, Amartya Sen was awarded the Nobel Prize in Economics in 1998.

Links

Neufeld et al. (1994) present an example of a voting cycle from the US Senate. Brams (1976, pp. 43-47) discusses the strategic dimensions of the US House voting cycle presented in this section. Campbell and Kelly (2000, 2003) explore the normative and strategic properties of majority rule in some depth. Arrow (1951a, 1963a) began the formal study of the criteria for determining how an alternative should be selected as a function of individual preferences, and his impossibility theorem is one of the most significant discoveries in the history of ideas. Campbell and Kelly (2002) prove that theorem and its close relatives and review the literature since Arrow. Kenneth Arrow was awarded the Nobel Prize in Economics in 1972 for his extensive and very deep contributions to economic theory.

Problem Set

(1) Prove that in the case of two alternatives, if majority rule is used to select one of the alternatives, supplemented by some tie-breaking rule when necessary, then whatever tie-breaking rule is employed, no coalition can manipulate.

(2) Example 7.3 presented a majority rule cycle with three alternatives and three individuals. Explain how one can construct a cycle with three alternatives and any odd number of individuals greater than one.

(3) List all the logically possible linear orders of the three alternatives x, y, z. (A linear order is one that can be represented as a column, with higher alternatives being preferred to lower ones; a linear order rules out the possibility that two distinct alternatives are indifferent to each other.) Now, identify all the families of single-peaked subsets of preferences.

(4) Suppose that an odd number of individuals have single-peaked preferences. The *median voter* is the one whose peak – i.e., most-preferred alternative – is to the left of exactly half the peaks of the other voters and is also to the right of

exactly half the peaks of the other voters. Explain why the median voter's peak will defeat every other alternative by a majority of votes.

(5) Does the set {xzy, zxy, zyx, yzx} of preferences over three alternatives x, y, z have the single-peak property? Explain. (The ordering xzy ranks x first, then z, then y last. The others are interpreted similarly.)

Each of the social choice functions in questions 6 through 16 is defined for every profile. If the rule can't be manipulated explain why. If the rule can be manipulated, demonstrate that fact with an example.

(6) The rule selects whichever of the alternatives ranked in the top two positions by person 1 is preferred by person 2.

(7) The rule selects person 1's top-ranked alternative or person 2's top-ranked alternative, whichever comes earlier in the alphabet.

(8) The rule selects the common top alternative if there is one. If there is not a common top then person 2's top-ranked alternative is selected.

(9) There are two feasible alternatives, x and y, and there are ten individuals. The rule selects the majority winner if there is one, and if there is a tie the rule selects the alternative that is preferred by person 1.

(10) There are two feasible alternatives, x and y, and there are n individuals. The rule selects y if all persons declare that they prefer x to y; otherwise the rule selects x.

(11) There are two feasible alternatives, x and y, and there are n individuals. The rule selects y if all persons declare that they prefer y to x; otherwise the rule selects x.

(12) There are two feasible alternatives, x and y, and there are six individuals. The rule selects the alternative that gets the most votes, but individuals 1, 2, and 3 are each allowed to cast three votes for their preferred alternatives, and individuals 4, 5, and 6 may each cast only two votes for their preferred alternatives.

(13) There are three individuals, 1, 2, and 3, and four alternatives, w, x, y, and z. If there is a plurality winner – i.e., an alternative at the top of the reported preference ordering of two or more individuals – then that alternative is selected. If there is no plurality winner then the alternative ranked second by person 1 is selected.

(14) There are three individuals, 1, 2, and 3, and four alternatives, w, x, y, and z. If there is a plurality winner then that alternative is selected. If there is no plurality winner then the rule selects whichever of the top ranked alternatives is alphabetically earliest.

(15) There are three individuals, 1, 2, and 3, and four alternatives, w, x, y, and z. The rule selects the alphabetically earliest alternative from the set of alternatives that are not ranked last by anyone. (There are three individuals and four alternatives, so at least one alternative will not be ranked last by anyone.)

(16) This time there are $n > 2$ individuals and $m > 3$ alternatives with n and m
arbitrary. The rule selects the alphabetically earliest alternative from the set
of alternatives that are ranked first by someone.

7.2 PREFERENCE REVELATION IN GENERAL

The previous section featured a number of voting rules. With unrestricted individual preferences, almost every rule gave individuals an incentive to profit from
misrepresenting their preferences in some situations. Only two things worked:
restricting the number of alternatives on the ballot and restricting the set of
admissible individual preferences. If there are only two alternatives on the ballot
then conventional majority rule induces truthful revelation of individual preference. But that approach will – except by accident – run afoul of efficiency when
there are actually three or more feasible alternatives.

What about arbitrarily restricting individual preferences? If we have a priori
information establishing that each person's preference ranking belongs to a particular family of single-peaked or value-restricted preferences, then we can apply
majority rule and know that there will be an alternative that will survive an election
when paired with any other alternative and that truthful revelation is a dominant
strategy for each person if no one is allowed to report a preference scheme that is
outside of the restricted family. This section investigates the possibilities for truthful revelation when there are three or more alternatives and we are unable to rule
out any ranking of the alternatives as a possible preference scheme for any individual. We prove that if each alternative is selected in at least one situation – perhaps
when everyone ranks that alternative at the top – then the only rules that induce
truthful revelation are rules that ignore the preferences of all but one individual.
Before stating this formally, we specify our framework.

At the very least, democracy means that decisions that have widespread social
consequences should be the result of a process in which individual assessments of
the alternatives have a bearing on the outcome – in a positive way. The society that
we wish to study can be anything from a small committee to an entire nation. Once
we have identified the society, the next step is to identify the policy options at issue.
These alternatives have a different character in different applications. If a college
class is selecting a president then the alternatives are the names of the eligible
candidates. If we are interested in a nation selecting a health care policy, then the
options are the various proposals under consideration. In most situations, one of
the options will be "no change" – that is, the status quo. We can even model the
market system in this abstract way, with each alternative being a particular configuration of production and consumption activities. The framework will be flexible
enough to embrace a panel of physicians deciding which patient is to receive a
kidney transplant when the next organ becomes available, or a panel of scientists
determining which experiments will be performed by a space probe of Saturn, or
the board of directors of a modern corporation deliberating on a proposed merger.
The analysis pertains to any group decision in which the individuals care about the
alternatives but there is rarely unanimous agreement about what should be done.

The group's decision should be a function of the individual preferences of the group members. Therefore, we need to model the individual assessments of the policy options, and we do this by representing the *order* in which each individual ranks the alternatives, as we did in Section 7.1. In this chapter, the social choice process does not use any information about the *intensity* of an individual's preference for one alternative over another. Consequently we only require information about the order of individual preference – i.e., where one alternative ranks relative to another. Does *x* rank above or below *y* in individual *i*'s preference scheme? In the next chapter we see that allowing additional preference input – specifically, information about intensity of preference – opens the door to a social choice procedure that induces truthful revelation even though it is sensitive to everyone's preferences. That procedure has significant drawbacks, however.

We say nothing about *why* the individuals have the preferences that they have. One person will be very selfish and rank the policy options according to their impact on the basket of goods and services that he himself will consume. Another may be altruistic, taking into account the impact on those less fortunate. Some individuals will not rank alternatives according to what they want but according to what they think society should have; in some people this normative judgement is selfishly based, and in others it is not. Whatever the basis of the individual's preference ordering of the alternatives it is what motivates the individual's participation in the decision process, and these orderings are the input in our model. The output is the decision rendered; a selection of one of the options as the decision taken by society. In other words, the *social choice rule* selects a feasible alternative as a function of individual preferences.

DEFINITION: *The Social Choice Framework*

There are *n* individuals and a given set *X* of feasible alternatives. *A profile p* assigns an ordering *p(i)* of the members of *X* to each individual *i*. The alternative that is most-preferred by individual *i* at profile *p* is said to be the *top* of *p(i)*. A *social choice rule g* selects a member *g(p)* of *X* for each profile *p*. We require *g(p)* to be defined for every logically possible profile *p* for which no individual is ever indifferent between two distinct alternatives and for which every individual's preference is transitive – the *unrestricted preferences* assumption. (Transitivity means that if *x* is preferred to *y* and *y* is preferred to *z* then it must be the case that *x* is preferred to *z*.) The rule *g is nonimposed* if for each member *x* of *X* there is some profile *p* such that *g(p) = x*.

A profile is interpreted as a record of the individual preferences in a particular situation. Sometimes the profile will represent the true preferences of the respective individuals, and sometimes it will represent the preferences *reported* by the individuals. No restriction is placed on the either the true or the reported preferences. In other words, the social choice rule must render a decision for each logically possible assignment of preference orderings to individuals. We would expect a social choice rule to select x at any profile for which everyone ranked x at the top. Nonimposition merely requires that there be *some* profile at which x is selected.

The social choice rule g is not necessarily a voting system – and we are certainly not restricting attention to rules that have actually been tried. In principle g could represent the market system, with $g(p)$ being the market equilibrium for the configuration of preferences represented by p. However, the theorem that we prove in this section applies only when the unrestricted preferences assumption is appropriate – that is, when every logically possible ordering of the feasible set is a conceivable individual ordering. This is certainly not the case for the allocation of private goods. Create outcome y from x by giving person 1's car to person 2. Standard economic models exclude preferences that have person 1 ranking y at the top, as the most-preferred alternative. However, the proof in this chapter makes use of such an ordering. Therefore, the proof is valid only for situations in which the unrestricted preferences assumption is appropriate. For instance, if the members of X represent different mixes of public projects that are financed with a given amount of tax revenue, then we cannot a priori rule out any ordering of X as a possible preference that an individual might have.

7.2.1 The Gibbard-Satterthwaite Theorem

We seek a nonimposed social choice rule that induces individuals to report their preferences truthfully. In other words, no individual can manipulate. A social choice rule for which truthful preference revelation is a dominant strategy is said to be *strategy proof.*

DEFINITION: *Strategy Proofness*

Given profile p we say that individual i can *manipulate* the social choice rule g at p if there exists a profile q such that $q(j) = p(j)$ for all $j \neq i$ and $g(q)$ ranks higher in $p(i)$ than $g(p)$ does. The social choice rule g is *strategy proof* if no individual can manipulate.

In interpreting the definition of manipulation we think of $p(i)$ as the true preference of individual i. By reporting $q(i)$ instead of $p(i)$ individual i might precipitate the selection of an alternative $g(q)$ that i prefers, according to his true preference $p(i)$, to the alternative $g(p)$ selected when i reports truthfully. We require $q(j) = p(j)$ for all $j \neq i$ because we cannot assume that others will change their reported preferences to suit individual i.

Here are two strategy-proof social choice rules: (i) Select two specific alternatives and label them x^* and y^*. The outcome is x^* unless the reported individual preference orderings have y^* ranking above x^* in a majority of cases, in which case y^* is the outcome. There may be many available alternatives other than these two, but only x^* and y^* can ever be selected. Why is this scheme strategy proof? Suppose that x^* wins under truthful revelation, but individual j prefers y^* to x^*. Then j has voted for y^* but x^* won nonetheless. Misrepresentation by j would result in another vote being cast for x^*, in which case x^* will still win. Similarly, if y^* wins under truthful revelation, but j prefers x^* there is nothing that j can do to prevent the election of y^*. In most situations there are more than two alternatives to consider but with this voting scheme the outcome must be either x^* or y^* in every case. Suppose there is a third alternative z, and everyone ranks z as most preferred. The outcome will not be efficient; everyone prefers z to the winner, which must be either x^* or y^*. This procedure is strategy proof but very unsatisfactory on efficiency grounds.

Our second strategy-proof procedure *is* efficient: (ii) there are any number of alternatives and the outcome is always the most-preferred alternative according to the reported preference scheme of person 1. No one other than person 1 can affect the outcome so no one other than person 1 has an incentive to manipulate. And it is in person 1's self-interest to ensure the selection of his most-preferred alternative so person 1 will always report truthfully. The procedure is strategy proof. It is obviously dictatorial and therefore completely unsatisfactory.

DEFINITION: *Dictatorship*

The social choice rule g is *dictatorial* if there is some individual i such that, for each profile p, $g(p)$ is the top-ranked member of $p(i)$. We say that individual i is a *dictator* in that case.

In plain words, an individual is a dictator if the rule *always* selects the alternative that the individual most prefers. If there are at least three feasible alternatives, a nonimposed social choice rule cannot be strategy proof if it is not dictatorial.

The Gibbard-Satterthwaite Theorem

Suppose that the feasible set has three or more members, preferences are unrestricted, and the social choice rule g is nonimposed. Then g is dictatorial if it is strategy proof.

Proof of this theorem for the case of two individuals and three alternatives is quite easy, and we take care of that in the next section. You may wish to stop there, in which case you will have a good grasp of the import of the theorem and an idea of how the general proof works.

7.2.2   Proof for Two Individuals and Three Alternatives

We assume in this section that the feasible alternatives are x, y, and z, and no others, and that persons 1 and 2 are the only individuals whose preferences are to be considered. We show that either person 1 or person 2 must be a dictator. That means that a strategy-proof rule must select an individual in advance, say individual 1, and always select 1's top-ranked alternative at every profile. We start with a profile p at which either person 1 or person 2's top alternative must be selected – because the third alternative is bottom ranked by both. (It is easy to show that an alternative can't be selected by a strategy proof rule if it is bottom ranked by everyone.) Then we show that the individual whose top-ranked alternative is selected at p must inevitably have absolute power. But even if strategy proofness implies that one individual has considerable power, why can that power ever be mitigated? Example 7.5 in the previous section shows what can go wrong.

The proof begins with the unanimity lemma: if both persons 1 and 2 have a common top-ranked alternative then that alternative must be selected if g is strategy proof. Then we use that lemma to show that strategy proofness implies that z will not be selected at a profile at which both persons rank z at the bottom.

Step 1: The Unanimity Lemma

If both 1 and 2 have x ranked at the top at p then g(p) = x if g is strategy proof and x is selected at some profile.

Proof:

Let q be a profile at which x is selected, and let p be a profile at which both persons 1 and 2 have x ranked at the top. Strategy proofness implies that g must select x when person 1's preference ordering is $p(1)$ and person 2 reports the ordering $q(2)$. That is, $g(p(1), q(2)) = x$. If we did not have $g(p(1), q(2)) = x$ then person 1 would have an opportunity to manipulate by reporting $q(1)$ because we know that $g(q(1), q(2)) = x$ and x is ranked at the top of $p(1)$. Therefore, strategy proofness implies $g(p(1), q(2)) = x$. That fact itself implies that strategy proofness requires that g select x when person 2's preference ordering is $p(2)$ and person 1 reports $p(1)$. That is, $g(p(1), p(2)) = x$. If we did not have $g(p(1), p(2)) = x$ then person 2 would have an opportunity to manipulate by reporting $q(2)$ because we know that $g(p(1), q(2)) = x$. Therefore, strategy proofness implies $g(p) = g(p(1), p(2)) = x$. ∎

Now we show that if both persons 1 and 2 have a common *bottom*-ranked alternative then that alternative must not be selected if g is strategy proof.

Step 2

If both persons 1 and 2 have z ranked at the bottom then g(p) ≠ z if g is strategy proof and nonimposed.

Proof:

If the two individuals have the same top-ranked alternative, then that alternative will be selected (by the unanimity lemma), and hence the common bottom-ranked alternative will not be selected. Suppose that the top-ranked alternatives are different, but the common bottom z is selected. Because both individuals rank z last, person 1's second choice is person 2's top choice, as in the case of Table 7.11. If person 1 misrepresents by reporting the same ordering as person 2 then there will be a common top which will be selected (by the unanimity lemma). Because person 1 ranks z last he prefers person 2's top alternative to z, contradicting the fact that g is strategy-proof. We have to abandon the supposition that a common bottom alternative is selected at some profile. ∎

Table 7.11 Profile p

$p(1)$	$p(2)$
X	y
Y	x
Z	z

Our two voters are Andre and Maggie. Profile p has each ranking z last, but they have different top-ranked alternatives. Because g will not select z at profile p it will select the top alternative of one of these two individuals. Let's refer to the individual whose top alternative is selected at p as person 1, and let's rename that individual's top alternative at p and call it x. The profile is displayed as Table 7.11. We now prove that g selects person 1's top alternative at *every* profile. In other words, person 1 is a dictator for g.

Step 3

If $g(p) = x$ for the profile p of Table 7.11 then $g(q) = x$ for the profile q of Table 7.12.

Proof:

If $g(q) = z$ then person 1 would have an opportunity to manipulate when the profile of true preferences is q, because, by the unanimity lemma, person 1 could then precipitate the selection of y by reporting an ordering with y at the top. Therefore, strategy proofness implies that $g(q) \neq z$.

Table 7.12 Profile q

$q(1)$	$q(2)$
x	y
y	z
z	x

If $g(q) = y$ then person 2 would have an opportunity to manipulate when the profile of true preferences is p of Table 7.11 because $g(p) = x$ and $q(1) = p(1)$, and person 2 prefers y to x at p according to 2's true preference $p(2)$. Therefore, strategy proofness implies that $g(q) \neq y$.

We have ruled out $g(q) = z$ and also $g(q) = y$. Therefore $g(q) = x$. ∎

Step 4

If $g(p) = x$ for the profile p of Table 7.11, then $g(r) = x$ for any profile r that has x ranked at the top for person 1.

Proof:

Note that x is ranked at the bottom by person 2 at the profile q of Table 7.12. Therefore, strategy proofness implies that x will be selected at any profile for which 1's reported ordering is $q(1)$ – that is, whenever person 1 has x at the top and z at the bottom. If in that situation there is an ordering that person 2 could report to secure the selection of an alternative other than x then 2 could manipulate at q, where person 2 prefers anything to x. Therefore, $g(s) = x$ for any profile s that has $s(1) = q(1)$.

Table 7.13 Profile t

$t(1)$	$t(2)$
y	z
x	y
z	x

If $g(r) \neq x$ and x is ranked at the top for person 1 then person 1 can manipulate at r by the argument of the previous paragraph, because person 1 can precipitate the selection of his or her most-preferred alternative x by reporting the ordering $q(1)$. (To make this claim we suppose that $r(1)$ is the true preference of person 1.) Therefore, we must have $g(r) = x$, at any profile r for which x is top-ranked by person 1.

We haven't established that person 1 is the dictator. So far, we only know that alternative x will be selected at any profile at which x is top ranked by person 1. Perhaps y will not be selected in some situation in which it is ranked first by person 1. If so person 1 is not a dictator. We now show that this can't happen. ∎

Step 5

If $g(p) = x$ for the profile p of Table 7.11, then $g(t) = y$ for profile t of Table 7.13.

Proof:

If $g(t) = x$ then person 2 would have an opportunity to manipulate when the profile of true preferences is t, because, by the unanimity lemma (step 1), person 2 can precipitate the selection of y by reporting an ordering with y at the top. Therefore, strategy proofness implies that $g(t) \neq x$.

Table 7.14 Profile u

$u(1)$	$u(2)$
y	z
z	y
x	x

If $g(t) = z$ then person 1 would have an opportunity to manipulate when the profile of true preferences is t by reporting an ordering with x on top. That would precipitate the selection of x (by step 4) and at t person 1 prefers x to z. Therefore, strategy proofness implies that $g(t) \neq z$.

We have ruled out $g(t) = x$ and also $g(t) = z$. Therefore $g(t) = y$. ∎

Step 6

If $g(p) = x$ for the profile p of Table 7.11, then $g(u) = y$ for profile u of Table 7.14.

Proof:

If $g(u) \neq y$ then person 1 would manipulate when the profile of true preferences is u by reporting $t(1)$ of step 5. (Note that $u(2)$ and $t(2)$ are identical.) Therefore, strategy proofness implies that $g(u) = y$.

Now we complete the proof of the Gibbard-Satterthwaite Theorem by applying steps 2, 3, and 4 to the profile u (of step 6) to show that y is selected at *any* profile for which person 1 has y ranked at the top. (This time, y plays the role of x, and x plays the role of z. Note that x is bottom ranked for both persons at u.) Having established that, we use the arguments of steps 5 and 6 to show that z is selected at the profile with y at the bottom for both persons, z at the top for person 1, and x at the top for person 2. Having established that, we can apply steps 2, 3, and 4 again to show that z is selected at any profile at which person 1 has z ranked at the top. Because x, y, and z are the only three alternatives, we then have proved that individual 1 is a dictator.

The top alternative of either Andre or Maggie is selected at profile p of Table 7.11. We chose to use "person 1" as the new name for whichever individual that is, and "alternative x" as the new name for that person's most-preferred alternative. That individual must be a dictator for g.   ∎

Every strategy-proof and nonimposed rule is dictatorial if there are three alternatives and two individuals.

Remark 1. Nonimposition played a role in the proof right at the beginning when we assumed that x is selected at some profile. Similarly, the proof depends on the assumption that y is selected at some profile, and so is z. (The rule that selects x at *every* profile is obviously strategy proof, and so is the rule that *never* selects z but selects x when both individuals prefer x to y and otherwise selects y.)

Remark 2. With only two individuals, there will be profiles at which x is first and y is second for one person and the other has y first and x second, as in the case of profile p of Table 7.11. One of the two individuals must be favored in that instance, and once that happens strategy proofness forces the rule to give that individual absolute power. However, the Gibbard-Satterthwaite Theorem is not special to the case $n = 2$. If $n > 2$ there will be favoritism of some individual at some profile, but it will be more subtle. Nevertheless, strategy proofness will still force the rule to give the favored individual absolute power. For instance, begin with profile α that has x at the top for everyone and y second. Then x will be selected. Now, move y to the top and x down to second place for one individual at a time. When we are finished we will be at profile β that has y first and x second for everyone, and hence y will be selected at β. We started with x being selected and finished with y. At some intermediate stage we must have switched the ordering of x and y for one individual and caused the selection to change from x to y. That individual is given special treatment at that point, and strategy proofness will imply that that person is a dictator.

Sources

This remarkable theorem was discovered independently in the 1970s by the philosopher Alan Gibbard and the economist Mark Satterthwaite (Gibbard, 1973; Satterthwaite, 1975).

Links

See Section 7.3.2 on voters and economic agents. There is a vast literature on the preference revelation problem. Significant surveys include Chapter 10 of Kelly (1988), Chapter 1 of Saari (1994), Barberà (2001, 2004), Jackson (2001), and Maskin and Sjöström (2002).

Problem Set

(1) Consider the following social choice rule defined for two individuals, 1 and 2, and three alternatives x, y, z: The individuals report a preference ordering of the three alternatives, and if one of the alternatives is ranked at the top of both reported preference orderings then that alternative is the selected outcome; otherwise person 1's top-ranked alternative is the outcome. (Assume that two distinct alternatives are never indifferent in anyone's preference ordering.) Prove that truthful revelation is a dominant strategy for this social choice rule. Does this contradict the Gibbard-Satterthwaite theorem? Explain.

Questions 2 and 3 each pertain to a different social choice function. In each case determine whether truthful revelation is a dominant strategy. If it is not, demonstrate that fact with an example. If truthful revelation is a dominant strategy prove that it is.

(2) There are three feasible alternatives and three individuals. The rule is based on the total number of votes received by each alternative when the Borda rule (Example 7.10) is used to rank the alternatives. The alternative with the largest total score is selected. If the three alternatives have the same score then x is selected. If there are exactly two alternatives with the highest score, then whichever of those two alternatives comes before the other in the alphabet is selected.

(3) As in the previous question the alternative with the largest total Borda score is selected, but if two or more alternatives are tied for the highest score then whichever of those alternatives ranks highest in the reported preference ordering of person 1 is selected.

Questions 4–7 each pertain to a different social choice function with unknown properties *except* that truthful revelation is a dominant strategy. You can't assume that the rule is dictatorial, or is majority rule, or any other rule. You can't assume that it is defined for every profile. You only know that the rule can't be manipulated and whatever additional properties are given in stating the question. Profiles P, Q, R, S, and T are displayed in Table 7.15.

Table 7.15

P(1)	P(2)	Q(1)	Q(2)	R(1)	R(2)	S(1)	S(2)	T(1)	T(2)
x	y	x	y	y	x	x	x	y	z
y	x	y	z	x	z	y	z	x	y
z	z	z	x	z	y	z	y	z	x

(4) Alternative x is selected at profile P, and whenever there is a common top alternative that common top is selected. Determine the alternative that is selected at profile Q and explain why it must be selected.

(5) Alternative x is selected at profile R. Determine the alternative that is selected at profile S and explain why it must be selected.

(6) Alternative x is selected at any profile at which person 1 has x at the top, and whenever there is a common top alternative that common top is selected. Determine the alternative that is selected at profile T and explain why it must be selected.

(7) Alternative y is selected at profile R. Determine the alternative that is selected at profile T and explain why it must be selected.

7.3   GENERAL PROOF OF THE GIBBARD-SATTERTHWAITE THEOREM

The most accessible evidence for the fact that people *do* attempt to manipulate is the observation that in a three-candidate election we often choose not to vote for our most-preferred candidate when that candidate has little chance of being elected. In that situation we often vote for our second choice, in an attempt to prevent the candidate whom we rank last from being elected. But what's wrong with *that*? It probably makes the election more responsive to individual preferences. Then let's take that kind of behavior as given and build it into the definition of the rule g. In other words, let $g(p)$ be the outcome as a result of an equilibrium configuration of strategies by the n individuals. The Gibbard-Satterthwaite Theorem tells us that even *that* rule can be manipulated.

7.3.1   A Concise General Proof

There are n individuals, named 1, 2, $\ldots$, n. There are at least three alternatives, comprising the set X. The proof consists mainly in creating a new profile from an old one by moving some alternative (or alternatives) around in one or more individual orderings. We will do this in a way that allows us to say something precise about the alternative selected at the new profile. For instance, suppose that $g(p) = x$, alternative x is at the top of $p(1)$, and we create profile r from p simply by keeping x at the top of person 1's ordering but we change the way that the alternatives ranking below x are ordered relative to each other. Strategy-proofness of g implies that $g(r) = x$. Otherwise, person 1 could manipulate at r by reporting $p(1)$, resulting in profile p at which x is selected. (Note that $r(1)$ ranks x above every other alternative.) We can say more: suppose that $g(p) = x$ and x ranks somewhere in the middle of $p(1)$. Now create profile r from p simply by changing the way that the alternatives ranking below x in $p(1)$ are ordered relative to each other, and by changing the way that the alternatives ranking above x in $p(1)$ are ordered relative to each other. Then $g(r) = x$ by strategy proofness: if $g(r) = y \neq x$ and y ranks above x in $p(1)$ then person 1 could manipulate at p by reporting $r(1)$. And if $g(r) = y \neq x$ and y ranks below x in $p(1)$ then y also ranks below x in $r(1)$, so person 1 could manipulate at r by reporting $p(1)$. Our first lemma generalizes this.

Lemma 1 (Monotonicity)

Suppose that g is strategy-proof and x is selected at profile p. Then g(r) = x for any profile r such that, for each individual i and each alternative y, alternative y ranks above x in p(i) if y ranks above x in r(i).

Proof:

Suppose that $g(p) = x$ and, for each individual i, an alternative y ranks above x in $p(i)$ if it ranks above x in $r(i)$. Let p' be obtained from p by replacing $p(1)$ with $r(1)$. Suppose that $g(p') = z \neq x$. If z ranks below x in $p'(1) = r(1)$ then person 1 can manipulate g at p' by reporting $p(1)$. If z ranks above x in $p'(1)$ then by hypothesis z ranks above x in $p(1)$, in which case person 1 can manipulate g at p by reporting $p'(1)$. Therefore, $g(p') = x$. The same argument shows that $g(p'') = x$ if $g(p') = x$ and p'' is obtained from p' by replacing $p'(2) = p(2)$ with $r(2)$. We have $g(p'') = x$, and we continue in this fashion, replacing $p(i)$ with $r(i)$, one individual at a time. At each stage x must be selected by the above argument, and thus x must be selected at the next stage. Therefore, when all $p(i)$ have been replaced we have $g(r) = x$. ∎

Why is this called the monotonicity lemma? Because it includes the special case for which r is obtained from p by moving some alternative x up in the ranking of some individual.

Because each alternative is chosen at *some* profile, we can use monotonicity to show that an alternative is selected by g at any profile that has everyone ranking that alternative at the top.

Lemma 2 (Unanimity)

If some alternative x ranks at the top of r(i) for every individual i then g(r) = x.

Proof:

There is some profile p such that $g(p) = x$. Compare p and r: For each individual i and each alternative y, we have y ranking above x in $p(i)$ if y ranks above x in $r(i)$. This holds because no alternative ranks above x in $r(i)$. Therefore, Lemma 1 implies that $g(r) = x$. ∎

DEFINITION: *Moving Alternatives Up and Down*

When we say that the ordering $r(i)$ is obtained by moving y up (resp., down) in $p(i)$ we mean that $r(i)$ is the same as $p(i)$ except that y occupies a higher (resp., lower) position in $r(i)$ than in $p(i)$. (The ordering of $X\backslash\{y\}$, the set of alternatives exclusive of y, is the same for $r(i)$ as for $p(i)$.) When we say that $r(i)$ is obtained from $p(i)$ by moving y to the top we mean that the ordering $r(i)$ ranks y above all other alternatives, with x ranking above z in $r(i)$ if and only if x ranks above z in $p(i)$, for any x and z distinct from y.

The final lemma establishes that if x is selected and we change the profile so that some alternative y moves up in some or all individual orderings then alternative y must be selected at the new profile if x is not chosen there.

Lemma 3

If $g(p) = x$ and profile r is obtained from p by moving some alternative y up in some or all $p(i)$ then $g(r) = x$ or y.

Proof:

Suppose that $g(r) = z$ but $x \neq z \neq y$. Compare r and p: Arbitrary alternative b ranks above z in $p(i)$ if it ranks above z in $r(i)$. Then $g(p) = z$ by monotonicity (Lemma 1), because $g(r) = z$. This contradicts the fact that $g(p) = x \neq z$. We must abandon the supposition that $g(r)$ does not equal x or y. ∎

Now we use the lemmas to establish that g is dictatorial.

Proof of the Gibbard-Satterthwaite Theorem:

Choose any two alternatives x and y and any profile p such that x ranks at the top of $p(i)$ and y ranks at the bottom for each individual i. Then $g(p) = x$ by Lemma 2 (Unanimity).

Create p'' from p by moving y to the top for each individual, one person at a time in numerical order. By Lemma 3, at each stage the selected alternative will be either x or y. By Lemma 2 (Unanimity), we have $g(p'') = y$. Let individual j be the first person for whom the selected alternative changes from x to y as a result of j's reported ordering changing from $p(j)$ to $p''(j)$, which has y ranked at the top. (Once the selected outcome changes from x to y it must remain at y, by Lemma 1, as other individual orderings are modified by moving y to the top.) We will show that j is a dictator for g. From now on we let j denote this individual who is *pivotal* for the sequence of changes taking us from p to p''.

Let q be the profile obtained from p by moving y to the top for the first $j-1$ individuals, with $q(i) = p(i)$ for all $i \geq j$. Let r be the profile obtained from q by moving y to the top for $q(j) = p(j)$. We have $g(q) = x$ and $g(r) = y$ by the previous

Table 7.16

$q(j-1)$	$q(j)$	$q(j+1)$	$r(j-1)$	$r(j)$	$r(j+1)$	$s(j-1)$	$s(j)$	$s(j+1)$
y	x	x	y	y	x	y	y	⋮
x			x	x			x	⋮
⋮	⋮	⋮	⋮	⋮	⋮	⋮	⋮	⋮
								x
	y	y			y	x		y
	$g(q) = x$			$g(r) = y$			$g(s) = y$	

Table 7.17

$t(j-1)$	$t(j)$	$t(j+1)$	$u(j-1)$	$u(j)$	$u(j+1)$	$v(j-1)$	$v(j)$	$v(j+1)$
y	x			x			x	
	y	⋮	⋮	z	⋮	⋮	z	⋮
⋮	⋮			y			y	
		x	z		z	z		z
x		y	y	⋮	x	y	⋮	y
		x			y	x		x
	$g(t) = x$			$g(u) = x$			$g(v) = x$	

paragraph. (Profiles q, r, and s are displayed in Table 7.16. For each profile it is implicit that, for each $i < j$ individual i's ordering is modified in the same way that $j-1$'s was, and for $i > j$ individual i's ordering is modified in the same way that $j+1$'s was.

Create profile s from r by moving x down to the bottom for each $i < j$ and by moving x down to second last position, just above y, for each $i > j$, with $s(j) = r(j)$. Then $g(s) = y$ by monotonicity (Lemma 1) because $g(r) = y$ and when we create s from r alternative y does not change its ranking relative to any other alternative for any individual. Now create t from s by simply moving x above y for individual j. (Table 7.17) Because $s(j)$ has y in first place and x second, we create $t(j)$ from $s(j)$ by moving x to the top. Then $g(t) = x$ or y by Lemma 3. Suppose that $g(t) = y$. Create q' from q by moving y up to second position for individual j. Then $g(q') = x$ by Lemma 1. Compare t and q'. (Consult Table 7.17: q' is the same as q, except that we replace $q(j)$ with $t(j)$.) For each individual i, alternative y has the same position in $q'(i)$ relative to the other alternatives as it does in $t(i)$. Therefore, $g(t) = y$ and Lemma 1 imply $g(q') = y$, contradicting the fact that $g(q') = x$. We have to drop the supposition that $g(t) = y$. We must have $g(t) = x$.

Choose any alternative z other than x or y. (There are at least three alternatives.) Create profile u from t by moving y down to second last position, just above x, and z down to third last position, just above y, for each $i < j$, and by moving z to second position, just between x and y, for individual j, and then for all $i > j$ moving z down to third last position, just above x which is just above y (Table 7.17). We have $g(u) = x$ by Lemma 1 (Monotonicity) because $g(t) = x$ and in moving from t to u we do not change the position of x relative to any other alternative for any individual.

Now, create v from u by moving y up just above x to second last position for each $i > j$ (Table 7.17). We have $g(v) = x$ or y by Lemma 3. At profile v, alternative x ranks last for each $i \neq j$ and x ranks at the top of $v(j)$. Suppose that $g(v) = y$. Create v' from v by moving z to the top for each individual. This does not change the ranking of y relative to any other alternative for any individual. Therefore, $g(v') = y$ by Lemma 1 (Monotonicity). But z ranks at the top of $v'(i)$ for each individual i and thus $g(v') = z$ by Lemma 2 (Unanimity). This contradiction forces us to abandon the supposition that $g(v) = y$. Therefore, $g(v) = x$.

We have established the existence of a profile v such that $g(v) = x$, the alternative ranking at the top of $v(j)$ and at the bottom of $v(i)$ for all $i \neq j$. This implies that x is selected at any profile p' at which x ranks at the top of $p'(j)$. To prove this, create v'' from v by replacing $v(i)$ with $p'(i)$ for all $i \neq j$, one individual at a time in numerical order. When we replace $v(1)$ with $p'(1)$ alternative x will still be selected, or else individual 1 could manipulate at v by reporting $p'(1)$ because x is at the bottom of $v(1)$. Similarly, for any other $i \neq j$ alternative x will still be selected when we replace $v(i)$ with $p'(i)$ because it was selected before we replaced $v(i)$. Otherwise, individual i could manipulate before the replacement because x is at the bottom of $v(i)$. Therefore, strategy-proofness of g implies that $g(v'') = x$. Finally, create p' from v'' by replacing $v''(j) = v(j)$ with $p'(j)$, which has x on top. We have $g(p') = x$ because $g(v'') = x$, and if $g(p') \neq x$ then person j could manipulate at p' by reporting $v''(j)$.

We have established that alternative x is selected whenever person j reports an ordering with x on top. Say that individual j is *decisive* for x. But x was an arbitrary alternative. Therefore, we have proved that for every alternative there is an individual who is decisive for that alternative. But we can't have person h decisive for alternative b and some $k \neq h$ decisive for some $c \neq b$. (Consider a profile r' with b on top of $r'(h)$ and c on top of $r'(k)$. We have $g(r') = b$ because h is decisive for b, and $g(r') = c$ because k is decisive for c, a contradiction.) Nor can we have some person h decisive for alternative b and some $k \neq h$ also decisive for b. (That would imply that any individual who is decisive for some $c \neq b$ will either be someone other than h or someone other than k, giving us two different individuals who are decisive for two different alternatives.) Therefore, there is a single individual who is decisive for every alternative. That person is obviously a dictator. Therefore, g is dictatorial. ∎

7.3.2   Voters and Economic Agents

We have often referred to the individuals in our model as voters. But the model is very abstract. Is there any reason why the social choice function g couldn't be the market mechanism, with $g(p)$ identifying the market outcome (equilibrium) that emerges when individual preferences are specified by the profile p? The answer is concealed in the proof of the Gibbard-Satterthwaite theorem which employs a variety of profiles, including some that have arbitrary outcome x ranked first for every individual. But there is no such profile in economic models that incorporate private goods, if only implicitly via income taxes. Suppose that x is a specification of the private goods consumption of each individual and x gives both Brendan and Lilly a generous amount of each of the commodities that contribute significantly to individual welfare. (In particular, neither is desperately poor.) If y is identical to x except that y gives Brendan a little bit less of some good and Lilly a little bit more of that good then Lilly will prefer y to x. When preferences satisfy the assumptions of standard economic models there will be no profile at which some feasible alternative ranks first for every individual. The proof offered in this chapter is invalid when the preferences come from a standard economic model.

Sources

This remarkable theorem was discovered independently in the 1970s by the philosopher Alan Gibbard and the economist Mark Satterthwaite (Gibbard, 1973; Satterthwaite, 1975). The proof presented in this section is based on Reny (2001). Alternative proofs have been provided by Barberà (1983); Benoit (2000); and Sen (2001), among others.

Links

Although the proofs offered in this chapter are invalid when individual preferences come from a standard economic model, it has been shown that strategy-proofness remains elusive in that context. In a pure exchange economy strategy-proofness and efficiency are in conflict (Zhou, 1991b; Serizawa, 2002; Serizawa and Weymark, 2003). See also Section 11.4.1 of Chapter 11 in this book. Strategy-proofness is unattainable in a model with pure public goods (Zhou, 1991a). See also Section 8.4.1 of Chapter 8 in this book.

Problem Set

Each of the first four questions refers to a profile displayed in Table 7.18.

(1) Whenever both individual have the same top-ranked alternative that top-ranked alternative will be selected. Which alternatives *cannot* be selected at profile P?

(2) Whenever the individuals have different top-ranked alternative but the same second-ranked alternative that second-ranked alternative will be selected. Which alternative *must be* selected at Q?

Table 7.18

$P(1)$	$P(2)$	$Q(1)$	$Q(2)$	$R(1)$	$R(2)$	$S(1)$	$S(2)$
W	X	W	X	W	Z	W	Z
X	Z	Z	Y	X	W	X	X
Y	Y	X	Z	Y	X	Y	Y
Z	W	Y	W	Z	Y	Z	W

(3) Whenever both individual have the same top-ranked alternative that top-ranked alternative will be selected. Alternative X will be selected whenever person 1 ranks X on top. Which alternative *must be* selected at profile R?

(4) Alternative X is selected whenever person 2 ranks X last and person 1 reports the ordering $S(1)$ on the left. Which alternative *must be* selected at profile S?

Each of the last three questions defines a social choice function that is different for each question, and each is defined for every profile. If the rule can't be manipulated explain why. If the rule can be manipulated, demonstrate that fact with an example.

(5) There are n individuals and m alternatives, with n and m arbitrary except that $n > 2$ and $m > 3$. Given arbitrary profile p, For each alternative x there is an integer $k(x)$ such that x is in position $k(x)$ for some individual, and is ranked no lower than $k(x)$ for any individual. (For instance, if x is at the top for everyone, then $k(x) = 1$. If x is ranked second by someone and first by everyone else then $k(x) = 2$.) If there is a single alternative x such that $k(x) < k(y)$ for every other alternative y then the rule selects x. If two or more alternatives share this distinction then the rule selects the alternative from that set that ranks highest in person 1's reported preference ordering.

(6) This rule is the same as that of question 5 except that if there is a tie for the smallest $k(x)$ value then the rule selects the alphabetically earliest of these tied alternatives.

(7) There are m alternatives and an even number n of individuals, with $m = 3$ and $n \geq 4$. The group $\{2, 3, \ldots, n\}$ chooses by majority rule from the top two alternatives in the reported preference ordering of person 1.

7.4   THE REVELATION PRINCIPLE

A social choice rule must elicit information about individual preferences so that the outcome of the process will reflect these preferences in the appropriate way. If individuals have an incentive to misrepresent their preference the purpose of the rule is defeated. Is there any social choice procedure that is not vulnerable to this kind of manipulation? To increase the chance of an affirmative answer let us broaden the definition of a social choice rule to include *mechanisms*.

There are three or more alternatives. A mechanism requires individual i to announce some message m_i. This message could be a complete description of i's preference scheme; it could be the name of some alternative; it could be both; it could be a list of numbers. Nothing is ruled out, but each particular mechanism will be based on some kind of message. In addition, the mechanism specifies which message is to be reported by i for each possible preference scheme. (For instance, the market system asks you to choose a consumption plan that maximizes your individual welfare subject to your budget constraint.) Let $\sigma_i(R)$ denote the message that i is required to send when i's true preference ordering is R. Finally, the mechanism specifies the outcome, or winner, for each possible configuration of messages transmitted by the voters. Let μ be the outcome function. The function μ specifies an outcome $\mu(m)$ in feasible set X for each profile $m = (m_1, m_2, \ldots, m_n)$ of individual messages.

DEFINITION: *Social Choice Mechanism*

A mechanism specifies the type of message, and the set of available messages, for each individual i. It also specifies the behavioral rule σ_i for each i, and the function μ to identify the outcome. A *direct revelation* mechanism requires each individuals to report his or her preference ordering.

The social choice rules of Sections 7.1–7.3 are direct revelation mechanisms.

The referee observes $i's$ message m_i, but cannot tell whether m_i equals $\sigma_i(R)$ when R is $i's$ true preference scheme. That is because R cannot be observed. If it were verifiable by an outside observer there would be no need for a mechanism in the first place. The only way to ensure that individual i sets $m_i = \sigma_i(R)$ is to design the mechanism so that i always has an incentive to do so. We want this to be a *dominant strategy*. That is, for every possible preference scheme R that i might have and whatever messages the others report, there is no message m_i that i could send that would result in an outcome that ranks higher in the ordering R than the outcome that results when i reports $\sigma_i(R)$, given the messages of the others. A mechanism with this property (for each individual i) is said to be *strategy proof*.

DEFINITION: *Strategy-Proof Mechanism*

The mechanism is strategy proof if for each individual i, and each admissible preference scheme for that individual, submitting the message specified by σ_i is a dominant strategy.

Suppose that we have a strategy-proof mechanism μ that is defined at every profile. We can use it to define a strategy-proof direct revelation mechanism (social choice rule) g by setting $g(p) = \mu(m)$ for any profile p, where $m_i = \sigma_i(p(i))$ for each i. Suppose that μ is nondictatorial. This means that for any individual i there is an assignment p of preferences to individuals such that

$$\mu(\sigma_1(p(1)), \sigma_2(p(2)), \ldots, \sigma_n(p(n)))$$

is not the alternative ranked at the top of $p(i)$. But then for any individual i there is an assignment p of preferences such that $g(p)$ is not the alternative ranked at the top of $p(i)$. In other words, g is not dictatorial. Suppose that μ is nonimposed in the sense that for each feasible alternative x in X there is some profile p such that $\mu(\sigma_1(p(1)), \sigma_2(p(2)), \ldots, \sigma_n(p(n))) = x$. Then g is also nonimposed, non-dictatorial, strategy-proof, and defined at every profile. We have contradicted the Gibbard-Satterthwaite Theorem. Therefore, every strategy-proof mechanism that is defined at every profile is either imposed or dictatorial. This observation is known as the revelation principle.

The Revelation Principle

The Gibbard-Satterthwaite Theorem extends from direct revelation mechanisms to mechanisms in general.

Public Goods and Preference Revelation

This chapter investigates preference revelation in a standard economic model. There is a commodity that can be consumed jointly and simultaneously by the entire community – a fireworks display, for instance. To produce this *public good*, resources have to be diverted from the production of commodities for private consumption. In our model, as in the real world, efficiency requires a positive amount of some public good to be produced. But there is a point beyond which an increase in the supply of the public good leads to an inefficient outcome. Clearly, identification of an efficient outcome depends on individuals revealing their preferences. In this context truthful revelation of individual preference is problematic because one can consume the public good without contributing to the financing of it.

More generally, agent A's action generates a *positive spillover* if some other agent B directly benefits as a result of that action. For example, if A removes weeds from his own property, then neighbor B's grass will have fewer weeds because one source of seed has been eliminated. In this case, most of the benefit of A's effort is reaped by A, so we say that the spillover is incomplete. However, if C produces a fireworks display then everyone else in town will have just as good a view of it as C and hence the spillover is complete. When the agent creating the spillover benefit is not compensated for the positive effect on the welfare of others, we refer to it as an *externality*. Important examples include the containment of a virulent disease by a health organization, the retardation of global warming or ozone depletion by international treaty, and publication of information concerning public safety.

Our aim is to provide the individual decision maker with incentive to consider the benefit that others derive from his or her actions. The decision maker can be a single individual or household, or a region within a country, or even a country itself. When one country takes costly measures to reduce its output of carbon dioxide any resulting retardation of global warming is a benefit that is captured by every country. When a province or a state within a single country imposes restrictions on the firms within its borders to reduce the amount of sulphur dioxide dumped into the air, the benefits are enjoyed throughout the country – to a degree. Pollution in the air above one region can flow to other areas.

When the spillover is complete, as in the fireworks case, we refer to the commodity generating it as a *pure public good*. A public good is created when one individual or institution's action generates widespread benefit, and it is impossible (or very costly) for the agent creating the benefit to be compensated by those receiving it. Most cases that economists treat as a pure public good fall short of the ideal in one way or another, but the polar case is a useful laboratory device for investigating noncooperative behavior.

DEFINITION: *Pure Public Good Versus Pure Private Good*

A commodity is a pure *public* good if it is possible for every member of the community to consume every unit of the good that has been produced, and the utility derived by anyone is independent of the number of individuals who avail themselves of the opportunity to consume the good. It is a pure *private* good if and only if one person can benefit from the consumption of a unit of that good.

By definition, any amount of a public good that is made available to one individual or group can be simultaneously enjoyed by everyone in the community, although not everyone receives the same level of benefit. The higher is the community's level of consumption of the public good X the more input must be devoted to its production, and hence the larger is the community's sacrifice of private goods due to the diversion of resources to the production of X. However, the production technology does not require any individual's sacrifice to be proportional to his or her benefit from consuming the public good. (An individual who makes no contribution at all to the financing of X is said to be a *free rider*, because that person consumes the same amount of X as someone who did contribute.)

Truthful preference revelation is very hard to elicit because of the free rider problem, but efficiency requires the amount of public good X produced to be a function of reported preferences, and hence so is the share of the financing of X contributed by each individual. Without very carefully designed incentives, individuals will be able to misrepresent their preference scheme in a way that significantly reduces their share of the cost of financing the public good – and hence leaves a lot of disposable income for purchasing private goods – without appreciably reducing the level of X available for consumption. This would give that person a net increase in utility, relative to truthful revelation. (With a large number of individuals, the loss of one person's contribution to the financing of X will have a tiny effect on the amount of X produced.)

Public goods can be found in outer space: there are so many man-made satellites that signal interference, collisions, and falling debris can cause harm. Monitoring from outer space is a public good that can provide health benefits, as well as warnings of asteroid and comet collisions, and benefits from hurricane tracking (Sandler, 2004, p. 235).

The previous chapter examined public sector decision making in a very abstract model. In this chapter we endow the model with much more structure, including a production function and resource constraints, and by employing individual utility functions with classical economic properties.

8.1 THE ECONOMIC MODEL

The hypothesis of the Gibbard-Satterthwaite Theorem of Chapter 7 assumes that any logically possible ordering of the alternatives is a plausible preference scheme for any individual. An explicitly economic model places restrictions on individual preferences. For example, if everyone has more of every good when the economy is in state x than when it is in state y we can rule out individual preferences that have y ranking above x. Also, indifference curves are often assumed to be bowed in towards the origin, disqualifying many preference schemes. Perhaps such restrictions on the domain of admissible preferences will lead to a model with more potential for truthful revelation of preferences. We explore this possibility in a simple model with one public good.

A public good is a commodity from which everyone in the community jointly benefits. A pure public good is an ideal case in which every amount produced is consumed in equal measure by all, even though varying levels of benefit are realized. Consider, for example, street lights. In this case the community is the group of residents on one street. Street lights reduce crime. Consider the placement of lights on a typical city street. Would the residents be served best by having one light in front of each house, one light for the entire street, or some intermediate number? The decision *should* depend on householders' preferences, which will take into consideration the benefit in terms of crime reduction from the various plans and the nature and quantity of the goods and services that could be produced instead of a street lamp.

Having the government take the initiative for the project does not automatically solve the problem. The central authority must uncover enough preference information to determine when an increase in the production of the public good would not yield enough benefit to justify the required sacrifice of other commodities. This is by no means a simple matter. It is one virtue of the market mechanism that for a wide range or goods and services this process of accumulating essential information about household preferences is accomplished simply and neatly. (See Chapter 11, or the brief treatment in Section 3.1 of Chapter 3.)

Australia's dog fence is 3,307 continuous miles of wire mesh, running essentially from one Australian coast to the other. The fence keeps the wild dingo dogs from killing the sheep. The dingoes are on the north side of the fence, and more than 120 million sheep are on the south side (O'Neil, 1997). A failure to repair a hole anywhere in the fence eventually puts all of the sheep in jeopardy.

In the case of any commodity for which the benefits are confined to one individual – that is, a pure private good – a consumer does not derive any benefit unless he or she pays for the good, and the higher the price, the higher the benefit that must be realized for the consumer to justify the purchase. When a good provides benefits to the wider community – not only to the individual making the purchase decision – a very high level of overall community benefit can be sacrificed when each individual determines that *his or her* benefit is not great enough to justify paying the purchase price.

8.1.1   A Continuum of Public Projects

We investigate the possibility of achieving an efficient outcome in the presence of public goods by means of a simple model with two commodities, a pure public good X and a pure private good Y. Each individual i's utility has the quasi-linear form $U_i(x, y_i) = B_i(x) + y_i$ where x is the level of output of the public good and y_i is individual i's consumption of the private good. Therefore, if y_i changes to $y_i + \Delta y_i$ but x remains the same, the change in the individual's utility is

$$\Delta U_i = B_i(x) + y_i + \Delta y_i - [B_i(x) + y_i] = \Delta y_i.$$

In brief, if x does not change, then for each individual i we have $\Delta U_i = \Delta y_i$.

There are n individuals, and each individual i is endowed with ω_i units of the private good Y at the beginning of the period and zero units of the public good. The private good can either be consumed or used as an input in the production of the public good. (We could interpret x as code for a particular allocation of resources that specifies every detail except the amount y_i of the private good Y delivered to each individual i.) Let $g(x)$ denote the amount of good Y required to produce x units of the public good. The amount of the private good Y available for consumption is $\theta - g(x)$, where θ specifies the amount of Y available initially. That is, $\theta = \omega_1 + \omega_2 + \cdots + \omega_n$.

DEFINITION: *The Public Good Model*
There are n individuals, and each individual i has a utility function of the form $U_i = B_i(x) + y_i$, where x is the amount of the public good produced and y_i is i's consumption of the private good. The production of x units of the public good requires $g(x)$ units of the private good as input, leaving a total of $\theta - g(x)$ units of the private good available for consumption. (A total of θ units of the private good are available initially.) We often let N denote the set of all individuals.

∂8.1.2 Efficiency

Section 2.5.1 of Chapter 2 characterized efficiency with quasi-linear utility: an outcome that leaves everyone with a positive amount of the private good is efficient if and only if it maximizes total utility. But the proof of that claim does not guarantee an individual's consumption of the private good is nonnegative. This section characterizes efficient outcomes subject to the constraint that no one's consumption of Y can fall below zero. That is, $y_i \geq 0$ must hold for each individual i at any feasible allocation. An allocation is said to be *interior* if all consumption levels are strictly positive. We show that an interior allocation is efficient if and only if it maximizes total utility.

DEFINITION: *Interior Allocation*
If $x > 0$ and $y_i > 0$ for each individual i we say that the allocation is interior.

Total utility is $\sum_{i \in N} U_i(x, y_i) = \sum_{i \in N} (B_i(x) + y_i) = \sum_{i \in N} B_i(x) + \sum_{i \in N} y_i$.

When we maximize the sum of individual utilities we have to respect the resource constraint, $\sum_{i \in N} y_i \leq \theta - g(x)$. Efficiency obviously implies that this will be satisfied as an equality, and hence $\sum_{i \in N} y_i = \theta - g(x)$. Therefore, we want to maximize

$$\sum_{i \in N} B_i(x) + \theta - g(x),$$

a function of a single variable x. Let $f(x)$ denote this function. That is, $f(x)$ is total individual utility after incorporating the resource constraint.

First-Order Condition for Efficiency of an Interior Allocation when Utility is Quasi-Linear
Assume that B_i' is positive for every nonnegative level of output of the public good. If $x^* > 0$, and $y_i > 0$ for each individual i, and the allocation (x^*, y) is efficient then $f'(x^*) = 0$, where f denotes the function $\sum_{i \in N} B_i(x) + \theta - g(x)$.

Proof:

$U_i = B_i(x) + y_i$. If we change x by an amount dx, and then y_i by an amount dy_i then

$$dU_i = B'_i(x)dx + dy_i.$$

We will show that dx and dy_i can be chosen so that $\sum_{i \in N} dy_i = -g'(x)dx$ and $dU_i > 0$ for each i. Because $-g'(x)dx$ is the change in the amount of Y available for consumption when x changes by dx, we will wind up with a feasible allocation. Consequently, $dU_i > 0$ for each individual i implies that the original allocation is not efficient.

Note that $f'(x) = \sum_{i \in N} B'_i\left(x\right) - g'(x)$. Suppose that $f'(x) > 0$ at allocation (x, y). We show that each individual j's utility can be increased. We have

$$\sum_{i \in N} B'_i(x) - g'(x) > 0, \qquad [1]$$

and thus

$$1 - \frac{g'(x)}{B'_1(x) + B'_2(x) + \ldots + B'_n(x)} > 0 \qquad [2]$$

(There are n households. If $g'(x) > 0$ then then the sum of the $B'_i(x)$ is positive by [1]. Therefore, we can divide [1] by the sum of the $B'_i(x)$ without changing the direction of the inequality.)

For arbitrary individual j, multiply both sides of [2] by $B'_j(x)$. Because $B'_j(x) > 0$ the direction of the inequality doesn't change. We get

$$B'_j(x) - \frac{B'_j(x)}{B'_1(x) + B'_2(x) + \ldots + B'_n(x)} g'(x) > 0. \qquad [3]$$

For $dx > 0$ we can multiply through by dx, yielding

$$B'_j(x)dx - \frac{B'_j(x)}{B'_1(x) + B'_2(x) + \ldots + B'_n(x)} g'(x)dx > 0 \qquad [4]$$

Now, let

$$t_j = \frac{B'_j(x)}{B'_1(x) + B'_2(x) + \ldots + B'_n(x)} \qquad [5]$$

be individual j's share of the cost of increasing x. That is, we let $dy_j = -t_j \times g'(x)\,dx$. Note that [5] implies that $\sum_{i \in N} t_i = 1$. Therefore, $\sum_{i \in N} dy_i = -g'(x)\,dx$.

Inequality [4] establishes that $dU_j(x) = B'_j(x)dx - t_j g'(x)dx$ is strictly positive. We have constructed a new feasible allocation that gives everyone more utility than the original allocation at which $f'(x) > 0$. The original allocation is not efficient. (Strictly speaking, we have actually proved that there is some $dx > 0$ sufficiently small such that the constructed allocation is feasible and gives everyone more utility than the original allocation *and* each y_i will still be positive.)

Now, suppose that $f'(x) = \sum_{i \in N} B'_i(x) - g'(x) < 0$. The inequalities in [1], [2], and [3] are reversed as a result. After replacing the greater than sign > in [3] with the less than sign <, when we multiply through by $dx < 0$ we will change the direction of the inequality again, yielding [4], with the left-hand side again positive. With t_j given by [5], *we reduce x* to $x + dx$ and increase individual *j*'s consumption of Y by $-t_j \times g'(x)\, dx$. This will be possible for some $dx < 0$ sufficiently small in absolute value, because $x > 0$. An argument parallel to the one of the previous paragraph shows that everyone's utility will increase if dx is sufficiently close to zero. The new level of consumption of Y is guaranteed to be positive, because this time we are reducing the amount of Y that is used in producing X, and this adds to an individual's private good consumption. ∎

The cost shares specified by [5] are critical if we are to increase everyone's utility by moving from x toward x^*, the value of x at which $f'(x) = 0$. If instead we insist on equal cost shares, then those who derive little marginal benefit from X will suffer a net decline in utility when we increase x. And with equal shares, individuals who have a high marginal benefit from X will find their net utility falling when x is reduced. But if $f'(x)$ is not zero there is *some* system of cost shares that will allow everyone to benefit from a change in the allocation in the appropriate direction. Making all individuals' cost shares proportional to their marginal benefits will always work.

Finally, we assume the *classical second-order condition*: decreasing marginal benefit from X and increasing marginal cost of producing X.

The Classical Second-Order Condition

Assume that $g''(x) \geq 0$ for all x, and for every individual i, $B''_i(x) \leq 0$ holds for all x. In addition, either $g''(x) > 0$ for all x or else for some individual i, $B''_i(x) < 0$ holds for all x.

This condition implies that the value of x that maximizes total utility is unique, and that $f'(x) = 0$ must hold if f is maximized by an allocation for which $x > 0$ and $y_i > 0$ for each i.

Characterization of Efficiency of an Interior Allocation when Utility is Quasi-Linear

Assuming the classical second-order condition, an interior allocation (x, y) for which $B'_i(x) > 0$ holds for all x and each individual i is efficient if and only if it maximizes total utility. Moreover, there is a unique level x^* such that every efficient interior allocation satisfies $x = x^*$. We refer to x^* as the efficient level of x.

Proof:

In *any* model, whether there is a divisible private good or not, and whether preferences are quasi-linear or not, any allocation that maximizes total utility is efficient. (If outcome F maximizes total utility then there can be no feasible outcome G that gives one person more utility than F and does not leave anyone else with less utility than F. If there were such an outcome G it would provide more total utility than F, contradicting the fact that F maximizes total utility.) Therefore, it remains to prove that with a divisible private good and quasi-linear individual utility, the *only* interior allocations that are efficient and leave everyone with a positive amount of the private good are the allocations that maximize total utility.

We have seen that in this context efficiency implies that x maximizes

$$\sum_{i \in N} U_i \ (x, y_i) = \sum_{i \in N} B_i \ (x) + \theta - g(x) \equiv f(x).$$

Note that $f'(x) = \sum_{i \in N} B_i'(x) - g'(x)$, and hence the classical second-order condition implies that $f''(x) < 0$ holds for all x. Therefore, f has a unique global maximum, say at x^*. In addition, $f'' < 0$ implies that $f'(x) > 0$ holds if $0 < x < x^*$. Therefore, $0 < x < x^*$ and $y_i > 0$ for all i implies that allocation (x, y) is not efficient because it violates the first-order condition for efficiency. Similarly, $f'' < 0$ implies $f'(x) < 0$ if $x > x^*$, and thus $x > x^*$ and $y_i > 0$ for all i implies that (x, y) is not efficient, again by the first-order condition for efficiency. Therefore, assuming $y_i > 0$ for all i, allocation (x, y) is not efficient unless $x = x^*$ and $\sum_{i \in N} y_i = \theta - g(x)$. ∎

We have demonstrated that $f'(x) = 0$ is necessary and sufficient for efficiency, given the second-order condition plus $x > 0$, $y_i > 0$ for each i, and $\sum_{i \in N} y_i = \theta - g(x)$. Because $f(x) = \sum_{i \in N} B_i(x) + \theta - g(x)$, we have $f'(x) = \sum_{i \in N} B_i'(x) - g'(x) = 0$ at an efficient outcome. This is known as the *Samuelson efficiency condition.* In words, the *sum* of the marginal utilities from X must equal the marginal cost of X at an efficient allocation.

Samuelson Efficiency Condition

$$\sum_{i \in N} B_i'(x) = g'(x).$$

If this condition is satisfied by a unique value of x we refer to that value as the Samuelson level (or efficient level) of the public good.

If the classical second-order condition is satisfied, and x^* is the efficient level of the public good, and $\sum_{i \in N} y_i = \theta - g(x^*)$ also holds, then $\sum_{i \in N} U_i$ is maximized subject to the resource constraint and thus the allocation is efficient. The amount of Y available for consumption is $\theta - g(x^*)$. *Total* utility is unchanged if we redistribute that amount of Y among the n individuals. (For instance, if we increase y_1 by δ units and reduce y_2 by δ units we don't affect total utility.) Because total utility remains the same after redistribution, total utility is still maximized and hence the new allocation is efficient. (*Any* allocation that maximizes total utility is efficient in *any* model.) Therefore, assuming the classical second-order condition, an allocation at which all consumption variables are positive is efficient if and only if it provides exactly x^* units of the public good, where x^* satisfies the Samuelson condition, and uses exactly $g(x^*)$ units of Y in producing the public good, and redistributes the remaining amount of Y to consumers.

Example 8.1 Two Individuals and Constant Marginal Cost

Individual 1's utility function is $U_1(x, y_1) = 10 - 10(x+1)^{-1} + y_1$ and 2's utility function is $U_2(x, y_2) = 15 - 15(x+1)^{-1} + y_2$. Each unit of the public good is produced by employing 1 unit of the private good as input. Thus, $g(x) = x$. A total of 120 units of the private good is available initially ($\theta = 120$):

$$U_1 + U_2 = 25 - \frac{25}{x+1} + y_1 + y_2 = 25 - \frac{25}{x+1} + 120 - x$$

Therefore, we maximize $f(x) = 25 - 25(x+1)^{-1} + 120 - x$. We have $f'(x) = 25(x+1)^{-2} - 1$. The second derivative of f is $-50(x+1)^{-3}$, which is negative for all $x \geq 0$. Thus if we set $f'(x) = 0$ we get a unique global maximum.

$25(x+1)^{-2} - 1 = 0$ implies $25 = (x+1)^2$ and hence $x^* = 4$. The efficient level of the public good is 4. Therefore, at an efficient outcome we have $y_1 + y_2 = 120 - 4 = 116$. An interior allocation is efficient if and only if $x = 4$ and $y_1 + y_2 = 116$.

∂8.1.3 Competitive Market Equilibrium

Why can't we leave the selection of a public project to the market system? Competitive markets will yield an efficient outcome *if* we create a market for each spillover effect. For instance, there would have to be one market in which the benefit conferred on agent 1 by agent 2's actions would be priced. However, most of these markets would be thin, with few agents. When markets are thin there will be a strong incentive to deviate from the competitive rules. What about having the public good itself traded in a conventional market? A simple example will show why this usually leaves us far from an efficient outcome.

Example 8.2 Three Individuals and Constant Marginal Cost

Suppose $U_1 = \ln(x+1) + y_1$, $U_2 = 2\ln(x+1) + y_2$, $U_3 = 3\ln(x+1) + y_3$, and $g(x) = x$. Each agent is endowed with eight units of the private good. The Samuelson level of the public good solves

$$\frac{1}{x+1} + \frac{2}{x+1} + \frac{3}{x+1} = 1.$$

Hence, $x^* = 5$.

What is the competitive equilibrium for Example 8.2? Let P_X be the price of the public good, with P_Y denoting the price of private good. The production of x units of the public good will cost $P_Y \times x$ because x units of Y will be employed as input. The revenue from x units of the public good will be $P_X \times x$ and profit will be

$$P_X \times x - P_Y \times x = (P_X - P_Y)x.$$

If $P_X > P_Y$ then profit can be made arbitrarily large by producing an arbitrarily large amount of X. The supply of the public good will exceed the demand, so we can't have an equilibrium at which P_X exceeds P_Y. If $P_Y > P_X$ then the firm will take a loss if x is positive, and the loss is larger the larger is x. When $P_Y > P_X$ the firm maximizes profit by setting $x = 0$. In that case, the demand for the public good will exceed supply if even one consumer has a positive demand for X. Therefore, competitive market equilibrium requires $P_X = P_Y$, and for convenience we let the price of each good be $1.

For the economy of Example 8.2, when $P_X = 1 = P_Y$, and individual i purchases x_i units of the public good and consumes y_i units of the private good, we must have $x_i = 8 - y_i$. (The individual begins with 8 units of Y but sells $8 - y_i$, units at $1 each. The money from the sale is used to buy x_i units of the public good.) Because $x_i = 8 - y_i$, we can replace y_i in individual i's utility function of Example 8.2 with $8 - x_i$.

A competitive market equilibrium $(x^*, x_1^*, x_2^*, x_3^*, y_1^*, y_2^*, y_3^*)$ must satisfy the following five conditions:

x_1 maximizes $\ln(x_1 + x_2^* + x_3^* + 1) + 8 - x_1$ subject to $0 \le x_1 \le 8$.

x_2 maximizes $2\ln(x_1^* + x_2 + x_3^* + 1) + 8 - x_2$ subject to $0 \le x_2 \le 8$.

x_3 maximizes $3\ln(x_1^* + x_2^* + x_3 + 1) + 8 - x_3$ subject to $0 \le x_3 \le 8$.

$y_1^* = 8 - x_1^*, y_2^* = 8 - x_2^*, \ y_3^* = 8 - x_3^*.$

$x^* = x_1^* + x_2^* + x_3^*.$

If the inequality $x_i \le 8$ doesn't hold then y_i is negative because $y_i = 8 - x_i$. Note that the last two conditions imply that the total consumption of the private good equals 24 minus the amount of the private good needed to produce x^* units of the public good. To maximize individual i's utility subject to $0 \le x_i \le 8$ we exploit the fact that if the marginal benefit to i of consuming another unit of X exceeds the marginal cost to i (which is 1) then i will demand more X. However, if the marginal benefit to i is less than i's marginal cost then i will reduce x_i, unless it is already 0.

Set $x^* = 2$, $x_1^* = 0 = x_2^*$, and $x_3^* = 2$. If $y_1^* = 8 = y_2^*$ and $y_3^* = 6$ the five conditions are satisfied, and we have a competitive equilibrium. Moreover, this is the only competitive equilibrium because the five necessary conditions for market equilibrium imply that

$$1/(x^* + 1) \le 1, 2/(x^* + 1) \le 1, \quad \text{and} \quad 3/(x^* + 1) \le 1,$$

with the first of these inequalities holding as an equality if $x_1^* > 0$, the second holding as an equality if $x_2^* > 0$, and the third holding as an equality if $x_3^* > 0$. Obviously, only the third can hold as an equality if all three are satisfied. Can we

Table 8.1

	Competitive equilibrium	Revised outcome
U_1	ln3 + 8 = 9.099	ln6 + 7.5 = 9.292
U_2	2ln3 + 8 = 10.197	2ln6 + 7= 10.584
U_3	3ln3 + 6 = 9.296	3ln6 + 4.5 = 9.875

have all three holding as a strict inequality? If so, the five equilibrium conditions imply that $x_1^* = x_2^* = x_3^* = 0$ and hence $x^* = 0$. This implies $3/(x^*+1) > 1$, a contradiction. Therefore, $3/(x^* + 1) = 1$ and hence $x^* = 2$. It follows that $1/(x^*+1) < 1$ and $2/(x^*+1) < 1$ and thus $x_1^* = x_2^* = 0$. Agents 1 and 2 are *free riders*. They each benefit from the 2 units of the public good financed by agent 3 without contributing themselves.

The competitive equilibrium is not efficient: *if* 5 units of the public good were produced and the Y consumption of 1, 2, and 3 were reduced by 0.5, 1, and 3.5 units respectively we would have a feasible allocation. Table 8.1 shows each agent's utility at each allocation. Utility is higher for each agent at the new allocation than it is at the competitive equilibrium, confirming that the latter is not efficient. (Table 8.1: note that y_i reductions of 0, 1, and 4 on individuals 1, 2, and 3 respectively would also serve to demonstrate the inefficiency of the competitive equilibrium.)

We have assumed that at a competitive equilibrium one agent cannot collect a payment from another for the benefit that the former confers on the latter by purchasing public goods. Therefore, all agents must pay the competitive price if they want to contribute to the production of the public good. Agents for which the marginal benefit of the public good is low will prefer to spend their income on other commodities, and enjoy – for free – whatever amount of the public good is financed by others.

Under special circumstances, the market system can provide close to the efficient level of the public good. In the case of a lighthouse there is a very narrow range of payoff functions and technologies that need to be considered, and for each of these there is a unique efficient number of lighthouses: zero is too little and two is too much. One lighthouse is the socially optimal number. This means that only the question of viability remains to be settled. Any scheme that collects enough revenue to finance the operation of the lighthouse will do. Typically, however, there is a wide range of output levels that could conceivably be efficient. Each is efficient for some plausible configuration of individual preferences and real cost function, and the market system would often be far from that level.

In the seventeenth century the English Crown gave a private firm the exclusive right to collect a port tax if it erected and maintained a lighthouse (Coase, 1974). However, even though the private provision of the public good was viable under this arrangement, the monopoly firm would exclude ships that did not derive enough benefit from using the port to justify paying the fee. If those firms were allowed to use the facility their payoff would increase, and the payoffs of other agents would be unchanged. The monopoly equilibrium is inefficient, but not woefully so in this case.

8.1.4 Voluntary Contributions

The previous subsection demonstrated that when a public good is allocated by the market system the outcome is usually inefficient. At some level of X below the efficient level, no individual will want to purchase an additional unit of the public good because the cost to the individual decision maker would exceed the benefit to that individual. But because of the spillover effects, the total benefit to the community of an additional unit of X will exceed the total cost. We run into the same problem if individuals are asked to contribute voluntarily to a fund that will be used to purchase the public good. If each individual J determines how much to contribute by comparing the benefit he or she gets from another dollar spent on the public good to the utility J would have gained by using the dollar to buy more private goods for personal consumption, then the fund will not collect enough money to finance the efficient level of X.

We can prove our claim that voluntary contributions will not support the efficient level of X by reinterpreting Example 8.2 of the previous subsection: instead of interpreting x_i as the amount of X purchased by individual i, we can interpret x_i as the amount of money that individual i voluntarily contributes to the fund. With either version the amount of the public good consumed by each person is the sum of the x_i, and individual i's consumption of the private good is the amount that i started with minus x_i. For the utility functions of Example 8.2, individuals 1 and 2 will contribute nothing and individual 3 will contribute \$2. Exactly two units of the public good will be made available but the efficient level is five.

Here is a somewhat different example to illustrate the inefficiency of a system of voluntary contributions.

Example 8.3 Cleaning the Neighborhood

A and B are neighbors. Each is bothered by the amount of debris (or carbon dioxide if A and B are countries) that motorists discharge. If A supplies e_A units of effort to cleaning up then A and B will each derive $2e_A$ units of benefit. Similarly, if B supplies e_B units of effort to pollution abatement then A will receive $2e_B$ units of benefit from that activity, and so will B. We assume that each unit of effort expended by an agent reduces the agent's utility by 3 units. Therefore, the payoff to A when B supplies e_B units of effort to cleanup and A supplies e_A units of effort is $U_A = 2(e_A + e_B) - 3e_A = 2e_B - e_A$ and B's payoff is $U_B = 2e_A - e_B$.

If $e_A = e_B = 1$, then the payoff to each is $2 \times (1 + 1) - 3 \times 1 = 1$. However, we have here a continuum version of the prisoner's dilemma game: Each player i chooses a number e_i between 0 and 1 inclusive, and for any choice of e_j by the opponent j, the response that maximizes player i's payoff is $e_i = 0$, *treating e_j as a constant*. Clearly, $e_A = 0$ is a dominant strategy for A, and $e_B = 0$ is a dominant strategy for B. However, if $e_A = 0 = e_B$ then each player's payoff is 0, but each gets a payoff of 1 from the cooperative outcome $e_A = 1 = e_B$.

On Earth Day (April 22, 1990), celebrants in Central Park, New York City, left behind 150 tons of garbage.

The pursuit of self-interest is self-defeating in this case. If the two individuals interact repeatedly over time then the cooperative outcome can be sustained as an equilibrium. (See Sections 1.5.7 and 1.7.2 of Chapter 1.) However, Example 8.3 is intended as a metaphor for the interaction of *many* individuals. If one commuter decides to take public transportation instead of a car – to reduce air pollution – that commuter cannot assume that it will motivate others to do the same.

Many experiments have been designed to test the Nash prediction of zero voluntary contributions. In fact, around half the efficient level of the public good is typically reached in these experiments, although the level diminishes somewhat when the subjects repeat the experiment.

∂8.1.5 Average Cost Taxation

A consequence of the Samuelson efficiency condition is that *any individual* has the ability to determine the level of output of the public good if efficiency is guaranteed. Suppose, for instance, that individual 1 wants exactly 9 units of X to be produced. Suppose also that $g'(9) = 15$ and $B_2'(9) + B_3'(9) + \cdots + B_n'(9) = 13$. Then if individual 1 reports a benefit function B_1 such that $B_1'(9) = 2$ the Samuelson condition is satisfied at $x = 9$. There are lots of functions that would work – for instance, $B_1(x) = 12\sqrt{x}$. We refer to this ability of each individual to control the level of X as *unilateral decisiveness*.

DEFINITION: *Unilateral Decisiveness*

For any individual i and any level x of public good output, given the utility functions reported by the other individuals, there exists a utility function such that i can guarantee that the Samuelson efficiency condition is satisfied at x simply by reporting that utility function.

Why would we ever have an equilibrium – of any scheme for determining the quantity of X produced – if each individual can control the level of output? A successful allocation mechanism must give each individual an incentive to demand the level of output of X that satisfies the Samuelson condition with respect to the true individual preferences, even though the individual cannot know what those true preferences are, apart from his or her own. In short, individuals must have an incentive to report truthfully. This will not happen if the individual cost shares are equal, as we are about to see. Suppose there are n individuals, and each must sacrifice one-nth of the total amount of the private good necessary to produce the public good.

DEFINITION: *Average Cost Taxation*

Each individual i reports his or her benefit function B_i, and the value of x that satisfies Samuelson condition is then produced. Individual i's consumption of the private good is reduced by $g(x)/n$ units if n is the total number of individuals.

The problem with average cost taxation is that individuals who derive relatively little benefit from the public good will want relatively little of it to be produced, if they have to pay the same share of the cost as everyone else. Consequently, they will not report their true benefit functions. Similarly, those who get a high level of benefit will submit benefit functions that impart an upward bias to the output of the public good.

Example 8.4 Two Individuals

Individual 1's utility function is $U_1(x, y_1) = 10 - 10(x+1)^{-1} + y_1$, individual 2's utility function is $U_2(x, y_2) = 15 - 15(x+1)^{-1} + y_2$, and $g(x) = x$. Each individual begins with 60 units of the private good ($\omega_1 = \omega_2 = 60$). This is the setup of Example 8.1. The efficient level of X is 4. To see if truthful revelation is a dominant strategy, we can exploit the unilateral decisiveness property and see how much X each individual will "demand."

Maximize $U_i = \alpha - \alpha (x+1)^{-1} + 60 - 0.5x$. The first derivative is $\alpha(x+1)^{-2} - 0.5$. The second derivative is negative for all $x \geq 0$. When we set the first derivative equal to 0 we get $(x+1)^2 = 2\alpha$. Therefore, $x = \sqrt{2\alpha} - 1$. Individual 1, with $\alpha = 10$, will want 3.47 units of X to be produced and individual 2, with $\alpha = 15$, will want 4.48 units. Will both reveal their benefit functions truthfully? Suppose that individual 2 reports his true utility function. Because individual 1 wants $\sqrt{20} - 1$ units of X and $B_2'(\sqrt{20} - 1) = 15/20$ she only has to report the benefit function $5 - 5(x + 1)^{-1}$, for which marginal benefit is $5/20$ when $x = \sqrt{20} - 1$. Hence, individual 1 will not report truthfully.

∂8.1.6 **Benefit Taxation**

Absent positive or negative spillovers, a *competitive* market equilibrium is efficient. All individuals choose a consumption plan at which their marginal rate of substitution for any pair of goods consumed is equal to the ratio of the respective prices. Consequently, the price paid by consumers is proportional to the benefit that they derive from the good at the margin. With a public good in our model, we can imitate the market system by imposing a tax on each individual that is proportional to the benefit that is derived from the public good at the margin.

Specifically, we require individuals to report their benefit functions B_i, and these are used to determine the level x^* of the public good that satisfies the Samuelson condition. This will require a total sacrifice of $g(x^*)$ units of the private good. Each individual i contributes the fraction t_i of that cost by having i's consumption of the private good reduced by $t_i \times g(x^*)$. We want t_i to be proportional to i's marginal benefit of X at x^*, and we also want the cost shares to sum to unity.

DEFINITION: *Benefit Taxation*

Each individual i reports his or her benefit function B_i, and the Samuelson condition is then used to identify x^*, the efficient level of X. Individual i's consumption of the private good is reduced by $t_i \times g(x^*)$, where

$$t_i = \frac{B_i'(x^*)}{B_1'(x^*) + B_2'(x^*) + \ldots + B_n'(x^*)}.$$

The benefit tax mechanism is successful on one level: *assuming* truthful revelation, each individual will want the efficient level of the public good to be produced. To confirm this we maximize $U_i = B_i(x) + \omega_i - t_i \times g(x)$. We have

$$\frac{dU_i}{dx} = B_i'(x) - \frac{B_i'(x^*)}{B_1'(x^*) + B_2'(x^*) + \ldots + B_n'(x^*)} \times g'(x).$$

Note that the second derivative is negative. The Samuelson condition implies $B_1'(x^*) + B_2'(x^*) + \ldots + B_n'(x^*) = g\prime(x^*)$ so we can write

$$\frac{dU_i(x^*)}{dx} = B_i'(x^*) - B_i'(x^*),$$

which equals zero. Therefore, U_i is maximized at x^*, the efficient level of X, assuming that the benefit functions are reported truthfully. We will *not* get truthful revelation, however, because an individual can report a benefit function for which marginal benefit is zero at every value of x. In that case the individual's tax rate will be zero. The individual will get less benefit from the public good because the level of X will be lower than if he or she had reported truthfully, but in most cases that will be more than offset by the increased consumption of the private good due to a reduced tax burden.

Example 8.5 The Benefit Tax Mechanism with Three Agents

Let $U_1 = x + y_1$, $U_2 = 2x + y_2$, $U_3 = 5x + y_3$, and $g(x) = 0.5x^2$. Each agent is endowed with 24 units of the private good. Because $g'(x) = x$, the efficient level x^* of the public good solves $1 + 2 + 5 = x$, and thus $x^* = 8$. If each i reports his or her benefit function truthfully, then 8 units of the public good are produced, and person 1's share of the cost is ⅛. Therefore, $U_1 = 8 + 24 - ⅛ \times ½ \times 8^2 = 28$ under truthful revelation. To show that the three individuals will not all report truthfully at equilibrium we suppose that persons 2 and 3 do report their true benefit functions. Let's calculate U_1 when person 1 reports the benefit function "$B_1(x) = 0$ for all x." The resulting Samuelson condition is $0 + 2 + 5 = x$, and hence 7 units of X will be produced. In that case $U_1 = 7 + 24 - 0 \times ½ \times 7^2 = 31$, which is higher than 1's utility under truthful revelation.

One might object that individuals 2 and 3 can also play the game. That's true, but we have at least shown that truthful revelation is not a dominant strategy for each individual. But let's see what happens when everyone plays strategically. Perhaps a Nash equilibrium of the benefit tax mechanism will precipitate a level of X that is not too far from the actual efficient level.

Example 8.6 Nash Equilibrium of the Benefit Tax Mechanism

There are n individuals, each with the utility function $U_i = x + y_i$. We have $g(x) = 0.5x^2$ and each agent is endowed with ω_i units of the private good. For computational convenience, we assume that each individual i is known to have a utility function of the form $U_i = \alpha_i x + y_i$, but the exact value of α_i is hidden information. Because $g'(x) = x$, the Samuelson (or efficient) level must satisfy $\alpha_1 + \alpha_2 + \cdots + \alpha_n = x$, where α_i is the benefit parameter *reported* by individual i. Therefore, $x^* = n$ under truthful revelation, and that is the efficient level of the public good. But we need to find the equilibrium level of X when each person plays strategically. Our calculations will be simplified by the fact that the individuals have identical utility functions, but we can't exploit that fact until *after* we maximize individual utility. Otherwise we will ascribe to a single person the ability to control the strategies of others.

Let α be the benefit parameter reported by person i, and we let β denote the sum of the benefit parameters reported by everyone else. Then $x = \alpha + \beta$. Therefore, individual i will choose α to maximize

$$U_i = \alpha + \beta + \omega_i - [\alpha/(\alpha+\beta)] \times \frac{1}{2}(\alpha+\beta)^2 = \alpha + \beta + \omega_i - \frac{1}{2}\alpha(\alpha+\beta)$$

because person i's tax rate is $\alpha/(\alpha+\beta)$. The first derivative of i's utility as a function α is $1 - \alpha - \frac{1}{2}\beta$ and the second derivative is negative. Therefore, we maximize U_i by setting $1 - \alpha - \frac{1}{2}\beta = 0$. *Now* we can exploit the fact that the individuals are identical and will make identical decisions. Because β is the sum of the $n - 1$ reported benefit parameters other than individual i's we have $\beta = (n - 1)\alpha$. Therefore

$$1 - \alpha - \frac{1}{2}(n - 1)\alpha = 0,$$

the solution of which is $\alpha = 2/(n + 1)$. Each individual's true benefit parameter is 1 but each will report the benefit parameter $2/(n + 1)$ at equilibrium. As a result, only $n \times [2/(n + 1)] = 2n/(n + 1)$ units of the public good will be produced. Fewer than 2 units of the public good will be available at the benefit tax equilibrium, but the efficient level is n. For large n there is a vast difference between the benefit tax equilibrium and the efficient allocation.

We have tried the market system, average cost taxation, and the benefit tax mechanism. Are there any public decision schemes that perform better than the market system with respect to the allocation of public goods? The rest of this chapter is devoted to this question. Although the model that we use is extremely simple, it incorporates enough features of resource allocation with public goods to enable us to bring out the strategic nuances.

Sources

The efficiency condition for public goods is derived by Samuelson (1954). In 1970 Paul Samuelson received the Nobel prize for this and many other breakthroughs in almost every branch of economic theory. Anderson (2001) reviews the experimental evidence on the provision of public goods. Arrow (1970) demonstrated that the competitive equilibrium is efficient *if* there is a market for each spillover effect.

Links

Cornes and Sandler (1996, Chapter 8) thoroughly explore the inefficiency of competitive equilibrium when there are positive spillovers. As the number of players increases in Example 8.3, the gap between the individual payoff when everyone cooperates and the individual payoff when each plays the dominant strategy also increases (Sandler, 1992; Cornes and Sandler, 1996, p. 163).

Problem Set

The first three questions pertain to an economy with three individuals. A total of 100 units of the private good is available initially.

(1) $U_1 = x + y_1$, $U_2 = 2x + y_2$, and $U_3 = 9x + y_3$. The production technology is represented by the real cost function $g(x) = x^2$. Determine the efficient level of output of the public good.

(2) $U_1 = 2\sqrt{x} + y_1$, $U_2 = 4\sqrt{x} + y_2$, and $U_3 = 6\sqrt{x} + y_3$. When 1 unit of Y is used as input, 1 unit of X is obtained as output. Determine the efficient level of output of the public good and characterize the set of efficient outcomes.

(3) $U_1 = 2\sqrt{x} + y_1$, $U_2 = 4\sqrt{x} + y_2$, and $U_3 = 18\sqrt{x} + y_3$. When 1 unit of Y is used as input exactly one-third of a unit of X is obtained as output.

    (A) Determine the efficient level of output of the public good and characterize the set of efficient outcomes.

    (B) Assume that the current allocation has $x = 9$, $y_1 = 18$, $y_2 = 15$, and $y_3 = 40$. The output level $x = 9$ is not consistent with efficiency. Show that some individuals will be made worse off by a move to the efficient level of X if the reduction in the consumption of the private good Y resulting from the increase in the production of X is shared equally by the individuals.

    (C) Assume that the current allocation has $x = 9$, $y_1 = 18$, $y_2 = 15$, and $y_3 = 40$ as in part B. The output level $x = 9$ is not consistent with efficiency. Show that everyone can be made better off by a move to the efficient level of X by some assignment of cost shares to the individuals. In other words, show that the reduction in the consumption of the private good Y resulting from the increase in the production of X can be assigned to individuals in a way that leaves everyone better off.

(D) Assume that the current allocation has $x = 9$, $y_1 = 33$, $y_2 = 30$, and $y_3 = 10$. The output level $x = 9$ is not consistent with efficiency. Show that it is *not* possible to make everyone better off by a move to the efficient level if y_3 is not allowed to fall below 0.

(E) Assume that the current allocation has $x = 9$, $y_1 = 33$, $y_2 = 30$, and $y_3 = 10$ as in part D. The output level $x = 9$ is not consistent with efficiency. Show that it *is* possible to increase x by *some* amount in a way that leaves everyone better off than with $x = 9$.

For questions 4–7 each of the three individuals has an endowment of 40 units of the private good.

(4) $U_1 = 1\sqrt{x} + y_1$, $U_2 = 2\sqrt{x} + y_2$, and $U_3 = 3\sqrt{x} + y_3$. Each unit of X requires 1 unit of Y as input.

(A) Characterize the allocation that is defined by transferring all of the private good to person 3 and then choosing x to maximize 3's utility subject to the production constraint.

(B) Is this allocation efficient? Explain.

(C) Does this allocation satisfy the Samuelson condition? Support your answer with a simple proof.

(D) Explain how an allocation can be efficient without satisfying the Samuelson condition.

(5) Each individual's preferences can be represented by the utility function $15\ln(x + 1) + y_i$. When 1 unit of Y is used as input exactly one-third of a unit of X is obtained as output.

(A) What is the marginal social cost of X?

(B) Can an allocation for which $x = 9$ be efficient if each individual has a positive amount of the private good? If so, explain why; if not, prove it with a numerical example.

(C) Can an allocation for which $x = 29$ be efficient? If so, explain why; if not, prove it with a numerical example.

(6) $U_1 = \sqrt{x} + y_1$, $U_2 = 4\sqrt{x} + y_2$, $U_3 = 5\ln(x + 1) + y_3$. The real cost of production is given by the function $g(x) = 5x$.

(A) What is the marginal social cost of X?

(B) Characterize the set of efficient allocations.

(7) $U_1 = 6\sqrt{x} + y_1$, $U_2 = 12\sqrt{x} + y_2$, $U_3 = 18\sqrt{x} + y_3$, with $\omega_i = 200$ for each i. Let P denote the price of X. Normalize so that the price of Y is \$1. When 1 unit of Y is used as input exactly one-third of a unit of X is obtained as output. What would be the competitive equilibrium price of X in a private ownership market economy with both goods being allocated by the market system? Will the outcome be efficient? If so, explain why; if not, prove it with a numerical example.

(8) Explain why the Samuelson condition would not be satisfied at equilibrium if the level of the pure public good were determined by demand and supply forces in a competitive market – that is, if it were allocated the way private goods are allocated in the market system.

(9) Let $B_i(x) = 2\sqrt{x}$ for each $i = 1, 2, \ldots, n$, with $g(x) = x$. Find the equilibrium level of x under benefit taxation when *each* individual reports the benefit function that gives him or her the maximum utility given the reports of others.

(10) There are two individuals, and each is endowed with 12 units of the private good. Let $U_1 = 6x + y_1$, and $U_2 = 6x + y_2$. If $g(x) = \frac{1}{2}x^2$ then the Samuelson condition is satisfied by $x = 12$. But 12 units of the public good require 72 units of the private good as input. The economy has only 24 units of the private good. What has gone wrong with our reasoning?

(11) Suppose that the benefit tax mechanism is used. Prove that for any specification of B_1 and g, person 1 maximizes utility by reporting truthfully *if* he or she is certain that every other individual i will report that $B_i(x)$ is constant – that is, that benefit does not increase when x increases.

Questions 12–14 concern the following special case of our model: $U_i = a_i x + y_i$ for each i. The production of x units of the public good requires $\frac{1}{2} x^2$ units of the private good as input. An allocation is determined by having each i report a benefit parameter β_i, producing $\beta_1 + \beta_2 + \ldots + \beta_n$ units of the public good and collecting a total of $\frac{1}{2}(\beta_1 + \beta_2 + \ldots + \beta_n)^2$ units of the private goods from households. Specification of the mechanism is complete when we determine by how much each household's consumption of the private good is reduced to obtain the $\frac{1}{2}(\beta_1 + \beta_2 + \ldots + \beta_n)^2$ units that are needed for the production of the public good. (Note that we use a_i to denote individual i's true benefit parameter, with β_i representing the reported benefit parameter.)

(12) Suppose that each individual i's consumption of the private good is reduced by $\frac{1}{2}\beta_i(\beta_1 + \beta_2 + \ldots + \beta_n)$ units. Suppose that $\beta_2 + \beta_3 + \ldots + \beta_n = 2$. If $2 > a_1 > 0$ then person 1 is better off reporting a benefit parameter of 0 than reporting the true parameter a_1. But what is person 1's best strategy? What value of β_1, person 1's reported benefit parameter, maximizes U_1 given $a_1 > 0$ and the fact that the benefit parameters reported by the others sum to 2?

(13) Suppose that each individual i's consumption of the private good is reduced by $\frac{1}{2}\beta_i(\beta_1 + \beta_2 + \ldots + \beta_n)$ units. Assume that $a_1 = 3$ and $a_i = 1$ for all $i > 1$. Prove that we have a Nash equilibrium if person 1 reports a benefit parameter of 3 and everyone else reports a benefit parameter of 0.

(14) Assume that $n = 2$, $U_1 = 4x + y_1$, $U_2 = 3x + y_2$, and $\omega_1 = \omega_2 = 20$. Each consumer gets half of the profit of economy's only firm, which uses Y as input to produce X. Specifically, x units of the public good require $\frac{1}{2}x^2$ units of the private good as input. Suppose that the public good is allocated by the private market system, so that the public good is supplied by a price-taking, profit-maximizing firm to utility-maximizing individuals. Show that $x = 4$ at the competitive market equilibrium. (Hint: begin by determining the firm's supply as a function of the price P of its output. For convenience, fix the price of the private good at unity.)

(15) There are two individuals, with $\omega_1 = 200$ and $\omega_2 = 100$. The production of x units of the public good requires $1.5x^2$ units of the private good as input. The public good is produced by a single firm, and each individual gets half the firm's profit. Let $U_1 = 48\sqrt{x} + y_1$, and $U_2 = 30\sqrt{x} + y_2$. At a competitive equilibrium of the private ownership market economy we have the following: the price of X is 12, and the price of Y is 1. Individual 1 buys 4 units of X and individual 2 buys 0 units of X. Find the value of y_1 and y_2 at equilibrium and confirm that we do indeed have an equilibrium.

(16) Prove that the competitive market equilibrium of Section 8.1.3 really is an equilibrium by showing that all consumers are maximizing utility given their budget constraints, the firm is maximizing profit given the equilibrium price, and demand equals supply for each good.

8.2 THE PIVOTAL MECHANISM

A successful mechanism for determining the output of the public good must come to terms with the unilateral decisiveness principle. (See Section 8.1.5 for the definition.) The pivotal mechanism succeeds by making it costly for an individual to shift the level of X away from the value that maximizes total utility *under truthful revelation*. Remarkably, the *pivotal mechanism* gives the individual the incentive to seek the value of X that maximizes total utility even though no individual knows the benefit function of any other agent!

What makes this mechanism work is that the cost to the individual of changing the level of X equals the cost imposed on the rest of society by that change. Before defining this scheme we recall the role played by social cost pricing in the Vickrey (second-price) auction of a single indivisible asset (Section 6.2 of Chapter 6). There are n individuals $i = 1, 2, \ldots n$, and i's reservation value for the asset is V_i. Suppose that $V_1 > V_i$ for all $i > 1$. Submitting a bid equal to one's reservation value is a dominant strategy, so that each V_i will be known to the auctioneer after the bids have been recorded. If the asset is a Picasso painting then the costs of production are zero, and we don't have to worry about taxing the community to underwrite its production. But giving the painting to individual i entails an opportunity cost because others are denied the utility that it would have provided. The cost to the community is V_1 when the painting is given to anyone but person 1, because V_1 is the maximum utility that can be generated by an alternative assignment. If person 1 does get the asset then the cost to the rest of the group is V_h, where h denotes the individual with the second-highest reservation value. Moreover, V_h is the price that will be paid by person 1 when everyone submits a bid equal to his or her true reservation value. No one else pays anything. In that case, we can say that the Vickrey auction requires all participants to pay a fee equal to the cost that their participation has imposed on the rest of society. Anyone whose reservation value is not the highest pays nothing because the outcome would have been the same without his or her participation. Without the high-reservation-value person the asset would have gone to the one with the next highest reservation value so the second-highest reservation value is the amount that the high-reservation-value person pays. The pivotal mechanism for determining the output of a public good also imposes a charge on each individual equal to the cost that his or her participation imposes on the rest of society.

8.2.1 The Model

As in Section 8.1, there are n individuals; each utility function has the quasi-linear form $U_i(x, y_i) = B_i(x) + y_i$ ($i = 1, 2 \ldots, n$) where x is the level of output of the public good and y_i is individual i's consumption of the private good. Each individual i is endowed with ω_i units of the private good Y, a unit of which can either be consumed or used as an input in the production of the public good, X. The production of x units of the public good requires $g(x)$ units of Y as input. The amount of the private good Y available for consumption is $\theta - g(x)$, where θ specifies the amount of Y available initially. That is, $\theta = \omega_1 + \omega_2 + \ldots + \omega_n$.

Instead of explicitly tracking the level of the public good, we feature a *public project* that not only specifies the level of X but also determines how much of the cost of producing the public good is borne by each individual.

DEFINITION: *Public Project*

A typical public project F specifies the menu x_F of public goods produced and, for each individual i, the amount $c_i(F)$ by which i's consumption of the private good falls as a result of the diversion of some of the private good from consumption to use as input in producing the public good.

Focusing on public projects simplifies the analysis in two ways. First, feasibility is implicit because we will assume that all the projects under consideration can actually be carried out with available resources and technology. Second, the utility of each individual from each project is determined because $U_i(F) \equiv B_i(x_F) + \omega_i - c_i(F)$ is the utility derived from project F by individual i. (If i's share of the cost were not specified then i's utility from a given level of X would be unknown.) Clearly, i will prefer project F to project G if and only if $U_i(F) > U_i(G)$. In words, i prefers F to G if and only if F yields more benefit to i net of the effect on i's consumption of the private good. The project need not even be quantifiable; it might specify how a particular industry is to be regulated.

It will not be necessary to explicitly specify how i's private consumption is reduced by a particular project, but to the extent that resources *are* diverted to produce X there will have to be a reduction in the total community consumption of Y, and this will inevitably be borne by individuals, although there is a wide variety of ways in which the distribution of this burden can be determined. Whatever specific formula is used is captured by the cost functions c_i. The cost of producing the public good could be shared equally. Alternatively, each person's cost share could be proportional to his or her wealth, and so on. Different projects could employ different cost sharing formulas. In fact the only difference between projects F and G might be the cost functions employed. That is, F and G might specify precisely the same set of governments activities, and hence the same government expenditure, but employ different formulas to specify how the necessary revenue is to be collected.

The public projects under consideration could generate *negative* individual benefit. For instance, F and G could be alternative proposals for storing nuclear waste. F might put the storage facility in your neighborhood, and G in mine. All of the claims that we make for the pivotal mechanism are valid in cases where the public project reduces the utility of some individuals. Fairness would have to be taken into consideration, in addition to efficiency, but this book only treats the problem of arriving at an efficient outcome in the presence of asymmetric information.

The pivotal mechanism – which is defined in the next subsection – will collect a surtax from each individual equal to the cost that the individual's participation imposes on the rest of society. This surtax would be over and above the sacrifice of Y specified by the cost function c_i. Because the surtax involves the private good, it has efficiency implications. However, our initial goal is project efficiency, by which we mean the selection of the project that maximizes total utility *before* any surtaxes are imposed.

DEFINITION: *Project Efficiency*
A mechanism for selecting a single public project from a given set of projects satisfies project efficiency if it always selects from that set the project that maximizes total utility.

We are assuming quasi-linear preferences, so maximization of total utility is necessary and sufficient for efficiency. (We assume that $y_i > 0$ will hold for each i.)

We use $V_i(F)$ to denote i's net benefit $B_i(x_F) - c_i(F)$ from project F. Because $U_i(F) = B_i(x_F) + \omega_i - c_i(F)$ we have $U_i(F) = V_i(F) + \omega_i$. Let $\sum_{i=1}^{n} V_i(F)$ denote the sum of the net benefit levels V_i from project F. That is,

$$\sum_{i=1}^{n} V_i(F) = V_1(F) + V_2(F) + \ldots + V_n(F).$$

Then $\sum_{i=1}^{n} U_i(F) = \sum_{i=1}^{n} V_i(F) + \sum_{i=1}^{n} \omega_i$. Therefore, for any two projects F and G we have

$$\sum_{i=1}^{n} V_i(F) + \sum_{i=1}^{n} \omega_i > \sum_{i=1}^{n} V_i(G) + \sum_{i=1}^{n} \omega_i$$

if and only if $\sum_{i=1}^{n} V_i(F) > \sum_{i=1}^{n} V_i(G)$. Therefore, project efficiency is equivalent to maximizing $\sum_{i=1}^{n} V_i$.

8.2.2 Two Options

Two public projects have been presented to the community for consideration. (Section 8.2.4 concerns the choice of x from a continuum.) The two proposals are F and G, and individuals are asked to report the net benefit that they receive from each project. The project that generates the higher level of total utility is adopted and carried out.

DEFINITION: *Project Selection by the Pivotal Mechanism*

Each i is asked to report $V_i(F)$ and $V_i(G)$. Project F is adopted if $\sum_{i=1}^{n} V_i(F) \geq \sum_{i=1}^{n} V_i(G)$, otherwise G is adopted.

Each individual is also required to pay a surtax equal to the cost that his or her participation has imposed on the rest of society. Typically, individual i's surtax will be zero because the winning project would have generated more total utility even if i's net benefit function had not been included.

For any project P and any individual j we let $\sum_{i \neq j} V_i(P)$ denote the sum of $V_i(P)$ over all individuals i *except* individual j.

DEFINITION: *The Surtax Imposed by the Pivotal Mechanism*

Suppose that $\sum_{i=1}^{n} V_i(F) > \sum_{i=1}^{n} V_i(G)$, and hence F is selected. If $\sum_{i \neq j} V_i(G) > \sum_{i \neq j} V_i(F)$ then individual j pays a surtax equal to the difference, which is $\sum_{i \neq j} V_i(G) - \sum_{i \neq j} V_i(F)$. If $\sum_{i \neq j} V_i(F) \geq \sum_{i \neq j} V_i(G)$ then j's surtax is zero.

The role of the surtax is to induce each individual to reveal his or her net benefit function V_i truthfully. When the pivotal mechanism is employed, *truthful revelation is a dominant strategy for each individual,* as we show.

Again, suppose that F is the winning project: that is, $\sum_{i=1}^{n} V_i(F) > \sum_{i=1}^{n} V_i(G)$. Individual j would not have to pay a surtax if $V_j(G) > V_j(F)$ because even with j's participation total net benefit from F exceeds total net benefit from G and thus when we exclude V_j total net benefit from F must exceed total net benefit from G. Nevertheless, the *threat* of a surtax will prevent agent j from overstating the net benefit that he or she gets from G in order to precipitate the selection of G.

Even when F is the winning project and $V_j(F) > V_j(G)$, individual j will not have to pay a surtax if there is more total net benefit from F than from G when V_j is excluded. The only one who pays a surtax is the individual j who gets greater net utility from the winning project, and the other project would have been selected had V_j not been included. Even so, the surtax is not so large as to induce individual j to deviate from truthful revelation to the extent of understating j's net benefit from the winning project to precipitate the selection of the other project and thus escape the surtax. We test these claims with an example before providing a proof.

Table 8.2 True Net Benefit Levels

	Soren	Rosie	Edie
Project F	10	19	30
Project G	15	10	40
Surtax	0	0	4

Example 8.7 A Community of Three Individuals

The first two rows of Table 8.2 give the net benefit V_i derived by each person from each project. If each individual reports truthfully, project G will be adopted because it yields a total net benefit of 65, versus 59 for F. Although Soren prefers G to F he does not pay a surtax because G would still win (by 50 to 49) without Soren's participation. Rosie does not pay a surtax because the outcome she prefers was not selected. But Edie pays a surtax because without her participation the outcome would have been F, which yields a total net benefit to the rest of the community of 29, versus 25 for G. The surtax that Edie pays is the difference, which is 4.

Clearly, Soren has no incentive to deviate from the truth: His preferred outcome is selected without his having to pay a surtax. He can only change the outcome by causing F to be selected, and then he would have to pay a surtax (of 1). Rosie could cause her preferred outcome F to be selected by overstating her net utility from F by 7 or more, but then Rosie would have to pay a surtax of $(15 + 40) - (10 + 30) = 15$. Rosie's net benefit is 10 when G is selected, and it would be $19 - 15 = 4$ if she misrepresented her preference to ensure the victory of F. Clearly, this would not be to her advantage. Edie could avoid the surtax of 4 by understating her preference for G (or overstating her preference for F) but her net benefit when she tells the truth is $40 - 4 = 36$, which is greater than her net benefit when she misrepresents her preference to avoid the surtax. (Her net benefit from F is only 30.)

In fact there is no situation in which anyone has an incentive to misrepresent his or her preference.

Pivotal Mechanism Theorem for the Binary Case
Truthful revelation is a dominant strategy for each individual and each specification of the individual net benefit functions.

Proof:

Without loss of generality, assume that F is selected when everyone reports truthfully. That is, $\sum_{i=1}^{n} V_i(F) \geq \sum_{i=1}^{n} V_i(G)$. Therefore, *if* individual j has to pay a surtax it will equal

$$\sum_{i=1}^{n} V_i(G) - V_j(G) - [\sum_{i=1}^{n} V_i(F) - V_j(F)].$$

We represent this surtax as $\sum_{i \neq j} V_i(G) - \sum_{i \neq j} V(F)$, the total net benefit from G of everyone in society except j minus the total net benefit from F derived by everyone in society except for j. We examine individual j's decision in three cases, with $\sum_{i=1}^{n} V_i(F) \geq \sum_{i=1}^{n} V_i(G)$. holding in each case.

Case 1: Individual j gets at least as much net benefit from F as from G, and F provides more total net benefit even when V_j is excluded. In symbols, $V_j(F) \geq V_j(G)$ and $\sum_{i \neq j} V_i(F) \geq \sum_{i \neq j} V_i(G)$. There is no incentive for j to change the reported V_j to ensure the selection of G. That could lower j's utility even without a surtax, although j would surely have to pay one if $\sum_{i \neq j} V_i(F) > \sum_{i \neq j} V_i(G)$.

Case 2: Individual j gets more net benefit from F than from G, but G provides more total net benefit when V_j is excluded.

That is, $V_j(F) > V_j(G)$ and $\sum_{i \neq j} V_i(G) \geq \sum_{i \neq j} V_i(F)$. This means that under truthful revelation individual j pays a surtax of $\sum_{i \neq j} V_i(G) - \sum_{i \neq j} V_i(F)$. Could individual j increase his or her utility by deviating from truthful revelation sufficiently to pre-cipitate the selection of G? That would allow j to escape the surtax, but j would realize less net benefit from G than from F: Because $\sum_{i=1}^{n} V_i(F) \geq \sum_{i=1}^{n} V_i(G)$ we have

$$\sum_{i \neq j} V_i(F) + V_j(F) \geq \sum_{i \neq j} V_i(G) + V_j(G), \qquad [6]$$

which implies

$$V_j(F) - [\sum_{i \neq j} V_i(G) - \sum_{i \neq j} V_i(F)] \geq V_j(G). \qquad [7]$$

In words, the net benefit that j gets from F minus the tax surcharge is at least as great as j's net benefit from G. In fact, the net benefit that j gets from F minus the tax surcharge is strictly greater than j's net benefit from G when $\sum_{i \neq j} V_i(G)$ is strictly greater than $\sum_{i \neq j} V_i(F)$. (The inequalities $\geq$ in [6] and [7] will be replaced by $>$ when $\sum_{i \neq j} V_i(G) > \sum_{i \neq j} V_i(F)$.) Therefore, j cannot improve on truthful revelation by pre-cipitating the selection of G.

Case 3: Individual j gets more net benefit from G than from F.

We have $V_j(G) > V_j(F)$. Individual j would prefer to see G adopted but if j were to overstate the net benefit that he or she received from G then j would surely have to pay a surtax if G were selected. That is because F is selected when j reports truthfully, even though $V_j(G) > V_j(F)$, and so it must be the case that $\sum_{i \neq j} V_i(F) > \sum_{i \neq j} V_i(G)$, and thus j would have to pay a surtax equal to $\sum_{i \neq j} V_i(F) - \sum_{i \neq j} V_i(G)$. if he or she caused G to be selected. Moreover,

$$\sum_{i \neq j} V_i(F) + V_j(F) \geq \sum_{i \neq j} V_i(G) + V_j(G)$$

implies

$$V_j(F) \geq V_j(G) - [\sum_{i \neq j} V_i(F) - \sum_{i \neq j} V_i(G)]. \qquad [8]$$

Therefore, j will not get more net benefit from G after paying the surtax than j gets from F. Hence j cannot improve on truthful revelation in this case. ∎

We have demonstrated that truthful revelation is a dominant strategy for each individual. Social cost pricing provides the incentive for individuals to submit their true net benefit functions. In effect, the individual is induced to maximized total net benefit. When F maximizes total utility under truthful revelation the individual has an incentive to ensure that F is selected because [7] holds in case 2 and [8] holds in case 3. Each is equivalent to $\sum_{i=1}^{n} V_i(F) \geq \sum_{i=1}^{n} V_i(G)$.

8.2.3   Defects of the Pivotal Mechanism

The surtaxes provide just the right incentive for individuals to report their benefit schedules truthfully. The surtax makes it costly for i to overstate the benefit from his or her preferred project in an attempt to prevent the other from being selected. And because the surtax is independent of i's report, *as long as it does not cause the outcome to change*, there is no incentive to understate one's benefit as there is with benefit taxation. But the surtaxes result in the accumulation of a government budget surplus. (The surplus is 4 in Example 8.6.)

This budget imbalance is inevitable if the incentive to report truthfully is to be maintained! The government could return the surplus to the community but that would alter the incentives and would in fact result in truthful revelation being inferior to some other strategy in some situations. We can demonstrate this by means of the net benefit functions of Example 8.6.

Example 8.8 Equal Sharing of the Surplus

Suppose that the budget surplus were shared equally by the three individuals. The true net benefit functions are as given in Table 8.2 of Example 8.6. If Rosie were to report $V_R(F) = 24$ and $V_R(G) = 10$ then G would still be selected, this time by 65 "votes" to 64. However, the surtax paid by Edie would increase from 4 to 9, and Soren would have to pay a surtax of $24 + 30 - (10 + 40) = 4$. This means that Rosie would receive a one-third share of a \$13 surplus instead of a one-third share of a \$4 surplus. Her utility would increase from $10 + 4/3$ to $10 + 13/3$ as a result. Misrepresentation pays in this case.

By definition, the government budget surplus is the sum of the individual surtaxes. Truthful revelation is a dominant strategy only when the government budget surplus is not rebated to the community. This means that the pivotal mechanism does not yield efficient outcomes even though it satisfies project efficiency: The other efficiency requirement, $\sum_{i=1}^{n} y_i = \sum_{i=1}^{n} \omega_i - g(x)$, is violated because the surtaxes by individuals are payments over and above what is required to purchase the input needed to produce the public good. Only $g(x)$ units of Y are needed to produce x units of X, but $\sum_{i=1}^{n} y_i$ falls short of $\sum_{i=1}^{n} \omega_i - g(x)$ by the amount of the surplus, which is positive or zero. However, if the number of individuals is large then the surplus will be close to zero on average – because the probability that an individual's participation changes the outcome will be low if the number of voters is large. By the same token, if the probability that an individual's participation will have any effect on the outcome is virtually zero then there is little incentive to participate in the first place. Thus, the budget surplus problem vanishes only when a more subtle incentive problem emerges.

Perhaps more serious is the fact that the pivotal mechanism can leave someone worse off than if the mechanism had not been used at all.

Table 8.3 True Net Benefit Levels

	Soren	Rosie	Edie
Project F	20	30	40
Project G	30	25	31
Surtax	0	1	5

Example 8.9 Participation Can be Harmful

As usual, Table 8.3 reveals the true net benefit levels for the respective individuals. Suppose that F is the status quo, with no change in the government's provision of public goods, and G is the consequence of government funding of a project to explore Mars. The status quo will be retained if the pivotal mechanism is used to elicit information about individual preference, but the surtaxes that are necessary to induce truthful revelation leave Edie worse off than if proposal G had not been considered. There is no change in the status quo, but it costs Edie one-eighth of her initial net benefit for the pivotal mechanism to determine that the status quo should prevail.

Another problem is that the mechanism is vulnerable to manipulation by *coalitions* – even coalitions of two people.

Example 8.10 Two-Person Manipulation of the Pivotal Mechanism

The true net benefit functions are displayed in Table 8.4. If individuals report truthfully G would be selected even though the majority prefers F to G. (G gets 90 "votes" and F gets 80.) If Rosie and Edie collude and each agree to cast 300 "votes" for F then F will be selected without either having to pay a surtax. This is confirmed by Table 8.5. Rosie does not pay a surtax because F would win without her, and Edie does not pay a surtax for the same reason. Each gets a net benefit of 30 as a result of this ploy, and that is 20% higher than the net benefit that each receives with truthful revelation and the outcome G.

Although a single individual cannot manipulate the pivotal mechanism, it is extremely vulnerable to manipulation by a pair of individuals acting in concert. We can augment Example 8.9 by adding a large number n of individuals who have the same net benefit function as Soren. As long as Rosie and Edie each report a net benefit for F of more than $20(n + 1) + 25$ then F will be selected and neither of the collaborators will have to pay a surtax. Rosie and Edie could successfully collude even if there were millions of other voters.

We are unable to offer a single public decision mechanism that has almost all of the properties that are important for efficient and democratic public policies. In some cases the market mechanism may precipitate a better outcome than any

Table 8.4 True Net Benefit Levels

	Soren	Rosie	Edie
Project F	20	30	30
Project G	40	25	25
Surtax	10	0	0

Table 8.5 Reported Net Benefit Levels

	Soren	Rosie	Edie
Project F	20	300	300
Project G	40	25	25
Surtax	0	0	0

In the United States, the agencies responsible for liquidating failed property and casualty insurance companies recover only 33 percent of the book value of the companies' assets on average and only 41 percent of the liquid assets. Part of the problem is that the state regulatory agents whose job it is to liquidate the assets of an insolvent insurance company pay their own expenses first and do not have much incentive to maximize the proceeds from the sale of assets (Hall, 2000).

collective choice process, especially if the degree of spillover is moderate and the cost of exclusion is low. (The cost of exclusion is low if, as in the case of a lake with a single access road, individuals who don't pay a user fee can be prevented from enjoying the public good. In the case of mosquito control, the cost of exclusion is high.) However, if exclusion is costly and the degree of spillover is high, then the political process has a chance of outperforming the market system, but a lot will depend on the incentives provided to key personnel: public provision of the good will require appropriate effort by the relevant government officials. This effort cannot be taken for granted because of another private information problem – hidden action. Just as there is a possibility that the mechanic hired to repair your car will shirk and charge you for work that was not done, so government employees — including professors — can contribute less than their best effort.

This is not to suggest that the private ownership market economy does not have its own hidden action problems. However, the preference revelation problem for the allocation of private goods - commodities with very limited spillovers - disappears as the number of agents gets arbitrarily large, but it gets worse in a model featuring public goods.

8.2.4   A Continuum of Options

We return to the case in which x is a real number, interpreted as the level of output of the public good. A project is a specification of the quantity x along with the amount $c_i(x)$ by which each individual i's consumption of the private good is reduced to obtain the input of Y needed to produce x. Of course, $\sum_{i=1}^{n} c_i(x) = g(x)$, where $g(x)$ is the amount of the private good Y required as input to produce of x units of the public good. We wish to elicit an individual's entire benefit function $B_i(x)$ so that the level of x that maximizes $\sum_{i=1}^{n} [B_i(x) + \omega_i - c_i(x)]$, or total utility, can be identified. Note that

$$\sum_{i=1}^{n} B_i(x) + \sum_{i=1}^{n} \omega_i - \sum_{i=1}^{n} c_i(x) = \sum_{i=1}^{n} B_i(x) - g(x) + \sum_{i=1}^{n} \omega_i,$$

which expresses total utility as a function of x.

Social cost pricing is the key to the success of the pivotal mechanism, which requires each agent i to report i's net benefit function $V_i(x) = B_i(x) - c_i(x)$ and then produces the efficient project. When x varies along a continuum, the calculation of the cost to the rest of society of an individual's participation is more complicated than in the two-option case, but the principal is the same. Note that $\sum_{i=1}^{n} V_i(x) = \sum_{i=1}^{n} B_i(x) - g(x)$, so that $\sum_{i=1}^{n} V_i(x)$ is maximized at the efficient level of x under truthful revelation.

DEFINITION: *The Pivotal Mechanism*

If R_j is the net benefit function reported by agent j and x^* maximizes the sum of the reported functions, then x^* units of X are produced and each individual j's consumption of Y is reduced by $c_j(x^*)$. In addition, each individual j pays a surtax of

$$t_j = \sum_{i \neq j} R_i(x^j) - \sum_{i \neq j} R_i(x^*),$$

where x^j is the value of x that maximizes $\sum_{i \neq j} R_i(x)$.

When the reported net benefit functions are the true ones, the efficient level of the public good is produced. Therefore, the pivotal mechanism satisfies project efficiency. (It would be fully efficient if it were not necessary to collect the surtaxes.) It is easy to see that t_j is the cost to the rest of society of individual j's participation: the surtax t_j is equal to the maximum total utility that the rest of society could realize without consulting j's preferences minus the total utility that the rest of society receives with j's preferences included and the adoption of project x^*.

We next establish that truthful revelation is a dominant strategy for each individual in every possible situation, even when x can vary along a continuum. In fact, the following proof is very general and applies to any set of feasible public projects: whatever benefit functions are reported by others, arbitrary agent j cannot gain by reporting a net benefit function that is not j's true $V_j = B_j - c_j$. In other words, there is no function R_j that will precipitate a higher level of utility for j *according to j's true benefit function V_j* than the utility level that results from reporting that true V_j.

Pivotal Mechanism Theorem for the General Case

Truthful revelation is a dominant strategy for each individual and each specification of the individual net benefit functions.

Proof:

We temporarily adopt the unilateral decisiveness principle of Section 8.1.5: for any value of x, an arbitrary individual can guarantee that x is selected as the level of the public good by reporting the appropriate net benefit function. Consider arbitrary individual j. Let $R_1, R_2, \ldots, R_n$ be the reported benefit functions, with V_j denoting agent j's true benefit function. Given the mechanism's cost rules, what value of x maximizes j's utility?

$$U_j = V_j(x) + \omega_j - t_j = V_j(x) + \omega_j - \sum_{i \neq j} R_i(x^j) + \sum_{i \neq j} R_i(x)$$

$$= V_j(x) + \sum_{i \neq j} R_i(x) + \omega_j - \sum_{i \neq j} R_i(x^j).$$

Because $\omega_j - \sum_{i \neq j} R_i(x^j)$ is independent of j's reported net benefit function, it can be treated as a constant from the standpoint of j's maximization problem. Therefore,

The pivotal mechanism has been tested in laboratory settings. Surprisingly, the efficient outcome emerged only 70 percent of the time, even though truthful revelation is a dominant strategy (Attiyeh et al., 2000). This might be due to the mechanism's vulnerability to collusion.

the value of x that maximizes U_j is also the value of x that maximizes $V_j(x) + \sum_{i \neq j} R_i(x)$. What reported net benefit function by individual j will lead to the value of x that maximizes $V_j(x) + \sum_{i \neq j} R_i(x)$? If j submits $R_j(x)$ then the value of x selected will be the one that maximizes $R_j(x) + \sum_{i \neq j} R_i(x)$. Clearly, j can do no better than setting $R_j(x) = V_j(x)$. This is the case *even if* individual j could force any value of x to be produced. Therefore, without unilateral decisiveness individual j would still want the same x. In other words, reporting the true $V_j(x)$ is a dominant strategy (The dominant strategy property follows from the fact that we have demonstrated that setting $R_j(x) = V_j(x)$ is a best response by j whatever the net benefit functions $R_i(x)$ reported by the other individual, whatever their motivation.)   ∎

8.2.5   Relation to the Gibbard-Satterthwaite Theorem

Truthful revelation is a dominant strategy for each individual when the pivotal mechanism is used to select a public project. Why does that not contradict the Gibbard-Satterthwaite Theorem (Sections 7.2.2 or 7.3.1 of Chapter 7)? That theorem establishes that there does not exist a non-dictatorial incentive scheme for inducing truthful revelation when there are more than two possible outcomes. The pivotal mechanism is even invulnerable to manipulation when there is a continuum of possible outcomes. And the pivotal mechanism is certainly not dictatorial. To confirm that, suppose that there are n individuals and person j's net benefit from project A is 10 and it is 0 from all other projects. Each of the other individuals gets a net benefit of 20 from project Z and 0 from all other projects including A. The pivotal mechanism will select Z, but j prefers A to Z and hence j is not a dictator.

The key difference between the framework of the Gibbard-Satterthwaite Theorem and that of the pivotal mechanism is that the latter assumes quasi-linear preferences, with each person's utility being independent of the private goods consumption of other individuals. The Gibbard-Satterthwaite Theorem, however, requires a social choice rule to select an outcome for each logically possible ordering of the feasible alternatives by the individuals. Because the success of the pivotal mechanism depends on surtaxes, these additional payments must be part of the model. Once they are included we can no longer assume that any logically possible ordering is an admissible preference scheme for an individual. For one thing, the outcome that sees project K carried out with individual j paying a surtax of \$100 will never be preferred by j to the adoption of K without any additional payment by j. However, the proof of the Gibbard-Satterthwaite Theorem employs profiles in which the outcome "K plus a \$100 payment by j" is at the top of j's preference ordering. In short, the proof of the Gibbard-Satterthwaite Theorem does not go through on the domain of preference profiles for which the pivotal mechanism induces truthful revelation.

Sources

The pivotal mechanism was discovered independently by Groves (1973) and Clarke (1971). (See also Tideman and Tullock, 1976.)

Links

Rob (1982) proved that the budget surplus is virtually zero with a large number of individuals. Green and Laffont (1979) have a simpler proof but they make stronger assumptions about the probability distribution of voter utilities.

Problem Set

(1) Does the pivotal mechanism select the option that is preferred by a majority when there are only two feasible options? Explain.

(2) Consider the case of three individuals, Soren, Rosie, and Edie, and two public projects F and G. Table 8.6 gives the benefit derived by each person from each project – that is, the benefit net of the taxes assessed to command the resources necessary to construct the project.

Table 8.6. True Net Benefit Levels

	Soren	Rosie	Edie
Project F	10	20	30
Project G	15	10	40

(A) What project would be undertaken if the pivotal mechanism were employed *and* individuals reported their net benefit figures truthfully? Calculate the surtax for each individual.

(B) Show that none of the three individuals has an incentive to misrepresent his or her benefit schedule in this setting. What does it mean to say that truthful revelation of preference is a dominant strategy in this case?

(C) What is the size of the government budget surplus associated with your answer to question A?

(3) Repeat question 2 for the payoffs of Table 8.7.

Table 8.7 True Net Benefit Levels

	Soren	Rosie	Edie
Project F	4	30	24
Project G	10	20	30

(4) Table 8.8 gives you the true net benefit levels for each of *three* public projects F, G, and H for each of three individuals. Repeat question 2 for this case.

Table 8.8 True Net Benefit Levels

	Soren	Rosie	Edie
Project F	5	18	33
Project G	10	25	18
Project H	15	10	28

(5) Suppose that the pivotal mechanism is augmented by having the surplus returned to the community by giving each individual a fraction of the surplus that is proportional to the net benefit that the individual gets from the project that is selected. (If A is selected and the sum of the $V_i(A)$ is 100 then individual j get the fraction $V_j(A)/100$ of the surplus.) *By means of a specific numerical example,* show that truthful revelation is no longer a dominant strategy.

(6) The pivotal mechanism is employed, and the individuals pay equal shares of the cost of funding public projects before calculating surtaxes. For the case $B_i(x) = a_i x$ $(i = 1, \ldots, n)$ with $a_i > 0$ and $g(x) = \frac{1}{2}x^2$, show that the pivotal mechanism induces individual 1 to report his or her true a_1.

(7) The pivotal mechanism is employed, and the individuals pay equal shares of the cost of funding public projects before calculating surtaxes. There are three individuals, with $B_1(x) = 2\sqrt{x}$, $B_2(x) = 4\sqrt{x}$, and $B_3(x) = 12\sqrt{x}$, For A and B below determine the outcome generated by the pivotal mechanism when $g(x) = x$. Specify the level of output of the public good, the share of the cost of financing that public good that is borne by each individual, and the surtax paid by each person. Compute the utility of each person at the pivotal equilibrium and compare it with the utility that each enjoys when no public goods are produced and everyone simply consumes his or her own endowment. What does this comparison reveal about the properties of the pivotal mechanism?

   (A) $\omega_1 = \omega_2 = \omega_3 = 168$.

   (B) $\omega_1 = 40$, $\omega_2 = 100$, and $\omega_3 = 60$.

(8) The pivotal mechanism is employed, $g(x) = x$, and the individuals pay equal shares of the cost of funding public projects before calculating surtaxes. For $n = 3$ and $B_1(x) = a\sqrt{x}$, $B_2(x) = \delta\sqrt{x}$, $B_3(x) = \lambda\sqrt{x}$, and arbitrary ω_i, show that person 2's pivotal surtax is zero if $\delta = (a + \lambda)$. What is the underlying intuition?

(9) Consider the following modification of the pivotal mechanism: use the same rule for determining the level of output of the public good but change the surtax formula for each individual j by dropping the term $\sum_{i \neq j} R_i(x^j)$. Prove that truthful revelation is still a dominant strategy. Assume that the efficient level of x is positive. Prove that the government budget is always in deficit as a result of the modified tax formula.

(10) Show that the pivotal mechanism defined in Section 8.2.2 is actually a special case of the mechanism defined in Section 8.2.4. In other words, prove that

when there are only two options the surtax formula of Section 8.2.4 agrees with that of Section 8.2.2.

(11) Rework the problem of allocating a single indivisible object to a group of n individuals by using the framework and notation of this section. Now, show that the allocation rule and surtax rule defined by the Vickrey auction coincides with the respective formulas of the pivotal mechanism.

8.3 GROVES MECHANISMS

Social cost pricing is the key to the success of the pivotal mechanism. Each individual pays a surtax equal to the cost that the individual's participation imposes on the rest of society. Even when no one is pivotal, and no surtaxes are collected, the *threat* of a surtax prevents individuals who would be disappointed with the outcome from tilting it in another direction. But it is not the level of the surtax per se that provides the incentive for truthful revelation, it's the fact that the difference between the surtax paid by individual j when j reports truthfully and surtax paid when j deviates is equal to the change in the cost that j imposes on the rest of society. This fact suggests a generalization of the pivotal mechanism by adding surtaxes (that may be positive or negative) that are independent of the agent's own report.

8.3.1 The Model

There are n individuals, indexed by $i = 1, 2, \ldots, n$. There is a given (possibly infinite) set $Q = \{q, q', q'', \ldots\}$ of feasible public projects. Each individual i has a payoff function $U_i = V_i(q) - t_i$, where V_i is a real valued function on Q and t_i is a payment by agent i to the government. If t_i is negative then individual i receives $-t_i$ dollars from the government. We refer to V_i as i's *net benefit function*: $V_i(q)$ is i's benefit from q minus i's share of the total cost of producing q. We continue to assume that V_i is known only to individual i.

When we focus only on the set of feasible projects, with private goods off stage, selecting the project that maximizes total net benefit does not guarantee an efficient outcome. For one thing, some of the private good left over after a sufficient amount has been allocated to financing the adopted project might be wasted, and hence not available for private consumption. Moreover, any surtaxes that are collected will render the entire outcome inefficient if these surtaxes cannot be returned to the private sector without destroying the incentive for truthful revelation. Therefore, we refer to an outcome as *project-efficient* if total net benefit is maximized.

DEFINITION: *Project Efficiency*

If q^* is feasible (i.e., it belongs to Q) and $\sum_{i=1}^{n} V_i(q^*) \geq \sum_{i=1}^{n} V_i(q)$ holds for all q in Q we say that q^* is project-efficient.

This definition is justified by Section 2.5.1 of Chapter 2: with quasi-linear preferences an outcome that leaves everyone with a positive amount of the private good is efficient if and only if it maximizes total utility.

Example 8.11 Retardation of Global Warming

Each agent i is a country and each $q \in Q$ is a proposal to reduce global warming by $x(q)$ percent by imposing an adjustment cost $c_i(q)$ on each $i \in N$. Then $V_i(q) = B_i(q) - c_i(q)$, where $B_i(q)$ is the benefit that country i receives from q. Suppose, for instance, that the function B_i is the same for each $i \in N$ (or that each B_i is known). The cost functions c_i are unknown, however, and a central authority wants to learn each country's true cost function so that the burden of adjustment can be imposed on the low-cost countries. We will see that it is possible to design an incentive scheme to induce each agent to report truthfully, in spite of the apparent incentive to claim to be a high-cost country so that the burden will fall elsewhere.

In many applications there are only two projects under discussion, the status quo and a new proposal:

Example 8.12 The Binary Choice Model

The agents can be countries, or individuals in a small community at the other extreme. $Q = \{0,1\}$, where 0 represents the status quo and 1 is the new proposal. We can let V_i be a *number* – the difference between i's benefit at the new proposal and at the status quo. If $\sum_{i=1}^{n} V_i > 0$ then $q^* = 1$ (only the new proposal is project efficient), and if $\sum_{i=1}^{n} V_i < 0$ we have $q^* = 0$ (only the status quo is project efficient).

An important special case of the general framework is the resource allocation model with pure public goods.

Example 8.13 The Public Goods Model of Section 8.1

Each individual i is characterized by a utility function U_i representing i's preferences, and an endowment ω_i of a private good. The utility function is defined over the space of consumption plans, and agent i's plan (x, y_i) specifies the amount $x \geq 0$ of a public good available to all and i's consumption $y_i \geq 0$ of a single private good Y. We further simplify by assuming that utility is quasi-linear: For each $i \in N$ there is a real-valued function B_i defined on the set of nonnegative real numbers, such that $U_i(x,y_i) = B_i(x) + y_i$. We complete the model by including a real cost function g that specifies the amount $g(x)$ of the private good required for the production of x units of the public good.

An *allocation* (x, y) identifies the level of the public good and the vector $y = (y_1, y_2, \ldots, y_n)$ of private good consumption levels. Allocation (x, y) is *feasible* if $x \geq 0$, $y \geq 0$, and

$$\sum_{i=1}^{n} y_i + g(x) \leq \sum_{i=1}^{n} \omega_i,$$

the *resource constraint*. In words, the amount of the private good allocated to agents plus the amount used up in producing the public good cannot exceed the sum of the endowments. Each feasible allocation (x, y) corresponds to the project q for which $x(q) = x$ and $c_i(q) = \omega_i - y_i$. (The set Q is implicit.) The benefit function is $V_i(q) = B_i[x(q)] - c_i(q)$. The Samuelson condition is

$$B_1' (x) + B_2' (x) + \ldots + B_n' (x) = g'(x).$$

Our framework can even be used to model the distribution of indivisible private goods. We illustrate with the case of a single indivisible asset.

Example 8.14 Allocation of a Single Indivisible Asset

Q is the set of n-tuples $(q_1, q_2, \ldots, q_n)$ such that q_i is either 0 or 1 for each i, and $\sum_{i=1}^{n} q_i = 1$. (Agent i gets the asset if and only if $q_i = 1$.) If v_i is agent i's reservation value for the asset, then $V_i(q) = v_i$ if $q_i = 1$, and $V_i(q) = 0$ if $q_i = 0$. If the "asset" is undesirable then v_i is negative. For instance, $q_i = 1$ means that garbage (or toxic waste) is stored in region i.

8.3.2 The Mechanisms

We can generalize the surtaxes of the pivotal mechanism to generate the large family of Groves mechanisms. The difference between the surtaxes paid by arbitrary individual j arising from alternative reported net benefit functions is still equal to the difference between the respective costs imposed on the rest of society. That will allow us to apply the proof that truthful revelation is a dominant strategy for the pivotal mechanism to this much larger family. This more general approach employs *marginal* social cost pricing.

DEFINITION: *Marginal Social Cost Pricing*

Marginal social cost pricing is used if alternative decisions D' and D'' each impose costs on the individual J making the decision and the difference between that J's cost arising from the choice of D' and the cost arising from the choice of D'' is equal to the total cost incurred by everyone but J as a result of D' minus the total cost incurred by everyone but J as a result of D''.

If the rest of the group derives benefit from j's action, then the cost of j's action is negative. That is, individual j receives a payment, and marginal social cost pricing requires the difference between j's stipend when j adopts D' and j's stipend when j adopts D'' to be equal to the total benefit realized by the rest of the group as a result of D' minus the total benefit realized by the rest of the group as a result of D''.

A Groves mechanism selects the project that maximizes total net benefit according to the reported net benefit functions and then imposes surtaxes that embody marginal social cost pricing. That gives us a great deal of latitude, however, in determining the surtax formulas. There is a large family of Groves mechanisms; one for each specification of the surtax formulas.

DEFINITION: *Groves Mechanism*

Each individual i reports a net benefit function R_i, and the project q^* that maximizes $\sum_{i=1}^{n} R_i(q^*)$ is adopted. Each individual j pays a surtax of

$$t_j = \Phi_j(R_1, R_2, \ldots, R_{j-1}, R_{j+1}, \ldots, R_n) - \sum_{i \neq j} R_i(q^*)$$

where Φ_j is independent of j's report. Each specification of the Φ_j defines a different Groves mechanism.

We can let Φ_j depend on the messages of individuals other than i and the mechanism will still have the dominant strategy property. The key is that the social cost of a *change* in an agent's message will be reflected in a change in that agent's transfer.

It remains to show that truthful revelation is a dominant strategy for each individual in every possible situation. That is, whatever benefit functions are reported by others, arbitrary agent j cannot gain by reporting a net benefit different from j's true $V_j = B_j(q) - c_j$. In other words, given the reports of others, there is no function R_j that will precipitate a higher level of utility for j according to j's true benefit function V_j than the utility level that results from reporting that true V_j.

Strategy-Proofness Theorem for Groves Mechanisms
   Truthful revelation is a dominant strategy for each individual.

Proof:

Consider the decision of individual 1. Let R_1, R_2 R_3, ..., R_n be the reported net benefit functions, with V_1 denoting agent 1's true net benefit function. The mechanism's cost rules imply

$$U_1 = V_1(q) - t_1 = V_1(q) - \Phi_1(R_2, R_3, \ldots, R_n) + \sum_{i \neq 1} R_i(q)$$

Because $\Phi_1(R_2, R_3, \ldots, R_n)$ is independent of 1's reported net benefit function, it can be treated as a constant from the standpoint of 1's maximization problem. Therefore, the project q that maximizes U_1 is also the q that maximizes $V_1(q) + \sum_{i \neq 1} R_i(q)$, and that can be achieved if agent 1 reports V_1. Therefore, individual 1 cannot profit from misrepresenting his or her net benefit function. The same argument will work for the other individuals.   ∎

Source

This section is based on Groves (1973).

Links

For the public goods model of Section 8.1 (and Example 8.3) any mechanism for which truthful revelation is a dominant strategy is a Groves mechanism for some choice of the functions Φ_i. This was established by Green and Laffont (1977, 1979). Walker (1978) proved the same result for a much narrower family of preferences. (Walker's theorem is stronger because a mechanism is required to operate successfully over a narrower range of cases.) Danilov and Sotskov (2002, pp. 99–104) work out the extreme assumptions needed to guarantee the existence of a Groves mechanism that always leads to a balanced government budget.

8.4 EFFICIENCY AND INCENTIVE COMPATIBILITY

Because of the surtaxes that are collected in some situations, the pivotal mechanism does not guarantee budget balance, and hence it does not guarantee an efficient outcome, even though it satisfies *project* efficiency. We now consider whether there exists *any* mechanism that induces truthful revelation and yields efficient outcomes without sometimes leaving an individual with less utility than if the mechanism had not been used at all. In Section 8.4.1, we prove that there is no such mechanism. In Section 8.4.2, we relax the incentive compatibility requirement and exhibit a mechanism for which a Nash equilibrium always yields an efficient outcome.

We seek a mechanism for determining the level of output x of a single public good, along with the consumption y_i of a single private good by each individual i. There are n individuals, and each i is endowed with ω_i units of the private good. (If the public good is not produced at all then individual i consumes $y_i = \omega_i$.) Individual i's preferences are represented by a quasi-linear utility function $U_i(x) = B_i(x) + y_i$. The production of x units of the public good requires $g(x)$ units of the private good to be used as input. Therefore, a feasible outcome (or allocation) must satisfy

$$y_1 + y_2 + \ldots + y_n \leq \omega_1 + \omega_2 + \ldots + \omega_n - g(x).$$

Efficiency can be satisfied by giving all of the private good to one individual, say j, and then choosing the output of the public good that maximizes j's utility subject to the requirement that j's consumption of the private good equal the total amount available initially minus what has to be used as input in the production of the public good. The outcome would be efficient because it maximizes j's utility, and thus any change would lower it. In other words, it would be impossible to increase anyone's utility without making someone else worse off. This procedure would also satisfy our requirement that truthful revelation is a dominant strategy: individual j clearly has no incentive to misrepresent his or her preference scheme. No one else can profit from misrepresentation either, because no one else's preferences have any influence on the outcome. A simple way of preventing a mechanism from going to such a dreadful extreme is to require it to select a level of output of the public good that leaves all individuals at least as well off as they were before the mechanism was employed. We refer to this as the *participation constraint*.

DEFINITION: *Participation Constraint*

For each individual i, utility at equilibrium must be at least as high as i's utility when i consumes 0 units of the public good and ω_i units of the private good. Formally,

$$B_i(x) + y_i \geq B_i(0) + \omega_i$$

where x is the output of the public good at equilibrium and y_i is i's consumption of the private good at equilibrium.

The participation constraint disqualifies absurd mechanisms such as the dictatorial scheme of the previous paragraph.

∂8.4.1 Dominant Strategy Equilibrium

We simplify by assuming that there are only two individuals and that the production of x units of the public good requires x^2 units of the private good as input: $g(x) = x^2$. We also assume that $\omega_1 = 2.5 = \omega_2$. In addition, we limit the benefit functions $B_i(x)$ to those of the form $\beta_i \ln(x + 1)$, where β_i can be any positive constant. Note that the first derivative of i's benefit function $B_i(x)$ is $\frac{\beta_i}{x+1}$, which is positive for all $x \geq 0$. Applying Section 8.1.2 to the present case, if $y_1 > 0$ and $y_2 > 0$ then the outcome is efficient only if it maximizes total utility subject to $y_1 + y_2 = \omega_1 + \omega_2 - g(x) = 5 - x^2$. This gives us a very simple model, but even so we prove that there exists no mechanism for which truthful revelation is a dominant strategy, the participation constraint is satisfied, and the outcome is efficient.

We will prove that the participation constraint does in fact imply $y_1 > 0$ and $y_2 > 0$, and thus to characterize the efficient outcomes for the reported benefit functions we maximize

$$\beta_1 \ln(x+1) + \beta_2 \ln(x+1) + 5 - x^2. \qquad [9]$$

The first derivative of this function is

$$\frac{\beta_1}{x+1} + \frac{\beta_2}{x+1} - 2x, \qquad [10]$$

and the second derivative is

$$-\beta_1(x+1)^{-2} - \beta_2(x+1)^{-2} - 2$$

which is negative for all values of x. Setting [10] equal to 0 and solving for x yields

$$2x^2 + 2x - \beta_1 - \beta_2 = 0,$$

And thus

$$x^* = -0.5 + 0.5\sqrt{1 + 2\beta_1 + 2\beta_2}, \qquad [11]$$

the efficient level of x. (There is a second root for which $x < 0$, but it is of no interest in this case.) Therefore, an efficient allocation for which $y_1 > 0$ and $y_2 > 0$ must satisfy $x = x^*$ and $y_1 + y_2 = 5 - (x^*)^2$. And if those conditions are satisfied the outcome is efficient because it maximizes total utility.

We now have enough background to consider whether it is possible to design incentives in such a way that individuals will report their benefit parameters β_i truthfully. We show that it is impossible to do so without violating efficiency or else making someone worse off than he or she was before the public good was provided.

Impossibility Theorem

If truthful revelation is a dominant strategy for a mechanism, it will either fail to deliver an efficient outcome for some specifications of the individual benefit functions or else violate the participation constraint for some specifications of the individual benefit functions.

Proof:

We begin with the case $\beta_1 = \beta_2 = 2$. Then by [11]

$$x^* = -0.5 + 0.5\sqrt{1 + 4 + 4} = 1.$$

Suppose that the mechanism delivers x units of the public good and leaves individuals 1 and 2 with y_1 and y_2, respectively, of the private good. Because we cannot rule out $y_1 = 0$ or $y_2 = 0$ at this stage we can only be sure that efficiency implies $x \leq 1$, as we now show.

Because the second derivative of [9] is negative it has a unique global maximum at $x^* = 1$. If $x > 1$ we can increase total utility by reducing x to $x^* = 1$. The private good thereby released can be divided equally between the two individuals to increase the utility of each. (Consult Section 8.1.2 if necessary.)

We have $x \leq 1$ at an efficient outcome. Suppose in addition that $y_i = 0$. Then i's utility cannot be greater than

$$2\ln(1 + 1) < 1.4 < 2.5 = \omega_i$$

Therefore, the participation constraint implies that $y_1 > 0$ and $y_2 > 0$. It follows that efficiency implies $x = x^* = 1$. This requires 1 unit of the private good as input so we must have $y_1 + y_2 = 5 - 1 = 4$. Therefore, either $y_1 \leq 2$ or $y_2 \leq 2$. Without loss of generality, assume that $y_1 \leq 2$.

We conclude the proof by showing that when individual 1's benefit parameter is $\beta_1 = 2$ he or she can get a higher level of utility by reporting $\beta_1 = 2/9$ than by reporting truthfully. Let x', y'_1, and y'_2 denote the equilibrium when $\beta_1 = 2/9$ and $\beta_2 = 2$. Note that when $\beta_1 = 2/9$ and $\beta_2 = 2$ condition [11] becomes $x^* = 2/3$. Therefore, efficiency implies $x' \leq 2/3$ in that case. (If $x' > x^*$ total utility can be increased by reducing x' to $2/3$. The private good thereby released can be distributed to the two individuals to increase the utility of each.) The participation constraint implies

$$(2/9)\ln(\tfrac{2}{3}+1)+y_1 \ge (2/9)\ln(x'+1)+y_1' \ge 2.5 \qquad [12]$$

when person 1 reports $\beta_1 = 2/9$. (The mechanism can do no better than work with the benefit functions that it is given, and thus it must provide an outcome that is efficient with respect to those functions.) Now, [12] implies

$$y_1' \ge 2.5 - (2/9)\ln(5/3) > 0.$$

But $y_1' > 0$ and efficiency imply $x' = \tfrac{2}{3}$. (Because $\beta_2 = 2$ we have already established $y_2' > 0$.) Finally, $x = \tfrac{2}{3}$ and $y_1 \ge 2.5 - (2/9)\ln(5/3)$ imply

$$U_1 = 2\ln(x'+1)+y_1' \ge 2\ln(5/3)+2.5-(2/9)\ln(5/3) > 3.40. \qquad [13]$$

When person 1 truthfully reports $\beta_1 = 2$ we have $y_1 \le 2$ and $x \le 1$ thus

$$U_1 = 2\ln(x+1)+y_1 \le 2\ln 2+2 < 3.39. \qquad [14]$$

Statement [14] establishes that person 1's utility is less than 3.39 with the true benefit parameter $\beta_1 = 2$, but [13] shows that his or her utility will be higher than 3.40 with the reported $\beta_1 = 2/9$. Therefore, person 1 can manipulate when $\beta_1 = 2 = \beta_2$. ∎

Note that our proof is valid for any mechanism, whether it asks individuals to report their benefit functions directly or uses a more subtle system of messages. No mechanism can satisfy all three properties because efficiency and the participation constraint imply that truthful revelation is not a dominant strategy for all specifications of the preference parameters. This is unfortunate because an individual's preference information is hidden from others, and hence a mechanism must work well for a wide range of individual preferences, and these preferences are unknown when the community chooses or designs a mechanism.

8.4.2 Nash Equilibrium

A dominant strategy is a best response to *anything* that one's rivals might do. A strategy is a component of a Nash equilibrium if it is merely a best response to what others are *currently* doing. Typically, a Nash equilibrium is not a dominant strategy equilibrium. The latter is much more demanding. Therefore, we relax the requirement that truthful revelation be a dominant strategy for each individual and simply ask for a Nash equilibrium that is efficient. We also impose the participation constraint.

We assume that for each output level q of the public good the cost share $c_i(q)$ of each individual i is exogenously given. Then $V_i(q) = B_i(q) - c_i(q)$ is i's net benefit function. We assume that $c_i(0) = 0$ for each i. In words, if the public good is not produced, then no one is charged.

As in the case of the market process (studied in Section 8.1.3), each individual i has an opportunity to add an amount x_i to the amount of the public good available to all. But we now employ a mechanism that differs from the market mechanism in two important respects: first, the individual is allowed to *reduce* the output of the public good. In other words, x_i can be negative. At equilibrium,

$x_1 + x_2 + \cdots x_n$ units of the public good are provided. (There are n individuals, and in this section we assume that $n \geq 3$.) Second, individual i's consumption of the private good is *not* reduced by x_i multiplied by the price of the public good. That doesn't lead to an efficient outcome, as we saw in Section 8.1.3. For our new mechanism, if $q = x_1 + x_2 + \ldots x_n$ units of the public good are produced, individual i's consumption of the private good is reduced by $c_i(q)$ but i receives a *transfer payment* of $x_{i+1} - x_{i-1}$ multiplied by the amount of the public good produced. An individual's transfer could be negative, in which case that individual pays that amount of money into a fund that is used to give positive transfers to others. We use the term transfer payment to emphasize that each dollar received by someone is a dollar paid by someone else.

DEFINITION: *Walker's Mechanism*

Each individual i announces a real number x_i and $x_1 + x_2 + \cdots + x_n$ units of the public good are produced, with each individual's share of the cost determined in advance. We will refer to x_i as individual i's demand for the public good. Given the demands, each individual i receives a transfer payment of

$$(x_{i+1} - x_{i-1}) \times (x_1 + x_2 + \ldots + x_n).$$

(If $i = n$ then $i + 1$ is interpreted as individual 1. If $i = 1$ then individual $i - 1$ is person n.)

Equilibrium Theorem for Walker's Mechanism

A Nash equilibrium of the Walker mechanism is efficient and it satisfies the participation constraint.

Proof:

The participation constraint is satisfied at equilibrium because one of the strategies available to individual i is to set x_i equal to the negative of the sum of the x_j over all $j \neq i$. That will result in $x = 0$, $y_i = \omega_i$, and $U_i = \omega_i$. If the individual adopts a different strategy, it must be because it will yield more utility. At a Nash equilibrium, where each individual is employing a best response strategy, individual i's utility must be at least ω_i. Hence, the participation constraint is satisfied. For this subsection only we let x denote $(x_1, x_2 \ldots, x_n)$, the list (or vector) of demands. The total is denoted $\sigma(x)$. That is, $\sigma(x) = x_1 + x_2 + \ldots + x_n$ is the total amount of the public good produced if x constitutes a Nash equilibrium. Let $m_i(x)$ denote i's transfer payment.

Let $x = (x_1, x_2 \ldots, x_n)$ be a Nash equilibrium. We show that the outcome is efficient. First, we establish budget balance. In other words, the transfer payments sum to 0. Individual i's transfer is $m_i(x) = (x_{i+1} - x_{i-1}) \times \sigma(x)$. Then for all x,

$$\frac{1}{\sigma(x)} \times [m_1(x) + m_2(x) + \ldots + m_n(x)]$$

$$= x_2 - x_n + x_3 - x_1 + \ldots + x_1 - x_{n-1}$$

$$= x_2 + x_3 + \ldots + x_{n-1} + x_n + x_1$$

$$- [x_n + x_1 + x_2 + \ldots + x_{n-2} + x_{n-1}] = 0 \qquad [15]$$

The transfer payments do sum to 0.

We prove that the equilibrium is *weakly* efficient by showing that any outcome that gives everyone more utility than the Nash equilibrium x is not feasible. Consider the output level q of the public good, and transfer payments $s_1, s_2, \ldots s_n$ Suppose that for each individual i

$$V_i(q) + s_i > V_i(\sigma(x)) + m_i(x).$$

Individual i could have adopted a strategy that resulted in q units of the public good being provided. Specifically, given the demand x_j of each $j \neq i$, if i demands $d_i^i = q - [\sigma(x) - x_i]$ then we have $\sigma(d^i) = q$ if we set $d_j^i = x_j$ for all $j \neq i$. By definition of Nash equilibrium, individual i chose to demand x_i instead of d_i^i and hence we must have

$$V_i(\sigma(x)) + m_i(x) \geq V_i(\sigma(d^i)) + m_i(d^i) = V_i(q) + m_i(d^i)$$

Then for each i,

$$V_i(q) + s_i > V_i(\sigma(x)) + m_i(x) \geq V_i(q) + m_i(d^i).$$

Therefore, $V_i(q) + s_i > V_i(q) + m_i(d^i)$. It follows that $s_i > m_i(d^i)$ for each i. (The output of the public good is the same in the two situations, so the preferred outcome must give individual i a higher transfer payment.) Therefore,

$$s_1 + s_2 + \ldots + s_n > m_1(d^1) + m_2(d^2) + \ldots + m_n(d^n). \qquad [16]$$

But we have $\sigma(d^i) = q, d_{i+1}^i = x_{i+1}$, and $d_{i-1}^i = x_{i-1}$ for each individual i. Therefore,

$$m_i(d^i) = (x_{i+1} - x_{i-1}) \times q,$$

which implies that $m_1(d^1) + m_2(d^2) + \ldots + m_n(d^n) = 0$ by [15]. Therefore, [16] implies

$$s_1 + s_2 + \ldots + s_n > 0.$$

The transfer payments $s_1, s_2, \ldots, + s_n$ are not feasible because they have a positive sum. Anyone who "receives" a negative transfer actually pays that amount of money. Because $s_1 + s_2 + \ldots + s_n > 0$, the amount of money received exceeds the amount paid in. This means that the outcome that provides q units of the public good, along with transfer payments $s_1, s_2, \ldots, s_n$, is not feasible. We have shown that no feasible outcome can give everyone more utility than the Nash equilibrium.

Could there be a feasible outcome that gives, say, individual j more utility without leaving anyone else with less utility? No. If that were possible, then individual j could give a tiny amount of commodity Y to everyone else and we would then have a feasible outcome that gave everyone strictly more utility than the Nash equilibrium. But we have just proved that that is impossible. Therefore the Nash equilibrium is efficient. ∎

∂Example 8.15 Three Individuals

The production of q units of the public good requires q units of the private good as input. Suppose that $c_i(q) = \frac{1}{3}q$ for each i. In words, each individual pays a third of the cost of the producing the public good. The respective utility functions are

$$U_1 = \ln(q+1) + y_1, \ U_2 = 2\ln(q+1) + y_2, \ U_3 = 3\ln(q+1) + y_3.$$

The transfers are

$$m_1 = (x_2 - x_3)q, \quad m_2 = (x_3 - x_1)q, \quad m_3 = (x_1 - x_2)q.$$

The efficient level of the public good is value of q that maximizes

$$\ln(q+1) + 2\ln(q+1) + 3\ln(q+1) + \omega_1 + \omega_2 + \omega_3 - q.$$

The first derivative is $6/(q+1) - 1$, and when we set this equal to 0 we get $q = 5$, the efficient amount of the public good. (The second derivative is negative.) Person i pays $\frac{1}{3}q$ as her share of the cost of producing q, and i receives a transfer of $(x_{i-1} - x_{i+1})q$.

Therefore i pays a total of $(\frac{1}{3} + x_{i+1} - x_{i-1})q$. At a Nash equilibrium of the Walker mechanism

Given x_2 and x_3, x_1 maximizes $\ln(x_1 + x_2 + x_3 + 1) + \omega_1 + (-\frac{1}{3} + x_2 - x_3)(x_1 + x_2 + x_3)$

Given x_1 and x_3, x_2 maximizes $2\ln(x_1 + x_2 + x_3 + 1) + \omega_2 + (-\frac{1}{3} + x_3 - x_1)(x_1 + x_2 + x_3)$

Given x_1 and x_2, x_3 maximizes $3\ln(x_1 + x_2 + x_3 + 1) + \omega_3 + (-\frac{1}{3} + x_1 - x_2)(x_1 + x_2 + x_3)$

The respective first-order conditions are

$$\frac{1}{x_1 + x_2 + x_3 + 1} - \frac{1}{3} + x_2 - x_3 = 0,$$

$$\frac{2}{x_1 + x_2 + x_3 + 1} - \frac{1}{3} + x_3 - x_1 = 0,$$

$$\frac{3}{x_1 + x_2 + x_3 + 1} - \frac{1}{3} + x_1 - x_2 = 0.$$

We know that the Nash equilibrium is efficient, and thus $x_1 + x_2 + x_3 = 5$. Therefore, the three equations simplify to the following:

$$\frac{1}{6} - \frac{1}{3} + x_2 - x_3 = 0.$$

$$\frac{2}{6} - \frac{1}{3} + x_3 - x_1 = 0.$$

$$\frac{3}{6} - \frac{1}{3} + x_1 - x_2 = 0.$$

The second equation yields $x_3 = x_1$, and the third is $x_2 - x_1 = 1/6$. Because $x_1 + x_2 + x_3 = 5$ we need to solve

$$x_2 - x_1 = \frac{1}{6} \text{ and } 2x_1 + x_2 = 5.$$

The solution is $x_1 = 29/18$, $x_2 = 32/18$, and $x_3 = 29/18$. These values give us the transfers $m_1 = (1/6)q$, $m_2 = 0$, and $m_3 = -(1/6)q$. Now, substitute these transfers into the respective individual utility functions and then show that $q = 5$ maximizes each of the following functions

$$\ln(q + 1) + \omega_1 - q/3 + q/6$$

$$2\ln(q + 1) + \omega_2 - q/3 + 0q/6$$

$$3\ln(q + 1) + \omega_3 - q/3 - q/6$$

The purpose of the transfers is to adjust each individual's marginal cost of acquiring an additional unit of the public good so that everyone wants the same amount of the public good. That guarantees that a Nash equilibrium exists. By having the transfers sum to zero we not only balance the government's budget, we precipitate an efficient outcome at equilibrium.

The average cost taxation mechanism of Section 8.1.5 always yields an efficient outcome at equilibrium. Unlike the Walker mechanism, however, a Nash equilibrium almost never exists. That's because each individual's marginal cost of acquiring an additional unit of the public good is exogenously determined by average cost taxation – independently of anyone's preferences. We illustrate with a final example.

∂Example 8.16 Average Cost Taxation

The setup is the same that of Example 8.14 except that we employ average cost taxation instead of the Walker mechanism. We have $c_i(q) = \frac{1}{3}q$ for each individual i but there are no transfers. If a Nash equilibrium exists and it leads to the production of q units of output, then q maximizes each of the three functions

$$\ln(q + 1) + \omega_1 - q/3$$

$$2\ln(q + 1) + \omega_2 - q/3$$

$$3\ln(q + 1) + \omega_3 - q/3$$

The respective first-order conditions are:

$$\frac{1}{q+1} - \frac{1}{3} = 0, \frac{2}{q+1} - \frac{1}{3} = 0, \text{ and } \frac{3}{q+1} - \frac{1}{3} = 0.$$

(The second derivative is negative in each case.) The equation for persons 1, 2, and 3, are satisfied by $q^1 = 2$, $q^2 = 5$, and $q^3 = 8$ respectively. The three equations can't be satisfied simultaneously. If this constituted an equilibrium each individual i would maximize U_i by reporting a benefit function that resulted in $x = q^i$. There is no Nash equilibrium.

Sources

The impossibility theorem of Section 8.4.1 was discovered and proved by Leonid Hurwicz (1972) for the case of pure private goods. It was Hurwicz who taught economists how to investigate the role of incentives in general equilibrium resource allocation models. He received the Nobel Prize in 2007. This chapter presents the theorem of Roberts (1979) for the standard public goods model. The mechanism of Section 8.4.2 was devised by Walker (1981).

Links

Campbell and Truchon (1988) provide a complete characterization of efficient outcomes, allowing for the possibility that the private goods consumption of one or more individuals is zero. See Walker (1980) for a more thorough investigation of the possibility of using dominant strategies to identify an efficient outcome. The Nash equilibria for Walker's mechanism are Lindahl equilibria, and the existence of a Lindahl equilibrium is proved in Foley (1970) and Milleron (1972). See Corchón (1996) and Repullo (1987) for a general treatment of Nash implementation. Chen (2008) discusses the performance of mechanisms in a laboratory setting.

Problem Set

(1) Design a mechanism that satisfies the participation constraint and is invulnerable to manipulation by any individual. (Of course, the equilibria won't always be efficient.)

(2) Design a mechanism that satisfies the participation constraint and that always yields equilibria that are efficient. (Of course, some individual can manipulate the mechanism in some situations.)

(3) Rework Example 8.14 with $c_1(q) = \frac{1}{4}q$ instead of $c_1(q) = \frac{1}{3}q$, $c_2(q) = \frac{1}{4}q$ instead of $c_2(q) = \frac{1}{3}q$, and $c_3(q) = \frac{1}{2}q$ instead of $c_3(q) = \frac{1}{3}q$

(4) Rework Example 8.15 with $U_1 = \beta_1\ln(q+1)$, $U_2 = \beta_2\ln(q+1)$, and $U_3 = \beta_3\ln(q+1)$. Find a condition on the benefit parameters β_1, β_2, β_3 for which a Nash equilibrium of the average cost mechanism exists.

(5) Repeat question 3 but with $c_1(q) = \lambda_1 q$, $c_2(q) = \lambda_2 q$, and $c_3(q) = \lambda_3 q$, where λ_1, λ_2, and λ_3 are given fractions that sum to 1.

Matching

This chapter examines allocation problems for which the desired "commodities", such as dormitory rooms, are only available in discrete units and each "consumer" wants one unit and *only* one unit. Moreover, allocating a desired object to the highest bidder is unacceptable, as it would be in the case of an offer of admission to a good university. The objective is to match each student with a room (or a university), or available kidneys with the patients on a transplant waiting list, and so forth.

Suppose that an economics department has a given number of students (i.e., majors) and professors, and the objective is to assign each student a professor-advisor. In this case both sides of the match have preferences: students like some professors better than others, and the professors can rank the students. There are problems for which only one side of the match has preferences: students have preferences for dormitory rooms, but the rooms don't have preferences for students.

We can also classify matching problems according to whether we can have outcomes at which an agent is paired with more than one agent of the opposite type, as in the case of college admissions. Each student is placed with only one college, but each college admits many students. Both types have preferences: each student can rank the colleges, and the colleges have preferences for students – if only for students with high test scores.

The first allocation problem that we study is a *marriage model*, for which there are two types of agents: there is a set of W types and a set of M types. Each member of each type has a preference ordering for the members of the other type, and each agent is matched with at most one member of the other type. The problem of matching students and advisors can be a marriage model. A student will have at most only one advisor, and if there is a department rule limiting a professor to at most one advisee then we have a marriage model. Our objective is not to classify allocation problems, however, but to *solve* them by designing satisfactory allocation procedures.

If there are ten agents of each type then the marriage model has 36,288,000 possible solutions – not including cases where at least two agents are unmatched. (We allow preferences that declare "I'd rather be unmatched than paired with *him.*") Some of the arrangements are efficient, but many will not be. Clearly, we want an outcome that at least passes the efficiency test. We also want an economical procedure for matching the agents. we don't want to employ an algorithm that consumes vast amounts of time and money. We also want to respect individual rights. We don't want to match agent α with agent β if α would prefer being unmatched to having β as a partner. Respecting rights opens the door to the possibility of manipulation. By declaring that she would rather be unmatched than paired with β, when that is not in fact true, agent α may force the procedure to give her a match that she prefers to the one that she would have had if she had reported her preferences truthfully. Therefore, we also look for matching procedures that are incentive compatible, in the sense that they induce truthful revelation of preferences.

To simplify the discussion we assume throughout that all agents have preferences that are strict, in the sense that they are never indifferent between two agents of the opposite type; one will be strictly preferred to the other. For the most part, we assume that all agents care only about their own match. In other words, agent a's welfare is unaffected by matches that do not involve a.

9.1   ONE-TO-ONE MATCHING

An economics department has a set of majors, each of whom is referred to as type M. There is also a set of professors, the type W agents. Some of the majors want to do an honors thesis, and that requires having a professor as an advisor. Each thesis writer needs only one advisor, and the department has a rule preventing a professor from advising more than one student. Each professor has encountered each student in one or more classes, so the professors have preferences for the students. And the students certainly have preferences for the professors. Hence, we have a marriage model, the subject of this section.

9.1.1   Preferences and Assignments

The end product of the process is an *assignment*, which pairs each W-type with at most one M-type, and each M-type with at most one W-type.

DEFINITION: *An Assignment*

A specific assignment $\pi = (AZ, BY, \ldots)$ is a set of pairs, denoting that A is matched with Z, agent B with Y, and so on. We refer to AZ as a *match*. If an agent is not matched with anyone we say that that he or she is *single*.

We would expect an agent to be unmatched if he or she is unacceptable to every agent of the opposite type, but there might well be other situations in which an agent is single.

DEFINITION: *Unacceptable Agents*

A is unacceptable to X if they are of opposite type and X would rather be single (i.e., unmatched) than be paired with A.

An agent may be acceptable to a vast number of agents of the opposite type but still be unmatched – if, for example, all of the agents who found A acceptable secured partners that they found more desirable than A.

We are obviously using W and M as mnemonics for women and men. We do not recommend our matching procedure for real-world marriages. Our objective is to improve the assignment procedure in cases such as the student–advisor relationship. This is problematic because, in general, there will be no obvious best assignment, as our first example reveals.

Example 9.1 Two Agents of Each Type

The two *W* types are *A* and *B*, and the two *M* types are *Y* and *Z*. *A* prefers *Y* to *Z* and *B* prefers *Z* to *Y*. It is possible to give each *W* her first choice. However, *Y* prefers *B* to *A* and *Z* prefers *A* to *B*. It is also possible to give each *M* his first choice. There are only two possible assignments, but neither gives every agent his or her first choice: the assignment $\pi = (AY, BZ)$ gives each *W* her first choice but each *M* gets his second choice. And $\pi' = (AZ, BY)$ gives each *M* his first choice while each *W* gets her second choice.

Of course, individual preferences are central to our study of matching. A complete specification of the individual preferences is called a *profile*, and is usually denoted as *p*. The profile *p* of Example 9.1 specifies $p(A) = YZ$, $p(B) = ZY$, $p(Y) = BA$, and $p(Z) = AB$.

DEFINITION: *Preference Profile*

A profile *p* specifies the preference ordering *p(N)* of each agent *N*. (The ordering *p(N)* ranks agents of the opposite type.) We can express *p(N)* as a column, with each agent being strictly preferred to agents ranked lower in the column. We can also express *p(N)* as the row *ABCD . . . E*, indicating that *A* is preferred to every other agent, *B* is preferred to every agent other than *A* or *B*, and so on.

Whatever matching process is used, the outcome will depend on the nature of agent preferences. We may want to reject allocation schemes that fail to take advantage of the opportunity to improve the welfare of two agents by pairing them with each other, instead of giving each an undesirable match. In fact, we may want to give a pair of agents the right to reject an assignment if they would be better off with each other than with their assigned partners. We say that those agents *block* the assignment in question, and that the assignment is not stable.

DEFINITION: *Blocking Pair*

If π is an assignment we say that *AX* blocks π at profile *p* if *A* is a *W*-type and *A* prefers *X* to the *M*-type assigned to her by π (or *A* is unmatched at π and *X* is acceptable), and *X* is an *M*-type and *X* prefers *A* to the *W*-type assigned to him by π (or *X* is unmatched at π and *A* is acceptable).

If the matching process delivers unstable assignments, and participation in the process is voluntary, agents who can block will get together and make their own arrangements. This lack of participation by some agents can motivate others to circumvent the process by arranging their own matches, making the formal matching process less satisfactory.

DEFINITION: *Stable Assignment*

π is a stable assignment at profile p if there is no blocking pair, and no agent prefers being single to the partner assigned to him or her by π.

Identifying stable assignments can be tedious, but the process can often be simplified somewhat by searching for *perfect matches*, which are pairs of agents who like the other best.

DEFINITION: *A Perfect Match*

AX is a perfect match if A is a W-type, X is an M-type, and A prefers X to every other M and X prefers A to every other W.

Clearly, if AX is a perfect match then every stable assignment must pair A with X; otherwise AX could block.

Table 9.1

A	*B*	*C*	*X*	*Y*	*Z*
Y	*X*	*X*	*B*	*B*	*A*
X	*Z*	*Z*	*C*	*A*	*B*
Z	*Y*	*Y*	*A*	*C*	*C*

Example 9.2 An Unstable Assignment

$W = \{A, B, C\}$ and $M = \{X, Y, Z\}$ with the preferences as specified in Table 9.1. Agent A prefers Y to X and X to Z (and of course, Y to Z). The preferences of the others are interpreted similarly. the assignment $\pi = (AY, BZ, CX)$ is not stable because B would rather have X than Z, and X would rather have B than C.

The data from seven regional labor market for new physicians and surgeons in the United Kingdom provide striking evidence that centralized matching processes that do not guarantee stability do not perform better than the decentralized processes that they replaced. The matching processes differ from region to region. Roth (1991).

Every stable outcome is efficient. We provide a formal proof, but it is easy to convince oneself that stability implies efficiency: If π is not efficient then we can make one person, say A, better off without hurting anyone. If A's new partner Z is not harmed then Z must prefer A to his partner at π, and hence AZ can block π. In other words, an assignment that is not efficient can't be stable. That's equivalent to saying that every stable outcome is efficient.

Efficiency Theorem

Every stable assignment is efficient.

Proof:

Suppose that π is a stable assignment, but π' is another assignment that A prefers to π. To establish that π is efficient, we need to show that some agent is worse off at π' than at π. Suppose that π pairs A with X but π' pairs A with Y, whom A prefers to X. (We know that A prefers X to being single because π is stable.) If Y prefers being matched with A to his situation under π, then π wouldn't be stable, because AY can block. Therefore, stability of π implies that Y is worse off at π' than at π.

Suppose, however, that A is single at π. Then at π' agent A must have a match, say with Y, because A prefers π' to π. If Y is single at π and Y prefers a match with A to being single then π cannot be stable because A and Y would each prefer the match AY to their situation under π. Because π is stable, if Y is single at π then he prefers being single to a match with A and thus Y is worse off at π' than at π. Suppose, then, that Y is matched at π, to B. If Y prefers A to B then π cannot be stable because then A and Y each prefer π' to π. Because π is stable, it must be the case that Y prefers B to A, and hence Y is worse off under π' than under π.

We have exhausted all the possibilities. Therefore, if some agent prefers π' to π then someone would be harmed by a move from π to π'. Hence π is efficient.   ■

It is not the case that every efficient assignment is stable, as we demonstrate with the next example.

We have acknowledged the possibility that an agent may prefer to remain single rather than to be matched with a particular agent of the opposite type. This is captured by the column representing the agent's preference ordering by simply omitting the unacceptable agents. For the agent preferences as displayed in Table 9.2, if in fact there are no agents missing from the reported preference orderings then A finds Z unacceptable, B finds both X and Z unacceptable, and so on.

Table 9.2

A	B	C	X	Y	Z
Y	Y	Z	A	A	C
X	⋮	⋮	⋮	B	⋮

Example 9.3 An Efficient Assignment that is Not Stable

$W = \{A, B, C\}$ and $M = \{X, Y, Z\}$ with the preferences as specified Table 9.2. Consider the assignment $\pi = (AX, BY, CZ)$. It is not stable because both A and Y prefer the match AY to the one that each has at π. However, it is efficient because if we begin with π and modify A's match then A will be worse off unless we replace AX with AY. But if we do that we make X worse off. If we modify B's match at π then we make B worse off, and if we modify C's match at π we make C worse off. The vertical dots in Table 9.2 represent missing preference information. Note that π remains efficient and unstable no matter how the table is completed.

9.1.2   The Deferred Acceptance Algorithm

The following *Deferred Acceptance Algorithm (DAA)* always generates a stable outcome: we select one of the types, which we'll call W. Each W agent proposes to the M type at the top of her preference ordering – the M that she most prefers, in other words. At the next stage each M provisionally accepts the W agent that he most prefers of all the acceptable agents that proposed to him and rejects all other proposals. At the next stage each rejected W type proposes to the M that ranks next highest in her preference ordering. At that point there could be some Ms with two or more proposals. Each M type then rejects all proposals but the one from an acceptable W that ranks higher in his preference ordering than any other agent from which he has received a proposal. This means that he may reject an agent that he provisionally accepted at a previous stage. If an agent C is rejected by an agent Z at some stage then C cannot propose again to Z at a later stage. The algorithm continues alternating proposals by Ws with rejections or provisional acceptances by Ms until we reach a round T at which no agent is rejected, except perhaps an agent who has been rejected by every M-type that is acceptable to her. Then T is the terminal stage of the algorithm. The algorithm is a *deferred* acceptance procedure because acceptances are not binding until the terminal round.

DEFINITION: *The Deferred Acceptance Algorithm (DAA)*

One of the types is selected to do the proposing, call it W. At each stage each W proposes to the M that ranks highest among the agents who have not rejected her at a previous stage, and each M rejects every proposal except the one that he likes best. The algorithm terminates at any round in which the only proposers who received rejections at the end of that round have been rejected by all acceptable agents of the opposite type. We let $\pi(p)$ denote the outcome of the DAA at profile p. When the algorithm terminates each proposer will have at most one provisional acceptance which then becomes the agent's match. A proposer who has been rejected by every acceptable agent of the opposite type will be single, as will an agent who received no proposals.

Table 9.3

A	B	C	D	E	S	T	X	Y	Z
Y	T	Z	S	Y	D	E	A	C	B
S	Y	X	T	S		B	E	D	A
X	X	S	X	X		A	C	A	E
T	Z			Z	T		D	B	
Z	S			Y		C			

Example 9.4 Deferred Acceptance with Five Agents of Each Type

Let $W = \{A, B, C, D, E\}$ and $M = \{S, T, X, Y, Z\}$ with the preferences as specified in Table 9.3. Note that each W is acceptable to some M and each M is acceptable to some W. Note also that S would only consent to a match with D. Every other W is unacceptable to S. Agents C, Y, and Z each find that two of the agents are unacceptable. With the Ws proposing, at the end of the first round Y and Z have each received a proposal from an unacceptable agent (E and C respectively) so those proposals are rejected. The algorithm's four rounds are displayed in Table 9.4. An agent who rejects a proposal appears in bold, under the name of the rejected agent, in the row for the round in which the rejection takes place. In round 2, agents C and E propose to X and S respectively, resulting in E's rejection by S who finds E unacceptable. E proposes to X in round 3 because X ranks third in E's preference ordering and E has now been rejected by her two highest ranking Ms. Now X has two proposals, from C and E, so X rejects C and provisionally accepts E. In round 4 agent C proposes to S, the next and last agent in her preference ordering, and is rejected because C is unacceptable to S. At the end of round 4 there is no agent who has more than one proposal, and C has been rejected by every agent that is acceptable to her. The assignment is $\pi^* = (AY, BT, DS, EX)$. Agents C and Z are single.

It is easy to confirm that π^* of Example 9.4 is stable: A, B, and D each receive her most-preferred match, so none of these W-types can belong to a blocking pair. None of C's acceptable Ms would prefer C to his match at π^*. (Z doesn't have a match but finds C unacceptable.) E prefers Y and S to X but neither finds E acceptable, and hence E can't be a member of a blocking pair. A blocking pair would have to contain a W-type, so π^* cannot be blocked and hence must be stable. (Alternatively, one could go through the list of Ms to show that no M-type can be a member of a blocking pair.)

9.1.3 Stability and Optimality of the Deferred Acceptance Algorithm

This section explains the sense in which the DAA favors the proposers and shows that the deferred acceptance algorithm always yields a stable assignment.

Intuitively, the outcome of the DAA is stable because each proposer approaches the agent that she likes best, and hence no proposer could be part of a blocking pair. There is rivalry, however, when two or more proposers have the same agents at the

Table 9.4

Round	Proposers				
	A	*B*	*C*	*D*	*E*
1	*Y*	*T*	**Z**	*S*	*Y*
2	*Y*	*T*	*X*	*S*	**S**
3	*Y*	*T*	**X**	*S*	*X*
4	*Y*	*T*	**S**	*S*	*X*

top of their preference orderings. Therefore, our intuition only goes so far. We need a *proof* of stability.

Stability Theorem

The deferred acceptance algorithm yields a stable assignment whichever type does the proposing.

Proof:

Let's refer to the proposers as W-types and let π^* be the outcome of the *DAA*. We show that no M-type X is part of a blocking pair. Suppose that X is single at π^* but prefers A to being single. Then A never proposed to X, otherwise X *would* be matched – with A or someone that X prefers to A. Suppose, on the other hand, that X is paired with B by π^*, but X prefers A. Again we can say that A never proposed to X, otherwise X would have rejected B. Therefore, if X prefers a match with A to his situation at π^* we can say that A never proposed to X. If X is unacceptable to A then AX certainly cannot block π^*. If X is acceptable to A then, because A did not propose to X, the assignment π^* must pair X with a W-type that X prefers to A, and thus AX cannot block π^*. ∎

Typically the deferred acceptance algorithm yields a different assignment when the W-types propose than when the M-types propose. (Of course, if every agent is part of a perfect match then the *DAA* gives everyone his or her perfect match regardless of who does the proposing.) Because the proposers take the initiative, we suspect that the Ws do better when they propose that when the Ms propose, and vice versa. Recall Example 9.1: when A and B propose each gets her most-preferred M-type, and when Y and Z propose each gets his most-preferred W-type. In general, a proposer is not guaranteed her ideal mate. For one thing, two proposers could have the same most-preferred agent. But a proposer will never prefer another *stable* assignment to the outcome of the *DAA*, as we now show.

DEFINITION: *Optimal Assignments*

Assignment π is W-optimal if there is no stable assignment that some W-type prefers to π. It is M-optimal if there is no stable assignment that some M-type prefers to π.

Our proof that the *DAA* is proposer-optimal makes use of the notion of an achievable match, which is a match that an agent has at *some* stable outcome.

DEFINITION: *Achievable Match*

If A and X are opposite types then AX is an achievable match for A (and for X) at profile p if there is a stable assignment that pairs A with X, in which case we say that X is achievable for A, and vice versa.

Note that an achievable match is defined independently of the matching process.

Optimality Theorem

The outcome of the deferred acceptance algorithm is W-optimal when the W-types propose and it is M-optimal when the M-types propose.

Proof:

Let the proposers be A, B, C, . . ., and let X, Y, Z, . . . denote agents of the opposite type. If A is rejected by X in round 1 of the *DAA* then AX is not achievable for A: suppose that A and B each propose to X in round 1, and A is rejected because X prefers B to A. Because B has proposed to X in round 1 we know that X is B's most-preferred match. Therefore, if any assignment matches A and X it is blocked by BX. Hence, at the end of round 1 no proposer A is rejected by an agent X such that AX is achievable.

Suppose that we have established that no proposer is rejected by an achievable agent in round t of the *DAA* or in any previous round. (This is the induction hypothesis.) We prove by contradiction that no proposer is rejected by an achievable agent in round $t + 1$. Suppose, to the contrary, that A is rejected by Y at the end of round $t + 1$ because Y prefers B to A and has a proposal from B, but A and Y are paired at some stable assignment π. By definition every proposer is paired with an achievable type at π. By the induction hypothesis, individual Y is B's most-preferred achievable agent – because B must have proposed to Y, and if B was rejected in some previous round of the *DAA* it cannot have been by an achievable agent. It follows that BY blocks π, a contradiction.

We have established that no proposer is rejected by an achievable agent at the end of round $t = 1$, and we have proved that if no proposer is rejected by an achievable agent at the end of any of the first t rounds, then no proposer is rejected by an achievable agent at the end of any of the first $t + 1$ rounds. This establishes that no proposer is rejected by an achievable agent at the end of any round. But if a proposer is never rejected by an achievable agent then the *DAA* pairs the proposer with her most-preferred achievable agent. It follows that if π^* is the outcome of the *DAA* and π is another stable assignment then no proposer prefers π to π^*. (Every match from π^* is achievable, and so is every match from π.) ∎

9.1.4 Strategy

We turn to the question of incentive compatibility. Is it possible for agent J to wind up with a better match by rejecting agent N and accepting N' when J actually prefers N to N'? If J is one of the proposers, is it possible for J to benefit by proposing to N' instead of N even though J actually prefers N and has not been rejected by N'? A simple way to address these questions is to suppose that all agents submit their preference orderings to a referee who then uses the reported preferences to work out the outcome of the *DAA*. Would submitting the true preference ordering be a dominant strategy?

DEFINITION: *Strategy Proofness*

A matching process is strategy proof if for each specification of the agent preferences truthful revelation is a dominant strategy for each agent. (Truthful revelation is a dominant strategy for J if, regardless of the preferences of the other agents, reporting a preference ordering that is different from his true ordering can never precipitate a match that J prefers, *according to his true preferences*, to the one that results from reporting his true preference ordering.)

It is easy to show that the *DAA* is not strategy-proof.

Example 9.5 A Non-Proposer Benefits from Misrepresentation

A, B, and C are the Ws and the Ms are X, Y, and Z. The true individual preferences are displayed in Table 9.5. If the Ws propose, then truthful revelation by everyone results in the match $\alpha = (AX, BZ, CY)$, as Table 9.6 confirms. (A rejection is noted in bold. In round 1 both A and C propose to X who then rejects C and provisionally accepts A. Therefore, X is in bold in the round 1 row of Table 9.6. In round 2 agent C applies to Y. B has applied to Z in round 1, so there are no rejections at the end of round 2, the final round.) If X had deviated from truthful revelation by reporting $p(X) = BCA$ then we would work out the *DAA* by applying Table 9.7. (Note that everyone has the same preference in Table 9.7 as in Table 9.5 except for X who has $P(X) = BAC$ in the latter.) The *DAA* yields $\beta = (AZ, BX, CY)$ for the preferences of Table 9.7, as confirmed by Table 9.8. (Again, an agent who rejects a proposal appears in bold, under the name of the rejected agent, in the row for the round in which the rejection takes place.) Note that X prefers BX to AX according to his *true* preference scheme.

Table 9.5

A	B	C	X	Y	Z
X	Z	X	B	A	A
Z	X	Y	A	B	B
Y	Y	Z	C	C	C

Table 9.6

	Proposer		
Round	*A*	*B*	*C*
1	*X*	*Z*	**X**
2	*X*	*Z*	*Y*

Table 9.7

A	*B*	*C*	*X*	*Y*	*Z*
X	*Z*	*X*	*B*	*A*	*A*
Z	*X*	*Y*	*C*	*B*	*B*
Y	*Y*	*Z*	*A*	*C*	*C*

Table 9.8

	Proposer		
Round	*A*	*B*	*C*
1	**X**	*Z*	*X*
2	*Z*	**Z**	*X*
3	*Z*	*X*	**X**
4	*Z*	*X*	*Y*

Table 9.9

A	*B*	*C*	*X*	*Y*	*Z*
X	*Z*	*X*	*B*	*A*	*A*
Y	*X*	*Y*	*A*	*B*	*B*
Z	*Y*	*Z*	*C*	*C*	*C*

What happened? By rejecting *A* at the end of round 1, even though *X* prefers *A* to *C*, agent *X* caused *A* to propose to *Z* in round 2 and that resulted in *Z* rejecting *B*, making agent *B* ultimately available for *X*, who gets his most-preferred match by misrepresenting his preference ordering.

Not only is the *DAA* not strategy proof, but there is *no* strategy-proof matching mechanism that always generates a stable assignment. A constant rule is strategy-proof but not stable. (A constant rule generates an assignment *γ* that is independent of agent preferences. Suppose that *γ* matches *A* and *X*. If agent preferences are such that *A* prefers *Y* to *X* and *Y* prefers *A* to every other agent of the opposite type – and to being single – then *AY* blocks *γ*.) Serial choice is strategy-proof but not stable. (The serial choice mechanism matches *A* with her most-preferred agent of the opposite type. It then matches *B* with the agent *B* likes best from the set of agents exclusive of A's partner, and then it matches C with the agent C likes best from the set of all agents except for A's and B's partners, and so on. Strategy-proofness of serial choice is proved in Section 9.2.4.) Dictatorship is not well defined for the matching model. Assigning A to her most-preferred agent of the opposite type does not identify a single assignment. (Dictatorship *is* strategy-proof in any context for which it is well defined.)

Impossibility Theorem

There exists no matching process that produces a stable assignment at every preference profile and never gives any agent a chance to benefit by submitting a preference ordering that is different from his or her true preference ordering.

The claim is valid whether or not the assignment is generated by an algorithm or some other process.

Proof:

There are three agents of each type: the Ws are A, B, and C and the Ms are X, Y, and Z. Consider the profile of agent preferences in Table 9.5. There are only two stable assignments in this case:

$$\alpha = (AX,\ BZ,\ CY)\ \text{and}\ \beta = (AZ,\ BX,\ CY).$$

We begin by confirming that α is stable: Agents A and B each get their most-preferred partner and thus neither can be part of a blocking pair. And CX is the only match preferred to α by C, but X prefers α to a match with C. And β is stable because both X and Z get their most-preferred W type. Therefore, neither X nor Z can be a member of a blocking pair. Agent Y prefers a match with A or B to a match with C, but both A and B prefer β to a match with Y. Because each agent prefers a match with anyone of the opposite type to being single, β cannot be blocked. Therefore, assignment β is stable.

Next we show that α and β are the *only* stable assignments for these preferences. Consider a different assignment π. If π does not yield CY then it must produce either AY or BY. (If A is single at π then π is not stable because A prefers Y to being single and Y prefers A to anyone else. If B is single at π then π is not stable because B prefers X to being single and X prefers B to anyone else.) But if π contains AY it is not stable because A prefers Z to Y, and Z prefers A to anyone else. (AZ blocks.) And if π contains BY it is not stable either because B prefers X to Y, and X prefers B to anything else. (BX blocks.) We have shown that π contains CY, and thus there are only two ways to match A and B with X and Z. One of these leads to α and the other leads to β. (There can be no unmatched agents in an assignment that is stable for these preferences, because each agent prefers a match to anyone of the opposite type to being single.)

Note that A and B each prefer α to β, and X and Z each prefer β to α. Let **M** be any matching process that generates a stable assignment for each specification of agent preferences. Suppose that **M** results in β when applied to the preferences of Table 9.5. Now apply **M** to the preferences of Table 9.9. Note that Table 9.9 is the same as Table 9.5 except that we have changed the preferences of A. The only stable assignment for Table 9.9 is α, as we now show. Let π be a stable assignment for the preferences of Table 9.9. If π does not match C and Y then it must yield either AY or BY. But if π produces BY it is not stable because B prefers X to Y, and X prefers B to anything else. Therefore, π matches A and Y if it doesn't match C and Y. Therefore, either

$$\pi = (AY, BX, CZ) \text{ or } \pi = (AY, BZ, CX).$$

The former is not stable for the preferences of Table 9.9 because Z prefers B to C, and B prefers Z to X. (BZ blocks.) The latter is not stable because X prefers A to C, and A prefers X to Y. (AX blocks.) Therefore, π must match C and Y. Consequently, $\pi = \beta$ or $\pi = \alpha$. But β is not stable for Table 9.9 because A prefers Y to Z, and Y prefers A to C. (AY blocks.) It follows that α is the only stable assignment for Table 9.9. (Confirm that α *is* stable.) Therefore, α is the output of **M** for the preferences of Table 9.9. Note that β matches A with Z and α matches A with X, and A prefers X to Z according to A's true preferences, the preference ordering of Table 9.5. Because the only difference between the two tables is the reported preference scheme of agent A, it follows that **M** is not strategy proof if the true agent preferences are given in Table 9.5 and β is selected: agent A can profit by misrepresenting her preference ordering. Specifically, if she were to report the preference scheme of the first column of Table 9.9 then she would precipitate the selection of an outcome that she prefers to the one that is generated by **M** under truthful revelation.

We know that β and α are the only stable assignments for Table 9.5, and strategy proofness implies that **M** cannot select β. Therefore, if **M** is strategy proof and always yields a stable outcome it must generate assignment α for Table 9.5. Now, apply **M** to the preferences of Table 9.7, which is the same as Table 9.5 except for the preferences of X. We show that β is the only stable assignment for Table 9.7 by supposing that π is an arbitrary stable assignment for that preference profile. If π does not match C and Y then it must yield either AY or BY. But if π yields AY it is not stable because A prefers Z to Y, and Z prefers A to anything else. Therefore, π results in BY if it does not match C and Y, in which case either $\pi = (AX, BY, CZ)$ or $\pi = (AZ, BY, CX)$. The former is not stable for Table 9.7 because Z prefers B to C, and B prefers Z to Y. (BZ blocks.) The latter is not stable because X prefers B to C, and B prefers X to Y. (BX blocks.) Therefore, π matches C and Y, and hence $\pi = \beta$ or $\pi = \alpha$. The previous paragraph established that **M** must select α at Table 9.5. But α is not stable for Table 9.7 because X prefers C to A, and C prefers X to Y. Therefore, β is the only stable assignment for Table 9.7, and thus **M** must select β for that preference profile. But α matches X with A and β matches X with B, and X prefers B to A according to his preference ranking in Table 9.5. Tables 9.5 and 9.7 are identical except for the reported preference scheme of agent X. Therefore, **M** is not strategy proof because when the true agent preferences are the ones given in Table 9.5, agent X can profit by misrepresenting his preference ordering. Specifically, if he were to report the preference scheme of the fourth column of Table 9.7 then he would precipitate the selection of an outcome that he prefers to the one that is selected under truthful revelation.

We have shown that **M** is not strategy proof. But **M** was an *arbitrary* procedure that always generated a stable assignment for any specification of agent preferences. Therefore, we have shown that every strategy-proof procedure will precipitate an unstable outcome in some situations. Equivalently, if a procedure always delivers a stable assignment under truthful revelation then truthful revelation cannot be a dominant strategy for every agent.   ∎

The optimality theorem of Section 9.1.3 comes close to establishing that no *proposer* can profit by misrepresenting his or her preferences if an assignment is determined by the *DAA*. There is no *stable* assignment that a proposer prefers to the *DAA* outcome, so there is no deviation from truthful revelation by a proposer that leads to a stable assignment that he or she prefers to the one that results from truthful revelation. However, when an agent contemplates a change in strategy, to see if it will precipitate a preferred outcome, we cannot expect the agent to restrict consideration only to strategies that lead to an assignment that is stable with respect to the true preferences. Nevertheless, it *is* the case that the *DAA* is immune to manipulation by proposers, whether the assignment gives rise to a stable outcome or not.

Proposer Strategy-Proofness Theorem
If the DAA is employed then no proposer can benefit by deviating from truthful revelation

---

If all agents were to submit their preference orderings to a referee, and the referee then applied the *DAA* to the stated preferences, resulting in the assignment π^*, then submitting the true preference ordering is a dominant strategy for every proposer. We do not prove this because the optimality theorem reveals enough of the intuition behind the proof that the *DAA* is invulnerable to manipulation by any proposer.

We have only employed examples in which the number of W types equals the number of M types. All of our arguments can be extended to the general case by adding "dummy" agents: If there are more Ws than Ms just add a sufficient number of Ms to make the two sets equal in size. Assign the degenerate preference scheme to these new Ms, so that they prefer being single to being matched with any W. Similarly, if the Ms outnumber the Ws we can add a sufficient number of dummy Ws. Why does this work? Because none of the original arguments depend on the absence of such agents. Also, no dummy agent will have a match at any stable outcome, so it's just as if the dummy agent didn't exist.

Sources

David Gale and Lloyd Shapley Gale wrote the seminal paper on matching (Gale and Shapley, 1962). Alvin Roth extended their results and applied them to a wide range of allocation problems. Shapley and Roth were awarded the Nobel Prize in Economics in 2012. (David Gale died in 2008.) This section is based on Roth (1982).

Links

Roth and Sotomayor (1990) provide an extensive discussion of matching. Roth (2015) is a superb, informal, and very readable introduction to matching. Vulkan et al. (2013) touch on many aspects of matching that are not treated in this section or in either of the aforementioned books.

Problem Set

(1) Suppose there are three Ws and three Ms. Specify the preferences however you like, except that each agent finds every one of the opposite type to be acceptable, and there is at least one inefficient outcome. Identify the efficient outcomes and the inefficient ones.

(2) Suppose that there are n individuals of each type and $n > 3$. A, B, and C each prefer X, Y, and Z to every other member of the opposite type, and X, Y, and Z each prefer A, B, and C to every other member of their opposite type. Prove that every stable outcome has to match A with X or Y or Z, and the same is true for B and C.

(3) Prove that the unstable assignment $\pi = (AY, BZ, CX)$ of Example 9.2 is efficient.

(4) Assume that there are three Ws and three Ms. Specify the preferences of each agent so that the *DAA* generates the same match when the Ms propose as when the Ws propose.

(5) For the special case of two agents of each type, prove that truthful revelation is not a dominant strategy for each agent if the *DAA* is used to arrive at an assignment and an agent can declare that he would rather be single than matched with a particular agent of the opposite type, even when that is not true.

(6) For each of the preferences of Tables 9.1, 9.2, and 9.3 determine the assignment precipitated by the *DAA* when the Ms propose.

(7) For the case of two agents of each type, suppose that each M is acceptable to each W, and each W is acceptable to each M. Prove that no agent can benefit by misrepresenting his or her preferences, except by declaring that some acceptable agent of the opposite type is unacceptable.

(8) In proving that there is no matching algorithm that always yields a stable outcome and for which truthful revelation is a dominant strategy for every agent for every specification of individual preferences, we employed a situation with exactly three agents of each type. Assume that every agent would prefer to be matched with anyone of the opposite type to being single, and extend the proof to the general case, with $m > 3$ type W agents and $n > 3$ type M agents.

9.2   SCHOOL ADMISSIONS

The problem of assigning students to schools is one for which schools are matched with more than one student, although each student can be matched with at most one school. Each student has a preference ordering of the schools and each school has a preference ordering of the students. The school system could be the set of public schools in a municipality, or even the set of colleges in a particular country. However, the results discussed in this section have been more widely applied to city public schools than to colleges. This section can be read independently of the others, but familiarity with the previous section is recommended.

9.2.1   The Basics

We will refer to the students as A, B, C, etc., or on occasion as S_1, S_2, S_3, etc. There are m schools, named X, Y, Z, . . ., or C_1, C_2, C_3, . . . (C for college). Each school X has a capacity (or quota) q_X. It can admit fewer than q_X students, but it doesn't have room for more. There are n students, each seeking to attend one of the schools, preferably the school he or she considers best. An assignment specifies the set of students admitted to each school so that no student is assigned to more than one school, and no school is asked to admit more students than it can accommodate.

DEFINITION: *The School Admissions Problem*

C_1, C_2, . . ., C_m is the set of schools, and each school C_j has a capacity q_j. S is the set of students. Each school has a preference ordering for students, and each student has a preference ordering for schools. An *assignment* $\pi = (C_1 S_1, C_2 S_2, . . ., C_m S_m)$ assigns a set S_j of students to school C_j (for $j = 1, 2, . . ., m$) such that no student is assigned to more than one school and S_j has no more than q_j members for each school C_j. The pair $C_j S_j$ is called a *match*.

If a school would not accept a particular student under any circumstances we say that the student in question is unacceptable to that school. Similarly, if a student would not be willing to attend a particular school, even if it meant not attending school at all, then that school is unacceptable to that student.

DEFINITION: *Acceptability*

If a school X would prefer not to admit student A even if its student population fell short of its capacity, then we say that A is unacceptable to X, and we incorporate that fact into the school's preference ordering by omitting student A from its ranking. Similarly, if a student B would prefer being unmatched to attending school Y we say that Y is unacceptable to B, and Y will be omitted from B's preference ranking.

We have to be careful in defining a school's preference for one set of students over another.

DEFINITION: *Student and School Preferences*

Student A prefers assignment π' to π'' if the school assigned to A by π' ranks higher in A's preference ordering than the school assigned to A by π''. Each college has a preference ordering of individual students, and we say that college X prefers the *set* of students S' to the set S'' if we can create S' from S'' by eliminating one student from S'' and replacing her with a student that ranks higher in X's preference ordering or by adding an acceptable student. College X also prefers S' to S'' if it has room for another student and we can create S' from S'' by adding an acceptable student. We say that school X prefers assignment π' to π'' if X prefers the set of students assigned to it by π' to the set of students assigned to it by π''.

Note that the definition does not give complete information. Suppose that X prefers A to B, B to C, and C to D. We can't determine if it prefers the set $\{A, D\}$ to the set $\{B, C\}$. But we will have all the information we need.

We adapt the notion of stability to the school admissions problem in the obvious way: an assignment π is stable if there is no student–school pair such that the student would prefer the school to the one to which the student was assigned by π, and the school would rather have that student than one of the students assigned to it by π.

DEFINITION: *Blocking Pair*

AZ blocks the assignment π if student A prefers school Z to the school to which A is assigned by π (or A prefers Z to being unmatched if A is unmatched by π) and school Z prefers student A to one of the students assigned to Z by π (or A is acceptable to Z and π has assigned fewer than q_Z students to Z.).

Of course, we say that π is stable if it cannot be blocked.

DEFINITION: *Stable Assignment*

Assignment π is stable if there exists no student–school pair that blocks π.

Suppose that preferences are such that there is a student B and a school Y such that B prefers Y to every other school and Y prefers at most $q_Y - 1$ students to B. Then every stable assignment must enroll B in school Y, otherwise BY blocks π. That fact sometimes makes it easier to identify stable assignments.

Table 9.10

A	B	C	X	Y	Z
Y	X	X	B	B	A
X	Z	Z	C	C	B
Z	Y	Y	A	A	C

Example 9.6 Finding the Stable Assignments

The students are A, B, and C and the schools are X, Y, and Z. Each school has room for exactly one student: $q_X = q_Y = q_Z = 1$. The preferences are specified by Table 9.10. Every stable assignment must include BX because X is B's top choice and B is X's top choice. That leaves A and C to be assigned to schools Y and Z, and there are only two ways to do that, given the unit capacity of each school. Therefore,

$$\pi^S = (AY, BX, CZ), \text{ and } \pi^C = (AZ, BX, CY)$$

are the only assignments that could be stable. And π^S is in fact stable, because A and B each get their most-preferred match, and although C prefers X to Z, school X does not prefer C to B. The assignment π^C is also stable, because X and Z each enroll its most preferred student and, although Y prefers B to C, student B prefers X to Y. Note that π^C favors the schools and π^S favors the students, in a sense to be made precise in the next section.

9.2.2 Who Takes the Initiative, Students or Schools?

A simple extension of the deferred acceptance algorithm allows us to define a procedure that always yields a stable assignment: the *student optimal deferred acceptance (SODA)* algorithm requires the students to do the "proposing." The schools respond by accepting or rejecting. In standard terminology, students apply for admission to the schools. Acceptance is deferred in that it is not binding until the algorithm has terminated. (We will prove that *SODA* delivers an assignment that no student prefers to any other stable assignment, hence the term "student optimal.") At the outset, each student applies to his or her most-preferred school. Then each school X provisionally accepts the q_X students from its applicant pool that rank highest in that school's preference ordering. (Unacceptable students are not included in a school's preference ranking.) If fewer than q_X acceptable students have applied then X provisionally admits all of the applicants that it finds acceptable. Applicants that are not provisionally admitted are rejected. Once a student is rejected by a school she can't reapply to the same school at a subsequent stage. At the next stage all rejected students apply to the school that ranks next highest in their preference orderings – except in the case of a student who has been rejected by all schools that the student finds acceptable, in which case he or she drops out of the running and will be unmatched. Each school will now have a new, augmented, set of applicants, and it provisionally accepts all the students that rank highest in its preference ordering, up to its capacity. (A school's augmented set of applicants includes all students who have been provisionally accepted by that school in a previous round and who have not subsequently been rejected, along with all new applicants to the school.) A school provisionally admits all of the applicants that it finds acceptable if fewer than its quota of students – i.e., capacity – have applied. The process continues in this fashion until no student is rejected at the end of a round, except perhaps a student who has been rejected by every school that is acceptable to her – that is, every school that the student finds preferable to being unmatched. At this point each student that is currently provisionally accepted by a school is firmly accepted by that school, resulting in a stable assignment.

Example 9.7 The *SODA* Outcome

We begin with the agents and the preferences of Table 9.10 of Example 9.6. The stable assignments are $\pi^S = (AY, BX, CZ)$ and $\pi^C = (AZ, BX, CY)$. (A, B, and C are the students.) It is easy to see that *SODA* results in π^S, which is stable, by the argument of Example 9.6: in the first stage A applies to school Y, and B and C both apply to X. Then X accepts B and rejects C, because X prefers B to C. At the next stage C applies to Z, her second-ranked school and Z accepts C, its only applicant. We now have A provisionally accepted by Y, B provisionally accepted by X, and C provisionally accepted by Z. The algorithm terminates with these becoming binding acceptances, resulting in π^S.

The *SODA* adaptation of the *DAA* has the students taking the initiative by "proposing" – by applying to schools. Now we consider the *college optimal deferred acceptance* (*CODA*) algorithm in which the schools do the "proposing." (A college in this case could be a school at any level, but we need an acronym that distinguishes students from schools.) That is, a school takes the initiative by offering admission to the students that rank at the top of its preference ordering until it reaches capacity. Each student then responds by rejecting every school except the one that the student most prefers out of all the schools that have offered admission. Some schools will then have openings. Such a school will then offer admission to the students, in order of school preference, from whom they have not previously received rejections and who are not provisionally accepted by that school. Students with multiple admission offers will then choose the most preferred offer and reject the others, and so on.

Example 9.8 The *CODA* Outcome

We return to the setup of Table 9.10 of Example 9.6. The stable assignments are

$$\pi^S = (AY, \ BX, \ CZ) \text{ and } \pi^C = (AZ, \ BX, \ CY)$$

and we saw that *SODA* results in π^S. Now we show that the *CODA* output is π^C. In the first stage, schools X and Y both offer admission to B, while Z offers admission to A. School Z is provisionally accepted by A, but Y is rejected by B in favor of X. At the next stage school Y offers admission to C and will not be rejected because C has no other offers. In that case, A is assigned to school Z, B is assigned to X, and C is assigned to Y, resulting in π^C. Student B is indifferent between π^C and π^S because they give B the same match. However, A and C each prefer π^S to π^C, while schools Y and Z each prefer π^C to π^S. School X is indifferent between the two because its student intake is the same in either case.

To ensure that you have a clear picture of *SODA* and *CODA* we present a simple example for which the schools have room for more than one student.

Example 9.9 *SODA* and *CODA* Compared

There are four students, A, B, C, and D, and two schools X, and Y, each with room for two students. Both schools are acceptable to each student, but A and B prefer Y to X and C and D prefer X to Y. College X ranks the students in alphabetical order: $p(X) = ABCD$. But $p(Y) = DCBA$. Then *SODA* assigns C and D to X and A and B to Y. (In round 1 each student applies to her preferred school. As a result, each school has two applications, and the algorithm terminates.) In each round of the *CODA* algorithm a school X is required to fill its quota q_X by offering admission to enough students to reach its capacity, as long as there are sufficient acceptable students who have not previously rejected X. In round 1 of *CODA* school X offers admission to A and B and Y offers admission to D and C. No student has more than one offer, so *CODA* terminates with A and B placed in X and C and D placed in Y.

To establish that *SODA* and *CODA* yields stable assignments regardless of the agent preferences we simply adapt the stability proof for one-to-one matching from Section 9.1.3.

School Admissions Stability Theorem
The SODA and CODA versions of the deferred acceptance algorithm each yield a stable assignment for any specification of student and college preferences.

Proof of *SODA* Stability:
We show that no college X can be part of a blocking pair: suppose that X has exactly m students enrolled by π^S, the output of *SODA*, but m is less than q_X, the capacity of X, and student A is acceptable to X but is not assigned to X by π^S. Then A never applied to X, otherwise X would have more than m students, including A or some student that X prefers to A. Suppose, on the other hand, that X is at capacity at π^S, A is not enrolled in X, but X would prefer to have student A in place of B who is assigned to X By π^S. Again, we can say that A never applied to X, otherwise X would have rejected B. Therefore, if X prefers enrolling A to its situation at π^S we can say that A never applied to X. If X is unacceptable to A then AX certainly cannot block

π^S. If X is acceptable to A then, because A did not apply to X, the assignment π^S must enroll A in a school that she prefers to X. If A finds X unacceptable then she prefers being unmatched to being assigned to X. Thus AX cannot block π^S.   ∎

Proof of *CODA* Stability:

We show that no student A can be part of a blocking pair: Suppose that A is unmatched at π^C, the output of *CODA*, but prefers admission to college X to being single. Then X never offered admission to A, otherwise A *would* be matched – with X or some college that A prefers to X. Suppose, on the other hand, that A is enrolled in college Y by by π^C, but A prefers X. Again we can say that X never proposed to A, otherwise A would have rejected Y. Therefore, if A prefers enrollment in X to her situation at π^C we can say that X never proposed to A. If A is unacceptable to X then AX certainly cannot block π^C. If A is acceptable to X then, because X did not propose to X, the assignment π^C must assign q_X students to X, *and* each of those students is preferred to A by X. Thus AX cannot block π^C.   ∎

The above general proof establishes stability of the *DAA* for the marriage model, in which each agent has a capacity of 1. The following definition of optimality is a natural extension of the marriage model definition.

DEFINITION: *Optimal Assignments*

Assignment π is student optimal if there is no stable assignment that some student prefers to π. It is school optimal if there is no stable assignment that some school prefers to π.

Refer to Examples 9.7 and 9.8: Recall that $\pi^S = (AY, BX, CZ)$, the output of *SODA*, and $\pi^C = (AZ, BX, CY)$, the output of *CODA* for the preferences of Table 9.10. Under π^S student A is assigned to her most-preferred school, and so is B. Student C would rather be enrolled in X than Z, but there is no stable outcome that matches C and X because π^S and π^C are the only stable assignments. Under π^C school X enrolls its most-preferred student, and so does Z. School Y would prefer student B to C but there is no stable assignment that matches B and Y.

We could adapt the proof of optimality of the *DAA* (Section 9.1.3) but we leave that chore to the reader and simply state the result:

School Admissions Optimality Theorem

The outcome of SODA is student optimal and outcome of CODA is school optimal.

Because the marriage model is a special case of the school admissions problem, it follows from the discussion of strategy proofness in Section 9.1.4 that there is no school admissions procedure that always yields a stable outcome and which cannot be manipulated by a student or school deviating from its true preference ordering. However, it's unsatisfactory to have the proof based on a setup with only three students and three schools. To generalize, begin with the three students A, B, and C and the three schools X, Y, and Z employed in the proof in Section 9.1.4. Now add any number m of schools C_1, C_2, ..., C_m with respective capacities q_1, q_2,..., q_m that can be as large as you like. We also add n students S_1, S_2, ..., S_n such that $n = q_1 + q_2 + \ldots + q_m$. Have each new student prefer each new school C_j to X and Y and to Z. Have each new school C_j prefer each new student S_i to A and to B and to C. Therefore, every stable assignment will assign each new student to one of the new schools, which are now full. It remains to determine how A, B, and C are to be assigned to X, Y, and Z. At this point we continue with the proof from Section 9.1.4.

Impossibility Theorem for School Admissions:

For any procedure that always yields a stable outcome, there will be preference profiles at which some student or school can benefit by deviating from its true preferences.

The optimality theorem establishes that no *student* can profit by misrepresenting his or her preferences *if* the outcome is determined by *SODA* and the deviation from truthful revelation by the student results in another *stable* assignment. However, this does not prove that deviation from truthful revelation by a student can never precipitate an assignment, *whether stable or not*, that is preferred by that student to the one that emerges from truthful revelation. We merely state without proof the more general result.

Proposer Strategy-Proofness Theorem

If the SODA algorithm is employed then no student can benefit by deviating from truthful preference revelation. If the CODA algorithm is employed then no college can benefit by deviating from truthful preference revelation.

If all students were to submit their preference orderings to a referee, and the referee then applied the *SODA* algorithm to those preferences and to the preferences submitted by schools, then submitting the true preference ordering is a dominant strategy for every student.

9.2.3   When Test Scores Generate School Preferences

The previous subsection adapted the deferred acceptance algorithm to the school admissions problem. Now we consider the matching process when the school preferences are generated by student test scores only. In their final year of high school students take a number of different tests. There may be only two kinds of tests, quantitative and verbal, but there may be more. Each school uses one of the tests to rank the students, and different schools may use different tests.

If there are hundreds (perhaps thousands) of schools, we are not supposing that each student has to write hundreds of tests before applying to school. Several (perhaps a hundred or more) schools can use the same test to rank the students. Some of the "tests" can even be weighted averages of the components of a singe test.

Example 9.10 Four Colleges and Two Tests

The four schools are E (engineering school), H (humanities only), L (liberal arts), and M (pre-medicine). The two tests are *quantitative* and *verbal*. Let $q(s)$ and $v(s)$ be the respective scores of student s on the quantitative and verbal tests. Let $\sigma_C(s)$ be the summary score assigned to student s by college C. A reasonable supposition is that

$$\sigma_E(s) = q(s), \sigma_H(s) = v(s), \sigma_L(s) = 0.5q(s) + 0.5 \; v(s),$$
$$\text{and } \sigma_M(s) = 0.75q(s) + 0.25 \; v(s).$$

If the schools rank students according to the test scores they don't need to participate in the placement process. The state (or some other agency) can act as proxy for each school, assigning the q_j students with the top scores on test j to school C_j, and then have each student respond by rejecting the admissions offers from all but one school – the one that the student most prefers from the schools to which he or she has been assigned, and so on.

Does a student always have an incentive to get the highest possible test score when *CODA* is used? No! The following is an example in which a reduction in a student's test score results in the student being reassigned to a school that she prefers to the one in which she would have been placed with a higher score.

Example 9.11 A Lower Test Score can Mean a Better School when *CODA* is Used

There are two schools, X and Y, and two students, A and B. Each school has room for only one student. Student A prefers X to Y and B prefers Y to X. There are two tests, quantitative and verbal. School X uses the quantitative score and Y uses the verbal score. The original test scores are displayed in Table 9.11. In the first round of *CODA* student B is offered admission to X (because B's quantitative score is higher than A's), and A is offered admission to Y (because A's verbal score is higher than B's). Because A does not receive an offer of admission from a preferred school, A accepts Y, and B accepts X because B does not have any other offer. That is the final assignment.

Table 9.11

Student	Quantitative score	Verbal score
A	80	90
B	90	80

Table 9.12

Student	Quantitative score	Verbal score
A	80	70
B	90	80

Suppose, however, that A had done less well on the verbal test, resulting in the scores reported in Table 9.12. Note that B's scores have not changed. With this second set of scores, student B is offered admission to both X and Y, because B has a higher score than A on both the quantitative and verbal test. Both schools have reached capacity, so there are no initial offers to A. Then B responds by choosing her preferred school, which is Y. School X now has a vacancy, and it makes an offer of admission to the student with the next highest quantitative score, and that of course is A. Student A accepts X's offer, and the algorithm terminates with A going to X and B going to Y. With the original test scores A was matched with Y. Clearly, student A prefers the match that results when A gets the lower test score.

What happened? A's lower test score resulted in both schools initially offering admission to B. This gives B a role in the process, and because B's preferences are different from A's student B rejects the school that A wants. Let's say that a matching process is *responsive* if it never punishes a student for getting a higher score. Example 9.11 shows that *CODA* is not responsive. However, *SODA is* responsive, although we do not prove that here.

DEFINITION: *Responsiveness*

A matching process is responsive if there is no preference profile p and no profile σ of test scores at which some student A is assigned to college X, although A would be assigned to Y with σ' and $p(A)$ ranks X higher than Y and σ' is identical to σ except that with σ' student A gets a higher score on one of the tests and the same score as σ on every other test. (Every other student has the same test scores at σ' as he or she has at σ.)

We have serious reservations about an assignment procedure is not responsive. *Fairness* also deserves consideration. We say that a student placement algorithm is unfair if some student prefers some school to the one to which the student was admitted *and* the student has a higher score on the test used by the preferred school than someone who was actually admitted to that school. It is also unfair if the student was not assigned to any school by the algorithm but has a higher test score for a school that is acceptable to her than someone admitted to that school.

DEFINITION: *Fairness*

Assignment π is fair if there is no student A and no school X such that A prefers X to the school to which A is assigned by π (or A prefers X to being unmatched if π does not assign A to any school) and A has a higher score on the test used by X than some student actually admitted to X or X has unused capacity. We say that the student placement algorithm itself is fair if for every specification of student preferences and test scores the resulting assignment is fair.

Unfortunately, fairness and efficiency are incompatible in some situations, regardless of the algorithm employed. We demonstrate this by means of a simple example.

Example 9.12 Fairness and Efficiency Cannot Both be Satisfied

There are three students, A, B, and C, and two schools, X and Y, each with room for only one student. (One of the students will not be able to attend school.) Student A prefers Y to X, and the other two prefer X to Y as shown in Table 9.13.

School X uses a quantitative test score and Y uses a verbal test score. The student scores are displayed Table 9.14. We show that the only fair assignment π has A enrolled in X and C enrolled in Y. The assignment is not fair if A isn't enrolled in any school because A has the highest quantitative score, and thus will have a higher quantitative score than whoever is enrolled in school X. Similarly, the assignment can't be fair if C is not enrolled in any school because C has the highest verbal score. Therefore, a fair assignment either assigns A to X and C to Y, or else A to Y and C to X. But the latter isn't fair because B has a higher quantitative score than C. The assignment π that assigns A to X and C to Y is the only fair one in this case. However, π is not efficient because A prefers Y to X and C prefers X to Y. Therefore, if A and C switch assignments they will each be better off than at π. Student B is unaffected by the switch, so we will have made two individuals better off without harming the other person, and hence π is inefficient. If an algorithm precipitates the lone fair assignment in this situation it will not deliver an efficient outcome, and if it delivers an efficient outcome it won't be fair.

Table 9.13

A	B	C
Y	X	X
X	Y	Y

Table 9.14

Student	Quantitative score	Verbal score
A	90	80
B	80	70
C	70	90

Table 9.15

	Proposer		
Round	A	B	C
1	Y	X	**X**
2	**Y**	X	Y
3	X	**X**	Y
4	X	**Y**	Y

Note that the example employs a slightly less demanding fairness criterion than given in the definition box.

The *CODA* algorithm selects the fair assignment for Example 9.12: X will offer admission to A, the high scorer on the quantitative test, and Y will offer admission to C, the high scorer on the verbal test. Because each of these students has only one offer, each accepts and the algorithm terminates with A being assigned to X and C assigned to Y. This is also the outcome of the *SODA* algorithm, as Table 9.15 shows: In the first round A applies to Y and B and C each apply to X. School X will accept B and reject C because B has a higher quantitative score than C. (The **X** under proposer C in the first row of the table is bold to denote a rejection.) Then C will apply to Y on the second round, and Y will now have applications from both A and C. Because C has a higher verbal score than A, student A will be rejected by Y, which will provisionally accept C. Student A will now apply to X and be accepted because A has a higher quantitative score than B, its other applicant. Because B is rejected by X, B will apply to Y and be rejected because C has a higher verbal score than B. The algorithm now terminates because B has been rejected by both schools, and A and C have both been rejected by their top-ranked schools. *SODA* assigns A to X and C to Y, the only fair assignment for this problem.

It's easy to see why *SODA* always delivers a fair outcome. If student J prefers school Y to Z then J will apply to Y before Z. If J has a higher score on the test used by Y than student K then Y would never reject J before rejecting K. In other words, if Y rejects J then it will also reject K before the *SODA* algorithm terminates.

As we have seen (Examples 9.7 and 9.8 for instance), *SODA* and *CODA* typically do not produce the same outcome, but neither guarantees an efficient outcome, as Example 9.12 and the subsequent paragraph establish. However, in any situation the fair outcome π^S generated by *SODA* will weakly dominate every other fair assignment π from an efficiency standpoint. That is, every student will either prefer the school assigned to him or her by π^S to the one assigned to him or her by π, or else the student will be indifferent because he or she has the same match in both cases.

9.2.4 Single-Test Placement

An interesting special case of the student placement problem has the schools all using the same test score. We call this the *single-test placement problem*. There will be a single stable assignment if we use the test scores to generate a school's ranking of students. A simple way of finding the stable assignment is by means of the *serial choice algorithm*: the student with the highest test score announces his or her most-preferred school, and the student is permanently assigned to that school. The student with the next highest ranking is assigned to that student's most-preferred school, and so on until a school is full – that is, has reached its capacity. That school is dropped from the list of available schools. The student with the highest score, of all those students who have not yet been matched with a school, then chooses his or her most-preferred school from the set of schools that have not yet reached capacity. The algorithm proceeds in this fashion, with the students choosing in order of test score and with a school being removed from the list of available schools as soon as it is full.

DEFINITION: *The Serial Choice Algorithm (SCA)*

The n students are ranked $S_1, S_2, \ldots, S_n$ according to their scores on the single test σ. That is, $\sigma(S_1) > \sigma(S_2) > \ldots > \sigma(S_{n-1}) > \sigma(S_n)$. Let Σ denote the set of all schools, with Σ^t representing the set of available schools at stage t. At stage t student S_t chooses the school that she most prefers from Σ^t. We have $\Sigma^1 = \Sigma$, with $\Sigma^t = \Sigma^{t-1}$ if no school in Σ^{t-1} reached its capacity as a result of the choice of S_{t-1}. If school X did reach its capacity q_X at stage $t-1$ then we remove X from Σ^{t-1} to arrive at Σ^t. The algorithm terminates when each of the n students has chosen or each school has reached its capacity, whichever comes first. Each student who has had an opportunity to choose is matched with the school that he or she selected.

Example 9.13 *SODA* = *CODA* = *SCA* with a Single Test

There are five students, A, B, C, D, and E and two schools X, and Y, each with room for two students. B, C, and E prefer X to Y but A and D prefer Y to X. Each school ranks the students in alphabetical order: $p(X) = p(Y) = ABCDE$. (We give the name A to the student with the highest score, B has the next highest score, and so on.) If *SCA* is used A chooses first and selects Y. B goes next and chooses X, then C chooses X, followed by D choosing Y. The two schools are now full, which leaves E unmatched. The *SCA* assignment π^* is (AY, BX, CX, DY). If *SODA* is employed then each student applies to her preferred school in round 1, leaving X with three applications. Student E is rejected by X so E applies to Y in round 2. Now Y has three applications, and it will reject E. *SODA* terminates with $\pi^S = (AY, BX, CX, DY) = \pi^*$. In round 1 of *CODA* schools X and Y, with identical preferences, both offer admission to A and B. Student A will reject X and B will reject Y at the end of round 1. Both schools now have one opening and both will offer admission to C, who will reject Y which will offer admission to D in round 3. Now there is no student with more than one offer. *CODA* terminates with the assignment $\pi^C = (AY, BX, CX, DY) = \pi^* = \pi^S$.

It is easy to show that the *SCA* is both strategy proof and responsive when all schools use the same test.

Single-Test Strategy-Proofness and Responsiveness Theorem for the SCA

When applied to the student placement model with a single test score the serial choice algorithm is strategy proof, and it never punishes students for improving their test scores.

Proof:

Clearly, in this single-test model it never benefits a student to lower his or her score. That would only result in a lower ranking, and a later choice, perhaps from a smaller list of schools. Certainly, there would be no school *added* to the list available by the time the student had a chance to select. The order of choice by the higher ranking students will not have changed, so they will make the same selections, and hence the set of schools available to a student will either shrink or stay the same if the student's test score falls. Given that a lower score will give a student lower priority but will not otherwise affect the order in which people choose, a student cannot profit from a lower score. Therefore, the *SCA* is responsive.

Now, given the test scores, can there be any benefit to students from misrepresenting their preferences when the *SCA* is employed? No. In this case, misrepresenting one's preference ranking of schools can't change the set of schools from which a student is able to choose, because it can't affect the order in which students choose. Therefore, misrepresentation of preference will either have no effect on a student's welfare, because the school that ranks highest in the available set still ranks highest according to the false preference ordering, or else it results in the student being assigned to a less desirable school – less desirable in terms of the student's true preferences. We have proved that the *SCA* is strategy proof when a single test used by all schools. ■

We conclude this section by proving that the student placement problem in which all schools use the same test score has only one stable assignment, and that it is the one generated by the *SCA*. We already know that the assignments precipitated by the either *SODA* or *CODA* algorithms are stable. It follows that the *SODA* and *CODA* algorithms yield the same outcome for this special model.

Uniqueness Theorem for Single Test Placement

The assignment π^* generated by the serial choice algorithm applied to the student placement model with a single test score is the only stable assignment for that model. And π^* is also generated by the SODA and the CODA algorithms.

Proof:

We begin by proving that π^* is stable, and then we show that it is the only stable assignment. Let $S_1, S_2, \ldots, S_n$ be the ranking of students by test score, with the lower numbered students getting higher scores. Because the *SCA* gives S_1 his or her most-preferred school out of the set of all schools, no student–school pair involving S_1

can block π^*. Suppose that for the first t students $S_1, S_2, \ldots, S_t$ there is no school that can join with one of these t students to block π^*. Could student S_{t+1} join with some school to block π^*? No. None of the schools that receive one of the first t students would prefer to have S_{t+1} instead of one of the students with a higher score. Of the schools still available at the time S_{t+1} had an opportunity to choose, none would be preferred by S_{t+1} to the one assigned by π^* because the *SCA* allowed S_{t+1} to select the school that she most preferred from among those available. Therefore, no school-student pair involving S_{t+1} could block π^* because either S_{t+1} would prefer the school assigned by π^* or the school would prefer each of the students assigned to it by π^* to S_{t+1}. We have proved that S_1 cannot be part of a student–school pair that blocks π^*, and that if none of the first t students can be part of a student–school pair that blocks π^*, then that also must hold for the first $t + 1$ students – that is, the $t + 1$ students with the highest scores. It follows that no student S_t, for any value of t, can be part of a blocking pair, and hence π^* is stable.

Next we show that π^* is the only stable assignment. We assume that π is an arbitrary stable assignment and prove that $\pi = \pi^*$: obviously, stability implies that π gives S_1 his or her most-preferred school, which we'll call C^*. That follows from the fact that S_1 has the highest score and hence is at the top of the preference ranking of every school. (If π does not assign S_1 to C^* then the pair consisting of S_1 and C^* can block π.) Now suppose that we can prove that any stable assignment π assigns student S_m to his or her most preferred school in $\sum^m$, for $m = 1, 2, \ldots, t$. (The set $\sum^m$ of schools available to S_m is the set determined by the *SCA*.) Then stability of π implies that S_{t+1} can only be assigned to a school in $\sum^{t+1}$. (If S_{t+1} is assigned to a school C_j not in $\sum^{t+1}$ then some higher ranking student S_i must be assigned to C_j by π^* but not by π because if S_{t+1} prefers C_j to her match at π then C_j must have been full at stage $t+1$. In that case the student-school pair consisting of S_i and C_j can block π, contrary to the supposition that π is stable.) Because stability of π implies that π can only send student S_{t+1} to a school in $\sum^{t+1}$, and π^* sends S_{t+1} to his or her most preferred school in $\sum^{t+1}$, any other assignment consistent with all of the top t students getting their most-preferred schools from their available sets (as determined by the *SCA*) would assign S_{t+1} to a school that was less desirable to him or her than the school C_h to which S_{t+1} is assigned under π^* and would leave C_h with a student with a lower test score than S_{t+1} (or an empty seat), in which case S_{t+1} and C_h would block π. Therefore, π must also assign S_{t+1} to the school in $\sum^{t+1}$ that S_{t+1} most prefers.

Here's what we have so far: if π is stable then it must assign S_1 to S_1's most-preferred school, and if for any t the assignment π assigns S_m to S_m's most-preferred school in the set $\sum^m$ for $m = 1, 2, \ldots, t$, then if π is stable it must assign S^{t+1} to his or her most-preferred school in $\sum^{t+1}$. We can increase t one stage at a time to establish that a stable assignment must assign students to schools in precisely the way that the *SCA* does. That is $\pi = \pi^*$.

We have proved that π^*, the assignment generated by the *SCA*, is the unique stable assignment for the student placement model with a single test. Because both *SODA* and *CODA* generate stable assignments, we then conclude that *SODA*, *CODA*, and *SCA* precipitate the same outcome. ∎

9.2.5 Recent Reform of Public School Choice

Early in the new century, widespread parental dissatisfaction with the admissions process for public schools in Boston and New York led authorities to ask economists Atila Abdulkadiroğlu, Parag Pathak, and Alvin Roth for advice on redesigning the systems, both of which received a failing grade from parents. Of course, the welfare of students and parents could be increased if a substantial increase in resources were made available. But could the school placement process be redesigned in a way that improved matches generally, *given* the existing resources? Experience with the deferred acceptance algorithm inspired the consultants to redesign the system in a way that improved outcomes for almost everyone concerned.

We begin with the New York City story. The process of assigning students to public high schools received the most attention. As with the deferred acceptance algorithm, the old system began with students ranking schools in order of preference. (They were allowed to rank as many as twelve schools.) But the old system had little else in common with the *DAA*. It had two basic problems: only a small fraction of the students were placed in schools that they considered best or second best. Because so many pupils received multiple offers of admission and had to take time to deliberate there were about 30,000 students each year who were not assigned to any of the dozen schools that they had ranked, and had to be placed by the administration. The second problem was that parents were reluctant to submit their true preference ordering for schools for fear that if they were truthful about the school they liked best their child would be passed over and in the process lose the opportunity to be placed in the school that ranked second.

The economists recommended a new matching process based on *SODA*. (Practical and political considerations made it necessary to modify *SODA* in a number of ways.) The result was a great success. The number of students who weren't assigned to any of the schools that they had ranked fell from 30,000 to 3,000. Moreover, parents could safely submit their true preference orderings. *SODA* does not punish a student for ranking her preferred school first, regardless of how unrealistic that is. If A were rejected by her top choice X at the end of round 1 *SODA* would then apply to A's second ranked school Y in round 2. (This is all done by computer software.) Then if A were qualified enough she would be admitted to Y when *SODA* terminated. In terms of our jargon, *SODA* is strategy-proof for students. With the old system A risked being stuck with her third choice by listing her most-preferred school X first: Often A's second ranked school Y would be full of less qualified students after round 1 – full of students who ranked Y first.

Boston also replaced its old system with a modified deferred acceptance algorithm based on *SODA*. The old assignment process used immediate acceptance, which can penalize a student for submitting her true preferences, as the next example demonstrates.

Example 9.14 Immediate Versus Deferred Acceptance

There are three students, A, B, and C. The three schools X, Y, and Z each has room for only one student. A likes X best and Y second best. B likes Y best and Z second best and C likes X best. Suppose that X prefers C to A, and Y prefers A to B. (We don't need any more preference information to determine the output of both immediate acceptance and of *SODA*.) In the case of both deferred acceptance and immediate acceptance, A and C apply to X in round 1 and B applies to Y. With both algorithms X rejects A, at the end of round 1, but with immediate acceptance B is enrolled in Y and C is placed in X, leaving A to be placed in Z, her third choice. What happens with *SODA*? When A is rejected by X at the end of round 1 she applies to Y, her second choice, at the beginning of round 2. Now Y has two applications, one from A and one from B. Then Y rejects B, who then applies to Z, her second choice, and *SODA* terminates with the assignment (AY, BZ, CX). A gets a better match with *SODA*, and so does Y.

A Boston school does not generate its own ranking of students. Hence, the schools do not have preferences. Instead, *SODA* works with student rankings that are determined for the school by the board of education. These rankings are called *priorities*. Typically, different schools will be given different student rankings, although they will have a lot in common, unlike our next example with three students and three schools.

Example 9.15 *SODA* can be Inefficient with School Priorities Instead of Preferences

There are three students, A, B, and C, and three schools, X, Y, and Z, each with room for only one student. The rankings are displayed in Table 9.16. In working out *SODA* the school's priority is treated as its preference ordering. In round 1 students A and C apply to Y and B applies Z. Then Y rejects C because A has higher priority. Then C applies to Z in round 2. Because Z now has applications from B and C it will reject B with the lower priority. Then B applies to Y in round 3. Y will then reject A who has lower priority at school Y than B. Then A applies to X, which gives us the *SODA* outcome: $\pi^S = (AX, BY, CZ)$. This is not efficient because if B and C switch schools each will get a preferred placement.

Table 9.16

Student Preferences			School Rankings		
A	B	C	X	Y	Z
Y	Z	Y	A	B	C
X	Y	Z	B	A	A
Z	X	X	C	C	B

Example 9.15 does not contradict the efficiency theorem of Section 9.1.2 because the priority rankings that play the role of school preferences are not in fact preferences, and are imposed by a central authority. Therefore, in determining whether an assignment is efficient only the preferences of students are considered. (If we *did* treat the school rankings of Table 9.16 as preferences then when we modify π^S by having B and C switch schools the two schools involved, Y and Z, will be made worse off, and we can show that π^S *is* efficient.) If, however, the priority rankings imposed on schools are influenced by correlation between the strengths of a school and the ability of a student, as when a child who excels at mathematics is given high priority at a school that emphasizes science, the priority rankings are not irrelevant to efficiency.

Sources

This section is based on Roth and Sotomayor (1990) and Roth (2015). Examples 9.11 and 9.12 are from Balinski and Sönmez (1999), who prove, among other things, that the fair outcome generated by *SODA* will weakly dominate every other fair assignment from an efficiency standpoint. Example 9.15 is from Erdil and Ergin (2013).

Links

See Abdulkadiroğlu et al. (2005a) for a thorough discussion of the New York City high school match, and Abdulkadiroğlu et al. (2005b) for the Boston story. See Ergin and Sönmez (2006) for more on the original "Boston mechanism." American college sororities use a matching process that does not generate stable outcomes (Mongell and Roth, 1991). Chen and Sönmez (2006) give a study of school choice in a laboratory setting.

Problem Set

(1) There are six students, $A, B, C, D, E,$ and F, and three colleges, $X, Y,$ and Z, each with room for two students. The student preferences are given in Table 9.17 and the college preferences are given in Table 9.18. Work out the assignment generated by *SODA*. Demonstrate that it is stable.

(2) Work out the assignment generated by *CODA* for the data of question 1. Demonstrate that it is stable.

(3) There are six students, $A, B, C, D, E,$ and F, and three colleges, $X, Y,$ and Z, each with room for two students. The test scores are displayed in Table 9.19 and the student preferences are given in Table 9.20. Work out the assignment

Table 9.17

A	B	C	D	E	F
X	X	Z	Z	Y	X
Y	Y	Y	Y	X	Z
Z	Z	X	X	Z	Y

Table 9.18

X	Y	Z
B	A	A
A	F	B
C	C	C
D	E	F
E	D	D
F	B	E

Table 9.19

Student	Quantitative score	Verbal score
A	90	80
B	85	90
C	80	70
D	75	60
E	70	75
F	65	85

Table 9.20

A	B	C	D	E	F
X	X	Z	Z	Y	X
Y	Y	Y	Y	X	Z
Z	Z	X	X	Z	Y

determined by *CODA* if college *X* were to use the quantitative score and *Y* and *Z* each used the verbal test score.

(4) Assume the data of question 3, but this time assume that colleges *X* and *Y* use the quantitative test score, and *Z* uses the verbal score. Work out the assignment determined by the *CODA*.

(5) Prove that when school preferences are generated by a single test score then an assignment is stable if and only if it is efficient.

(6) Prove that when school preferences are generated by a single test score then the *SCA* is fair.

9.3 HOSPITALS AND DOCTORS

Thousands of physicians who have just graduated from medical school need to be placed with hospitals who will employ them as residents. This is obviously an extremely important matching problem. It is a variant of the school admissions problem because each doctor will wind up at only one hospital, but most hospitals will employ more than one resident. In the United States about 20,000 doctors are matched with about 4,000 residency programs each year.

In 1952 a matching algorithm was first used in the United States to place physicians in residency programs. The US internship program began about half a century before that. In the early 1900s the hospital demand for graduating doctors was significantly larger than the supply. (The interns represented cheap labor.) Hospitals negotiated directly with medical students, offering internships to some and being either accepted or rejected by each student receiving an offer. Competition for newly minted physicians resulted in hospitals approaching medical students earlier and earlier in their programs. By 1944 appointments were being made two years before graduation. This meant that matches between hospitals and doctors were based on far less information than a hospital would have if it waited until late in the graduating year to approach a student. No individual hospital had an incentive to wait because other hospitals would have already contracted with the best doctors. Because of the strong incentive to beat the competition to a student's door, efforts by the medical community to halt the process did not avail. Adding to the overall dissatisfaction with this decentralized market process was the fact that it was not uncommon for doctors to renounce a contract when a better opportunity presented itself at a later date. (A hospital that was rejected by the doctor to whom it made its first offer would often find that its second choice had already accepted a position elsewhere.) And when a contract *was* honored it often resulted in a bad match: the student might have changed his intended specialty by the time he graduated, and the hospital to which he was under contract might not have a strength in the new specialty. Or the hospital might find that a different graduate would, after all, be a better hire. The problem was not just one of frustration by doctors and hospitals but also of inefficient resource allocation.

Problems continued to plague this labor market even after 1945 when medical schools agreed not to release information about students prior to an agreed date. Hospitals forced doctors to accept or reject an offer without giving them sufficient time to deliberate. (A hospital worried that if it gave a doctor a reasonable amount of time to respond to an offer it could lose a chance to hire its second ranked doctor if the earlier offer were rejected.) Frustration on both sides of the market had reached a high enough level by the early 1950s that students and hospitals agreed to the creation of a centralized clearinghouse. The National Resident Matching Program (NRMP) was born.

9.3.1   When Most Doctors were Men

About 50 percent of the current graduates of US medical schools are women. In Sections 9.1 and 9.2 we did not find it necessary to keep track of gender. We didn't have to know what fraction of the agents were women. That would also be true of the market for medical residents were it not for the fact that a significant number of medical school graduates are married to other physicians. Therefore, a successful matching process must accommodate *couples*. Prior to 1970 there were few women doctors and very few doctors married to doctors. This section explains the matching process that evolved in that era and was used until the mid-1990s when it was re-designed to allow couples to express a preference.

DEFINITION: *The Residency Matching Problem*

There is a given set of hospitals and a given number of physicians seeking residency in a hospital. Each hospital H has a number q_H of vacancies to fill and has a preference ordering for physicians. Each physician has a preference ordering for hospitals. An *assignment* π places each doctor in at most one hospital and no hospital H is assigned more than q_H new doctors.

The National Intern Matching Program (NIMP, now called the National Resident Matching Program) was set up in 1950 as a clearing house that employed an algorithm to match doctors and hospitals. Hospitals would submit their preference orderings of graduating medical students to the clearing house, and the students would submit their individual rankings of hospitals. One important criterion was *stability*: when the final assignment is determined there should be no hospital and no doctor who would each prefer being matched with the other to the assignment determined by the algorithm.

DEFINITION: *Stable Assignment*

We say that *DJ blocks* the assignment π if π assigns doctor D to hospital H and doctor E to hospital J, and D prefers J to H and J prefers D to E. Assignment π is stable if there is no blocking pair.

The algorithm went through a trial and error phase. The initial NIMP proposal was intended to favor doctors: the first round would match doctor–hospital pairs such that each ranked the other first. In round 2 a hospital that ranked physician B second would be matched with B if he ranked that hospital first and B had not been placed in round 1 and the hospital had a vacancy at the end of round 1. Round 3 would match hospital H with physician C if H ranked C first and C ranked H second, and C had not been matched in a prior round and H still had at least one vacancy. Round 4 would match a hospital with a doctor if each ranked the other second, and the doctor had not been matched in a prior round and the hospital still had a vacancy.

A complete ranking by either hospital or doctor would be prohibitively costly, so the algorithm works with partial rankings. Our examples employ a small number of doctors and hospitals so we employ complete rankings. We begin by illustrating the trial algorithm that was proposed.

Example 9.16 Three Hospitals and Three Doctors

The doctors are D, E, and F, and the hospitals are H, I, and J. We assume that each hospital wishes to hire one and only one resident. Table 9.21 displays the preference rankings of each. Doctor D prefers H to I and I to J (and, of course, H to J). The columns for E and F are interpreted similarly. Hospital H ranks doctor E first, then F, and then D. And so on. The trial algorithm begins by searching for a hospital-resident pair such that each gives the other first-place rank. There are no such pairs for this table, so we proceed to the second stage in which we search for a hospital that ranks a doctor second when that same doctor ranks that hospital first. There are two such matches: E and I, and F and H. Then doctor E is assigned to hospital I, and F is assigned to H. Then J and D are paired by default. The assignment is $\pi = (DJ, EI, FH)$.

Note that hospital J is D's last choice. D would have faired better to have (untruthfully) ranked I in first place, as we now show.

Example 9.17 Preference Misrepresentation by a Doctor

Assume that the true preferences are as specified in Table 9.21 of Example 9.16, but the reported preferences are those of Table 9.22, which is the same as Table 9.21 except for the fact that D has switched the ordering of H and I. Because the trial algorithm begins by searching for a hospital-resident pair such that each gives the other first-place rank, we now have D matched with I, and D prefers I to hospital J according to D's true preference ordering, although D is assigned to J when D reports his true preference ranking

Table 9.21

D	E	F	H	I	J
H	I	H	E	D	F
I	J	J	F	E	E
J	H	I	D	F	D

Table 9.22

D	E	F	H	I	J
I	I	H	E	D	F
H	J	J	F	E	E
J	H	I	D	F	D

Essentially, the problem with the original proposal was that by listing his true first choice a doctor could miss an opportunity to be matched with his second choice. Because the trial algorithm sometimes gives physicians incentive to misrepresent their first choice of hospital, it was revised in response to student objections. The rule that was actually employed in the first year of centralization begins by searching for a hospital–resident pair for which each ranks the other first, as before. If there are no such pairs, the algorithm searches for a match between a *hospital's* first choice and a *doctor's* second choice. The next stage matched a hospital with a doctor if the doctor ranked that hospital third and the hospital ranked the doctor first. And so on.

Example 9.18 Example 9.16 with the Revised Algorithm

The true preferences are the ones given in Table 9.21 of Example 9.17. There are no hospital–resident pairs such that each ranks the other first. But hospital I ranks D first and D ranks I second, so D and I are paired. Similarly, hospital J ranks F first, and F ranks J second. Therefore F is assigned to J, leaving E and H to be paired by default. The algorithm produces $\pi = (DI, FJ, EH)$. Although the trial algorithm assigned D to his lowest ranked hospital, the revised version matched D and I.

Although the revised algorithim eliminated the incentive of a physician to misrepresent his most-preferred residency program, it is not the case that truthful revelation is a dominant strategy for every agent. Recall the impossibility theorem of Section 9.1.4: no strategy-proof matching mechanism exits when both types have preferences. However, the revised algorithm – the one that was actually employed to match doctors and hospitals – makes successful preference misrepresentation by doctors very unlikely. One can prove that no physician can ever gain by misrepresenting his first choice. Consider the example, with Table 9.21 displaying the true preferences. If D deviates from truthful revelation and ranks I first then D and I are matched in round 1, and that gives D the same assignment as truthful revelation. If D ranks J first and I second then D gets assigned to I in round 2. If D ranks J first and H second then D is matched with I in round 3. (I is the only hospital that doesn't rank D last.) What about E? Under truthful revelation E is assigned to his lowest ranked hospital, H. If E ranks H first then he is assigned to H in round 1. If E ranks H second he's assigned to H in round 2. If E ranks J first and I second then he's matched with H in round 3. We leave it to the reader to examine the incentives of agent F.

A doctor can't gain by misrepresenting the hospital that he likes best. And it would risky to misrepresent the preference ordering of the other hospitals. One would have to know a lot about the preferences of the hospitals and the other doctors to do it advantageously.

The algorithm was modified from time to time to repair defects that came to light.

9.3.2 Couples

Married couples became involved in the matching process in significant numbers in the 1970s. Couples would sometimes decline job offers that were generated by the algorithm, and they began to completely bypass the clearinghouse. (Participation is voluntary.) Some hospitals responded by entering into direct negotiation with couples in the belief that they could land better doctors than if they used the clearinghouse. As a result, some students found that their assigned hospitals wouldn't hire them. In 1983 the NRMP modified the algorithm to allow couples to express their preference for hospitals as a pair. In 1995 the economist Alvin Roth was asked to redesign the system, which he did along with Elliott Peranson, who had long been the NIMP's technical mastermind. The new matching process is called the Roth-Peranson algorithm.

The matching mechanism that had been in use since 1952 is a version of the deferred acceptance algorithm in which the hospitals did the proposing. The Roth and Peranson algorithm begins by assigning individual doctors – those not registered as part of a couple – with the doctors doing the proposing. (*SODA* instead of *CODA*. See Section 9.2.1.) When that phase of the algorithm terminates, blocking pairs, involving hospitals and *couples*, are then identified. Each blocking pair P is eliminated, one pair at a time, by assigning the doctor to the hospital with which he or she forms part of the block P. This second stage typically results in some displaced students who had been matched in the first phase. The displaced students are matched in the final phase of the algorithm.

The next example shows that it is possible for every assignment to be blocked if every doctor belongs to a couple. (If there are no couples with preferences the deferred acceptance algorithm always yields a stable outcome, no matter who does the proposing.)

Example 9.19 is extreme for two reasons: the number of hospitals and doctors is small, and a large fraction of the doctors (100 percent in the case of the example) are married to other doctors. With more realistic numbers, there is almost always at least one stable assignment. This has been determined theoretically, and also empirically from observations of applications of the Roth-Peranson algorithm to many other labor markets.

Example 9.19 Every Assignment is Blocked

There are four doctors, A, B, C, D, and four hospitals, H, I, J, K, each with one opening. But A and B apply as a couple and so do C and D. Therefore, there is one preference ordering for the couple AB and one for CD. Hospital and couple preferences are displayed in Table 9.23. There are 24 possible assignments: Four ways to place a doctor with H, and for each of these there are three doctors not yet assigned and hence three ways to place a doctor with I. That leaves two doctors not yet placed, and hence two ways to fill the vacancy at J ($4 \times 3 \times 2 = 24$). (A couple's preference ordering is read from left to right: AB's first choice is for A to be assigned to H and B to be assigned to I. AB's last choice is for A to be assigned to I and B to be assigned to H. AB's second choice is for A to be assigned to K and B to be assigned

Table 9.23

	Couple preferences												Hospital preferences			
													H	*I*	*J*	*K*
													D	D	B	B
AB	HI	KH	KJ	KI	HK	HJ	JK	JH	JI	IJ	IK	IH	B	C	C	D
CD	KI	KJ	KH	JH	JI	JK	IK	IH	IJ	HI	HK	HJ	A	B	A	A
													C	A	D	C

to *H*. Hospital *H* prefers *D* to *B*, *B* to *A*, and *A* to *C*.) Each of the twenty-four assignments can be blocked by some couple–hospital pair. We treat only four assignments, leaving it to the reader to show that each of the others can be blocked.

(*AH, BI, CJ, DK*) is blocked by couple *CD* and hospital *I* because *I* prefers *D* to *B* and *CD* prefers *JI* to *JK*.

(*AK, BH, CI, DJ*) is blocked by couple *CD* and hospital *H* because *H* prefers *D* to *B* and *CD* prefers *IH* to *IJ*.

(*AJ, BK, CH, DI*) is blocked by couple *AB* and hospital *H* because *H* prefers *A* to *C* and *AB* prefers *HK* to *JK*.

(*AI, BJ, CK, DH*) is blocked by couple *CD* and hospital *I* because *I* prefers *D* to *A* and *CD* prefers *KI* to *KH*.

If the hospitals had preferences for couples instead of individuals there would be no blocking. We could use the school admissions model with each couple treated as a single "student".

Sources
This section is based on Roth (1984) and Roth (2015).

Links
See Roth (1990) for a discussion of the market for medical school graduates in the United Kingdom. Roth and Peranson (1999) discuss changes in the assignment algorithm from several important perspectives. Kojima et al. (2013) show why there will almost always exist a stable assignment if the number of participants is realistically large. They also demonstrate that it is very unlikely that a participant could successfully manipulate the Roth-Peranson algorithm by misrepresenting its preference if the number of participants is large.

Problem Set

(1) Determine all the stable assignments for the preferences of Example 9.16.

(2) Assume that there are three doctors and three hospitals, with each hospital intent on hiring exactly one doctor. Use the *CODA* algorithm of Section 9.2

to represent the revised hospital–doctor assignment. Show that it precipitates a stable assignment for every specification of hospital and doctor preferences.

(3) Assume that there are three doctors and three hospitals, with each hospital intent on hiring exactly one doctor. Use the *CODA* algorithm of Section 9.2 to represent the revised hospital–doctor assignment. Prove that physicians never have incentive to rank their true most-preferred hospital lower than first.

(4) Example 9.19 listed four of the twenty-four possible assignments. List the other twenty and find at least one doctor–hospital blocking pair for each.

9.4   ALLOCATING DORMITORY ROOMS

There are n students and n dormitory rooms, and each student has a preference ordering over the set of rooms. To simplify the discussion, we assume that no student is indifferent between two different rooms.

The allocation problem is typically applied to a situation in which some of the students already have rooms. If the student has to choose between retaining his or her present room for the next academic year or participating in the new allocation of rooms and possibly winding up with one that is less desirable than the one given up then the student has to make a decision in the presence of uncertainty. Therefore, individual preferences will be represented initially in terms of utility functions, so that we can compute and compare the expected utility of different strategies. We distinguish between students who already occupy rooms and those who are new to the matching process.

DEFINITION: *The Room Assignment Problem*

Σ is the set of n students and Π is the set of n rooms. Each student S has a utility function U_S defined over the rooms. Student S prefers strategy σ to strategy σ' if and only if the expected utility from σ exceeds the expected utility from σ'. We assume that $U_S(\sigma') = U_S(\sigma)$ if and only if σ' and σ assign the same room to S. The (partial) assignment π_0, placing some students in rooms, is the status quo. If SR belongs to π_0 it means that room R is currently occupied by student S. An assignment π specifies the room assigned to each student. Each student has one and only one room and no room is occupied by more than one student.

If SR belong to π_0 then the room allocation scheme that we employ may or may not give S the right to keep R, and if S does relinquish claim on R the allocation scheme may or may not guarantee that S will wind up with a room that is at least as good as R. The room allocation scheme may or may not satisfy the following *participation constraint*.

For every SR in π_0 the expected utility realized by S when S participates in the scheme is at least as high as $U_S(R)$.

9.4.1 A Commonly Used Scheme

The first allocation scheme that we consider gives any student who already occupies a room the right to hold on to that room. That means that a student can choose not to participate in the matching mechanism, in which case he is re-assigned to his current room. Many colleges and universities use the *serial choice with no guarantee* mechanism. At the outset each student who already occupies a room has to declare whether he wants to participate. If he does not participate he retains his current room for the next year. If he does participate he cannot have his current room again next year if it is not on the menu when it is his turn to choose – i.e., if it has already been chosen by somebody else. Students who do not presently occupy rooms, or who have waived their right to occupy their current room for another year, are given numbers. Student number 1 chooses a room from the set of available rooms, and the one that is chosen is removed from the list of available rooms. The second student chooses from the set of currently available rooms, and that choice is removed from the list. Then the third student makes a choice, and so on.

DEFINITION: *Serial Choice with No Guarantee (SCNG)*
If SR belongs to π_0 then S must decide whether to keep room R or participate in the matching scheme. Let Π_1 denote the set of rooms that are either not currently occupied or are presently occupied by a student who has agreed to give up his or her room and participate in the scheme. Σ_1 is the set of students who do not have a room or who have given up the room that they had – i.e., given up the right to occupy their present room again next year. The members of Σ_1 are numbered, $S_1, S_2, \ldots, S_m$. Student S_1 has highest priority, and S_2 is next, and so on. Student S_1 chooses his or her most-preferred room from Π_1, and that room is removed from the list, resulting in the available set Π_2. Then S_2 chooses from Π_2, and the selected room is withdrawn, resulting in the available set Π_3. At stage t student S_t chooses from Π_t, where Π_t is obtained from Π_{t-1} by removing the room chosen by S_{t-1}.

The numbering of students can be determined entirely by chance, with each having the same probability of being selected to go first. This random allocation can be modified, say by giving seniors and/or those with a high GPA a higher probability of receiving a low number. But any set of priority numbers can result in an inefficient assignment if the matching process does not satisfy the participation constraint, as our first example demonstrates.

Table 9.24

Room	U_A	U_B	U_C
X	10	12	12
Y	12	10	10
Z	1	1	1

Example 9.20 Inefficiency of the *SCNG* with Three Students and Three Rooms

We allocate rooms using the *SCNG* algorithm. The three students are A, B, and C. The rooms are X, Y, and Z. Student A currently occupies X, and the other two rooms are unoccupied. The utility functions are given by Table 9.24. We have $U_A(X) = 10$, $U_A(Y) = 12$, $U_A(Z) = 1$, and so forth. A has to decide whether to hold on to X or participate in the allocation scheme. We assume that the priority ordering is determined by a draw from a uniform probability distribution. In plain words, three pieces of paper are placed in a hat, each one bearing a name of a student. A slip of paper is removed at random, and the student whose name is on the slip is first, and the second student is the one whose name is drawn next. There are six possible orderings, namely *ABC, ACB, BAC, BCA, CAB*, and *CBA* and each has the same chance of determining priority. Therefore, the probability of each ordering is 1/6. If A retains room X then A's utility will be 10, because $U_A(X) = 10$. If A participates in the allocation scheme then $U_A = 12$ if A chooses first or second. (B or C will choose X if it is available.) But if A goes last then $U_A = 1$, and this will happen with two of the six possible orderings of the students. Therefore, A's expected utility is

$$4U_A(Y)/6 + 2U_A(Z)/6 = 48/6 + 2/6 = 8\frac{1}{3}$$

if A participates in the lottery. This is less than the expected utility of claiming room X for the next year. Therefore, A will opt out, and Y will be assigned to either B or C, with Z going to the one who does not get Y. This outcome is inefficient because if A changes rooms with the person who got Y both individuals will be better off and the third individual will not be affected.

Suppose that A opted out (as she has every incentive to do) and B chooses before C. Then B will choose Y resulting in the inefficient assignment (AX, BY, CZ). If A and B switch the new assignment (AY, BX, CZ) increases the utility of both A and B with C being unaffected. What's the problem? Why couldn't the housing authority just let two students switch rooms when that benefitted both? It could, and it should. But with a realistic number of students it would be extremely costly for someone to identify another student who wanted to trade. Hundreds of other tenants would probably have to be contacted before finding one who wanted to exchange rooms. It would be far better to have a matching process that guaranteed that an efficient outcome would result from the self-interested behavior of the participants.

If there are no existing tenants, as would be the case with a freshman dorm, then the *SCNG* procedure always leads to an efficient outcome.

Theorem

SCNG is efficient if there are no existing tenants.

Proof:

Student S_1 gets his or her most-preferred room, so any change in S_1's assignment will reduce that student's utility. Given that we can't change S_1's assignment and that S_2 gets the first choice of the rooms available after S_1 makes a selection, we can't change the assignment of rooms to S_1 or S_2 without making one of those students worse off. Suppose that we have established that we can't change the room assignment of any of the first t students without making one of them worse off. It follows that we can't change the room assignment of any of the first $t + 1$ students without making one of them worse off: student $t + 1$ chose her most-preferred room from the set of rooms available after the first t students make their choices. If we give $t + 1$ a different room (from the one in which the *SCNG* placed her) then either she will get one of the rooms assigned to one of the first t individuals, making one of them worse off, or we will give $t + 1$ a room that *she* likes less well than the one that she chose when participating in the *SCNG*. ∎

Versions of serial choice with random determination of the order of choice are employed at many US universities, including Michigan, Princeton, Rochester, and Stanford (in their graduate residences) and Carnegie-Mellon, Duke, Harvard, Northwestern, University of Pennsylvania, William and Mary, and Yale (in their undergraduate dormitories). Many different randomization procedures are employed, with variations even across undergraduate colleges at Yale. At Duke, Harvard, Northwestern, Pennsylvania, and William and Mary incumbent students are permitted to opt out of the allocation process and retain their current rooms (Abdulkadiroğlu and Sönmez, 1999).

Where in the proof did we use the fact that none of the rooms is currently occupied? It was implicit in the assumption that an individual had only one strategy, namely to chose one of the rooms from the available set. When a student already occupies a room there is another choice – not participating in the matching process.

It is obvious that no student can profit by misrepresenting his or her preferences if the *SCNG* is employed and there are no existing tenants – that is, none of the rooms is already occupied. We formally test for strategy proofness by supposing that all students submit their utility functions to a referee who then uses these functions to work out the outcome of the *SCNG*. Would submitting the true utility function be a dominant strategy?

DEFINITION: *Strategy Proofness*

A matching process for determining an assignment of rooms is strategy proof if for each specification of the true student utility functions, reporting truthfully is a dominant strategy for each student.

Theorem

SCNG is strategy-proof if there are no existing tenants.

Proof:

Student S_1 gets his or her most-preferred room under truthful revelation, so S_1 has no incentive to misrepresent his or her preferences. In general, student S_t gets whichever room in Π_t maximizes the utility function that S_t reports, and *the utility function that S_t reports has no effect on the order in which students choose.* Therefore, S_t's report cannot affect the set of rooms from which he or she is allowed to choose: The dominant strategy for S_t is to report his or her true utility function and get the room in Π_t that S_t actually likes best.   ∎

Note that it suffices for all students to report their preference orderings of rooms. A utility representation is not necessary. But the students who currently occupy a room make expected utility calculations to see if they should participate.

9.4.2 An Efficient Procedure

The possibility of winding up with an inferior room if you give up the one that you currently hold can lead to inefficiency. Therefore, we modify the *SCNG* algorithm by removing the potential penalty for relinquishing a room. We begin with the assumption that only one of the rooms is occupied before the assignment process begins. The new allocation scheme, called the *serial choice with guarantee (SCG1)* algorithm, proceeds in the same fashion as *SCNG*, except that *all* students are numbered, perhaps by lottery, and if at some stage someone claims a room that you occupy you get to take that student's place in line, which means that it is now your turn to choose. You can reclaim your own room or take a better one if one is available. It is the possibility of getting a better room if someone chooses yours, and the right to reclaim your room if nothing better is available, that guarantees an efficient outcome.

DEFINITION: *Serial Choice with Guarantee (SCG1)*

All students are numbered. Let Π_1 denote the set of all rooms and let Π_t be the set of rooms that have not been selected prior to stage t. The algorithm proceeds according to the rules of *SCNG*, with student S_t choosing from Π_t at stage t, until we reach a stage t at which S_t claims a room that is currently occupied by a student who has not yet chosen. Suppose S_t chooses the room occupied by S_j and $j > t$. The algorithm is suspended while the ordering of students is changed, with S_j replacing S_t as the next student to choose, and then S_t chooses after S_j, with priority ordering otherwise unaffected. If S_j does not reclaim her current room X then X remains on the menu for the next student in line and the room actually chosen by S_j is removed from the menu.

The *SCG1* circumvents *SCNG*'s potential inefficiency in the case of Example 9.20: the priority *BCA* would lead to an initial choice of room X by B. Because X is occupied by A the priority is changed to *ABC*. That means that A will choose Y, and then B will choose X, and C gets Z. Similarly, if C were to go first and choose X then the priority would change to *ACB* with A being assigned to Y. With *SCG1* and the data of Example 9.20 student A winds up with Y for all six initial orderings of the students and A's expected utility is 12 which exceeds the utility of retaining room X.

Theorem
SCG1 is efficient if only one room is currently occupied.

Even if an existing tenant were allowed to opt out, the *SCG1* would precipitate an efficient outcome because of the guarantee that participation would not diminish a student's utility. That guarantee increases participation and forestalls any inefficiency. Rather than proving this we generalize the *SCG1* algorithm to include the possibility that more than one room is currently occupied and then establish efficiency of the more general version.

If there are two or more rooms that are already occupied we have to adjust *SCG1* to deal with possible *cycles*. A cycle occurs when A claims the room currently occupied by B, who then takes A's turn and claims the room currently occupied by C, who goes ahead of both B and A and claims the room currently occupied by A.

DEFINITION: *A Serial Choice Cycle*
A cycle is a set Π_t of $m+1$ rooms and a sequence $S_t S_{t+1} \ldots S_{t+m-1} S_{t+m}$ of $m+1$ students such that the first choice of S_t from Π_t is the room occupied by S_{t+1}, the first choice of S_{t+1} from Π_t is the room occupied by S_{t+2}, and so on, with the first choice of student S_{t+m-1} from Π_t being the room occupied by S_{t+m} and the first choice of S_{t+m} from Π_t being the room occupied by S_t.

If *ABCA* is a cycle the revised algorithm gives A's room to C, C's room to B, and B's room to A. In other words, each member of a cycle gets the room that he wanted. Each gets the room he likes best from the set rooms that were available when the cycle began.

DEFINITION: *Serial Choice with Guarantees (SCG) in General*

Let $S_1, S_2, \ldots, S_n$ denote the priority ranking (of all students), with Π_1 being the set of all rooms. Let Π_t denote the set of rooms that have not been selected prior to stage t. (Rooms that had already been occupied when the algorithm started will belong to Π_t if and only if they have not yet been newly assigned to someone by the algorithm.) Student S_t chooses from Π_t. If the chosen room was originally unoccupied then it is assigned to S_t and removed from the set of available rooms, resulting in Π_{t+1}, the new set of available rooms. If S_t does choose a room that is currently occupied, say by student S', *and S' has not already chosen a room*, the algorithm searches for a cycle. If there is no cycle, the ordering of students is changed, with S' now having highest priority (among the remaining students) and S_t second. The algorithm now resumes with S' choosing from Π_t. If S' does not choose her current room X then X remains on the menu for the next person in line, and the room actually chosen by S' is removed from the menu. If a cycle is found then all students in the cycle are assigned their chosen rooms, and all those rooms are removed from Π_t to constitute the set Π_{t+1} of rooms available at the next stage.

As we did in the earlier sections, we investigate incentive compatibility by supposing that all students give their preference ordering to a referee, who then uses the reported preferences to work out the assignment determined by the algorithm.

The outcome of the SCG is strategy proof: students that are part of a cycle get their most-preferred rooms from the set of rooms available when the cycle is identified. No member of a cycle can benefit by not reporting her true preference ordering. At each stage the student whose turn it is to choose gets the room that ranks higher in her reported preference ordering than any other available room, and no student can affect the order in which he or she chooses, or the set of rooms available, by changing his or her reported preference ordering. Therefore, if the student's first choice is not currently occupied, she can do no better than report her true preference ordering. What about the case of a student A who slips one position in the queue because A has chosen the room occupied by B, but A and B are not part of a cycle? If A forestalls the switch in priority by choosing a room that is *not A's* most-preferred (in the set of available rooms) A will do no better than under truthful revelation by asking for his second choice. Under truthful revelation she will get her second choice anyway if B retains his current room (and then A chooses), but A would lose the opportunity of getting her most-preferred room (i.e., B's current room) if she didn't ask for it and B would not have re-claimed his current room if he had chosen before A.

Would submitting the true preference ordering be a dominant strategy in general? (A strategy is dominant if, for any configuration of strategies played by others, there is no alternative strategy that would give the decision taker a higher payoff.)

DEFINITION: *Strategy Proofness*

A matching mechanism for determining an assignment of rooms to students is strategy proof if for each specification of the student preferences truthful revelation is a dominant strategy for each agent.

We have informally demonstrated that the SCG passes this test. Now we provide a rigorous proof:

Theorem

The SCG is strategy proof, however many rooms are already occupied.

Proof:

Consider arbitrary student σ_t, where $\sigma_1, \sigma_2, \ldots, \sigma_n$ is the ordering in which the students actually chose as a result of applying the SCG to the original priority ranking $S_1, S_2, \ldots, S_n$. Let Φ_t be the set of available rooms when student σ_t has an opportunity to choose. All other rooms have been assigned by the time σ_t has a turn. Clearly, Φ_1 is the set of all rooms, so σ_1 (who might not be S_1) gets the room that is at the top of σ_1's true preference ordering, whether or not σ_1 is part of a cycle. Clearly, σ_1 has no incentive to misrepresent his or her preference ordering – i.e., to choose a room that is not most preferred according to σ_1's true preference scheme. Similarly, student σ_t has no incentive to choose anything but his or her most-preferred alternative in Φ_t: Student σ_t can't do anything to change the set of rooms that are available at the time he makes his choice. If σ_t is part of a cycle under truthful revelation then he gets the room he likes best in Φ_t. And if σ_t is not part of a cycle under truthful revelation he still gets the room he likes best in Φ_t. Since t was arbitrary, we have established that the SCG induces truthful revelation by all students, whatever their priority rankings.

∎

Have we contradicted the theorem of Section 9.1.4? No. That result pertains to a matching problem in which both sides have preferences. But the dormitory rooms don't have preferences for students.

Example 9.21 Application of the SCG Algorithm

There are five students, A, B, C, D, and E, and five rooms, V, W, X, Y, and Z. Three of the rooms are presently occupied: W by student B, X by student C, and Y by student D. All five students will participate in the allocation scheme because all three

Table 9.25

A	B	C	D	E
W	Z	W	W	X
V	⋮	Y	Z	Y
⋮		⋮	X	W
				V
			⋮	Z

tenants are guaranteed rooms that are at least as attractive as the ones they currently occupy. Assume that the priority ordering is *ABCDE*. Table 9.25 displays the students' preferences. We have given only a partial preference ordering for the first four students because we don't need any more information to work out the details of the SCG in this case.

Student *A* goes first and chooses *W*, which is already occupied by *B*, so the priority immediately changes to *BACDE*. Then *B* goes first and chooses *Z*, which is not occupied, so room *Z* is assigned to *B* and removed from the menu. *A* then chooses *W*, which is *not* occupied by someone waiting for a turn to choose, so *W* is assigned to *A* and removed from the list of available rooms. The available rooms are now *V*, *X*, and *Y* with *C*, *D*, and *E*, in that order, waiting to choose. Student *C* chooses *Y*, which is occupied by *D*, and *D* would choose *X*, which is occupied by *C*. We have a cycle, and thus room *Y* is assigned to *C* and *X* is assigned to *D*. That leaves room *V* to be assigned to student *E*. Then $\pi^* = (AW, BZ, CY, DX, EV)$ is the resulting assignment.

Is π^* of Example 9.21 efficient? *A* and *B* each wind up with the room that he or she prefers to every other room. Therefore, if we change the assignment in a way that changes the room assigned to *A* we will make *A* worse off, or if we assign a different room to *B* we will make *B* worse off. Therefore, in searching for an assignment that makes at least one person better off than π^* and no one worse off we have to restrict attention to the assignment of rooms *V*, *X*, and *Y* and to students *C*, *D*, and *E*. The SCG assignment π^* gives *C* the room that she most prefers from *V*, *X*, and *Y*. Therefore, if we change the room assignment of *A*, *B*, or *C* then we will make one of those three worse off. Similarly, the SCG assignment π^* gives *D* the room that *D* most prefers, subject to the constraint that *A* and *B* have to get *W* and *Z*, respectively. Therefore, if we change the room assignment of *A*, *B*, *C*, or *D* we will make one of those students worse off. It follows that if we do not assign room *V* to student *E* then we will inevitably leave *A*, *B*, *C*, or *D* worse off than they are at the SCG assignment π^*. Therefore, if π^* is our starting point, we cannot make one of the five students better off without leaving at least one of them worse off. Therefore, π^* is efficient. In general the SCG always delivers an efficient outcome.

Theorem

The SCG always produces an efficient assignment.

Proof:

Let S_1, S_2, ..., S_n and σ_1, σ_2, ..., σ_n and Φ_t be defined as in the proof of strategy-proofness. Let π^* be the assignment produced by SCG. We show that we cannot alter π^* without making one of the students worse off. Clearly, student σ_1 gets the room at the very top of σ_1's preference ordering, whether or not σ_1 and S_1 are the same. Therefore, we can't change the room assigned to σ_1 by π^* without making σ_1 worse off. Suppose we have proved that we cannot change the room assigned to σ_j by π^* for any $j \leq t$ without making one of the students σ_1, σ_2, ..., σ_t worse off. It follows that we cannot alter π^* without making one of the students σ_1, σ_2, ..., σ_t, σ_{t+1} worse off: if we are not to make one of the first $t + 1$ students worse off then we know that we can't change the room assigned by π^* to one of the first t students. Therefore, if we are not to make one of the first $t + 1$ students worse off, the set of rooms available for σ_{t+1} is precisely the same as the set available under the SCG. And σ_{t+1} gets the room he likes best in Φ_{t+1} under *SCA*, whether he is part of a cycle or not. We can't change σ_1's room assignment without making someone worse off, and we have just shown that if we can't change σ_t's assignment without making one of the first t students worse off then we can't change σ_{t+1}'s assignment without making one of the first $t + 1$ students worse off. Therefore, we can't modify π^* without making someone worse off.   ∎

Return to Example 9.21. Could one of the students have been assigned a better room (according to his or her own preferences) by making a different choice than the one that lead to π^*? Because A and B both wind up with the rooms that they prefer to every other room, neither could have profited by deviating from truthful revelation. There is nothing that C can do to change the set of rooms available when it is C's turn to choose, and because the SCG gives C his or her most-preferred room from that set individual C cannot profit by misrepresenting his or her preferences. The same can be said of D. Student E goes last, and there is nothing that E can do to get an earlier choice. Therefore, student E cannot profit by deviating from truthful preference revelation.

Source

The section is based on Abdulkadiroğlu and Sönmez (1999). Example 9.21 is from that article.

Links

Zhou (1990) proves that there is no strategy-proof allocation scheme that treats individuals symmetrically and always yields an efficient outcome. Chen and Sönmez (2002) test *SCNG* and SCG. The latter is significantly more likely to result in an efficient allocation in laboratory settings with human subjects. See also Chen and Sönmez (2004).

Problem Set

(1) We proved that if there are no existing tenants then the outcome of the *SCNG* is always efficient. The proof was quite simple. Why doesn't it work when some of the rooms *are* already occupied?

(2) For each possible priority ordering determine the assignment generated by the *SCNG* for Example 9.21 if none of the three rooms is originally occupied – the case of a freshman dorm, for instance.

(3) There are five students, *A, B, C, D*, and *E*, and five rooms, *V, W, X, Y*, and *Z*. Agent *A* already occupies room *Y*, and no other room has a tenant before the new room assignments are determined. The order in which students choose is determined by a random draw from a uniform probability distribution, and then the *SCNG* algorithm is employed. Specify a utility function for student *A* and preference orderings for the other students so that *A* decides not to participate in the lottery and the resulting outcome of the *SCNG* is inefficient for at least one priority ranking.

(4) For the case of five students and five rooms, specify the student preferences so that the SCG assigns all their most preferred rooms, regardless of how many rooms are occupied and who occupies them. Explain your answer.

(5) Work out the assignment for the SCG when the priority ranking is *EDCBA* and three of the rooms are already occupied – *W* by *B, X* by *C*, and *Y* by *D*. The preferences of the five students for the five rooms are given by Table 9.24.

(6) Repeat question 5 but with the priority ranking *ACEBD* instead of *EDCBA*.

(7) Modify *SCG1* so that when S_t chooses the room currently occupied by S_j and $j > 1$ then S_t and S_j change places in line. Show that truthful revelation of preference is not a dominant strategy for this modified algorithm.

9.5 KIDNEY TRANSPLANTS

End-stage renal disease, also called chronic kidney disorder, can be treated with dialysis or by transplanting another kidney into the patient. Transplanting is the better treatment method because it offers a greater probability of success. Moreover, dialysis can be exhausting. It is so time consuming that it prevents some patients from holding down a job.

Transplants depend on the availability of kidneys from either a cadaver or a live donor. Most transplanted organs are taken from cadavers, but a significant number are provided by live donors. There is a substantial gap between the demand for organs and the supply, and the gap is growing. There are black markets in kidneys, some of which are beyond dreadful.

We are born with two kidneys, but need only one. That makes it possible for a living individual to donate a kidney to someone with kidney disease who would die if a healthy organ were not transplanted. An organ from a cadaver can also be transplanted successfully if it is healthy, is a good match, and is harvested immediately after death. In 2015 there were over 100,000 patients in the United States on the waiting list for a transplant. Over 16,000 kidney transplants were performed in the US in 2008, and slightly over a third of these involved a live donor, with the remaining kidneys harvested from a cadaver. Every year about 6% of the people on the waiting list die before a kidney becomes available, and between 1% and 2% become too ill to qualify for a transplant.

In India the "donors" are often illiterate young women who don't fully understand the risks and who receive only a small fraction of the large sums paid by the recipients.

A kidney exchange program designed by economists Alvin Roth, Tayfun Sönmez, and Utku Ünver has vastly increased the number of lives saved through transplants. Their procedure was inspired by an algorithm for reassigning individuals to offices, so we'll start with that.

9.5.1 The Top Trading Cycle Algorithm

Each member of the economics department has an office, and no office is occupied by more than one person. There is general dissatisfaction with the current office assignment and the university administration will allow the professors to reassign themselves, provided that each department member endorses the new arrangement.

A meeting to discuss the possible assignments would be *very* time consuming: if there are five professors, there are 120 different office arrangements. With ten individuals there are 3,628,800 possible assignments. Can we devise a simple algorithm that takes as input each individual's preference ordering of the offices and delivers a new office assignment with the following properties: no individual is made worse off (the participation constraint), the new assignment cannot be improved upon (efficiency), and no one can gain by misrepresenting her preferences (strategy-proofness).

DEFINITION: *The Participation Constraint, Efficiency, and Strategy-Proofness*

Participation constraint: No individual is assigned an office that is less desirable – in terms of that individual's own preferences – than the office she currently occupies.

Efficiency: No other assignment would make at least one person better off without making someone worse off.

Strategy-proofness: No individual could benefit by submitting an ordering other than her true preference ordering.

A successful algorithm has these three properties whatever the initial assignment and whatever the individual preferences.

The following *Top Trading Cycle* algorithm does the job: each individual points to the office she likes best. If there is a *cycle* – with *A* pointing to the office currently occupied by *B* for instance, *B* pointing to the office currently occupied by *C, C* pointing to the office currently occupied by D, and D pointing to the office currently occupied by A – then each person *in the cycle* is assigned the office to which she pointed. That means that each person in the cycle moves to the office that she prefers above all others. What about individuals who are not part of a cycle? We start the algorithm again with a new set of individuals – those who were not part of a cycle, and hence did not receive a new assignment – and the offices that they currently occupy. When we apply the algorithm a second time there will be new cycles: someone who did not get an assignment in the first round but who pointed to an office that *was* assigned in the first round will have to point to a different office in round 2. (Offices that were assigned in round 1 are taken off the menu for round 2.) Anyone who is part of a round 2 cycle will get an assignment in round 2, namely the office that she pointed to in round 2. The algorithm proceeds in this way until all offices have been assigned. (What if Z is left at the end with no assignment? In that case only Z's current office will not have been assigned. In the final round that will be the only office on the menu, and hence that will be the office to which Z points. There is a one-person cycle.)

DEFINITION: *Cycle*

$X_1 \rightarrow X_2 \rightarrow X_3 \rightarrow \ldots X_{m-1} \rightarrow X_m \rightarrow X_1$ is a cycle if X_1 likes X_2's current office best, X_2 likes X_3's current office best, and so on. In general, X_t likes X_{t+1}'s office best for all $t \leq m-1$, and X_m likes X_1's office best. If X_j likes her current office better than any other we have the *trivial cycle* $X_j \rightarrow X_j$.

There *will be* a cycle: consider three individuals A, B, and C, and their offices. If A points to her own office then we have the cycle $A \rightarrow A$. Suppose that A points to B's office. If B points to A's office we have the cycle $A \rightarrow B \rightarrow A$. If B points to her own office then we obviously have a cycle. But suppose that $A \rightarrow B \rightarrow C$. If $C \rightarrow A$ we have the cycle $A \rightarrow B \rightarrow C \rightarrow A$. If $C \rightarrow B$ then $B \rightarrow C \rightarrow B$ is a cycle. The only remaining possibility is $C \rightarrow C$, a trivial cycle.

Theorem: Existence of a Cycle

If each person points to one and only one office there will be at least one cycle.

Proof:

Choose any individual, and let that person be designated X_1. If X_1 points to the office that she currently occupies then we have the cycle $X_1 \rightarrow X_1$. Otherwise, let X_2 denote the person occupying the office to which X_1 points. If $X_2 \rightarrow X_2$ we have a cycle. If $X_2 \rightarrow X_1$ then we have the cycle $X_1 \rightarrow X_2 \rightarrow X_1$. But if X_2 points to a third person, whom we will call X_3, we will have a *chain* $X_1 \rightarrow X_2 \rightarrow X_3$. We keep going in this fashion until we find a chain $X_1 \rightarrow X_2 \rightarrow X_3 \rightarrow \ldots X_{m-1} \rightarrow X_m \rightarrow$ such that $X_m \rightarrow X_j$ for some $j < 1$, in which case we have identified the cycle $X_j \rightarrow X_{j+1} \rightarrow X_{j+2} \rightarrow \ldots X_{m-1} \rightarrow X_m \rightarrow X_j$. But suppose there is a total of K individuals and offices, and we have exhausted them all, resulting in the chain $X_1 \rightarrow X_2 \rightarrow X_3 \rightarrow \ldots X_{K-1} \rightarrow X_K$, and $X_j \rightarrow X_i$ does not hold for any $j \leq K$ and $i < j$. But X_K must point to *some* office, and if it's not the office currently occupied by any other individual then X_K must point to her own office, in which case $X_K \rightarrow X_K$ is a cycle. There will always be at least one cycle, and there may be more than one. ■

DEFINITION: *Top Trading Cycle (TTC) Algorithm*

There is a given set of individuals along with their current offices. A new assignment of offices is generated by having each individual point to the office that she likes best. Then cycles are identified, and each member of a cycle is assigned to the office to which she pointed. Individuals and offices not assigned in this way comprise the starting point for a second application of the algorithm. The algorithm proceeds in this way until all individuals receive their new assignments.

Example 9.22 Nine Individuals and Nine Offices

The individuals are $A, B, C, D, F, G, H, J, K$. An office will be identified by the name of the individual currently occupying it. Figure 9.1 is the result of round 1: J likes A's current office best, A likes B's current office best, and so on.

There are two cycles in round 1: $B \rightarrow C \rightarrow D \rightarrow B$ and $F \rightarrow G \rightarrow F$. At the end of round 1, B gets C's current office, C gets D's office, and D gets B's office. And F and G switch offices.

Individuals J, A, H, and K did not receive an office assignment in round 1. Round 2 is a new application of the algorithm, but only with J, A, H, and K and their offices (Figure 9.2). Cycles are again identified and each member of a cycle gets the office that she "pointed to." To see how round 2 plays out, we need the individual preferences. They are given in Table 9.26, which does not display the entire ordering, but just enough to allow us to work out the new assignment. (Table 9.26 displays the most-preferred office of each of the nine individuals, allowing us to identify the cycles in round 1. It also displays the second choices of A and H, the two individuals whose first choices were an office that was assigned in round 1 but who did not themselves get a round 1 assignment.)

Individuals B, C, D, F, and G received their assignments in round 1. Therefore, only A, H, J, and K participate in round 2. The only cycle is $AHJA$ (Figure 9.2).

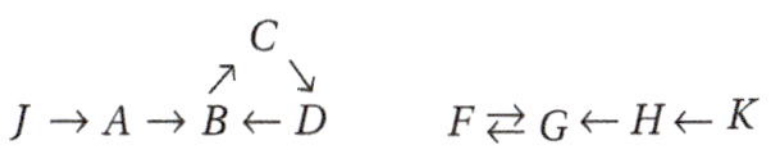

$$J \rightarrow A \rightarrow B \overset{\nearrow C \searrow}{\underset{}{\leftarrow D}} \qquad F \rightleftarrows G \leftarrow H \leftarrow K \qquad \qquad A \overset{\nearrow H \searrow}{\underset{}{\leftarrow J}} \leftarrow K$$

Figure 9.1 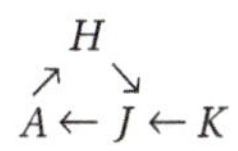   **Figure 9.2**

Table 9.26

A	B	C	D	F	G	H	J	K
B	C	D	B	G	F	G	A	F
H							J	

(*A* points to *H*, not *B*, because *B*'s office is no longer on the menu.) Each of those individuals gets a new assignment: *A* gets *H*'s current office, *H* gets *J*'s, and *J* gets *A*'s. Round 3 involves only *K* and *K*'s current office. Of all nine offices, *K*'s current office may or may not rank last in *K*'s preference ordering. But, of all of the offices currently available – only *K*'s current office in this example – *K*'s current office is the one that *K* likes best. We have a trivial cycle: *K* points to her present office, which will thus be her "new" match.

By checking individual preferences for Example 9.22, it's easy to confirm that no individual prefers her old office to her new office. We next prove that the Top Trading Cycle algorithm satisfies our three properties in general – however many individuals there are and whatever the individual preferences are.

Theorem

The Top Trading Cycle algorithm satisfies the participation constraint.

Proof:

If individual *N* gets her assignment in round *t* then *N*'s current office was not re-assigned in any previous round, otherwise *N* would have been part of a cycle in a previous round and would have received her new assignment prior to round *t*. Therefore, if *N* gets her new office in round *t*, her current office is one of the available ones. If *N* does not point to her current office, it's because there's another office – from the set of offices that have not yet been reassigned – that *N* likes better. Therefore, *N*'s new office cannot rank below her current office in her preference ordering.   ∎

Theorem

The Top Trading Cycle algorithm always yields an efficient assignment.

Proof:

Let R_1 be the set of individuals who received their assignments in round 1. Each of these gets the office she likes best. Therefore, we cannot change the room assignment of any one in R_1 without making that individual worse off.

For any round *t* let R_t denote the set of individuals who get their room assignment in round *t*. Suppose that we have proved that we can't change the room assignment of anyone in R_j, for any $j \leq t$, without harming someone who received her new assignment in one of the first t rounds. (An individual is harmed by a change if she prefers the old office to the new one.) It follows that we can't change the assignment of any person in R_j, for any $j \leq t + 1$, without harming someone who received her new assignment in one of the first $t + 1$ rounds, as we now show: If N gets her new assignment in round $t + 1$, then N gets the room she likes best of all the rooms currently occupied by the individuals in $R_{t + 1}$. Therefore, the only way to change N's assignment without making her worse off is to give her a room that the Top Trading Cycle algorithm allocated to someone in R_j for some $j \leq t$. But that, according to our supposition, will make some individual in R_k worse off for some $k \leq t$.

We have proved that if we can't change the assignment determined by the TTC of anyone in R_j for some $j \leq t$ without harming some individual who received her assignment in one of the first t rounds, then we can't change the assignment of anyone who received her assignment in one of the first $t + 1$ rounds without harming someone who received her assignment in one of the first $t + 1$ rounds. Because we have also proved that we can't change the assignment of anyone in R_1 without harming someone in R_1 our proof that the TTC algorithm always yields an efficient outcome is complete. (Start with $t = 1$, and increase t one round at a time until everyone has received a new room assignment.)   ∎

What about the possibility of manipulating the algorithm by submitting a preference ordering that is different from one's true ordering? Obviously, no individual in R_1 can benefit by misrepresenting her preferences because the TTC gives each member of R_1 her most-preferred room. But even a person who gets her new room assignment in the last round is unable to get a better room by contriving to get an assignment in an earlier round, as we now show.

Theorem
   The Top Trading Cycle algorithm is strategy-proof.

Proof:

Suppose that individual N receives her new room assignment in round $t > 1$. We show that she cannot benefit by misrepresenting her preferences. Individual N can't gain by getting an assignment *later* than round t because the set of available rooms would then be a subset of the rooms available in round t. (If an individual is not part of a cycle until round t she can't affect the assignments made prior to round t.) Suppose that she misrepresents her preferences in a way that gives her a room assignment in round t^* and $t^* < t$. Can N break into a cycle in round t^*? Suppose we have $X_1 \rightarrow X_2 \rightarrow X_3 \rightarrow \ldots X_{m-1} \rightarrow X_m \rightarrow X_1$ and $N \neq X_j$ for any $j \leq m$. None of the people in the cycle points to N so, no matter what preference ordering she submits, N cannot create a cycle involving some of these X_j by pointing to one of them. Is there another way that N can N create a cycle in round t^*? Yes, but not in a way that gives her a better room assignment that would result from truthful revelation. Suppose that $X_1 \rightarrow X_2 \rightarrow X_3 \rightarrow \ldots X_{m-1} \rightarrow X_m \rightarrow$ is a *chain* in round t^*

with $X_i \neq X_j$ for all distinct i and j and, say, $N = X_3$. Then if X_3 points to X_1 instead of X_4 we have the cycle $X_1 \rightarrow X_2 \rightarrow X_3 \rightarrow X_1$, in which case N is assigned to X_1 in round t^*. (Note that N cannot create a cycle involving X_j for any $j > 3$.) But the rooms of X_1, X_2, and X_3 would be available in round t under truthful revelation because none of them is part of a cycle in round t^* when $N (= X_3)$ reports truthfully. Therefore, none of their rooms would be assigned in round t^*. *Of the rooms available* in round $t^*+ 1$, X_2 would still be the first choice of X_1 and X_3 would still be the first choice of X_2. We can repeat this claim for every subsequent round until we get to round t: any room that N could get by misrepresenting her preferences would be on the menu in the round in which N would get her new assignment under truthful revelation, and hence could not be superior, according to N's true preferences, to the room that she would get by revealing those preferences truthfully.   ∎

9.5.2 Transplant Cycles

A patient has to be healthy enough to survive the transplant surgery, and the new kidney has to be compatible with the recipient. There has to be compatibility of both blood type and tissue. The four blood types are O, A, B, and AB. (The labels have to do with the presence or absence in the blood of two proteins, A and B. Type O blood has neither, and type AB has both.) A donor with O-type blood is compatible with anyone. An A is compatible with an A and an AB recipient. Bs are compatible Bs and ABs. An AB donor can give his kidney to an AB recipient only. Tissue compatibility is more subtle and is based on the possibility of tissue rejection by the recipient, which will occur if antibodies against the donor's tissue types form in the blood of the recipient. During childbirth a mother can be exposed to some of her husband's proteins carried by the child. If she develops antibodies to those proteins, her husband would not be tissue compatible, and his kidney would not be a good match for her, even if the two had the same blood type. (The probability of tissue incompatibility between two individuals *selected at random* has been estimated at about 11%.)

We postpone until the next section the discussion of transplanting kidneys from a cadaver, and the kinds of complex exchanges that are possible when A's spouse (who is a bad match for A) donates a kidney to B, and A receives a cadaver kidney. This section explores the possibility of exchanges of kidneys involving recipient-donor pairs in which each donor is a bad match for the patient she would like to benefit.

The simplest kind of exchange is bilateral. Patient P needs a new kidney and has a willing donor D, and potential recipient P' has a willing donor D'. But D is incompatible with P and D' is incompatible with P'. If D is a good match for P' and D' is a good match for P then each patient can receive a healthy kidney – P from D' and P' from D. Each of the four individuals gets his or her desired outcome. Donor D made a sacrifice that resulted in a new lease on life for P, the person that she wanted to help. Similarly, D' got the result that he wanted and that his sacrifice made possible. Recipient P is obviously far better off than when the only hope for a transplant was D's kidney, and similarly for P'.

The first kidney exchange in the US took place in 2000, and for a time bilateral exchanges were the only ones that the medical community would authorize. But many more patients can be helped if exchanges involving three or more patient–donor pairs are permitted, as the next two examples demonstrate.

Example 9.23 Only Two-Way Exchanges are Permitted

There are fourteen patient–donor pairs, and we number them 1 through 14. We also identify the blood type of each member of each pair. For instance, PAB_7 refers to the patient from pair 7 who has blood type AB, and DA_7 is the donor who arrived with patient 7 and she has blood type A. The donor of each of the first nine pairs has a blood type that is incompatible with his or her patient. These pairs are . . .

$(PA_1, DAB_1), (PB_2, DAB_2), (PO_3, DA_3), (PO_4, DA_4), (PO_5, DB_5), (PA_6, DB_6),$
$(PA_7, DB_7), (PA_8, DB_8), (PB_9, DA_9)$

Each patient in each of the remaining five pairs is tissue-incompatible with the donor who arrived with that patient. These pairs are . . .

$(PA_{10}, DA_{10}), (PA_{11}, DA_{11}), (PA_{12}, DA_{12}), (PB_{13}, DO_{13}), (PAB_{14}, DO_{14}).$

You can check each of the first nine pairs to confirm the blood incompatibility, but the tissue incompatibility of the last five is an artifact of the example. To keep things simple we assume that there is no tissue incompatibility between any patient and any donor who arrived with a different patient. With these fourteen patient–donor pairs, no more than four transplants can be arranged if only two-way exchanges are allowed. Here are four possibilities:

$DB_7 \rightarrow PB_9$ and $DA_9 \rightarrow PA_7$ (Donor 7 gives a kidney to patient 9, etc.)
$DA_{11} \rightarrow PA_{10}$ and $DA_{10} \rightarrow PA_{11}$
$DB_6 \rightarrow PB_{13}$ and $DO_{13} \rightarrow PA_6$
$DAB_1 \rightarrow PAB_{14}$ and $DO_{14} \rightarrow PA_1$

Example 9.24 Three-Way Exchanges are Also Possible

The fourteen patient–donor pairs are the ones of Example 9.23, with the same incompatibilities. It is now possible to give eleven patients a new kidney by implementing the following two-way exchange

$$DB_7 \rightarrow PB_9 \text{ and } DA_9 \rightarrow PA_7$$

and these three-way exchanges:

$DA_{10} \rightarrow PA_{11}$ and $DA_{11} \rightarrow PA_{12}$ and $DA_{12} \rightarrow PA_{10}$
$DO_{13} \rightarrow PO_3$ and $DA_3 \rightarrow PA_6$ and $DB_6 \rightarrow PB_{13}$
$DO_{14} \rightarrow PO_4$ and $DA_4 \rightarrow PA_1$ and $DAB_1 \rightarrow PAB_{14}$

Confirm that no patient receives a transplant from a donor with incompatible blood or tissue. Four patients receive a new kidney with the transplants of Example 9.23. If three-way exchanges are allowed that number increases by almost 200 percent, to eleven.

It's again the case that no patient receives a transplant from a donor with an incompatible blood type. Note that if only the pairs 3, 5, and 12 presented themselves for surgery no transplants could be performed if only bilateral exchanges were allowed.

Surprisingly, with a large population all of the potential transplants can be realized even if cycles are restricted to fewer than five patient–donor groups.

We now have a parallel to the room allocation problem of Section 9.5.1. The donor kidneys play the role of the rooms and the occupants are the patients awaiting a healthy kidney. Instead of a professor pointing to the room that he likes best, each patient points to the kidney that is the best match for him or her. (The patients themselves don't "point". The patient's medical team identifies the donor kidney that would be the best match for their patient.) Cycles are then identified and each patient in a cycle receives the kidney to which he or she pointed. (Patients in round 2 cycles will probably have to wait: the matches in those cycles are typically not good enough.) The resulting network of transplants is efficient: no subgroup can arrange their own kidney exchange to the benefit of every patient in the subgroup. It is also strategy-proof: a patient's medical team cannot give the patient a better match by pointing to a donor kidney that is not the best one for their patient.

9.5.3 Transplant Chains

Let's see how the availability of cadaver kidneys enhances the way that successful exchanges can take place. We must also recognize the presence of a significant number of *non-directed donors*. These are individuals who do not know anyone with chronic kidney disease, but seek to help someone in need.

A chain is a sequence of transplants involving patient-donor pairs as well as a patient who is not paired with a donor, and such that at least one patient receives a kidney from either a non-directed donor or a cadaver. There may even be one patient who receives a non-directed donor kidney and another who receives a cadaver kidney.

Example 9.25 A Chain with Four Transplants

There is one non-directed donor D_0, three patient-donor pairs, (P,D), (P',D'), (P'',D''), and one patient P_W who is first on the waiting list for a cadaver kidney and does not have a donor. D_0 is a good match for P, D is a good match for P', D' is a good match for P'' and D'' is a good match for P_W. None of the paired donors is a good match for the patient with whom she is paired. That leads to the following transplant chain:

$$D_0 \to P,\ D \to P',\ D' \to P'',\ D'' \to P_W.$$

A patient P and his paired donor may be content to have P go to the head of the queue for a cadaver kidney if there is a potential chain that does not promise a live kidney for P but leads to transplants of donor kidneys for others.

Surgeries involving *cycles*, such as $D \to P'$, $D' \to P''$, $D'' \to P$, are always performed simultaneously to avoid the tragedy that would result from D'' rene-

---

Example 9.26 A Chain Ending with the Cadaver Waiting List

There are three patient–donor pairs, (P,D), (P',D'), (P'',D''). D is a good match for P', D' is a good match for P'' but D'' is not a good match for P. The following chain would benefit all three patients: $D \to P'$, $D' \to P''$, and P is put at the top of the waiting list for a cadaver kidney.

---

ging on her promise to donate a kidney to P, having been notified that the kidney donated by D' has already been transplanted in P'', the patient that D'' sought to help. D would have given one of her kidneys to P' but D's sibling P is not going to benefit. *Chains* do not have that vulnerability.

In July of 2007 twenty-eight year old Matt Jones of Michigan started a chain of sixteen transplants by donating a kidney to a stranger in Phoenix. Over a *three year period*, sixteen transplants were performed, involving thirty-one (living) people. The last donor in the chain gave a kidney to someone on the waiting list for a cadaver kidney. That patient wasn't paired with a donor, and the chain ended (Roth, 2015, p.44).

Consider Example 9.26 once again. After nondirected donor D_0 gave his kidney to P in January the medical team searched for a patient for which D's kidney would be suitable. They found P', and the transplant of D's organ into P' took place in March. After the surgery, D' reneged on his promise to donate a kidney to a stranger. Patient P'' is bitterly disappointed, as is his sibling D''. But P'' is no worse off that he was before the chain was identified. He's back where he started, hoping for an implant from a cadaver or a chain in which he could become involved. D'' still has her kidney and thus has the potential for helping P'' by being part of a new chain (or a cycle).

Sources

The *TTC* algorithm is due to Shapley and Scarf (1974). The rest of the section is based on Roth (2015) and Roth et al. (2004). Examples 9.23 and 9.24 are from Sönmez and Ünver (2013). Roth et al. (2007) prove that with a large population all of the potential transplants can be realized even if cycles are restricted to fewer than five patient–donor groups.

Links

Sönmez and Ünver (2013) present a thorough discussion of the many sophisticated theorems on kidney exchanges. Su and Zenios (2006) and Votruba (2003) have other perspectives on kidney allocation. Blair and Kaserman (1991) argue that the supply of cadaver kidneys could be substantially increased by very simple (and ethical) changes in public policies and law.

Problem Set

(1) The top trading cycle algorithm satisfies the participation constraint, efficiency, and strategy-proofness. For each of the three properties design a different reassignment mechanism that doesn't satisfy it, but satisfies the other two.

(2) Prove that the *TTC* outcome of Example 9.22 is efficient however one completes the specification of the individual preferences.

(3) Suppose that the individual rankings of the offices are identical. Prove that the *TTC* algorithm does not put anyone in a different office from the one that she currently has.

(4) Suppose that there is a total of K individuals and offices. For each positive $m \leq K$ specify individual preferences so that there are exactly m cycles in round 1.

(5) For the data of Example 9.23 find other sets of bilateral exchanges that result in four transplants.

(6) For the data of Example 9.23 find other sets of exchanges that result in eleven transplants.

9.6   LUNG TRANSPLANTS

A person is born with two lungs. The right one has three lobes and the left has two. A healthy adult can sacrifice one of these lobes and remain active and healthy – but will have to stop running marathons. The sacrifice of two lobes exposes the donor to grave risks, and hence a lung transplant from living individuals requires two donors. The patient's diseased lungs are removed and each is replaced with a lobe from the right lung of one of the donors. Accordingly, the new lungs will be smaller than normal. They will get larger over time but new tissue will not develop. (New tissue *will* grow when a diseased liver is replaced by part of a donor's liver.) The recipient of a successful lung transplant will have significant limitations but can live a relatively normal life.

The lung donor's blood type must be compatible with that of the recipient. The probability that compatibility will be achieved when the search for a willing donor is confined to the patient's close circle of friends and relatives is lower for lung transplants than for kidney transplants because of the former's two-donor requirement. That makes the creation of a clearing house to facilitate lung *exchanges* that much more valuable. A lung exchange involving patients Alex and Zena occurs when one (or two) of the volunteers who expressed a willingness to donate to Alex have a lobe transplanted into Zena, and Alex receives a lobe from one (or two) of the volunteers who were willing to donate to Zena.

DEFINITION: *Two-Way Lung Exchange*

There are two patients, P_1 and P_2. Individual P_1 arrives with donors D and E, and P_2 arrives with donors F and G. A two-way exchange occurs when (i) D and E each donate a lobe to P_2 and F and G each donate a lobe to P_1, or (ii) D and F each donate a lobe to P_1 and E and G each donate a lobe to P_2.

Case (ii) would arise when one of P_1's willing donors is blood-type compatible with P_1 and the other is not, and only one of P_2's willing donors is compatible with P_1, and the incompatible P_1 donor is compatible with P_2, and the P_2 donor who does not give a lobe to P_1 is compatible with P_2. Before illustrating with an example we review blood-type compatibility.

The four blood types are O, A, B, and AB. (The labels have to do with the presence or absence in the blood of two proteins, A and B. Type O blood has neither, and type AB has both.) Donors with O-type blood are compatible with anyone. An A is compatible with both A and AB recipients. And Bs are compatible Bs and ABs. An AB donor can only give a lobe to an AB recipient.

If an AB donor were to give a lobe to a type A patient, the recipient's immune system, with antibodies to the B protein, would treat the AB tissue as an invader and attack it. If an A-type patient has two willing donors, with blood types O and A, then he or she will not be part of an exchange. Each of the donors is compatible with the patient. Note that an O-type patient can only receive a lobe from an O-type donor. The patient's immune system would attack an A protein and also a B protein.

A lung transplant also requires size compatibility: the donor must be at least as heavy as the recipient. We will ignore size compatibility to focus on the more complicated blood-type scenarios.

DEFINITION: *A Lung Exchange Candidate and an Exchange Pool*

A candidate arrives with two donors, and will be represented as a triple $X - Y - Z$, where X is the patient and Y and Z are his two donors. Each of the individuals will be identified by blood type, thus: $B_1 - B - A$, indicating that patient 1 has blood type B and two willing donors with blood types B and A. Then $A_2 - O - B$, is patient 2, with blood type A and two donors with blood types O and B. Obviously, $X - Y - Z$ is the same as $X - Z - Y$. An *exchange pool* is the set of triples that present themselves as candidates.

It will be obvious to anyone who remembers high school permutations and combinations that arranging lung exchanges when there are hundreds of needy patients will be far too time consuming without an efficient algorithm. The complexity of the task is reduced somewhat by the special status of AB and O blood types. (An AB can donate only to an AB patient, and an O patient can receive a lobe only from an O donor.)

Example 9.27 A Two-Way Exchange

Patients $B_1 - B - A$ and $A_2 - O - B$ will each have to participate in an exchange because each has an incompatible donor. In this case they comprise a successful two-way exchange with patient 1's donor A giving a lobe to patient 2 and 2's donor B giving a lobe to 1. (Patient 1's B donor gives a lobe to 1 and Patient 2's O donor gives a lobe to 2.)

Exchange Eligibility Theorem

Only six types of patients will participate in a two-way exchange:
$$A - A - B, A - O - B, A - B - B, B - B - A, B - O - A, \text{ and } B - A - A.$$

Proof:

An AB-type patient is compatible with any donor. Therefore, no AB patient is a candidate for *any* exchange. (Only patients who arrive with two donors are eligible for an exchange, and any AB patient with two donors already has two compatible donors.) The absence of AB patients in the exchange pool means that no patient with an AB *donor* is a candidate for any exchange. Therefore, there won't be any AB donors in the exchange pool. (No patient in the exchange is type AB, and thus no AB donor can be matched with any patient in the pool.) In symbols, if $X - Y - Z$ participates in an exchange we have $X \neq AB$, $Y \neq AB$, and $Z \neq AB$.

To show that no O-type patient can participate in a *two-way* exchange suppose to the contrary that $X - Y - Z$, and $O - V - W$ engage in a two-way exchange. If Y can donate to the O-patient then $Y = O$, in which case Y is also compatible with X. If Y cannot donate to O then Y must be compatible with X if X participates in the two-way exchange. (Every participant in an exchange receives two lobes. If O is in a two-way exchange with X, and Y is not compatible with O or X then O and X cannot both receive two lobes.) Similarly, Z must also be compatible with X. Therefore, X would not be part of an exchange with $O - V - W$ after all because X already has two compatible donors.

We have shown that any patient in a two-way exchange is either an A or B, and no donor in such an exchange can be an AB. That leaves the six cases listed in the hypothesis. (Recall that $X - Y - Z$ is the same as $X - Z - Y$.) ∎

Note that in a two-way exchange every A-type patient has at least one B donor, which means that an A patient must exchange with a B patient. (An A patient X cannot accept tissue from his B donor, nor can any other A patient accept tissue from X's B donor.) Similarly, a B patient must exchange with an A patient. The $A - B - B$ patients will have to exchange both donors, and hence can participate in a two-way exchange only with $B - A - A$. The economists Haluk Ergin, Tayfun Sönmez, and Utku Ünver have devised a simple algorithm that will maximize the number of two-way exchanges in any pool of patients. In other words, if exchanges can be no more complicated than two-way, the Ergin-Sönmez-Ünver algorithm maximizes the number of transplants.

Why would exchanges be limited to the two-way cases? Because even with a two-way exchange six separate surgeries are involved – the two patients and the four donors. And they must be performed simultaneously to eliminate the possibility that donor D, who arrived with patient P_1, reneges on his promise to donate a lobe to P_2 after P_1 had already received the transplant provided by one of the donors who arrived with P_2. A three-way exchange will require nine simultaneous surgeries! Although the first lung transplant using a *living* donor took place in 1990, and the first *kidney* exchange was performed in 2000, no lung exchanges have been performed anywhere in the world. However, the medical community initially resisted the idea of a kidney exchange. There is reason to hope that lung exchanges will gain acceptance. Accordingly, we briefly consider exchanges involving more than two patients.

Example 9.28 An Essential Three-Way Exchange

$B_1 - A - A$, $A_2 - A - B$, and $A_3 - A - B$ are the only patients in the pool. Patient 1 can participate in an exchange only if 2 and 3 are both involved because 1 needs two new donors. Moreover, patients 2 and 3 cannot implement a two-way exchange because each needs an additional lobe from an A type. Therefore, there will be no transplants unless there is a three-way exchange, with patients 2 and 3 each receiving a lobe from one of the A donors arriving with patient 1, who receives a lobe from each of the B donors.

Ergin, Sönmez, and Ünver have also devised an algorithm that allows both two-way and three-way exchanges. Subject to a modest assumption on the distribution of blood-type combinations in the pool, it maximizes the number of transplants that are possible, given the pool. They have also proved that no pool requires exchanges larger than six-way in order to identify an optimal matching. Our final example demonstrates that there *are* pools for which optimality requires a six-way exchange.

Example 9.29 An Essential Six-Way Exchange

The patients are:

$$A_1 - O - B \,\&\, B_2 - O - A \,\&\, B_3 - O - A \,\&\, O_4 - O - B \,\&\, O_5 - O - B \,\&\, O_6 - O - B$$

Figure 9.3 specifies the exchange. The arrow under a donor points to the name (i.e., number) of the patient who receives a lobe from that donor. To confirm that every patient receives two lobes check that every patient number appears under two different arrows.

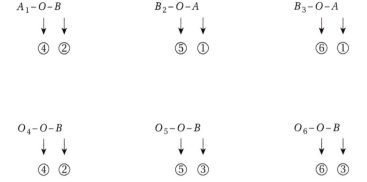

Figure 9.3

Why can't the six patients be accommodated by means of two (or three) smaller exchanges? Although patients 1 and 2 could obviously participate in a two-way exchange, the only way for *each* of the six patients to receive a transplant is to have a six-way exchange.

A six-way exchange is essential for the pool of Example 9.29

Unless there is a six-way exchange, one of the patients will be denied a transplant.

Proof:

None of the O patients can spare his O donor because there are three O patients who need a total of six O donors. (Remember, only an O donor is compatible with an O patient.) That requires the participation of patients 1, 2, and 3 if 4, 5, and 6 are each to have a successful transplant. Moreover, patient 1 can be successfully transplanted only if the A donors of 2 and 3 each contribute to A, because neither of 2 or 3's O donors can contribute to 1 without one of the O patients being denied a transplant. In other words, 1 must be in the same exchange as 2 and 3. And patient 4 must receive a lobe from one of the O patients of 1, or 2, or 3, and hence 1, 2, 3, and 4 have to be in the same exchange. Similarly, 1, 2, 3, and 5 have to be in the same exchange, and so do 1, 2, 3, and 6.   ∎

Ergin, Sönmez, and Ünver show that optimality can be achieved in any pool without employing exchanges that have more than six patients, provided that the pool satisfies their modest distribution assumption.

Source

This section is based on Ergin et al. (2017).

Links
See Roth (2015) for a discussion of the gradual acceptance of kidney exchanges by transplant physicians.

Problem Set
Specify all of the six-way exchanges that maximize the number of transplants for the pool of Example 9.29.

10

Networks

Networks can be tiny – your circle of very close friends, for instance. They can be vast, as in the case of the individuals and institutions connected to you and to each other through the world wide web. The internet has not only given us an extraordinary increase in the number of sources from which we can obtain information. It has also increased the value of that information, in part because of the great increase in the number of sources of information available to the compilers of any web site that you visit. (Of course, the web has also greatly increased the number of sources of *mis*information.) Until the arrival of the internet, an increase in the number of sources of information brought with it a substantial increase in the cost of widespread comparison shopping: one had to sacrifice a significant amount of time to visit rival retailers. By contrast, the web has vastly reduced the cost of acquiring information from any one source, and thus has made it possible to comparison shop extensively at almost no cost. (Transactions involving rare books have increased more than a hundred-fold since the advent of the internet, because search costs have virtually dropped to zero. In the previous century collectors of rare books had to wait for the arrival of annual catalogues. These catalogues were costly and infrequently updated because of the cost and the time commitment required of their compilers.)

Nathan Rothschild added millions to his fortune when the news of Wellington's victory over Napoleon at Waterloo reached him, via carrier pigeon, before any other stock trader (Malkiel, 2003, p. 196). The installation of a telegraph cable on the ocean floor in the nineteenth century allowed London to communicate with Australia in four days. It had taken seventy days by surface mail (Fulcher, 2004, pp. 82–83).

The internet may be the network that comes to mind first, but it is probably not the most important one. That is obviously the case in parts of the third world where there is no access to the web. Instead, networks that rely on information transmission by word-of-mouth are used to locate sources of safe drinking water, to provide access to birth control information, and for AIDS prevention campaigns, to name but a few crucial examples.

It is usually necessary to model the network that includes you and your close friends as a large network that includes the people you are connected to indirectly, such as a friend of a friend. Hence, it will also include a friend of a friend of a friend. Many of the people connected to your closest friends are unknown to you, but should be included in the network model because the information gleaned by a friend from one of her friends is indirectly available to you, although that second-hand information will typically not be as reliable as that which arrives directly from a friend.

The theoretical and empirical study of networks that began in the twentieth century has flourished in the new century. *Social and Economic Networks* by Matthew Jackson is perhaps the most valuable and influential of the introductory treatments (Jackson, 2008). It cites 675 articles and books on the subject. This explosion of interest is due in part to the fact that the analysis of network structure and its implications is fascinating, but more importantly to the fact that there are many public policy dilemmas that cannot be adequately analyzed without due regard for the ambient network. Research has centered on the question of how networks form and evolve, and how, and to what extent, the resulting network structure contributes to individual welfare generally.

Consider a recent program for providing microfinance to a set of forty-three villages in Karnataka, a state in southern India. (*Microfinance* involves making small loans on favorable terms to small business that would not otherwise have access to banking services.) A key step is the dissemination of information about the availability of the loans. How does the pattern of diffusion of information affect participation in the program? The relevant network for examining this question is one in which each household is linked to the households of kin, or those with which they exchange favors or advice, etc. Suppose one estimates the probability that a household will take advantage of the loan opportunity by means of a regression model in which the probability that a household will avail itself of microfinance is a function of household characteristics and the fraction of a household's friends and associates who participate in the program, without embedding the model in the appropriate network. The regression results will show that participation in the program by one's contacts has a significant effect on that probability. That simple approach fails to distinguish between cases in which information about the program did not reach arbitrary household *J* even though *J* has a number of friends who participated in the program, and cases in which information did reach *J* which nonetheless chose not to participate. When that distinction is made, by means of a properly formulated network model, the endorsement effect – having close friends who participate in the program – is no longer statistically significant. The first model appears to show that such participation is important, but the network model reveals that the transmission of information about the existence program is key, and that is obviously correlated with participation. The network model takes into account a family's *position* in the network, allowing one to identify a household *J* that is some "distance" from the household *H* that receives the information first, but who nonetheless has a high probability of receiving the information because *J* is in close contact with several households who themselves are in close contact with *H*. It is possible then to estimate the probability of a participating household passing the information on to its neighbors and the probability of an informed but non-participating household sharing the information. The former probability is about ten times greater than the latter. The straightforward regression analysis shows a statistically significant peer effect in part because a household is more likely to be informed about the program if it has neighbors who have taken advantage of it. The network model is much more likely to suggest successful policies for widespread dissemination of information than the straightforward regression model.

Recent research has uncovered a long list of social and economic phenomena that arise from network effects: Patterns of criminal activity, voting patterns, diffusion of innovations, purchase decisions, peer effects in school performance, the role of personal contacts in choosing which jobs to apply for, trade (the subject of Section 10.4), and research alliance among firms (the subject of Section 10.5), among others. The literature on social and economic networks is vast. This chapter merely scratches the surface.

The next section introduces the elements of formal network models. Section 10.2 analyses one family of network models – those for which the benefit that an agent derives from a given network depends on proximity to other agents. It gives some indication of how networks are evaluated, particularly from the standpoint of stability and efficiency. Section 10.3 is a brief detour to presents the basics of Cournot equilibrium, used in Sections 10.4 and 10.5.

Source
The discussion of microfinance in India is from Banerjee et al. (2013).

Links
Jackson (2008) is a thorough survey and introduction to the study of social and economic networks. Goyal (2007) is less comprehensive but also highly recommended. Useful surveys of the field include Jackson (2004, 2011, and 2014).

10.1 GRAPHS AND NETWORKS

10.1.1 Terminology
The individuals or institutions that are related to each other are represented as *nodes* on a graph. A node can even represent a single country. A node will be called an *agent* when we do not need to be specific, and is represented as a dot in the diagram. The relationship between two agents, say i and j, is represented diagrammatically by a line between nodes i and j. We use N to denote the set of all nodes, and g to represent a particular graph, as in Figure 10.1 for which $N = \{1, 2, 4, 5, 6, 7\}$. We say that i and j are *linked*, and that ij is a *link*, if the graph representing the network has a line from i to j. If there is no such line then i and j are not linked.

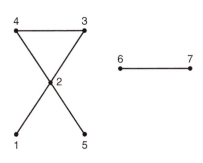

Figure 10.1

There are many applications for which the relationship is directed as when i and j are web pages and i has a link to j but j does not have a link to i. In that case the line connecting i and j is an arrow pointing at j.

However, this brief chapter will not cover many significant aspects of network theory. In particular we will ignore directed graphs.

DEFINITION: *Graphs and Networks*

A network is represented by a graph g on a set of nodes N with some (not usually all) pairs of nodes connected by a line. Two nodes that are so connected are said to be linked. We can represent g algebraically by setting $g_{ij} = 1$ if there is a link between i and j and $g_{ij} = 0$ if there is no such link. If $g_{ij} = 1$ we let $g - ij$ denote the new graph obtained from g by removing the link ij and leaving g otherwise unchanged. If $g_{ij} = 0$ we let $g + ij$ denote the new graph obtained from g by adding link ij without otherwise changing g.

Two nodes that are not linked may be *connected* in the sense that there is an agent h such that i and h are linked, and so are h and j. In that case we say that there is a *path* between i and j. A path can have more than two links. The network in Figure 10.1 has no link between 3 and 5, but there is a path from 3 to 5. In fact, there are two paths between 3 and 5: Node 3 is linked to 4 which is linked to 2 which is linked to 5. And 3 is linked to 2 which is linked to 5. The number of links in the shortest path between i and j is called the *distance* between i and j. In Figure 10.1 there is no path of any length between 6 and 5, or between 7 and 5. The subgraph consisting of $\{6, 7\}$ and the line connecting them is called a *component* of the entire graph. The following two properties characterize a component C of an arbitrary graph g:

(i) There is a path between every pair of nodes in C, and

(ii) if i belongs to C and ij is a link in g then j also belongs to C.

Note that (i) and (ii) imply that every path between two nodes of C involves only nodes from C. Note also that a component C of g is a *maximal* connected sub-network of g in the following sense: If we create C' from C by adding to C even one node from g that does not belong to C then C' is not connected. If g itself is a component of g we say that g is *connected*, in which case there is a path between any two nodes of g. Of course, if g is connected then g is its only component.

DEFINITION: *Path, Distance, Connectedness, and Component*

A path between two nodes i and j is a sequence $i_1, i_2, \ldots, i_k$ of nodes such that $i_1 = i$, $i_k = j$, and $i_h i_{h+1}$ is a link for $1 \leq h < k$. The distance between i and j is the number of links in the shortest path between i and j. (If ij is itself a link then the distance between i and j is 1.) A graph is connected if there is a path between any two distinct nodes. The graph g' for the set of nodes N' is a component of g if the N' is a subset of N, g' is connected, every link of g' is a link of g, and there is no link between any node in N' and one that does not belong to N'.

If the network has a link between nodes 5 and 2, a link between 2 and 3, and a link between 3 and 4 (as in Figure 10.1) we will let 5234 denote the path from 5 to 4 that uses those links. Of course, the distance between 5 and 4 in Figure 10.1 is not 3 because 524 is also a path between 5 and 4.

A *star* is a network in which one agent, the center, has a link to every other agent but no agent other than the center has a link to any agent other than the center. A star is a minimal connected network in the sense that no connected network has fewer links than the star, which has $n - 1$ links (Figure 10.2). The line of Figure 10.2 is also a connected network with $n - 1$ links, but unlike the star, if $n > 3$ there are pairs of agents that are more than two links from each other. If $n = 2$ or 3 every line is a star.

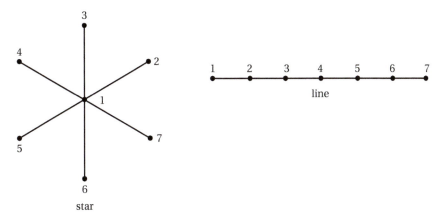

Figure 10.2

10.1.2 The Component Structure

Uncovering the component structure of a network is often the lever that we use to uncover fundamental properties of a particular family of networks. We begin our analysis with an algorithm for identifying components.

The Component Search Algorithm (CSA)

Arbitrarily choose some agent in N, and call this agent #1. If 1 is not linked to any other member of N, then $\{1\}$ is a component of the network. Otherwise, arbitrarily choose some agent that is linked to 1 and call it node #2. Continue in this fashion: at stage t we will have a set $J_t = \{1, 2, \ldots, t\}$ of t agents such that each member of J_t is linked to at least one other member of J_t. If every agent in N who is linked to some member of J_t also belongs to J_t then we stop. If there is some agent in N, say $t + 1$, who is not in J_t but is linked to some member of J_t let J_{t+1} denote the set $\{1, 2, \ldots, t, t + 1\}$. Because N is finite we will reach a stage T, the *terminal stage*, such that each member of J_T is linked to at least one other member of J_T, and there is no agent in N who is linked to some member of J_T but does not itself belong to J_T.

Theorem

   J_T, *the output of the CSA, is a component of the network.*

Proof:

We merely have to show that there is a path entirely within J_T from any member of J_T to any other member of J_T. (By definition of the terminal stage, no node not belonging to J_T is linked to a member of J_T.) Obviously there is a path between 1 and 2 that remains in $\{1, 2\}$. Suppose that we have established that there is a path between any two members of J_t that remains in J_t. We want show that that implies that there is a path between any two members i and j of J_{t+1} that remains in J_{t+1}. That is certainly the case if i and j are both in J_t. Suppose that $j = t + 1$. Then there is a link between h and $t+1$ for some h in J_t. Then there is a path π from i to h that is entirely within J_t, and hence entirely within J_{t+1}, because both are in J_t. It follows that there is a path π' between i and $t + 1$ that is entirely within J_{t+1}: Just add the link from h to $t+1$ to π. We have established that J_t must be connected for each $t \leq T$, and hence J_t is connected, which means that it is a component of the network. ∎

Component Lemma

If $T < n$ then the network has at least two components, where T is the final stage of any application of the CSA, and n is the number of nodes in the network. If a network has only one component it must have at least $n-1$ links.

Proof:

J_T is a component, and if $T < n$ there is some j belonging to N but not to J_T. With j as the first node apply the CSA to find the component C containing j. (It may be $\{j\}$.) No member of C has a link to a member of J_T, otherwise the CSA would have stopped at stage T. In other words, C is a component of the network.

If there is only one component then $T = n$. At the first stage the CSA identifies one link between two nodes. At each stage t an additional link is identified, and that link does not belong to any previous stage because it involves a node that was not employed at any previous stage. Therefore, the terminal stage T has identified $T-1$ links. ∎

Note that a line has exactly $n-1$ links, as does a star (Figure 10.2).

10.1.3 Efficiency and Stability

An agent will receive a *payoff* from a particular network, depending on the nature and number of the links involving that agent. Some networks also provide a payoff to an agent that also depends on the paths leading from that agent, as when one obtains information from a friend of a friend – information that may be discounted when it has traveled along two or more links. We let $u_i(g)$ denote the payoff to i from network g.

Let $\sum u_i(g)$ denote the sum of the payoffs over all agents. Given a set of nodes N the network g is efficient if there is no other network g' on N that gives one agent a higher payoff than g and every agent at least as high a payoff as g. It is standard in network theory to use the term efficient more narrowly to refer to a network that maximizes the total payoff. Of course, maximization of the total payoff always yields an efficient outcome (Section 1.4 of Chapter 1). This book applies the term *TU-efficient* to a network that maximizes the total utility (or payoff).

DEFINITION: *TU-Efficient Network*

Given the set of nodes N, the network g on N is TU-efficient if $\sum u_i(g) \geq \sum u_i(g')$ for every network g' on N.

If a connected network g has n nodes and exactly $n-1$ links then either g is a star or else there is a pairs of nodes that are at a distance greater than 2 from each other. To illustrate, suppose $n = 3$. If g is connected it is either a triangle or a star. ($N = \{1,2,3\}$.) Suppose that 12 is a link. If the network does not include 23 it must include 13 because there is a path from 1 to 3. Therefore, if it does not include 23 it is a star with 1 at the center. If the network includes 12 and 23 then it either includes 31, in which case it is a triangle, or else it does not include 31, in which case it is a star with 2 at the center. When $n = 3$ a triangle has n links and a star has $n-1$ links.

Lemma on Connected Networks

If g is a connected network with n nodes and exactly $n-1$ links, and each node is at most distance 2 from any other node, then g is a star.

Proof by Induction:

We know that the claim is true if $n = 3$, because in that case a connected network is either a star or a triangle and the latter has three links. Consider the following claim:

$H(n)$: any connected network with n nodes and exactly $n-1$ links is a star if each node is at most distance 2 from any other.

We conclude the proof by showing that $H(n-1)$ implies $H(n)$.

The first step is to establish that if every node in a network g has at least two links then g must have at least n links. Suppose that g has fewer than n links. We show that some node has less than 2 links. Let L denote the set of nodes with less than two links. If 1 has no links then 1 belongs to L. If 1 is linked, say with 2, and 12 is the only link involving 2 then 2 belongs to L. If 2 has a second link, say with 3, but 23 is the only link involving 3 then 3 belongs to L. We continue in this fashion, extending the path 123. If we reach a stage $123 \ldots j-1, j$ such that $j-1, j$ is the only link involving j then we will have found a member of L. Otherwise, we establish that the $n-3$ links 12, 23, 34, $\ldots$, plus the link between $n-2$ and $n-1$ in addition to the link between $n-1$ and n, constitutes a path. That path has $n-1$ links. But g has fewer than n links. Therefore, 12 must be the only link involving 1. It follows that that if every node in a network g has at least two links then g must have at least n links.

Suppose that $H(n-1)$ is true. Given network g with n nodes and exactly $n-1$ links there must be a node, call it α, that has only one link, say $\alpha\beta$. Then $g-\alpha\beta$ is a star because it has exactly $n-1$ nodes and exactly $n-2$ links. (Although α is a node in $g-\alpha\beta$ we can ignore it because it is not linked to any other member of $g-\alpha\beta$.) If β is the center of $g-\alpha\beta$ then g is a star with center β. If β is not the center of $g-\alpha\beta$ then β is linked to the center, which we call λ. Because $n \geq 4$ there is some node γ that is different from α, β, and λ. The distance from α to γ is 3, contrary to our hypothesis. (Because $g-\alpha\beta$ is a star the only path from α to γ is $\alpha\beta\lambda\gamma$.) It must be the case that β is the center of $g-\alpha\beta$, and hence g itself is a star. This completes the proof by induction: The claim $H(n)$ is true for $n = 3$, and if it is true for one value of n it is true for $n + 1$. ∎

The lemma also applies to components of a network because a component is a maximal connected sub-network: if C is a component with k nodes and exactly $k-1$ links, and each node of C is at most distance 2 from any other node in C, then C is a star.

Networks evolve as agents (represented by nodes) create and eliminate links. We typically expect this process to reach a stage at which no agent (represented by a node) has an incentive to eliminate a link, and there is no pair of agents who are not linked but could mutually benefit by becoming linked. In that case we say that the current network is stable. The test for stability is different from the test for efficiency: if i receives a higher payoff from $g-ij$ than from g, and g is the current network, agent i has an incentive to break the link ij. That could result in a lower payoff for j. Even if j also benefits from the elimination of ij it is possible that other agents benefitted indirectly from that link and are adversely affected by its elimination. The test that is used for network stability is appropriate in contexts where an individual has the right to break a link to another agent regardless of its effect on others. It also implicitly assumes that two agents can form a link if it is in their mutual interest to do so - regardless of its effect on others.

Nash equilibrium does not fully capture what we mean by *network* stability. Consider the simplest case: two agents who would each benefit by being linked. That link constitutes a Nash equilibrium because an individual would see his payoff fall (to zero) if he unilaterally broke the link. But the empty network is also a Nash equilibrium if the consent of both agents is required for link formation. No individual could benefit by acting alone because link formation requires a move by both of the agents in question. Network models are employed when we want to incorporate the effects of communication among individuals, and we assume that if a pair of agents can mutually benefit, net of any connection costs, by becoming linked they will exchange information and stake the steps necessary to form the link.

We say that g is *pairwise stable* if there is no pair of agents i and j who are not linked but who would both benefit by being linked and there is no pair of linked agents i and j such that either i or j would benefit if the link were severed.

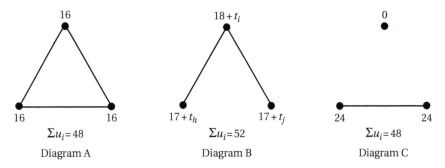

Figure 10.3

DEFINITION: *Stable Network*

The network g on N is pairwise stable if for all distinct i and j in N such that $g_{ij} = 0$ we have

$$u_j(g + ij) < u_j(g) \text{ if } u_i(g + ij) > u_i(g)$$

and for all i and j in N such that $g_{ij} = 1$ we have

$$u_i(g) \geq u_i(g - ij) \text{ and } u_j(g) \geq u_i(g - ij).$$

This definition is appropriate only for models for which mutual consent is required for a link to be forged or sustained. In other words, if one member of a pair of linked agents can increase his or her payoff by breaking the link, the other agent is unable to prevent that from happening. And if a link with i would increase the payoff to j the link cannot be formed without the consent of i, consent that would presumably not be forthcoming if the link would reduce i's payoff.

Example 10.1 Incompatibility of TU-Efficiency and Pairwise Stability

$n = 3$. All of the possible networks, except the empty one, are represented by Figure 10.3. The number at each node specifies the payoff of the agent represented by that node for the network represented by the diagram. (All links are formed in network A and each agent gets a payoff of 16.) Each diagram represents six networks, depending on where we place the numbers 1, 2, and 3, which are the names of the agents. Diagram B includes the possibility of transfers t_h, t_i, and t_j. Feasibility requires that $t_h + t_i + t_j = 0$. Set $t_h = t_i = t_j = 0$ initially. Network B is the only TU-efficient one, with total utility of 52. Total utility is 48 for A and for C. But B, a star, is not pairwise stable: If agent i, the center, breaks one of the links then i's payoff increases from 18 to 24. Can we specify transfers t_h, t_i, and t_j so that B is stable? It will not be stable if h and j have an incentive to form the link hj, resulting in A at which h and j each have a payoff of 16. Therefore, pairwise stability of B requires

$$17 + t_h \geq 16 \text{ and } 17 + t_j \geq 16. \text{ Equivalently, } t_h \geq -1 \text{ and } t_j \geq -1.$$

Pairwise stability of B also requires $18 + t_i \geq 24$ because agent i, the center of the star B, receives a payoff of 24 (Diagram C) if one of B's links is broken. (Remember, C represents six networks; one for each assignment of the agents to the three nodes.) Therefore, $t_i \geq 6$ if B is stable. But now we have $t_h + t_i + t_j \geq -1 - 1 + 6 = 4$, which is infeasible.

Note that the payoffs for the networks of Example 10.1 are partly the result of externalities: the payoff to agent i when he or she is linked to h and also to j is different in the presence of the link hj than in a network that includes ih and ij but not hj.

Link

The first two chapters of Jackson (2008) are a comprehensive introduction to the terminology and elements of network analysis.

Problem Set

(1) Prove that if every node of g has exactly one link then n is even and g has a total of $\frac{1}{2}n$ links.

(2) Prove that if every node of g has at least two links then g has at least n links.

(3) Prove that a star is a minimal connected network in the sense that no other connected network has fewer than $n-1$ links.

(4) Prove that g is a minimal connected network if and only if for every link ij of g the network $g-ij$ is not connected.

(5) Prove that if $n = 3$ the line and the triangle are the only connected networks.

(6) Suppose that C is a subgraph of g and that for every link ij of g the node i belongs to C if and only if j belongs to C. Prove that if g is connected then g itself is its only component.

10.2   DISTANCE-BASED PAYOFFS

The contribution an agent makes to the welfare of someone else is typically greater, the shorter the distance between the two. The simplest way to capture this to let b_t denote the payoff to agent i from another agent j who is at the end of the path from i to j and the shortest path between i and j has t links. Then b_t is positive for each t and $b_t > b_{t+1}$ for all t. There is a cost $c > 0$ of forming a link and both of the linked agents pay that cost, which is the same for all pairs of agents. A special case is obtained by setting $b_t = \delta_{t-1}$ for all $t > 1$, where δ is a given number δ such that $0 < \delta < 1$.

DEFINITION: *The Distance-Based Payoff Model*

The model is defined by the parameters b_t (for $t = 1, 2, \ldots$) and c. The payoff u_i to an agent i with exactly k links is $k(b_1 - c)$ plus, for each $t > 1$,

$b_t \times$ the number of agents at distance t from agent i.

When necessary we will write $u_i(g)$ to identify the network for which the individual payoffs are calculated.

Example 10.2 Distance-Based Payoffs for Figure 10.1

Agent 1 has one link and is distance 2 from 3, 4, and 5. Therefore, $u_1 = b_1 - c + 3b_2$. Similarly, $u_5 = b_1 - c + 3b_2$. Agent 3 has two links (34 and 32) and is distance 2 from 1 and from 5. Therefore, $u_3 = 2(b_1 - c) + 2b_2$. Similarly, $u_4 = 2(b_1 - c) + 2b_2$. Finally, $u_2 = 4(b_1 - c)$ and $u_6 = (b_1 - c) = u_7$. Total utility, $\sum u_i$, is $12(b_1 - c) + 10b_2$.

10.2.1 Efficiency

Given the set of nodes N, the network g on N is *TU-efficient* if $\sum_{i \in N} u_i(g) \geq \sum_{i \in N} u_i(g')$ for every network g' on N (Section 10.1.3).

Let g_0 denote the *empty network*, which has no links. Every pair of nodes is linked in the *complete network* which we denote by g_C. Let g_S denote a *star network*. (Given a set of n nodes, all stars will have the same shape, but different nodes at the center.) Recall that $\sum u_i(g)$ denotes the sum of utilities over all nodes i of the network g. Obviously $\sum u_i(g_0) = 0$. And $u_i(g_C) = (n-1)(b_1-c)$ for all i, which means that $\sum u_i(g_C) = n(n-1)(b_1 - c)$.

To calculate $\sum u_i(g_S)$ assume that node 1 is the center of the star. Therefore each $i \neq 1$ is connected to 1 but not to any other node. We have $u_1(g_S) = (n - 1)(b_1 - c)$. For $i > 1$ there is a link to 1 and a path of length 2 to any other $j > 1$. Then

$$u_2(g_S) = b_1 - c + (n - 2)b_2$$

and $u_i(g_S) = u_2(g_S)$ for all $i > 2$. Therefore, to calculate $\sum u_i(g_S)$ we multiply $u_2(g_S)$ by $(n - 1)$ and add $(n - 1)(b_1 - c)$.

Therefore,

$$\sum u_i(g_S) = (n - 1)(b_1 - c) + (n - 1)[b_1 - c + (n - 2)b_2] \text{ or}$$
$$\sum u_i(g_S) = 2(n - 1)[b_1 - c + \tfrac{1}{2}(n - 2)b_2] \tag{1}$$

In the distance-based payoff model only star networks are TU-efficient, apart from the two extreme cases for which either the empty network is the only TU-efficient one, because the cost of forming a link is high relative to the benefits, or the complete network is the only TU-efficient one, because the cost of forming a link is low relative to the benefits.

Efficiency Theorem for Distance-Based Payoffs

(1) *The complete network is the only TU-efficient one if $b_2 < b_1 - c$.*

(2) *The empty network is the only TU-efficient one if $b_1 + \frac{1}{2}(n-2)b_2 < c$.*

(3) *If $b_1 - b_2 < c < b_1 + \frac{1}{2}(n-2)b_2$ a star is the only TU-efficient network.*

Proof:

Suppose that $b_2 < b_1 - c$. Because $b_t < b_2$ for all $t > 2$ we have $b_t < b_1 - c$ for all $t > 1$. If i and j are not linked in g then we can create the network $g+ij$ by adding the link ij. The utility of i will increase by at least $b_1 - c - b_2$, which is positive, and the utility of j will also increase by at least $b_1 - c - b_2$. This follows from the fact that u_i and u_j each increase by $b_1 - c$ when we link them, but if g has a path between i and j then we also subtract b_t if the shortest path between the two had length t. For every node h different from i and j the addition of the link ij cannot reduce u_h: either u_h does not change, because the addition of ij does not shorten the length of the shortest path from h to any other node, or it increases by $b_s - b_t$ every time we replace some path of length t with a path of length s for some $s < t$. Therefore, $\sum u_i(g+ij) > \sum u_i(g)$. We can continue increasing total utility by adding links. Hence, the complete network is the only TU-efficient one when $b_2 < b_1 - c$.

We assume that $b_2 > b_1 - c$ for the remainder of the proof. To prove 2 and 3 we suppose that C is a component of network g. We will show that if C has more than one node and it is not a star then we can increase total utility by modifying the network to make the set of nodes in C comprise a star, while leaving the network unchanged outside of C. (Total utility will increase but it will not necessarily be positive.)

Let k denote the number of nodes in C. Then C has a total of $k(k-1)/2$ pairs of nodes. (There are k ways to choose the first member of a pair, and having chosen it there are $k-1$ ways to choose the second member of the pair. This gives a total of $k(k-1)$ *ordered* pairs. But $\{i, j\}$ is the same pair as $\{j, i\}$, so there are $\frac{1}{2}k(k-1)$ two-element subsets of C.) Suppose that C has m links. These links contribute $2m(b_1 - c)$ to total utility. (If i and j are linked then $(b_1 - c)$ is counted once in u_i and again in u_j.) And because C has m links there are $\frac{1}{2}k(k-1) - m$ pairs of nodes that are not linked and hence are connected by a path of length 2 or more. If i and j are linked, that link adds $2(b_1 - c)$ to total utility. If the distance t between i and j is greater than 2 then the path between those two nodes adds $2b_t$ to total utility: we add b_t for u_i and again for u_j. Therefore, if we let U_C represent the sum of the individual utilities over C for the given network g we have

$$U_C \leq 2m(b_1 - c) + [k(k-1) - 2m]b_2. \qquad [2]$$

(Because $b_t < b_2$ for $t > 2$ the right-hand side of [2] overstates U_C when the distance t between i and j is greater than 2 for some pair of nodes in C.)

A star network on C that includes all the nodes of C, but only the nodes of C, will have a total utility of

$$S_C = 2(k-1)[b_1 - c + \tfrac{1}{2}(k-2)b_2] \qquad\qquad [3]$$

obtained from [1] by substituting k for n. Then

$$S_C - U_C \geq 2[m - (k-1)][b_2 - (b_1 - c)] \qquad\qquad [4]$$

which is derived by subtracting the right-hand side of [2] from [3] and simplifying. The Component Lemma from Section 10.1.2 establishes that $m \geq k - 1$. (Set $k = n$ in the statement of the lemma, where k is the number of nodes and m is the number of links.) When $b_2 > b_1 - c$ and $m > k - 1$ both terms on the right-hand side of [4] will be positive, and hence $S_C > U_C$.

If $m = k - 1$ and C is not a star then, by the lemma on connected networks, at least one pair of nodes in C are at a distance greater than 2 from each other. In that case the right-hand side of [2] is strictly greater than U_C because b_2 will overstate the value of a path in at least one case. It follows that $S_C > U_C$ if $m = k - 1$ and C is not a star assuming that $b_2 > b_1 - c$.

We have established that when $b_2 > b_1 - c > 0$ and g is TU-efficient then each component of g with more than one node is a star.

We next rule out the possibility that a TU-efficient network can have two components if both have more than one node. That will imply that a TU-efficient network is either a star or the network in which each component is a single node. (Of course, if each component is a single node then the network is empty.)

Suppose that C_1 and C_2 are two different components of g with k_1 and k_2 nodes respectively, and at least one of them is a star. We will show that total utility will increase if we combine these components into a single star with $k_1 + k_2$ nodes. We can assume that $k_1 \geq k_2$. (If $k_2 > 1$ also holds, and g is TU-efficient then, by the argument above, both C_1 and C_2 are stars.) Let S^+ denote the sum of the utilities over the two components. (Recall that a component of a network has no links from the component to nodes outside of the component, and hence the utility of a node in the component is independent of the network outside of the component.) Using [1] again, and substituting k_j for n we get

$$S^+ = 2(k_1 - 1)[b_1 - c + \tfrac{1}{2}(k_1 - 2)b_2] + 2(k_2 - 1)[b_1 - c + \tfrac{1}{2}(k_2 - 2)b_2].$$

(If C_2 is not a star then $k_2 = 1$ and thus C_2 contributes nothing to S^+.) Simplify by letting α denote $b_1 - c$ with β representing $\tfrac{1}{2}b_2$. Then

$$\tfrac{1}{2}S^+ = (k_1 - 1)[\alpha + (k_1 - 2)\beta] + (k_2 - 1)[\alpha + (k_2 - 2)\beta].$$

Now create two new stars by removing one node from C_2 and adding it to C_1, resulting in one star with $k_1 + 1$ nodes and another with $k_2 - 1$ nodes. Let S^* denote the sum of the utilities over the two new stars.

$$\tfrac{1}{2}S^* = k_1[\alpha + (k_1 - 1)\beta] + \max\{0, (k_2 - 2)[\alpha + (k_2 - 3)\beta]\}.$$

Then $\tfrac{1}{2}S^* - \tfrac{1}{2}S^+ \geq 2(k_1 - k_2 + 1)\beta = (k_1 - k_2 + 1)b_2$ after simplifying. Because b_2 is positive and $k_1 \geq k_2$ the number $(k_1 - k_2 + 1)$ is positive, establishing that $S^* > S^+$. We have increased total utility. We can continue in this fashion, moving nodes into the larger component and increasing utility. This will end when the two components

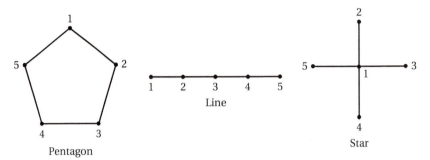

Figure 10.4

have been transformed into a one-star component. We can continue in this way until we have a network which is itself a star. But we have not shown that this star network has more utility than the network in which each component is a single node. The latter has a total utility of zero. Therefore, we have shown that when $b_2 > b_1 - c > 0$, if the star network has positive total utility then it is TU-efficient, but if it has negative total utility then the only TU-efficient network is empty.

The final question is, "When does the star network have negative total utility?" From [1] we have

$$\sum u_i(g_S) = 2(n-1)[b_1 - c + \tfrac{1}{2}(n-2)b_2].$$

Therefore, if $n > 1$ then $\sum u_i(g_S)$ is positive if and only if $b_1 - c + \tfrac{1}{2}(n-2)b_2 > 0$, which is equivalent to $b_1 + \tfrac{1}{2}(n-2)b_2 > c$. Therefore, we can state that if $b_1 - b_2 < c < b_1 + \tfrac{1}{2}(n-2)b_2$ then star networks are the only TU-efficient ones, but if $b_1 + \tfrac{1}{2}(n-2)b_2 < c$ only the empty network is TU-efficient. ∎

Note that if $n > 3$ a line cannot be TU-efficient, nor can any graph that is not a star and is neither complete nor empty.

Example 10.3 Total Utility of the Star, Pentagon, Line, and Complete Networks for n = 5

$n = 5$, $b_1 = 4$, $b_2 = 4-\delta$ (for $0 < \delta < 2$), $b_3 = 2$, $b_4 = 1$, and $c = 3$. We calculate total utility for the complete network and the three networks of Figure 10.4.

Complete network: $u_1 = 4(b_1 - c) = 4(1) = 4$. Therefore, $\sum u_i = 5u_1 = 20$.

Star with 1 at the center: $u_1 = 4(b_1 - c) = 4$ and $u_2 = b_1 - c + 3b_2 = 1 + 3(4-\delta) = 13-3\delta$.

Hence, $\sum u_i = u_1 + 4u_2 = 56-12\delta$.

Pentagon: $u_1 = 2(b_1 - c) + 2b_2 = 2(1) + 2(4-\delta) = 10-2\delta$ and $\sum u_i = 5u_1 = 50-10\delta$.

Line : $u_1 = u_5 = b_1 - c + b_2 + b_3 + b_4 = 1 + 4 - \delta + 2 + 1 = 8 - \delta$.

$u_2 = u_4 = 2(b_1 - c) + b_2 + b_3 = 2(1) + 4 - \delta + 2 = 8 - \delta$, and

$u_3 = 2(b_1 - c) + 2b_2 = 2(1) + 2(4 - \delta) = 10 - 2\delta$. Then

$$\sum u_i = 2u_1 + 2u_2 + u_3 = 42 - 6\delta.$$

Note that the parameters of this example satisfy $b_1 - b_2 < c < b_1 + \frac{1}{2}(n-2)b_2$, the condition that implies that a star is the only TU-efficient network. In fact, because $c < b_1$ for the given parameters the condition will be satisfied for any value of n. Note also that $\delta < 2$ implies that $56 - 12\delta$ exceeds both $50 - 10\delta$ and $42 - 6\delta$.

The next example revisits the four networks of Example 10.3 with a different set of parameters. In fact we have $c > b_1$, which means that individuals can have positive utility only if distant associations provide a big enough payoff to offset the loss incurred when a link is established.

Example 10.4 Total Utility of the Star, Pentagon, Line, and Complete Networks When $b_1 < c$

$n = 5$, $b_1 = 3$, $b_2 = 2$, $b_3 = 1$, $b_4 = \frac{1}{2}$, and $c = 4$. Three of the networks are given by Figure 10.4.

Complete network: $u_1 = 4(b_1 - c) = 4(-1) = -4$. Therefore, $\sum u_i = 5(-4) = -20$.

Star with 1 at the center: $u_1 = 4(b_1 - c) = -4$ and $u_2 = b_1 - c + 3b_2 = -1 + 3(2) = 5$. Hence, $\sum u_i = u_1 + 4u_2 = 16$.

Pentagon: $u_1 = 2(b_1 - c) + 2b_2 = 2(-1) + 2(2) = 2$ and $\sum u_i = 5u_1 = 10$.

Line : $u_1 = u_5 = b_1 - c + b_2 + b_3 + b_4 = -1 + 2 + 1 + \frac{1}{2} = 2\frac{1}{2}$.

$u_2 = u_4 = 2(b_1 - c) + b_2 + b_3 = -2 + 2 + 1 = 1$, and

$u_3 = 2(b_1 - c) + 2b_2 = 2(-1) + 2(2) = 2$. Then $\sum u_i = 2u_1 + 2u_2 + u_3 = 9$.

Note that we still have $c < b_1 + \frac{1}{2}(n-2)b_2$ in this case, and hence stars are the only TU-efficient networks. But none is stable. The center agent can increase its payoff by breaking its link with another agent, a consequence of the fact that link formation reduces utility by 1 *and* the center does not benefit from another agent's links because other agents are linked only to the center. It would not be correct to say that in the case of a star network all of the costs of network formation are borne by the center because both agents pay c when they form a link. But it is the case that when c exceeds b_1 the center of any star will have an incentive to break links. With the parameters of Example 10.4 no agent $i > 1$ can gain from breaking its link with the center because of the indirect benefit received through the center's links with other agents.

10.2.2 Stability

The test of stability employed in this chapter is appropriate for networks that give an agent – whether a person or firm or country – the right to unilaterally sever a link if that link ceases to be of benefit to that agent. It also presumes that two agents who would mutually benefit by linking would have the right to do so. (Recall the formal definition in Section 10.1.3.)

Example 10.5 Stability Calculations for Examples 10.3 and 10.4

For the parameters of Example 10.3:

Complete network: If agent 1 breaks the link 12 then $\Delta u_1 = -(4-3)+4-\delta = 3-\delta$ which is positive. (The link 12 is removed but 1 is still connected to 2 via 132.) The complete network is not stable.

Star: If the center 1 breaks the link 12 then $\Delta u_1 = -(4-3) < 0$. (No path of length 2 or more is added.) If agent 2 breaks the link 12 then there is no path from 2 to any other agent and thus $\Delta u_2 = -(13 - 3\delta) < 0$. If 2 and 3 establish the link 23 then $\Delta u_3 = 4 - 3 - (4-\delta) = \delta - 3 < 0$. (The path 213 is no longer the shortest path from 2 to 3.) The star is stable.

Pentagon: If agent 1 forms a link with 3 then $\Delta u_1 = 4 - 3 - (4-\delta) < 0$. (The path 123 is no longer the shortest path from 1 to 3, and the distance from 1 to 4 is still 2.) If agent 1 breaks the link 12 then $\Delta u_1 = 1 - (4-3) + 2 - (4-\delta) = \delta - 2 < 0$. (The path 15432 becomes the shortest path from 1 to 2 and 1543 replaces 123 as the shortest path from 1 to 3.) The pentagon is stable.

Line: If agents 1 and 4 form 14 then 14 replaces 1234 as the shortest path from 1 to 4 and 145 replaces 12345 as the shortest path from 1 to 5. It follows that $\Delta u_1 = 4 - 3 - 2 + 4 - \delta - 1 = 2 - \delta > 0$. The line is not stable in this case.

For the parameters of Example 10.4:

The *complete network* is not stable: If agent i breaks the link with j then $\Delta u_i = 2 - (b_1 - c) = 3$. (If $i \neq k \neq j$ then ikj becomes the shortest path between i and j, but ik remains the shortest path between i and k.)

The *star* is not stable: If agent 1, the center, breaks the link 12 then $\Delta u_1 = -(b_1 - c) = 1$. (For $j \geq 3$ the link $1j$ is still the shortest path between 1 and j.)

The *pentagon* is not stable: If 1 breaks the link 12 then u_1 increases from $2(b_1 - c) + 2b_2 = 2$ to $(b_1 - c) + b_2 + b_3 + b_4 = 2\frac{1}{2}$.

The *line* is not stable: If agent 2 breaks the link 21 then $\Delta u_2 = -(b_1 - c) = 1$. (The link 21 imposes a net cost on agent 2 but does not provide any benefit in terms of 1's link to other agents: Agent 1 is linked only to agent 2.)

The following theorem does not completely characterize stable networks for distance-based utility, but it does identify some conditions under which stability may, or may not, hold.

Stability Theorem for Distance-Based Utility

Assume that $c \geq 0$ and $b_2 > 0$.

(1) *If $b_1 - c > b_2$ only the complete network is pairwise stable.*

(2) *If $b_1 - b_2 < c < b_1$ then every star is pairwise stable.*

(3) *If $b_1 < c$ then every node in a pairwise stable network has either zero links or at least two links. Therefore, if $b_1 < c < b_1 + \frac{1}{2}(n - 2)b_2$ there exists no pairwise stable and TU-efficient network.*

Proof:

(1) Suppose that $b_1 - c > b_2$.

Then $b_1 > c$ because $b_2 > 0$. If i and j are not linked in g create the network $g+ij$ by adding the link ij. The utility of i will increase by at least $b_1 - c - b_2$. That follows from the fact that a path from i to j, which added at most b_2 to u_i is replaced by a link, which adds $b_1 - c$. Of course, $b_1 - c - b_2$ is positive. Similarly, the utility of j will increase. Therefore, the complete network is the only pairwise stable one in this case.

(2) If $b_1 - b_2 < c < b_1$ and g is a star it is pairwise stable:

Let n be the center of the star. If $n = 2$ then the star is simply the link 12. If the link is broken then u_1 and u_2 will each fall by $b_1 - c$, which is positive. Therefore, a star is pairwise stable if $n = 2$. Suppose that $n > 2$ and n is the center of the star. If we create the network $g+12$ by adding the link 12 we will add $b_1 - c - b_2$ to u_1. (The shortest path between 1 and 2 in g has distance 2. The path contributes b_2 to u_1 and to u_2. Hence, the addition of the link removes b_2 but adds $b_1 - c$ to each of those payoffs.) But $b_1 - b_2 < c$ is equivalent to $b_1 - c - b_2 < 0$. Therefore, no agent can increase utility by forming a link with an agent who is not the center of g. Can the center n increase u_n by breaking a link with another agent i? That would cause u_n to fall by $b_1 - c$, which is positive. (It would not change the distance between n and any node other than i.) If $i \neq n$, the center, then $u_i(g) = b_1 - c + (n-2)b_2$, which is positive because $b_1 - c + (n-2)b_2 > b_1 - c > 0$ if $n > 2$. If the link with the center is broken u_i will fall to zero. Therefore, g is pairwise stable.

(3) Suppose that $b_1 < c$ and i has only one link, with j.

Then u_j will increase if j's link with i is broken because u_j will increase by $c - b_1$ which is positive. The link with i provided no benefit to j via i's links to other agents because i was linked only with j. Therefore, if g is a pairwise stable network and $b_1 < c$ then every node has at least two links unless it has zero links. (A node can't have exactly one link if g is pairwise stable.) If $b_1 < c$ then $b_1 - b_2 < c$. If $c < b_1 + \frac{1}{2}(n-2)b_2$ also holds then a star is the only TU-efficient network (via the efficiency theorem in Section 10.2.2.) Every node except the center of a star has exactly one link, and thus a star is not pairwise stable when $b_1 < c < b_1 + \frac{1}{2}(n-2)b_2$.   ■

Example 10.6 Instability of the Network of Figure 10.1 when $b_1 - b_2 < c < b_1$

If $b_1 - b_2 < c < b_1$ agent 3's payoff increases when the link with 4 is broken: u_3 will increase by $-(b_1 - c) + b_2$ which is positive because $b_1 - b_2 < c$. (When the link with 4 is broken agent 3 will lose $b_1 - c$, the benefit from that link, but will gain b_2 from the path 324.) We could also demonstrate the instability of the network by pointing out that both u_6 and u_3 will increase when a link between 6 and 3 is forged: u_6 will gain $b_1 - c > 0$ from the link with 3, and $2b_2$ from the paths 632 and 634, and $2b3$ from the paths 6321 and 6325. Agent 3 will gain $b_1 - c + b_2$ from the link 36 and the path 367.

Problem Set

(1) For $n = 5$, $b_1 > b_2 > b_3 > b_4$, and $c < b_1$ determine the range of values of b_1, b_2, b_3, b_4, and c for which: the complete network is efficient; the star network is efficient, the pentagon is efficient; the line is efficient.

(2) For $n = 5$, $b_1 > b_2 > b_3 > b_4$, and $c > b_1$ determine the range of values of b_1, b_2, b_3, b_4, and c for which: the complete network is efficient; the star network is efficient, the pentagon is efficient; the line is efficient.

(3) For $n = 5$, $b_1 > b_2 > b_3 > b_4$, and $c < b_1$ determine the range of values of b_1, b_2, b_3, b_4, and c for which: the complete network is stable; the star network is stable, the pentagon is stable; the line is stable.

(4) For $n = 5$, $b_1 > b_2 > b_3 > b_4$, and $c > b_1$ determine the range of values of b_1, b_2, b_3, b_4, and c for which: the complete network is stable; the star network is stable, the pentagon is stable; the line is stable.

10.3   COURNOT EQUILIBRIUM

We present the simplest version of the Cournot model. It abstracts from almost everything but the strategic interaction of the firms in a single industry. There are n identical but independent firms producing a homogeneous product. This means that a unit of the good produced by one firm is a perfect substitute for a unit produced by any other firm. The market demand function is $Q = A - P$, where Q is the total quantity demanded at price P. The parameter A is a constant. Demand will be zero when P is greater than or equal to A. Each firm has a constant average and marginal cost of c. Fixed cost is zero. Consider the production strategy of a single firm X. Let R denote the total output of every firm but X. The firms are independent, which means that they do not collude to keep prices and profits high. The individual firm will react to R by choosing its output level q to maximize its own profit, *given R*, and given the market demand function. From the latter we have $q + R = A - P$ and hence

$$q = A - R - P. \qquad [5]$$

We solve [5] to get the industry price as a function of X's output and the output of the other firms in the industry:

$$P = A - R - q.$$

Because X cannot control R — we're assuming that the firms do not collude — it will be treated as a constant when X chooses its profit maximizing value of q. The cost of producing q units of output is cq, and hence the firm's profit is $Pq - cq$. Firm X will maximize

$$(P - c)q = (A - R - q - c)q = (A - R - c)q - q^2 .$$

The first derivative of this function is $A - R - c - 2q$. By setting this equal to zero and solving we get $q^* = \frac{1}{2}(A - R - c)$. (Note that the second derivative is negative. We can also obtain q^* from the formula for maximizing a quadratic.)

The firms are identical and hence will have identical output levels. Therefore, $R = (n - 1)q^*$. We have $q^* = \frac{1}{2}[A - (n-1)q^* - c]$, the solution of which is

$$q^* = \frac{A - c}{n + 1} \qquad [6]$$

If you set $R = (n-1)q$ *before* you maximize X's profit you ascribe to X the ability to control the output of every other firm, and the result of the maximization process will not be the industry equilibrium for *independent* firms.

The industry output Q^* at equilibrium is nq^* and hence

$$Q^* = \frac{n(A - c)}{n + 1} . \qquad [7]$$

P^*, the equilibrium price, is the solution to $A - Q^*$, and thus $P^* = A - \dfrac{n(A - c)}{n + 1} = \dfrac{An + A - nA + nc}{n + 1}$.

$$P^* = \frac{A + nc}{n + 1} \qquad [8]$$

Individual firm profit is

$$(P^* - c)q^* = \left(\frac{A + nc}{n + 1} - c\right)\left(\frac{A - c}{n + 1}\right) = \frac{(A + nc - nc - c)(A - c)}{(n + 1)^2} = \frac{(A - c)^2}{(n + 1)^2} \qquad [9]$$

Example 10.7 Four Firms

$A = 100$, $c = 15$, and $n = 4$. Therefore, $Q = 100 - P$. The individual firm's output is q and thus $P = 100 - q - R$, letting R denote the output of the other three firms. Individual firm profit is $(P - 15)q$ or $(100 - q - R - 15)q$, and when we maximize that we get $q^* = \frac{1}{2}(85 - R) = \frac{1}{2}(85 - 3q^*)$, the solution of which is $q^* = 17$. Therefore, total industry output is $4 \times 17 = 68$. The Cournot equilibrium price is $100 - 68 = 32$. The individual firm's profit is $(32 - 15)17 = 289$.

Consumer surplus is the gain in utility from obtaining a product that is available at price P. It is equal to the benefit that the commodity provides minus the cost PQ of acquiring the Q units demanded at the market price P. Therefore, it is the area below the demand curve and above a horizontal line P units above the quantity axis. (See Section 2.5.3 of Chapter 2 for justification of this claim.) If Q denotes the world demand for a commodity and $Q = A - P$ is the world demand function then $q = A - R - P$ is the demand of country X if R denotes the demand by the rest of the world. Figure 10.5 depicts this demand function D_X. Note that exactly zero units will be demanded by the residents of X if the price is $A - R$. And $A - R - q$ is the price at

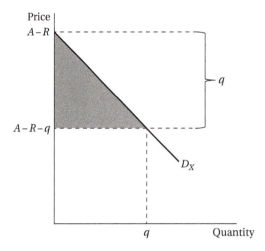

Figure 10.5

which the residents of X will demand exactly q units. The consumer surplus of X is the shaded area, which is a triangle. The base of the triangle is q and the height is $A - R - P = A - R - (A - R - q)$ which is also q (Figure 10.5). Therefore, the consumer surplus is $\frac{1}{2}q^2$.

Consumer Surplus Theorem

The consumer surplus derived from a good is $\frac{1}{2}q^2$ if the market demand function for the good has the form $q = a - p$, where a is a constant, p is the price, and q is the total quantity demanded.

Link

Any good intermediate microeconomics test will provide a more extensive treatment of Cournot equilibrium.

Problem Set

(1) Prove that if we set $R = (n-1)q$ *before* maximizing X's profit we will get the cartel outcome in the sense that we arrive at the price–quantity combination that maximizes total industry profit.

(2) Continue to assume zero fixed cost. Suppose that we do *not* assume that every firm has the same constant average and marginal cost c, but instead use c_i to denote firm i's (constant) average and marginal cost. Show that profit maximization implies that $q_i = \frac{1}{2}(A - R_i - c_i)$, where q_i is firm i's output and R_i is the total output of all firms other than i. Exploit the fact that $\sum q_i = (n-1)\sum R_i$, where summation is over all firms i, to derive the Cournot equilibrium price and the output of each firm. Confirm that demand equals supply.

(3) Show that the equilibrium of question 2 satisfies [6] and [8] above when $ci = c$ for every firm i.

10.4 BILATERAL TRADE

A majority of the regional trade agreements reached in the last quarter century are bilateral treaties, and commit the signatories to mutual free trade. Do such agreements inhibit the emergence of *global* free trade? We use a network model to address this question. The agents (or nodes) are individual countries.

10.4.1 The Trade Model

Let n denote the number of countries. There are at least three. Each country has one firm that is capable of serving the domestic market and also exporting to other countries. To simplify the calculations we assume that two countries i and j either have a free trade agreement with each other, allowing each to export to the other free of duty, or else i faces a tariff in country j that is so high that exporting to j is unprofitable and j faces a tariff imposed by country i that keeps j's goods out. In particular, a *free trade agreement* is bilateral: it must be adopted by both counties for either of the two to get free access to the other's market. The agreement is achieved at zero cost. A free trade agreement (FTA) between i and j does not provide any benefit to any other country, and i does not benefit from any FTA that j has with a third country.

Let $N = \{1, 2, \ldots, n\}$ denote the set of countries, with g denoting the network that is created by the matrix of FTAs. We set $g_{ij} = 1$ if i and j have an FTA with each other, and $g_{ij} = 0$ otherwise. The analysis will be easier to follow if we also set $g_{ii} = 1$ for each i in N. If $g_{ij} = 0$ then i cannot enter j's domestic market, nor can j enter i's market. Recall that g_C denotes the complete network ($g_{ij} = 1$ for each i and j) and g_O is the empty (autarky) network ($g_{ij} = 0$ for each i and j). Let $N_i(g)$ denote the set of countries that i supplies – the set of j in N such that $g_{ij} = 1$, with $n_i(g)$ representing the number of elements in $N_i(g)$. In other words $n_i(g)$ equals 1 plus the number of FTAs that country i has in network g. (The extra 1 accounts for the fact that i belongs to $N_i(g)$.)

We employ the Cournot model of competition (Section 10.3) to determine output and prices, and thereby social welfare in each country. The active firms in country i compete by setting quantities. Let Q_i denote the total output in i with P_i denoting price. The market demand function in country i is

$$Q_i = A - P_i \tag{10}$$

Let q_{ij} denote the amount of output supplied by country j's firm in country i. In particular, q_{ii} is the amount of output supplied by the domestic firm. Then Q_i is the sum of the q_{ij} over all j in $N_i(g)$. The marginal and average costs of production in each country are assumed to be constant and equal to c in each country. (There are no fixed costs.) The parameters A and c do not vary from country to country, and $A > c$.

DEFINITION: *The Trading Network Model*

N is the set of n countries and g is a trading network, with $g_{ij} = 1$ if i has an FTA with j or if $i = j$; otherwise $g_{ij} = 0$. We use $g+ij$ to denote the network that is formed when link ij is added to g. $N_i(g)$ is the set of countries j with which i has an FTA, including i itself, with $n_i(g)$ denoting the number of countries in $N_i(g)$. q_{ij} is the amount of output supplied by firm j in country i, and $Q_i = A - P_i$ is the demand function in i, where Q_i is the total amount demanded and P_i is price.

10.4.2 Efficient and Stable Trading Networks

From now on the network g will be implicit, allowing us to write N_i and n_i when there is no danger of confusion. The measure of *social welfare* in country i is consumer surplus (see Section 10.2) plus total profit earned by i's firm in the domestic market and in all foreign markets in which i is active, plus tariff revenue collected by country i. (A firm's revenue is a measure of the benefit that consumers derive from the firm's activities, and the firm's cost is a measure of the value to consumers of the output lost when resources are transferred to the firm in question. Therefore, the firm's profit is a measure of the *net* value to consumers of a firm's activities.)

Theorem on Social Welfare

If countries export only to countries with which they have an FTA then arbitrary country i's social welfare W_i is given by

$$W_i = \frac{[n_i(A - c)]^2}{2(n_i + 1)^2} + \sum_{j \in N_i} \frac{(A - c)^2}{(n_j + 1)^2}.$$

Proof:

There is no "tariff revenue" term because country i receives imports only from countries with which it has an FTA and no duty is imposed on goods from those countries.

The first term in W_i is consumer surplus. From [7] in Section 10.2 we have $Q_i = \frac{n_i(A-c)}{n_i+1}$ with consumer surplus equal to $\frac{1}{2}Q_i^2$ by the Consumer Surplus Theorem in Section 10.2.

The second term in W_i is the sum of the $\frac{(A-c)^2}{(n_j+1)^2}$, the profit earned by country i's firm in country j, over all countries j with which i has an FTA, plus profit in i's domestic market. (Recall [9].)   ∎

We now demonstrate that almost every pair of countries will sign an FTA. The only possibility other than universal free trade is that a single country is shut out of every market but its own, and all other countries trade freely with each other.

Stability Theorem

A pairwise stable trading network is either a complete network, or one with a component containing $n-1$ countries.

Proof:

Let g represent the network we are testing for stability. Suppose that countries i and j do not have an FTA. Then $g_{ij} = 0$. We compare the social welfare $W_i(g)$ with $W_i(g+ij)$, country i's welfare when the link ij is added to g. (Recall that $g+ij$ denotes the network that is formed when link ij is added to g.) With n_i and n_j representing the number of countries active in i and j respectively when the trading network is g, the addition of link ij causes each of those numbers to increase by 1. Therefore the addition of ij causes consumer surplus in i to increase by

$$\frac{[n_i+1)(A-c)]^2}{2(n_i+2)^2} - \frac{[n_i(A-c)]^2}{2(n_i+1)^2}.$$

(We have $n_i + 2$ in the denominator of the first term because the number of firms active in country i is now $n_i + 1$.) The profit earned by country i's firm in its domestic market changes by

$$\frac{(A-c)^2}{(n_i+2)^2} - \frac{(A-c)^2}{(n_i+1)^2},$$

a negative number. (The entry of firm j increases competition.) The addition of link ij adds $\frac{(A-c)^2}{(n_j+2)^2}$ to i's profit as a result of its participation in j's market. Therefore, $W_i(g+ij) - W_i(g)$ is

$$\Delta W_i = \frac{[(n_i+1)(A-c)]^2}{2(n_i+2)^2} - \frac{[n_i(A-c)]^2}{2(n_i+1)^2} + \frac{(A-c)^2}{(n_i+2)^2} + \frac{(A-c)^2}{(n_j+2)^2} \qquad [11]$$

We want to show that $\Delta W_i > 0$ if $n_i \geq 2$. To that end, multiply both sides of [11] by the positive number $\frac{2(n_i+1)^2(n_i+2)^2}{(A-c)^2}$ to obtain

$$(n_i+1)^4 - n_i^2(n_i+2)^2 + 2(n_i+1)^2 - 2(n_i+2)^2 + 2(n_i+1)^2\,(n_i+2)^2/(n_j+2)^2.$$

Because the last term is positive, it suffices to show that the following inequality holds when $n_i \geq 2$:

$$(n_i+1)^4 - n_i^2(n_i+2)^2 + 2(n_i+1)^2 - 2(n_i+2)^2 > 0. \qquad [12]$$

But that inequality reduces to $2\,n_i^2 - 5 > 0$, which is clearly satisfied when $n_i \geq 2$. (We can also establish that [12] holds for all $n_i \geq 2$ by showing that it holds for $n_i = 2$ and that the derivative with respect to n_i of the left-hand side of [12] is positive.)

The same calculation (with the subscripts i and j switched) shows that $\Delta W_j > 0$ if $n_j \geq 2$.

We have just demonstrated that a country that already has at least one trading partner can increase its level of welfare by adding a new *FTA* with another country. The welfare of both will increase if the second country already has a trading partner. What about two countries without any trading partners?

Consider the case of i and j such that $n_i = 1 = n_j$. We have

$$W_i(g) = W_j(g) = \tfrac{1}{2}\,\frac{(A-c)^2}{4} + \frac{(A-c)^2}{4} = \frac{3(A-c)^2}{8}.$$

If i and j form an FTA the welfare of each will now be

$$W_i(g+ij) = W_j(g+ij) = \tfrac{1}{2}\,\frac{[2(A-c)]^2}{9} + \frac{2(A-c)^2}{9} = \frac{4(A-c)^2}{9}.$$

And four-ninths exceeds three-eights: the link increases the welfare of both. Consumer surplus will increase in each country due to the increased supply of goods and the associated lower prices. Each country's profit from foreign sales will increase from zero to a positive number, although profit in the domestic market will fall due to the increased competition.

Suppose that g has more than two components. A pairwise stable trading network cannot have two singleton components. If g has more than two components and exactly one singleton component then it has at least two components C and D with two or more members each, in which case g cannot be pairwise stable: a country from C and one from D can sign an *FTA*, increasing the welfare of each. A pairwise stable trading network cannot have two components unless one of them is a singleton. Therefore, if a pairwise stable trading network is not complete it must have two components, one of which is a singleton and the other comprises all nations except the singleton component. ∎

Can we actually have a stable network in which one country J closes its domestic market to every other country, but there is free trade among the other countries? Although consumer surplus in J and J's profit from foreign sales will both increase if J enters an FTA with another country, the profit earned by J's firm in its domestic market falls — due to the increased competition - by more than enough offset the gains if foreign competition is robust and J's profits from sales abroad are sufficiently small.

Example 10.8 A Four-Country World

We only need to assume that $n \geq 4$ to show that an isolated country will be harmed by entering the free trade area. Let g denote the network in which country 1 is isolated and the remaining $n-1$ countries trade freely with each other. Then $g+12$ is the network in which country 1 establishes an *FTA* with 2, and the original *FTA*s remain in force. If we apply [11] to this situation, with $i=1$ and $j=2$, we have $n_i=1$ and $n_j=n-1$ and hence

$$\frac{\Delta W_1}{(A-c)^2} = -\frac{3}{72} + \frac{1}{(n+1)^2}$$

which will be negative if and only if $(n+1)2 > 24$. This inequality holds for integer values if and only if $n \geq 4$. Of course, competition in foreign markets is greater the larger is n.

Although we have proved that no trading network is pairwise stable unless it is complete or consists of two components, we need to confirm that the complete network actually *is* stable.

Theorem

The complete network is pairwise stable.

Proof:

The complete network g_C includes every possible link. Therefore, we merely have to confirm that no agent can benefit by *breaking* a link. The welfare of arbitrary country i in network g_C is

$$W_i(g_C) = \frac{[n(A-c)]^2}{2(n+1)^2} + \frac{n(A-c)^2}{(n+1)^2},$$

where n is the total number of countries. If i were to break the link with j then i's welfare would be

$$W_i(g-ij) = \frac{[(n-1)(A-c)]^2}{2n^2} + \frac{(A-c)^2}{n^2} + \frac{(n-2)(A-c)^2}{(n+1)^2}.$$

There will be $n-1$ countries exporting to i's domestic market, including i of course, and hence the second term is individual firm profit in that market. In addition, i will sell in $n-2$ foreign markets, each of which will have n countries supplying goods, accounting for the final term. (Country j will not export to country i but will be active in all other markets.)

We conclude by showing that $W_i(g_C) - W_i(g_C - ij)$ is positive.

$$W_i(g_C) - W_i(g_C - ij) = \frac{[n(A-c)]^2}{2(n+1)^2} + \frac{n(A-c)^2}{(n+1)^2} - \frac{[(n-1)(A-c)]^2}{2n^2}$$
$$- \frac{(A-c)^2}{n^2} - \frac{(n-2)(A-c)^2}{(n+1)^2}. \tag{13}$$

For positive n, expression [13] is positive if and only if

$$\frac{n^2 + 2n - 2(n-2)}{2(n+1)^2} > \frac{(n-1)^2 + 2}{2n^2}.$$

(Collect all the terms with $(n + 1)^2$ in the denominator and employ $2(n + 1)^2$ as a common denominator. Then collect all terms with n^2 or $2n^2$ as denominator and use $2n^2$ as a common denominator.) Multiply both sides of the previous inequality by $2n^2(n+1)^2$ to obtain the following equivalent statement

$$\left(n^2 + 4\right)\left(n^2\right) > \left(n^2 - 2n + 3\right)(n + 1)^2.$$

Cancelling will reduce this to $4(n - 2) > 3$, which will obviously hold if $n > 2$. (Recall that we assume $n \geq 3$ in this section.) Therefore, $W_i(g_C) > W_i(g_C - i_j)$ if $n > 2$.   ∎

Efficiency Theorem

The only TU-efficient trading network is the complete one.

Proof:

Let g represent the network being tested for TU-efficiency. *Individual* country welfare for g is

$$W_i(g) = \frac{[n_i(g)(A - c)]^2}{2(n_i(g) + 1)^2} + \sum_{j \in N_i(g)} \frac{(A - c)^2}{(n_j(g) + 1)^2}.$$

Therefore, total world welfare generated by network g is

$$\sum_{i \in N} W_i(g) = \sum_{i \in N} \frac{[n_i(g)(A - c)]^2}{2(n_i(g) + 1)^2} + \sum_{i \in N}\sum_{j \in N_i(g)} \frac{(A - c)^2}{(n_j(g) + 1)^2} \qquad [14]$$

The second term in [14] can be written thus:

$$\sum_{i \in N} n_i(g) \frac{(A - c)^2}{(n_i(g) + 1)^2} \qquad [15]$$

That is a consequence of the fact that $n_i(g)$ is the total number of countries supplying country i, and $\frac{(A-c)^2}{(n_i(g)+1)^2}$ is the profit earned in i by each of these countries. (Note that $n_j(g)$ is in the denominator of the last term on [14] but $n_i(g)$ is in the denominator of [15].) When we sum [15] over N, the set of countries in the world, we get the total profit realized over the entire world. The second term of [14] is also total world profit: It is the profit obtained by country i over all of the markets in which it is active, summed over all i. Therefore, we can state that the total world welfare generated by network g is the sum of the terms $T_i(g)$ over all i in N, where $T_i(g)$ is defined by [16]:

$$T_i(g) = \frac{[n_i(g)(A - c)]^2}{2(n_i(g) + 1)^2} + n_i(g) \frac{(A - c)^2}{(n_i(g) + 1)^2} \qquad [16]$$

Total world welfare generated by the complete network g_C is obtained by summing individual country welfare $W_i(g_C)$ over all i in N. And

$$W_i(g_C) = \frac{[n(A-c)]^2}{2(n+1)^2} + n\frac{(A-c)^2}{(n+1)^2}.$$

It is easy to show that $W_i(g_C)$ is at least as large as $T_i(g)$ for arbitrary country i and strictly greater for at least one country: Substitute m for $n_i(g)$ in [16]. We have $n \geq m$. We need to show that $\frac{n^2}{2(n+1)^2} + \frac{n}{(n+1)^2} \geq \frac{m^2}{2(m+1)^2} + \frac{m}{(m+1)^2}$ holds. If we multiply both sides of that inequality by $2(n+1)^2(m+1)^2$ we get $(n^2+2n)(m+1)^2 \geq (m^2+2m)(n+1)^2$. After distributing and doing some cancelling we get the equivalent statement $n(n+2) \geq m(m+2)$, which obviously holds because $n \geq m$. Because $g \neq g_C$ we must have $n > n_i(g)$ for at least one i. Thus $W_i(g_C) > T_i(g)$ for at least one i with $W_i(g_C) \geq T_i(g)$ holding for all i. ∎

Source
This section is based on Goyal and Joshi (2006).

Link
The analysis is extended in Goyal (2007).

Problem Set
Each of these questions assumes that $n = 4$, $A = 10$, and $c = 1$.

(1) Calculate country 1's welfare for each of the following cases: A: $N_1(g) = \{1\}$. B: $N_1(g) = \{1,2\}$. C: $N_1(g) = \{1,2,3\}$. D: $N_1(g) = \{1,2,3,4\}$.

(2) Compute ΔW_1 when country 1 adds the link 14 for each of the following assumptions about the initial value of $N_1(g)$: A: $N_1(g) = \{1\}$. B: $N_1(g) = \{1,2\}$. C: $N_1(g) = \{1,2,3\}$.

(3) Compute ΔW_1 as a result of country 1 breaking the link 14 for each of the following assumptions about the initial value of $N_1(g)$: A: $N_1(g) = \{1,4\}$. B: $N_1(g) = \{1,2,4\}$. C: $N_1(g) = \{1,2,3,4\}$.

(4) Calculate total world welfare for each of the following cases: A: $N_i(g) = \{i\}$ for each country i. B: $N_1(g) = \{1,2\} = N_2(g)$ and $N_3(g) = \{3,4\} = N_4(g)$. C: $N_1(g) = \{1,2,3\} = N_2(g) = N_3(g)$ and $N_4(g) = \{4\}$. D: $N_1(g) = \{1,2,3,4\} = N_2(g) = N_3(g) = N_4(g)$.

10.5 R&D NETWORKS

There are many instances of collaboration on research and development by firms that are otherwise legally unrelated. In some cases the firms are direct competitors – rival suppliers of similar products. Other cases involve firms that manufacture quite different goods. This section treats the latter more thoroughly, with some observations in Section 10.5.4 on how the analysis differs when the firms operate in the same market.

10.5.1 Monopoly Profit Maximization

If firm X is a monopoly supplier to a market with demand function $Q = A - P$ it will charge price $P = A - Q$ if it decides to supply Q units of output. If it has constant marginal cost of m it will choose Q to maximize $(A - Q)Q - mQ$, which is revenue minus cost. (Assume that fixed cost is zero.) The first derivative of this function is $A - m - 2Q$. By setting this equal to zero and solving we get $Q^* = \frac{1}{2}(A - m)$. (Note that the second derivative is negative. We can also obtain Q^* from the formula for maximizing a quadratic.) The equilibrium price P^* is the solution to $A - Q^*$, and thus $P^* = A - \frac{A-m}{2}$ or $P^* = \frac{A+m}{2}$. It follows that

$$\text{profit} = \left[\frac{A+m}{2}\right] Q - mQ = \left[\frac{A-m}{2}\right] Q = \left[\frac{A-m}{2}\right]\left[\frac{A-m}{2}\right] \qquad [18]$$

if fixed cost is zero and the firm's R&D cost is also zero. (A positive fixed cost leaves marginal cost and marginal revenue unaffected, and thus it does not affect equilibrium prices or quantities, *provided* that revenue is sufficient to cover variable cost and fixed cost, including the opportunity cost of capital. Therefore, our "zero fixed cost" assumption can be substantially weakened.) Note this paragraph can be obtained from Section 10.3 by setting $n = 1$.

Consumer surplus is the gain in utility from obtaining a product that is available at price P. It is equal to the benefit that the commodity provides minus the cost PQ of acquiring the Q units demanded at the market price P. Therefore, it is the shaded area in Figure 10.5 – the area between the demand curve and a horizontal line P units above the quantity axis. (Set $R = 0$ and $q = Q$. R denotes the output of all the other firms in the industry. In the case of monopoly, X is the only firm and hence $R = 0$.) The height of the shaded area is Q and the base has length Q. Therefore, consumer surplus $= \frac{1}{2}Q^2$.

10.5.2 The Model

Let n denote the number of firms that could potentially collaborate on the research effort to reduce marginal cost. Let e_i denote the effort expended by firm i. Firm i will share its cost-reducing innovation with the other firms to which it is linked, via an agreement that may be more or less formal. As usual, g denotes the network: the R&D network in this case. If i and j are linked then the two firms will share the fruits of their individual discoveries. Research effort itself is costly, but leads to lower marginal cost of production. Specifically, marginal cost is initially c for each of the n firms, but it falls to

$$m_i(g) = c - e_i - \textstyle\sum_{j \in N_i(g)} e_j$$

for firm i, where $N_i(g)$ is the set of firms that have agreed to share the results of their R&D with i. To keep the calculations to a minimum we assume that fixed costs are initially zero, but the effort level e_i adds λe_i^2 to i's total cost. (Given e_i, the firm's R&D cost is independent of its output level, but the firm is free to change R&D expenditure.) We further simplify by restricting attention to networks for which $N_i(g)$ has the same number of firms for each of the n firms. In plain words, each firm is

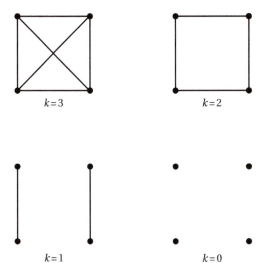

Figure 10.6

assumed to have a collaborative agreement with exactly k other firms. Figure 10.6 illustrates the possibilities for $n = 4$.

We seek the value of k that maximizes individual firm profit, and also the value of k that maximizes total welfare. The first step is to find the value of e_i that an independent profit maximizing firm will choose.

Each of the n firms is a monopoly in its own market, and each firm i is constrained by a market demand function, $Q_i = A - P_i$, that has the same functional form.

DEFINITION: *The Research Network Model*

N is the set of n monopolies and g is a research collaboration network. Let $N_i(g)$ denote the set of firms j with which i has agreed to share the results of its R&D. Firm i faces the market demand function $Q_i = A - P_i$, where P_i is the price set by i and Q_i is the quantity demanded. Each firm i contributes the effort e_i to R&D resulting in marginal cost $m_i(g) = c - e_i - \sum_{j \in N_i(g)} e_j$. The R&D effort level e_i adds λe_i^2 to i's total cost. Assume that $\lambda > \frac{1}{4}$.

10.5.3 A Network of Monopolies

The monopolist's profit is $\frac{(A-m)^2}{4}$ if no costly effort is devoted to R&D. (Recall [18].)

Let $\pi_i(g)$ be the profit of firm i as a function of e_i, given the network g. From [18] we have

$$\pi_i(g) = \frac{(A - m_i(g))^2}{4} - \lambda\, e_i^2 = \frac{(A - c + e_i + \sum_{j \in N_i(g)} e_j)^2}{4} - \lambda\, e_i^2,$$

a function of e_i. (Firm i cannot control the effort level of other firms. Therefore, we treat e_j as a constant for all $j \neq i$.) Then

$$\frac{d\pi_i(g)}{de_i} = (\tfrac{1}{4})2(A - c + e_i + \sum_{j \in N_i(g)} e_j) - 2\lambda e_i.$$

It follows that the second derivative is $\tfrac{1}{2} - 2\lambda$, which is negative by assumption. At this point we treat e_j, for $j \neq i$, as a constant because its value is not something that is under the control of firm i. We have

$$\frac{d\pi_i(g)}{de_i} = \tfrac{1}{2}(A - c + \sum_{j \in N_i(g)} e_j) + \tfrac{1}{2}(1 - 4\lambda)e_i.$$

Because $e_j \geq 0$ for every firm j, and assuming $A - c > 0$, we see that $\frac{d\pi_i(g)}{de_i}$ is positive when $e_i = 0$. (The model would not be interesting if $A - c$ were non-positive.) Therefore, profit is not maximized at the boundary point ($e_i = $ zero) and hence $\frac{d\pi_i(g)}{de_i} = 0$ at equilibrium, which yields

$$\tfrac{1}{2}(A - c + e_i + \sum_{j \in N_i(g)} e_j) - 2\lambda e_i = 0. \qquad [19]$$

Now we can incorporate the fact that each firm faces the same demand function $Q_i = A - P_i$ (in different markets), each has the same marginal cost function, and there is some k such that $N_i(g)$ has exactly k members for each firm i (our symmetry assumption). It follows that at equilibrium we will have $e_i = e_j$ for all j in $N_i(g)$. Therefore, the sum of the e_j over all j in $N_i(g)$ equals ke_i, and [19] simplifies to

$$\tfrac{1}{2}(A - c + e_i + ke_i) - 2\lambda e_i = 0$$

When we solve this for e_i we obtain

$$e_i(k) = \frac{A - c}{4\lambda - k - 1} \quad \text{and} \quad m_i(k) = c - \frac{(k+1)(A - c)}{4\lambda - k - 1} \qquad [20]$$

for arbitrary firm i. Note that we have incorporated our symmetry assumption by making e_i a function of k. (If we had set $e_j = e_i$ before taking the derivative we would be ascribing to firm i the power to control the effort level of firm j.)

Refer to k as the *level of collaboration* on R&D: by definition, if k increases then so does the number of firms with which arbitrary firm i shares the results of its research. It is clear from [20] that a firm will devote more effort to R&D if it collaborates with a greater number of monopolies. The reduction in the marginal cost of production more than offsets the addition to total cost of the additional R&D effort. That claim implies that marginal cost does indeed fall as the level of collaboration increases.

Theorem on Collaboration, Effort, and Cost
$e_i(k)$ increases as k increases, and $m_i(k)$ decreases as k increases.

Proof:

From [20] we see that the denominator of $e_i(k)$ decreases as k increases, while the numerator is unchanged. Therefore, $e_i(k)$ increases as k increases.

To show that $m_i(k)$ decreases as k increases we merely have to show that

$$c - \frac{(k+2)(A-c)}{4\lambda - k - 2} < c - \frac{(k+1)(A-c)}{4\lambda - k - 1}.$$

This will certainly hold if $4\lambda - k - 2 > 0$ because both denominators will be positive, and hence the positive fraction $(k+2)/(4\lambda - k - 2)$ will exceed the fraction $(k+1)/(4\lambda - k - 1)$. (The former has a larger numerator and a smaller denominator than the latter.)

We can avoid the assumption that $4\lambda - k - 2$ is positive (and hence so is $4\lambda - k - 1$) by simply computing the derivative $\frac{dm_i(k)}{dk}$. It is $-\frac{4\lambda(A-c)}{(4\lambda-k-1)^2}$, which is negative because $A > c$. ∎

Does an increase in the extent of collaboration on R&D unambiguously increase the total welfare resulting from the profit maximizing decisions of the n monopolies? We will use total producer surplus (i.e., profit) plus consumer surplus as our measure of welfare. A welfare measure must capture the benefit derived by consumers *net of the cost*. Marginal cost is incorporated in the measure of consumer surplus because it is reflected in the price. But fixed costs are not. We have to at least subtract the fixed cost of the R&D effort devoted to reducing marginal cost. (R&D effort is fixed in the sense that it is independent of the firm's level of output.)

Efficiency Theorem

Total welfare is increasing in the level k of collaboration.

Proof:

We begin by computing consumer surplus delivered by arbitrary firm i: Section 10.5.1 establishes that firm i's output Q_i is $\frac{1}{2}(A - m)$. Therefore, $Q_i^2 = \frac{(A-m_i(k))^2}{4}$.

Using [20] to substitute for $m_i(k)$ and $e_i(k)$ results in

$$Q_i^2 = \frac{\left(A - c + \frac{(k+1)(A-c)}{4\lambda-k-1}\right)^2}{4} = \frac{\frac{[(A-c)(4\lambda-k-1)+(k+1)(A-c)]^2}{(4\lambda-k-1)^2}}{4} = \frac{[4\lambda(A-c)]^2}{4(4\lambda-k-1)^2}$$

The denominator clearly decreases when k increases, and thus Q_i^2 increases as k increases. (The numerator is independent of k.) Therefore consumer surplus, $\frac{1}{2}Q_i^2$, increases when k increases. (See Section 10.3 for a proof that consumer surplus equals $\frac{1}{2}Q_i^2$.)

From [18], the profit of firm i is $\frac{(A-m_i(k))^2}{4}$ minus fixed cost. Fixed cost is just the cost of the firm's R&D effort. Hence, profit is

$$\frac{\left(A-c+\frac{(k+1)(A-c)}{4\lambda-k-1}\right)^2}{4} - \lambda e_i^2 = \frac{\frac{[(A-c)(4\lambda-k-1)+(k+1)(A-c)]^2}{(4\lambda-k-1)^2}}{4} - \lambda e_i^2 =$$

$$= \frac{[4\lambda(A-c)]^2}{4(4\lambda-k-1)^2} - \lambda\frac{(A-c)^2}{(4\lambda-k-1)^2} = \frac{\left(16\lambda^2-4\lambda\right)(A-c)^2}{4(4\lambda-k-1)^2}.$$

Arbitrary firm i's profit clearly increases as k increases. (Note that $16\lambda^2 - 4\lambda = 4\lambda(4\lambda-1)$ is positive because we have assumed that $\lambda > \frac{1}{4}$.)

For arbitrary firm i, both consumer and producer surplus increase as k increases. Therefore, total welfare (the sum of consumer and producer surplus over all n firms) is increasing in k. ∎

10.5.4 Collaboration by Firms in a Single Market

It is not rare for firms that are rival suppliers of a particular commodity – automobiles for instance – to collaborate on research and development. (Daimler-Chrysler conducted research on emissions control systems in conjunction with BMG Group and Volkswagen. Toyota has engaged in research on intake manifolds in collaboration with Daihatsu Motor Company. In both cases, other research was undertaken independently of the R&D partner. See Goyal, 2007, p. 248.)

When R&D partners I and J compete in the same market the cost-reducing effort by firm I has two effects on its own profit: the reduction in I's marginal cost tends to reduce I's profit, but it also reduces J's marginal cost and hence increases the competitive pressure on I, tending to lower I's profit. If the market is oligopolistic, the individual firm's R&D effort is lower the greater the level of collaboration, in contrast to the case of a network of independent monopolies. Social welfare is maximized at a level of collaborative activity that is positive but short of full collaboration.

Source

This section is based on Goyal and Moraga-González (2001).

Link

The analysis is extended in Goyal (2007). See Goyal and Moraga-González (2001) for the full treatment of collaboration involving firms in an oligopolistic market.

Problem Set

Each of these questions assumes that $n = 4$, $A = 10$, and $c = 1$.

(1) Calculate individual country welfare for each value of k from 0 to 3.

(2) Calculate total world welfare for each value of k from 0 to 3.

(3) Show that the network is not stable when $N_1(g) = \{1,2\} = N_2(g)$ and $N_3(g) = \{3,4\} = N_4(g)$.

General Competitive Equilibrium

This chapter takes an economy-wide perspective and seeks a mechanism that elicits private information about individual preferences and firm production recipes to deliver an efficient allocation of private goods and services. We assume away all other hidden information problems. In particular, every consumer is assumed to know the quality of every firm's output, every employer knows the abilities of every prospective employee, every lender knows the probability of default of every creditor, and so on. Every manager can be relied on to maximize profit. In fact there is no shirking by anyone.

The economy faces an impressive challenge – to induce truthful revelation of the remaining hidden information, specifically preferences and production functions. In fact, three of the five sections even assume away this hidden information problem, highlighting instead the transmission of information. Recall that an outcome is efficient if there is no other arrangement of production and consumption activities that makes one person better off without lowering the utility of anyone else. Identification of an efficient outcome would seem to require an enormous amount of information about all of the private characteristics. Therefore, even with most of the hidden information problems assumed away, identification of an efficient outcome by the market system is a remarkable accomplishment. Social cost pricing is the key.

In a private ownership market economy the consumer maximizes utility subject to a budget constraint, and this results in a chosen consumption plan at which the marginal rate of substitution (MRS) for each pair of commodities equals the price ratio for those goods. Therefore, the price ratio transmits information about one consumer's MRS to every other consumer and every firm. The budget constraint gives consumers the incentive to employ that information in their utility maximization calculations, as Section 11.1.4 demonstrates. Profit maximization by a firm in a competitive environment results in the equilibrium price of a commodity that is also equal to the marginal cost of producing that good. Therefore, prices transmit *marginal* information about consumer preferences and firm production recipes.

In spite of the fact that prices transmit only marginal information, we demonstrate in Sections 11.2 and 11.3 that this allows an efficient outcome to be identified in a wide range of circumstances. The first section is an informal examination of incentives at work in a capitalist economy. In Section 11.4, we look at one specific incentive issue – the ability of a trader to advantageously manipulate prices. The last section looks at the performance of the market system when there is a resource that is jointly and freely employed by several firms.

11.1 COMPETITION, PROPERTY RIGHTS, AND PROSPERITY

Competition between political parties makes it very difficult for a ruling party to conceal serious problems or to ignore them if they do come to light. Competition between firms reduces the likelihood that a firm can survive if it attempts to profit by deceiving consumers. Competition among firms in a private ownership market economy is also a key ingredient of efficiency and economic growth. We examine these claims briefly and informally in this section.

11.1.1 Competition and Reputation

The producer of a commodity has two sets of rivals. The obvious group consists of the other producers, but in a market economy consumers are the also firm's adversaries in the sense that, unless somehow constrained, the producer can increase profit by misleading its customers – about product quality, in particular. Product quality has many dimensions – durability, versatility, performance, operating cost, maintenance cost – and there are many opportunities for the unscrupulous manufacturer to reduce production costs by sacrificing quality while keeping up a good appearance. In a command economy, where profit maximization may not be a firm's chief goal, the workers in a production plant can still gain by misleading consumers about quality. Their task is easier if they do not have to maintain high quality.

What prevents a producer from succumbing to the temptation to gain at the expense of consumers? Regulation by a government agency sometimes plays an important role, even in a market economy. Far more important, typically, is the discipline of competition under capitalism. Modern technology requires a heavy initial capital outlay for the production of most goods and services. Competition among the owners of capital keeps the rate of return on capital low enough so that the initial expenditure can be recovered only after many (or at least several) years of sustained production and sales. Therefore, the firm is not just interested in profit today. High current profit will lead to heavy losses in the future if present profits depend on duplicity, which is discovered and broadcast to consumers by word of mouth, by consumer research firms, and by the media. When consumers have the option of buying from a firm's competitors, the temptation to sacrifice both consumer welfare and the firm's future is held in check to a great extent. Warranties also play a role. If other firms provide a comprehensive warranty, then firm X must do the same to stay afloat. If X were to deceive customers by manufacturing low-quality items and passing them off as high-quality products, it would suffer heavy losses in the future as items are returned for replacement or repair under the warranty.

In some cases it is not easy to discover that the consumer has been misled. Consider housing construction. Defects may not show up for years, but when they do they can be extremely costly – wiring that causes fires, a leaky roof, and so forth. It will be very difficult for consumers to determine that construction company X produces houses that are more defect prone than those of other firms. The same is true for the suppliers of health care. And warranties won't work well in either case. A meaningful warranty on a new house would have to be long lived, but that presents *the construction firm* with a hidden information problem. Warranties remain in force as long as the consumer undertakes proper maintenance. This is easy to monitor in the case of new cars, which can be brought back to the dealer for periodic inspections, but is very difficult in the case of new houses. More significant is the fact that it becomes harder to define "proper maintenance" as time passes. And if maintenance requirements can't be specified, contracts cannot be written conditional on maintenance taking place. But if the home owner is not penalized for failure to keep the house in good repair then the owner has much less incentive

In spite of the difficulties we've identified, construction companies are not heedless of their reputation. Nevertheless, housing construction is typically regulated by the government as well as by the market. Because the cost of mistakes or fraud can be enormous, there is a case for government regulation even if defects could be eventually attributed to the producer. It is no coincidence that regulation is more stringent in Florida and California, where hurricanes and earthquakes are a constant worry.

In the 1980s in some areas of the former East Germany 90 percent of children suffered respiratory disease. Pollution-related cancers and infant mortality soared in Czechoslovakia during the 1970s and 1980s. During the same period, 95 percent of Polish rivers were polluted and the leukemia rate was soaring (*Business Week*, March 19, 1990, pp. 114, 115).

to invest in preventive care. A serious moral hazard problem prevents long-term warranties from being offered.

For a wide range of goods and services, competition among producers does force the individual firm to be concerned with its reputation. It is the lack of competition in the manufacture of appliances in the former Soviet Union that accounts for the explosion of thousands of television sets per year in Russia (see Milgrom and Roberts, 1992, p. 13).

Competition and reputation also have an important role to play in the political realm, of course. One reason why pollution reached grim proportions in Eastern Europe by 1990 is that the lack of political competition made it relatively easy for ministers responsible for the environment to conceal problems and thereby minimize the probability of being sacked. Politicians in multiparty, democratic countries also have an interest in covering up, but political rivals and a competitive press make it much more difficult to escape detection. "It is significant that no democratic country with a relatively free press has ever experienced a major famine ... This generalization applies to poor democracies as well as to rich ones" (Sen, 1993, p. 43). A. K. Sen has demonstrated that even in severe famines there is enough food to sustain the entire population of the affected region, and that leaders who must seek reelection are far more likely to take the steps necessary to see that food is appropriately distributed. The incentives confronting political leaders have life and death consequences for millions.

11.1.2 Responsiveness of Competitive Markets

A lot of creativity can be traced to market forces. A firm has to improve its product and bring new products to market; not just respond to a rival's innovation but anticipate what its rivals might do. "Catch-up" is a risky game to play. A firm is much more likely to survive and prosper if it takes its rivals by surprise. Each firm in an industry wants to be first with an innovation. The greater the competition in the industry, the more desperately a firm will strive to be the front runner. Several times a day you encounter evidence of the resulting creativity of markets. Even if you confine attention to the realm of information technology you can quickly recall quite a number of product innovations that owe their existence as much to some firm's fear of losing ground to others as to the ingenuity of someone's mind.

Modern printers receive several jobs more-or-less simultaneously from different workers. A contemporary printer builds a stack of documents, but will stagger the various jobs to reduce the probability that when A collects her output she unknowingly walks away with B's document. Competition between the printer manufacturers had much to do with that. Before the US government broke AT&T's monopoly hold on telephone service the telecom firm would not allow customers to use non-AT&T equipment. More significantly, they were under no pressure to provide useful services to customers – such as a telephone ringer that could be turned off when the baby is asleep. (My wife and I put thick tape around the bell.) Now that the suppliers of telephone services face vigorous competition, all kinds of useful features are available.

Beverage cans are made from two pieces of aluminum. A very thin disk is stamped to form the bottom and sides. The top is a separate disk that is crimped onto the sides. Because the contents are under pressure and the top is scored to allow the pop top to tear open when the consumer applies force, the top must be substantially thicker than the sides, adding to the cost of producing the can. Consequently, in the 1970s the sides of the can were tapered near the top to reduce the surface area of the top disk (Petrosky, 1996, p. 102). Think about the intricate web of market forces that inspired that innovation.

Pre-Industrial Revolution economies did not offer any consumer goods that were not also available in ancient Rome. The rate of economic growth over the 1500 years prior to the Industrial Revolution was essentially zero. Contrast that with the impressive stream of innovations that we enjoy. The flow of goods and services per capita from the world's mature capitalist economies is from several hundred percent to several thousand percent higher than 150 years ago. Why?

Capitalist, or free market, economies provide incentives that promote growth. Entrepreneurs are motivated to devote their energies to productive outlets, rather than to activities that merely transfer wealth from one pocket to another, as when an individual acquires land from a grateful monarch for services rendered. The rule of law plays a key role: contracts are enforced and property is protected from arbitrary expropriation.

11.1.3 Why not China?

Why did the Industrial Revolution start in England and a few other countries in Western Europe in the late eighteenth century and not much earlier in China?

Most of the following Chinese inventions are from the T'ang and Sung dynasties (618–906 AD and 960–1126 AD, respectively): paper, movable type, compasses, water wheels, sophisticated water clocks, gunpowder, spinning wheels, mechanical cotton gins, hydraulic trip hammers, ship construction techniques that permitted larger and more seaworthy vessels, sternpost rudders, superior sail designs, porcelain, umbrellas, matches, toothbrushes, and playing cards (Baumol, 1993, p. 42).

So many fundamental technological breakthroughs are of ancient Chinese origin.

There is no question that China had sufficient technical know-how for sustained economic growth. But it lacked a political and legal environment capable of nurturing and sustaining private enterprise. The monarch claimed the right to all property, and this right was used to raise money to solve budget difficulties or finance wars. "Private" property could be confiscated at any time. Also, the state thwarted private enterprise, and when it didn't succeed in stopping a venture it would often confiscate the fruits of inventive activity, as it did with paper, printing, and the bill of exchange. Consequently, any wealth that a merchant did succeed in accumulating was typically used to purchase land or invest in the enterprise of becoming a scholar-official. (English property owners led the world in extracting property right guarantees from their monarch.)

The Chinese scholar-official, called a Mandarin, held a position in what we would today call the civil service. A Mandarin occupied a far more prestigious position in Chinese society than even an extremely successful merchant or industrialist. One could not become a Mandarin without passing the astonishingly difficult civil service exams, and these required years of preparation, study, and tutoring. Families devoted lavish amounts of effort and resources in the attempt to get their children through these exams. The Mandarin's pay was low, however, and this led to corruption: he often extorted money from the people under his jurisdiction to boost the return on the investment in his education. Neither land purchase nor extortion is a productive investment from society's standpoint.

11.1.4 To Make a Long Story Short

The market mechanism is *decentralized*: each consumer is motivated by self-interest, as is each owner of a firm and each company manager. How could an efficient outcome possibly emerge from such apparent chaos?

Example 11.1 Two Individuals with Straight-Line Indifference Curves

Individual 1's utility function is $U_1 = 4a + b$, where a is the amount of good A and b is the amount of good B consumed by person 1. Individual 2's utility function is $U_2 = 5x + 2.5y$, where x and y denote person 2's consumption of commodities A and B, respectively. Suppose that $\Delta a = 1$. In words, person 1's consumption of A increases by 1 unit. Then

$$\Delta U_1 = 4a + 4 + b + \Delta b - (4a + b) = 4 + \Delta b.$$

(The Greek letter Δ denotes change.) Therefore, if $\Delta b = -4$ then $\Delta U_1 = 0$. In other words, 4 units of commodity B is the maximum that person 1 would be willing to sacrifice to obtain 1 more unit of A. Now, let $\Delta x = -1$. Then

$$\Delta U_2 = 5x - 5 + 2.5y + 2.5\Delta y - (5x + 2.5y) = -5 + 2.5\Delta y$$

If $\Delta y = +2$ then $\Delta U_2 = 0$. We see that 2 units of commodity B are the minimum compensation that person 2 needs for the loss of 1 unit of A. Finally, suppose that

$$\Delta a = 1 = -\Delta x \text{ and } \Delta b = -3 = -\Delta y.$$

In words, person 2 gives 1 unit of good A to person 1 in exchange for 3 units of good B. Then person 1 sacrifices less than the maximum that she would be prepared to give up to get another unit of A. And person 2 receives more than the minimum amount required to compensate him for the loss of a unit of A. It follows that the utility of both increases: $\Delta U_1 > 0$ and $\Delta U_2 > 0$. We have increased the utility of both consumers without affecting the consumption of anyone else. (Production plans are unchanged – it's just a matter of two people trading.) We conclude that the original outcome was not efficient.

The only thing that could undermine the argument of Example 11.1 is the possibility that $b < 3$ or $x < 1$ initially, but b and x are both positive. Then for some positive number δ we have $b > 3\delta$, and $x > \delta$, and if

$$\Delta a = \delta = - \Delta x \quad \text{and} \quad \Delta b = - 3\delta = - \Delta y$$

we have

$$\Delta U_1 = 4\Delta a + \Delta b = \delta > 0 \quad \text{and} \quad \Delta U_2 = 5\Delta x + 2.5\Delta y = 2.5\delta > 0.$$

The assumption that both individuals have linear utility functions is quite extreme, but it is very easy to generalize the argument, as we do now.

Example 11.2 Indifference Curves that are Curved

The commodity bundle (10, 8) provides 10 units of commodity A and 8 units of B. Suppose that the straight line $4a + b = 48$ is tangent at (10, 8) to person 1's indifference curve through (10, 8). Suppose that the equation of the tangent to individual 2's indifference curve through (7, 6) at the bundle (7, 6) itself is $5x + 2.5y = 50$. Therefore, for $\delta > 0$ sufficiently small we can set

$$\Delta a = \delta = - \Delta x \quad \text{and} \quad \Delta b = - 3\delta = - \Delta y$$

and thus $\Delta U_1 > 0$ and $\Delta U_2 > 0$. The tangent line approximates the indifference curve, but it is an extremely good approximation in a region very close to the tangency point. Therefore, we can use the argument of Example 11.1 if δ is sufficiently small. We have increased the utility of both consumers without affecting the consumption of anyone else, and hence the original outcome is not efficient.

By definition, an individual's MRS at a commodity bundle is the negative of slope of the tangent to the indifference curve at that bundle. For Examples 11.1 and 11.2, the slope of $4a + b = 48$ is -4. The slope of $5x + 2.5y = 50$ is $-5/2.5 = -2$. Therefore, person 1's MRS at (10, 8) is 4 and 2's MRS at (7, 6) is 2. Because these marginal rates are not equal we were able to engineer a trade between the two individuals that made both better off and that had no effect on anyone else's consumption. If the original allocation of goods and services is efficient, this won't be possible. We have discovered an important necessary condition for efficiency.

Efficiency Theorem 1: Necessary Condition for Efficiency
If two consumers have a positive amount of each of two commodities then if their
marginal rates of substitution are not equal the economy-wide allocation of
goods and services is not efficient.

Why should we worry about inefficiency if individuals can get together and trade to rectify the situation, as in Examples 11.1 or 11.2? Because there are millions of consumers, and hence an astronomical number of trades that may have to be arranged to move the economy toward an efficient outcome. Moreover, the two individuals may be two thousand miles apart. It is vital that an economic system get the allocation of commodities right the first time. The market system does: each consumer maximizes utility subject to the budget constraint, and that results in equality between the individual's MRS and the price ratio. At individual 1's chosen consumption plan his or her MRS will equal p_A/p_B, where p_A is the price of A and p_B is the price of B. That means that when other consumers determine their own utility-maximizing consumption plans they will take individual 1's MRS into consideration because the price ratio p_A/p_B will play a central role. Because budget-constrained utility maximization implies $MRS_1 = p_A/p_B = MRS_2$, where MRS_i denotes individual i's MRS, person 1's MRS plays a central role in person 2's utility-maximization exercise and vice versa. Of course, this can be said of any pair of individuals who consume some of each of the two goods in question.

To summarize: the price ratio transmits information about one consumer's MRS to all other consumers, and the budget constraint gives each the incentive to use this information in his or her planning. This incentive derives from the fact that the price ratio p_A/p_B is the amount of commodity B that the individual could have purchased with the amount of money it takes to purchase one unit of commodity A. That opportunity cost will play a central role in the utility-maximizing individual's decision making. This information and incentive role of prices is one reason for the high-level performance of the private ownership market economy.

Now let's consider the production of goods and services. Reinterpret Examples 11.1 and 11.2 with individual 1 as *firm* 1, and individual 2 as *firm* 2. In that case, $U_1(a, b)$ is firm 1's output when it employs a units of input A and b units of input B. Similarly, $U_2(x, y)$ is firm 2's output when it employs x units of A and y units of B. (The two firms may produce very different commodities.) If the firms do not have identical marginal rates of technical substitution (*RTS*; i.e., their isoquants do not have identical slopes at the respective input bundles employed) then they can trade inputs in a way that increases the output of both firms. This extra output can be used to increase someone's utility without affecting that of anyone else: there is no increase in the amount of any input employed.

Efficiency Theorem 2: A Second Necessary Condition for Efficiency

If two firms employ a positive amount of each of two inputs and if their marginal rates of technical substitution (RTS) are not equal, the economy-wide configuration of production and consumption activities is not efficient.

Note that cost minimization – one consequence of profit maximization – by a firm in the market system implies that each firm's employment of inputs equates the input price ratio p_A/p_B to the firm's *RTS*. Efficiency requires $RTS_1 = RTS_2$ for any two firms 1 and 2. In the market system, $RTS_1 = p_A/p_B = RTS_2$ and thus $RTS_1 = RTS_2$. The input price ratio transmits information to each firm about the *RTS* of each other firm, and the profit motive – via cost minimization – gives each firm the incentive to use that information. To activate the profit motive, of course, we have to give consumers ownership shares in the firms. They will then have an incentive to motivate the managers of firms to maximize profit.

Suppose that we arrive on the scene just after the market mechanism reaches an equilibrium: each consumer has maximized utility subject to the budget constraint, each firm has maximized profit, given the prices, and demand equals supply for every good. Let's test the efficiency of the equilibrium by trying to divert resources from the production of commodity *B* to the production of commodity *A* to see if we can make some individuals better off without harming anyone else. Specifically, we'll withdraw a specific package *R* of resources (inputs) from the production of *B* and use them to produce more *A*. Suppose that this results in the loss of ∇b units of *B* and an increase of Δa units of *A*. (Because Δb is negative we let ∇b represent its absolute value.) Now, suppose that this change in the economy-wide output of goods and services allows us to rearrange everyone's consumption in a way that increases everyone's utility. But all consumers have maximized utility subject to their budget constraints. It must be that the bundles, which yield higher utility, were not chosen because they were not affordable – that is, too expensive. If this is true for each consumer, it must be true in the aggregate. Therefore, $p_A\Delta a > p_B\nabla b$, where p_A and p_B denote the equilibrium prices of *A* and *B*, respectively. In words, the total amount of money that would have been saved by reducing *B* consumption is insufficient to finance the total increase in *A* consumption.

We know that $p_A\Delta a > p_B\nabla b$ and that the change in production was brought about by moving a set *R* of resources from firms that produce *B* to firms that produce *A*. This implies that firms have not maximized profit, contradicting the supposition that we started from equilibrium. Why does $p_A\Delta a > p_B\nabla b$ contradict profit maximization? If each firm maximizes profit, given the prices, then total, economy-wide profit must be maximized at equilibrium. However, the transfer of the set *R* of resources from *B* firms to *A* firms will not change total *cost* in the economy. Cost will be lower in the industry producing commodity *B* but will be higher by the same amount in industry *A*. However, revenue has increased because $p_A\Delta a > p_B\nabla b$. If we can increase total revenue in the economy without increasing total cost, we can increase total profit. If that is possible at least one firm must initially have fallen short of profit maximization, contradicting the definition of equilibrium, which requires, among other things, profit maximization by each firm. (If each firm's profit is maximized then total profit is maximized.) We have proved that starting from an equilibrium of the market system it is not possible to change the composition of goods and services produced to make one person better off without making someone worse off.

We seem to have exhausted all the possibilities for improving on the outcome of the market system, without finding a source of inefficiency. Nothing succeeded, so the market equilibrium must be efficient. However, this subsection is far from rigorous enough to be called a proof. It does have the advantage of bringing out some of the intuition behind the remarkable performance of the private ownership market economy. The rigorous proof of efficiency comes in the next section.

Sources

Milgrom and Roberts (1992, p. 13) recount the story of exploding television sets in Russia. The paragraph on famines in Section 11.1.1 is based on Sen (1981). Hammons (2001) notes the existence of educational testing services for children educated at home. The discussion of economic growth in Section 11.1.2 is based on Chapter 1 of Baumol (2002). Section 11.1.3 on China is based on pages 31–44 in Baumol (1993).

Links

See Drèze and Sen (1989) for a thorough examination of the problem of hunger. Balazs (1964) is a classic study of the Mandarin class. The historian Prasannan Parthasarathi (2011) challenges the explanation for the industrial revolution taking root in England long before it did in China that we presented in Section 11.1.3 above.

Problem Set

(1) Individual 1's utility function is $U_1 = \alpha a + \beta b$, where α and β are positive constants, a is the amount of the good A consumed by person 1, and b is the amount of good B. Individual 2's utility function is $U_2 = \rho x + \sigma y$, where ρ and σ are positive constants, and x and y denote person 2's consumption of commodities A and B, respectively.

   (A) Show that if α/β is not equal to ρ/σ then the two individuals have indifference curves with different slopes.

   (B) Show that if a, b, x, and y are all positive and the two individuals have different marginal rates of substitution then there is a trade between the two that raises the utility of each.

(2) The utility functions of individuals 1 and 2 are, respectively, $U_1 = ab$ and $U_2 = xy$, with a, b, x, and y as in question 1. Find the tangent to person 1's indifference curve through the commodity bundle (5, 3) at bundle (5, 3), and the tangent to person 2's indifference curve through (6, 9) at (6, 9). If you don't know calculus, a good approximation will suffice: draw an accurate indifference curve and use

a ruler to construct the tangent. Then find the equation that it represents. Use the arguments of Examples 11.1 and 11.2 to devise a trade between the two individuals that leaves both better off. Plug the new values of a, b, x, and y into the utility functions to confirm that $U_1(a, b)$ is now higher than $U_1(5, 3)$ and that $U_2(x, y)$ is now higher than $U_2(6, 9)$.

(3) Section 11.1.4 showed that if the transfer of resources from the production of commodity A to commodity B results in a change in the total production of A and B that could be used to make everyone better off, then $p_A \Delta a > p_B \nabla b$, where p_A and p_B denote the equilibrium prices of A and B, Δa is the increase in the output of A, and ∇b is the reduction in the output of B. Show that $p_A \Delta a > p_B \nabla b$ holds even if the change in production can be used to make just one consumer better off without making any other consumer worse off, assuming that before the change is made consumers have maximized utility subject to their respective budget constraints.

11.2 THE ARROW-DEBREU ECONOMY

This section establishes the efficiency of the model of a private ownership market economy developed by K. J. Arrow and G. Debreu, who first worked out the fundamental properties of general equilibrium. It is sometimes referred to as the Arrow-Debreu-McKenzie model in belated recognition of the seminal contribution of Lionel McKenzie. (See Weintraub, 2014).

11.2.1 The Model

We begin with the pure exchange version: production has already taken place. As a result, each consumer has an abundance of some commodities and a dearth of others. The individual supplies some goods to the market and uses the resulting income to buy other goods. This *exchange economy* is at equilibrium when the prices have adjusted to the point where supply equals demand in each market simultaneously.

DEFINITION: *n-Person Exchange Economy*

There are n consumers, indexed by $i = 1, 2, \ldots, n$, and there are ℓ commodities, named $c = 1, 2, \ldots, \ell$. Individual i's consumption plan is a vector (list) $x_i = (x_{i1}, x_{i2}, \ldots, x_{i\ell})$ that specifies the consumption of x_{ic} units of each commodity c. Individual i is endowed with the ℓ-vector $\omega_i = (\omega_{i1}, \omega_{i2}, \ldots, \omega_{i\ell})$ that specifies the amount ω_{ic} of each commodity c that i possesses before trade takes place. An *allocation* x is an assignment of a commodity bundle x_i to each individual i, and it is *feasible* if

$$x_{1c} + x_{2c} + \cdots + x_{nc} \leq \omega_{1c} + \omega_{2c} + \cdots + \omega_{nc}$$

holds for each commodity c. The preference scheme of individual i is represented by a utility function U_i.

To simplify the notation we let $x_1 + x_2 + \ldots + x_n \leq \omega_1 + \omega_2 + \ldots + \omega_n$ represent the statement "$x_{1c} + x_{2c} + \ldots + x_{nc} \leq \omega_{1c} + \omega_{2c} + \ldots + \omega_{nc}$ for each commodity c."

A *price system* is an ℓ-vector $p = (p_1, p_2, \ldots, p_\ell)$ specifying the price p_c of each commodity c. A *competitive equilibrium* of this economy is a price-allocation pair (p, x) such that for each individual i the consumption plan specified for i by allocation x maximizes i's utility subject to i's budget constraint, and the total consumption of each good equals the total endowment of that good – that is, demand equals supply for each commodity. Individual i's *budget constraint* is

$$p_1 x_{i1} + p_2 x_{i2} + \cdots + p_\ell x_{i\ell} \leq p_1 \omega_{i1} + p_2 \omega_{i2} + \cdots + p_\ell \omega_{i\ell}$$

We assume that the individual sells all of the goods in i's endowment ω_i for an amount of money $p_1 \omega_{i1} + p_2 \omega_{i2} + \ldots + p_\ell \omega_{i\ell}$. This money is then used to buy a new collection $(x_{i1}, x_{i2}, \ldots, x_{i\ell})$ of goods and services.

Example 11.3 Buying Back Some of your Endowment

There are two commodities ($\ell = 2$). Individual 1's endowment is $\omega_1 = (12, 0)$. That is, person 1 holds 12 units of the first good and 0 units of the second good before markets open. If $p_1 = 2$ and $p_2 = 5$ then the individual's budget constraint is $2x_{11} + 5x_{12} \leq 24$. The consumption plan $(7, 2)$ is affordable because $2 \times 7 + 5 \times 2 = 24$. If the individual demands $(7, 2)$ we portray him or her as selling the entire endowment for $24 and then using $14 of that to buy back 7 units of commodity 1. The remaining $10 is used to purchase 2 units of commodity 2. In fact, the consumer would simply sell 5 units of commodity 1 for $10 and then use that money to buy 2 units of the second good.

A homeowner "buys back" her own house every period, in the sense that she could sell it at current market value and then use the proceeds to buy something else, now or in the future. The decision about what to consume in the current period is not unrelated to the value of her house.

DEFINITION: *Competitive Equilibrium of an Exchange Economy*

The price system p and allocation x constitute a competitive equilibrium if for each individual i the consumption plan x_i maximizes U_i subject to i's budget constraint, and $x_1 + x_2 + \ldots + x_n = \omega_1 + \omega_2 + \ldots + \omega_n$, which means that demand equals supply for each commodity.

Now let's add production to the model. There are ℓ commodities and n individual consumers (or households) as in the exchange economy. In addition there are m firms. We let $I = \{1, 2, \ldots, n\}$ denote the set of households and let $J = \{1, 2, \ldots, m\}$ denote the set of firms. An allocation assigns a consumption plan to each individual and a production plan to each firm. Each individual has an initial endowment and a preference scheme, represented by a utility function. Each firm j has a technology set T_j that specifies the production plans that the firm is able to carry out.

DEFINITION: *The Arrow-Debreu Economy with Production*

There are n consumers and ℓ commodities. Each individual i has an initial endowment vector ω_i. Also, individual i may own shares in one or more firms. We let α_{ij} be the fraction of firm j owned by individual i. We let the utility function U_i represent the preference scheme of individual i. An allocation (x, y) specifies a consumption plan x_i for each individual i and a production plan y_j for each firm j. The production plan $y_j = (y_{j1}, y_{j2}, \ldots, y_{j\ell})$ specifies a positive, zero, or negative number y_{jc} for each commodity c. If $y_{jc} > 0$ then the production plan y_j yields y_{jc} units of commodity c as output but if $y_{jc} < 0$ the plan y_j requires $|y_{jc}|$ units of commodity c as input. This sign convention allows us to distinguish inputs from outputs and to represent profit straightforwardly.

Given the price system $p = (p_1, p_2, \ldots, p_\ell)$ the production plan $y_j = (y_{j1}, y_{j2}, \ldots, y_{j\ell})$ yields a profit of

$$p_1 y_{j1} + p_2 y_{j2} + \cdots + p_\ell y_{j\ell},$$

which we write as py_j for short. If $y_{jc} > 0$ then $p_c y_{jc}$ is the revenue resulting from the sale of y_{jc} units of commodity c at price p_c. If $y_{jc} < 0$ then $|y_{jc}|$ units of commodity c are employed as input at a cost of $p_c \times |y_{jc}|$. When we *add* $p_c y_{jc}$ into the firm's profit calculation we are subtracting $p_c \times |y_{jc}|$ from revenue.

Example 11.4 The Profit Calculation

There are two commodities, and the firm's technology simply requires the employment of 2 units of commodity 1 for each unit of output of commodity 2. The production plan $y_1 = (-10,5)$ employs 10 units of commodity 1 as input and produces 5 units of commodity 2 as output. If $p_1 = 3$ and $p_2 = 9$ then the firm's profit is $p_1 y_{11} + p_2 y_{12} = 3 \times -10 + 9 \times 5 = 15$.

Let's keep track of a particular commodity c. Given the allocation (x, y), the net output of c is $\sum_{j \in J} y_{jc}$. Because y_{jc} is a negative number when j uses c as an input, the expression $\sum_{j \in J} y_{jc}$ gives us the total output of c by the production sector less the total amount of c used as input by firms. Therefore, $\sum_{j \in J} y_{jc}$ is the net output of commodity c. It is possible to have $\sum_{j \in J} y_{jc} < 0$. This would be inevitable if c were labor: all firms use labor as an input but it is not produced by any firm. Labor would be supplied by households, of course, and if ω_{ic} denotes household i's endowment of labor then $\sum_{i \in I} \omega_{ic} + \sum_{j \in J} y_{jc}$ is equal to the total endowment of labor in the economy less the total amount used as input. Therefore, $\sum_{i \in I} \omega_{ic} + \sum_{j \in J} y_{jc}$ is the total amount of labor available to households as leisure for consumption. And $\sum_{i \in I} x_{ic}$ is obviously the total amount of leisure consumed by the household sector. Therefore, any allocation (x, y) must satisfy

$$\sum_{i \in I} x_{ic} \le \sum_{i \in I} \omega_{ic} + \sum_{j \in J} y_{jc}$$

if commodity c is labor.

Consider another commodity c for which $\sum_{j \in J} y_{jc}$ is positive. The allocation (x, y) leads to positive net output of c, and is added to the households' endowment $\sum_{j \in J} \omega_{ic}$ of c (if any) to determine the total amount of c available for consumption. This total again is $\sum_{j \in J} \omega_{jc} + \sum_{j \in J} y_{jc}$ and again we see that an allocation must satisfy

$$\sum_{i \in I} x_{ic} \le \sum_{i \in I} \omega_{ic} + \sum_{j \in J} y_{jc}.$$

We refer to this inequality as the *material feasibility* condition, and it must hold for each commodity c.

An allocation must also satisfy the *firm-level* feasibility conditions. Firm j's technology must be capable of turning the inputs specified by y_j into the outputs specified by y_j. Recall that T_j is the set of production plans that are technologically feasible for firm j. If y_j belongs to T_j there is no guarantee that j will actually be able to obtain the inputs required by y_j. There might be excess demand for one input, making it unavailable to some firms. This will not happen if the material feasibility condition holds, but that is guaranteed to hold only at equilibrium. The individual firm cannot be expected to worry about the economy-wide material feasibility condition.

DEFINITION: *Feasibility*

The allocation (x, y) is feasible if

$$\sum_{i \in I} x_{ic} \le \sum_{i \in I} \omega_{ic} + \sum_{j \in J} y_{jc}$$

holds for every commodity c (material feasibility), and in addition the production plan y_j belongs to the technology set T_j, for each firm j (firm-level feasibility).

Example 11.5 Feasibility in a Simple Economy

There are two commodities, one individual, and one firm. It follows that $a_{ij} = 1$. (Individual 1 owns the firm and hence the rights to the firm's profit.) The individual's endowment is $\omega_1 = (48,0)$. The firm's production technology is specified by the equation " output $= 2\sqrt{\text{input}}$." Suppose the allocation (x, y) specifies the consumption plan $x_1 = (32, 8)$ and the production plan $y_1 = (-16, 8)$, which employs 16 units of commodity 1 as input and produces 8 units of commodity 2 as output $(8 = 2\sqrt{16})$. If $p_1 = 1$ and $p_2 = 4$ then the firm's profit is 16, and the consumer's budget constraint $x_{11} + 4x_{12} \le \omega_{11} + 4\omega_{12} + 16$ is satisfied. The allocation $((32, 8),$ $(-16, 8))$ is feasible because $(-16, 8)$ is in the firm's technology set, and in addition

$$32 = 48 - 16 \text{ and } 8 = 0 + 8.$$

At equilibrium, each firm maximizes profit, given prices and its technology set, all consumers maximize utility given their budget constraints, and every market clears (i.e., the demand for each good equals its supply). Suppose that the prices are given by $p = (p_1, p_2, \dots, p_\ell)$.

Profit maximization is easy to characterize: recall that $p_1 y_{j1} + p_2 y_{j2} + \dots + p_\ell y_{j\ell}$, which we denote by $py_{j,}$ is j's profit from the production plan y_j. Then the plan y_j maximizes profit if y_j belongs to T_j and $py_j \ge pz_j$ holds for all z_j in T_j. In words, the plan y_j is feasible for the firm, and no other feasible plan yields higher profit.

Derivation of the consumer's budget constraint requires a little work. If x_i is individual i's consumption plan then expenditure is clearly $p_1 x_{i1} + p_2 x_{i2} + \dots + p_\ell x_{i\ell}$ which we write as px_i for short. What is i's income? Income from the sale of i's endowment is just $p\omega_i = p_1\omega_{i1} + p_2\omega_{i2} + \dots + p_\ell\omega_{i\ell}$, but i may also have profit income. Household i owns the fraction α_{ij} of firm j so i will receive that fraction of j's profit and hence will receive $\alpha_{ij}py_j$ in total from firm j. If we add this term over all firms j we get i's total profit income, namely $\sum_{j \in J} \alpha_{ij} py_j$. Therefore, i's total income is $p\omega_i + \sum_{j \in J} \alpha_{ij} py_j$, and hence i's budget constraint is

$$px_i \le p\,\omega_i + \sum_{j \in J} \alpha_{ij}\, py_j.$$

DEFINITION: *General Competitive Equilibrium*

The price system p and allocation (x, y) constitute a competitive equilibrium if for each individual i the consumption plan x_i maximizes U_i subject to i's budget constraint; for each firm j the production plan y_j belongs to T_j, the set of feasible production plans for firm j; and no member of T_j yields a higher profit than y_j *given* the price regime p. Finally, all markets clear, which means that

$$\sum_{i \in I} x_{ic} = \sum_{i \in I} \omega_{ic} + \sum_{j \in J} y_{jc}$$

holds for each commodity c. We refer to this last property as *market clearance.*

Before presenting an example of general equilibrium we identify a property of a simple family of utility functions that is used frequently.

DEFINITION: *Cobb-Douglas Utility Function*

Cobb-Douglas utility functions have the form $U(a, b) = a^\alpha b^\beta$ where a is the consumption of the first good, b is the consumption of the second good, and α and β are positive constants.

Note that with Cobb-Douglas utility if the price of either good is zero then there will be unlimited demand for that good and demand will certainly exceed supply. Therefore, both prices will be positive at equilibrium. It follows that, unless the individual's endowment is zero, he or she will have a positive income and hence can afford a positive amount of each good. Consequently, utility will be positive. But if $a = 0$ or $b = 0$ then utility is zero. (With Cobb-Douglas preferences, $U(0, b) = 0 = U(a, 0)$.) That can't be a utility-maximizing strategy. Therefore, the consumer will demand a positive amount of each good at equilibrium. It follows that the consumer's marginal rate of substitution will equal the price ratio at the consumption plan demanded.

We exploit the equality of the MRS and the price ratio without explicitly invoking it every time we use a Cobb-Douglas utility function.

Example ∂11.6 Competitive Equilibrium in a Simple Economy with Production

The setup is identical to that of Example 11.5: there are two commodities, one individual, and one firm. Individual 1's preference is represented by the utility function $U_1 = x_{11} \times x_{12}$, and 1's endowment is $\omega_1 = (48,0)$. Individual 1 owns the firm, so it follows that $\alpha_{ij} = 1$. The firm's production technology is given by "output $= 2\sqrt{\text{input}}$." We show that $p_1 = 1$ and $p_2 = 4$ are competitive equilibrium prices. The production plan $y_1 = (-16, 8)$ results in a profit of $1 \times -16 + 4 \times 8 = 16$. To confirm that $(-16, 8)$ is profit maximizing given the prices, let q denote the amount of input employed. Then the firm will produce $2\sqrt{q}$ units of the second good. The firm's profit is

$$4 \times 2\sqrt{q} - 1 \times q$$

and the first derivative of profit is

$$\frac{4}{\sqrt{q}} - 1.$$

(Note that the second derivative is negative.) When we set the first derivative equal to 0 and solve for q we get $q = 16$. Then no other feasible production plan gives a higher profit than $(-16, 8)$.

The consumer's budget constraint is $x_{11} + 4x_{12} \leq 1 \times 48 + 16$. (The right-hand side is the value of the individual's endowment plus profit.) The consumption plan $x_1 = (32, 8)$ maximizes U_1 subject to the budget constraint. To confirm this we set

$$MRS = \frac{x_{12}}{x_{11}} = \frac{p_1}{p_2} = \frac{1}{4}.$$

Then $x_{11} = 4x_{12}$ and hence the budget equation $x_{11} + 4x_{12} = 64$ reduces to $2x_{11} = 64$, and thus the chosen consumption plan has $x_{11} = 32$. Because $x_{11} = 4x_{12}$ we have $x_{12} = 8$. (If you don't know calculus, you can take my word that the MRS is the amount of the second good divided by the amount of the first good. To use calculus to derive the MRS, begin with the utility function $U = ab$. Hold utility constant at k. The equation of the associated indifference curve is $ab = k$, and we can solve this for b, yielding $b = ka^{-1}$. The derivative db/da is $-ka^{-2}$. Because $k = ab$ we can write

$$\frac{db}{da} = -ka^{-2} = -(ab)a^{-2} = -\frac{b}{a}$$

The MRS is the negative of this derivative. That is, the MRS is the negative of the slope of the indifference curve. The derivative can also be computed by applying the implicit function theorem to $u_1(x, y) = k$.)

The demand for commodity 1 is $x_{11} = 32$, and the supply is $\omega_{11} + y_{11} = 48 - 16$. The demand for commodity 2 is $x_{12} = 8$, and the supply is $\omega_{12} + y_{13} = 0 + 8$. Therefore, both markets clear. (Alternatively, set $x_{11} = 64 - 4x_{12}$ and maximize $(64 - 4x_{12})x_{12}$.)

11.2.2 Welfare Theorem for an Exchange Economy

Every competitive equilibrium of the n-person exchange economy is weakly efficient. That is, there is no feasible allocation that gives everyone more utility than the equilibrium. An important implicit assumption is that for each individual i the utility function U_i depends only on i's consumption plan $x_i = (x_{i1}, x_{i2}, \ldots, x_{i\ell})$ and hence is independent of any other individual's consumption of any commodity. A concluding remark shows that we can actually claim that the equilibrium is efficient, not just weakly efficient.

Welfare Theorem

> *A competitive equilibrium of the n-person exchange economy is efficient.*

Proof:

We begin by showing that every allocation that gives everyone more utility than the equilibrium violates the material feasibility condition $x_1 + x_2 + \ldots + x_n \leq \omega_1 + \omega_2 + \ldots + \omega_n$ Let the price system p and the allocation x constitute a competitive equilibrium. Suppose that the allocation z satisfies $U_i(z_i) > U_i(x_i)$ for each individual i. Because x_i maximizes U_i subject to i's budget constraint

$$p_1 x_{i1} + p_2 x_{i2} + \cdots + p_\ell x_{i\ell} \leq p_1 \omega_{i1} + p_2 \omega_{i2} + \cdots + p_\ell \omega_{i\ell}$$

the consumption plan z_i was not affordable when x_i was chosen. That is,

$$p_1 z_{i1} + p_2 z_{i2} + \cdots + p_\ell z_{i\ell} > p_1 \omega_{i1} + p_2 \omega_{i2} + \cdots + p_\ell \omega_{i\ell}$$

for each individual i. It follows that

$$\begin{aligned}
&p_1(z_{11} + z_{21} + \cdots + z_{n1}) + p_2(z_{12} + z_{22} + \cdots + z_{n2}) + \cdots \\
&\quad + p_c(z_{1c} + z_{2c} + \cdots + z_{nc}) + \cdots + p_\ell(z_{1\ell} + z_{2\ell} + \cdots + z_{n\ell}) \\
&> p_1(\omega_{11} + \omega_{21} + \cdots + \omega_{n1}) + p_2(\omega_{12} + \omega_{22} + \cdots + \omega_{n2}) + \cdots \\
&\quad + p_c(\omega_{1c} + \omega_{2c} + \cdots + \omega_{nc}) + \cdots + p_\ell(\omega_{1\ell} + \omega_{2\ell} + \cdots + \omega_{n\ell}).
\end{aligned}$$

In words, the total market value of consumption exceeds the total market value of the commodities available for consumption. That strict inequality is inconsistent with the following material feasibility requirement:

$$z_{1c} + z_{2c} + \cdots + z_{nc} \leq \omega_{1c} + \omega_{2c} + \cdots + \omega_{nc}$$

which must hold for each commodity c. (If the total consumption of commodity c is less than or equal to the total endowment of c, then the market value of the amount of consumption of commodity c provided by z must be less than or equal to the market value of the total endowed amount of c. In that case, the total market value of consumption at z, over all commodities, cannot exceed the total market value of all endowments.) We have proved that the competitive equilibrium allocation is weakly efficient: there is no *feasible* allocation that gives everyone more utility than the competitive equilibrium. ∎

Suppose that we had a feasible allocation z that gave *one* individual i more utility than the equilibrium allocation x and gave everyone else at least as much utility as x. Then we can construct a feasible allocation z' that gives everyone strictly more utility than x, contradicting what we have just proved. To construct z' from z we merely take a small amount of some commodity away from individual i, but we confiscate a sufficiently small amount so that i still has more utility than at x. Then we divide the amount taken from i among the remaining individuals. The resulting allocation z' will give each more utility than at z, and hence strictly more utility than at x. And z' is feasible because it is constructed from z simply by redistributing a little bit of one of the commodities. Because we have already proved that there is no feasible allocation that makes everyone better off than at the competitive equilibrium we have demonstrated that the competitive equilibrium is in fact efficient, not just weakly efficient.

The previous paragraph incorporates two implicit assumptions: first, individual i's preference ordering is continuous: if i strictly prefers z_i to x_i and we reduce z_i by some sufficiently small amount the resulting consumption plan will still be strictly preferred to x_i. Second, any individual's utility will increase if that person's consumption of any commodity increases, however small that increase.

Note that our proof is valid even when one or more consumers is at a corner of his or her budget line, with marginal rates of substitution unequal to the equilibrium price ratio, and even when marginal rates of substitution are not defined. The proof does not even depend on the representation of individual preference by a utility function: if individual i prefers z_i to x_i, and x_i was chosen at equilibrium, then z_i must have been too expensive. The rest of the proof follows without modification. It is a *very* general argument. The key assumptions are that agents take prices as given and that preferences are *self-regarding* – each individual cares only about his or her own consumption.

11.2.3 The Welfare Theorem in the General Model

Now we add production to the model and show that a competitive equilibrium of the Arrow-Debreu economy is efficient, provided that every commodity that affects individual utility is traded in a competitive market – the *completeness of markets* assumption. Completeness of markets means that for every possible realization of every random event there is a market in which one can purchase or sell a unit of any good contingent on that realization. Completeness also requires that for every future date there is a market in which anyone can purchase or sell a unit of any good for delivery at that date. It also entails the assumption that if individual or firm K's actions affect the welfare of other agents – think of pollution – then there is a market that causes this side effect to be brought to bear on K's decision making via K's budget constraint (if K is a consumer) or K's profit (if K is a firm).

DEFINITION: *Complete Set of Markets*
Every commodity that affects some individual's welfare is traded in a competitive market.

A complete set of markets would be astronomical in number. We never have anything close to completeness in the real world. Nevertheless, the Arrow-Debreu economy with complete markets is a valuable framework within which to study resource allocation. It is also an important benchmark case. For one thing, it helps us identify what has gone wrong when the economy is not efficient.

Welfare Theorem for an Economy with Production
If markets are complete then a competitive equilibrium of the Arrow-Debreu economy is efficient.

Proof:

We begin by showing that an allocation that gives everyone strictly more utility than the competitive equilibrium cannot be feasible. Let (p, x, y) be the competitive equilibrium. Suppose that the allocation (x', y') gives everyone more utility. Then $U_i(x_i') > U_i(x_i)$ for each consumer i. But x_i maximizes U_i subject to the budget constraint. This means that x_i' was not affordable when x_i was chosen. Therefore

$$px_i' > p\omega_i + \sum_{j\in J}\alpha_{ij}py_j.$$

This is true for each i, so it will remain true when we sum over all individuals. That is,

$$\sum_{i\in I}px_i' > \sum_{i\in I}p\omega_i + \sum_{i\in I}\sum_{j\in J}\alpha_{ij}py_j.$$

Now $\sum_{i\in I}\sum_{j\in J}\alpha_{ij}py_j$ is equal to $\sum_{j\in J}py_j\sum_{i\in I}\alpha_{ij}$. But for firm j the sum $\sum_{i\in I}\alpha_{ij}$ is the sum of all the ownership shares in firm j and that total must equal 1. Therefore, $\sum_{i\in I}\sum_{j\in J}\alpha_{ij}py_j$ equals $\sum_{j\in J}py_j$, which is the total profit in the economy at equilibrium. Therefore, we can state

$$\sum_{i \in I} p x_i' > \sum_{i \in I} p \omega_i + \sum_{j \in J} p y_j. \tag{1}$$

If y_j' does not belong to T_j for some firm j then the allocation (x', y') is not feasible. If each y_j' does belong to T_j, then because y_j maximizes j's profit given p we must have $p y_j \geq p y_j'$ for each firm j. Therefore, $\sum_{j \in J} p y_j \geq \sum_{j \in J} p y_j'$. This inequality and [1] gives us

$$\sum_{i \in I} p x_i' > \sum_{i \in I} p \omega_i + \sum_{j \in J} p y_j' \tag{2}$$

However, [2] is inconsistent with material feasibility of (x', y'): If we did have $\sum_{i \in I} x_{ic}' \leq \sum_{i \in I} \omega_{ic} + \sum_{j \in J} y_{jc}'$ for each commodity c, then by virtue of the fact that $p_c \geq 0$ we would have

$$p_c \sum_{i \in I} x_{ic}' \leq p_c \sum_{i \in I} \omega_{ic} + p_c \sum_{j \in J} y_{jc}' \tag{3}$$

for each c. When we add each side of [3] over all commodities we get

$$\sum_{i \in I} p x_i' \leq \sum_{i \in I} p \omega_i + \sum_{j \in J} p y_j' \tag{4}$$

a direct contradiction of [2]. (Statements [3] and [4] are equivalent because $p \sum_{i \in I} x_i'$ is equal to $p_1 \sum_{i \in I} x_{i1}' + p_2 \sum_{i \in I} x_{i2}' + \ldots + p_\ell \sum_{i \in I} x_{i_\ell}'$, and the other terms of [2] can be similarly expressed.) Therefore, there can be no feasible allocation that gives everyone more utility than the competitive equilibrium. ∎

We have shown that any allocation that gives everyone more utility than the competitive equilibrium must violate one of the feasibility conditions. In other words, there is no feasible allocation that would give everyone more utility than the market equilibrium. If there were a feasible allocation (x', y') that gave *one* individual i more utility than the equilibrium and gave no one any less utility we could construct a feasible allocation (x'', y'') from (x', y') by taking a sufficiently small amount of some commodity away from individual i in a way that still leaves person i strictly better off than at the equilibrium. If we divide the amount confiscated from i among the remaining individuals we will have made everyone better off than at the equilibrium, contradicting what we have just proved. Therefore, the competitive equilibrium is in fact efficient, not just weakly efficient. (The second-to-last paragraph of Section 11.2.2 discloses the implicit assumptions that make this argument work.)

To complete the demonstration that the Arrow-Debreu economy performs efficiently we must prove that an equilibrium actually exists. Example 11.9 of Section 11.3 shows that existence cannot be taken for granted. However, if individual preferences exhibit diminishing MRS and production processes have diminishing marginal products, then a competitive equilibrium will exist. That is, *if* agents take prices as given, there will be an equilibrium and it will be efficient – assuming complete markets. The existence question is explored briefly in Section 11.3 and the assumption of price-taking behavior is the subject of Section 11.4. We conclude this section by showing what goes wrong when markets are not complete.

11.2.4 Externalities

A competitive equilibrium of the private ownership market economy will not likely be efficient if one person's consumption directly affects the welfare of someone else, which we refer to as an *externality*.

DEFINITION: *Externality*

An externality is present when some agent A's actions directly affect the welfare of another agent B but the system does give A an incentive to bring the effect on B to bear on A's decision making.

Let's see why externalities undermine the efficient operation of competitive markets.

Example 11.7 A Two-Person Exchange Economy with Externalities

The endowments are $\omega_1 = (0, 16)$ and $\omega_2 = (16, 0)$, with

$$U_1 = x_{11} \times x_{12} - 3x_{21} \quad \text{and} \quad U_2 = x_{21} \times x_{22}.$$

Person 1 is adversely affected by the other person's consumption of the first good. Person 1 cannot control the choice of person 2 so when 1 maximizes utility he or she must take x_{21} as given. That is, x_{21} will be treated as a constant in person 1's decision making. Therefore, to find the chosen consumption plans we can employ the utility functions $U_1 = x_{11} \times x_{12}$ and $U_2 = x_{21} \times x_{22}$. The MRSs are x_{12}/x_{11} for person 1 and x_{22}/x_{21} for person 2. Each consumer will maximize utility by setting the MRS equal to the price ratio. (The MRS is derived at the end of Example 2.4. Note that individual utility would be 0 if the individual consumed 0 units of one of the goods.) Therefore we have

$$\frac{x_{12}}{x_{11}} = \frac{p_1}{p_2} = \frac{x_{22}}{x_{21}}.$$

At a competitive equilibrium we have demand equaling supply, and thus

$$x_{11} + x_{21} = 16 \quad \text{and} \quad x_{12} + x_{22} = 16$$

These equations and $x_{12}/x_{11} = x_{22}/x_{21}$ give us

$$\frac{x_{12}}{x_{11}} = \frac{16 - x_{12}}{16 - x_{11}}.$$

Cross multiplying yields $x_{11} = x_{12}$. Because $x_{12}/x_{11} = p_1/p_2$ we have $p_1/p_2 = 1$, or $p_1 = p_2$. Consumer 1's budget constraint is $p_1 x_{11} + p_2 x_{12} = 16p_2$ because 1's endowment consists of 16 units of good 2. Because $p_1 = p_2$ and $x_{11} = x_{12}$ the budget constraint reduces to $2p_1 x_{11} = 16p_1$, the solution of which is $x_{11} = 8$. Then $x_{11} = 8 = x_{12}$. Because market clearance requires $x_{11} + x_{21} = 16$ and $x_{12} + x_{22} = 16$ we also have $x_{21} = 8 = x_{22}$. At equilibrium each individual's consumption plan is (8, 8), but $U_1 = 40$ while $U_2 = 64$.

Is the equilibrium of Example 11.7 efficient? Because 1's utility increases when 2's consumption of the first good falls, it should be possible to make both people better off than they are at the equilibrium by transferring some of the first good from person 2 to person 1 and some of the second good from person 1 to person 2. Specifically, transfer 0.5 units of the first good from person 2 to 1, and 0.6 units of the second good from person 1 to 2. The new utility levels will be

$$U_1 = 8.5 \times 7.4 - 3 \times 7.5 = 40.4 \quad \text{and} \quad U_2 = 7.5 \times 8.6 = 64.5$$

Both individuals have a higher level of utility than at equilibrium, proving that the equilibrium allocation was not even weakly efficient.

When there are consumption externalities the proof of the first welfare theorem breaks down at the start. If U_i depends on the consumption of other individuals as well as on i's consumption then it is no longer true that if i prefers the feasible allocation b' to the equilibrium then the market value of i's consumption at b' must exceed i's income. It may be changes in the consumption of others, changes that are beyond i's control, that make b' superior to the equilibrium in i's estimation. For example at the equilibrium prices $p_1 = p_2$ the basket (8.5, 7.4) is *cheaper* for person 1 than the equilibrium basket (8, 8). But the latter was the best that person 1 could do given his or her budget constraint *and* given the choice (8, 8) of person 2. But 1 prefers (8.4, 7.4) to the equilibrium in part because of the changes in the other person's consumption.

In general, negative externalities are created when the decision of a consumer or firm imposes costs on society that are not costs to the decision maker. In most cases the market system uses prices to transmit information about social costs and benefits. But when an agent's decision imposes a cost on society that is not incorporated in a price that the agent pays, then vital information, necessary for efficiency, is not transmitted to the decision-making agent. Even if the agent receives the information from other sources, if it does not affect his or her spending power then the agent has no *incentive* to take those costs into consideration.

Consider what happens when social costs *are* incorporated into the price: Labor accounts for 70–75 percent of all costs of production in mature capitalist economies. The labor used

Microevolution of antibiotic-resistant microbes has resulted from the widespread administration of antibiotics to humans. (We also indirectly consume the antibiotics that are routinely given to livestock and used in commercial food preparation.) When a physician prescribes an antibiotic the patient benefits, but an imperceptible amount of harm is done to the rest of the population. *Widespread* over-prescription of antibiotics in wealthy nations is of enormous significance. It created a giant experiment with a vast number of opportunities for microbes to mutate. They have done so with great success. In the 1990s the World Health Organization warned that the high level of resistance to drugs that were once extremely effective in treating common infectious diseases will soon precipitate a global crisis. Our antibiotics could soon be rendered useless (Kmietowicz, 2000). By 2012 the problem had become dire, with the emergence of "nightmare" superbugs such as Carbapenem-Resistant-Enterobacteriacea (CRE). It kills half of those seriously infected and has the ability to transmit its resistance to otherwise treatable bacteria. The targets of CRE are hospital patients with compromised immune systems. (See the Centers for Disease Control at www.cdc.gov.)

by a firm is clearly a cost to society – if it were not used by the firm it could be employed productively elsewhere. The firm using labor has to pay wages that are a function of its workers' potential contribution to production in general – a consequence of all firms bidding for the use of productive factors. That gives the firm incentive to economize on the use of labor. This contributes to efficiency. More strikingly, the firm has a strong incentive to reduce the size of its wage bill (more than 70 percent of total cost) by inventing labor-saving equipment. If capital equipment lowers the labor requirement per unit of output, it raises the total output of a given labor force. And of course, output per worker, and hence consumption per worker, has risen dramatically over the decades and centuries. And all because the firm's use of labor is a cost to society that is brought to bear on the firm's decision by means of a price – the wage rate.

If the costs of pollution could be incorporated into the prices that bear on the decisions of firms and consumers, the same powerful force for innovation would be unleashed. Each household would strive to avoid the social costs of its polluting: by altering activities to reduce the amount of waste discharged into the water and air and by purchasing products that lower total social cost by incorporating pollution reduction technology. Knowing this, some firms would have a strong incentive to invent pollution abatement technology and others to invest in that technology when it became available. And to the extent that the activities of firms result in waste being discharged into the water and air, if this cost to society were converted to a cost paid by the polluting firms there would be a strong incentive for firms to avoid these costs by investing in technology to reduce waste by-products. (This is discussed at greater length in Section 3.2 of Chapter 3.) When output prices do not incorporate pollution costs manufacturers will typically not offer two versions of a product even if the more expensive one is better for the environment and hence is costlier to manufacture. Firms know that a consumer has a strong incentive to buy the less expensive model because *one* household's pollution – or lack thereof – does not have an appreciable effect on the environment, but does have an appreciable effect on the left-hand side of the budget equation.

The presence of significant *positive* externalities also results in an inefficient market equilibrium. For example, when someone considers purchasing fireworks for a private independence day celebration that person doesn't take into consideration the benefit that his or her neighbors will derive from the display. But that spillover benefit should clearly be counted – by someone – as a benefit to society. But the decision makers consider only the benefit to themselves.

Example ∂11.8 One Private Good and One Public Good

Commodity 1 is a *pure public good* – any amount of it provided for one person or group benefits everyone in the community. Commodity 2 is a conventional private good that can be consumed directly or used to produce the public good. Each unit of the public good requires 1 unit of the private good as input. If we let the price of the private good be unity then the price of the public good will also be unity in a competitive equilibrium, because the marginal cost of producing the public good is constant at 1. Therefore, the equilibrium price ratio is 1. Now, suppose that there are three consumers, each is endowed with 50 units of the private good and 0 units of the public good, and each has the utility function $6\sqrt{q} + t_i$, where q is the amount of the public good produced and t_i is the amount of the private good consumed by individual i. If the public good – for example, fireworks, or disease control – were only available on the private market then each consumer would optimize by equating marginal benefit and the price ratio. Therefore, $\frac{3}{\sqrt{q}} = 1$ at equilibrium. We solve this for $q = 9$. The total amount of the public good purchased in the community is 9 units, and everyone benefits from each of the 9 units, whether individuals purchased much or little of the good. Suppose that each individual buys 3 units of the public good. Is this outcome efficient? Individual utility is $U_i = 6\sqrt{9} + 50 - 3 = 65$ for each i. However, if the community could somehow arrange for $q = 81$ and have each i's consumption of the private good reduced by an additional $\frac{1}{3} \times 72 = 24$ to collect the input necessary to produce 72 additional units of the public good, then $U_i = 6\sqrt{81} + 50 - 27 = 77$, which is much higher *for each individual* than utility at the private market equilibrium. The market equilibrium is not efficient.

Sources

The foundations of modern general equilibrium theory were laid by Kenneth J. Arrow, Gerard Debreu, and Lionel McKenzie. See Arrow (1951b), Arrow and Debreu (1954), McKenzie (1954), and Debreu (1959). Weintraub (2014) tells that story superbly. Arrow was awarded the Nobel Prize in 1972, and Debreu in 1983.

Links

McKenzie (2002) is an excellent treatment of modern general equilibrium theory, from its inception in the middle of the twentieth century to the latest research. Weintraub (2014) also tells that story superbly. See Stiglitz (1993) for more on why markets can't even be approximately complete. For a fuller treatment of the technical side of the Arrow-Debreu model – existence of equilibrium, in particular – see Campbell (1987), especially pages pp. 39–47, Chapter 7, and Appendixes 2 and 3. To see why the completeness of markets assumption rules out externalities see Campbell (1987, pp. 56–60). Some economists claim that hidden information problems, particularly those related to contract enforcement, are so severe that the Arrow-Debreu model has nothing to teach us (Gintis, 2000, pp. 46, 136, 140). This section does implicitly assume that contracts can be costlessly enforced. Even so, we learn that the private ownership market economy orchestrates production and consumption activities in a way that obviates the need for an astronomical number of welfare-improving trades.

Problem Set

For each of these questions (a, b) denotes the bundle consumed by person 1 and (x, y) is the bundle consumed by person 2.

(1) Compute the competitive equilibrium of the two-person, two-commodity exchange economy with utility functions

$$u_1(a, b) = a^2 b \quad \text{and} \quad u_2(x, y) = xy^2$$

and endowments $(0, 3)$ for person 1 and $(3, 0)$ for person 2.

(2) The *second* theorem of welfare economics asserts that under certain modest conditions on preferences and technology sets, every efficient allocation is a competitive equilibrium allocation *for some redistribution of initial endowments – and profit shares, if the model includes production.* Verify the second welfare theorem for the following two-person, two-commodity exchange economy:

$$u_1(a, b) = ab \quad \omega_1 = (0, 1)$$
$$u_2(x, y) = xy \quad \omega_2 = (1, 0).$$

That is, identify all of the efficient allocations and then prove that each is a competitive equilibrium outcome for some distribution of the total endowment $(1,1)$.

(3) Consider the following simple two-person, two-commodity exchange economy:

$$u_1(a, b) = ab \quad \text{and} \quad \omega_1 = (0, 1),$$
$$u_2(x, y) = x + lny \quad \text{and} \quad \omega_2 = (2, 2).$$

(Recall that lny is the function whose first derivative is y^{-1}. The marginal utility of Y is $1/y$.) Find the competitive equilibrium for this economy. Is the competitive equilibrium allocation efficient? Explain.

(4) Solve the following two-person, two-commodity exchange economy for the competitive equilibrium:

$$u_1 = ab \quad \text{and} \quad \omega_1 = (1, 1),$$
$$u_2 = xy + b \quad \text{and} \quad \omega_2 = (1, 0).$$

Is the equilibrium outcome efficient? Explain briefly.

(5) Consider the following simple two-person, two-commodity exchange economy:

$$u_1 = ab - x \quad \text{and} \quad \omega_1 = (0, 1),$$
$$u_2 = xy + a \quad \text{and} \quad \omega_2 = (1, 0).$$

(A) Explain carefully why $p_1 = 1 = p_2$ and $a = b = x = y = \frac{1}{2}$ define a competitive equilibrium.

(B) Is this competitive equilibrium allocation efficient? Explain your answer.

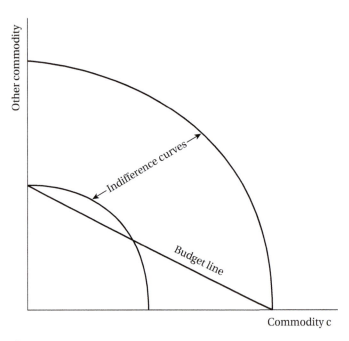

Figure 11.1

11.3   NONCONVEX ECONOMIES

What can we say about economies in which individual preferences do not have the diminishing marginal rate of substitution property? The proof of the welfare theorem does not make any assumptions about the *MRS*. As long as there is a complete set of markets a *competitive* equilibrium is efficient. *But will a competitive equilibrium exist?* Yes, if preferences have the diminishing MRS property. (Production functions also have to have a nonpositive second derivative, but we only look at exchange in this section.)

11.3.1   Nonconvexity in the Arrow-Debreu Economy

The easiest way to uncover the difficulties that can arise without the diminishing MRS property is to examine a *one-person* exchange economy with two commodities.

Example 11.9 Nonexistence of Equilibrium with Increasing MRS

There are two commodities and one individual (and no production). The individual's consumption plan is a bundle (a, b), and the utility function is $U = a^2 + b^2$. The equation of an indifference curve is $a^2 + b^2 = k$, where k is a given positive constant. This is the equation of a circle with center at the origin. Therefore, the MRS increases as we slide down the indifference curve (Figure 11.1). The consumer is endowed with one unit of each good. Demand can equal supply in each market only if the consumer demands one unit of each good. It is easy to show that there is no price system at which this can happen.

Everything hinges on the fact that $(\alpha + \beta)^2 = \alpha^2 + 2\alpha\beta + \beta^2 > \alpha^2 + \beta^2$ if α and β are both positive. This has implications for demand. The consumer will want to spend all of his or her income on one of the goods. Accept the truth of this assertion for a moment. Then there can be no equilibrium at any price regime: the demand for one of the goods will be zero but there is positive supply of that good (Figure 11.1). (And there will be excess demand for the commodity on which the consumer spends all of the income.) Therefore, our demonstration that there is no equilibrium will be complete once we show that all of the income will be spent on one good.

Suppose that $p_2 \geq p_1$. (The second good is at least as expensive as the first good.) Suppose also that $a > 0$ and $b > 0$. We have $U(a,b) = a^2 + b^2$, but if the individual reduces b to zero then $p_2 b$ dollars will be released that can be used to buy $\Delta a = p_2 b / p_1$ additional units of good 1. Because $p_2 \geq p_1$ we have $\Delta a \geq b$, which means that the new level of consumption of the first good is at least $a + b$. Because $ab > 0$ we have

$$U(a + \Delta a, 0) \geq (a+b)^2 = a^2 + b^2 + 2ab > a^2 + b^2 = U(a+b).$$

Utility has increased. Similarly, if $p_1 > p_2$ *and* $a > 0$ then the consumer can increase utility by reducing expenditure on the first good to zero and using the money thereby released to buy more of the second good. Therefore, the consumer will spend all of the money on the cheaper good, and if the prices are equal the consumer will not care which good he or she buys but will prefer either extreme to any affordable consumption plan with a positive amount of each good. The consumer will never demand a positive amount of *both* goods, but the supply of each is positive. Therefore, there can be no price system at which demand equals supply.

The problem revealed by Example 11.9 is a lot worse than the lack of existence of an equilibrium: there is no price system at which supply and demand are *approximately* equal in each market: if $p_1 < p_2$ then the consumer will spend all income on the first good. The demand for the second good will then be zero, but the supply is 1. The consumer's income is $p_1 + p_2$, so the consumer will buy $(p_1 + p_2)/p_1$ units of good 1. Therefore, the demand for the first good will exceed 2 because $p_2/p_1 > 1$. Of course, if $p_2 < p_1$ then the individual will demand 0 units of good 1 and more than 2 units of good 2. (If $p_1 = p_2$ the consumer will get 2 units of one good and 0 units of the other.) For any price system, the demand for one of the goods will be zero, which is well below the supply, and the demand for the other good will be at least double the supply.

It is remarkable that we can exhibit a failure of markets to clear at any price regime, even in an approximate sense, by means of a simple economy having only one consumer and two goods. It is easy to extend this example to one that has many commodities, and the reader is invited to do so. Of course, the fact that there is only one consumer is far from realistic. Is it essential for the nonexistence of equilibrium?

Example 11.10 Two Consumers, Each with Increasing MRS

This exchange economy consists of two consumers, each identical to the individual of Example 11.9. If $p_1 = p_2$ then each individual's income is $p_1 + p_2 = 2p_1$. (One's endowment consists of 1 unit of each good.) The consumers will spend all of that income on one of the goods and will receive $2p_1/p_1 = 2$ units of that commodity, whichever it is. The utility of the bundle that maximizes utility subject to the budget constraint is $4 = 2^2 + 0 = 0 + 2^2$. The individuals will be indifferent between the affordable bundles $(2, 0)$ and $(0, 2)$. If one of the consumers demands $(2, 0)$ and the other demands $(0, 2)$ then the total demand for each good will be 2. The total supply of each good is also 2, because each individual is endowed with 1 unit of each good. We have a competitive equilibrium, because each individual has maximized utility subject to the budget constraint and each market clears.

For any even number of consumers, each identical to the individual of Example 11.9, there will be a competitive equilibrium with $p_1 = p_2$. If half of the consumers spend all of their income on the first good and the rest spend all of their income on the other good, then demand will equal supply for each good. However, there can be no exact equilibrium with an odd number of consumers. Consider first the case of a three-person economy.

Example 11.11 Three Identical Consumers, each with Increasing MRS

Each of the three individuals are identical to the one of Example 11.9. If $p_1 > p_2$ or $p_1 < p_2$ then all individuals will spend all of their income on the cheaper good. The demand for the other good will be 0, but its supply will be 3. The demand for the cheaper good will be greater than 6, but the supply is only 3. (For instance, if $p_1 = 2$ and $p_2 = 3$ then income is 5, so each person will demand $5/2 = 2.5$ units of good 1. The demand for good 1 is $3 \times 2.5 = 7.5$.) If $p_1 = p_2$ then a consumer will either buy 2 units of good 1 and 0 units of good 2, or vice versa. Table 11.1 shows that the closest we can get to market clearance is for one consumer to spend all income on one of the goods and the other two to spend all their income on the other good. We will get an excess supply of the former of 1 and an excess demand for the latter. The excess

Table 11.1

Number who buy only the first good	Demand for the first good	Demand for the second good
0	0	6
1	2	4
2	4	2
3	6	0

demand is a smaller fraction of total demand than in the case of the one-person economy of Example 11.9. Also, excess supply is a smaller fraction of total supply than in the one-person economy, but there is still a significant gap between demand and supply.

With an odd number n of identical consumers, we cannot have exact market clearance with increasing MRS preferences. Here's why: let t be the number of consumers who spend all of their income on good 1, and let s be the number who spend all of their income on good 2. If $p_1 < p_2$ then $t = n$ and $s = 0$, so we are far from equilibrium. Similarly, if $p_1 > p_2$ then $t = 0$ and $s = n$. If $p_1 = p_2$ then t and s can both be positive. In fact, each individual is indifferent between $(2, 0)$ and $(0, 2)$ so t and s can be any two integers such that $t + s = n$. Because n is odd, we cannot have $t = s$. If demand equals supply for the first good we will have $n = $ supply $=$ demand $= 2t$ and thus $n = 2t$ which implies that n is even. When n is odd, we have to drop the supposition that demand equals supply at equilibrium.

If the number of traders is large then we are guaranteed a general equilibrium in a practical sense, if not in an exact sense, regardless of the nature of individual preferences.

Example 11.12 An Odd but Large Number of Consumers

Each of the n individuals is identical to the one of Example 11.9. Let $t = \frac{1}{2}n$. Then both $t + \frac{1}{2}$ and $t - \frac{1}{2}$ are integers. If $p_1 = p_2$ we can have $t + \frac{1}{2}$ individuals each spend all of their income on one of the goods and $t - \frac{1}{2}$ individuals each spend all of their income on the other good (Table 11.2). The supply of each good is $n = 2t$. Therefore, the closest we can get to market clearance involves demand exceeding supply for one of the goods by 1 and supply exceeding demand by 1 unit for the other good. When the number n of individuals is large, the supply n of each good is large, in which case a difference between demand and supply of 1 unit is trivial. We have an approximate equilibrium, which, for practical purposes, is sufficiently close to market clearance.

11.3.2 Indivisibilities: Assigning Students to Courses

A number of major law schools and graduate schools of business in the US use auctions to allocate students to courses. Business schools at U. C. Berkeley,

Table 11.2

Number who buy only the first good	Demand for the first good	Demand for the second good
$t + \frac{1}{2}$	$2t + 1$	$2t - 1$
$t - \frac{1}{2}$	$2t - 1$	$2t + 1$

Table 11.3

Students	Courses and Bids		
	A	B	C
Maria	50	38	12
Heidi	48	22	30
Isaac	47	28	25
Nora	45	35	20

Columbia, Michigan, Northwestern, and Yale employ variants of the following auction.

Each student is given 100 *registrar dollars*, often called bidding points, and is required to use that endowment to bid for courses. A student is expected to bid more of this "money" for courses for which he or she has greater desire, but the total amount bid cannot exceed the 100 point budget. The bids are then ranked from highest to lowest. If Danielle bids 25 for course A and 11 for course B then any bid greater than 25 for any course will rank above Danielle's bid for A, and any bid lower than 11 will rank below her bid for B. The allocation begins by assigning the student with the highest bid to the course that is targeted by that bid. Then the student with the next highest bid is assigned to the course targeted by that person's bid. And so on, until a course is full. That course is then removed from the menu, and the next highest bid for a course that is still on the menu is then considered. When a student has filled his or her schedule any remaining bids by that individual are removed from the list.

Example 11.13 Four Students and Three Courses

Maria, Heidi, Isaac, and Nora must each take two courses. Course A has three openings, B has two openings, and C has four openings. The bids are displayed in Table 11.3. Maria bids 50 for A, Heidi bids 48 for A and 22 for B, and so on. Maria's bid of 60 is the highest of all the bids, and is considered first. She is assigned to course A. The next highest bid is Heidi's 48, also for A, and she is also given a seat in A. Isaac's bid of 47 (for A) is next and he is given the a seat in course A, which is now full. The next bid on the list is Nora's bid of 45 for course A, but it is not honored because A is full. We then consider the next bid after 45: Maria's bid of 38 for B. Maria is given a seat in course B, and her schedule is now full; and we can ignore her other bid (of 12 for C). After 38 comes Nora's bid of 35 for B, and thus she is given the remaining seat in course B, which is now full. Next comes Heidi's bid of 30 for C, so Heidi is enrolled in course C, completing her schedule. Isaac's bid of 28 for B is next, but that course is full so the bid is unsuccessful. We turn to Isaac's bid of 25 for C: Isaac gets a seat in course C, and he now has a full schedule. Nora's bid of 20 for C is successful: she is assigned to C. Each student now has a full schedule, and no course is over-enrolled: Maria will take A and B, Heidi and Isaac will both take A and C, and Nora will take B and C. (There will be an empty seats in C.)

We can characterize the outcome of this auction in terms of market clearing prices: if $p_A = 47$, $p_B = 35$, and $p_C = 20$ and a student can enroll in a course if and only if her bid for that course is at least as high as the price of that course we have market clearing prices. Each student with a limited income of 100 will demand precisely the courses that are assigned to that individual by the auction. Note that the price of C is zero because the auction does not fill that course. In general, the market clearing price of a course is the lowest bid for that course among the students who are given a seat in that course by the auction.

Although the auction is fairly widely used, it is also fairly widely resented by the students involved. There are three main criticisms: it is seen as unfair, especially by students who were not able to get into any of the "good" courses even though others were assigned to many of them. It also forces students to behave strategically, even though the course assignment auction has the flavor of the Vickrey auction. (The price paid by a winner in a Vickrey auction is equal to the highest of the unsuccessful bids.) Unlike a conventional auction, the money that is spent bidding for courses has no value in the ambient economy. Therefore, over-bidding for a course has a much different implication for an agent's overall welfare. The course auction can be inefficient.

Student dissatisfaction with course auctions lead economists Eric Budish and Judd Kessler to design an allocation mechanism based on the Arrow-Debreu economy. The Wharton School of Business at the University of Pennsylvania adopted it in the fall term of 2013. As in the course auction, each student is given a budget of registrar dollars which they spend on courses. A student demands a course by spending some of her money on it, but the demand is indirect. Students submit their preferences and the allocation software uses that preference information to work out their demand functions. Prices adjust until demand equals supply for each course, except that a course which does not fill at equilibrium will have a price of zero. The demand for a course is just the number of students who have used enough of their money to pay the price for that course. The supply of a course is the limit placed on enrollment by the administration. Submitting preferences is not straightforward because course A can be more or less desirable if B is taken at the same time – to some degree, B can be a complement to, or a substitute for, A.

Example 11.14 Two Students and Four Courses

Danielle and Christopher have the same preferences: A is the best course, taught by the star professor, B is considered almost as good, but a little less desirable. Course C is not at all desirable, but one would take it if were the only way to fill out one's schedule. The same applies to D, but it is considered even less beneficial than C. Each student must take exactly two courses, and each course has room for only one student. Preferences are separable in the sense that if Y is preferred to Z then, for any course X, having X and Y is better than having X and Z. It follows that each student has the following preference scheme:

$$AB \succ AC \succ AD \succ A \succ BC \succ BD \succ B \succ CD \succ D$$

The symbol $\succ$ is read "is strictly preferred to." If Christopher and Danielle have equal incomes then there are no market clearing prices. Either both will demand a seat in A or no one will. Note that preferences are nonconvex because the "goods" are not divisible.

Equilibrium can be attained if the incomes are almost equal, but not exactly equal. Specifically, set Christopher's income at 101 and Danielle's at 100. Then $p_A = 101$, $p_B = 80$, $p_C = 20$, and $p_D = 0$ will clear each market. Christopher will demand courses A and D. His expenditure will be 101, equal to his income. He would prefer to have A and B, or even A and C, but can't afford either combination. Danielle will demand B and C. Any schedule that includes A will be out of her reach – i.e., too expensive. Note that Danielle does not do badly. She gets a course that is almost as sought after as A, and her other course is considered better than D, which Christopher has to take to fill his schedule. Note also that we would also get market clearance if Danielle has the larger income. The registrar could toss a coin to determine who gets the slightly larger income. The Budish-Kessler mechanism is fairer than the course auction in two senses: any advantage that the mechanism gives to one student is slight, and every student has the same chance of obtaining that slight advantage. By contrast, the course auction would too often give both of the popular courses to the student with the superior strategy. The mechanism performed well in laboratory experiments according to measures of efficiency and fairness.

Sources
Section 11.3.2 is based on Sönmez and Ünver (2010) and Budish and Kessler (2016). Example 11.13 is from the former. Example 11.14 is from Budish (2011).

Links
Anderson et al. (1982) show that under very general conditions there will be an approximate equilibrium of an n-person exchange economy, and that the percent by which demand is less than supply or is greater than supply approaches zero as n increases without limit. Even for modestly large n, the gap between demand and supply is virtually zero (as a fraction of total supply).

Problem Set
(1) Consider a one-person exchange economy with two goods, A and B. Let $U_1 = a^2 + b$ and $\omega_1 = (1, 1)$ be the utility function and endowment, respectively. Prove that this economy does not have a competitive equilibrium. (Hint: write down the budget equation and then use it to solve for b as a function of a. Substitute this expression for b in the utility function, and then draw the graph of utility as a function of a.)

(2) For each of the following one-person exchange economies determine the efficient allocation (or allocations) and see if there is *any* price system and income level at which the consumer will choose an efficient outcome.

    (A) $U_1 = 2a^2 + b^2$ and $\omega_1 = (1, 1)$.

    (B) $U_1 = a^2 + b^2$ and $\omega_1 = (1, 2)$.

(3) For each of the three economies of the first two questions, demonstrate that there is an approximate competitive equilibrium when there is a large number of individuals identical to person 1.

11.4 EFFICIENCY AND INCENTIVE COMPATIBILITY

We have seen that a complete set of markets results in a competitive equilibrium of the private ownership market economy that is efficient. The assumption that each individual and firm takes the prices as given was key. Each individual or firm calculates a best response to the given prices, without considering how a different response might affect prices, perhaps in a direction favorable to the decision maker. In this section we consider the appropriateness of the price taking assumption. In Section 11.4.4 we establish that it is rational for each agent to take market prices as given *if* there is a large number of suppliers of each good and many consumers.

Many goods are produced by only a handful of firms, however. In such cases the individual producer can profit by exploiting the fact that a change in its supply will have an effect on prices. This is easy to understand, but we nevertheless work through a specific example in Section 11.4.1, in part to clarify what we mean by price taking on the one hand and exploiting one's market power on the other hand.

We will see that a departure from price taking behavior can be viewed as a misrepresentation of the agent's hidden characteristic – preference in the case of a consumer and the production technology in the case of a firm. Because it is possible for a supplier to profit from misrepresentation in the private ownership market economy when there are few rival producers, we are led to ask if there are alternative economic systems that are invulnerable to misrepresentation. Sections 11.4.2 and 11.4.3 are devoted to this question, which is also addressed at the end of Section 11.4.1.

The sensible approach would seem to be to put the spotlight on the individual firm and trace the effects of a misrepresentation of its production technology back to individual consumer welfare. For instance, in the case of the Arrow-Debreu economy we would chart how a firm's misrepresentation affected its profit, then how the incomes of the firm's shareholders were affected, and finally how that impacted shareholder utility. That makes our task much more complicated, however, so we confine attention to pure exchange for which the suppliers are individual households, and the supplies are the individual endowments. This gives us a much more direct connection between agents' misrepresentations – of preference schemes – and individual utility.

11.4.1 Dominant Strategy Equilibrium

Consumers' hidden (private) characteristics are their preference schemes. What does misrepresentation of preference mean in the context of the market system?

Consumers are never asked to report their utility functions or preferences. They *are* asked to submit a list of demands that maximize individual utility, given the current prices. If a consumer misrepresents his or her preferences by demanding a basket of goods that is not utility maximizing, there will be no way for anyone else to detect this misrepresentation.

We can, however, view the market system as a mechanism in which each consumer is asked to submit his or her utility function to a referee, who then computes the resulting demand functions. The individual demand functions are then fed into a computer which calculates the equilibrium configuration of prices. The demand functions are used to determine individual consumption of each good at the equilibrium prices, and the resulting baskets of goods and services are delivered to the consumers. The question we are addressing can be stated this way: would it ever be to anyone's advantage to submit a false utility function to the referee? We are about to see that the answer is "yes". An appropriately chosen false utility function will induce demands that cause prices to change in a way that leaves the individual with more utility – according to her true utility function – than she would have realized under truthful revelation. The consumer will have benefitted by deviating from the rules of the game, and no one will know that she has deviated.

Can an individual consumer in fact influence prices by altering his or her demands? The intuition is that this power is negligible when there is a realistically large number of consumers, as Section 11.4.4 confirms. This section shows how misrepresentation can be profitable when the number of consumers is small. This will prepare us for the large numbers case by clarifying what is meant by misrepresentation of preference.

Example 11.15 A Two-Person, Two-Commodity Exchange Economy

Person 1's endowment is $\omega_1 = (0, 1)$ and 2's endowment is $\omega_2 = (1, 0)$. The utility functions are

$$U_1 = ab \quad \text{and} \quad U_2 = xy.$$

assuming that a typical allocation assigns the consumption plan $\theta_1 = (a, b)$ to person 1 and $\theta_2 = (x, y)$ to person 2. The competitive equilibrium is easy to compute: individual 1's MRS is b/a and individual 2's MRS is y/x. (See the end of Example 11.6 for the derivation of the MRS.)

Because each individual has a positive amount of each good at equilibrium each individual's MRS is equal to the price ratio. Therefore, b/a equals the price ratio, which equals y/x. Therefore, $b/a = y/x$. But $a + x = 1$ and $b + y = 1$ at equilibrium (market clearance). Therefore,

$$\frac{b}{a} = \frac{1-b}{1-a},$$

and if we cross multiply we get $a - ab = b - ab$, which implies $a = b$. Now, (a, b) and the endowment point $(0, 1)$ are both on 1's budget line and thus $p_1a + p_2b = p_2$ which implies $p_1/p_2 = (1-b)/a$. Therefore,

$$\frac{b}{a} = \frac{1-b}{a},$$

which implies $b = \frac{1}{2}$, and therefore $a = \frac{1}{2}$ because $a = b$. Finally, $x = y = \frac{1}{2}$. The equilibrium price ratio equals each MRS at equilibrium. Because $b/a = 1$ the price ratio is 1 at equilibrium. That is, $p_1 = p_2$. We have found the competitive equilibrium: The prices are equal and each individual's consumption plan is $(\frac{1}{2}, \frac{1}{2})$. Note that each individual's income at equilibrium is $p_1 = p_2$.

A consumption plan (a,b) satisfies the budget equation $p_1 a + p_2 b = p_1 \omega_1 + p_2 \omega_2$ if and only if it satisfies $\lambda p_1 a + \lambda p_2 b = \lambda p_1 \omega_1 + \lambda p_2 \omega_2$ for arbitrary positive constant λ. Therefore, we can multiply both sides of the budget equation by $\lambda = 1/p_1$. In calculating an equilibrium set of prices we are free to simplify the task by setting $p_1 = 1$. (This remains true when production is added to the model: the plan y^* maximizes the firm's profit (for price regime $p_1, p_2, \ldots, p_\ell$) over all plans in the technology set T if and only if y^* maximizes profit for price regime $\lambda p_1, \lambda p_2, \ldots, \lambda p_\ell$. Moreover, when all prices are multiplied by λ a firm's profit is multiplied by λ, and hence both the left-hand side *and* the right-hand side of an individual's budget equation is multiplied by λ when all prices are multiplied by λ.)

DEFINITION: *Price Taking Behavior*

An individual is a price taker if at each price regime he or she demands the consumption plan that maximizes utility subject to the budget constraint, without taking into consideration how different demands might have affected prices.

By definition of a *competitive* equilibrium, each person takes the price regime as given. In the case of Example 11.15, $(\frac{1}{2}, \frac{1}{2})$ is the unique utility-maximizing consumption plan of all those plans (a, b) satisfying the budget constraint $1a + 1b = 1$. But each individual has a monopoly in the supply of one of the goods, and each individual supplies half of his or her endowment at the competitive equilibrium. Each can be expected to know that the price of the good he or she supplies will increase if the supply is reduced. That is, the individuals will surely not behave as price takers in this economy – our price taking assumption is unfounded. We offer a proof by contradiction. The argument makes use of Figure 11.2.

Figure 11.2 represents person 2's utility in terms of person 1's consumption (a, b). This means that an indifference curve for person 2 is the set of plans (a, b) such that $U_2(1 - a, 1 - b)$ is constant. In the present case, $U_2 = xy$, so an indifference curve for person 2 is the set of plans (a, b) such that $(1 - a) \times (1 - b)$ is constant.

Suppose that person 2 always acts as a price taker. This means that 2's demand vector (x, y) will always be the one that maximizes U_2 subject to the budget constraint $p_1 x + p_2 y = p_1$. (Person 2's income is p_1 because 2 is endowed with 1

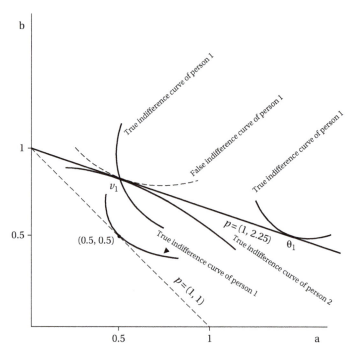

Figure 11.2

unit of the first good.) Let's see if person 1 can profit from preference misrepresentation. The intuition is simple. If person 1 demands the vector v_1 and at that point 1 demands more of good 2, the good that 1 supplies, than the straightforward utility-maximization exercise would predict, then the price of good 2 will be kept high. This will be utility maximizing in a more sophisticated sense. Let's see why.

Suppose that $p_1 = 1$ and $p_2 = 2.25$, and person 2 demands $v_2 = (1, 1) - v_1$, where v_1 is given in Figure 11.2. (The budget line is the flatter of the two lines in the diagram.) Both markets clear because $v_1 + v_2 = (1, 1) = \omega_1 + \omega_2$. Note, however, that at the competitive demand vector θ_1 person 1 would be on a higher indifference curve than the one through v_1. *If person 1 could be sure of having the order θ_1 filled* then ordering θ_1 would be the better strategy, given the prices $p_1 = 1$ and $p_2 = 2.25$. But person 1 can be sure that the order θ_1 *won't* be filled. Markets clear when person 1 undersupplies the second good by ordering v_1 for herself and because θ_1 specifies a lower demand (i.e., higher supply) for the second good, we will have excess supply of the second good when person 1 orders θ_1 and person 2 orders v_2. The price of the second good will have to fall, and this means that individual 1 can't have θ_1 after all.

The *competitive* equilibrium allocation gives each person the basket (½, ½). Recall Example 11.15. The associated equilibrium prices are $p_1 = 1 = p_2$. At a higher price for good 2, say $p_2 = 2.25$, person 2 will demand less of good 2. Person 2's demand under price system $p = (1, 2.25)$ is v_2, which is identified by the point v_1 in Figure 11.2. The vector v_1 is what would be left for person 1 if person 2 were given the basket v_2. If person 1 were to demand the vector that maximizes U_1 given the price vector $p = (1, 2.25)$ then 1 would demand θ_1 as shown in Figure 11.2. As we have seen, markets won't clear when person 1's consumption plan is θ_1 and person 2's plan is $v_2 = (1,1) - v_2$. The total demand for good 1, the good on the horizontal axis, exceeds 1, which is the supply of 1. Therefore, p_1/p_2 will increase. If person 1 continued to behave competitively – that is, take prices as given – then the economy would wind up back at the competitive equilibrium with each person receiving $(\frac{1}{2}, \frac{1}{2})$. But if person 1 were to demand v_1 when $p_1 = 1$ and $p_2 = 2.25$ and person 2 demands v_2 then both markets would clear because $v_2 = (1, 1) - v_1$, and hence $v_1 + v_2 = (1, 1)$. The economy would be in equilibrium because there would be no tendency for prices to change: demand and supply would be equal in both markets. And because markets clear, all consumers would be able to carry out their plans. Moreover, v_1 gives individual 1 more utility than $(\frac{1}{2}, \frac{1}{2})$ according to 1's true preferences! The next example makes this concrete by working out v_2 and θ_1.

Example 11.16 Misrepresentation in the Economy of Example 11.15

To obtain v_2 we want to maximize $U_2 = xy$ subject to $1x + 2.25y = 1$, because person 2 has 1 unit of good 1 to sell at a price of \$1. Clearly, utility maximization implies

$$MRS = \frac{y}{x} = \frac{p_1}{p_2} = \frac{1}{2.25} = \frac{4}{9}.$$

Then $9y = 4x$. We also have $1x + 2.25y = 1$, which is equivalent to $4x + 9y = 4$. When we substitute $4x$ for $9y$ we get $4x + 4x = 4$, which implies $x = \frac{1}{2}$. Then $y = 4x/9 = 2/9$. Therefore, $v_2 = (1/2, 2/9)$. It follows that if consumer 1 demands $v_1 = (1/2, 7/9)$ when $p_1 = 1$ and $p_2 = 2.25$ and 2 demands v_2 then both markets will clear and person 1's utility will be

$$U_1 = \frac{1}{2} \times \frac{7}{9} = \frac{7}{18},$$

which is more than

$$U_1 = \frac{1}{2} \times \frac{1}{2} = \frac{1}{4},$$

the utility that person 1 realizes by announcing his or her true utility-maximizing demand at every turn.

When $p_1 = 1$ and $p_2 = 2.25$ the true utility-maximizing demand θ_1 of person 1 satisfies $b/a = 4/9$ or $9b = 4a$. Because 1's budget constraint at this price regime is $a + 2.25b = 2.25$, or $4a + 9b = 9$, person 1 would set $8a = 9$. In that case, $a = 9/8$ and thus $b = 1/2$. The consumption plan $(9/8, 1/2)$ yields $U_1 = 9/8 \times 1/2 = 9/16$, which is even greater than $7/18$. However, consumer 1 could never realize the utility level $9/16$ because markets wouldn't clear. If the consumers continued to takes prices as given, the excess demand for good 1 when person 1 demanded the bundle $(9/8, 1/2)$ would cause the price of the first commodity to rise relative to the second, pushing the price regime toward the equilibrium where $p_1 = p_2$. But when the two prices are equal person 1's utility is considerable less than $9/16$ or even $7/18$. This explains why it is in person 1's interest to demand v_1 when $p_1 = 1$ and $p_2 = 2.25$, even though the indifference curve through v_1 is not tangent to the budget constraint, as Figure 11.2 shows. (There is *some* indifference curve tangent to the budget line at v_1 - the broken curve of Figure 11.2 - so individual 1 can always claim that he or she is following the rules.)

Note that person 1 misrepresents U_1 by demanding 7/9 of a unit of commodity 2, instead of 1/2 a unit that would be demanded if person 1 were passively maximizing utility subject to the budget constraint. Because person 1 is a monopoly supplier of good 2, by *demanding* 7/9 units person 1 is under supplying commodity 2. That causes its price to be significantly higher than the competitive level and allows person 1 to purchase a bundle that yields more utility than the competitive equilibrium would yield.

Deviating from price taking behavior can be interpreted as preference misrepresentation: by demanding v_1, individual 1 is in effect claiming that 1's preference scheme generates the broken indifference curve in Figure 11.2 instead of the solid curve. In terms of the algebra (Example 11.16), individual 1 is in effect announcing the utility function $U_1 = (4\sqrt{2a})/9 + b$. (Confirm that a price taker with this utility function will demand $v_1 = (1/2, 7/9)$ when $p_1 = 1$ and $p_2 = 2.25$. The MRS is $4/9\sqrt{2a}$.) We have demonstrated that truthful revelation is not a dominant strategy in the case of the Arrow-Debreu model of the private ownership market economy.

Perhaps a different resource allocation mechanism would induce truthful revelation of individual preference in a two-person exchange economy. We'll be wasting our time attempting to design one. There is no allocation mechanism for which truthful revelation is a dominant strategy, equilibrium outcomes are efficient, and all individuals are guaranteed at least as much utility as they would get simply by consuming their endowments and not participating in the economy. Section 8.4.1 of Chapter 8 proves this for economies that include a public good. We do not present the corresponding proof for exchange economies with private goods only, but instead, relax our incentive compatibility requirement and simply ask for a mechanism that yields efficient outcomes at each Nash equilibrium.

11.4.2 Nash Equilibrium

Instead of seeking a resource allocation mechanism for which truthful revelation is a dominant strategy, let's merely ask for one in which Nash equilibria always exist and Nash equilibrium outcomes are always efficient.

Example 11.17 Two Individuals and Two Feasible Outcomes

There are two agents and two possible outcomes, x and y. We only need to know whether an individual prefers x to y or the converse. (For simplicity we ignore the possibility of indifference between x and y. We can think of each outcome as specifying the amounts of a large number of commodities to be consumed by each person.) Then there are four possible individual preference schemes:

$$(x, x), (x, y), (y, x), \text{ and } (y, y).$$

We refer to each of these as an *environment*. At (x, x) each person prefers x to y. At (x, y) person 1 prefers x to y, but 2 prefers y to x. Person 1 prefers y to x at (y, x), but 2 prefers x to y. And they both prefer y to x at (y, y).

We show how demanding is the requirement that a Nash equilibrium exists for every specification of individual preferences and that every equilibrium give rise to an efficient outcome. Consider an arbitrary mechanism, which is simply a specification of the set of strategies available to each individual and a function f, which determines whether the outcome is x or y, given the chosen strategies. That is, if consumer 1 plays s_1 and 2 plays s_2 then the outcome $f(s_1, s_2)$ is either x or y. We require that for each of the four possible environments of Example 11.17 a Nash equilibrium (s_1, s_2) exists, and $f(s_1, s_2)$ is efficient with respect to the underlying preferences.

Note that efficiency is a very modest requirement in this context. Both outcomes are efficient for the environments (x, y) and (y, x). Only x is efficient for (x, x) and only y is efficient for (y, y). Our framework is very abstract: the outcomes x and y could refer to almost anything. For instance, each could specify the private goods consumption of each of the two agents, or they could specify a set of public policies, or output levels of specific public goods.

The Hurwicz-Schmeidler Theorem

For the economy of Example 11.17, if a mechanism has a Nash equilibrium for every environment, and every Nash equilibrium is efficient, then it must give one individual the power to force the mechanism to deliver his or her most-preferred outcome in every environment, in which case we call that person a dictator.

Proof:

Let (s_1, s_2) be a Nash equilibrium for (x, y). Assume that $f(s_1, s_2) = x$. (We treat the case $f(s_1, s_2) = y$ last.) Because (s_1, s_2) is an equilibrium and 2 prefers y to $x = f(s_1, s_2)$ it must be the case that $f(s_1, \beta) = x$ for every strategy β available to person 2. Now, let (t_1, t_2) be a Nash equilibrium for (y, x). If $f(t_1, t_2) = y$ then we must have $f(t_1, \beta) = y$ for every strategy β available to person 2 because (t_1, t_2) is an equilibrium for (y, x) and 2 prefers x to y at (y, x). Therefore, person 1 can ensure that the outcome is x by playing s_1 and can guarantee that the outcome is y by playing t_1, in which case 1 is a dictator.

Suppose, then, that $f(t_1, t_2) = x$. Then (s_1, s_2) is a Nash equilibrium for (x, y), with $f(s_1, s_2) = x$, and (t_1, t_2) is a Nash equilibrium for (y, x), with $f(t_1, t_2) = x$. We now show that (s_1, t_2) is an equilibrium for (y, y), and that $f(s_1, t_2) = x$, contradicting efficiency: if $f(\alpha, t_2) = y$ for some strategy α available to person 1, then (t_1, t_2) would not be an equilibrium for (y, x). Therefore, we have $f(\alpha, t_2) = x$ for all α available to person 1. In

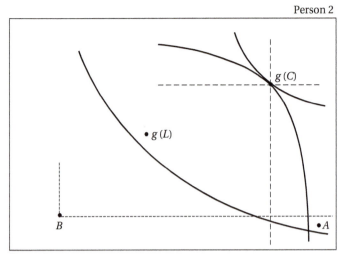

Person 2

$g(C)$

• $g(L)$

B • A

Person 1

Figure 11.3

particular, $f(s_1, t_2) = x$. If $f(s_1, \beta) = y$ for some strategy β available to person 2, then (s_1, s_2) is not an equilibrium for (x, y). Therefore, $f(s_1, \beta) = x$ for all β. We have established that (s_1, t_2) is an equilibrium for (y, y), although $f(s_1, t_2) = x$. (Recall that $f(s_1, \beta) = x$ for every strategy β available to person 2, including $\beta = t_2$.) Therefore, existence and efficiency of equilibrium require $f(t_1, t_2) = y$ and hence person 1 is a dictator.

We began the proof by assuming that $f(s_1, s_2) = x$ and concluded that person 1 is a dictator. There is only one other possibility: $f(s_1, s_2) = y$. In that case, an analogous argument will reveal that person 2 is a dictator.   ∎

11.4.3 Subgame-Perfect Nash Equilibrium

We can circumvent the Hurwicz-Schmeidler Theorem of the previous section by allowing one person to threaten to punish the other player for employing a strategy that would precipitate an inefficient outcome. A threat has to be credible if we are to take the resulting equilibrium seriously. According, we employ subgame-perfect Nash equilibrium. (See Section 1.5.7 of Chapter 1.) This allows us to demand more from a resource allocation mechanism than mere efficiency. We assume that a social choice function g is given. In other words, g specifies the socially optimal outcome for each specification of individual preferences.

Example 11.18 A Very Simple Resource Allocation Problem

We assume an exchange economy with two people and two private goods. The width of the box in Figure 11.3 is the total amount of good 1 available in this economy, and the height of the box is the total amount of good 2. A point such as B

in the box specifies the consumption of each individual: person 1 gets an amount of good 1 equal to the distance of B from the left-hand edge of the box, and an amount of good 2 equal to the height of B from the bottom of the box. Person 2 gets everything not allocated to person 1. Specifically, person 2's consumption of good 1 is the distance of B from the right-hand edge of the box, and 2's consumption of good 2 is the distance of B from the top of the box.

The individual's preferences can be represented by standard utility functions. Suppose there are two possible scenarios, called *environments:*

Environment C: Both individuals have the Cobb-Douglas utility function $U_C(x, y) = xy$, where x is the amount of good 1 consumed and y is the amount of good 2 consumed.

Environment L: Both individuals have the Leontief utility function $U_L(x, y) =$ min$\{x, y\}$.

Person 1's utility function U_C is represented in Figure 11.3 by the solid indifference curves that bend in toward the origin. U_C is higher for person 1 at any point above an indifference curve than it is at any point on the curve. Person 2's utility function U_C is represented by the solid indifference curves that bend up and away from the origin. As we move northeast in the diagram, person 2's utility decreases and 1's utility increases.

U_L for person 1 is represented in Figure 11.3 by means of the L-shaped broken-line indifference curves, with U_L increasing as we move northeast in the box. For the environment L, person 2's indifference curves are the broken line curves that are L-shaped when the diagram is rotated 180°. (Turn the book upside down.) With the diagram in its normal position, person 2's utility increases as we move southwest.

The social choice function g identifies the outcomes $g(C)$ and $g(L)$ in Figure 11.3 as socially optimal for environments C and L respectively.

The rest of this subsection examines the possibility of implementing g. That is, we wish to design an economic system – a *mechanism* – whose equilibrium for each environment E is the outcome $g(E)$ specified by g.

DEFINITION: *Implementation*

A mechanism specifies a set of strategies available to each participant in the economy. The mechanism implements the social choice rule g if, for each environment E for which g specifies an outcome $g(E)$, the equilibrium of the mechanism at environment E is precisely $g(E)$.

We begin by showing that it is impossible to implement the rule g defined by Example 11.18 if we require each *ordinary* Nash equilibrium to yield $g(C)$ in environment C and $g(L)$ in environment L.

Impossibility Theorem for Example 11.18

There exists no mechanism for implementing the social choice rule g of Example 4.4 in ordinary Nash equilibrium.

Proof:

Suppose to the contrary that we have a mechanism whose Nash equilibria in environments C and L yield, respectively, outcomes $g(C)$ and $g(L)$. Let (s_1, s_2) be a Nash equilibrium for environment C. Then (s_1, s_2) must be an equilibrium for environment L as well. If to the contrary there is some strategy α available to person 1 such that $U_L(\alpha, s_2) > U_L(g(C)) = U_L(s_1, s_2)$ then $U_C(\alpha, s_2) > U_C(g(C))$ must also hold, contradicting the fact that (s_1, s_2) is a Nash equilibrium for environment C. This follows from the fact that person 1's indifference curve through $g(C)$ for the utility function U_L (the broken curve) is strictly above person 1's indifference curve through $g(C)$ for the utility function U_C (the solid curve), except at $g(C)$ itself of course (Figure 11.3). In other words, for any consumption plan Z for person 1, if $U_L(Z) > U_L(g(C))$ then $U_C(Z) > U_C(g(C))$. Therefore, if (s_1, s_2) is a Nash equilibrium for environment C then there is no α available to person 1 such that (α, s_2) gives person 1 higher utility than $U_L(g(C))$.

Similarly, there can't be any strategy β available to person 2 such that (s_1, β) results in 2 receiving more utility than $U_L(g(C))$: Figure 11.3 shows that any outcome Z that person 2 prefers to $g(C)$ according to U_L is southwest of 2's broken-line indifference curve through $g(C)$ and hence southwest of 2's solid indifference curve through $g(C)$, and thus person 2 would prefer Z to $g(C)$ according to U_C. If (s_1, β) gave person 2 more utility than $g(C)$ according to U_L, then (s_1, β) would give person 2 more utility than $g(C)$ according to U_C, contradicting the supposition that (s_1, s_2) is a Nash equilibrium for C. Therefore, (s_1, s_2) must be a Nash equilibrium for environment L as well.

We have contradicted the claim that the mechanism implements g. The strategy pair (s_1, s_2) precipitates the outcome $g(C)$ and is a Nash equilibrium for L. But $g(C) \neq g(L)$ as shown by Figure 11.3. Therefore, there is no mechanism that implements g in ordinary Nash equilibrium.   ∎

It is clear from Figure 11.3 that we could perturb the indifference curves in environment L just a little so that they have a negative slope at every point and there is no kink where the slope is not defined.

We now show that g can be implemented by an *extensive form* mechanism with subgame-perfect Nash equilibrium as our equilibrium concept. Specifically, at least one equilibrium exists for each environment and all subgame-perfect equilibria for environment C precipitate the outcome $g(C)$, and all subgame-perfect equilibria for environment L precipitate the outcome $g(L)$.

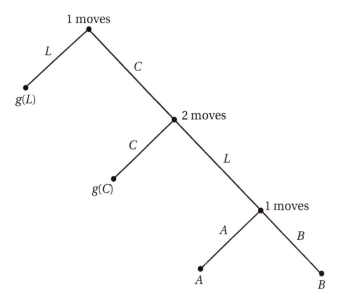

Figure 11.4

Example 11.19 A Simple Mechanism with Subgame-Perfect Equilibria that are Optimal

Stage 1 *Person 1 announces either L or C.*
If person 1 announces L the outcome is $g(L)$ and there is no further play.
If person 1 announces C then player 2 makes a move at stage 2.

Stage 2 *Person 2 agrees or disagrees with player 1.*
If person 2 agrees that C is the true state then the outcome is $g(C)$ and there is no further play. If person 2 disagrees then player 1 makes the next and last move at stage 3.

Stage 3 *Person 1 chooses either outcome A of Figure 11.3 or outcome B of Figure 11.3.* The mechanism is represented as Figure 11.4.

Before working out the subgame-perfect Nash equilibria for each of the two environments, L and C, we point out that in either situation both people will know which is the true environment. That's because each person knows that they have identical preferences in each environment. The mechanism designer (i.e., the consultant hired by the government) can exploit the fact that in each environment each consumer knows the other's utility function. That makes it easier to design a successful mechanism. However, neither the designer nor the government will know which of the environments is the true one – because individual preference is hidden information.

Analysis of Example 11.19

First, suppose that the true state is L, which means that both have Leontief preferences. Person 1 prefers $g(C)$ to $g(L)$, but if 1 announces C at stage 1 then player 2 will challenge, knowing that 1 will choose B over A at stage 3 because 1 prefers B to A in environment L. Because person 2 prefers B to $g(C)$ in environment L, the challenge would be 2's best response. *If* person 1 threatened to choose A in stage 3 then person 2 would be forced to accept $g(C)$ and we would have a Nash equilibrium. But it is not subgame perfect – that is, it is not in person 1's interest to carry out this threat if stage 3 were actually reached. The only subgame-perfect Nash equilibrium results in $g(L)$. It has person 1 announcing L at stage 1 and declaring that he or she would choose B if stage 3 were reached, while person 2 declares her intention to challenge in stage 2 if person 1 announces C at stage 1.

Finally, suppose that the true state is C, and hence both consumers have Cobb-Douglas preferences. Person 1 has no incentive to announce L and take $g(L)$ unless he fears that 2 would challenge at stage 2. But then person 1 would be forced to choose between A and B, and he would pick A, which gives more utility than B according to U_C, and A is worse for 2 than $g(C)$. Therefore, even if both A and B are worse for player 1 than $g(L)$, a threat by 2 to challenge C at stage 2 unless 1 announces L in stage 1 would not be credible, because if push came to shove the challenge would precipitate A, which gives 2 less utility (in terms of U_C) than $g(C)$. Therefore, the only subgame-perfect equilibria in this environment results in $g(C)$. This is sustained by having person 1 announce C at stage 1, declaring that he would choose A if stage 3 were reached, while 2 announces that she would accept C at stage 2.

Example 11.18 and the discussion that follows it demonstrates that there are social choice functions that can be implemented in subgame-perfect Nash equilibrium but not in Nash equilibrium.

11.4.4 Price Taking

Now we consider an individual consumer's ability to manipulate prices in a private ownership market economy when the total number of individuals is large. Intuition tells us that an individual's power is negligible when there is a realistically large number of consumers.

Recall the definition of price taking behavior from Section 11.4.1: a trader is a *price taker* if he or she always demands a basket that maximizes utility *given* the price regime. Section 11.4.1 showed that price taking behavior is not a dominant strategy. Now we show that the gain from deviating from price taking behavior is virtually zero if the number of consumers is large. Specifically, we show that the gain from deviating goes to zero as the number of traders gets arbitrarily large. We demonstrate this by assuming a large number of individuals identical to person 1 of Example 11.15, and a large number identical to person 2.

Example 11.20 Many Traders of Each Type

There are t individuals i with $U_i = ab$ and $\omega_i = (0, 1)$ and t individuals j with $U_j = xy$ and $\omega_j = (1, 0)$. We call the former type 1 and the latter type 2. We show that the ability of a single type-1 consumer to manipulate prices becomes negligible as t becomes sufficiently large. We begin by determining the demand functions: for convenience, let's normalize and set the price of the second good equal to unity, with P denoting the price of the first good. For a type 1 individual, utility maximization implies $MRS = b/a = p_1/p_2 = P$, and thus $b = Pa$. (Refer back to Example 11.6 for the derivation of the MRS.) The budget constraint is $Pa + b = 1$ because a type-1 person is endowed with 1 unit of the second good, whose price is \$1. The solution to $b = Pa$ and $Pa + b = 1$ is

$$a = \frac{1}{2P} \quad \text{and} \quad b = \frac{1}{2}$$

These are the demands of a type-1 person as a function of the price ratio P, *assuming price taking behavior.* A type-2 consumer sets $MRS = y/x = P$. We have $y = Px$. The budget constraint is $Px + y = P$. (A type-2 person has 1 unit of good 1 to sell at price P.) The two equations $y = Px$ and $Px + y = P$ yield

$$x = \frac{1}{2} \quad \text{and} \quad y = \frac{P}{2},$$

the demand functions of a price taking type-2 person.

If everyone is a price taker, and $P = 1$, we have $a = \frac{1}{2} = x$, and thus the total demand for commodity 1 would be $t \times \frac{1}{2} + t \times \frac{1}{2} = t$, which equals the total supply. (The type 2s each supply 1 unit of good 1.) And when $P = 1$ we have $b = \frac{1}{2} = y$. The total demand for commodity 2 would be $t \times \frac{1}{2} + t \times \frac{1}{2} = t$, which equals the total supply. (The type 1s each supply 1 unit of good 2.) Therefore, $P = 1$ is the market clearing price ratio, *assuming price taking behavior.*

Now, suppose that everyone takes price as given and announces their true utility-maximizing demand vectors *except* for one type-1 person, whom we refer to as person m. The total demand for good 1 from everyone except person m is $(t - 1) \times (1/2P) + t \times \frac{1}{2}$. The total supply of the first good is exactly t, so even before we add the demand of person m we see that the following inequality is a necessary condition for market equilibrium:

$$\frac{t - 1}{2P} + \frac{t}{2} \leq t. \tag{5}$$

This must hold because demand will exceed supply if $(t - 1)/2P + t/2 > t$, whatever m announces, and market forces will cause the price to change. Note that statement [5] is equivalent to

$$P \geq \frac{t - 1}{t}. \tag{6}$$

Similarly, the aggregate demand for the second good is at least $(t - 1) \times \frac{1}{2} + t \times \frac{1}{2}P$. Exactly t units of the second good are supplied, so even without the demand of person m we must have

$$\frac{t - 1}{2} + \frac{tP}{2} \leq t; \tag{7}$$

otherwise the demand for good 2 would exceed the supply, even without including person m, and the prices would change. Statement [7] is equivalent to

$$P \leq \frac{t+1}{t}. \tag{8}$$

Then [6] and [8] together yield

$$\frac{t-1}{t} \leq P \leq \frac{t+1}{t}. \tag{9}$$

If t is even reasonably large, then both $(t-1)/t$ and $(t+1)/t$ will be very close to unity. Therefore, whatever person m's demands, the market price ratio P will be very close to the *competitive* equilibrium price.

Example 11.15 featured an exchange economy with $t = 1$: one type-1 consumer and one type-2 consumer. Each individual is a monopoly supplier of one of the goods and hence has the ability to affect the market clearing price to advantage. Example 11.20 shows that when there is a large number of suppliers of each commodity, no individual can manipulate the price to any significant degree. Inequality [9] shows that any utility gain to the individual who deviates from price taking will be swamped by the cost of learning enough about aggregate demand to be able to manipulate the price in an advantageous way.

Sources

Hurwicz (1972) showed that price taking is not a dominant strategy and proved that there is *no* allocation mechanism for which truthful revelation is a dominant strategy, equilibrium outcomes are efficient, and each individual is guaranteed at least as much utility as he or she would get simply by consuming his or her endowment and not participating in the economy. The theorem and proof of Section 11.4.2 are due to Hurwicz and Schmeidler (1978). The mechanism of Section 11.4.3 is from Moore and Repullo (1988). The proof that a single individual's ability to manipulate prices vanishes as the number of traders increases, which we illustrated with an example in Section 11.4.4, is due to Roberts and Postlewaite (1976).

Links

Jackson (2001) and Maskin and Sjöström (2002) provide extensive discussions of the incentive issues sketched in this section.

Problem Set

(1) Show that the ability of a *type*-2 person to manipulate prices in the economy of Example 11.19 becomes negligible as t becomes sufficiently large.

(2) Consider an exchange economy with two goods and $n = 2t$ individuals. The first t individuals have the utility function $U = a^2b$ and endowment $\omega = (1, 0)$. The other individuals have the utility function $U = xy$ with endowment $\omega = (0, 1)$. Show that the ability of a single individual to influence the price ratio is negligible if t is sufficiently large.

11.5   COMMON PROPERTY RESOURCES

Suppose that each of n firms has free access to a resource from which it can extract a marketable commodity such as fish. If we assume that the amount harvested by any entrepreneur depends on the effort expended by that agent *and* also on the effort of all others, and if we assume in addition that output per unit of effort declines as the total effort of all fishers increases, then we have the classical common property resource model in which the pursuit of self-interest leads to an inefficient rate of extraction in the short run and insufficient conservation in the long run. Let's examine the short run problem.

We need to identify the efficient rate of extraction. Let e_i be the effort expended by firm i on the lake, which is the common resource. That is, e_i denotes the number of hours of fishing per week spent by the workers in boat i. Let $e = e_1 + e_2 + e_3 + \ldots + e_n$ represent the total effort. For simplicity, assume that effort is undertaken at a constant opportunity cost of c: One hour of fishing on the lake involves the sacrifice of c fish that could have been obtained by fishing in the ocean for one hour. (Alternatively, c is the opportunity cost of leisure.) If $T(e)$ denotes the total number of units of output (e.g., fish harvested) from all entrepreneurs as a function of total effort then $A(e) = T(e)/e$ is the average product, which we assume declines as e increases. Therefore, marginal product $M(e)$ is less than $A(e)$ for each level of e. (This is quite intuitive. If the grade that you get in your next course is higher than your GPA then your GPA will rise, but if the your next grade is lower than your current GPA that average will fall. You don't need calculus to follow this section, but if you want to use calculus then, of course, $M(e)$ is the first derivative of $T(e)$.)

∂ Let $t(x)$ be any real-valued function. Then the average, $t(x)/x$, is itself a function of x, which we name $a(x)$. Take the derivative of $a(x)$:

$$
\begin{aligned}
a'(x) &= x^{-1}t'(x) - t(x)x^{-2} \\
&= \frac{t'(x) - [t(x)/x]}{x} = \frac{t'(x) - a(x)}{x}.
\end{aligned}
$$

Then the average is falling (a' is negative) if and only if $t'(x) < a(x)$. But t' is the marginal. Therefore, the average is falling if and only if the marginal is less than the average.

Figure 11.5 illustrates a particular case: the efficient level of effort e^* is at the intersection of the marginal product curve $M(e)$ and the constant opportunity cost line c. Although average product exceeds marginal product at e^*, and hence the equilibrium is at e^+, an increase in effort beyond e^* will add less to output than to cost. This generalizes.

Efficiency Theorem for a Common Property Resource
 The efficient level of effort equates marginal product and marginal opportunity cost, and the efficient rate of extraction of fish is $x^* = T(e^*)$.

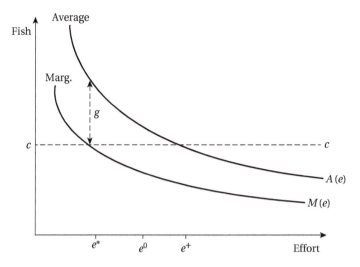

Figure 11.5

Proof:

If e is the actual amount of effort expended and $M(e) < c$ then one unit of effort transferred *from* the lake *to* the ocean will increase the community's consumption of fish by $c - M(e)$. There won't be any increase in cost in the form of additional input employed. Therefore, the gain $c - M(e)$ can be distributed in a way that makes some individuals better off without reducing anyone's utility. This means that $M(e) \geq c$ must hold if the outcome is efficient. But if we actually have $M(e) > c$ then one unit of effort transferred from the ocean to the lake will increase fish consumption by $M(e) - c$, and we can use the extra output to increase the utility of some people without making anyone worse off. Therefore, efficiency implies $M(e) = c$.   ∎

Let's determine the *actual* - that is, equilibrium - extraction rate when the resource is available to anyone without a user charge, in which case the only cost to an individual entrepreneur as a result of expending a unit of effort in extraction is the opportunity cost c. It turns out that the equilibrium occurs at e^+ in Figure 11.5 where *average* product equals marginal cost, and that is *above* the efficient level of input (or effort).

Equilibrium Theorem for a Common Property Resource
  If the resource is available for a user charge of zero then average product equals marginal cost at equilibrium, resulting in an inefficient outcome.

Proof:

Suppose that the current total input level is some amount e^0 below the point where $A(e)$ equals c. Suppose that firm i now increases its input slightly. The addition to the total catch per unit of additional input will be $M(e^0)$, the marginal product at e^0. *Society* would be better off if that additional unit of effort were employed in fishing the ocean where the yield would be c fish per unit of effort instead of $M(e^0)$. But the individual firm owner has no incentive to maximize social welfare. In the case of a common property resource the harvest per boat tends to be the average harvest. Even though the average harvest falls as a single firm increases its input level, the total harvest tends to be shared evenly by all boat owners. If the individual boat's catch equals the average output then it pays the boat's owner to increase the input level as long the extra harvest at the margin by the particular boat, which will be close to the average output, is greater than the private cost at the margin, which is c in this case. Therefore, harvesting will continue until average product is equal to marginal cost, or $A(e) = c$. This defines the equilibrium e^+ in Figure 11.5. ∎

If the government imposed a user charge of g dollars per hour spent fishing on the lake then the private marginal cost to an individual boat will now be $c + g$ and self-interest will drive entrepreneurs to harvest up to the point where average product equals $c + g$. In other words, $A(e) = c + g$ characterizes the equilibrium that results when there is a user charge of g. If g is set equal to $A(e^*) - c$ then $A(e) = c + g$ implies $e = e^*$ and the efficient outcome is attained (Figure 11.5 again).

Example ∂11.21 Output is Proportional to the Square Root of Effort

Let q denote output. The production function is $q = 20\sqrt{e}$, where e is total effort over all firms. The opportunity cost of a unit of effort is 1. Consumer welfare is maximized by maximizing $20\sqrt{e} - e$. The first derivative is $10/\sqrt{e} - 1$, and when we set that equal to 0 we get $e^* = 100$, the efficient level of effort. (Confirm that the second derivative is negative for all $e > 0$.) To determine the equilibrium effort level when the user cost of the resource is 0, we equate the average product to 1. Average product $= 20\sqrt{e}/e = 20/\sqrt{e}$. When we equate this to 1 we get $e^+ = 400$. Suppose that we currently have $e = 100$. Consider the position of entrepreneur F contemplating adding 200 units of effort. (F's initial effort level is zero.) That would yield 200 units of output on the ocean. When devoted to fishing the lake it causes output to increase from $20\sqrt{100}$ to $20\sqrt{300}$, an increase of only 146.4. However, F's yield is determined by average product. Total output will be $20\sqrt{300}$ of which F gets two-thirds because F supplies two-thirds of the effort, and $\frac{2}{3} \times 20\sqrt{300} = 230.9$ is better than the 200 available to F on the ocean.

The efficient outcome would be realized if the right to use the lake is held by a profit-maximizing firm, even though that owner had no interest in steering the economy to an efficient outcome. This is true whether the owner is a single individual or the entire community.

Monopoly Equilibrium Theorem

If the right to use the common property resource is held by a monopoly and that owner's costs are fixed, profit is maximized by charging a user fee that resulted in efficient use at equilibrium.

Proof:

Let's find the profit-maximizing fee f per unit of effort – that is, per hour on the lake. Assume that the costs of setting and collecting the fee are independent of the intensity of economic activity on the lake. That is, the costs of the lake owner are fixed, at k, say. Then the lake owner's profit is $fe - k$. The functions fe and $fe - k$ are maximized by the same value of e.

Let's determine the equilibrium value of e when the users of the lake must pay the lake's owner a fee of f per hour of use: Individual users will increase effort until the total value, e, satisfies $A(e) = c + f$. The profit-maximizing owner will maximize fe subject to $A(e) = c + f$. Because $f = A(e) - c$ at equilibrium, the owner of the lake will maximize $A(e)e - ce$, which equals $T(e) - ce$, or total product minus total variable cost. We have already examined this case. The function $T(e) - ce$ will be maximized when marginal product equals marginal cost, at e^*.   ∎

Profit maximization by the owner of the lake leads to the efficient outcome. Free, unrestricted use, does not.

Notice that the social optimum can be realized by private ownership or by government directive. (Verify that $f = g$.) Which approach goes further toward promoting social welfare? Perhaps it doesn't matter whether society chooses the public or private remedy for correcting the inefficiency. They yield the same outcome, e^*. Is there any difference between the two regimes?

In both cases the principal delegates the crucial job to an agent. The public approach requires the state to impose a user fee. The principal is the society, and the agent is a government body (the regulator) that is given the job of computing the efficient fee g and enforcing it. Acquiring the necessary information about marginal and average product is not an easy task. What assurance is there that the regulator will devote the necessary effort to this task? Who monitors the regulator? We can ask the same question of the private solution. It works only if

Wild salmon feed and grow off the southwest coast of Greenland and Faroe Islands before returning to spawn in their native rivers. The salmon population in these rivers has declined precipitously as a result of ocean net fishing. When salmon are caught they don't return to the rivers to spawn. Because there are private property rights in the ocean netting of salmon off Greenland and Faroe Islands it is possible to restore the wild salmon population without impoverishing the ocean fishermen. The property rights consist of individual boat quotas, which can be bought and sold. A boat can't harvest salmon unless it holds a quota, which is an entitlement to harvest a given number of fish. The Atlantic Salmon Federation compensates fishermen for not exercising their netting rights, resulting in a much greater number of salmon returning to spawn. By contrast, the US government has spent more than $35 million to restock Atlantic coastal rivers with salmon, to little effect (Anderson and Leal, 1997, pp. 156–157).

the owner of the lake maximizes profit. But owners typically hire an agent, called a manager, to carry out this task for them. The manager's personal welfare is his or her chief concern, and that is not perfectly aligned with the interests of the owners. But the manager is monitored by the capital market in a capitalist economy. If the manager's activities do not provide a satisfactory rate of return on the firm's capital equipment and resources then a takeover would be profitable for someone who has access to an agent who *can* get the most out of the inputs.

Moreover, there is usually better information on the performance of agents in the private sector than in the government sector. Almost all of the relevant data can be reduced to a single number: rate of return on capital. Another reason why government agents can be harder to motivate is that their budget constraints are typically softer than those that govern firms in the private sector. However, if a private firm anticipates that the government will come to its rescue, the discipline effect of its budget constraint will soften. In the late 1970s the US government gave massive assistance to the Chrysler Corporation when it was on the verge of bankruptcy. Similarly, the US government used the "too big to fail" rationale to assist some large banks in the 1980s. It rescued General Motors in 2007 by purchasing a controlling interest in GM. See Section 3.5 of Chapter 3 for contemporary "too big to fail" stories.

The preceding paragraph hardly scratches the surface, but it gives an indication of the kind of issues that have to be settled before one can decide whether the public or private remedy is better in a particular case.

Link

Ostrom (1990) is a thorough treatment of the theory and history of common property resources. (Elinor Ostrom received the Nobel Prize in Economics in 2009.) Hannesson (2004) is a superb analysis of our use of the ocean; not the largest common property, but second only to the air that we breathe.

Problem Set

(1) Confirm that the profit-maximizing fee f set by the monopoly owner of the common property resource is equal to the fee g that the government would charge to elicit an efficient outcome.

(2) Suppose that $16\sqrt{e}$ units of output result when a total of e units of effort are supplied. The opportunity cost of e units of effort is $\frac{1}{2}e^2$. Determine the efficient level of effort and the equilibrium level of effort when the resource is freely available.

(3) Show that the constant opportunity cost assumption is critical to our demonstration that profit maximization will lead to efficiency.

References

Abdulkadiroğlu, Atila, and Tayfun Sönmez. (1999). House allocation with existing tenants. *Journal of Economic Theory* 88: 233–260.

—— (2003). School choice: A mechanism design approach. *American Economic Review* 93: 729–747.

Abdulkadiroğlu, A., P. Pathak, and A. E. Roth. (2005a). The New York City high school match. *American Economic Review, Papers and Proceedings* 95: 363–367.

Abdulkadiroğlu, A., P. Pathak, A. E. Roth, and T. Sönmez. (2005b). The Boston public school match. *American Economic Review, Papers and Proceedings* 95: 368–371.

Admati, A., and M. Hellwig. (2013). *The Bankers' New Clothes: What's Wrong with Banking and What To Do about it.* Princeton University Press.

Aghion, P., M. Dewatripont, C. Hoxby, A. MasColell, and A. Sapir. (2010). Governance and performance of universities: Evidence from Europe and the US. *Economic Policy* 25: 7–59.

Akerlof, G. A. (1970). The market for "lemons": Qualitative uncertainty and the market mechanism. *Quarterly Journal of Economics* 84: 488–500.

Akerlof, G. A., and P. Romer. (1994). Looting: The economic underworld of bankruptcy for profit. *Brookings Papers on Economic Activity* 2: 1–73.

Akerlof, G. A., A. Rose, J. Yellen, and H. Hessenius. (1991). East Germany in from the cold: The economic aftermath of currency union. *Brookings Papers on Economic Activity* 1: 1–87.

Alchian, A., and H. D. Demsetz. (1972). Production, information costs, and economic organization. *American Economic Review* 62: 777–795.

Allen, D. A., and D. Lueck. (2002). *The Nature of the Farm: Contracts, Risk, and Organization in Agriculture.* Cambridge, MA: MIT Press.

Allen, Franklin, and Gale, Douglas. (2000). Corporate governance and competition. In *Corporate Governance*, ed. Xavier Vives. Cambridge University Press. 23–84.

Anderson, L. R. (2001). Public choice as an experimental science. In *The Elgar Companion to Public Choice*, ed. W. F. Shughart and L. Razzolini. Cheltenham, UK: Edward Elgar. 497–511.

Anderson, R. M., M. A. Khan, and S. Rashid. (1982). Approximate equilibrium with bounds independent of preferences. *Review of Economic Studies* 44: 473–475.

Anderson, T. L., and D. R. Leal. (1997). *Enviro-Capitalists: Doing Good While Doing Well.* New York: Rowman and Littlefield.

Aoki, Masahiko. (2000). Information and governance in the Silicon Valley model. In *Corporate Governance*, ed. Xavier Vives. Cambridge University Press. 169-195.

Arnott, R., T. Rave, and R. Schob. (2005). *Alleviating Urban Traffic Congestion*. Cambridge, MA: MIT Press.

Arrow, K. J. (1951a). *Social Choice and Individual Values*. 1st edn. New York: Wiley.

(1951b). An extension of the basic theorems of classical welfare economics. In *Proceedings of the Second Berkeley Stigl Symposium on Mathematical Statistics and Probability*, ed. J. Neyman. Berkeley, CA: University of California Press. 507-532.

(1963a). *Social Choice and Individual Values*. 2nd edn. New York: Wiley.

(1963b). Uncertainty and the welfare economics of medical care. *American Economic Review* 53: 941-973.

(1970). The organization of economic activity: Issues pertinent to the choice of market versus non-market allocation. In *Public Expenditures and Policy Analysis*, ed. R. H. Haveman and J. Margolis. Chicago: Markham.59-73.

(1971). *Essays in the Theory of Risk-Bearing*. Chicago: Markham.

(1979). The property rights doctrine and demand revelation under incomplete information. In *Economics and Human Welfare*, ed. M. Boskin. New York: Academic Press.23-39.

(1984). The economics of agency. In *Principals and Agents: The Structure of Business*, ed. J. Pratt and R. Zeckhauser. Boston: Harvard Business School Press. 37-51.

Arrow, K. J., and G. Debreu. (1954). Existence of equilibrium for a competitive economy. *Econometrica* 22: 265-290.

Ashenfelter, O. (1989). How auctions work for wine and art. *Journal of Economic Perspectives* 3: 23-36.

Attiyeh, G., R. Franciosi, and M. Isaac. (2000). Experiments with the pivotal process for providing public goods. *Public Choice* 102: 93-112.

Axelrod, R. (1984). *The Evolution of Cooperation*. New York: Basic Books.

Autor, D. H., L. F. Katz, and A. B. Krueger. (1998). Computing inequality: Have computers changed the labor market? *Quarterly Journal of Economics* 113: 1169-1213.

Ayres, Ian, and S. D. Levitt. (1998). Measuring positive externalities from unobservable victim precaution: An empirical analysis of Lojack. *Quarterly Journal of Economics* 112: 43-77.

Baker, George. (2002). Distortion and risk in optimal incentive contracts. *Journal of Human Resources* 37: 728-751.

Baker, George, Robert Gibbons, and K. J. Murphy. (2002). Relational contracts and the theory of the firm. *Quarterly Journal of Economics* 117: 39-84.

Balazs, E. (1964). *Chinese Civilization and Bureaucracy*. New Haven: Yale University Press.

Ballou, Dale, and Michael Podgursky. (1997). *Teacher Pay and Teacher Quality*. Kalamazoo, MI: W. E. Upjohn Institute for Employment Research.

(2001). Merit pay symposium: Let the market decide. *Education Next* 1, Spring: 16-25.

Banerjee, A., A. G. Chandrasekhar, E. Duflo, and M. O. Jackson. (2013). The diffusion of microfinance. *Science* 341: 6144.

Banerjee, A., and E. W. Eckard. (2001). Why regulate insider trading? Evidence from the first great merger wave (1897-1903). *American Economic Review* 91: 1329-1349.

Barberà, S. (1983). Strategy-proofness and pivotal voters: A direct proof of the Gibbard-Satterthwaite theorem. *International Economic Review* 24: 413–418.

(2001). An introduction to strategy proof social choice functions. *Social Choice and Welfare* 18: 619–653.

(2004). Strategy proofness. In *Handbook of Social Choice and Welfare*, Vol. 2, ed. K. J. Arrow, A. K. Sen, and K. Suzumura, Amsterdam: Elsevier. Ch. 24.

Basu, Kaushik. (1994). The traveler's dilemma: Paradoxes of rationality in game theory. *American Economic Review: Papers and Proceedings* 84: 391–395.

Baumol, W. J. (1993). *Entrepreneurship, Management, and the Structure of Payoffs*. Cambridge, MA: MIT Press.

(2002). *The Free-Market Innovation Machine*. Princeton University Press.

(2012). *The Cost Disease: Why Computers Get Cheaper and Health Care Doesn't*. New Haven: Yale University Press.

Bebchuk, L. A., J. M. Fried, and D. I. Walker. (2002). Managerial power and rent extraction in the design of executive compensation. *University of Chicago Law Review* 69: 751–846.

Bebchuk, L. A., and J. M. Fried. (2004). *Pay Without Performance: The Unfilled Promise of Executive Compensation*. Cambridge, MA: Harvard University Press.

Becker, G. S., and R. A. Posner. (2009). *Uncommon Sense: Economic Insights, from Marriage to Terrorism*. University of Chicago Press.

Benoit, J.-P. (2000). The Gibbard-Satterthwaite theorem: a simple proof. *Economics Letters* 69: 319–322.

Bernstein, P. (1992). *Capital Ideas*. New York: The Free Press.

Bertrand, M., and S. Mullainathan. (2000). Agents with and without principals. *American Economic Review* 90: 203–208.

(2001). Are CEOs rewarded for luck? Agents without principals are. *Quarterly Journal of Economics* 116: 910–932.

(2003). Enjoying the quiet life. *Journal of Political Economy* 111: 1043–1075.

Bichler, Martin. (2001). *The Future of e-markets: Multidimensional Market Mechanisms*. Cambridge University Press.

Binmore, K. (1992). *Fun and Games*. Lexington, MA: D.C. Heath.

Binmore, K., and J. Davies. (2001). *Calculus: Concepts and Methods*. Cambridge University Press.

Binmore, K., and P. Klemperer. (2002). The biggest auction ever: The sale of British 3G telecom licenses. *Economic Journal* 112: C74–C96.

Binmore, K., and L. Samuelson. (1992). Evolutionary stability in repeated games played by finite automata. *Journal of Economic Theory* 57: 278–305.

Blair, R. D., and D. L. Kaserman. (1991). The economics and ethics of alternative cadaveric organ procurement policies. *Yale Journal on Regulation* 8: 403–452.

Blair, R. D., and F. Lafontaine. (2011). *The Economics of Franchising*. Cambridge University Press.

Blinder, A. S. (2013). *After the Music Stopped: The Financial Crisis, the Response, and the Work Ahead*. New York: The Penguin Press.

Borda, J.-C. (1781). *Memoire sur les elections au scrutins*. Histoire de l Academie Royale des Sciences.

Brams, S. J. (1976). *Paradoxes in Politics: An Introduction to the Nonobvious in Political Science*. New York: The Free Press.

Brickley, J. A., J. L. Coles, and R. L. Terry. (1994). Outside directors and the adoption of poison pills. *Journal of Financial Economics* 35: 371–390.

Budish, Eric. (2011). The combinatorial assignment problem: Approximate competitive equilibrium from equal incomes. *Journal of Political Economy* 119: 1061–1103.

Budish, Eric, and J. B. Kessler. (2016). *Bringing real market participants' real preferences into the lab: Changing the course allocation mechanism at Wharton.* Booth School of Business, University of Chicago.

Calvert, R. L. (1986). *Models of Imperfect Information in Politics.* Chur, Switzerland: Harwood Academic Publishers.

Camerer, C. F., L. Babcock, G. Lowenstein, and R. H. Thaler. (2004). Labor supply of New York City cab drivers: One day at a time. In *Advances in Behavioral Economics*, ed. C. F. Camerer, G. Lowenstein, and M. Rabin, 533–547. Princeton University Press.

Cameron, S., and J. Heckman. (1993). The nonequivalence of high school equivalents. *Journal of Labor Economics* 11: 1–47.

Campbell, D. E. (1987). *Resource Allocation Mechanisms.* New York: Cambridge University Press.

Campbell, D. E., and J. S. Kelly. (2000). A simple characterization of majority rule. *Economic Theory* 15: 689–700.

(2002). Impossibility theorems in the Arrovian framework. In *Handbook of Social Choice and Welfare*, Vol. 1, ed. K. J. Arrow, A. K. Sen, and K. Suzumura, 35–94.

(2003). A strategy-proofness characterization of majority rule. *Economic Theory* 22: 557–568.

Campbell, D. E., and M. Truchon. (1988). Boundary optima in the theory of public goods supply. *Journal of Public Economics* 35: 241–249.

Carlin, Wendy, and Colin Mayer. (2000). How do financial systems affect economic performance? In *Corporate Governance*, ed. Xavier Vives. Cambridge University Press.137–160.

Carmichael, H. L. (1988). Incentives in academics: Why is there tenure? *Journal of Political Economy* 96: 453–472.

(1989). Self-enforcing contracts, shirking, and life-cycle incentives. *Journal of Economic Perspectives* 3: 65–83.

(2001). Tenure promotes honest hiring. *Policy Options* 22: 10–14.

Carmichael, H. L., and B. W. McLeod. (2000). Worker cooperation and the ratchet effect. *Journal of Labor Economics* 18: 1–19.

Carr, Jack L., Frank Mathewson, and N. C. Quigley. (1995). Stability in the absence of deposit insurance: The Canadian banking system 1890–1966. *Journal of Money, Credit and Banking* 27: 1137–1158.

Chen, Yan. (2008). Incentive-compatible mechanisms for pure public goods: A survey of experimental research. In *The Handbook of Experimental Economics Results*, Vol. 1, ed. C. R. Plott and V. Smith. New York: Elgar Publishing Co. 625–643.

Chen, Yan, and Tayfun Sönmez. (2002). Improving efficiency of on-campus housing: An experimental study. *American Economic Review* 92: 1669–1686.

(2004). An experimental study of house allocation mechanisms. *Economics Letters* 83: 137–140.

(2006). School choice: An experimental study. *Journal of Economic Theory* 127: 202–231.

Chiappori, P.-A. and B. Salanié. (2003). Testing contract theory: A survey of some recent work. In *Advances in Economics and Econometrics: Invited Lectures to Eighth World Congress of the Econometric Society*, ed. M. Dewatripont, L. Hansen, and S. Turnovsky. Cambridge University Press.115–149.

Chichilnisky, G., and G. Heal. (1993). Global environmental risks. *Journal of Economic Perspectives* 7: 65–86.

(1999). Catastrophe futures: Financial markets for unknown risks. In *Markets, Information, and Uncertainty: Essays in Economic Theory in Honor of Kenneth J. Arrow*, ed. G. Chichilnisky. New York: Cambridge University Press.120–140.

Choi, Y. J., J. Chen, and Y. Sawada. (2015). Life insurance and suicide: Asymmetric information revisited. *B. E. Journal of Economic Analysis and Policy* 15: 1127–1149.

Clarke, E. H. (1971). Multipart pricing of public goods. *Public Choice* 8: 19–73.

Coase, R. H. (1960). The problem of social cost. *Journal of Law and Economics* 3: 144–171.

(1974). The lighthouse in economics. *Journal of Law and Economics* 17: 357–376.

Comment, Robert, and G. W. Schwert. (1995). Poison or placebo: Evidence on the deterrence and wealth effects of modern antitakeover measures. *Journal of Financial Economics* 39: 3–43.

Condorcet, Marquis de. (1785). *Essai sur la'application de l'analyse à la possibilité des décisions rendues à la pluralité des voix*. Paris: Imprimerie Royale. (Reprinted in 1972 by Chelsea Publishing Co., New York.)

Conley, J., and D. Diamantaris. (1996). Generalized Samuelson and welfare theorems for nonsmooth economies. *Journal of Public Economics* 59: 137–152.

Cook, C. (1990). A survey of perestroika. *The Economist*, April, p. 6.

Cooter, R. D., and T. S. Ullen. (1994). *Law and Economics*. 2nd edn. Glenview, IL: Scott, Foresman.

Corchon, L. C. (1996). *The Theory of Implementation of Socially Optimal Decisions in Economics*. London: Macmillan Press.

Cornes, R., and T. Sandler. (1996). *The Theory of Externalities, Public Goods, and Club Goods*. 2nd edn. New York: Cambridge University Press.

Costa, D. L. (1998). *The Evolution of Retirement*. University of Chicago Press.

Cramton, P., and J. A. Schwartz (2000). Collusive Bidding: Lessons from The FCC spectrum auctions. *Journal of Regulatory Economics* 17: 229–252.

Cramton, P., and S. Kerr. (1999). The distributional effects of carbon regulation. In *The Market and the Environment*, ed. Thomas Sterner, Chapt. 12. Cheltenham, UK: Edward Elgar.

Cramton, P., R. Gibbons, and P. Klemperer. (1987). Dissolving a partnership efficiently. *Econometrica* 55: 615–632.

d'Aspremont, C., and L.-A. Gerard-Varet. (1979). Incentives and incomplete information. *Journal of Public Economics* 11: 25–45.

Dana, J. D. (1998). Advance-purchase discounts and price discrimination in competitive markets. *Journal of Political Economy*. 106: 395–422.

Danilov, V. I., and A. I. Sotskov. (2002). *Social Choice Mechanisms*. Berlin: Springer.

Debreu, G. (1959). *Theory of Value*. New York: Wiley.

Demsetz, H. (1968). Why regulate utilities? *Journal of Law and Economics* 11: 55–65.

Demirgüç-Kunt, A., and E. J. Kane. (2002). Deposit insurance around the globe. Where does it work? *Journal of Economic Perspectives* 16: 175–195.

Dewatripont, Mathias, and Jean Tirole. (1994). *The Prudent Regulation of Banks.* Cambridge, MA: MIT Press.

Diamond, Peter. (1992). Organizing the health insurance market. *Econometrica* 60: 1233–1254.

Dixit, A. K. (2004). *Lawlessness and Economics: Alternative Modes of Governance.* Princeton University Press.

Downs, A. (1957). *An Economic Theory of Democracy.* New York: Harper & Row.

Dranove, David. (2000). *The Economic Evolution of American Health Care.* Princeton University Press.

Drèze, J., and A. K. Sen. (1989). *Hunger and Public Action.* Oxford University Press.

Duflo, E., R. Hanna, and S. Ryan (2012). Incentives work: Getting teachers to come to school. *American Economic Review* 102: 1241–1278.

Dutta, P. K. (2000). *Strategies and Games.* Cambridge, MA: MIT Press.

Dyer, D., and J. H. Kagel. (2002). Bidding in common value auctions: How the commercial construction industry corrects for the winner's curse. In *Common Value Auctions and the Winner's Curse*, ed. J. H., Kagel, and D. Levin. Princeton University Press. 349–393.

Dyson, George. (2012). *Turing's Cathedral: The Origins of the Digital Universe.* New York: Pantheon Books.

Easterbrook, F. H. (1984). Insider trading as an agency problem. In *Principals and Agents: The Structure of Business*, ed. J. Pratt and R. Zeckhauser. Boston, MA: Harvard Business School Press, 81–100.

(1986). Manager's discretion and investor welfare: Theories and evidence. *Delaware Journal of Corporate Law* 9: 540–567.

Ehrenberg, R. G. (2000). *Tuition Rising: Why College Costs So Much.* Cambridge, MA: Harvard University Press.

Erdil, A, and H. Ergin. (2013). Improving efficiency in school choice. In *The Handbook of Market Design*, ed. Nir Vulkan, Alvin E. Roth, and Zvika Neeman. Oxford University Press. 170–188.

Ergin, Haluk, and Tayfun Sönmez. (2006). Games of school choice under the Boston mechanism. *Journal of Public Economics* 90: 215–237.

Ergin, Haluk, Tayfun Sönmez, and M. U. Ünver. (2017). Dual-donor organ exchange. *Econometrica*, forthcoming. Available at www.stanford.edu/group/SITE/Unver.pdf, accessed December 1, 2015.

Farber, H. S. (2005). Is tomorrow another day? The labor supply of New York City cab drivers. *Journal of Political Economy* 113: 46–82.

Farrell, J. (1987). Information and the Coase theorem. *Journal of Public Economics* 1: 113–129.

Fay, S., E. Hurst, and M. J. White. (2002). The household bankruptcy decision. *American Economic Review* 92: 706–718.

Fisman, Ray, and Eduard Miguel. (2008). *Economic Gangsters: Corruption, Violence, and the Poverty of Nations.* Princeton University Press.

Foley, D. (1970). Lindahl's solution and the core of an economy with public goods. *Econometrica* 38: 66–72.

Frank, R. H. (2004). *What Price the Moral High Ground? Ethical Dilemmas in Competitive Environments.* Princeton University Press.

(2007). *The Economic Naturalist: In Search of Explanations for Everyday Enigmas.* New York: Basic Books.

Freeman, R. B., and M. M. Kleiner. (2005). The last American shoe manufacturer: Decreasing productivity and increasing yields in the shift from piece rates to continuous flow production. *Industrial Relations* 44: 301–330.

Freixas, Xavier, and J.-C. Rochet. (1997). *The Microeconomics of Banking*. Cambridge, MA: MIT Press.

Friedman, B. M., and F. H. Hahn. (1990). *Handbook of Monetary Economics*, Vol. 2. Amsterdam: Elsevier Science.

Friedman, J. (1971). A non-cooperative equilibrium for supergames. *Review of Economic Studies* 38: 1–12.

Fudenberg, D., and J. Tirole. (1991). *Game Theory*. Cambridge, MA: MIT Press.

Fudenberg, D., and E. S. Maskin. (1986). The folk theorem in repeated games with discounting or with incomplete information. *Econometrica* 54: 533–554.

Fulcher, James. (2004). *Capitalism: A Very Short Introduction*. Oxford University Press.

Gale, D., and L. S. Shapley. (1962). College admissions and the stability of marriage. *American Mathematical Monthly* 69: 9–15.

Gambetta, Diego. (1993). *The Sicilian Mafia*. Cambridge, MA: Harvard University Press.

Ghahramani, Saeed. (2002). *Fundamentals of Probability*. 2nd edn. New Jersey: Prentice Hall.

Gibbard, A. (1973). Manipulation of voting schemes: A general result. *Econometrica* 40: 587–602.

Gibbons, R. (1992). *Game Theory for Applied Economists*. Princeton University Press.

Gintis, Herbert. (2000). *Game Theory Evolving: A Problem-Centered Introduction to Modeling Strategic Interaction*. Princeton University Press.

Gladwell, Malcolm. (2008). *Outliers: The Story of Success*. New York: Little, Brown and Company.

Goeree and Holt. (2001). Ten little treasures of game theory, and ten intuitive contradictions. *American Economic Review* 91: 1402–1422.

Goldsmith, Jack, and Tim Wu. (2006). *Who Controls the Internet: Illusions of a Borderless World*. Oxford University Press.

Goyall, Sanjeev. (2007). *Connections: An Introduction to the Economics of Networks*. Princeton University Press.

Goyall, Sanjeev and S. Joshi. (2006). Bilateralism and free trade. *International Economic Review* 47: 749–778.

Goyall, Sanjeev and J. L. Moraga-González. (2001). R & D networks. *RAND Journal of Economics* 32: 686–707.

Green, J., and J.-J. Laffont. (1977). Characterization of satisfactory mechanisms for the revelation of preferences for public goods. *Econometrica* 45: 427–438.

(1979). *Incentives in Public Decision Making*. Amsterdam: Elsevier.

Gribbin, John, and Mary Gribbin. (1997). *Richard Feynman: A Life in Science*. New York: Dutton.

Grossman, S. J., and O. Hart. (1980). Take-over bids, the free-rider problem, and the theory of the corporation. *Bell Journal of Economics* 11: 42–64.

(1982). Corporate financial structure and managerial incentives. In *The Economics of Information and Uncertainty*, ed. J. McCall. University of Chicago Press. 109–140.

Grove, Hugh, Tom Cook, and Jon Goodwin. (2004). Enron red flags. *Journal of Financial Education*. 30: 90–110.

Groves, T. (1973). Incentives in teams. *Econometrica* 41: 617–631.

Gruber, J., and M. Owings. (1996). Physician financial incentives and Caesarian section delivery. *RAND Journal of Economics* 27: 99-123.

Hall, B. H. (1988). The effect of takeover activity on corporate research and development. In *Corporate Takeovers: Causes and Consequences*, ed. A. J. Auerbach. University of Chicago Press. 69-96.

Hall, B. J. (2000). Regulatory free cash flow and the high cost of insurance company failures. *Journal of Risk and Insurance* 67: 415-438.

Hall, B. J., and K. J. Murphy. (2000). Optimal exercise prices for risk averse executives. *American Economic Review* 90: 209-214.

   (2002). Stock options for undiversified executives. *Journal of Accounting and Economics* 33: 3-42.

   (2003). The trouble with stock options. *Journal of Economic Perspectives* 17: 49-70.

Hall, B. J., and J. Liebman. (1998). Are CEOs really paid like bureaucrats? *Quarterly Journal of Economics* 113: 653-691.

Hammons, C. W. (2001). School at home. *Education Next* 1: 48-55.

Hannesson, Rögnvaldur. (2004). *The Privatization of the Ocean*. Cambridge, MA: MIT Press.

Hansmann, Henry. (1996). *The Ownership of Enterprise*. Cambridge University Press.

Hanushek, E. A. (2002). The seeds of growth. *Education Next* 2, Fall: 10-17.

Harford, Tim. (2006). *The Undercover Economist: Explaining Why the Rich are Rich, the Poor are Poor - and Why You Can Never Buy a Decent Used Car*. Oxford University Press.

Harrison, B. (1993). Taking the high road to growth. *Technology Review* October: 68.

Hart, Oliver. (1995). *Firms, Contracts, and Financial; Structure*. Oxford University Press.

Haubrich, Joseph. (1994). Risk aversion, performance pay, and the principal-agent problem. *Journal of Political Economy* 102: 258-276.

Healy, Paul and Palepu Krishna. (2003). The fall of Enron. *Journal of Economic Perspectives*. 17: 3-26.

Heckman, James J. (2013). *Giving Kids a Fair Chance: A Strategy That Works*. Cambridge University Press.

Hendel, I., and Alessandro Lizzeri. (1999). Adverse selection in durable goods markets. *American Economic Review* 89: 1097-1115.

Herstein, I. N., and J. Milnor. (1953). An axiomatic approach to measurable utility. *Econometrica* 21: 291-297.

Hicks, J. R. (1939). *Value and Capital*. London: Clarendon Press.

Hill, Christopher. (1986). The political dilemma for Western governments. In *Terrorism and International Order*, ed. Lawrence Freedman, Christopher Hill, Adam Roberts, R. J. Vincent, Paul Wilkinson, and Philip Windsor. London: Routledge and Kegan Paul.

Hirshleifer, J., and J. G. Riley. (1992). *The Analytics of Uncertainty and Information*. Cambridge University Press.

Holmström, B. (1979a). Moral hazard and observability. *Bell Journal of Economics* 10: 74-91.

   (1979b). Groves' schemes on restricted domains. *Econometrica* 47: 1137-1144.

Holmström, B., and S. N. Kaplan. (2001). Corporate governance and merger activity in the US: Making sense of the 1980s and 1990s. *Journal of Economic Perspectives* 15: 121-144.

(2003). The state of US corporate governance: What's right and what's wrong. *Journal of Applied Corporate Finance* 16: 8–20.

Hoxby, C. M. (2001a). Changing the profession: How would school choice affect teachers? *Education Next* 1, Spring: 57–63.

(2001b). Rising tide: New evidence on competition and the public schools. *Education Next* 1, Winter: 68–74.

(2002). Would school choice change the teaching profession? *Journal of Human Resources* 38: 846–891.

(2003). School choice and school productivity. In *The Economics of School Choice*, ed. C. M. Hoxby. University of Chicago Press. 287–341.

(2014). *Covering the costs*. In *What Lies Ahead for America's Children and their Schools*, eds. C. E. Finn and R. Sousa. Palo Alto: Houver Institution Press. 149–176.

Hsiao, W C., P. Braun, P. Dunn, and E. R. Becker. (1988). Resource-based relative values: An overview. *Journal of the American Medical Association* 260 (16): 2418–2424.

Hurwicz, L. (1972). On informationally decentralized systems. In *Decision and Organization*, ed. C. B. McGuire and R. Radner. Amsterdam: Elsevier.297–336.

Hurwicz, L., and D. Schmeidler. (1978). Construction of outcome functions guaranteeing existence and Pareto optimality of Nash equilibria. *Econometrica* 46: 1447–1474.

Hurwicz, L., and M. Walker. (1990). On the article nonoptimality of dominant-strategy allocation mechanisms: A general theorem that includes pure exchange economies. *Econometrica* 58: 683–704.

Illing, G., and U. Klüh. (2003). *Spectrum Auctions and Competition in Telecommunications*. Cambridge, MA: MIT Press.

Jackson, M. O. (2001). A crash course in implementation theory. *Social Choice and Welfare* 18: 655–708.

(2004). A survey of models of network formation: Stability and efficiency. In *Group Formation in Economics; Networks, Clubs and Coalitions*. Gabrielle Demange and Myrna Wooders, eds. Cambridge University Press, 11–57.

(2008). *Social and Economic Networks*. Princeton University Press.

(2011). An overview of social networks and economic applications. In *The Handbook of Social Economics*, ed. J. Benhabib, A. Bisin, and M.O. Jackson. Amsterdam, North Holland Press.

(2014). Networks in the understanding of economic behaviors. *Journal of Economic Perspectives* 28: 3–22.

Jaffee, Dwight, and Joseph Stiglitz. (1990). Credit rationing. In *Handbook of Monetary Economics*, Vol. 2, ed. B. M. Friedman, and F. H. Hahn. Ch. 1, 837–888.

Jarrell, G. A., J. A. Brickley, and J. M. Netter. (1988). The market for corporate control: The empirical evidence since 1980. *Journal of Economic Perspectives* 2: 49–68.

Jensen, M. C. (1986). Agency costs of free cash flow, corporate finance, and takeovers. *American Economic Review* 76: 323–329.

(1988). Takeovers: Their causes and consequences. *Journal of Economic Perspectives* 2: 1–48.

(1993). The modern industrial revolution, exit, and the failure of internal control systems. *Journal of Finance* 48: 831–880.

Jensen, M. C., and Kevin J. Murphy. (1990a). CEO incentives: It's not how much you pay, but how. *Harvard Business Review* 68: 138–153.

(1990b). Performance pay and top-management incentives. *Journal of Political Economy* 98: 225–264.

Joskow, P. L., Schmalensee, Richard, and Bailey, E. M. (1998). The market for sulfur dioxide emissions. *American Economic Review* 88: 669–685.

Kagel, J. H., and D. Levin. (2002a). *Common Value Auctions and the Winner's Curse*. Princeton University Press.

(2002b). Bidding in common-value auctions: A survey of experimental research. In *Common Value Auctions and the Winner's Curse*, ed. J. H. Kagel, and D. Levin. Princeton University Press. 1–84.

Kahn, C., and G. Huberman. (1988). Two-sided uncertainty and up-or-out contracts. *Journal of Labor Economics* 6: 423–445.

Kandel, E., and E. P. Lazear. (1992). Peer pressure and partnerships. *Journal of Political Economy* 100: 801–817.

Kane, E. J. (1989). *The S & L Insurance Mess: How Did It Happen?* Washington, DC: Urban Institute Press.

Kanter, R. M. (1989). *When Giants Learn to Dance*. New York: Simon and Schuster.

Karush, W. (1939). *Minima of Functions of Several Variables with Inequalities as Side Constraints*. MSc Dissertation. Dept. of Mathematics, Univ. of Chicago, Chicago, Illinois.

Katzner, D. W. (1970). *Static Demand Theory*. New York: Macmillan.

Kelly, J. S. (1988). *Social Choice Theory*. Berlin: Springer-Verlag.

Kirby, K. N., M. Santiesteban, and G. C. Whinston. (2003). Impatience and grades: Delay-discount rates correlate negatively with college GPA. DP-63, Williams Project on the Economics of Higher Education, Department of Economics, Williams College. Available at www.williams.edu/wpehe/downloads.html, accessed December 15, 2005.

Klemperer, Paul. (1998). Auctions with almost common values. *European Economic Reviews* 42: 757–769.

(1999). Auction theory: A guide to the literature. *Journal of Economic Surveys* 13: 227–286. (Reprinted as Chapter 1 in Klemperer, 2004.)

(2002a). What really matters in auction design. *Journal of Economic Perspectives* 16: 169–189. (Reprinted as Chapter 3 in Klemperer, 2004.)

(2002b). How (not) to run auctions: The European 3G telecom auctions. *European Economic Review* 46: 829–845. (Reprinted as Chapter 7 in Illing and Klüh, 2003.)

(2003). *Why every economist should learn some auction theory* In *Advances in Economics and Econometrics: Invited Lectures to Eighth World Congress of the Econometric Society*, Vol. 1, ed. Mathias Dewatripont, L. Hansen, and S. Turnovsky. Cambridge University Press. 25–55. (Reprinted as Chapter 2 in Klemperer, 2004.)

(2004). Auctions: Theory and Practice. Princeton, N. J.: Princeton University Press.

Kmietowicz, Zosia. (2000). WHO warns of threat of "superbugs." *British Medical Journal* 320: 1624.

Kohler, Heinz. (1977). *Scarcity and Freedom: An Introduction to Economics*. Lexington, MA: D. C. Heath.

Kojima, F., P. A. Pathak, and A. E. Roth. (2013). Matching with couples: Stability and incentives in large markets. *Quarterly Journal of Economics* 128: 1585–1632.

Koopmans, T. C. (1957). *Three Essays on the State of Economic Science*. New York: McGraw-Hill.

Kotlikoff, L. J., and S. Burns. (2004). *The Coming Generational Storm: What You Need to Know About America's Economic Future*. Cambridge, MA: MIT Press.

Kotowitz, Y. (1989). Moral hazard. In *Allocation, Information, and Markets*, ed. J. Eatwell, M. Milgate, and P. Newman. New York: Norton.207–213.

Krauss, L. M. (1993). *The Fear of Physics*. New York: Basic Books.

Kremer, M., and R. Glennersten. (2004). *Strong Medicine: Creating Incentives for Pharmaceutical Research on Neglected Diseases*. Princeton, NJ/Cambride, MA: Princeton University Press/MIT Press.

Kreps, D. M. (1988). *Notes on the Theory of Choice*. Boulder, CO: Westview Press.

(1990). *Game Theory and Economic Modeling*. Oxford University Press.

Kreps, D. M., P. Milgrom, J. Roberts, and R. Wilson. (1982). Rational cooperation in the finitely repeated prisoners' dilemma. *Journal of Economic Theory* 27: 245–252.

Krishna, Vijay. (2002). *Auction Theory*. San Diego, CA: Academic Press.

Krueger, A. B., and A. Mas. (2004). Strikes, scabs, and tread separation: Labor strife and the production of defective Bridgestone/Firestone tires. *Journal of Political Economy* 112: 253–289.

Kuhn, H. W., and A. W. Tucker. (1950). Nonlinear programming. In *Proceedings of the Second Berkeley Symposium on Mathematical Statistics and Probability*, ed. Jerzy Neyman. Berkeley, CA: University of California Press.481–492.

Laffont, J.-J. (1994). The new economics of regulation ten years after. *Econometrica* 62: 507–537.

Laffont, J.-J., and D. Martimort. (2002). *The Theory of Incentives: The Principal-Agent Model*. Princeton University Press.

Laffont, J.-J., and J. Tirole. (1987). Auctioning incentive contracts. *Journal of Political Economy* 95: 921–937.

(1993). *A Theory of Incentives in Procurement and Regulation*. Cambridge, MA: MIT Press.

Lazear, E. P. (1979). Why is there mandatory retirement? *Journal of Political Economy* 87: 1261–1284.

(1992). Compensation, productivity, and the new economics of personnel. In *Research Frontiers in Industrial Relations*, ed. D. Lewin, O. Mitchell, and P. Sherer. Madison, WI: Industrial Relations Research Association.341–380.

(2000). Pay, performance, and productivity. *American Economic Review* 90: 1346–1361.

(2003). Teachers for the new century. *Hoover Digest* 1: 20–23.

Lee, D. R. (1988). Free riding and paid riding in the fight against terrorism. *American Economic Review* 78: 22–26.

Leland, H. E. (1992). Insider trading: Should it be prohibited? *Journal of Political Economy* 100: 859–887.

Leibenstein, Harvey. (1966). Allocative efficiency vs. X-efficiency. *American Economic Review* 56: 392–415.

Leibenstein, Harvey. (1976). *Beyond Economic Man*. Cambridge, MA: Harvard University Press.

Leontief, W. W. (1936). Composite commodities and the problem of index numbers. *Econometrica* 4: 39–59.

Levin, Jonathan. (2013). The economics of internet markets. In *Advances in Economics and Econometrics: Invited Lectures to Ninth World Congress of the Econometric Society*, ed. D. Acemoglu, M. Arellano, and E. Dekel. Cambridge University Press.

Levin, Jonathan, and Tadelis, Steven. (2005). Profit sharing and the role of professional partnerships. *Quarterly Journal of Economcs* 120: 131–171.

Lichtenberg, F. R. (1992). *Corporate Takeovers and Productivity*. Cambridge, MA: MIT Press.

Litan, R. E. (1991). Comment on T. Romer and B. R. Weingast's article, "Political foundations of the thrift debacle." In *Politics and Economics in the Eighties*, ed. Alberto Alesina. University of Chicago Press. 209–214.

Lucking-Reiley, David. (2000a). Vickrey auctions in practice: From nineteenth-century philately to twenty-first century e-commerce. *Journal of Economic Perspectives* 14: 183–192.

(2000b). Auctions on the internet: What's being auctioned, and how. *Journal of Induxtrial Economics* 48: 227–252.

MacCormick, John. (2012). *Nine Algorithms that Changed the World: The Ingenious Ideas that Drive Today's Computers*. Princeton University Press.

Makowski, L., and J. M. Ostroy. (1987). Vickrey-Clarke-Groves mechanisms and perfect competition. *Journal of Economic Theory* 42: 244–261.

(1991). *The margin of appropriation and an extension of the first theorem of welfare economics*. Los Angeles, CA: Department of Economics, UCLA working paper.

(1993). General equilibrium and market socialism: Clarifying the logic of competitive markets. In *Market Socialism: The Current Debate*, ed. P. K. Bardhan and J. E. Roemer. New York: Oxford University Press.69–88.

Malatesta, P., and R. Walking. (1988). Poison pill securities: Stockholder wealth, profitability, and ownership structure. *Journal of Financial Economics* 20: 347–376.

Malkiel, B. G. (2003). *A Random Walk Down Wall Street*. 8th edn. New York: Norton.

Mann, D. P., and J. P. Wissink. (1988). Money-back contracts with double moral hazard. *Rand Journal of Economics* 19: 285–292.

(1990a). Hidden actions and hidden characteristics in warranty markets. *International Journal of Industrial Organization* 8: 53–71.

(1990b). Money-back warranties vs. replacement warranties: A simple comparison. *American Economic Review* 80: 432–436.

Manne, H. G. (1965). Mergers and the market for corporate control. *Journal of Political Economy* 73: 110–120.

(1966). *Insider Trading and the Stock Market*. New York: The Free Press.

Mas-Colell, A., M. D. Whinston, and J. R. Green. (1995). *Microeconomic Theory*. New York: Oxford University Press.

Maskin, E. S. (1994). The invisible hand and externalities. *American Economic Review* 84: 333–337.

(2003). *Auctions and efficiency*. In *Advances in Economics and Econometrics: Invited Lectures to Eighth World Congress of the Econometric Society*, Vol. 1, ed. Mathias, Dewatripont, L. Hansen, and S. Turnovsky. Cambridge University Press. 1–24.

Maskin, E., and T. Sjöström. (2002). Implementation theory. In *Handbook of Social Choice and Welfare*, Vol. 1, ed. K. J. Arrow, A. K. Sen, and K. Suzumura. Amsterdam: Elsevier. Ch. 5.

McAfee, R. P. (2002). *Competitive Solutions*. Princeton University Press.

McAfee, R. P., and John McMillan. (1988). *Incentives in Government Contracting*. University of Toronto Press.

McConnell, J. J., and C. J. Muscarella. (1986). Corporate capital expenditure decisions and the market value of the firm. *Journal of Financial Economics* 14: 399–422.

McKelvey, R. D., and T. R. Palfrey. (1992). An experimental study of the centipede game. *Econometrica* 60: 803–836.

McKenzie, L. W. (1954). On equilibrium in Graham's model of world trade and other competitive systems. *Econometrica* 22: 147–161.

(2002). *Classical General Equilibrium Theory.* Cambridge, MA: MIT Press.

McMillan, John. (1992). *Games, Strategies, and Managers.* Oxford University Press.

(1994). Selling spectrum rights. *Journal of Economic Perspectives* 8: 13–29.

(1997). Markets in transition. In *Advances in Economics and Econometrics: Theory and Applications*, Vol. 2, ed. D. M. Kreps and K. F. Wallis. Cambridge University Press, 210–239.

(2002). *Reinventing the Bazaar: A Natural History of Markets.* New York: W.W. Norton.

McPhee, J. (1966). *Oranges.* New York: Farrar, Straus, and Giroux.

Megginson, W. L., and J. M. Netter. (2001). From state to market: A survey of empirical studies on privatization. *Journal of Economic Literature* 39: 321–389.

Milgrom, P. R. (1987). Auction theory. In *Advances in Economic Theory Fifth Worlds Congress*, ed. T. Bewley. Cambridge University Press. 1–32.

(1989). Auctions and bidding: A primer. *Journal of Economic Perspectives* 3: 3–32.

(2004). *Putting Auction Theory to Work.* Cambridge University Press.

Milgrom, P. R., and J. Roberts. (1992). *Economics, Organization, and Management.* Englewood Cliffs, NJ: Prentice Hall.

Miller, G. J. (1992). *Managerial Dilemmas: The Political Economy of Hierarchy.* Cambridge University Press.

Milleron, J.-C. (1972). Theory of value with public goods: A survey article. *Journal of Economic Theory* 5: 419–477.

Mirlees, J. (1971). An exploration in the theory of optimal income taxation. *Review of Economic Studies* 38: 175–208.

(1974). Notes on welfare economics, information, and uncertainty. In *Essays in Economic Behavior under Uncertainty*, ed. M. Balch, D. McFadden, and S. Wu. Amsterdam: North Holland Press. 243–258.

(1976). The optimal structure of incentives and authority within an organization. *Bell Journal of Economics* 7: 105–131.

(1999). The theory of moral hazard with unobservable behavior, part 1. *Review of Economic Studies* 66: 3–22.

Mishel, L., and J. Bernstein. (1992). Declining wages for high school and college graduates. Working paper. Washington, DC: Economic Policy Institute.

Mishkin, F. S. (1992). *Money, Banking, and Financial Markets.* New York: Harper Collins.

Moe, Terry. (2001). Hidden demand. *Education Next* 1, Spring: 48–55.

Molho, Ian. (1997). *The Economics of Information: Lying and Cheating in Markets and Organizations.* Oxford, UK: Blackwell Publishers.

Mongell, S., and A. E. Roth. (1991). Sorority rush as a two-sided matching mechanism. *American Economic Review* 81: 441–464.

Moore, J., and R. Repullo. (1988). Subgame perfect implementation. *Econometrica* 56: 1191–1220.

Murphy, K. J. (1999). Executive compensation. In *Handbook of Labor Economics*, ed. O. Ashenfelter and D. Card. Amsterdam: Elsevier. 2485–2563.

(2002). Explaining executive compensation: Managerial power versus the perceived cost of stock options. *University of Chicago Law Review* 69: 847–869.

Myerson, R. B. (1981). Optimal auction design. *Mathematics of Operations Research* 6: 58–73.

(1999). Nash equilibrium and the history of economic theory. *Journal of Economic Literature* 37: 1067–1082.

Nalebuff, Barry, and Ian Ayres. (2003). *Why Not?* Boston, MA: Harvard Business School Press.

Nasar, Sylvia. (1998). *A Beautiful Mind*. New York: Simon and Schuster.

Naughton, Barry. (2007). *The Chinese Economy: Transitions and Growth*. Cambridge, MA: MIT Press.

Neufeld, J. L., W. J. Hausman, and R. B. Rapoport. (1994). A paradox of voting: Cyclical majorities and the case of Muscle Shoals. *Political Research Quarterly* 47: 423–438.

Novshek, W. (1993). *Mathematics for Economists*. San Diego, CA: Academic Press.

Olson, Mancur. (1993). *Why is economic performance even worse after communism is abandoned? Unpublished mimeographed material*. Fairfax, VA.: George Mason University, Center for the Study of Public Choice.

(2000). *Power and Prosperity: Outgrowing Communist and Capitalist Dictatorships*. New York: Basic Books.

O'Neil, Thomas. (1997). Australia's dog fence. *National Geographic* 191 (4): 18–37.

Osborne, M. J. (2004). *An Introduction to Game Theory*. New York: Oxford University Press.

Osborne, M. J., and A. Rubinstein. (1990). *Bargaining and Markets*. San Diego, CA: Academic Press.

Ostrom, E. (1990). *Governing the Commons: The Evolution of Institutions for Collective Action*. Cambridge University Press.

Parthasarathi, P. (2011). *Why Europe Got Rich and Asia Did Not: Global Economic Divergence, 1600–1850*. Cambridge University Press.

Perry, T., and M. Zenner. (2000). CEO compensation in the 1990s: Shareholder alignment or shareholder expropriation? *Wake Forest Law Review* 35: 142–144.

Petrosky, Henry. (1992). *To Engineer Is Human: The Role of Failure in Successful Design*. New York: Vintage Books.

Petrosky, Henry. (1996). *Invention by Design: How Engineers Get from Thought to Thing*. Cambridge, MA: Harvard University Press.

Phlips, Louis. (1981). *The Economics of Price Discrimination*. New York: Cambridge University Press.

Poundstone, W. (1992). *Prisoner's Dilemma*. New York: Doubleday.

Prendergast, Canice. (1999). The provision of incentives in firms. *Journal of Economic Literature* 37: 7–63.

Prowse, Stephen. (1995). Corporate governance in an international perspective: A survey of corporate control mechanisms among large firms in the US, UK, Japan, and Germany. *Financial Markets, Institutions and Instruments* 4: 1–63.

Radner, R. (1991). Dynamic games in organization theory. *Journal of Economic Behavior and Organization* 16: 217–260.

(1992). Hierarchy: The economics of managing. *Journal of Economic Literature* 30: 1382–1415.

Rajan, R. G. (2010). *Fault Lines: How Hidden Fractures Still Threaten the World Economy*. Princeton University Press.

Rajan, R. G., and Zingales, L. (2000). The governance of the new enterprise. In *Corporate Governance*, ed. Xavier Vives. Cambridge University Press.201–227.

Rapoport, A. (1989). Prisoner's dilemma. In *Game Theory*, ed. J. Eatwell, M. Milgate, and P. Newman. New York: Norton.199–204.

Reichl, Ruth (2005). *Garlic and Sapphires: The Secret Life of a Critic in Disguise*. New York: Penguin Books.

Reinhardt, U. E., P. S. Hussey, and G. F. Anderson. (2004). US health care spending in an international context. *Health Affairs* 23: 10–25.

Reny, P. J. (2001). Arrow's theorem and the Gibbard-Satterthwaite theorem: A unified approach. *Economics Letters* 70: 99–105.

Repullo, R. (1987). A simple proof of Maskin's theorem on Nash implementation. *Social Choice and Welfare* 4: 39–41.

Riley, J. G. (1989). Signalling. In *Allocation, Information, and Markets*, ed. J. Eatwell, M. Milgate, and P. Newman. New York: Norton.287–294.

(2000). Silver signals: Twenty-five years of screening and signaling. *Journal of Economic Literature* 39: 432–478.

(2012). *Essential Microeconomics*. Cambridge University Press.

Riley, J. G., and W. Samuelson. (1981). Optimal auctions. *American Economic Review* 71: 381–392.

Rob, R. (1982). Asymptotic efficiency of the demand revealing mechanism. *Journal of Economic Theory* 28: 207–220.

Roberts, D. J. (1979). Incentives in planning procedures for the provision of public goods. *Review of Economic Studies* 46: 283–292.

Roberts, J., and A. Postlewaite. (1976). The incentive for price-taking behavior in large exchange economies. *Econometrica* 44: 115–127.

Romer, T., and B. R. Weingast. (1991). Political foundations of the thrift debacle. In *Politics and Economics in the Eighties*, ed. Alberto Alesina and G. Carliner. University of Chicago Press. 175–209.

Rosenthal, R. (1981). Games of perfect information, predatory pricing, and the chain store paradox. *Journal of Economic Theory* 25: 92–100.

Ross, S. (1973). The economic theory of agency: The principal's problem. *American Economic Review* 63: 134–139.

Roth, A. E. (1982). The economics of matching: Stability and incentives. *Mathematics of Operations Research* 7: 617–628.

(1984). The evolution of the labor market for medical interns and residents: A case study in game theory. *Journal of Political Economy* 92: 991–1026.

(1990). New physicians: A natural experiment in market organization. *Science*, December 14: 1524–1528.

(1991). A natural experiment in the organization of entry-level labor markets: Regional markets for new physicians and surgeons in the UK. *American Economic Review* 81: 415–40.

(2015). *Who Gets What - And Why*. Boston, MA: Houghton Mifflin Harcourt.

Roth, A. E., and E. Peranson. (1999). The redesign of the matching market for American physicians: Some engineering aspects of economic design. *American Economic Review* 89: 748–780.

Roth, A. E., and M. A. O. Sotomayor. (1990). *Two-Sided Matching: A Study in Game-Theoretic Modeling and Analysis.* Cambridge University Press.

Roth, A. E., and X. Xing. (1994). Jumping the gun: Imperfections and institutions relating to the timing of market transactions. *American Economic Review* 84: 992–1044.

Roth, A. E., T. Sönmez, and U. Ünver. (2004). Kidney exchange. *Quarterly Journal of Economics* 119: 457–488.

(2007). Efficient kidney exchange: Coincidence of wants in markets with compatability-based preferences. *American Economic Review* 97: 828–851.

Rothschild, M., and J. E. Stiglitz. (1976). Equilibrium in competitive insurance markets: An essay on the economics of imperfect information. *Quarterly Journal of Economics* 80: 629–649.

Rubinstein, A. (1986). Finite automata play the repeated prisoners' dilemma. *Journal of Economic Theory* 39: 83–96.

(1998). *Modeling Bounded Rationality.* Cambridge, MA: MIT Press.

Ryngaert, M. (1988). The effect of poison pill securities on shareholder wealth. *Journal of Financial Economics* 20: 377–417.

Saari, D. G. (1994). *Geometry of Voting.* Berlin: Springer-Verlag.

Samuelson, P. A. (1954). The pure theory of public expenditure. *Review of Economics and Statistics* 36: 387–389.

Samuleson, W. (1984). Bargaining under asymmetric information. *Econometrica* 52: 995–1005.

(1985). A comment on the Coase conjecture. In *Game-Theoretic Models of Bargaining,* ed. A. Roth. Cambridge University Press. 321–339.

Sandler, T. (1992). *Collective Action: Theory and Applications.* Ann Arbor: University of Michigan Press.

(2004). *Global Collective Action.* Cambridge University Press.

Sappington, D. E. M. (1991). Incentives in principal-agent relationships. *Journal of Economic Perspectives* 5: 45–66.

(1993). Designing incentive regulation. Working paper no. 93-94-10. University of Florida, College of Business Administration.

Sappington, D. E. M., and D. L. Weisman. (1996). *Designing Incentive Regulation for the Telecommunications Industry.* Cambridge, MS: MIT Press.

Satterthwaite, M. A. (1975). Strategy-proofness and Arrow's conditions: Existence and correspondence theorems for voting procedures and social welfare functions. *Journal of Economic Theory* 10: 187–217.

Scherer, F. M. (1988). Corporate takeovers: The efficiency arguments. *Journal of Economic Perspectives* 2: 69–82.

Schmalensee, Richard, P. L. Joskow, A. D. Ellerman, J. P. Montero, and E. M. Bailey. (1998). An interim evaluation of sulphur dioxide emissions trading. *Journal of Economic Perspectives* 12: 53–68.

Schmalensee, Richard, T. M. Stoker, and R. A. Judson. (1998). World carbon dioxide emissions: 1950-2050. *Review of Economics and Statistics* 80: 15–27.

Scotchmer, Suzanne. (2004). *Innovation and Incentives.* Cambridge, MA: MIT Press.

Segerfeldt, Frederik. (2003). *Water for Sale: How Business and the Market Can Resolve the World's Water Crisis*. Washington, DC: The Cato Institute.

Sen, A. K. (1966). A possibility theorem on majority decisions. *Econometrica* 34: 491–499.

(1981). *Poverty and Famines: An Essay on Entitlement and Deprivation*. Oxford University Press.

(1993). The economics of life and death. *Scientific American May*: 40–47.

Sen, Arunava. (2001). Another direct proof of the Gibbard-Satterthwaite theorem. *Economics Letters* 70: 381–385.

Serizawa, S. (2002). Inefficiency of strategy-proof rules for pure exchange economies. *Journal of Economic Theory* 106: 219–241.

Serizawa, S., and J. Weymark. (2003). Efficient strategy-proof exchange and minimum consumption guarantees. *Journal of Economic Theory* 109: 246–263.

Shapiro, Carl, and H. R. Varian. (1999). *Information Rules*. Cambridge, MA: Harvard Business School Press.

Shapley, Lloyd, and Herb Scarf. (1974). On cores and indivisibilities. *Journal of Mathematical Economics* 1: 23–37.

Sheffrin, S. M. (1993). *Markets and Majorities*. New York: The Free Press.

Shiller, R., and A. N. Weiss. (1999). Home equity insurance. *Journal of Real Estate Finanace and Economics* 19: 21–47.

Shleifer, Andrei. (2000). Discussion. In *Corporate Governance*, ed. Xavier Vives. Cambridge University Press.134–136.

Shleifer, A., and R. W. Vishny. (1986). Large shareholders and corporate control. *Journal of Political Economy* 294: 461–481.

(1988). Value maximization and the acquisition process. *Journal of Economic Perspectives* 2: 7–20.

(1997). A survey of corporate governance. *Journal of Finance* 52: 737–783.

Shoven, J. B., S. B. Smart, and J. Waldfogel. (1992). Real interest rates and the savings and loan crisis: The moral hazard premium. *Journal of Economic Perspectives* 6: 155–167.

Singh, Simon. (1999). *The Code Book: The Science of Secrecy from Ancient Egypt to Quantum Cryptography*. New York: Random House.

Smith, Mark B. (2003). *A History of the Global Stock Market: From Ancient Rome to Silicon Valley*. University of Chicago Press.

Sobel, Dava. (2005). *Longitude*. New York: Walker Publishing Company.

Sönmez, Tayfun, and M. U. Ünver. (2010). Course bidding at business schools. *International Economic Review* 51: 99–167.

(2013). Market design for kidney exchange. In *The Handbook of Market Design*, ed. Nir Vulkan, Alvin E. Roth, and Zvika Neeman. Oxford University Press. 93–137.

Spence, A. M. (1973). *Market Signalling: Information Transfer in Hiring and Related Processes*. Cambridge, MA: Harvard University Press.

Stavins, R. N. (1998). What can we learn from the grand policy experiment? Lessons from SO_2 allowance trading. *Journal of Economic Perspectives* 12: 69–88.

Stern, S., and P. Todd. (2000). A test of Lazear's mandatory retirement model. *Research in Labor Economics* 19: 253–273.

Sternberg, T. (1991). *FDIC auctions of failed banks: One way to measure the acquirer's surplus*. Berkeley: University of California, Haas School of Business.

Stiglitz, J. E. (1974). Incentives and risk sharing in sharecropping. *Review of Economic Studies* 41: 219–255.

    (1975). Incentives, risk, and information: Notes toward a theory of hierarchy. *Bell Journal of Economics* 6: 552–579.

    (1993). Market socialism and neoclassical economics. In *Market Socialism: The Current Debate*, ed. P. K. Bardhan, and J. E. Roemer. New York: Oxford University Press.21–41.

    (2000). The contributions of the economics of information to twentieth-century economics. *Quarterly Journal of Economics* 115: 144–1178.

    (2010). *Free Fall: America, Free Markets, and the Shrinking of the World Economy.* New York: W. W. Norton.

Stiglitz, J. E., and A. Weiss. (1981). Credit rationing in markets with imperfect information. *American Economic Review* 71: 393–410.

Stoft, Steven. (2008). *Carbonomics: How to Fix the Climate and Charge it to OPEC.* Bakersfield, CA: Diamond Press.

Strang, Gilbert. (1991). *Calculus.* Wellesley, MA: Wellesley-Cambridge Press.

Su, Xuanming, and S. A. Zenios. (2006). Recipient choice can address the efficiency-equity trade-off in kidney transplantation: A mechanism design approach. *Management Science* 52: 1647–1660.

Sutton, J. (2000). *Marshall's Tendencies: What Can Economists Know?* Cambridge, MA: MIT Press.

Thaler, R. H. (1992). *The Winner's Curse: Paradoxes and Anomalies of Economic Life.* New York: The Free Press.

Thompson, D. N. (1971). *Franchise Operations and Antitrust.* Lexington, MA: D.C. Heath.

Tideman, T. N., and G. Tullock. (1976). A new and superior principle for collective choice. *Journal of Political Economy* 84: 1145–1159.

Tirole, J. (1988). *The Theory of Industrial Organization.* Cambridge, MA: MIT Press.

Trinkaus, John and Joseph Giacalcone. (2005). The silence of the stakeholders: Zero decibel level at Enron. *Journal of Business Ethics.* 58: 237–248.

Ullen, T. S. (1994). *Rational victims – rational injurers: Cognition and the economic analysis of tort law.* Unpublished mimeographed material. Department of Economics, University of Illinois at Urbana-Champaign.

Varian, H. R. (2000). Differential pricing and efficiency. *First Monday* June: 1–6.

    (2007). Position auctions. *International Journal of Industrial Organization* 25:1163–1178.

Vickrey, W. (1945). Measuring marginal utility by reactions to risk. *Econometrica* 13: 319–333.

    (1961). Counterspeculation, auctions, and competitive sealed tenders. *Journal of Finance* 16: 8–37.

Vives, Xavier. (2000). Corporate governance: Does it matter? In *Corporate Governance*, ed. Xavier Vives. Cambridge University Press.1–21.

Von Neumann, J., and O. Morgenstern. (1944). *Theory of Games and Economic Behavior.* Princeton University Press.

Votruba, M. E. (2003). *Essays on the allocation of public resources.* Doctoral dissertation. Department of Economics, Princeton University.

Vulkan, Nir, A. E. Roth, and Z. Neeman. (2013). *The Handbook of Market Design*. Oxford University Press.

Waldrup, M. M. (1992). *Complexity*. New York: Simon and Schuster.

Waldspurger, C. A., T. Hogg, B. A. Huberman, J. O. Kephart, and S. Stornetta. (1992). Spawn: A distributed computational economy. *IEEE Transactions on Software Engineering* 18: 103–117.

Walker, M. (1978). A note on the characterization of mechanisms for the revelation of preferences. *Econometrica* 46: 147–152.

(1980). On the nonexistence of a dominant strategy mechanism for making optimal public decisions. *Econometrica* 48: 1521–1540.

(1981). A simple incentive compatible scheme for attaining Lindahl allocations. *Econometrica* 49: 65–71.

Weinberg, Samantha. (2003). *Pointing from the Grave*. New York: Hyperion.

Weintraub, E. R. (1982). *Mathematics for Economists*. Cambridge University Press.

(2014). *Finding Equilibrium: Arrow, Debreu, McKenzie and the Problem of Scientific Credit*. Princeton University Press.

Wen, Quan. (1994). The "folk theorem" for repeated games with complete information. *Econometrica* 62: 949–954.

Wheelan, Charles. (2002). *Naked Economics: Undressing the Dismal Science*. New York: W. W. Norton.

White, Lawrence J. (1991). *The S & L Debacle: Public Policy Lessons for Bank and Thrift Regulation*. New York: Oxford University Press.

White, M. J. (1999). What's wrong with US personal bankruptcy law and how to fix it. *Regulation* 22. Available at www.cato.org/pubs/regulation/regv22n3/reg22n3.html, accessed December 15, 2005.

Williams, S. R., and R. Radner. (1995). Efficiency in partnership when the joint output is uncertain. In *The Economics of Informational Decentralization*, ed. J. Ledyard, Boston: Kluwer.79–99.

Woessman, Ludger. (2001). Why students in some countries do better. *Education Next* 1, Summer: 67–74.

Wolak, F. A. (2002). Making sense of the Enron nonsense. Stanford Institute for Economic Policy Research policy brief, Stanford University. Available at http://stanford.edu/papers/briefs/policybrief_may02.html, accessed December 15, 2005.

Yermack, David. (1997). Good timing: The CEO stock option awards and company news announcements. *Journal of Finance* 52: 449–476.

Zeckhauser, R. (1970). Medical insurance: A case study of the tradeoff between risk spreading and appropriate incentives. *Journal of Economic Theory* 2: 10–26.

Zhou, Lin. (1990). On a conjecture by Gale on one-sided matching problems. *Journal of Economic Theory* 52: 123–135.

Zhou, Lin. (1991a). Impossibility of strategy-proof mechanisms in economies with pure public goods. *Review of Economic Studies* 58: 107–119.

(1991b). Inefficiency of strategy-proof allocation mechanisms in pure exchange economies. *Social Choice and Welfare* 8: 247–257.

Zimbalist, Andrew. (2004). *May the Best Team Win: Baseball Economics and Public Policy*. Washington, DC: Brookings Institution Press.

Author Index

Subject Index